# management
## A REAL WORLD APPROACH

# management:
## A REAL WORLD
## APPROACH

**Andrew Ghillyer**
Vice President of Academic Affairs
Argosy University, Tampa, Florida

 **McGraw-Hill**
**Higher Education**

Boston   Burr Ridge, IL   Dubuque, IA   New York   San Francisco   St. Louis
Bangkok   Bogotá   Caracas   Kuala Lumpur   Lisbon   London   Madrid   Mexico City
Milan   Montreal   New Delhi   Santiago   Seoul   Singapore   Sydney   Taipei   Toronto

# McGraw-Hill
# Higher Education

MANAGEMENT: A REAL WORLD APPROACH
Published by McGraw-Hill, a business unit of The McGraw-Hill Companies, Inc., 1221 Avenue of the Americas, New York, NY, 10020. Copyright © 2009 by The McGraw-Hill Companies, Inc. All rights reserved. No part of this publication may be reproduced or distributed in any form or by any means, or stored in a database or retrieval system, without the prior written consent of The McGraw-Hill Companies, Inc., including, but not limited to, in any network or other electronic storage or transmission, or broadcast for distance learning.

Some ancillaries, including electronic and print components, may not be available to customers outside the United States.

This book is printed on acid-free paper.

1 2 3 4 5 6 7 8 9 0 WCK/WCK 0 9 8

ISBN 978-0-07-337701-8
MHID 0-07-337701-5

Vice president/Editor in chief: *Elizabeth Haefele*
Vice president/Director of marketing: *John E. Biernat*
Sponsoring editor: *Natalie J. Ruffatto*
Developmental editor: *Kristin Bradley*
Senior marketing manager: *Keari Bedford*
Lead media producer: *Damian Moshak*
Media producer: *Benjamin Curless*
Director, Editing/Design/Production: *Jess Ann Kosic*
Project manager: *Christine M. Demma*
Senior production supervisor: *Janean A. Utley*
Designer: *Marianna Kinigakis*
Senior photo research coordinator: *Jeremy Cheshareck*
Photo researcher: *Keri Johnson*
Media project manager: *Mark A. S. Dierker*
Typeface: *10.5/13 New Aster*
Compositor: *ICC Macmillan Inc.*
Printer: *Quebecor World Versailles Inc.*
Cover credit: The Northern Trifid, also known as NGC 1579, located in the constellation Perseus, © Stock Trek Images/Finch Stock
Credits: The credits section for this book begins on page 445 and is considered an extension of the copyright page.

**Library of Congress Cataloging-in-Publication Data**

Ghillyer, Andrew.
    Management : a real world approach / Andrew Ghillyer.
        p. cm.
    Includes index.
    ISBN-13: 978-0-07-337701-8 (alk. paper)
    ISBN-10: 0-07-337701-5 (alk. paper)
    1. Management. I. Title.
    HD31.G47 2009
658—dc22                           2007042913

The Internet addresses listed in the text were accurate at the time of publication. The inclusion of a Web site does not indicate an endorsement by the authors or McGraw-Hill, and McGraw-Hill does not guarantee the accuracy of the information presented at these sites.

www.mhhe.com

# dedication

To Princess Megan

# BRIEF contents

# contents

## 《 part 2

## Planning and Leadership  109

# A SPECIAL NOTE TO
# students

My goal in writing this book, as the title implies, is to take a more "real world approach" to the subject of management. What will this mean for you as we embark on this journey together? The historical material will still be reviewed in order to help you understand where this still very young profession of management has come from. The foundational academic theories will also be covered so that you can become comfortable with the unique terminology that often makes managerial communication more intimidating than it needs to be. Don't think of these theories or models as formulas or equations to be learned by heart. They are simply attempts to capture management practices in a way that allows businesses to replicate successful behavior and new managers to learn what has worked for others in the past. As you progress through the book, you will develop a better understanding of the behavior demonstrated by managers you have worked with, and you will also develop a better sense of the style of management that works best for you.

To help you along this path, I have placed the material in a world that should be familiar to you. The case studies and exercises involve companies that you know—Best Buy, Wal-Mart, The Gap, UPS, and several others— and the challenges and opportunities those companies are facing have been deliberately selected as examples of what you may face as you begin your career. In addition, we will be getting to know a young man named Tony Davis as he begins his management career with the Taco Barn organization. Each chapter in the book begins and ends with a "World of Work" section where Tony deals with a management issue in his restaurant. As a new manager, Tony is enthusiastic and eager to do well, but as you will see, the decisions that managers have to make can often bring unexpected consequences. As you follow Tony's career in each chapter, you will be asked to think about how you would have acted if you were in Tony's place and had to face a similar situation in your job.

At the same time, you may find yourself wondering if there is a "right" answer to a particular question or situation, and often there may not be. As you explore the world of management, you will soon realize that there are often more gray areas than clearly defined black and white ones. Company policies and procedures dictate many decisions that managers make, but in some instances the decisions you will be required to make will need to be based on the specific situation you are facing at the time. As you review examples of these situations in the book with your professor and your fellow students, keep an open mind and try to learn from your classmates who may have different perspectives and engage them in reasoned and respectful discussions. Experienced managers will tell you that you never stop learning in the profession of management. You will learn from different situations every day. You are about to begin a journey that will help you prepare for a successful management career— I look forward to working with you!

Warmest Regards,

**Andy Ghillyer**

# ABOUT THE
# author

**Dr. Andrew Ghillyer** is the Vice President of Academic Affairs for Argosy University in Tampa. Dr. Ghillyer's past experience includes Chief Operating Officer (COO) of a civil engineering software company and Director of International Business Relations for a global training organization. Dr. Ghillyer received his doctorate in Management Studies from the University of Surrey in the UK. His professional credentials span over 24 years of operational management experience across a wide range of industries, markets, and cultures. He is a published author in the field of service quality, and has an established track record of growth and achievement in both corporate and entrepreneurial environments. Dr. Ghillyer also served on the Board of Examiners for the Malcolm Baldrige National Quality Award for the 2007 Award year. His first McGraw-Hill book, entitled: *Business Ethics: A Real World Approach,* was published in January 2007.

# APPROACHING MANAGEMENT . . .

McGraw-Hill Career Education is pleased to introduce *Management: A Real World Approach* by Andrew Ghillyer. As the title implies, this book is about the "real world" of management, and was written for students who aspire to be shift supervisors, team leaders, managers, or beyond during the course of their careers. We know that many students already work full or part time, and some of them may already hold management positions. This text offers a practical approach, balancing academic theory and practitioner application with explanations and examples that today's students will find interesting and accessible. We provide the appropriate material to develop a broader understanding of the management discipline—how it developed historically; how academic research has led to the development of commonly accepted management models; and how "real-time" implementation of managerial skills continues to challenge researchers.

The key objective of this book, as well as the student and instructor support, is to present management in a less intimidating and more topical manner, which has been achieved by emphasizing the application of material via a variety of exercises—both hypothetical and real life—for students to review and apply in their own environments.

## . . . ONE STEP AT A TIME!

*Management: A Real World Approach* breaks the overarching themes students need to know into four practical sections that students can use.

### Part 1: Foundations

This section provides a general introduction to the topic of management by presenting a working definition of management and examining the management process from the perspectives of tasks, roles, and skills. A brief history of management is reviewed in order to help students understand from where this still very young profession has come. Critical skills—communication and decision making—are reviewed in detail as a baseline for the introduction of other managerial skills.

### Part 2: Planning and Leadership

Following the general introduction, we move to the standard planning, leading, organizing, and controlling management model. Planning and strategic management are reviewed as critical components for the longer-term development of an organization and as a required balance to the day-to-day operational skills of a manager. Leadership and culture are then reviewed as crucial elements in the development of a productive work environment. The role of a manager in "walking the talk" and modeling the organizational culture is discussed in detail.

## Part 3: Organization and Control

Moving into the operational paradigm, we focus on the organizational responsibilities of management by reviewing the organization of work, structure, and people, and then we review the challenges involved in motivating people and in maintaining control at both the managerial and operational levels.

## Part 4: The Future of Management

After reviewing the broader topics within the management discipline, we focus on areas that are likely to occur in the responsibilities of managers as we move further into the twenty-first century—specifically diversity, global management, and the management of change. The book concludes with a review of three areas that present the greatest potential for significant change: the continued growth of technology, virtual management, and the increased emphasis on the ethical and social responsibilities of management.

# CHAPTERS THAT TAKE EXAMPLES BEYOND THE CLASSROOM . . .

Each of the 14 chapters follows a common structure with a range of assessment and progress measurement options for instructors to use.

### Learning Objectives

Each chapter begins with a list of **learning objectives.** These objectives are tied directly to the content and help students better understand what they will be studying in each.

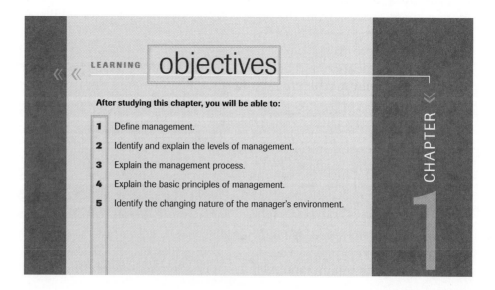

LEARNING « « objectives

After studying this chapter, you will be able to:

1. Define management.
2. Identify and explain the levels of management.
3. Explain the management process.
4. Explain the basic principles of management.
5. Identify the changing nature of the manager's environment.

CHAPTER « 1

## Key Terms

Developing a strong business vocabulary is one of the most important and useful aspects of this course. To assist you, all **key terms** in the book are highlighted in boldface type. Key terms are also defined in the margins, and page references to these terms are given at the end of each chapter. A full glossary is located in the back of the book. You should rely heavily on these learning aids in adding these terms to your vocabulary.

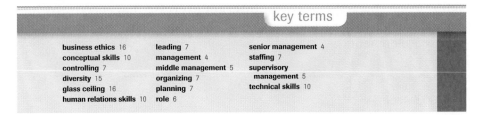

key terms

| | | |
|---|---|---|
| **business ethics** 16 | **leading** 7 | **senior management** 4 |
| **conceptual skills** 10 | **management** 4 | **staffing** 7 |
| **controlling** 7 | **middle management** 5 | **supervisory** |
| **diversity** 15 | **organizing** 7 | **management** 5 |
| **glass ceiling** 16 | **planning** 7 | **technical skills** 10 |
| **human relations skills** 10 | **role** 6 | |

## Progress Check Questions

**Progress check questions** related to each section throughout the chapters allow frequent student assessment of comprehension. These questions work in conjunction with the section outlines and the learning objectives for the chapter.

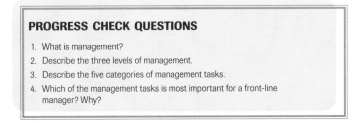

### PROGRESS CHECK QUESTIONS

1. What is management?
2. Describe the three levels of management.
3. Describe the five categories of management tasks.
4. Which of the management tasks is most important for a front-line manager? Why?

## Case Incidents

Two **case studies** per chapter reinforce key learning outcomes with challenging management scenarios.

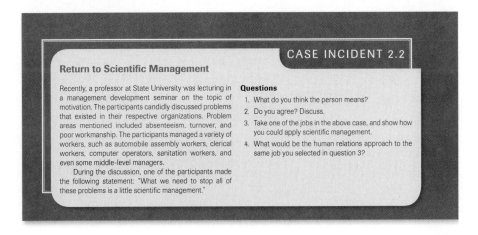

CASE INCIDENT 2.2

**Return to Scientific Management**

Recently, a professor at State University was lecturing in a management development seminar on the topic of motivation. The participants candidly discussed problems that existed in their respective organizations. Problem areas mentioned included absenteeism, turnover, and poor workmanship. The participants managed a variety of workers, such as automobile assembly workers, clerical workers, computer operators, sanitation workers, and even some middle-level managers.

During the discussion, one of the participants made the following statement: "What we need to stop all of these problems is a little scientific management."

**Questions**

1. What do you think the person means?
2. Do you agree? Discuss.
3. Take one of the jobs in the above case, and show how you could apply scientific management.
4. What would be the human relations approach to the same job you selected in question 3?

## Review Questions

At the end of each chapter, **review questions** reinforce key learning outcomes.

## Internet Exercises

To encourage the development of Internet skills—specifically search skills—each chapter features an **Internet exercise** that encourages students to locate and review useful Web sites for their ongoing management development.

## Team Exercises

Each chapter includes a **team-based exercise** to encourage presentation and team skills. Questions for these exercises also ask students to document the process of team development and the challenges involved in achieving a successful outcome in a team environment.

### review questions

1. Management has often been described as a universal process, meaning the basics of management are transferable and applicable in almost any environment. Do you believe a good manager in a bank could be equally effective in a college or university? Explain your reasoning.

2. How does one decide who is and who is not a manager in a given organization? For example, is the operator of a one-person business, such as a corner grocery store, a manager? Explain.

3. Do you think management can be learned through books and study or only through experience?

4. Consider your own personality, skills, and work experience. Do you think you would make a good manager? Why or why not?

### internet exercise

Visit the Web site for the American Management Association (www.amanet.org). Find a course on supervisory skills, and summarize the content of that course: What does the training include? What is the training designed to do for the skills of the course participants?

### team exercise

Divide into groups of two or three. Select a managerial policy change from the list on p. 20, and prepare the following:

1. A formal memo to be sent to all employees as an e-mail notifying them of the change in policy.

## Discussion Exercises

In line with the commitment to topical material, each chapter offers two detailed case studies featuring companies that are known to the students. The cases present management situations that are more "big picture" in scope, but the end-of-case questions encourage students to focus on the impact of those big picture decisions on the lower levels of the organizational pyramid.

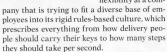

**discussion exercise 1.1**

### For UPS Managers, a School of Hard Knocks

*Execs Share the Kind of Gritty Life Experiences of Some Workers*

**A**t United Parcel Service Inc., rules are not to be broken. Without them, UPS could never move 13.5 million packages to their destinations on time each day. But two years ago, Mark J. Colvard, a UPS manager in San Ramon, Calif., had to decide whether or not to break one of those rules. A driver needed time off to help a sick family member, but under company rules he wasn't entitled to any time off. If Colvard went by the book, the driver would probably take the days anyway and be fired. If Colvard gave him the time off, he would catch flak from his other drivers. Colvard wound up giving the driver two weeks, took some heat for it, and kept a valuable employee. Six months earlier, Colvard admits, he would have gone the other way.

What changed his approach? A month he spent living among migrant farmers in McAllen, Tex., as part of an unusual UPS management training experience called the Community Internship Program (CIP). After building housing for the poor, collecting clothing for the Salvation Army, and working in a drug rehab center, Colvard said he was able to identify with employees facing crises back home. And that, he says, has made him a better manager. "My goal was to make the numbers, and in some cases that meant not looking at the person but looking at the bottom line," says Colvard. "After that one-month stay, I immediately started reaching out to people in a different way."

CIP began in 1968 as the brainchild of UPS founder James Casey, who wanted to open up the eyes of UPS's mainly white managers to the poverty and inequality exploding into violence in many cities. By now, nearly 1,200 current and former middle managers have moved through the program. And it has developed into an essential part of the UPS tradition, teaching managers the crucial skill of flexibility at a company that is trying to fit a diverse base of employees into its rigid rules-based culture, which prescribes everything from how delivery people should carry their keys to how many steps they should take per second.

UPS needs rules, but it also needs managers capable of bending them when necessary. "We've got 330,000 U.S. employees," says Don B. Wofford, the CIP coordinator and a graduate of the program. "There are all kinds of personalities and all kinds of diversity. We need managers who can manage those individuals."

# ...AND INTO THE REAL WORLD!

## World of Work

At the beginning and end of each chapter students will spend some time with Tony Davis, a newly promoted restaurant manager for the Taco Barn organization, as he embarks on his management career and learns more about **The World of Work.** Tony receives his formal appointment as unit manager in Chapter 1 and proceeds through a series of challenges relating directly to the chapter material as the book progresses. The hypothetical situations are based on real examples in a restaurant manager's life, and each vignette provides sufficient information for any student (even the rare few without fast-food or restaurant credentials in their brief careers) to propose solutions to Tony's problems. As Tony's story builds from chapter to chapter, students can monitor his growing confidence as a manager, plus the material provides a useful transition from one chapter to the next, along with the opportunity for instructors to revisit and refresh material at the beginning of each class. For those instructors that use journaling as part of their class work, Tony's regular progress updates can be aligned to the students' increasing comfort level with the more abstract management models in the book.

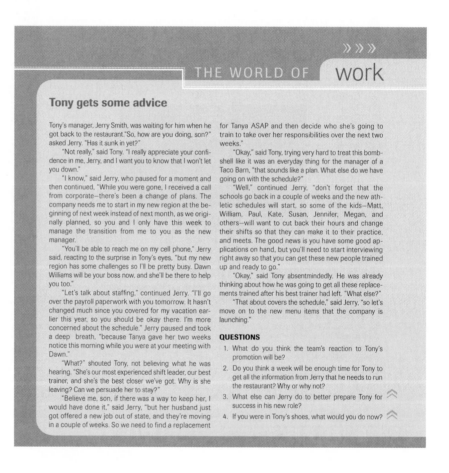

THE WORLD OF **work**   » » »

### Tony gets some advice

Tony's manager, Jerry Smith, was waiting for him when he got back to the restaurant. "So, how are you doing, son?" asked Jerry. "Has it sunk in yet?"

"Not really," said Tony. "I really appreciate your confidence in me, Jerry, and I want you to know that I won't let you down."

"I know," said Jerry, who paused for a moment and then continued, "While you were gone, I received a call from corporate—there's been a change of plans. The company needs me to start in my new region at the beginning of next week instead of next month, as we originally planned, so you and I only have this week to manage the transition from me to you as the new manager.

"You'll be able to reach me on my cell phone," Jerry said, reacting to the surprise in Tony's eyes, "but my new region has some challenges so I'll be pretty busy. Dawn Williams will be your boss now, and she'll be there to help you too."

"Let's talk about staffing," continued Jerry. "I'll go over the payroll paperwork with you tomorrow. It hasn't changed much since you covered for my vacation earlier this year, so you should be okay there. I'm more concerned about the schedule." Jerry paused and took a deep breath, "because Tanya gave her two weeks notice this morning while you were at your meeting with Dawn."

"What?" shouted Tony, not believing what he was hearing. "She's our most experienced shift leader, our best trainer, and she's the best closer we've got. Why is she leaving? Can we persuade her to stay?"

"Believe me, son, if there was a way to keep her, I would have done it," said Jerry, "but her husband just got offered a new job out of state, and they're moving in a couple of weeks. So we need to find a replacement

for Tanya ASAP and then decide who she's going to train to take over her responsibilities over the next two weeks."

"Okay," said Tony, trying very hard to treat this bombshell like it was an everyday thing for the manager of a Taco Barn, "that sounds like a plan. What else do we have going on with the schedule?"

"Well," continued Jerry, "don't forget that the schools go back in a couple of weeks and the new athletic schedules will start, so some of the kids—Matt, William, Paul, Kate, Susan, Jennifer, Megan, and others—will want to cut back their hours and change their shifts so that they can make it to their practice, and meets. The good news is you have some good applications on hand, but you'll need to start interviewing right away so that you can get these new people trained up and ready to go."

"Okay," said Tony absentmindedly. He was already thinking about how he was going to get all these replacements trained after his best trainer had left. "What else?"

"That about covers the schedule," said Jerry, "so let's move on to the new menu items that the company is launching."

#### QUESTIONS

1. What do you think the team's reaction to Tony's promotion will be?

2. Do you think a week will be enough time for Tony to get all the information from Jerry that he needs to run the restaurant? Why or why not?

3. What else can Jerry do to better prepare Tony for success in his new role?

4. If you were in Tony's shoes, what would you do now?

### Ethical Management

Even though many institutions now offer a separate business ethics course in their programs, we felt it was critical to emphasize the importance of **ethical management** practice in this text. As a result, each chapter features an ethical management dilemma for which students are presented with a scenario that requires a decision that may not present an immediately obvious solution. It serves to underline the likelihood of facing "right versus right" decisions at some point in a business career as opposed to the simpler "right versus wrong" decisions. The dilemmas are directly linked to the chapter material, and the questions ask students to relate the dilemma back to their own work experience.

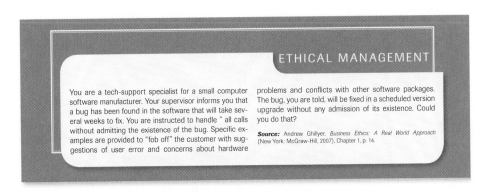

### ETHICAL MANAGEMENT

You are a tech-support specialist for a small computer software manufacturer. Your supervisor informs you that a bug has been found in the software that will take several weeks to fix. You are instructed to handle " all calls without admitting the existence of the bug. Specific examples are provided to "fob off" the customer with suggestions of user error and concerns about hardware problems and conflicts with other software packages. The bug, you are told, will be fixed in a scheduled version upgrade without any admission of its existence. Could you do that?

*Source:* Andrew Ghillyer, *Business Ethics: A Real World Approach* (New York: McGraw-Hill, 2007), Chapter 1, p. 14.

## Study Skills

Student learning does not end when he or she leaves the classroom. We know students often appreciate extra support. Each chapter provides helpful hints for students who aspire to learn and maintain good study habits. **Study Skills** boxes suggest proper study skills to help students thrive in their classes.

### Study Skills

#### Study Skills Are a Learned Behavior

What are your talents? What would you consider to be your greatest skills? Are you talented at singing, playing an instrument, playing sports, writing, painting, or renovating old cars?

Being good at studying is like anything you try: You might be better at some things than other things. Studying is a learned behavior like any engaged activity, and you can improve your study habits and performance with more practice.

Two key areas will help you become better at studying: *study preparation* and *study execution.*

Study preparation includes all the activities that help you get the most out of your reading and note taking. Study execution involves all the actions you take to stay on course to make sure you get the positive results you are seeking.

## Career Management

We also recognize the importance of supporting students as they transition from school to the professional world. Each chapter provides **Career Management** boxes with ideas to aid students in their journey into their careers and provide unique insights and activities that will help students succeed.

career management

### Understanding Career Planning

*Career planning* is a process by which an individual, in assessing an opportunity, creates a career plan for the future and develops the necessary objectives, resources, and procedures to achieve a desired outcome.

This career planning spirit motivates millions of people to obtain the necessary assistance to become successful professionals in the working world.

The question is: Why would you plan, develop, and set the standards for how your career will be achieved? Think about the possibilities of your becoming a high-level executive, a small business owner, or a manager of a company you would like to work for. For this to happen, it would require a career vision to set the objectives and guidelines to reach these lofty goals. Your work now can be a huge payoff in a career where you can find great success!

# STUDENT RESOURCES

### Student Online Learning Center

Our online site for the text gives students supplementary materials to help them better understand and master chapter material. The student **Online Learning Center** has **narrated PowerPoint slides** (which are also available for students to download to their MP3 players), extra chapter quizzes, extra review questions, and other supplemental text materials. You can access the Online Learning Center by visiting **www.mhhe. com/ghillyermangement.**

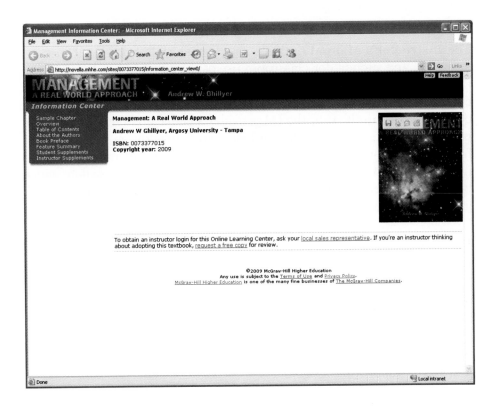

## Student Study Guide

The **Student Study Guide** includes worksheets, practice tests, and supplemental learning materials so students can reinforce their learning of the chapter concepts. The Student Study Guide is organized by chapter and learning outcome to assist students in understanding each chapter's goals and objectives. The guide is available in both a print version or as part of the online enhanced cartridge.

## Spanish Translations

Spanish-speaking students can take advantage of the **Spanish translations** of the glossary of key terms and online quizzes.

# INSTRUCTOR RESOURCES

## Online Learning Center–Instructor Content

The instructor's side of **Online Learning Center (OLC)** serves as a resource for instructors and has several features that support instructors in the creation of lessons. Included on the OLC are the Instructor's Manual (IM), which is organized by each chapter's learning objectives and includes page references, PowerPoint slides that include additional instructor teaching notes, the Asset Map, and other valuable materials.

## Instructor's Manual

The **Instructor's Manual** outlines course materials, additional in-class activities, and support for classroom use of the text and has been organized by learning outcome not only to give instructors a basic outline of the chapter but also to assist them in all facets of instruction. For every question posed in the text, the IM provides a viable answer. The text page numbers provide easy reference for instructors. In addition, the IM guides instructors through the process of integrating supplementary materials into lessons and assignments. The IM also includes sample syllabi, video notes, and student success insights. Ultimately, this will be an instructor's greatest advantage in using all materials to reach all learners.

## Test Bank

Every chapter provides a series of test questions, available in our Test Bank. Questions are organized by learning objective and Bloom's Taxonomy. A Test Table aligns questions with the content and makes it easy for you to determine the questions you want to include on tests and quizzes.

## Instructor PowerPoint Slides

PowerPoint slides created specifically for instructors include additional teaching notes and are tied directly to learning objectives. Each slide also includes a text page reference for your convenience.

### Asset Map

We know that instructors' time is valuable. To help you prepare, we have created an **Asset Map.** The Asset Map identifies by chapter, learning objective, and page number, exactly which supplements are available for you to use. Visit our Web site to preview how the Asset Map can help!

### Videos

Our instructor DVD includes videos for every chapter of the text. Teaching notes for the videos are located on the instructor's manual.

# ACKNOWLEDGMENTS

T his text represents the culmination of the combined efforts of a large number of people. Leslie Rue and Lloyd Byars generously provided the foundation material upon which this text has been built. Once again, McGraw-Hill/Irwin produced a "dream team" of dedicated and experienced professionals who shepherded this author and his text through the production process with unfailing enthusiasm and support. I would like to pay special mention to my editorial team, particularly Natalie Ruffatto and Kristin Bradley. In addition, Keari Bedford and Megan Gates' marketing vision for this text was a creative piece to this puzzle. I would also like to say a big thank you to Christine Demma for her tireless efforts in maintaining an oftentimes challenging schedule. Last, I would like to express my appreciation to the rest of the production team, Benjamin Curless, Janean Utley, and Marianna Kinigakis for their efforts behind the scenes.

McGraw-Hill and I would also like to acknowledge all the instructors whose valuable insights helped shape a text that we are all proud of:

Michele Adams, *Bryant & Stratton*

Mark Alexander, *Axia College of University of Phoenix*

Kristen Aust, *Bryant & Stratton*

Larry Banks, *Eagle Gate College Group*

Carl Bridges, *Lincoln Educational Services*

Linda Bruff, *Strayer University*

Gary Corona, *Florida Community College*

Pat DeBold, *Concord Career*

Nick DiMartina, *Bryant & Stratton College*

Jon Doyle, *Corinthian Colleges, Inc.*

Lowell Frame, *Indiana School of Business*

Jan Friedheim, *Education Systems & Solutions*

Steve Friedheim, *Education Systems & Solutions*

Maureen Frye, *Gibbs College*

Keeley Gadd, *National College*

Patricia Inkelar, *Everest College*

Pat Kapper, *CCA Board Member*

John Keim, *Heald*

Janet Kuser, *Fisher College*

Francis Maffei, *CTU*

Terrel Mailhoit, *Tidewater Tech*

Jaime Morely, *US Education*

John Olson, *ECPI*

Ken Pascal, *Art Institute of Houston*

Stephen Pearce, *Everest College*

Mary Ann Pelligrino, *IADT*

William Rava, *Bryant & Stratton*

Jack Risewick, *Bryant & Stratton*

Robert Roehrich, *NAU*

Linda Rose, *Westwood College*

David Schaitkin, *South Hills School of Business and Technology*

Angela Seidel, *Cambria-Rowe Business College*

Michael Shaw, *University of Phoenix*

Brenda Siragusa, *Corinthian College*

Rodo Sofranac, *Axia College of University of Phoenix*

Ronald Spicer, *CTU*

Bob Trewartha, *Minnesota School of Business*

Scott Warman, *ECPI*

Pete West, *Colorado Technical University Online*

Charlie Zaruba, *Florida Metropolitan University*

Michael Zerbe, *Stark State College*

Daphne Zito, *Katherine Gibbs School*

# PART ONE

## foundations

«  «

# WHAT IS MANAGEMENT?

**"Good management is the art of making problems so interesting and their solutions so constructive that everyone wants to get to work and deal with them."**

—Paul Hawken, author of *Growing a Business*

## The World of Work:  Tony gets a promotion

Tony Davis had been an employee of Taco Barn, Inc., for four years, and today he had a feeling that his 11 o'clock appointment with Dawn Williams, the regional manager for the area, would finally be his reward for four years of dedication and hard work.

Tony had started working in his local Taco Barn after school and decided to stay on after he graduated high school. Over the four years he had been trained in every area in the restaurant, from the correct use of cleaning supplies through food preparation and service, to working the cash register and taking the cash receipts to the bank at the end of the day. They had a good crew at this Taco Barn location—one of the best in the region, Tony thought. Their manager, Jerry Smith, "ran a tight ship," as he liked to say, but he treated his people well and was willing to work with you on your schedule if you had any special requests

for things like evening classes or sports practice or family commitments.

Since Taco Barn preferred to employ young people on a part-time basis, the rest of the crew added up to 18 people working a variety of hours and shifts. For the most part, everybody got on okay—no big fights or dramas—and everybody could be counted on to show up for his or her shift on time and ready to work. From what Jerry had told them about other locations in the Taco Barn chain, such productivity and reliability was rare.

At 11:05 the receptionist told Tony that Ms. Williams was ready for him and that he should go into her office. Meeting him at the door, Dawn shook his hand and asked him to take a seat.

"Tony, we've had our eye on you for a while now. Jerry tells me that you've become his right-hand man

# objectives

**After studying this chapter, you will be able to:**

**1** Define management.

**2** Identify and explain the levels of management.

**3** Explain the management process.

**4** Explain the basic principles of management.

**5** Identify the changing nature of the manager's environment.

---

at the restaurant, and he sees a great future for you with Taco Barn." Tony mumbled, "Thank you," and tried not to blush in response to the glowing praise.

"As you know," Dawn continued, "Taco Barn is a growing company, and we are always looking for locations to build new units. We built over 100 new units last year alone, and there are plans for us to start opening international units in the next few years. It's an exciting time to be with the organization, Tony."

"As we continue to grow," continued Dawn, "we need more regional managers to oversee new groups of restaurants, and new managers for both the new restaurants and the existing restaurants where managers have been promoted—and that, Tony, is where you come into the picture. Your team knows what a great job Jerry has done in building up that unit, and Taco Barn is finally recognizing that by giving him a regional management position across the other side of

the state. He and his wife will be moving to the same city as their daughter and grandkids, so it's working out well for everybody."

"Of course," Dawn continued with a broad grin on her face, "that leaves an opening for a unit manager, and both Jerry and I think you're ready for the job— what do you think?"

## QUESTIONS

1. Do you think Tony is ready for this promotion? Why or why not?

2. The team at Tony's location is performing well. Is there anything that he needs to change?

3. What skills do you think Tony will need to succeed in his new role? Refer to the 'management roles' section on page 8 for guidance here.

4. What should Tony do in his first week as manager?

# WHAT IS MANAGEMENT?

Organizations today operate in a world of constant change. Technology and society are changing more rapidly than ever before. Concern for the environment has forced companies to think about how their actions affect the quality of the air, land, and water. Competition is fiercer than ever because organizations from all over the world now try to sell their products and services to the same customers. Workplaces have become increasingly diverse, as minorities, women, and new immigrants participate in growing numbers. All these changes have created new challenges for managers.

## Defining Management

**Management** is the process of deciding the best way to use an organization's resources to produce goods or provide services. An organization's resources include its employees, equipment, and money. Although the definition is simple, the job of management is quite complex. Management must make good decisions, communicate well with people, make work assignments, delegate, plan, train people, motivate people, and appraise employees' job performance. The varied work of management is extremely difficult to master. Yet mastery of management is vital to organizational success.

## Levels of Management

All organizations, from one-person businesses to giant corporations, need managers. Small businesses may be managed by one or just a few managers. Large and medium-sized companies may have many levels of management.

## Senior Management

The highest level is known as **senior management.** Senior management has several important functions. First, it establishes the goals, or objectives, of the organization.[1] Second, it decides which actions are necessary to meet those goals. Finally, it decides how to use the organization's resources. This level of management usually includes the chairperson of the company's board of directors, the chief executive officer (CEO), the chief operating officer (COO), the chief financial officer (CFO), and the company's senior vice presidents. Senior managers are not involved in the company's day-to-day problems. Instead, they concentrate on setting the direction the company will follow.

## Middle Management

**Middle management** is responsible for meeting the goals that senior management sets. Middle managers can include department heads and district sales managers. This level of management sets goals for specific areas of the organization and decides what the employees in each area must do

Perceptions of management are changing. It is no longer inclusive to simply think of managers as powerful men sitting behind big desks.

**management**
The process of deciding the best way to use an organization's resources to produce goods or provide services.

**senior management**
The highest level of management, it establishes the goals, or objectives, of the organization, decides what actions are necessary to meet those goals, and decides how to use the organization's resources. Senior managers concentrate on setting the direction the company will follow.

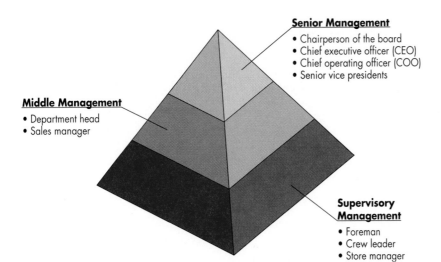

Senior Management
- Chairperson of the board
- Chief executive officer (CEO)
- Chief operating officer (COO)
- Senior vice presidents

Middle Management
- Department head
- Sales manager

Supervisory Management
- Foreman
- Crew leader
- Store manager

**figure 1.1**

THE MANAGEMENT PYRAMID

**middle management**
Responsible for implementing and achieving organizational objectives; also responsible for developing departmental objectives and actions.

**supervisory management**
Manages operative employees; generally considered the first level of management.

to meet those goals. For example, senior management might set a goal of increasing company sales by 15 percent in the next year. To meet that objective, middle management might develop a new advertising campaign for one of the organization's products or services.

## Supervisory Management

The front-line level of management is **supervisory management.** Supervisory managers make sure that the day-to-day operations of the organization run smoothly. They are in charge of the people who physically produce the organization's goods or provide its services. Forepersons, crew leaders, and store managers are all examples of supervisory managers.

Large companies usually have all three kinds of managers. At JCPenney, for example, supervisory managers run stores and departments within stores. These managers are responsible for making sure that the daily operations of the store run well. Middle managers oversee districts. These managers are responsible for making sure that all store managers within their district are performing well. Middle managers also may suggest ideas for increasing sales, improving service, or reducing costs within their districts. Senior managers include JCPenney's CEO and senior vice presidents. These managers make decisions about the company's policies, products, and organizational strategy. A decision to increase salaries throughout the company would be made by senior management, for example.

The three levels of management form a *hierarchy,* or a group ranked in order of importance. As can be seen in Figure 1.1, the management hierarchy is shaped like a pyramid, with very few senior managers at the top and many supervisory managers at the bottom. Figure 1.2 further describes the different levels of management.

JCPenney's is just one of many stores to use hierarchical management structures. What are the potential benefits and risks associated with this sort of structure?

**1. Senior Management**

Senior management is responsible for setting objectives for the organization, deciding what actions are necessary to meet them, and determining how best to use resources. This level of management usually includes the chairperson of the board of directors, the CEO, the COO, and the organization's senior vice presidents.

**2. Middle Management**

Middle management is responsible for achieving the goals set by senior management. Middle management includes department heads and district sales managers.

**3. Supervisory Management**

Supervisory management is responsible for the people who physically produce the organization's products or provide its services. Crew leaders and store managers are all examples of supervisors.

## THE MANAGEMENT PROCESS

**role**

Set of behaviors associated with a particular job.

If you are successful in your job it is very likely that you will be offered the opportunity to move up to a management position—probably in your own department at first and then to a position of managerial responsibility over more than one department. Here's where it gets tricky. Succeeding in a management role will require a lot more from you than just the skills and abilities that got you the promotion to begin with.

There are several ways to examine how management works. One way is to divide the *tasks* that managers perform into categories. A second way is to look at the *roles* that different types of managers play in a company. A **role** is a set of behaviors associated with a particular job. A third way is to look at the *skills* that managers need to do their jobs. Each of these ways of thinking about management will help you understand the management process.

### Management Tasks

Managers in all organizations—from small businesses to large companies—engage in basic activities. These activities can be divided into five categories:

**career management**

### Understanding Career Planning

*Career planning* is a process by which an individual, in assessing an opportunity, creates a career plan for the future and develops the necessary objectives, resources, and procedures to achieve a desired outcome.

This career planning spirit motivates millions of people to obtain the necessary assistance to become successful professionals in the working world.

The question is: Why would you plan, develop, and set the standards for how your career will be achieved? Think about the possibilities of your becoming a high-level executive, a small business owner, or a manager of a company you would like to work for. For this to happen, it would require a career vision to set the objectives and guidelines to reach these lofty goals. Your work now can be a huge payoff in a career where you can find great success!

1. **Planning.** A manager decides on goals and the actions the organization must take to meet them. A CEO who sets a goal of increasing sales by 10 percent in the next year by developing a new software program is engaged in planning.

2. **Organizing.** A manager groups related activities together and assigns employees to perform them. A manager who sets up a team of employees to restock an aisle in a supermarket is organizing.

3. **Staffing.** A manager decides how many and what kinds of people an organization needs to meet its goals and then recruits, selects, and trains the right people. A restaurant manager's staffing duties include interviewing and training waiters.

4. **Leading.** A manager provides the guidance employees need to perform their tasks, which helps to ensure that organizational goals are met. A manager leads by keeping the lines of communication open. Holding regular staff meetings where employees can ask questions about their projects and responsibilities is a good example of leading.

5. **Controlling.** A manager measures how the organization performs to ensure that financial goals are being met. Controlling requires a manager to analyze accounting records and to make changes if financial standards are not being met.

Many management activities overlap. Organizing, for example, is difficult without a plan. Keeping good employees on the job is difficult if a workplace is poorly organized and lacks leadership.

Figure 1.3 shows how different levels of management focus on different activities. Senior managers divide their time about equally among the five activities. Middle managers spend most of their time leading and controlling. Supervisory managers spend little time planning and a lot of time controlling.

**planning**
Process of deciding what objectives to pursue during a future time period and what to do to achieve those objectives.

**organizing**
Grouping activities, assigning activities, and providing the authority necessary to carry out the activities.

**staffing**
Determining human resource needs and recruiting, selecting, training, and developing human resources.

**leading**
Directing and channeling human behavior toward the accomplishment of objectives.

**controlling**
Measuring performance against objectives, determining the causes of deviations, and taking corrective action where necessary.

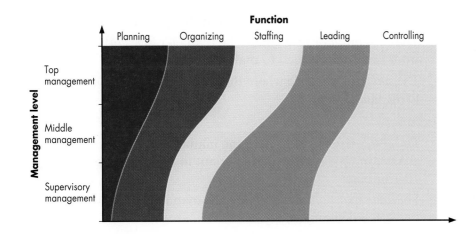

**figure 1.3**

RELATIVE AMOUNT OF EMPHASIS PLACED ON EACH FUNCTION OF MANAGEMENT

## PROGRESS CHECK QUESTIONS

1. What is management?
2. Describe the three levels of management.
3. Describe the five categories of management tasks.
4. Which of the management tasks is most important for a front-line manager? Why?

## Management Roles

Managers have authority, or power, within organizations and use it in many ways. To best use their authority, managers take on different roles. In the early 1970s Henry Mintzberg delivered a series of research reports that were based on the question: "How can management be improved and the skills of managers appropriately developed, without first understanding how managers spend their time?"

Mintzberg's research led him to identify 10 key managerial roles split into three categories (Fig. 1.4):[2]

Good managers understand the importance of the many roles they must play.

1. *Interpersonal:*
   - The *figurehead* role where the manager performs symbolic duties as head of the organization.
   - The *leader* role where he or she establishes the work atmosphere and motivates subordinates to act.
   - The *liaison* role where the manager develops and maintains networks of contacts outside the organization.

2. *Informational:*
   - The *monitor* role where the manager collects all types of information relevant and useful to the organization.
   - The *disseminator* role where the manager gives other people the information they need to make decisions.
   - The *spokesperson* role where the manager transmits information to the outside world.

3. *Decisional:*
   - The *entrepreneur* role where the manager initiates controlled change in the organization to adapt to the changing environment.
   - The *disturbance handler* where the manager deals with unexpected changes.

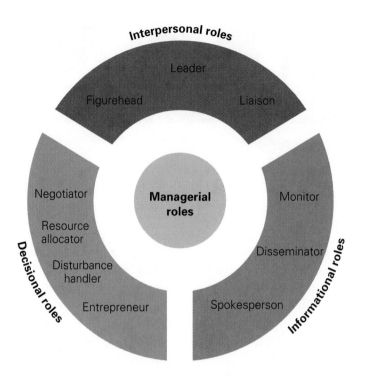

figure 1.4

MANAGEMENT ROLES

**Source:** Based on H. Mintzberg, *The Nature of Managerial Work* (New York: Harper & Row, 1973).

- The *resource allocator* role where the manager makes decisions on the use of organizational resources.
- The *negotiator* role where the manager deals with other individuals and organizations.

By spending time with five organizations and analyzing how their chief executives spent their time, Mintzberg identified one of the biggest challenges of managerial research.[3] His observations revealed that managers were more often called upon to be "in the moment" rather than focused on farsighted strategic plans. He found that their work often placed them as hostages to constant interruptions, jumping from subject to subject and problem to problem, rarely being allowed to give their undivided and uninterrupted attention to anything for any length of time.

## PROGRESS CHECK QUESTIONS

5. What are Mintzberg's three categories of managerial roles?
6. Describe and provide an example of five of the 10 managerial roles.
7. Think of a manager you work for currently (or have worked for in the past). How would you describe his or her combination of managerial roles?
8. Why are managers called upon to be 'in the moment'?

Successful managers understand the importance of balancing many skills.

**conceptual skills**

Involves understanding the relationship of the parts of a business to one another and to the business as a whole.

**human relations skills**

Are the ability to understand and work well with people. These skills enable managers to direct the social aspects of the work as well as the productivity of the work being performed.

**technical skills**

Involves being able to perform the mechanics of a particular job.

## Management Skills

A third way of looking at the management process is by examining the kinds of skills required to perform a particular job.[4] Three types of skills have been identified.

1. **Conceptual skills** are those that help managers understand how different parts of a company relate to one another and to the company as a whole. Decision making, planning, and organizing are managerial activities that require conceptual skills.

2. **Human relations skills** are those that managers need to understand and work well with people. Interviewing job applicants, forming partnerships with other companies, and resolving conflicts all require good human relations skills.

3. **Technical skills** are the specific abilities that people use to perform their jobs. Operating a word processing or financial spreadsheet program, designing a brochure, and training people to use a new budgeting system are all examples of technical skills that a manager would need to possess or train others to possess in order for the department to function effectively.

Not all management skills are easy to place in a single category. Most fall into more than one. In order to develop a company advertisement, for example, a manager must have conceptual, human relations, and technical skills. Managers would need conceptual skills to develop the advertisement's message. They would need human relations skills to assemble and motivate the team of people who would create the advertisement. Training the team by teaching them a computer graphics program would require technical skills.

All levels of management require a combination of these skills. Different skills are more important at different levels of management, as Figure 1.5 shows. Conceptual skills are most important at the senior management level. Technical skills are most important at the supervisory levels of management. Human relations skills are important at all levels of management.

## Study Skills

### Study Skills Are a Learned Behavior

What are your talents? What would you consider to be your greatest skills? Are you talented at singing, playing an instrument, playing sports, writing, painting, or renovating old cars?

Being good at studying is like anything you try: You might be better at some things than other things. Studying is a learned behavior like any engaged activity, and you can improve your study habits and performance with more practice.

Two key areas will help you become better at studying: *study preparation* and *study execution*.

Study preparation includes all the activities that help you get the most out of your reading and note taking. Study execution involves all the actions you take to stay on course to make sure you get the positive results you are seeking.

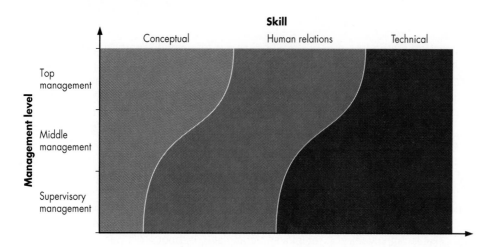

figure 1.5

MIX OF SKILLS USED AT
DIFFERENT LEVELS OF
MANAGEMENT

---

## PROGRESS CHECK QUESTIONS

9. Why is it important to understand the skills required to perform a particular job?
10. Give an example for each of the three managerial skills.
11. Find a job description for a management position from your local newspaper or a Web site such as Monster.com or CareerBuilder.com. How do the responsibilities outlined in that job description match-up to the three managerial skills?
12. Why are human relations skills important at all levels of management?

---

## THE MANAGEMENT AGREEMENT

If everything about management so far seems to be about power and responsibility, it's important to remember that a promotion to a managerial position will come with a price. You will get to do many new things, as we'll discover in later chapters, but there will also be many things that you will no longer be able to do.[5] As a manager, you will be expected to set the standard for your department and model the behavior you expect from your people. For that reason, you will no longer be able to do any of the following activities:

- Hang out with your employees as "one of the gang."
- Play favorites with your employees.
- Put yourself before them.
- Pass the buck on difficult assignments.
- Use your position to get even with your enemies.

## The Wadsworth Company

Last year, Donna Carroll was appointed supervisor of the small parts subassembly department of Wadsworth Company. The department employed 28 people. Donna had wanted the promotion and thought her 15 years of experience in various jobs at the company qualified her for the job.

Donna decided to have two group leaders report to her. She appointed Evelyn Castalos and Bill Degger to these new positions. She made it clear, however, that they retained their present operative jobs and were expected to contribute to the direct production goals of the department. Evelyn is ambitious and a highly productive employee. Bill is a steady, reliable employee.

Work assignment decisions were to be made by Evelyn. She took on this responsibility with great enthusiasm and drew up work-scheduling plans covering a period of one month. She believed productivity could be increased by 8 percent due primarily to work assignment improvements. She went regularly from workplace to workplace, checking the finished volume of work at each station. Bill assumed, at the suggestion and support of Donna, the task of training new employees or retraining present employees on new work coming into the department.

Donna spent most of her time preparing and reading reports. She made certain to be friendly with most of the other supervisors. She talked with them frequently and helped them fill out forms and reports required by their jobs. She also frequently circulated among the employees of her department, exchanging friendly remarks. However, when an employee asked a question concerning work, Donna referred the person to either Evelyn or Bill.

Some of the employees complained among themselves that the work assignments were unfair. They grumbled that favorites of Evelyn got all the easy jobs and, although the present volume of work had increased, no extra help was being hired. Several times the employees talked with Donna about this, but Donna referred them to Evelyn each time. Likewise, many of the employees complained about Bill's performance. They based their opinions on the apparent lack of knowledge and skill the new employees had after receiving training from Bill.

### Questions

1. Do you think Donna should have delegated the duties Evelyn and Bill are handling? Why or why not?
2. What difficulties do you see for Evelyn and Bill in being both group leaders and operative employees?
3. Do you consider Evelyn and Bill to be managers? Why or why not?
4. Is Donna doing the right thing in referring employee complaints back to Bill or Evelyn? Why or why not?

- Bring your personal problems to work.
- Lose your temper with your employees.
- Vent your frustrations with your boss to your employees.
- Ask others to do something that you wouldn't do.

To pursue the fulfilling and rewarding (both professionally and financially) job of a manager, you have to be willing to abide by this management agreement. As the saying goes, "with power comes responsibility," and the responsibilities of a manager can and will prevent you from doing things that you would normally prefer to do. If you get promoted from within a department as a new manager, one of the toughest challenges you can face is developing a new relationship with your former friends and colleagues who will now report to you.

## The Expansion of Blue Streak

Arthur Benton started the Blue Streak Delivery Company five years ago. Blue Streak initially provided commercial delivery services for all packages within the city of Unionville (population 1 million).

Art started with himself, one clerk, and one driver. Within three years, Blue Streak had grown to the point of requiring 4 clerks and 16 drivers. It was then that Art decided to expand and provide statewide service. He figured this would initially require the addition of two new offices, one located at Logantown (population 500,000) in the southern part of the state and one at Thomas City (population 250,000) in the northern part of the state. Each office was staffed with a manager, two clerks, and four drivers. Because both Logantown and Thomas City were within 150 miles of Unionville, Art was able to visit each office at least once a week and personally coordinate the operations in addition to providing general management assistance. The statewide delivery system met with immediate success and reported a healthy profit for the first year.

The next year, Art decided to expand and include two neighboring states. Art set up two offices in each of the two neighboring states. However, operations never seemed to go smoothly in the neighboring states. Schedules were constantly being fouled up, deliveries were lost, and customer complaints multiplied. After nine months, Art changed office managers in all four out-of-state offices. Things still did not improve. Convinced that he was the only one capable of straightening out the out-of-state offices, Art began visiting them once every two weeks. This schedule required Art to spend at least half his time on the road traveling between offices.

After four months of this activity, Art began to be get tired of the constant travel; operations in the two neighboring states still had not improved. In fact, on each trip Art found himself spending all his time putting out fires that should have been handled by the office managers.

Art decided to have a one-day meeting that all of his office managers would attend to discuss problems and come up with some answers. At the meeting, several issues were raised. First, all the managers thought Art's visits were too frequent. Second, most of the managers did not seem to know exactly what Art expected them to do. Finally, each of the managers believed he or she should have the authority to make changes in office procedures without checking with Art before making the change.

### Questions

1. Why do you think Blue Streak is struggling to grow?
2. Was it a good idea to change managers in all four out-of-state offices? Why or why not?
3. What suggestions would you offer to Art to improve his operation?
4. What management skills must Art master if he is to resolve his problems and continue to grow?

## PROGRESS CHECK QUESTIONS

13. Why is management such a difficult subject to study?
14. Why should a manager model the behavior he or she expects from his or her people?
15. Consider the list of behaviors you will have to give up to become a successful manager. Which one would be the hardest for you to give up? Why?
16. Think of your current job (or a job you have had in the past). How well does your manager abide by the "management agreement"?

# THE CHANGING NATURE OF THE MANAGER'S ENVIRONMENT

Anyone who follows the news on television, on the Web, or in a newspaper recognizes that rapid changes are occurring in lifestyles, resources, information availability, and the business environment. This section reviews some of these changes and examines their impact on management. The topics are covered in more detail in later chapters.

## Information Availability

Because of the increasing sophistication of communication systems and the rapid increase in the use of computers, new data and information are being provided at an accelerating rate. For example:

- Access to the Internet provides a wide array of information that previously was unavailable and/or difficult to obtain.
- Cell phones, e-mail, and video/teleconferencing enhance the opportunities for improved communications within businesses.
- The rapid increase in information availability increases technological change.

Increases in information availability and technological change require managers to have increased technical skills. Furthermore, these changes require more skilled and trained employees, which then increases the importance of the manager's role in training. Higher levels of skill and training require new approaches to motivation and leadership. Thus, the manager needs more skill in the human relations area.

## Attitude toward the Work Environment

Some forecasters predict that there will be more emphasis on the quality of work life in the future. The factors that can improve the quality of work life include:

1. Safe and healthy working conditions.
2. Opportunity to use and develop individual capabilities.
3. Opportunity for personal and professional growth.
4. Work schedules, career demands, and travel requirements that do not regularly take up family and leisure time.
5. The right to personal privacy, free speech, equitable treatment, and due process.

Because some of these factors fall within the scope of supervision, changes affecting them will have a direct impact on the manager's job.

Supervision of employees helps managers feel connected to their workers' personal and professional needs.

| GROUP | 1962 | 1980 | 1990 | 2000 | 2010 |
|---|---|---|---|---|---|
| Total | 40.5 | 34.6 | 36.6 | 39.3 | 40.6 |
| Men | 40.5 | 35.1 | 36.7 | 39.3 | 40.6 |
| Women | 40.4 | 33.9 | 36.4 | 39.3 | 40.6 |
| White | 40.9 | 34.8 | 36.8 | 39.7 | 41.3 |
| African American | (1) | 33.3 | 34.9 | 37.3 | 37.7 |
| Asian and other[2] | (1) | 33.8 | 36.5 | 37.8 | 38.7 |
| Hispanic origin[3] | (4) | 30.7 | 33.2 | 34.9 | 36.4 |
| White non-Hispanic | (4) | 35.0 | 37.0 | 40.4 | 42.2 |

**figure 1.6**

**MEDIAN AGES OF THE LABOR FORCE BY SEX, RACE, AND HISPANIC ORIGIN, SELECTED HISTORICAL YEARS AND PROJECTED 2010**

***Source:*** "Labor Force," *Monthly Labor Review,* November 2001, p. 36.

[1] Data not available before 1972.
[2] The "Asian and other" group includes (1) Asians and Pacific Islanders and (2) American Indians and Alaska Natives. The historic data are derived by subtracting "black" and "white" from the total; projections are made directly.
[3] Persons of Hispanic origin may be of any race.
[4] Data not available before 1980.

## Demographics

One of the more significant changes in today's environment is the increasing diversity of the American population. The latest demographic data show that the United States is becoming older and more diverse. Figure 1.6 shows the median age of the labor force by sex, race, and Hispanic origin for selected years and projected to 2010. Figure 1.7 shows the projected population by race to the year 2050. It is interesting to note that as of today Hispanics have grown to be the largest ethnic group.

## Diversity

**Diversity** in the workforce means including people of different genders, races, religions, nationalities, ethnic groups, age groups, and physical abilities. The increasing diversity of the workplace represents a major

**diversity**
Including people of different genders, races, religions, nationalities, ethnic groups, age groups, and physical abilities.

| DEMOGRAPHIC GROUP | 2010 | 2020 | 2030 | 2040 | 2050 | % CHANGE FROM 2010 to 2050 |
|---|---|---|---|---|---|---|
| White alone | 79.3 | 77.6 | 75.8 | 73.9 | 72.1 | −9.08% |
| African American alone | 13.1 | 13.5 | 13.9 | 14.3 | 14.6 | +11.45% |
| Asian alone | 4.6 | 5.4 | 6.2 | 7.1 | 8.0 | +42.5% |
| Hispanic (of any race) | 15.5 | 17.8 | 20.1 | 22.3 | 24.4 | +57.42% |
| All other races* | 3.0 | 3.5 | 4.1 | 4.7 | 5.3 | +76.67% |
| **Total** | **100.0** | **100.0** | **100.0** | **100.0** | **100.0** | |

Total % of Population

**figure 1.7**

**PROJECTED POPULATION OF THE UNITED STATES, BY DEMOGRAPHIC GROUP: 2010–2050**

***Source:*** U.S. Census Bureau, 2004, "U.S. Interim Projections by Age, Sex, Race, and Hispanic Origin," Internet Release Date: March 18, 2004.

*Includes American Indian and Alaska Native alone. Native Hawaiian and Other Pacific Islander alone, and two or more races.

Inequities in management exist for a variety of reasons. What can be done to address this issue?

**glass ceiling**

Refers to a level within the managerial hierarchy beyond which very few women and minorities advance.

**business ethics**

The application of standards of moral behavior to business situations - in other words, 'doing the right thing' in a business transaction.

social change in the United States. For many years, the managers of most large- and medium-sized U.S. organizations were almost exclusively white males. As recently as the 1960s and 1970s, women in the workforce filled primarily service and support roles, acting as secretaries, teachers, sales-clerks, and waitresses, for in-stance. Many minority workers were confined to menial jobs, such as custodial work and man-ual labor. In the last two decades of the twentieth century, however, more and more women and mi-norities joined the workforce. They also attained positions as high-level managers in organiza-tions of all sizes. Furthermore, they presently serve in senior-level management jobs in the federal, state, and local governments.

Despite these changes, most senior managers in the country are still white males. The problems women and minorities have had winning promotions to senior management positions has given rise to the term **glass ceiling,** which is the invisible barrier that prevents women and minorities from moving up in the organizational hierarchy.

## Business Ethics

**Business ethics** involves the application of standards of moral behavior to business situations—in other words, "doing the right thing" in a business transaction. In recent years, the increasing number of widely publicized business scandals—Enron, WorldCom, Tyco, HealthSouth, Adelphia Cable, and many others—has brought the issue of ethical business management to the top of the list of concerns for employees, customers, suppliers, and investors. Now, when looking at a company, they're not only looking at the quality of the product or service the company delivers but also asking whether the financial reports really reflect what is going on inside the company.

For managers, this new level of examination is now legally enforced through the Sarbanes-Oxley Act of 2002, which greatly increased the responsibilities managers must carry in accurately reporting on how the company is performing. In addition, many large organizations have added a new position to their senior management team—chief ethics officer—to ensure that the organization operates in an ethical manner.

You are a tech-support specialist for a small computer software manufacturer. Your supervisor informs you that a bug has been found in the software that will take several weeks to fix. You are instructed to "handle" all calls without admitting the existence of the bug. Specific examples are provided to "fob off" the customer with suggestions of user error and concerns about hardware problems and conflicts with other software packages. The bug, you are told, will be fixed in a scheduled version upgrade without any admission of its existence. Could you do that?

***Source:*** Andrew Ghillyer, *Business Ethics: A Real World Approach* (New York: McGraw-Hill, 2007), Chapter 1, p. 14.

In recognition of the increased emphasis on business ethics, each chapter will include an Ethical Management scenario for you to consider and discuss.

## CONCLUSION

The world of a business manager can be challenging and is without doubt constantly changing. In the next chapter, we look at how the job of management has developed over the years and how researchers have tried to build models of management behavior to help organizations and their employees better understand what it takes to be an effective manager.

MetLife is so committed to ethics in business that they agreed to be sole sponsor of the 2007 American Business Ethics Award (ABEA). How might this action be considered a reaction to the unethical management displayed by Andrew Fastow and others?

**MetLife**®

# Tony gets some advice

Tony's manager, Jerry Smith, was waiting for him when he got back to the restaurant. "So, how are you doing, son?" asked Jerry. "Has it sunk in yet?"

"Not really," said Tony. "I really appreciate your confidence in me, Jerry, and I want you to know that I won't let you down."

"I know," said Jerry, who paused for a moment and then continued, "While you were gone, I received a call from corporate—there's been a change of plan. The company needs me to start in my new region at the beginning of next week instead of next month, as we originally planned, so you and I only have this week to manage the transition from me to you as the new manager.

"You'll be able to reach me on my cell phone," Jerry said, reacting to the surprise in Tony's eyes, "but my new region has some challenges so I'll be pretty busy. Dawn Williams will be your boss now, and she'll be there to help you too."

"Let's talk about staffing," continued Jerry. "I'll go over the payroll paperwork with you tomorrow. It hasn't changed much since you covered for my vacation earlier this year, so you should be okay there. I'm more concerned about the schedule." Jerry paused and took a deep breath, "because Tanya gave her two weeks notice this morning while you were at your meeting with Dawn."

"What?" shouted Tony, not believing what he was hearing. "She's our most experienced shift leader, our best trainer, and she's the best closer we've got. Why is she leaving? Can we persuade her to stay?"

"Believe me, son, if there was a way to keep her, I would have done it," said Jerry, "but her husband just got offered a new job out of state, and they're moving in a couple of weeks. So we need to find a replacement for Tanya ASAP and then decide who she's going to train to take over her responsibilities over the next two weeks."

"Okay," said Tony, trying very hard to treat this bombshell like it was an everyday thing for the manager of a Taco Barn, "that sounds like a plan. What else do we have going on with the schedule?"

"Well," continued Jerry, "don't forget that the schools go back in a couple of weeks and the new athletic schedules will start, so some of the kids—Matt, William, Paul, Kate, Susan, Jennifer, Megan, and others—will want to cut back their hours and change their shifts so that they can make it to their practice, and meets. The good news is you have some good applications on hand, but you'll need to start interviewing right away so that you can get these new people trained up and ready to go."

"Okay," said Tony absentmindedly. He was already thinking about how he was going to get all these replacements trained after his best trainer had left. "What else?"

"That about covers the schedule," said Jerry, "so let's move on to the new menu items that the company is launching."

## QUESTIONS

1. What do you think the team's reaction to Tony's promotion will be?

2. Do you think a week will be enough time for Tony to get all the information from Jerry that he needs to run the restaurant? Why or why not?

3. What else can Jerry do to better prepare Tony for success in his new role?

4. If you were in Tony's shoes, what would you do now?

## key terms

| | | |
|---|---|---|
| **business ethics**  16 | **leading**  7 | **senior management**  4 |
| **conceptual skills**  10 | **management**  4 | **staffing**  7 |
| **controlling**  7 | **middle management**  5 | **supervisory management**  5 |
| **diversity**  15 | **organizing**  7 | |
| **glass ceiling**  16 | **planning**  7 | **technical skills**  10 |
| **human relations skills**  10 | **role**  6 | |

## review questions

1. Management has often been described as a universal process, meaning the basics of management are transferable and applicable in almost any environment. Do you believe a good manager in a bank could be equally effective in a college or university? Explain your reasoning.

2. How does one decide who is and who is not a manager in a given organization? For example, is the operator of a one-person business, such as a corner grocery store, a manager? Explain.

3. Do you think management can be learned through books and study or only through experience?

4. Consider your own personality, skills, and work experience. Do you think you would make a good manager? Why or why not?

## internet exercise

Visit the Web site for the American Management Association (www. amanet.org). Find a course on supervisory skills, and summarize the content of that course: What does the training include? What is the training designed to do for the skills of the course participants?

## team exercise

Divide into groups of two or three. Select a managerial policy change from the list on p. 20, and prepare the following:

1. A formal memo to be sent to all employees as an e-mail notifying them of the change in policy.

2. A 15-minute presentation to be delivered to key staff members (in this case your fellow students), outlining the reasons for the policy change and what the expected results will be.

**Policy Change Topics**

- The company on-site day care center is being closed to reduce costs.
- Parking spaces in the front of the building are now reserved for senior managers only. Employees must now park at the far end of the parking lot.
- Effective immediately, the entire company will be a nonsmoking area. No designated smoking areas will be provided.
- The company health gym will be closed immediately because no one is using it.
- The office cafeteria is being closed to make room for more office space.
- Access to the building is being restricted to employees only. Family and friends will now need to be signed in and issued visitor badges.

## For UPS Managers, a School of Hard Knocks

*Execs Share the Kind of Gritty Life Experiences of Some Workers*

At United Parcel Service Inc., rules are not to be broken. Without them, UPS could never move 13.5 million packages to their destinations on time each day. But two years ago, Mark J. Colvard, a UPS manager in San Ramon, Calif., had to decide whether or not to break one of those rules. A driver needed time off to help a sick family member, but under company rules he wasn't entitled to any time off. If Colvard went by the book, the driver would probably take the days anyway and be fired. If Colvard gave him the time off, he would catch flak from his other drivers. Colvard wound up giving the driver two weeks, took some heat for it, and kept

a valuable employee. Six months earlier, Colvard admits, he would have gone the other way.

What changed his approach? A month he spent living among migrant farmers in McAllen, Tex., as part of an unusual UPS management training experience called the Community Internship Program (CIP). After building housing for the poor, collecting clothing for the Salvation Army, and working in a drug rehab center, Colvard said he was able to identify with employees facing crises back home. And that, he says, has made him a better manager. "My goal

was to make the numbers, and in some cases that meant not looking at the person but looking at the bottom line," says Colvard. "After that one-month stay, I immediately started reaching out to people in a different way."

CIP began in 1968 as the brainchild of UPS founder James Casey, who wanted to open up the eyes of UPS's mainly white managers to the poverty and inequality exploding into violence in many cities. By now, nearly 1,200 current and former middle managers have moved through the program. And it has developed into an essential part of the UPS tradition, teaching managers the crucial skill of flexibility at a company that is trying to fit a diverse base of employees into its rigid rules-based culture, which prescribes everything from how delivery people should carry their keys to how many steps they should take per second.

UPS needs rules, but it also needs managers capable of bending them when necessary. "We've got 330,000 U.S. employees," says Don B. Wofford, the CIP coordinator and a graduate of the program. "There are all kinds of personalities and all kinds of diversity. We need managers who can manage those individuals."

**21**

Therefore, each summer UPS plucks 50 of its most promising executives from the company's 2,400 managers and brings them to cities across the country, where UPS partners arrange for daily community service projects aiding local populations. The problems encountered there—from transportation to housing, education, and health care—are the kinds of issues many UPS employees confront every day. By forcing managers to grapple with the same problems, UPS hopes to open their eyes to the difficulties many of their employees face, bridging the cultural divide that separates a white manager from an African-American driver or an upper-income suburbanite from a worker raised in the rural South. This is a necessity for UPS, where minorities—many from poor neighborhoods—make up 35 percent of the workforce and 52 percent of new hires. Three out of four managers, meanwhile, are white.

In 34 years, UPS has never scaled back the program, even during the cost cutting that accompanied September's terrorist attacks or the Teamsters strike in 1997. Excluding the cost of paying managers' salaries throughout the program, UPS's costs now amount to $10,000 per intern, or $13 million since CIP's inception. UPS concedes that it has no concrete evidence that the program works. But managers who have been through the UPS program say it made them more likely to search for unconventional solutions. Patti Hobbs, a division manager in Louisville who spent a month on New York's Lower East Side in 1998, remembers being impressed by the creative ideas of uneducated addicts for steering teens away from drugs. Realizing that the best solutions sometimes come from those closest to the problem, she immediately started brainstorming with the entire staff instead of just senior managers. Says Hobbs: "You start to think there's no one person, regardless of position, who has all the answers. The answers come from us all." One month living among the poor won't change the world. But it might help UPS managers see their employees as more than just a cog in a very efficient machine.

### Questions

1. Do you think other companies could benefit from programs like the Community Internship Program? Why or why not?

2. "UPS concedes that it has no concrete evidence that the program works." Why would a cost-conscious organization like UPS continue to fund this $13 million program without concrete evidence of its effectiveness?

3. What do you think the managers gain from participating in the CIP?

4. How would you implement a program like the CIP in your current job (or a job you have had in the past)? Provide specific evidence of the kinds of opportunities you would introduce and what the likely reaction of your fellow employees would be.

*Source:* Adapted from Louis Lavelle, "Management," *BusinessWeek Online,* July 22, 2002.

## New on the Job: Rookie Flubs

*The First Year Brings High Expectations That Can Quickly Deflate If You Make Some of These Beginner's Mistakes*

Few times in a young person's life are as stressful as the first year out of college. If all goes well, you land a dream job in your chosen profession. But now everything hangs in the balance. Do well in your rookie job, and it could put your career into overdrive. Your employer may shower you with promotions, pay raises, and increased responsibility, and you'll be able to leapfrog ahead of the competition in your next position. Do poorly, and you may be sent down to the minors. The good news: Barring any serious violations, relatively few people get completely sidetracked in their first year on the job, as most employers allow for a learning curve. The bad news is the reputation you make for yourself will be yours for a good long time—the corporate equivalent of your permanent academic record—coloring the way people see you for many years. Rookie mistakes are hard to avoid, but easy to learn from. Here's some advice to keep you sailing straight.

**Missing Face-time:** Face-time is your no. 1 prority. You want to do your job well, but almost as important as superior performance is making sure your superiors know you're working at the top of your game, and that's not always easy. One way to ensure this happens is to choose your assignments carefully. Pick projects that put you in contact with people who will add to your network and advance your career. Don't bury yourself in a long-term assignment where people can lose sight of you. Choose high-visibility projects where your strengths will shine. However, visibility is an advantage only if you have a unique skill that sets you apart from your peers. So spend some time assessing yourself and the competition.

**Tuning Out:** You probably networked your way in; now network your way up. Internal networking raises visibility, connects you with mentors, and gives you a deeper understanding of company culture and the needs of your employer that you can fill. This doesn't have to be complicated.

Identify someone high up in the corporate food chain who you don't normally interact with—your boss's boss, for instance—and talk to him about anything, from corporate goings-on to baseball scores. Stay behind at meetings to chat up the powers-that-be. Or volunteer to sit on a corporate committee or task force.

**Playing Prima Donna:** HR personnel weren't impressed with the young new recruit who called up complaining that the project he was put on was "too boring" and that he wanted off. He was immediately advised to "suck it up and be happy you're not getting coffee" by a senior manager at the company. Sticking with a job that may not be stellar at first is still worth your time. Besides visibility and experience, hanging tough through a job you don't want shows long-term commitment and puts you in a better position to land an assignment you do want.

**Dissing Support Staff:** Sheila Curran, the executive director of Duke University's Career Center, recalls a student who was called back for a second interview but wasn't hired because she was "dismissive" to the receptionist. The same kind of land mines lie in wait for new hires in their first year on the job. "Students don't realize that everyone from the people in the recruiting office to the person managing their on-site interview schedule may have a relationship that can help or hurt them, depending on how they're treated," Curran says.

**Overdoing It:** Show 'em what you're made of, but don't overreach. A better strategy for making a good first impression is to work on smaller projects that will allow you to exceed expectations. Volunteer to take over a project from a colleague who hands in a mediocre performance every year. He'll probably be grateful, and with a modest investment of your time you can do a far better job. Better yet, propose a new way of doing something that saves time or resources, expands the market for an existing product or service, or in some other way affects the bottom line. Even if your boss doesn't buy it, you just earned brownie points: You're now the person with all the bright ideas.

**Watching The Clock:** The big shots at your new company get to leave early for the beach on summer weekends, take two-hour lunches, and spend the afternoon on the golf course. But for mere mortals, the road to success is almost always paved with long hours and hard work. That means getting in early, leaving late, and eating lunch at your desk if necessary. Getting in before your boss and leaving after she does, if only by five minutes, is never a bad idea. If nothing else, it leaves her with the impression that you're devoted to your job. As with anything, there's a point at which working excessively long hours is counterproductive. If you've got very little on your plate, and you're still working an 80-hour week, you're no longer devoted to your job; you're incapable of managing your time, and possibly incompetent. As first impressions go, that's not a very a good one.

## Questions

1. Which of these six tips made the greatest impact on you? Why?

2. Which of these six tips made the least impact on you? Why?

3. Could you apply these tips in your current job (or a job you have held in the past)? Why or why not?

4. What other suggestions would you add to this list of recommendations for new hires?

***Source:*** Adapted from Paula Lehman, *BusinessWeek Online*, September 18, 2006.

# A BRIEF HISTORY OF MANAGEMENT

**"Those who cannot learn from history are doomed to repeat it."**

—George Santayana

## The World of Work: Tony considers his style

On the way home from the restaurant—soon to be *his* restaurant, Tony thought—the news of his promotion finally started to sink in. Jerry's promotion to regional manager didn't give either of them a lot of time to manage the transition, so the day had been filled with a lot of information—forms, rules, regulations, guidelines, and plenty of tips and tricks from Jerry on how to cope with the unexpected.

In the peace and quiet of his apartment, Tony started thinking back to his earlier days at the Taco Barn and to the many lessons he had learned from both Jerry and Dawn. They were very different in their approach to their jobs. Dawn was all about the numbers.

Whenever she visited the restaurant, she and Jerry would always end up huddled in one of the corner booths over her laptop screen or a spreadsheet printout discussing numbers—food costs, labor costs, and the figures for the latest marketing campaign to increase sales. Dawn always ended her visit by walking around and checking in with everyone to make sure they were doing okay. Since Jerry ran such a good crew, there were never any problems, but Tony wondered what Dawn's reaction would have been if she had found any.

Jerry's style always seemed to Tony to be more about the people than the numbers. He obviously hit

# LEARNING objectives

**After studying this chapter, you will be able to:**

**1** Explain the role of the Industrial Revolution in the development of managerial thought and identify the captains of industry and their role in management's evolution.

**2** Define scientific management, and outline the role Frederick W. Taylor played in its development.

**3** Identify and explain the human relations movement.

**4** Explain the systems approach.

**5** Explain the differences between Theory X, Theory Y, and Theory Z.

**6** Define the contingency approach to management.

**7** Explain the concepts of the search for excellence and the emphasis on quality.

**8** Understand what is required for an organization to move from good to great.

---

the financial targets that he needed to; otherwise he wouldn't have kept his job, thought Tony, but Jerry was always taking the time to work with his staff. He was hardly ever in his office—not that you could call the broom closet in the back of the kitchen an office. Jerry was always out in the kitchen working with the chefs or in the dining room, working with the servers before opening and checking on customers once the restaurant was open.

Tony suddenly realized that he would have to establish his own style of management now that he would be in charge of the restaurant. He had filled in for Jerry when he was on vacation a couple of times, but then he was really just minding the store until Jerry came back. This time was different—Tony was the manager now, and he wondered what kind of manager he should be.

**QUESTIONS**

1. Why should Tony be concerned about establishing his own style of management in the Taco Barn?

2. Which management style do you like better—Jerry's or Dawn's? Why?

3. Do you think Tony will choose Jerry's style or Dawn's? Why?

4. If you are currently in a management role, how would you describe your style? If you are working toward a management position, do you think you would be more like Dawn or Jerry? Why?

# THE HISTORY OF MANAGEMENT

Knowledge of the history of any subject is necessary to understanding where the subject came from, where it is now, and where it is going. Management is no exception. For example, how often have you read a news story covering a particular incident and formed an opinion only to change it when you understood the events leading up to the incident? Many of today's managerial problems began during the early management movement. Understanding the historical evolution of these problems helps the modern manager cope with them. It also helps today's managers develop a feel for why the managerial approaches that worked in earlier times do not necessarily work today. The challenge to present and future managers is not to memorize historical names and dates; it is to develop a feel for why and how things happened and to apply this knowledge to the practice of management.

Some forms of management have existed since the beginning of time. Ever since one human tried to direct another, management thought has been developing. The development of management as we know it is a relatively modern concept. The age of industrialization in the nineteenth century and the subsequent emergence of large corporate organizations called for new approaches to management.

# U.S. INDUSTRIAL REVOLUTION

**Industrial Revolution**

Starting in 1860, the U.S. Industrial Revolution encompassed the period when the United States began to shift from an almost totally farming-based society to an industrialized society.

As the name suggests, the U.S. **Industrial Revolution** encompassed the period when the United States began to shift from an almost totally farming-based society to an industrialized society. The year 1860 is generally thought of as the start of the Industrial Revolution in this country.

Daniel Wren has described the Industrial Revolution in America as having three components : power, transportation, and communication.[1] Many new inventions, such as the steam engine, allowed industries to expand and locate in areas that at one time were completely lacking in factories and other signs of progress. Industry was no longer dependent on water and horses for its power.

Transportation moved through periods of industrial and commercial traffic on canals, railroads, and eventually efficient road systems. However, progress always brings its own set of unique problems. Communication lines were extended, decisions had to be made within a rapidly changing framework, scheduling difficulties arose, and new markets developed. All these changes required new management skills.

Communication by way of the telegraph, telephone, and radio changed the way U.S. organizations functioned. Speed and efficiency dramatically increased. The trend away from an agricultural society forced many behavioral changes on the workers of the land. Schedules, work tasks, workloads, compensation, and safety were hotly debated issues well into the twentieth century.

# CAPTAINS OF INDUSTRY

Once industrialization began, it continued at a rapid pace. By the end of the nineteenth century, the economy had shifted from being mainly agricultural to being heavily involved with manufactured goods and industrial markets.[2]

John D. Rockefeller, James B. Duke, Andrew Carnegie and Cornelius Vanderbilt were the original *captains of industry.* Their collective contributions helped shape how we view business today.

During the last quarter of the nineteenth century, American business was dominated and shaped by captains of industry. These included John D. Rockefeller (oil), James B. Duke (tobacco), Andrew Carnegie (steel), and Cornelius Vanderbilt (steamships and railroads). In contrast to the nonjudgmental attitudes of previous generations, these individuals often pursued profit and self-interest above all else. Although their methods have been questioned, they did obtain results. Under these individuals, giant companies were formed through mergers in both the consumer and producer goods industries. They created new forms of organizations and introduced new methods of marketing. For the first time, nationwide distributing and marketing organizations were formed. The birth of the corporate giant also altered the business decision-making environment.

For the empire building and methods of the captains of industry, previous management approaches no longer applied. Government began to regulate business. In 1890, the Sherman Antitrust Act, which sought to check corporate practices "in restraint of trade," was passed.

By 1890, previous management methods were no longer applicable to U.S. industry. No longer could managers make on-the-spot decisions and maintain records in their heads. Corporations had become large scale, with national markets. Communication and transportation had expanded and spurred great industrial growth. Technological innovations contributed to industrial growth: The invention of the internal combustion engine and the use of electricity as a power source greatly increased industrial development at the close of the nineteenth century.

However, despite what seemed to be an ideal climate for prosperity and productivity, wages were low.[3] Production methods were crude, and worker training was almost nonexistent. There were no methods or standards for measuring work. Work had not been studied to determine the most desirable way to complete a task. The psychological and physical aspects of a job such as boredom, repetitiveness, and fatigue were not studied or even considered in the design of most jobs.

At this point in the development of management, the engineering profession made significant contributions. Engineers designed, built, installed, and made operative the production systems. It was only natural, then, for them to study the methods used in operating these systems.

## PROGRESS CHECK QUESTIONS

1. Explain why management did not emerge as a recognized discipline until the twentieth century.
2. Describe the three key components of the U.S. Industrial Revolution.
3. Who were the four leading captains of industry during this period?
4. What role did the captains of industry play in the development of modern organizations?

# SCIENTIFIC MANAGEMENT AND FREDERICK WINSLOW TAYLOR

The development of specialized tasks and of departments within organizations had come with the rapid industrial growth and the creation of big business. One person no longer performed every task but specialized in performing only a few tasks. This created a need to coordinate, integrate, and systematize the workflow. The time spent on each item could be significant if a company was producing several thousand items. Increased production plus the new need for integrating and systematizing the workflow led engineers to begin studying workflows and job content.

The spark generally credited with igniting the interest of engineers in general business problems was a paper presented in 1886 by Henry Towne, president of the Yale and Towne Manufacturing Company, to the American Society of Mechanical Engineers. Towne stressed that engineers should be concerned with the financial and profit orientations of the business as well as their traditional technical responsibilities.[4] A young mechanical engineer named Frederick Winslow Taylor was seated in the audience. Towne's talk sparked an idea in Taylor's mind for studying problems at Midvale Steel Company. During his years at Midvale, Taylor worked with and observed production workers at all levels. It did not take him long to figure out that many workers put forth less than 100 percent effort. Taylor referred to this tendency to restrict output as **soldiering.**

Taylor quickly saw that workers had little or no reason to produce more; most wage systems of that time were based on attendance and position. Piece-rate systems had been tried before but generally failed because of poor use and weak standards. Taylor believed a piece-rate system would work if the workers believed the standard had been fairly set and management would stick to that standard. Taylor wanted to use scientific and empirical methods rather than tradition and custom for setting work standards. Taylor's efforts became the true beginning of what would become known as **scientific management.**

Scientific management, as developed by Taylor, was based on four main principles:

- *The development of a scientific method of designing jobs to replace the old rule-of-thumb methods.* This involved gathering, classifying, and tabulating data to arrive at the "one best way" to perform a task or a series of tasks.

Timekeeping was fundamental to Frederick Winslow Taylor's theories on management.

**soldiering**

Describes the actions of employees who intentionally restrict output.

**scientific management**

Philosophy of Frederick W. Taylor that sought to increase productivity and make the work easier by scientifically studying work methods and establishing standards.

- *The scientific selection and progressive teaching and development of employees.* Taylor saw the value of matching the job to the worker. He also emphasized the need to study worker strengths and weaknesses and to provide training to improve employee performance.
- *The bringing together of scientifically selected employees and scientifically developed methods for designing jobs.* Taylor believed that new and scientific methods of job design should not merely be put before an employee; they should also be fully explained by management. He believed employees would show little resistance to changes in methods if they understood the reasons for the changes and saw a chance for greater earnings for themselves.
- *A division of work resulting in interdependence between management and workers.* Taylor believed if they were truly dependent on each other, cooperation would naturally follow.[5]

For both management and employees, scientific management brought a new attitude toward their respective duties and toward each other.[6] It was a new philosophy about the use of human effort. It emphasized maximum output with minimum effort through the elimination of waste and inefficiency at the operational level of the organization.[7] A methodological approach was used to study job tasks. This approach included research and experimentation methods (scientific methods). Standards were set in the areas of personnel, working conditions, equipment, output, and procedures.

The managers planned the work; the employees performed it. The result was closer cooperation between managers and employees.

The scientific study of work also emphasized specialization and division of labor. Thus, the need for an organizational framework became more and more apparent. The concepts of line and staff emerged. In an effort to motivate employees, wage incentives were developed in most scientific management programs. Once standards were set, managers began to monitor actual performance and compare it with the standards. Thus began the managerial function of control.

Scientific management is a philosophy about the relationship between people and work, not a technique or an efficiency device. Taylor's ideas and scientific management were based on a concern not only for the proper design of the job but also for the worker. This aspect has often been misunderstood. Taylor and scientific management were (and still are) attacked as being inhumane and aimed only at increasing output. In this regard, scientific management and Taylor were the targets of a congressional investigation in 1912.[8]

## Study Skills

### Rate Your Study Skills

Consider the following areas:

- Study knowledge (understanding the many approaches to good study habits).
- Study preparation (utilizing all the tools to get the most out of studying).
- Study execution (transforming all the techniques and skills into maximizing your results, usually shown by consistently getting good grades).

Based on the above, how would you rate your skills in these areas? Give yourself a grade:

- Study knowledge _____
- Study preparation _____
- Study execution _____

How does your report card look? Stay tuned.

The key to Taylor's thinking was that he saw scientific management as benefiting management and employees equally: Management could achieve more work in a given amount of time; the employee could produce more—and hence earn more—with little or no additional effort. In summary, Taylor and other scientific management pioneers believed employees could be motivated by economic rewards, provided those rewards were related to individual performance.

## Other Scientific Management Pioneers

Several followers and colleagues of Taylor helped to promote scientific management. *Henry Lawrence Gantt* worked with Taylor at both Midvale Steel and later at Bethlehem Steel. Gantt is best known for his work in production control and his invention of the Gantt chart, which is still in use today. The Gantt chart graphically depicts both expected and completed production. Gantt was also one of the first management pioneers to state publicly the social responsibility of management and business. He believed the community would attempt to take over business if the business system neglected its social responsibilities.[9]

    *Frank and Lillian Gilbreth* were important to the early management movement both as a husband-and-wife team and as individuals. The Gilbreths, inspired by Taylor and scientific research, were among the first to use motion picture films to study hand and body movements to eliminate wasted motion. Frank Gilbreth's major area of interest was the study of motions and work methods. Lillian Gilbreth's primary field was psychology. Following Frank's untimely death in 1924 (he was in his mid-50s), Lillian continued their work for almost 50 years until her death in 1972. During this time, Lillian's work emphasized concern for the worker, and she showed how scientific management should foster rather than stifle employees. Because of her many achievements (see Figure 2.1), Lillian Gilbreth became known as the First Lady of Management. By combining **time and motion study** and psychology, the Gilbreths contributed greatly to research in the areas of fatigue, boredom, and morale.

## Fayol's Theory of Management

Henri Fayol, a Frenchman, was the first to issue a complete statement on a theory of general management. Though popular in Europe in the early 1900s, the theory did not really gain acceptance in America until the late 1940s. Today, Fayol's greatest contribution is considered to be his theory of management principles and elements. Fayol identified the following 14 principles of management:

Lillian Gilbreth, the First Lady of Management, spent over 50 years of her life emphasizing concern for the worker and showing how scientific management should foster rather than stifle employees.

**time and motion study**
In order to find the 'one best way' to perform a task, Frederick Winslow Taylor began to measure individual tasks within jobs–measuring both the time taken to do the task and observing the motions involved. This area of research has since been incorporated into *ergonomics*.

**figure 2.1**

**LILLIAN M. GILBRETH:
FIRST LADY OF
MANAGEMENT**

*Source:* From Daniel A. Wren,
*Evolution of Management
Thought,* 4/e, 1994, p. 143.
Reprinted with permission of
John Wiley & Sons, Inc.

- First female member of the Society of Industrial Engineers (1921).
- First female member of the American Society of Mechanical Engineers.
- First female selected to attend the National Academy of Engineering.
- First woman to receive the degree of Honorary Master of Engineering (University of Michigan).
- First female professor of management at an engineering school (Purdue University, 1935).
- First female professor of management at Newark College of Engineering.
- First and only female recipient of the Gilbreth Medal (1931).
- First female awarded the Gantt Gold Medal.
- First and only recipient of the CIOS Gold Medal.
- Received over 20 honorary degrees and served five U.S. presidents as an adviser.

*Division of work:* Concept of specialization of work.

*Authority:* Formal (positional) authority versus personal authority.

*Discipline:* Based on obedience and respect.

*Unity of command:* Each employee should receive orders from only one superior.

*Unity of direction:* One boss and one plan for a group of activities having the same objective.

*Subordination of individual interests to the general interest:* A plea to abolish the tendency to place individual interest ahead of the group interest.

*Remuneration:* The mode of payment of wages was dependent on many factors.

*Centralization:* The degree of centralization desired depended on the situation and the formal communication channels.

*Scalar chain* (line of authority): Shows the routing of the line of authority and formal communication channels.

*Order:* Ensured a place for everything.

*Equity:* Resulted from kindness and justice.

*Stability of tenured personnel:* Called for orderly personnel planning.

*Initiative:* Called for individual zeal and energy in all efforts.

*Esprit de corps:* Stressed the building of harmony and unity within the organization.

Fayol developed his list of principles from the practices he had used most often in his own work. He used them as general guidelines for effective management but stressed flexibility in their application to allow for different and changing circumstances.

## Granddad's Company

J.R.V. Company, which manufactures industrial tools, was founded in 1905 by James R. Vail Sr. Currently, James R. Vail Jr. is the president of the company; his son Richard is executive vice president. James Jr. has run the company for the past 30 years in a fashion very similar to that of his father.

When the company was founded, James Sr. had been a big supporter of scientific management. He had organized the work very scientifically with the use of time and motion studies to determine the most efficient method of performing each job. As a result, most jobs at J.R.V. were highly specialized and relied on a high degree of division of labor. In addition, there was always a heavy emphasis on putting people in jobs that were best suited for them and then providing adequate training. Most employees are paid on a piece-rate incentive system, with the standards set by time and motion studies. James Jr. has largely continued to emphasize scientific management since he took over. All employees now receive two weeks of paid vacation and company insurance. Also, employees are generally paid an average wage for their industry. The present J.R.V. building was constructed in 1920, but it has had several minor improvements, such as the addition of fluorescent lighting and an employee lunchroom.

James Jr. is planning to retire in a few years. Recently, he and Richard, his planned successor, have disagreed over the management of the company. Richard's main argument is that times have changed and time and motion studies, specialization, high division of labor, and other company practices are obsolete. James Jr. counters that J.R.V. has been successful under its present management philosophy for many years and change would be "foolish."

### Questions

1. Do you agree with Richard? Why or why not?
2. Are the principles of scientific management applicable in today's organization? Explain your answer.
3. What are James Jr.'s reasons for keeping things the way they are?
4. What kind of changes do you think Richard would like to make?

---

Fayol's real contribution, however, was not the 14 principles themselves but his formal recognition and combination of these principles. In presenting his principles of management, Fayol was probably the first to outline what today are called the **functions of management.** In essence, he identified planning, organizing, commanding, coordinating, and controlling as elements of management. He most heavily emphasized planning and organizing because he viewed these elements as essential to the other functions. Recent translations and interpretations of some of Fayol's very early papers have further reinforced the fact that Fayol was ahead of his time in recognizing the role of administration (management) in determining the success of an organization.[10]

The works of Taylor and Fayol are essentially complementary. Both believed proper management of personnel and other resources is the key to organizational success. Both used a scientific approach to management. The major difference is in their orientation. Taylor stressed the management of work, whereas Fayol emphasized the management of organization.

**functions of management**

Fayol's summary of the key responsibilities of a manager - planning, organizing, commanding, coordinating, and controlling.

**PROGRESS CHECK QUESTIONS**

5. Define scientific management.
6. What were Taylor's four main principles of scientific management?
7. List Fayol's 14 principles.
8. Explain Fayol's five functions of management.

## THE HUMAN RELATIONS MOVEMENT

The Great Depression of 1929–32 saw unemployment in excess of 25 percent. Afterward, unions sought and gained major advantages for the working class. In this period, known as the Golden Age of Unionism, legislatures and courts actively supported organized labor and the worker. The general climate tended to emphasize understanding employees and their needs (as opposed to focusing on the methods used to conduct work). Figure 2.2 summarizes several of the most important pro-union laws passed during the 1920s and 1930s. A major research project, known as the Hawthorne studies, is generally recognized as igniting the interest of business in the human element of the workplace.[11]

### The Hawthorne Studies

The Hawthorne studies began in 1924 when the National Research Council of the National Academy of Sciences began a project to define the relationship between physical working conditions and worker productivity. The Hawthorne plant of Western Electric in Cicero, Illinois, was the study site. First, the researchers lowered the level of lighting, expecting productivity to decrease. To their astonishment, productivity increased. Over the next several months, the researchers repeated the experiment by testing many different levels of lighting and other variables. Regardless of the level of light, output was found to increase.

Baffled by the results, in early 1927 the researchers called in a team of psychologists from Harvard University led by Elton

Cicero, Illinois, home of the Hawthorne Plant of Western Electric, was the backdrop for studies that would revolutionize the interaction between management and employees.

| Railway Labor Act of 1926 | Gave railway workers the right to form unions and engage in collective bargaining; established a corresponding obligation for employers to recognize and collectively bargain with the union. |
| Norris–La Guardia Act of 1932 | Severely restricted the use of injunctions to limit union activity. |
| National Labor Relations Act of 1935 (Wagner Act) | Resulted in full, enforceable rights of employees to join unions and to engage in collective bargaining with their employer, who was legally obligated to do so. |
| Fair Labor Standards Act of 1938 | Established minimum wages and required that time-and-a-half be paid for hours worked over 40 in one week. |

**figure 2.2**

SIGNIFICANT PRO-UNION LEGISLATION DURING THE 1920s AND 1930s

Mayo. Over the next five years, hundreds of experiments were run involving thousands of employees. In these experiments, the researchers altered such variable elements as wage payments, rest periods, and length of workday. The results were similar to those obtained in the lighting experiments: Production increased, but with no obvious relationship to the environment. After much analysis, the researchers concluded that other factors besides the physical environment affected worker productivity. They found that employees reacted to the psychological and social conditions at work, such as informal group pressures, individual recognition, and participation in decision making.

The researchers also discovered that the employees responded positively to the attention paid to them by the researchers. This phenomenon has since become known as the **Hawthorne effect.** Yet another finding was the significance of effective supervision to both productivity and employee morale. While the methods used and the conclusions reached by the Hawthorne researchers have been questioned, they did generate great interest in the human problems in the workplace and focused attention on the human factor.[12]

**Hawthorne effect**
The positive behavior change demonstrated by employee when managers pay attention to them.

## Early Champions of Human Relations

*Mary Parker Follett* was not a businesswoman in the sense that she managed her own business. However, through her writings and lectures, she had a great impact on many business and government leaders. While concerned with many aspects of the management process, her basic theory was that the fundamental problem of any organization is to build and maintain dynamic yet harmonious human relations within the organization.[13] In 1938, Chester Barnard, president of New Jersey Bell Telephone for many years, published a book that combined a thorough knowledge of organizational theory and sociology.[14] Barnard viewed the organization as a social structure

## Return to Scientific Management

Recently, a professor at State University was lecturing in a management development seminar on the topic of motivation. The participants candidly discussed problems that existed in their respective organizations. Problem areas mentioned included absenteeism, turnover, and poor workmanship. The participants managed a variety of workers, such as automobile assembly workers, clerical workers, computer operators, sanitation workers, and even some middle-level managers.

During the discussion, one of the participants made the following statement: "What we need to stop all of these problems is a little scientific management."

### Questions

1. What do you think the person means?
2. Do you agree? Discuss.
3. Take one of the jobs in the above case, and show how you could apply scientific management.
4. What would be the human relations approach to the same job you selected in question 3?

and stressed the behavioral aspects of organizations. Effectively integrating traditional management and the behavioral sciences, Barnard's work had a great impact on managers and teachers of management.

## PROGRESS CHECK QUESTIONS

9. What were "the Hawthorne experiments"?
10. Explain "the Hawthorne effect."
11. Who were Elton Mayo, Mary Parker Follett, and Chester Barnard?
12. Why was the human relations movement important in the development of management theory?

## The Professional Manager

**professional manager**

A career person who does not necessarily have a controlling interest in the company for which he or she works. Professional managers realize their responsibility to three groups: employees, stockholders, and the general public.

The career manager, or **professional manager,** did not exist until the 1930s. Until this time, managers were placed into one of three categories: owner-managers, captains of industry, or financial managers. The owner-managers dominated until after the Civil War. The captains of industry controlled organizations from the 1880s to the turn of the century. The financial managers operated in much the same ways the captains of industry did, except that they often did not own the enterprises they controlled and operated. The financial managers dominated from around 1905 until the early 1930s, when the Great Depression severely weakened public confidence in business organizations.

In the late 1930s, the professional manager emerged. The professional manager is a career person who does not necessarily have a controlling interest in the enterprise for which he or she works. Professional managers realize their responsibility to three groups: employees, stockholders, and the public. With expanded technology and more complex organizations, the professional manager became more and more widespread.

## THE SYSTEMS APPROACH

The fragmentation period of the late 1950s and early 1960s was followed by an era of attempted integration. Many management theorists sought to use a systems approach to integrate the various management schools. A **system** is a set of connected elements that function as a whole.

The systems approach to management was viewed as "a way of thinking about the job of managing . . . [which] provides a framework for visualizing internal and external environmental factors as an integrated whole."[15] Under this approach, the organization can be seen as either an **open system** where it interacts with its external environment or a **closed system** where it has no interaction with its external environment. Most organizations are run as open systems, but even then they can make the mistake of ignoring their environment and acting as though they can operate independently of the world around them.

## THEORY X AND THEORY Y

In his 1960 book *The Human Side of Enterprise,* American social psychologist Douglas McGregor proposed a simple division of management styles that captured what he argued were fundamentally different ways of managing people:[16]

> **Theory X.** The controlling/authoritative manager believes that most employees don't like to work and will only work at the required level of productivity if they are forced to do so under the threat of punishment.
>
> **Theory Y.** The democratic/participative manager believes that employees can be trusted to meet production targets without being threatened and that they will often seek additional responsibilities because they enjoy the satisfaction of being creative and increasing their own skills.

Theory X and Theory Y managers have now become featured players in many management-training videos as the direct opposition of these management styles is reviewed. However, as managerial research progressed in the twentieth century, this division of styles was considered to be too simplistic, and a broader approach to management was proposed.

**system**
A system is an assemblage or combination of things or parts forming a complex or unitary whole.

**open system**
Under the systems approach to management, the organization is seen as an open system that is influenced by its internal and external environmental factors. The organization then, in turn, influences these same internal and external environmental factors; as a result, a dynamic relationship is created.

**closed system**
By contrast closed systems do not interact with their external environments.

**Theory X**
Argues there is a simple division of management styles that capture what are fundamentally different ways of managing people. Theory X managers manage in a very controlling and authoritative manner.

**Theory Y**
Managers believe employees can be trusted to meet production targets without being threatened, and that they will often seek additional responsibilities because they enjoy the satisfaction of being creative and increasing their own skills. As a result they manage in a democratic and participative manner.

# THE CONTINGENCY APPROACH

**contingency approach to management**

Theorizes that different situations and conditions require different management approaches.

The 1970s were characterized by the so-called contingency approach. In the **contingency approach to management,** different situations and conditions require different management approaches. Proponents believe there is no one best way to manage; the best way depends on the specific circumstances. Recognizing the rarity of a manager who thinks one way to manage works best in all situations, one might ask, "What is new about this approach?" What is new is that contingency theorists have often gone much further than simply saying, "It all depends." Many contingency theories outline in detail the style or approach that works best under certain circumstances. Contingency theories, many of which are discussed in this book, have been developed in areas such as decision making, organizational design, leadership, planning, and group behavior.

# THE JAPANESE MANAGEMENT MOVEMENT AND THEORY Z

**Theory Z**

Attempts to integrate American and Japanese management practices by combining the American emphasis on individual responsibility with the Japanese emphasis on collective decision making, slow evaluation and promotion, and holistic concern for employees.

The tremendous economic success many Japanese companies enjoyed following World War II drew worldwide attention to their management practices. As management scholars studied Japanese management, they identified certain characteristics that differed somewhat from traditional American approaches. In general terms, Japanese managers encouraged more employee participation in decision making, they showed a deeper concern for the personal well-being of employees, and they placed great emphasis on the quality of their products and services. Top management acted more as a facilitator of decision making than as an issuer of orders. The flow of information and initiatives from the bottom to the top of the organization was emphasized.

Realizing there were many valuable lessons to be learned from the Japanese, and in a direct acknowledgment to Douglas McGregor's Theory X and Theory Y, William Ouchi developed a theory, called **Theory Z,** that attempts to integrate American and Japanese management practices.[17] Theory Z combines the American emphasis on individual responsibility with the Japanese emphasis on collective decision making, slow evaluation and promotion, and concern for employees. Other factors recommended by Ouchi, such as length of employment and career path characteristics, represent

**career management**

## Developing Skills for a Successful Career

Career planning and development are comprehensive skills that cannot be obtained by a single learned experience. To capture the necessary skills to become competent in building your career, you must learn the many variety of tasks and, over time, apply this comprehensive learning.

What skills will you need to become "better" at developing and executing your career goals? The list might look like this:

- Leadership skills
- Team building skills
- Analytical skills
- Marketing skills
- Industry knowledge
- Management skills
- Problem-solving skills
- Planning skills
- Empathetic skills
- Technology skills

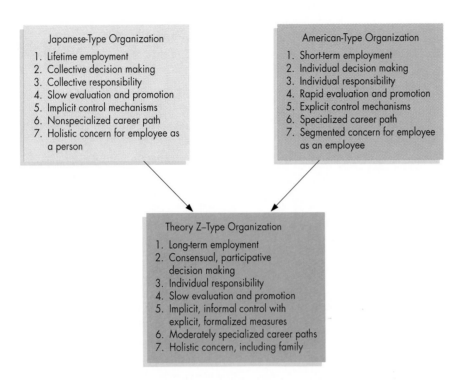

**figure 2.3**

**COMPARISON OF JAPANESE, AMERICAN, AND THEORY Z ORGANIZATIONS**

***Source:*** Adapted from William Ouchi, *Theory Z* (Reading, MA: Addison-Wesley Publishing, Inc., 1984), pp. 58, 71–88.

compromises between traditional American and Japanese practices. Figure 2.3 summarizes the profile of traditional American and Japanese organizations as well as Ouchi's Theory Z organization.

## THE SEARCH FOR EXCELLENCE

In 1982, Thomas J. Peters and Robert H. Waterman Jr. released a book, *In Search of Excellence,* which soon became, at the time, the best-selling management-related book ever published.[18] Working as management consultants at a time when Japanese management styles were receiving worldwide attention (in the late 1970s), Peters and Waterman asked, "Can't we learn something from America's most successful companies?" Using a combination of their own standards and six measures of financial success covering a 20-year period (1961 through 1980), the authors identified a final group of 36 American companies. According to the authors' measurements, these companies had demonstrated excellent performance over the 20-year period studied. Most of the 36 companies in the final group were well-known companies, such as IBM, McDonald's, Delta Air Lines, and Eastman Kodak. After interviewing each company in the group and analyzing their findings, Peters and Waterman identified eight "attributes of excellence," summarized in Figure 2.4.

While Peters and Waterman's work has been criticized as being overly subjective and not based on sound research methods, it has caused many managers to rethink their ways of doing things.[19] Specifically, Peters and Waterman reemphasized the value of on-the-job experimentation and

**figure 2.4**

**PETERS AND WATERMAN'S
EIGHT CHARACTERISTICS
OF EXCELLENT COMPANIES**

**Source:** Thomas J. Peters and
Robert H. Waterman, Jr., *In Search
of Excellence* (New York: Harper
& Row, 1982), pp. 13–16.

| CHARACTERISTICS OF EXCELLENCE | DESCRIPTION OF CHARACTERISTICS |
|---|---|
| 1. A bias for action | A tendency to get on with things; a willingness to experiment. |
| 2. Close to the customer | The provision of unparalleled quality/service; a willingness to listen to the customer. |
| 3. Autonomy and entrepreneurship | Encouragement of practical risk taking and innovation; tolerance of a reasonable number of mistakes as a part of the innovative process. |
| 4. Productivity through people | Rank-and-file employees are viewed as the root source of quality and productivity gains; employees are treated with respect and dignity; enthusiasm and trust are encouraged. |
| 5. Hands on; value driven | The company philosophy and values are clearly communicated; managers take a hands-on approach. |
| 6. Stick to the knitting | Companies diversify only into businesses that are closely related; emphasis is on internal growth as opposed to mergers. |
| 7. Simple form; lean staff | Companies have simple structure with clear lines of authority; headquarters staff is kept small. |
| 8. Simultaneous loose-tight properties | Autonomy is pushed down to the lowest levels, but at the same time certain core values are not negotiable. |

creative thinking, the need to place the customer first, and the need to treat employees as human beings.

However, as soon as two years after *In Search of Excellence* was published, at least 14 of the "excellent" companies highlighted by Peters and Waterman had lost some of their luster. Of the 14 companies that stumbled, 12 were unable to adapt to fundamental changes in their markets. Some maintain that being overly devoted to Peters and Waterman's eight characteristics, which do not emphasize reacting to broad economic and business trends, may have contributed to their problems. Others, including Peters and Waterman, argue that these companies ran into trouble because they strayed from the principles that had been key to their earlier successes. By the early 1990s, some of the stars of Peters and Waterman's original list, such as IBM, were also having difficulties. One company, Delta Air Lines, filed for bankruptcy protection in 2005. Some critics have also questioned the standards originally used by Peters and Waterman (continuous innovation, large size, and sustained financial performance over the 20-year period from 1961 to 1980) for selecting their "excellent" companies. Critics have also questioned whether the so-called excellent firms provided exceptional returns to stockholders in either the short run or the long run.

At least two lessons can be drawn from the experiences of these companies: (1) The excellent companies of today will not necessarily be the excellent companies of tomorrow and (2) good management requires much more than following any one set of rules.

## THE EMPHASIS ON QUALITY

Beginning in the late 1970s, gathering steam throughout the 1980s, and reaching its height in the early 1990s was an emphasis on overall quality of the product or service. The quality of American products and services had reached a low by the early 1970s. This phenomenon, coupled with the quality successes of the Japanese, forced managers to look to the quality issue as one way of improving the position of American products and services.

The major change that resulted from this increased attention to quality was a shift from finding and correcting mistakes or rejects to *preventing* them. This led to the development of total quality management (TQM), which is a management philosophy that emphasizes "managing the entire organization so that it excels in all dimensions of products and services that are important to the customer."[20] TQM is discussed in much more detail later in this book.

The emphasis on preventing mistakes is key to every company, but is potentially life-saving for this manager. Can you think of other fields in which the stokes extend beyond money?

## ETHICAL MANAGEMENT

The XYZ Corporation has been growing rapidly over the past three years. To help manage this growth, the CEO decides to create a new director level position. The position requires extensive business expertise, an understanding of the XYZ Corporation's industry, and exemplary strong people skills.

Two candidates remain after the final interviews: John, an external candidate with a strong business background, and Mary, a candidate from within the company, who also has the required skills. After two rounds of interviews, the vice president for human resources decides to offer the position to John. John considers the offer for several days, but decides to turn it down.

The vice president then meets with Mary and offers her the position. Upon hearing the offer, Mary pauses. She looks the VP straight in the eye and asks, "Was the job offered to John first?" How should the vice president respond?

**Source:** Adapted from "The Second Choice Asks a Hard Question," Institute for Global Ethics, www.globalethics.org.

# MOVING FROM GOOD TO GREAT

Following in the footsteps of Peters and Waterman's *In Search of Excellence,* Stanford University business professors Jim Collins and Jerry Porras published a book in 1994 entitled *Built to Last: Successful Habits of Visionary Companies* that took the business world by storm, selling over 3.5 million copies and replacing Peters and Waterman as the best-selling business book to date.[21] Arguing for the need to focus on creating a lasting organization by relying on "homegrown management," *Built to Last* (BTL) featured many well-known organizations such as Motorola, Disney, Ford, and Boeing—many of which have gone on to struggle in much the same way as many of Peters and Waterman's excellent organizations. The lessons here seem to be that excellence or superior vision can be very short term commodities and that managers can never rely on their current successes to guarantee future success.

In 2000 Collins and his team of researchers took another look at what it takes to turn a good organization into a great one with the publication of *Good to Great: Why Some Companies Make the Leap . . . and Others Don't*, a book that went on to sell over 2.5 million copies.[22] Starting with 1,435 companies and five years of research, the study produced 11 finalists that met Collins's standards as "great" companies that had made the move from good to great and maintained that status for a minimum of 15 years. One of the keys to making that move, Collins argued, was the **hedgehog concept,** by which managers focus on simple, basic principles that allow the company to focus on performance rather than pursuing several strategic projects at the same time. Figure 2.5 presents a comparison between *Built to Last* and *Good to Great* (GTG).

**hedgehog concept**

Drawn from Isaiah Berlin's essay "The Hedgehog and the Fox" in which "The fox knows many things but the hedgehog knows only one". In other words, great companies develop a simple core concept that guides all their future strategies, as opposed to chasing every new management fad or policy implementation.

**figure 2.5**

COMPARISON OF BUILT TO LAST VERSUS GOOD TO GREAT

|  | BUILT TO LAST<br>Successful Habits<br>of Visionary Companies | GOOD TO GREAT<br>Why Some Companies Make<br>the Leap and Others Don't |
|---|---|---|
| Author(s) | James C. Collins & Jerry I. Porras | James C. Collins |
| Published | 1994 | 2001 |
| Research Study | 18 visionary corporations measured against a control set of 18 comparison companies in a six year research study at the Stanford University Graduate School of Business | 21 business students from the University of Colorado spent 15,000 hours studying 11 companies identified as examples of great management using a similar control set of comparison companies |
| Recognized Companies | 3M, American Express, Boeing, Citicorp, Ford, General Electric, Hewlett-Packard, IBM, Johnson & Johnson, Marriott, Merck, Motorola, Nordstrom, Philip Morris, Procter & Gamble, Sony, Wal-Mart, Walt Disney | Abbott, Circuit City, Fannie Mae, Gillette, Kimberly-Clark, Kroger, Nucor, Philip Morris, Pitney Bowes, Walgreens, Wells Fargo |
| Key Concepts | • 12 shattered myths<br>• Clock Building, Not Time Telling<br>• Big Hairy Audacious Goals<br>• Good Enough Never Is | • Level 5 Leadership<br>• First Who . . . Then What<br>• The Hedgehog Concept |

## Tony selects a style

Tony had learned a lot from Jerry and he knew that he could always turn to his mentor for help and advice, even though Jerry would now be in charge of a region on the other side of the state. He liked Jerry's style of management—focused on the people who work in the restaurant as well as keeping the bosses happy by turning in good numbers. As Jerry always said, "You can't run the place on your own, Tony—if you don't have good people in your restaurant, you won't be able to take care of your customers. Without good people, you won't produce good food or happy diners, so take the time to hire the right employees, and when you find them, take good care of them so that they'll stay with you."

Tony believed in that approach—he had heard too many other unit managers complain about how hard it was to find good staff—but he also realized that a successful future with Taco Barn required you to turn in profitable numbers for your unit. In other words, if Dawn wasn't happy with his weekly numbers—sales, food cost, and labor cost—it wouldn't matter how happy his people were.

Tony also realized that if he were to move on in the future and become a regional manager like Jerry and Dawn, he had to make a name for himself within the organization. It didn't take him long to decide that being a popular manager with his staff wasn't going to be enough to get it done. He had to take care of the numbers, and if he could find a way to squeeze more profit out of his restaurant by increasing sales and reducing costs, then he would really be on his way. Sure, the employees might miss the old days with Jerry, but they would appreciate Tony's new approach and maybe even respect him as a mentor who could help them build a future with Taco Barn.

### QUESTIONS

1. Tony appears to have chosen a management style. How would you categorize that style based on the information in this chapter?

2. Is Tony right in thinking that better numbers will bring him more attention? Why or why not?

3. Do you think the Taco Barn employees will like the new Tony? Why or why not?

4. How would you advise Tony in this situation? What approach do you think he should follow? Why?

### PROGRESS CHECK QUESTIONS

13. Describe the contingency approach to management.
14. What are the differences between Theory X, Theory Y, and Theory Z?
15. Summarize the eight characteristics of excellent companies identified by Peters and Waterman in their book *In Search of Excellence.*
16. Explain Jim Collins's hedgehog concept.

## CONCLUSION

This chapter summarized some of the major events that affected management discipline from the nineteenth century to the present. But the discipline did not develop and mature at the same rate in all parts of the country. Similarly, it did not develop from a series of isolated events; rather it grew from a series of minor and major events.

In Chapter 3 we begin to examine the challenging mix of tasks and responsibilities that a manager needs to succeed in the modern business environment. Ironically, as we shall see, many of those tasks and responsibilities are fundamentally the same as those identified by the management scholars of a century ago.

## key terms

| | | |
|---|---|---|
| **closed system**  39 | **Industrial Revolution**  28 | **soldiering**  31 |
| **contingency approach to management**  40 | **time and motion study**  33 | **system**  39 |
| | **open system**  39 | **Theory X**  39 |
| **functions of management**  35 | **professional manager**  38 | **Theory Y**  39 |
| **Hawthorne effect**  37 | **scientific management**  31 | **Theory Z**  40 |
| **hedgehog concept**  44 | | |

## review questions

1. What are the benefits of understanding how management theory and practice has changed over the past 100 years? How could you use this information as a manager?
2. Why do you think many people have interpreted Taylor's scientific management principles as being inhumane?
3. What are the key differences between the principles of scientific management and the key elements of human relations management?
4. Would you describe your management style as that of a scientific principles manager or a human relations one? Why?

## internet exercise

Visit the Web site of the National Academies (comprised of four organizations: the National Academy of Sciences, the National Academy of Engineering, the Institute of Medicine, and the National Research Council) at www.nationalacademies.org.

1. Describe the history of the National Academy of Sciences and its expansion into the National Academies.

2. List the six major divisions of the National Academies.

3. What are the objectives of the Division of Behavioral and Social Sciences and Education (DBASSE)?

4. Select the "Featured Reports in Behavioral Sciences" page and summarize the description of one of the reports relating to a business topic.

## team exercise

### FINDING THE ONE BEST WAY

Suppose you have been assigned the simple task of stuffing 1,000 two-page flyers ($8\frac{1}{2} \times 11$ inches) into a normal size envelope ($4 \times 9\frac{1}{2}$ inches). The envelopes come in boxes of 250, and the flyer pages are in stacks of 1,000 each. The flyers must be stapled together, folded, and then placed into the envelopes.

a. Get a stapler, a few envelopes, and several $8\frac{1}{2} \times 11$ inch sheets of paper, and determine how you might accomplish this task. Identify where each component will be positioned and exactly how you will perform the task.

b. After you have tried your first method, see if you can determine any ways in which it might be improved.

c. Compare your method with others in your class.

d. Vote as a group on the "one best way" to perform the task.

### Questions

1. Were you able to improve your first method in step *b*?
2. Did you pick up further improvements from others in your class (step *c*)?
3. Were you able to agree on one best way (step *d*)?
4. How different was your original method from the final one best way?

# Face Time: The New Assembly Line

*In This Era of the "Knowledge Worker," Why Do So Many Managers Still Insist on Long Office Hours?*

**B**ack in the day, Henry Ford put out some fine automobiles and, while he was at it, revolutionized the workplace: He perfected the assembly line, which required workers to arrive at a designated time and work together in a complex, multitask operation. Good going, Henry!

A century later, sophisticated information technologies have given rise to the "knowledge worker"—a person whose chief contribution to a company is intellectual. In Ford's time, a great day on the assembly line occurred when employees worked *without* mistakes and accidents. In 2005, a good day is when a brilliant idea comes to mind that will help an organization leap ahead.

It's wonderful, slippery stuff, this knowledge work. Its tools are smooth and efficient minds that think and brainstorm nonstop— morning, evening, and suppertime, on the job or off. So, why do we so often manage knowledge workers as though they were assembly line folk?

## CHAINED TO A DESK

Why do we insist on what, in the current lingo, is known as "face time"? I define it as the love some managers have for the sight of workers sitting obediently at their desks hour after hour. Face time made perfect sense for factory workers, who literally had to stay on the line to do their jobs. But today, many of the people who are encouraged, prodded, and shamed into staying at the office from sunup to sundown could work—probably more productively—from almost anywhere.

Why? Because the assembly line of ideas chugs on night and day. Knowledge work is 24/7/365, and proceeds whether any one worker is well or unwell, present or absent, alive or dead.

In fact, one of the challenges of working in the knowledge economy is the difficulty of taking a vacation. You miss a couple of weeks of work, and you face catch-up frenzy upon return.

So, to hold knowledge workers to the same face-time requirements that Henry Ford used defies common sense. Although companies can use business results to evaluate sales managers, marketing gurus, telecommunications engineers, financial analysts, and most other office types, managers still love to ride herd on their work hours, too. And not just their work hours: Face-time addicts fixate on in-the-office work hours specifically. We all know that our employees jump back on their PCs after dinner at home, but somehow that doesn't count.

It's as though managers say to themselves: "Now that Fran is in charge of the product launch, the plan should be in great shape. Fran has a terrific track record and excellent relationships in the industry. Our weekly one-on-one will keep me up to date on her progress. She's also great about copying me on correspondence with our partners. But hey—if I can see her in the office every day from 6 a.m. to 8:30 p.m., I'll feel even better about how her project is going."

## A WOMAN'S PLACE

See? There's very little logic behind face-time addiction. For instance, who knows what you're really up to when your ear is glued to your phone? You could be tracking stock prices or talking to your bookie or wedding caterer. You could be doing any number of things. But, by gum, if your face is visible and your butt is in the chair, whatever you're doing must be work.

Face time for managers has turned into a crutch. It has less to do with managing people well than with making the boss feel better. Even when managers know that people are burned out, sick of one another's company, and grievously in need of a walk around the block—yo, they still insist on that face time.

## ABSURDITY PREVAILS

Employees buy into the face-time addiction, too. I remember saying to my boyfriend before we were married: "Pick me up at my office around 1:30." I meant 1:30 a.m. We lived in Chicago, so there were plenty of places to eat at that hour. I loved my job, for sure. But I also loved being an obsessed worker bee and essential to the company's success. Having kids knocked that fixation out of me right quick. But many people aren't so lucky. They go on working ungodly hours right up until retirement. And this is unfortunate, for three reasons:

One, it's unhealthy. Open the wellness section of any newspaper to read about what workplace stress is doing to Americans, and to the cost of health care.

Two, it reinforces the obviously disturbed notion that face time is what counts, even more than business results. It strengthens the absurd idea that more hours in the office will make the business run better.

Three, an unholy alliance of face-time-obsessed managers and face-time-addicted employees will create an environment where any balanced person will feel hated.

You think I'm exaggerating? In the booming 1990s, I worked for a fast-growing technology company, where a macho work ethic reigned supreme. The lengths to which workers would go to prove their loyalty struck me as almost sad.

## EXTREME FACE TIME

One evening, I watched a young man meet the Chinese restaurant delivery person at the side entrance. He returned to his office, opened the container, stuck a fork in the chicken chow mein, turned up his desk radio, and arranged his jacket over the back of his chair. Then, leaving his light on, the dinner on his desk, and his office door ajar, he went to his car.

A carton of food wasted! Well, not in his mind: He had bought himself an extra hour or two of face time, because if a higher-up walked by that open door, he'd be likely to think the employee was still working (just at the copier or in the men's room). I wanted to write BUSTED on the plastic fork, but that would have been cruel, and this person was already in a bad way: When an organization's culture goes gaga over face time, everyone suffers.

Am I anti-face time, then? No way. I think teamwork is essential, and time together as a group makes for a wonderful way to move ideas forward quickly. I just don't think it's an everyday essential, like vitamin C or calcium. Many companies balance face-time requirements and human requirements with something called core hours. They'll say: "We all have obligations outside of work, but we also need to see one another for some period every day. So let's all agree to be in the office from 10 to 3 Monday through Friday, while putting in a full week and getting lots of great stuff done."

## CUT THE CORD

Core hours are the ticket—as long as you don't establish them and then start quizzing people about where they were off to at 4:15 last Thursday.

## Questions

1. What are the three reasons why "working ungodly hours" can work against you?

2. What kind of "face time" does your boss expect at your current job (or a job you have held in the past)?

3. Have you ever felt pressure to put in more face time to keep up with your co-workers? How did you handle that pressure?

4. Is there a solution to the pressure of face time? How could you reassure your boss that you are being productive even when he can't see you every minute of the working day?

*Source:* Adapted from Liz Ryan, "Employment Trends," *BusinessWeek Online,* April 22, 2005.

## 3M: A Struggle between Efficiency and Creativity

*How CEO George Buckley Is Attempting to Balance both Discipline and Imagination*

Not too many years ago, the temple of management was General Electric. Former CEO Jack Welch was the high priest, and his disciples spread the word to executive suites throughout the land. One of his most highly regarded followers, James McNerney, was quickly snatched up by 3M after falling short in the closely watched race to succeed Welch. 3M's board considered McNerney a huge prize, and the company's stock jumped nearly 20 percent in the days after Dec. 5, 2000, when his selection as CEO was announced. The mere mention of his name made everyone richer.

McNerney was the first outsider to lead the inward-looking St. Paul Minnesota company in its 100-year history. He had barely stepped off the plane before he announced he planned to dramatically change the place. His playbook was classic GE. McNerney axed 8,000 workers (about 11 percent of the workforce), intensified the performance-review process, and tightened the purse strings at a company that had become an extravagant spender. He also brought in GE's famous Six Sigma program—a series of management techniques designed to decrease production defects and increase efficiency. Thousands of staffers became trained as

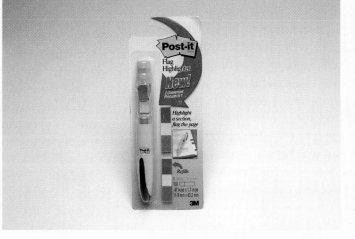

Six Sigma "black belt" specialists. The plan appeared to work: McNerney brought 3M's declining stock back to life and won rave reviews for bringing discipline to an organization that had become clumsy, inconsistent, and slow.

Then, four and a half years after arriving, McNerney abruptly left for a bigger opportunity, the top job at Boeing. Now his successors face a challenging question: whether the relentless emphasis on efficiency had made 3M a less creative company. That's a vitally important issue for a company whose very identity is built on innovation. After all, 3M is the birthplace of masking tape, Thinsulate, and the Post-it note. It is the invention machine whose methods were honored in the influential 1994 best seller *Built to Last* by Jim Collins and Jerry I. Porras. But those old hits have become distant memories. At the company that has always prided itself on drawing at least one-third of sales from products released in the past five years, today that fraction has slipped to only one-quarter. Those results are not coincidental. Efficiency programs such as Six Sigma are designed to identify problems in work processes—and then use thorough measurement to reduce variation and eliminate defects. When these types of initiatives become fixed in a company's culture, as they did at 3M, creativity can easily get squelched. After all, a breakthrough innovation is something that challenges existing procedures and norms.

## PROUD CREATIVE CULTURE

The tension that current CEO George Buckley is trying to manage—between innovation and efficiency—is one that's challenging CEOs everywhere. There is no doubt that the application of lean and mean work processes at thousands of companies, often through programs with obscure-sounding names such as ISO 9000 and Total Quality Management, has been one of the most important business trends of past decades. But as once-bloated U.S. manufacturers have shaped up and become profitable global competitors, the burden shifts to growth and innovation, especially in today's idea-based, design-obsessed economy. While process excellence demands precision, consistency, and repetition, innovation calls for variation, failure, and an element of luck. The very factors that make Six Sigma effective in one situation can make it ineffective in another. Traditionally, it uses exact statistical analysis to produce clear data that help produce better quality, lower costs, and more efficiency. That all sounds great when you know what outcomes you'd like to control. But what about when there are few facts to go on—or you don't even know the nature of the problem you're trying to define?

The pressures of Wall Street are another matter. Investors liked McNerney's approach to boosting earnings, which may have sacrificed creativity but made up for it in consistency. Profits grew, on average, 22 percent a year. In Buckley's first year, sales approached $23 billion and profits totaled $1.4 billion, but two quarterly earnings misses and a fading stock price made it a rocky ride. In 2007, Buckley seems to have satisfied many skeptics on the Street, convincing them he can fire up growth without killing the McNerney-led productivity improvements. Shares are up 12 percent since January.

It was one of the pillars of the "3M Way" that workers could seek out funding from a number of company sources to get their pet projects off the ground. Official company policy allowed employees to use 15 percent of their time to pursue independent projects. The company deliberately encouraged risk and tolerated failure. 3M's creative culture led the way for the one that is currently celebrated at Google. Perhaps all of that made it particularly painful for 3M's proud workforce to deal with the hard reality the company faced by the late '90s. Profit and sales growth were wildly erratic. It bungled operations in Asia amid the 1998 financial crisis there. The stock sat out the entire late '90s boom, budging less than 1 percent from September 1997 to September 2000. The flexibility and lack of structure, which had enabled the company's success, had also by then produced a bloated staff and inefficient workflow. So McNerney had plenty of cause to whip things into shape.

Under McNerney, the research & development (R&D) function at 3M was organized in ways that were unheard of in St. Paul, even though the guidelines would have looked familiar at many other organizations. Some employees found the constant analysis overwhelming. Steven Boyd, a PhD who had worked as a researcher at 3M for 32 years before his job was eliminated in 2004, was one of them. After a couple of months on a research project, he would have to fill in a "red book" with scores of pages worth of charts and tables, analyzing everything from the potential commercial application, to the size of the market, to possible manufacturing problems. Traditionally, 3M had been a place where researchers had been given plenty of room to pursue research down whatever alleys they wished. After the arrival of the new boss, the goal was to speed up and organize the progress of inventions into the new-product pipeline.

For a long time, 3M had allowed researchers to spend years testing products. Consider, for example, the Post-it note. Its inventor, Art Fry, a 3M scientist who's now retired, and others fiddled with the idea for several years before the product went into full production in 1980. Defenders of Six Sigma at 3M claim that a more systematic new-product introduction process allows innovations to get to market faster. But Fry, the Post-it note inventor, disagrees. In fact, he places the blame for 3M's recent lack of innovative sizzle squarely on Six Sigma's application in 3M's research labs. Innovation, he says, is "a numbers game. You have to go through 5,000 to 6,000 raw ideas to find one successful business." Six Sigma would ask, why not eliminate all that waste and just come up with the right idea the first time? That way of thinking, says Fry, can have serious side effects.

## REINVIGORATED WORKFORCE

Buckley, a PhD chemical engineer by training, seems to recognize the cultural consequences of a process-focused program on an organization whose fate and history is so bound up in inventing new stuff. "You cannot create in that atmosphere of imprisonment or sameness," Buckley says. "Perhaps one of the mistakes that we made as a company—it's one of the dangers of Six Sigma—is that when you value sameness more than you value creativity, I think you potentially undermine the heart and soul of a company like 3M." In recent years, the company's reputation as an innovator has been sliding. In 2004, 3M was ranked No. 1 on Boston Consulting Group's Most Innovative Companies list (now the *Busi-*

*nessWeek*/BCG list). It dropped to No. 2 in 2005, to No. 3 in 2006, and down to No. 7 this year.

To help get the creative juices flowing, Buckley is opening the money spout—raising spending on R&D, acquisitions, and capital expenditures. The overall R&D budget will grow 20 percent this year, to $1.5 billion. Even more significant than the increase in money is Buckley's reallocation of those funds. He's funneling cash into what he calls "core" areas of 3M technology, 45 in all, from abrasives to nanotechnology to flexible electronics. Quietly, the McNerney heritage is being revised at 3M. While there is no doubt the former CEO brought some positive change to the company, many workers say they are reinvigorated now that the corporate emphasis has shifted from profitability and process discipline to growth and innovation.

## Questions

1. Explain how the management styles of James McInerney and George Buckley compare to scientific management and human relations management.

2. Why would the use of "exact statistical analysis" reduce creativity?

3. Why would an organization "deliberately encourage risk"?

4. Do you think Buckley's plan will work? Why or why not?

*Source:* Adapted from Brian Hindo, "Inside Innovation," *BusinessWeek Online*, June 11, 2007.

# COMMUNICATION SKILLS

**"The most important thing in communication is hearing what isn't said."**

—Peter F. Drucker

## The World of Work: Under new management

Tony's transition week with Jerry Smith went very quickly. They spent time covering payroll, banking, food orders, and eventually planning out the schedule for the next month. Tony had covered a lot of these duties before when he covered for Jerry's vacation, but it felt different to be doing them as the new unit manager.

The schedule was the worst—trying to cover everybody's individual requests—only this many hours; only these days; wanting to be scheduled together because they car pool; needing time off for sports practice; canceling at the last minute because the babysitter didn't show—all these headaches made staffing the biggest block of Jerry's time, and Tony started to think

that there had to be a better way to do this. Jerry was a nice guy and did his best to accommodate all these requests, but Tony was starting to feel that people were beginning to take advantage of his flexibility.

After the fifth attempt at completing the schedule, Tony had decided that this would be the first opportunity for him to make some real changes and to show Jerry and his new boss Dawn Williams that he wasn't afraid to step up and put his stamp on this Taco Barn. Jerry ran a great unit, which was why he was being promoted to regional manager, but that didn't mean there wasn't room to improve. Tony believed that by setting a tougher standard on the schedule, he could

# objectives

**After studying this chapter, you will be able to:**

**1** Define communication, and explain why effective communication is an important management skill.

**2** Describe the interpersonal communication process.

**3** Understand the importance and appropriate use of written and oral communication.

**4** Identify the best means of communication as it pertains to specific situations.

**5** Explain the most common mechanisms for communicating within the organization.

**6** Understand the challenges of communication in international business activities.

CHAPTER

3

simplify the process and free up some time to work on other things in the restaurant. Plus, he thought, running the daily operations would be a lot easier if he didn't have to deal with schedule changes every time there was a change of shift. In addition, it would send a clear message to the rest of the staff that just because they used to be co-workers didn't mean that he was going to go any easier on them than Jerry ever did.

The next morning, as the lunch crew started clocking in for their shift, they noticed a new sign on the staff notice board on bright yellow paper:

*Effective immediately, there will be no changes to the schedule once posted. It is your responsibility to show up for your designated shift or find someone to cover for you if a problem or emergency prevents you from showing up.*
**Tony Davis, Unit Manager**

## QUESTIONS

1. Why is it so important for Tony to "put his stamp" on the Taco Barn as the new manager?

2. Did Tony make the right choice here? Why or why not?

3. What do you think the team's reaction will be?

4. What could Tony do differently here?

# COMMUNICATION AS A MANAGEMENT SKILL

**communication**
The act of exchanging information.

**Communication** is the act of exchanging information. It can be used to inform, command, instruct, assess, influence, and persuade other people. Communication skills are important in all aspects of life, including business.

Managers use communication every day. In fact, they spend as much as three-quarters of their time communicating (see Figure 3.1). Good managers develop effective communication skills. They use these skills to absorb information, motivate employees, and deal effectively with customers and co-workers. Good communication can significantly affect a manager's success.

Communicating effectively is an important management skill for several reasons:

- *Managers must give direction to the people who work for them.* Managers who fail to give clear guidance often find that employees perform their jobs poorly because they do not understand what is expected of them.
- *Managers must be able to motivate people.* Good managers use their ability to communicate to get other people excited about their jobs.
- *Managers must be able to convince customers that they should do business with them.* Effective communication is the key to convincing a customer to purchase a product or service. Without good communication skills, managers will find it difficult to attract customers, even if their companies' products or services meet the customer's needs.
- *Managers must be able to absorb the ideas of others.* Business managers interact with many people, including co-workers, customers, and suppliers. To be effective, they must be able to understand and accept other people's viewpoints.
- *Managers must be able to persuade other people.* Managers often have ideas that others oppose. To persuade other people to accept their ideas, managers must be able to communicate effectively.

## figure 3.1

**COMMUNICATING IN THE BUSINESS WORLD**

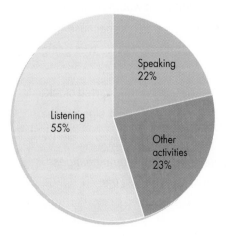

Speaking
22%

Listening
55%

Other
activities
23%

**figure 3.2**

**INTERPERSONAL
COMMUNICATION
PROCESS**

Sender → Initial message communicated both verbally and nonverbally. → Receiver

Event or condition generates information. This creates a message.

Perceives the message, derives meaning, and reacts to the message. The reaction creates a reply message to the sender.

Sender ← Reply message communicated both verbally and nonverbally (sometimes referred to as feedback).

Perceives message, derives meaning, and reacts to the message.

# INTERPERSONAL COMMUNICATION

Effective communication between individuals, especially between a manager and subordinates, is critical to achieving organizational objectives and, as a result, to managing people effectively. Estimates vary, but it is generally agreed that since managers spend much of their time with their subordinates, effective communication is critical to the wise and effective use of their time.

**Interpersonal communication** is an interactive process between individuals that involves sending and receiving verbal and nonverbal messages. The basic purpose of interpersonal communication is to transmit information so that the sender of the message is understood and understands the response of the receiver. Figure 3.2 diagrams this dynamic and interactive process. An event or a condition generates information. The desire to share the information, or inform another person about it, creates the need to communicate. The sender then creates a message and communicates it both verbally and nonverbally. The receiver, in turn, perceives and interprets the message and (hopefully) creates a reply message as a response to it. This reply message may generate a response by the sender of the initial message, and the process continues in this fashion.

Often, however, many factors interfere and cause this process to fail. Some causes of interpersonal communication failure are conflicting or inappropriate assumptions, different interpretations of the meanings of words (semantics), differences in perception, emotions either preceding or during communication, poor listening habits, inadequate communication skills, insufficient feedback, and differences in the interpretation of nonverbal communications.

> **interpersonal communication**
>
> An interactive process between individuals that involves sending and receiving verbal and nonverbal messages.

> The breakdown of communication is a problem that good managers try to address and avoid.

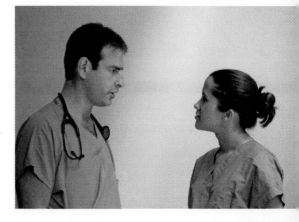

You have worked at the same company with your best friend for the last 10 years—in fact, he told you about the job and got you the interview. He works in the marketing department and is up for a promotion to marketing director—a position that he has been wanting for a long time. You work in sales and on your weekly conference call the new marketing director—someone recruited from outside the company—joins you. Your boss explains that although the formal announcement hasn't been made yet, the company felt it was important to get the new director up to speed as quickly as possible. He will be joining the company in two weeks, after completing his two weeks' notice with his current employer. Should you tell your friend what happened?

## Conflicting or Inappropriate Assumptions

Have you ever thought you were being understood when you were really not? This is a common mistake made by couples, teachers, superiors, and parents. If one assumes that communication is flowing as intended, one tends to move on with the dialogue without allowing feedback to indicate whether clarity of expression and communication has been achieved. Good managers and salespeople always seek verbal or nonverbal feedback, before continuing the communication process. Remember that interpretation of meaning can always be a problem when assumptions are involved. Messages such as "Stop," "Do this right now," and "Please don't" never seem to have the same meanings to children that the adult sender intended. Sound communication usually flows from ensuring that the sender and the receiver see and understand assumptions in the same way.

## Semantics

**semantics**

The science or study of the meanings of words and symbols.

**Semantics** is the science or study of the meanings of words and symbols. Words themselves have no real meaning. They have meaning only in terms of people's reactions to them. A word may mean very different things to different people, depending on how it is used. In addition, a word may be interpreted differently based on the facial expressions, hand gestures, and voice inflections used.

The problems involved in semantics are of two general types. Some words and phrases invite multiple interpretations. For example, Figure 3.3 shows different interpretations of the word *fix*. Another problem is that groups of people in specific situations often develop their own technical language, which outsiders may or may not understand. For example, physicians, government workers, and military employees are often guilty of using acronyms and abbreviations that only they understand.

Words are the most common form of interpersonal communication. Because of the real possibility of misinterpretation, words must be carefully chosen and clearly defined for effective communication.

An Englishman visits America and is completely awed by the many ways we use the word *fix*. For example,

1. His host asks him how he'd like his drink fixed. He meant *mixed*.

2. As he prepares to leave, he discovers he has a flat tire and calls a repairperson, who says he'll fix it immediately. He means *repair*.

3. On the way home, he is given a ticket for speeding. He calls his host, who says, "Don't worry, I'll fix it." He means *nullify*.

4. At the office the next day, he comments on the cost of living in America, and one of his colleagues says, "It's hard to make ends meet on a fixed income." She means *steady* or *unchanging*.

5. He has an argument with a co-worker. The latter says, "I'll fix you." He means *seek revenge*.

6. A colleague remarks that she is in a fix. She means *condition* or *situation*.

## figure 3.3

**INTERPRETATIONS OF THE WORD *FIX***

## Perception

**Perception** deals with the mental and sensory processes an individual uses in interpreting information she or he receives. Since each individual's perception is unique, people often perceive the same situation in different ways.

Perception begins when the sense organs receive a stimulus. The stimulus is the information received, whether it is conveyed in writing, verbally, nonverbally, or in another way. The sense organs respond to, shape, and organize the information received. When this information reaches the brain, it is further organized and interpreted, resulting in perception. Different people perceive the same information differently because no two people have the same personal experiences, memories, likes, and dislikes. In addition, the phenomenon of selective perception often distorts the intended message: People tend to listen to only part of the message, blocking out the rest for any number of reasons.

**perception**
The mental and sensory processes an individual uses in interpreting information received.

## PROGRESS CHECK QUESTIONS

1. What is communication?
2. Define interpersonal communication.
3. What is semantics?
4. What is perception, and what role does it play in communication?

## Emotions either Preceding or during Communication

Just as perception affects our cognitive processes during communication, emotions affect our disposition to send and receive the communication. Anger, joy, fear, sorrow, disgust, or panic (to mention only a few emotions) can all affect the way we send or receive messages. Emotional disposition is like the stage on which the communication piece plays its part: The stage can be perfectly prepared or in total disarray. The setting for the communication piece is obviously important. Communications during periods of high emotion usually have difficulty succeeding. Therefore, managers with good communication skills strive to manage the emotional as well as the physical communication environment.

# LEARNING TO COMMUNICATE

Managers communicate in writing and verbally. Before they can master either form of communication, they must be able to identify the audience, develop good listening skills, and understand the importance of feedback and nonverbal communication.

Anger can be a huge roadblock to communication. What can you do to avoid letting anger get the best of you?

## Understanding the Audience

Managers communicate with many different kinds of people. Hotel managers, for example, communicate with hotel guests, food and beverage managers, housekeepers, maintenance people, architects, travel agents, furniture salespeople, and many other types of people. They also may deal with senior management from the hotel's corporate office. Each of these groups of people represents a different audience.

To communicate effectively, managers need to determine their audience. Specifically, they need to be able to answer the following questions:

> *What does the audience already know?*
>
> *What does it want to know?*
>
> *What is its capacity for absorbing information?*
>
> *What does it hope to gain by listening? Is it hoping to be motivated? Informed? Convinced?*
>
> *Is the audience friendly or hostile?*

Hotel managers communicate with the hotel's housekeeping staff about complaints by guests. In doing so, they must inform the staff of the problem and motivate them to work harder to prevent complaints in the future. They would not need to

## Study Skills

### Keys to Good Study Habits

*Knowledge Is the Key to Performance*

What can I do to improve my study skills? Look at this following list to see what you might already be practicing for good study habits, and notice what might be areas that you have overlooked regarding keys to good study habits:

- Find a quiet place to study.
- Establish study time routines.
- Learn to prioritize and manage your time.
- Learn to become a better reader, writer, and listener.
- Maximize your memory and test taking skills.
- Reduce procrastination.
- Reduce test taking anxiety.

- Are you open to what other people say to you, or do you make up your mind about things before you hear other people's views?
- Do you become bored when other people speak?
- Do you interrupt people when they are speaking?
- Do you daydream at meetings?
- Are you hesitant to ask clarifying questions?

**figure 3.4**

ARE YOU A GOOD
LISTENER?

provide background material on the nature of the housekeeper's role. The audience already understands what that role includes.

If a lawsuit is filed against a hotel, managers of the hotel must inform senior management about the situation. In communicating with the hotel's senior management, they would describe what was being done to deal with the situation. They would also provide detailed background information that would allow the corporate officers to fully understand the situation.

## Developing Good Listening Skills

One of the most important skills a manager can develop is the ability to listen (see Figure 3.4). Good listening skills enable managers to absorb the information they need, recognize problems, and understand other people's viewpoints.

Managers need to learn to listen actively. Active listening involves absorbing what another person is saying and responding to the person's concerns (see Figure 3.5). Learning to listen actively is the key to becoming a good communicator.

Most people do not listen actively. Tests indicate that immediately after listening to a 10-minute oral presentation, the average listener has heard, comprehended, accurately evaluated, and retained about half of

1. **Listening**

   Knowing how to listen is an important part of dealing with customers. Using active listening skills helps managers understand why customers are dissatisfied.

2. **Responding**

   The way managers respond to complaints can be just as important as the way they solve the customer's problem. Businesspeople should always be courteous and friendly when dealing with customers. They should demonstrate interest in determining what went wrong and figuring out what they can do to solve the problem.

3. **Making Sure the Customers Are Satisfied**

   Managers need to determine whether they have satisfied the customers' needs. To do so, they must interpret the feedback they receive from the customers.

**figure 3.5**

USING ACTIVE LISTENING

what was said. Within 48 hours, the effectiveness level drops to just 25 percent. By the end of a week, listeners recall only about 10 percent or less of what they heard.

Managers need to work at being active listeners. Many people daydream or think about an unrelated topic when someone else is talking. Some people become angry by a speaker's remarks and fail to fully absorb what the person is saying. Others become impatient and interrupt, preferring to talk rather than listen.

Learning to listen actively involves the following steps:

- *Identify the speaker's purpose.* What is the speaker trying to achieve? Why is the speaker speaking?
- *Identify the speaker's main ideas.* Which of the points are the key points? Which points need to be addressed by the listener?
- *Note the speaker's tone as well as his or her body language.* Is the speaker angry? Nervous? Confident?
- *Respond to the speaker with appropriate comments, questions, and body language.* Use facial expressions and body language to express the emotions you want to express. Establish eye contact, sit up straight, and lean toward the speaker to show interest. Ask a question or make a comment from time to time to show that you are listening attentively.

## Feedback

Effective communication is a two-way process. Information must flow back and forth between sender and receiver. The flow from the receiver to the sender is called *feedback*. It informs the sender whether the receiver has received the correct message; it also lets the receiver know if he or she has received the correct message. For example, asking a person if she or he understands a message often puts the person on the defensive and can result in limited feedback. Instead of asking if a person understands a message, it is much better to request that the receiver explain what he or she has heard.

What are these students communicating nonverbally?

## Understanding the Importance of Nonverbal Communication

People have a great capacity to convey meaning through nonverbal means of expression. One form of nonverbal communication, called *paralanguage,* includes the pitch, tempo, loudness, and hesitations in the verbal communication. People also use a variety of gestures in nonverbal communication. In America, for example, one can raise an eyebrow to indicate disapproval, interest, concern, or attention. In Japan, however, that raised eyebrow would be considered an obscene gesture.

People also communicate nonverbally by how close they stand to each other. Body posture and eye contact also communicate messages. For example, lack of eye contact can communicate indifference or shyness.

In summary, nonverbal communication is an important supplement to verbal communication and sometimes can even change the meaning of verbal communication. Nonverbal communication is an effective way to communicate emotions. When combined with verbal communication, it gives managers powerful tools for transmitting information to employees.

# WRITTEN COMMUNICATION

Managers communicate in writing every day. They send e-mails, write letters, and draft reports. To communicate effectively, managers must be able to write clearly, concisely, and persuasively.

Before actually writing a business document, managers need to think about what they want to achieve. They must identify the purpose of the document, the audience, and the main point they want to convey. Using a form like that shown in Figure 3.6 can help them work through this stage of the writing process.

Proofreading is essential in effective communication of ideas.

## Principles of Good Writing

Many business managers have difficulty writing well. To improve their writing, managers can apply three basic principles:

- *Write as simply and clearly as possible.* Avoid writing in a way that is difficult to understand.

- *Be sure that the content and tone of the document are appropriate for the audience.* Do not waste readers' time communicating information they already know. However, do

**figure 3.6**

**IDENTIFYING THE PURPOSE, AUDIENCE, AND MAIN POINT OF A DOCUMENT**

**Purpose**
- Why am I writing this document?
- What action do I want the reader to take after reading it?

**Audience**
- Who will read this document?
- How much does the reader already know about the topic?
- How will the reader use the document?
- Are there any special sensitivities of which I should be aware?

**Main Message**
- What is the main message I want to convey in this document?
- How will I support that message?

not assume they are as familiar with the topic as you are. Always use a polite tone, especially when writing to customers.

- *Proofread the document.* If you are using a computer, use the spell-check function. If you are not using a computer, use a dictionary to check the spelling of words you do not know. Always read the document for incorrect grammar or usage.

---

### PROGRESS CHECK QUESTIONS

5. What is feedback, and how does it affect the communication process?
6. What are the four key steps of active listening?
7. Explain the importance of nonverbal communication in interpersonal communication.
8. What are the three basic principles of good writing?

---

## ORAL COMMUNICATION

Not all business communication is done in writing. In fact, most business communication is done orally.

Some oral communication is formal and takes place at meetings or interviews. Most oral communication is informal. It takes place in offices and hallways, next to the water cooler, in the cafeteria, and over the telephone.

### The Importance of Oral Communication

Communicating well verbally is important for managers. Successful managers use their oral communication skills to give clear instructions, motivate their staff, and persuade other people.

Being able to communicate effectively also is important because it can set the tone within a department or company. In some departments, managers say "good morning" to as many co-workers as they can. They invite their employees to discuss problems with them. In other departments, managers isolate themselves from lower-level employees and make no effort to communicate. These small differences can have a big effect on employee morale.

### Developing Oral Communication Skills

All businesspeople need to be able to speak effectively. Whether they are talking to a colleague or presenting a keynote address before thousands of people, they need to follow the same rules of thumb:

- *Make emotional contact with listeners by addressing them by name where possible.* When talking face to face, establish eye contact.

- *Avoid speaking in a monotone.* Use your voice to emphasize important words within a sentence.

- *Be enthusiastic and project a positive outlook.* Focus on what is going right, rather than what is going wrong.

- *Avoid interrupting others.* Even if you know what the other person is going to say, avoid cutting other people off or finishing their sentences for them.

- *Always be courteous.* Avoid getting angry when other people are talking, even if you disagree with what they are saying.

- *Avoid empty sounds or words, such as "uh," "um," "like," and "you know."* Sprinkling your speech with empty fillers will make you sound unprofessional.

### Career "Terminology" That Will Help

*"Knowledge Is the Key to Performance"*

Review the list of terms of how companies are structured, personal career qualities you must develop, how to find jobs, and what you can expect to do to get hired for a job.

*Looking inside companies*

Their structure can be slim and trim, layered, or a home office with satellites. Job listing and hiring come from the human resource department, which also posts job descriptions and benefits package information.

*How to find a job*

Jobs are found in wants ads, job Web sites, through personal contacts, or through employment agencies.

*Developing these skills as an aid in being hired*

Assessing self skills, learning career etiquette skills, developing career goals, filling out a job application, submitting a résumé, and executing a job interview.

---

### PROGRESS CHECK QUESTIONS

9. Explain the difference between formal and informal oral communication.

10. Successful managers use their oral communication skills in three primary ways. What are they?

11. List the six steps for effective oral communication

12. How could you improve your oral communication skills?

---

## CHOOSING THE BEST METHOD OF COMMUNICATION

Managers need to master both written and verbal communication skills. They also need to understand when to use each kind of skill. In general, verbal communication is most appropriate for sensitive communications, such as reprimanding or dismissing an employee. Written communication is most appropriate for communicating routine information, such as changes in company policies or staff. Choosing the best method

## Starting a New Job

Jack Smythe, branch manager for a large computer manufacturer, had been told by his marketing manager, Linda Sprague, that Otis Brown had just given two weeks' notice. When Jack had interviewed Otis, he had been convinced of his tremendous potential in sales. Otis was bright and personable, an MIT honor graduate in electrical engineering who had the qualifications the company looked for in computer sales. Now he was leaving after only two months with the company. Jack called Otis into his office for an exit interview.

**Jack:** Come in, Otis. I really want to talk to you. I hope I can change your mind about leaving.

**Otis:** I don't think so.

**Jack:** Well, tell me why you want to go. Has some other company offered you more money?

**Otis:** No. In fact, I don't have another job; I'm just starting to look.

**Jack:** You've given us notice without having another job?

**Otis:** Well, I just don't think this is the place for me!

**Jack:** What do you mean?

**Otis:** Let me see if I can explain. On my first day at work, I was told that formal classroom training in computers would not begin for a month. I was given a sales manual and told to read and study it for the rest of the day.

The next day, I was told that the technical library, where all the manuals on computers are kept, was in a mess and needed to be organized. That was to be my responsibility for the next three weeks.

The day before I was to begin computer school, my boss told me that the course had been delayed for another month. He said not to worry, however, because he was going to have James Crane, the branch's leading salesperson, give me some on-the-job training. I was told to accompany James on his calls. I'm supposed to start the school in two weeks, but I've just made up my mind that this place is not for me.

**Jack:** Hold on a minute, Otis. That's the way it is for everyone in the first couple of months of employment in our industry. Any place you go will be the same. In fact, you had it better than I did. You should have seen what I did in my first couple of months.

### Questions

1. What grade would you give Jack on this interview?
2. What suggestions do you have for Jack to help his company avoid similar problems of employee turnover in the future?
3. Should Jack find a way to make Otis change his mind? Why or why not?
4. Do you think Otis would change his mind and stay? Why or why not?

of communication will help you relay information in an appropriate and professional manner.

# COMMUNICATING WITHIN THE ORGANIZATION

In order to be an effective manager, the importance of the grapevine and e-mail must be understood.

## The Grapevine

**grapevine**
Informal channels of communication within an organization.

Many informal paths of communication also exist in organizations. These informal channels are generally referred to as the **grapevine.** During the

Civil War, intelligence telegraph lines hung loosely from tree to tree and looked like grapevines. Messages sent over these lines were often garbled; thus, any rumor was said to be from the grapevine. Grapevines develop within organizations when employees share common hobbies, hometowns, lunch breaks, family ties, and social relationships. The grapevine always exists within the formal organizational structure. However, it does not follow the organizational hierarchy; it may go from secretary to vice president or from engineer to clerk. The grapevine is not limited to nonmanagement personnel; it also operates among managers and professional personnel.

E-mail has become a major part of business communication. Be careful, however, not to rely too heavily upon it for sensitive communication. Radio Shack suffered from bad press and bad will when they laid off 400 employees via a mass e-mail in 2006.

The grapevine generally has a poor reputation because it is regarded as the primary source of distorted messages and rumors. However, management must recognize that the grapevine is often accurate. Management must also recognize that information in the grapevine travels more rapidly than information in the formal channels of communication. Finally, management must recognize the resilience of the grapevine. No matter how much effort is spent improving the formal channels of communication, grapevines will always exist.

Because the grapevine is inevitable, management should use it to complement formal channels of communication. In utilizing the grapevine, honesty is always the best policy. Rumors and distorted messages will persist, but honest disclaimers by management will stop the spread of inaccurate information.[1]

## E-mail

Especially valuable to communication in today's organizations is the use of electronic mail systems, or **e-mail,** provided by networked and online systems. The e-mail system provides for high-speed exchange of written messages through the use of computerized text processing and computer-oriented communication networks. The primary advantages of this system are that it saves time, eliminates wasted effort (such as unanswered or repeat phone calls), provides written records (if necessary) of communications without the formality of memos, and enables communication among individuals who might not communicate otherwise.

**e-mail**

The abbreviated version of 'electronic mail' refers to the system of sending and receiving messages over an electronic communications system.

## The Internet

The **Internet** is a global collection of independently operating but interconnected computers. Frequently referred to as the *information superhighway,* the Internet is actually a network of computer networks. Think of the Internet as comparable to the interstate highway system; just as the interstate system connects to different cities via many different routes, the Internet connects computers around the world via a number of different electronic pathways.

**Internet**

A global collection of independently operating, but interconnected, computers.

## Tardy Tom

On September 30, a large, national automobile-leasing firm in Columbus, Ohio, hired Tom Holland as a mechanic. Tom, the only mechanic employed by the firm in Columbus, was to do routine preventive maintenance on the cars. When he first began his job, he was scheduled to punch in on the time clock at 7 a.m. On October 30, Tom's supervisor, Russ Brown called him to his office and said, "Tom I've noticed during October that you've been late for work seven times. What can I do to help you get here on time?"

Tom replied, "It would be awfully nice if I could start work at 8 a.m. instead of 7 a.m."

Russ then stated, "Tom I'm very pleased with your overall work performance, so it's OK with me if your work-day begins at 8 a.m."

During the month of November, Tom was late eight times. Another conversation occurred similar to the one at the end of October. As a result of it, Tom's starting time was changed to 9 a.m.

On January 11, Russ Brown posted the following notice on the bulletin board:

*Any employee late for work more than two times in any one particular pay period is subject to termination.*

On January 20, Russ called Tom into his office and gave him a letter that read, "During this pay period, you have been late for work more than two times. If this behavior continues, you are subject to termination." Tom signed the letter to acknowledge that he had received it.

During February, Tom was late eight times and between March 1 and March 11, five times. On March 11, Russ notified Tom that he had been fired for his tardiness.

On March 12, Tom came in with his union representative and demanded that he get his job back. Tom alleged that there was another employee in the company who had been late as many times as he had, or more. Tom further charged that Russ was punching the time clock for this employee because Russ was having an affair with her. The union representative stated that three other people in the company had agreed to testify, under oath, to these facts. The union representative then said, "Russ, rules are for everyone. You can't let one person break a rule and penalize someone else for breaking the same rule. Therefore, Tom should have his job back."

### Questions

1. Was the manager communicating a message to Tom?
2. Should Tom get his job back? Why or why not?
3. What would you do if you were an arbitrator in this dispute?
4. How could Russ have handled this differently?

The real value of the Internet to managers is the information that it makes available. Through the Internet, managers can access massive amounts of information by accessing computers around the world that are linked together through the Internet. E-mail uses the Internet.[2]

### Intranets

**intranet**
A private, corporate, computer network that uses Internet products and technologies to provide multimedia applications within organizations.

An **intranet** is a private, corporate, computer network that uses Internet products and technologies to provide multimedia applications within organizations. An intranet connects people to people and people to information and knowledge within the organization; it serves as an "information hub" for the entire organization. Most organizations set up intranets primarily for employees, but they can extend to business partners and even customers with appropriate security clearance. Research has found that the biggest applications for intranets today are internal communications, followed by knowledge sharing and management information systems.[3]

# COMMUNICATION IN INTERNATIONAL BUSINESS ACTIVITIES

Communication in international business activities becomes more complicated in both the verbal and nonverbal communication processes. In verbal communication, the obvious problem of dealing with different languages exists. More than 3,000 languages are spoken, and about 100 of these are official languages of nations. English is the leading international language, and its leadership continues to grow. However, as anyone who has studied a modern language knows, verbally communicating with a person in another language complicates the communication process.

The nonverbal communication process is even more complicated. Cultural differences play a significant role in nonverbal communication. For example, in the United States, people tend to place themselves about three feet apart when standing and talking. However, in the Middle East, individuals are likely to stand only a foot or so apart while conversing. This closeness obviously could intimidate an American manager.

There are no simple answers to the problems in communicating in international business activities. However, there are two things the manager should do: (1) learn the culture of the people with whom he or she communicates and (2) write and speak clearly and simply. Most people will have learned English in school and will not understand jargon or slang. As expansion into international business continues, these simple rules will become increasingly important.

# CONCLUSION

In every function of management—planning, organizing, commanding, coordinating and controlling—communication skills can mean the difference between success and failure. In the next chapter we review another critical management skill: decision making.

With more than 31,000 locations worldwide, what was once a uniquely American franchise has become a worldwide commodity. What are some obstacles that might be created for a company like McDonald's?

## Tony gets some feedback

*Effective immediately, there will be no changes to the schedule once posted. It is your responsibility to show up for your designated shift or find someone to cover for you if a problem or emergency prevents you from showing up.*

**Tony Davis, Unit Manager**

Tony's new schedule policy started to create problems from the moment he posted the sign. First there were a few remarks about "Mr. Big" that Tony was sure were made deliberately as he walked by so that he could hear them. Then one or two employees started showing up late for their shifts with all kinds of excuses about buses being late, rides being late, or even oversleeping, as if they had suddenly forgotten how to set their alarm clock!

The first test of the policy came when Matt Crocker, a track star from the local high school, failed to show for his shift altogether. When Tony confronted him the next day, the explanation Matt offered was: "I'm sorry Tony but my coach changed the times for our track practice at the last minute, and I couldn't get to a phone to call you or find someone to cover for me. You know coach has done this before, and Jerry used to work with me on my schedule, but with your new policy, I didn't have a lot of options."

Tony was now left with a dilemma—should he make an example of Matt to enforce the policy? Or should he give the guy a break? "But," he thought, "if I give Matt a break, that will just encourage everyone else to ignore the policy, and I'll never cover my shifts. Pretty soon I'll be back to square one doing five versions of the schedule just like Jerry."

Tony decided to enforce the policy and took Matt off the schedule for the remainder of the week as a warning for not following the new policy. He felt bad about it but convinced himself that the tough decision would pay off in the long run.

The next morning two of the six folks scheduled for the morning shift failed to show up.

Fortunately it was a slow morning, and they were able to get the work done, but Tony was angry at what he saw as a direct challenge to his authority. As he sat angrily processing invoices in his office, Tanya, the shift leader, stopped by.

"Tony, can I talk to you for a minute?" Tanya asked.

"Sure," Tony said angrily.

"Look, I know it's my last week here and everything," continued Tanya, "but you have a real problem on your hands here, Tony. Being so strict about the schedule is really ticking some of your people off, and some are threatening to quit. They're even talking about calling Jerry to see if he can talk some sense into you. Did you ever think about asking them for suggestions or meeting with them to talk about the new schedule? Making such a dramatic change and then making an example of Matt like that looks to them like your new title is going to your head. He's been a good guy in the past, and it wasn't his fault that the coach changed the practice time."

### QUESTIONS

1. Should Tony have been surprised by the reactions of his crew?
2. Do you think the employees have the right to complain about the new schedule policy?
3. How could Tony have handled this differently?
4. What would you do now?

---

## key terms

**communication** 56
**e-mail** 67
**grapevine** 66

**Internet** 67
**interpersonal communication** 57

**intranet** 68
**perception** 59
**semantics** 58

## review questions

1. Give an illustration of a conflicting assumption.
2. What are the six basic "rules of thumb" of good oral communication?
3. Describe some ways the grapevine can be used effectively in organizations.
4. What is active listening?

## internet exercise

Visit Toastmasters International at www.toastmasters.org
Answer the following questions:

1. What is the Toastmasters Program, and how did it start?
2. What are the vision and mission of Toastmasters International?
3. Read the "Top 10 Tips for Public Speaking," and select the three tips that you found most useful.
4. Would you ever consider joining the Toastmasters Program? Why or why not?

## team exercise

**WHAT'S YOUR COMMUNICATION STYLE?**

Divide the class into pairs. Perform the exercise listed below, and then compare your results with your assigned partner.

Carefully read each statement and its four endings. Grade these by assigning a 4 to the ending that most describes you, a 3 to the next ending most like you, a 2 to the next ending most like you, and a 1 to the ending least like you. Once you have assigned a number, you may not use that number again in the set of four endings. For example, you may not assign a grade of 4 to both 1(a) and 1(b).

1. I am most likely to impress my co-workers as
   a. Down to earth, practical, and to the point.          a _____
   b. Emotional, sensitive to my own and others' feelings.  b _____
   c. Cool, logical, patient.                               c _____
   d. Intellectual and somewhat aloof.                      d _____

2. When I am assigned a project, I am most concerned that the project will be

   a. Practical, with definite results that will justify
      my time and energy on it.                                          a _____
   b. Stimulating, involving lively interaction with others.             b _____
   c. Systematically or logically develop.                              c _____
   d. Breaking ground and advancing knowledge.                          d _____

3. In reacting to individuals whom I meet socially, I am likely to consider whether

   a. They are assertive and decisive.                                  a _____
   b. They are caring.                                                  b _____
   c. They seem thorough and exact.                                    c _____
   d. They seem highly intelligent.                                    d _____

4. When confronted by others with a different opinion, I find it most useful to

   a. Pinpoint the key differences, and develop
      compromises so that speedy decisions can be made.                 a _____
   b. Put myself in the others' shoes, and try to
      understand their point of view.                                  b _____
   c. Keep calm and present my material clearly, simply,
      and logically.                                                   c _____
   d. Create new proposals.                                           d _____

5. Under pressure, I suspect I may come through to others as being

   a. Too concerned with wanting immediate action,
      and pushing for immediate decisions.                             a _____
   b. Too emotional and occasionally carried away by my
      feelings.                                                        b _____
   c. Highly unemotional, impersonal, too analytical
      and critical.                                                    c _____
   d. Snobbish, condescending, intellectually superior.               d _____

6. When lecturing to a group, I would like to leave the impression of being

   a. A practical and resourceful person who can show the
      audience how to, for example, streamline a procedure.            a _____
   b. A lively and persuasive individual who is in touch
      with the audience's emotions and moods.                          b _____
   c. A systematic thinker who can analyze the
      group's problems.                                                c _____
   d. A highly innovative individual.                                  d _____

Now transcribe the numbers that you wrote beside each ending to the appropriate spaces below. Total the columns for questions 1–3 and for questions 4–6. The initials at the bottom of the columns—S, F, T, and I—stand for the different communication styles: senser, feeler, thinker, and intuitor. The column with the highest total for questions 1–3 is your communication style under relaxed conditions, and the column with the highest total for questions 4–6 is your style under stress conditions. Once you have defined your particular style, check the table at the end of the exercise for the positive and negative traits associated with it. Note that you may have the positive traits without the negative ones or vice versa.

|     | a | b | c | d |     | a | b | c | d |
|-----|---|---|---|---|-----|---|---|---|---|
| 1.  | ___ | ___ | ___ | ___ | 4.  | ___ | ___ | ___ | ___ |
| 2.  | ___ | ___ | ___ | ___ | 5.  | ___ | ___ | ___ | ___ |
| 3.  | ___ | ___ | ___ | ___ | 6.  | ___ | ___ | ___ | ___ |
| **Total** | **S** | **F** | **T** | **I** | **Total** | **S** | **F** | **T** | **I** |

*Source:* Phyllis Kuhn, "Sharpening Your Communication Skills," *Medical Laboratory Observer,* March 1987. Used with permission from *Medical Laboratory Observer.* Copyright © 1987 by Nelson Publishing, Inc., www.mlo-online.com.

## Some Traits Linked to Each Communication Style

| **Positive** | **Negative** |
|--------------|--------------|
| *Intuitor* | |
| Creative | Fantasy-bound |
| Idealistic | Impractical |
| Intellectual | Too theoretical |
| *Feeler* | |
| Caring | Wishy-washy |
| Conscientious | Guilt-ridden |
| Persuasive | Manipulative |
| *Thinker* | |
| Exact, precise | Nitpicker |
| Deliberate | Rigid |
| Weighs all alternatives | Indecisive |
| *Senser* | |
| Decisive | Impulsive |
| Assertive | Aggressive |
| Enjoys producing quick results | Lacks trust in others' ability |
| Technically skillful | Self-involved, status seeking |

## The Secret Of BMW's Success

*BMW's Reputation for Innovation Can Be Traced to Its Equally Innovative Lateral Management Techniques*

At 4:00 p.m. on a Friday afternoon, when most German workers have long departed for the weekend, the mini-cafés sprinkled throughout BMW's sprawling R&D center in Munich are jammed with engineers, designers, and marketing managers deliberating so intently it's hard to hear above the din. Even the cappuccino machine is running on empty. It's an atmosphere far more Silicon Valley than Detroit. The intense employee buzz at BMW is hot management theory in action. Top consultants and academics say the kind of informal networks that flourish at BMW and the noise and borderline chaos they stimulate in big organizations are vital for innovation—especially in companies where knowledge sits in the brains of tens of thousands of workers and not in a computer server. Melding that brainpower, they say, is essential to unleashing the best ideas.

**HANDS ACROSS DIVISIONS.** BMW is one of a handful of global companies including Nokia and Raytheon that have turned to networks to manage day-to-day operations, overriding the classic management control pyramid. Those pioneering companies still turn to the management chain of command to set strategic goals, but workers have the freedom to forge teams across divisions and achieve targets in the best way possible—even if that way is unconventional. And they are encouraged to build ties across divisions to speed change.

**LIGHTNING-FAST CHANGES.** Speed and organizational agility is increasingly vital to the auto industry, since electronics now make up some 20 percent of a car's value—and that level is rising. BMW figures some 90 percent of the innovations in its new models are electronics-driven. That requires once-slow-moving automakers to adapt to the lightning pace of innovation and change driving the semiconductor and software industries. Gone is the era of the 10-year model cycle. Now automakers must ram innovation into high gear to avoid being overtaken by the competition. That's especially true in the luxury-auto leagues, where market leaders must pulse new innovations constantly onto the market, from podcasting for cars to infrared night vision systems. By shifting effective management of day-to-day operations to such human networks, which speed knowledge laterally through companies faster and better than old organizational models can, BMW has become as entrepreneurial as a tech startup, consultants say.

**MOBILE-PHONE MESSAGES.** BMW's ability to drive innovation even pervades its marketing division. To reach a younger crowd of potential buyers for its new 1 Series launch in 2004, BMW used mobile-phone messages as the main source of buzz, directing interested people to sign-ups on BMW's Web site for pre-launch test drives in August that year—something unheard of in the industry at the time. The experimental tactic worked: BMW sparked responses from 150,000 potential customers — and sales of the 1 Series took off when it was launched in September, 2004. In 2001, BMW stunned the advertising world by investing ad spending normally set aside for Super Bowl spots in short films that had nothing to do with telling consumers about its cars. The slick, professionally made films were pure entertainment, like its series of short films, *The Hire*, starring Clive Owens, and they cost a bundle: $25 million.

**BALANCING ACT.** The risky bet triggered serious anxiety at BMW's Munich headquarters. Few large companies are willing to embrace the lack of organizational clarity and vague structures that drive innovative ideas. At most companies, headquarters would have put a stop to the short-film idea, which has since been widely imitated. Researchers say most companies experiment with networks on a small scale and very few use the practice to full effect since doing so means an uncomfortable balancing act between hierarchy and discipline on one hand, and freewheeling networks that can veer toward near-chaos. But for innovation-driven companies, networks that enable entrepreneurial risk-taking are a silver bullet.

**IDEAS FIRST.** How does BMW manage discipline with creativity and keep the anarchy of networks from careening out of control? Workers at the Bavarian automaker are encouraged from their first day on the job to build a network or web of personal ties to speed problem-solving and innovation, be it in R&D, design, production, or marketing. Those ties run across divisions and up and down the chain of command. When it comes to driving innovation, forget formal meetings, hierarchy, and stamps of approval. Each worker learns quickly that pushing fresh ideas is vital. BMW's complex customized production system, the polar opposite of Toyota's standardized lines, is easier to manage if workers feel empowered to drive change. Like Dell Computer, BMW configures its cars to customers' orders, so each auto moving down the production line is different.

**FORGET OLD-SCHOOL RIGIDITY.** Making sure the system works without a hitch requires savvy workers who continually suggest how to optimize processes. By contrast, companies that don't have lateral quickness are crippled in fast-moving technology-driven industries. Rigid hierarchies that stifle fresh ideas and slow reaction times are one problem facing General Motors and Ford Motor. Once giants like GM were king, dominating the market with their huge volume and purchasing muscle. Big is no longer the ticket to success, and the slow-moving bureaucracies that big companies are saddled with are now a major handicap.

**KNOW THY CONSUMER.** BMW managers, by contrast, even talk about the "physics of chaos" and how to constantly nurture innovation and creativity by operating on the very edge of chaos without getting out of control. That's the industry's next *kaizen*—the art automakers will be forced to master in the 21st century.

The novel advertising scheme developed back in 2001 is a good example. Jim McDowell, then U.S. vice-president of marketing, was confident the project, dubbed "Big Idea," and kept under tight security in "War Room" No. 6 at BMW USA's Woodlake (N.J.) headquarters, would create just the kind of consumer buzz that BMW wanted—and would ultimately be more cost-effective for BMW than Super Bowl advertising. The idea was to give film directors a BMW car around which a compelling short film was to be made. Many of the tales centered on life-and-death chase scenes, but several were humorous or even melancholy. McDowell figured if *The Hire,* took off and the films were downloaded from BMW's Web site by 1 million to 2 million viewers, BMW would chalk up the same number of eyeballs as a snappy advertising campaign aired during the Super Bowl, but would reach a higher percentage of BMW-type customers.

**SNOWBALL EFFECT.** McDowell didn't take any half-measures. He went after talented directors such as John Frankenheimer *(The French Connection)* and Ang Lee *(Crouching Tiger, Hidden Dragon),* and signed up stars such as Madonna, Clive Owens, and Gary Oldman—giving them complete artistic freedom, aside from the BMW model that starred in each film. No advance advertising heralded the Internet launch of the films. The buzz started slowly with the first film but grew to avalanche proportions by the time Madonna's short comedy film about a cranky diva was released, overwhelming BMW's expectations and forcing the automaker to add

servers as fast as it could. But it didn't stop there. As the short-film gambit rocketed around the world, national TV broadcasters flooded McDowell's office with requests for interviews on CBS, *Entertainment Tonight*, and Fox News. The novelty of an automaker producing films fanned public interest and stoked downloads.

**"EXPERIMENTAL ENVIRONMENT."**
After one year, the number of viewers who had visited BMW's Web site to download *The Hire* shot to over 21 million, and with three more films added in 2002, it rocketed to 100 million, sparking a Harvard Business School case study. One million enthusiasts ordered a DVD with all eight films.

## Questions

1. How is communication "across divisions and silos" different from communication "up and down the hierarchy"?

2. Define the term "boundaryless corporation." You may want to do some research on Jack Welch and General Electric here.

3. If human networks "speed knowledge laterally through companies faster and better than old organizational models can," and employees are "encouraged from their first day on the job to build a network or web of personal ties to speed problem-solving and innovation," how does BMW ensure that the right decisions are made?

4. "Formal structures decide who to blame. Informal structures decide how to get things done." What are the implications of this philosophy for a BMW manager?

*Source:* Adapted from Gail Edmondson, "Innovation," *BusinessWeek Online,* October 16, 2006.

## What Works in Women's Networks

*How Two Corporations Crafted Organizations for Female Employees That Have an Actual Impact*

Corporate women's networks frequently get a bad reputation—for good reason. The groups frequently work on the fringes, hosting "lunch and learns" and book clubs that rarely provide the skills or exposure women need to rise in the ranks. Often, "these initiatives are run by people who don't really have much power," notes Claudia Peus, a visiting scholar at Massachusetts Institute of Technology's Sloan School of Manage-ment. When she interviewed more than 900 female executives about critical factors in their success, they ranked programs for the promotion of women last. "The spontaneous reaction was, 'They don't work.'" Yet such initiatives are flourishing. One reason is an eager-

ness on the part of talent-hungry employers to appear more female-friendly. Networks are cheap, usually relying on female volunteers and garnering little corporate funding. The groups may become little more than social gatherings, and have trouble attracting heavy hitters. But networks need not be feeble. They can be a magnet for recruiting and retaining top achiev-ers. Here's a look at some practices that work:

### GET CUSTOMERS IN ON THE ACT

Formed 10 years ago after a handful of senior fe-male employees had dinner with Jack Welch, the GE Women's Network has since grown to 40,000 active members worldwide. Its focus on leader-ship, advancement, and career-broadening op-portunities has helped GE get to the point where women now run businesses generating some $40 billion in sales, more than 20 percent of total rev-enues. One distin-guishing feature of the network: Its an-nual Leading & Learning summit that brings together about 150 top-level women, two-thirds of whom are cus-tomers or suppli-ers, to discuss a wide range of ideas and issues. Among the speakers at the May 2007 event: eBay Inc. CEO Meg Whitman, author Karenna Gore Schiff, play-wright Sarah Jones, Atlanta Mayor Shirley Franklin, and *Today* co-anchor Meredith Vieira. CEO Jeffrey R. Immelt also came, as he always does, to speak and spend a few hours with the participants. Within GE, the benefits of linking the company network to outsiders are many. One big positive is the exposure. "I don't get an awful lot of opportunities to interact with customers in my job," notes Tracie Winbigler, an executive vice-president at NBC Universal and co-chair of the network. "This gives me a chance to have more external focus." Another payoff to hosting such events is having customers form "a favorable impression of GE," adds co-chair Julie DeWane, who works as a general manager at GE Transportation. That's one reason why each geographic network "hub"—there are 140 of them around the world—is asked to participate in a range of community activities, from philanthropic ventures to other customer-oriented events. Network members in Europe now plan to hold a similar high-level summit there, and others are looking to extend the concept elsewhere.

## BRIDGE THE GENDER DIVIDE

Few women's networks can boast of a track record like that of Deloitte. Now in its 14th year, Deloitte's Initiative for the Retention and Advancement of Women, known as WIN, has been praised for its success in promoting women to the most senior ranks: 19.3 percent of partners are women, the highest percentage among the Big Four public accounting firms. That's up from 7 percent since WIN was started in 1993. One reason for its success? Many of the programs born out of Deloitte's women's initiative are geared toward both women and men. For instance, the firm is piloting a "mass career customization" program that will give every employee a framework for dialing up and down their hours, travel demands, and responsibilities as their personal needs change over the course of their careers. Unlike flextime or job-sharing policies, which men often avoid because of the stigma still associated with opting into them, everyone in the pilot locations will be enrolled in the program. Still, such initiatives have little direct impact on hard-charging audit partners whose idea of work-life balance is a three-day weekend after tax season. When asked, says Cathy Benko, the national managing director in charge of WIN, men almost always say that the women's initiative is important. "But then they'll stop, and if they continue, they'll say 'but it hasn't done anything for me.'" To help change that thinking, Benko came up with a new program two years ago called Women as Buyers. It would specifically help men with what mattered to them—winning more clients—while improving understanding between men and women at the firm. Noticing a lack of research on how executive women make decisions, the WIN team sponsored a yearlong study on the topic. It has been presenting its findings in four-hour workshops made up of two-thirds men and one-third women. The sessions remind men of simple differences such as client entertaining (women prefer breakfast to dinner, since they often have more evening responsibilities at home) and communication styles (just because a woman is nodding doesn't mean she agrees with you). While male executives may prefer consultants or accountants to sit by their side, women are more visual than men, the research found, and partners should face women executives in client meetings. And because women tend to see leadership roles as positions of responsibility rather than power, partners should think carefully about whom they parachute in to help sell services. The feedback from men has been overwhelmingly positive: More than 90 percent say the workshops were useful.

### Questions

1. Why do corporate women's networks get a bad reputation?

2. Why would GE's Women's Network want each geographic network "hub" to participate in a range of community activities?

3. How did Deloitte's WIN Workshop help improve understanding between women and men of the firm?

4. Think of the company you work for (or one you have worked for in the past). Would a network for women (or men) be successful? Why or why not?

*Source:* Adapted from Diane Brady and Jena McGregor, "Managing," *BusinessWeek Online,* June 18, 2007.

# DECISION-MAKING SKILLS

> "I have to be wrong a certain number of times in order to be right a certain number of times. However, in order to be either, I must first make a decision."

—Frank. N. Giampietro

## The World of Work: Tony tries another approach

Tony Davis's first attempt at putting his stamp on the Taco Barn hadn't gone well. All the time he had expected to gain by making the staff schedule less open to negotiation had been lost in finding coverage for employees who couldn't or didn't show for their assigned shifts. Tanya, his soon-to-be ex-shift leader had finally set him straight about the anger and frustration his new approach of "my way or the highway" was creating among his staff. His decision to make an example of Matt by keeping him off the schedule for a week after failing to show for his assigned shift was supposed to send a clear message of how serious Tony was about this scheduling issue. In reality, all he had succeeded in doing, as Tanya pointed out, was making the staff even angrier. Everyone thought Matt was a good guy who was struggling to balance his school and sports commitments as well as his work shifts. Punishing him for not calling in because his coach changed the time of the practice was, in their eyes, too harsh. Some had even suggested calling Jerry, the former store manager, to see if he could talk some sense into Tony.

"Great," said Tony, "here I am trying to make this place more efficient by freeing some time from my schedule to be more available in the restaurant, and my staff is screaming for Jerry to come back. Now what do I do? If I go back on the new policy, they'll see me as being weak and they'll complain about every new change from now on."

# objectives

## CHAPTER 4

**After studying this chapter, you will be able to:**

1 Explain the difference between decision making and problem solving.

2 Compare and contrast intuitive and rational approaches to decision making.

3 Explain the decision maker's environment and the conditions for making a decision.

4 Explain timing and participation as they relate to the decision-making process.

5 Identify methods for creative decision making.

6 Discuss management information systems.

"Why do you feel the need to be in the restaurant more, Tony?" asked Tanya, who was doing her best to help Tony work through this unexpected negative feedback. "You've got a good crew here—they don't need to be watched every minute of the day."

"It's not about watching them every minute of the day," replied Tony. "I know this is a good crew—so good in fact that a few of them could really do well as future managers with Taco Barn. Plus you're leaving, and until I replace your position, I need to be out there helping them, not sitting in the office working on the schedule for hours at a time."

"Did you ever think about telling them that, instead of making such a dramatic change and then making an example of Matt?" said Tanya. "It looks to them like your new title is going to your head when all you want to do is be more available to help them."

**QUESTIONS**

1. What assumptions did Tony make in introducing his new scheduling policy?

2. Which type of decision-making approach did Tony use here? Review the material on Intuitive and Rational approaches to decision-making for help here.

3. How could Tony change his interpersonal skills to fix this communication breakdown?

4. What should Tony do now?

# MAKING DECISIONS

Some authors use the term *decision maker* to mean *manager*. However, although managers are decision makers, not all decision makers are managers. For example, a person who sorts fruit and vegetables is required to make decisions, but not as a manager. However, all managers, regardless of their positions in the organization, must make decisions in the pursuit of organizational goals. In fact, decision making pervades all the basic management functions: planning, organizing, staffing, leading, and controlling. Although each of these functions requires different types of decisions, all of them require decisions. Thus, to be a good planner, organizer, staffer, leader, and controller, a manager must first be a good decision maker.

> **decision process**
>
> Process that involves three stages: intelligence, design, and choice.

Herbert Simon, a Nobel Prize winner, has described the manager's **decision process** in three stages: (1) intelligence, (2) design, and (3) choice.[1] The intelligence stage involves searching the environment for conditions requiring a decision. The design stage involves inventing, developing, and analyzing possible courses of action. Choice, the final stage, refers to the actual selection of a course of action.

The decision process stages show the difference between management and nonmanagement decisions. Non-management decisions are concentrated in the last (choice) stage. The fruit and vegetable sorter has to make a choice regarding only the size or quality of the goods. Management decisions place greater emphasis on the intelligence and design stages. If the decision-making process is viewed as only the choice stage, managers spend very little time making decisions. If, however, the decision-making process is viewed as not only the actual choice but also the intelligence and design work needed to make the choice, managers spend most of their time making decisions.

# DECISION MAKING VERSUS PROBLEM SOLVING

> **decision making**
>
> In its narrowest sense, the process of choosing from among various alternatives.

> **problem solving**
>
> Process of determining the appropriate responses or actions necessary to alleviate a problem.

The terms *decision making* and *problem solving* are often confused and therefore need to be clarified. As indicated earlier, **decision making,** in its narrowest sense, is the process of choosing from among various alternatives. A *problem* is any deviation from some standard or desired level of performance. **Problem solving,** then, is the process of determining the appropriate responses or actions necessary to alleviate a problem. Problem solving necessarily involves decision making, since all problems can be attacked in numerous ways and the problem solver must decide which way is best. On the other hand, not all decisions involve problems (such as the person sorting fruit and vegetables). However, from a practical perspective, almost all managerial decisions do involve solving or at least avoiding problems.

# THE INTUITIVE APPROACH TO DECISION MAKING

When managers make decisions solely on hunches and intuition (the **intuitive approach**), they are practicing management as though it were wholly an art based only on feelings. While intuition and other forms of judgment do play a role in many decision situations, problems can occur when managers ignore available facts and rely only on feelings. When this happens, managers sometimes become so emotionally attached to certain positions that almost nothing will change their minds. They develop the "don't bother me with the facts—my mind is made up" attitude. George Odiorne isolated the following emotional attachments that can hurt decision makers:

1. Fastening on unsubstantiated facts and sticking with them.
2. Being attracted to scandalous issues and heightening their significance.
3. Pressing every fact into a moral pattern.
4. Overlooking everything except what is immediately useful.
5. Having a preference for romantic stories and finding such information more significant than any other kind, including hard evidence.[2]

Such emotional attachments can be very real and can lead to poor decisions. They most often affect managers or decision makers who are "living in the past" and either will not or cannot modernize their thinking. An example is the manager who insists on making decisions just as the founder of the company did 40 years ago.

> **intuitive approach**
> Approach used when managers make decisions based largely on hunches and intuition.

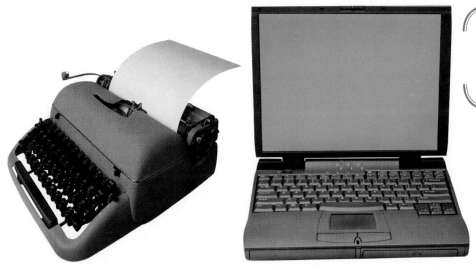

The inability to modernize can have serious consequences for a decision maker trying to make informed choices.

Odiorne offers two suggestions for managers and decision makers overwhelmed by emotional attachments.[3] First, become aware of biases and allow for them. Undiscovered biases do the most damage. Second, seek independent opinions. It is always advisable to ask the opinion of some person who has no vested interest in the decision. Intuition does play a role in decision making. The key is to not ignore facts when they are available.

# RATIONAL APPROACHES TO DECISION MAKING

Approaches to decision making that attempt to evaluate factual information through the use of some type of deductive reasoning are referred to as *rational approaches*. The following sections discuss two types of rational approaches:

## The Optimizing Approach

**optimizing approach**

Includes the following steps: recognize the need for a decision; establish, rank, and weigh criteria; gather available information and data; identify possible alternatives; evaluate each alternative with respect to all criteria; and select the best alternatives.

The physical sciences have provided a rational approach to decision making that can be adapted to management problems. The **optimizing approach** (sometimes called the *rational* or *scientific approach*) to decision making includes the following steps:

1. Recognize the need for a decision.
2. Establish, rank, and weigh the decision criteria.
3. Gather available information and data.
4. Identify possible alternatives.
5. Evaluate each alternative with respect to all criteria.
6. Select the best alternative.

Once the need to make the decision is known, criteria must be set for expected results of the decision. These criteria should then be ranked and weighed according to their relative importance.

Next, factual data relating to the decision should be collected. After that, all alternatives that meet the criteria are identified. Each is then evaluated with respect to all criteria. The final decision is based on the alternative that best meets the criteria.

## Limitations of the Optimizing Approach

The optimizing approach to decision making is an improvement over the intuitive approach, but it is not without its problems and limitations. The optimizing approach is based on the concept of the "economic man."

This concept proposes that people behave rationally and their behavior is based on the following assumptions:

1. People have clearly defined criteria, and the relative weights they assign to these criteria are stable.

2. People have knowledge of all relevant alternatives.

3. People have the ability to evaluate each alternative with respect to all the criteria and arrive at an overall rating for each alternative.

4. People have the self-discipline to choose the alternative that rates the highest (they will not manipulate the system).

Consider the following difficulties with the above approach. First, these assumptions are often unrealistic; decision makers do not always have clearly defined criteria for making decisions. Second, many decisions are based on limited knowledge of the possible alternatives; even when information is available, it is usually less than perfect. Third, there is always a temptation to manipulate or ignore the gathered information and choose a favored (but not necessarily the best) alternative.

Due to the limitations of the optimizing approach, most decisions still involve some judgment. Thus, in making decisions, the manager generally uses a combination of intuitive and rational approaches.

### Developing Habits for a Successful Career

By now you are familiar with the expression, "Good habits lead to good outcomes." How you handle daily duties, such as your job, school, eating and drinking choices, creates opportunities to develop good habits. Here is a list of habits that might help lead to personal and career success:

- Being on time
- Doing my best
- Listening
- Writing things down
- Consistent effort
- Positive attitude
- Completing all work
- Volunteering
- Even temperament
- Avoiding gossip
- Being trustworthy
- Working smart
- Exhibiting leadership
- Passion
- Character

## The Satisficing Approach

Believing the assumptions of the optimizing approach to be generally unrealistic, Herbert Simon, in attempting to understand how managerial decisions are actually made, formulated his **principle of bounded rationality.** This principle states, "The capacity of the human mind for formulating and solving complex problems is very small compared with the size of the problems whose solution *is* required for objectively rational behavior—or even for a reasonable approximation to such objective rationality."[4] Basically, the principle of bounded rationality states that human rationality has definite limits. Based on this principle, Simon proposed a decision model of the "administrative man," which makes the following assumptions:

1. A person's knowledge of alternatives and criteria is limited.

2. People act on the basis of a simplified, ill-structured, mental concept of the real world; this concept is influenced by personal perceptions, biases, and so forth.

**principle of bounded rationality**
Assumes people have the time and cognitive ability to process only a limited amount of information on which to base decisions.

3. People do not attempt to optimize but will take the first alternative that satisfies their current level of aspiration. This is called *satisficing*.

4. An individual's level of aspiration concerning a decision fluctuates upward and downward, depending on the values of the most recently identified alternatives.

**optimizing**

Selecting the best possible alternative.

**satisficing**

Selecting the first alternative that meets the decision maker's minimum standard of satisfaction.

**level of aspiration**

Level of performance that a person expects to attain; determined by the person's prior successes and failures.

The first assumption is a summary of the principle of bounded rationality. The second assumption follows naturally from the first. If limits to human rationality do exist, an individual must make decisions based on limited and incomplete knowledge. The third assumption also naturally follows from the first assumption: If the decision maker's knowledge of alternatives is incomplete, the individual cannot optimize but can only "satisfice." **Optimizing** means selecting the best possible alternative; **satisficing** means selecting the first alternative that meets the decision maker's minimum standard of satisfaction. Assumption four is based on the belief that the criteria for a satisfactory alternative are determined by the person's current level of aspiration. **Level of aspiration** refers to the level of performance a person expects to attain, and it is impacted by the person's prior successes and failures.

Figure 4.1 represents the satisficing approach to decision making. If the decision maker is satisfied that an acceptable alternative has been found, she or he selects that alternative. Otherwise the decision maker searches for an additional alternative. In Figure 4.1, the double arrows indicate a two-way relationship: The value of the new alternative is influenced by the value of the best previous alternative; the value of the best previous alternative is in turn influenced by the value of the new alternative. As the arrows indicate, a similar two-way relationship exists between the value of the new alternative and the current level of aspiration. The net result of this evaluation determines whether or not the decision maker is satisfied with the alternative. Thus, the "administrative man" selects the first alternative that meets the minimum satisfaction criteria and makes no real attempt to optimize.

## figure 4.1

**MODEL OF THE SATISFICING APPROACH**

***Source:*** Adapted from James G. March and Herbert A. Simon, *Organizations*, 1958, John Wiley & Sons.

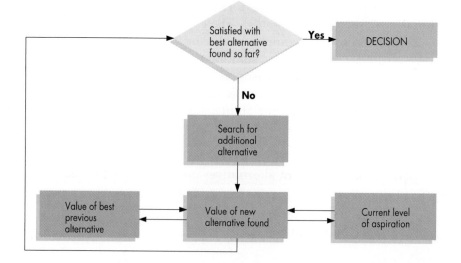

**PROGRESS CHECK QUESTIONS**

1. Explain the difference between decision making and problem solving.
2. Explain the intuitive approach to decision making.
3. What are the six steps in the optimizing approach to decision making?
4. Explain the satisficing approach to decision making.

## THE DECISION-MAKER'S ENVIRONMENT

A manager's freedom to make decisions depends largely on the manager's position within the organization and on its structure. In general, higher-level managers have more flexibility and freedom of choice. The patterns of authority outlined by the formal organization structure also influence the flexibility of the decision maker.

Another important factor in decision-making style is the purpose and tradition of the organization. For example, a military organization requires a different style of decision making than a volunteer organization does.

The organization's formal and informal group structures also affect decision-making styles. These groups may range from labor unions to advisory councils.

The final subset of the environment includes all of the decision maker's superiors and subordinates. The personalities, backgrounds, and expectations of these people influence the decision maker.

Figure 4.2 shows the major environmental factors within an organization that affect decision makers in an organization. In addition to these

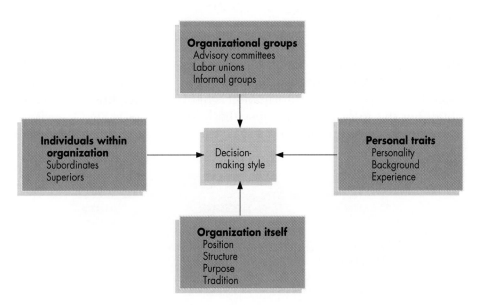

**figure 4.2**

ENVIRONMENTAL FACTORS INFLUENCING DECISION MAKING IN AN ORGANIZATION

major organizational factors, there are always other factors in the general environment that can influence a decision. Some of these factors might include industry norms, the labor market, the political climate, and competition. Successful managers must develop an appreciation for the different environmental forces that both influence them and are influenced by their decisions.

# CONDITIONS FOR MAKING DECISIONS

Decisions are not always made with the same amount of available information. The best decision often depends on what happens later. Consider the simple decision of whether to take an umbrella when going outside. The more desirable alternative is determined by whether or not it rains, but this is not under the control of the decision maker. Figure 4.3 gives combinations of alternatives and states of nature and their respective outcomes for the individual trying to decide whether or not to take an umbrella when going outside.

## Certainty

**situation of certainty**
Situation that occurs when a decision maker knows exactly what will happen and can often calculate the precise outcome for each alternative.

Knowing exactly what will happen places the decision maker in a **situation of certainty.** In such a situation, the decision maker can calculate the precise outcome for each alternative. If it is raining, the person knows the outcome of each alternative and therefore can choose the best alternative (take an umbrella). Rarely, however, are decisions made in today's organizations under a condition of certainty. A manager deciding between a delivery by air (taking a set time to arrive at a set cost) or one by truck (also taking a set time to arrive at a set cost) would be an example of a decision made under a condition of certainty.

## Risk

**situation of risk**
Situation that occurs when a decision maker is aware of the relative probabilities of occurrence associated with each alternative.

Unfortunately, the outcome associated with each alternative is not always known in advance. The decision maker can often obtain—at some cost—information regarding the different possible outcomes. The desirability of getting the information is figured by weighing the costs of obtaining the information against the information's value. A decision maker is in a **situation of risk** if certain reliable but incomplete

**figure 4.3**

UMBRELLA DECISION
ALTERNATIVES AND
OUTCOMES

| ALTERNATIVE | State of Nature | |
| --- | --- | --- |
| | NO RAIN | RAIN |
| Take umbrella | Dry, but inconvenient | Dry |
| Do not take umbrella | Dry, happy | Wet |

Dave, the newly appointed vice president of a manufacturing company, has just been informed that a team of internal auditors from the corporate head office will be arriving in two days. He prepares his staff as best he can. The day before the auditors arrive, one of his assistants discovers some disturbing news. It appears, he says, that Woody, a 30-year veteran of the plant, has been systematically altering accounts for years. Month by month, Woody has been shipping products to customers without billing them—and then billing customers without shipping anything.

Dave is stunned. Seeking an explanation, he learns that the practice has nothing to do with fraud. Woody wasn't lining his own pocket. He was simply trying to be helpful. His goal was to smooth out the cyclical nature of the orders so that, month by month, the figures sent to the home office appear level and consistent, with no peaks and valleys. Dave discovers that no money has been lost or gained: It all balances out in the end. And while the amount is not immense, the funds affected amount to perhaps 5 percent of the plant's annual earnings.

In one sense, Woody's adjustments have benefited Dave, who has already been complimented by his boss for his wise forecasts and for meeting his targets so accurately. But Dave also knows that if these practices were to come to light, Woody would be fired instantly—he himself, though ignorant of the practice until now, might have some tough explaining to do. After all, Woody has been fudging records and misstating corporate revenues to management, shareholders, and the IRS.

What should Dave do?

***Source:*** Adapted from "Smoothing the Factory's Accounts," Institute for Global Ethics, www.globalethics.org/resources/dilemmas/smoothing.htm.

---

information is available. In a situation of risk, some ideas of the relative probabilities associated with each outcome are known. If the weather forecaster has said there is a 40 percent chance of rain, the decision maker is operating in a situation of risk.

The precise probabilities of the various outcomes usually are not known. However, reasonably accurate probabilities based on historical data and past experiences often can be calculated.

When no such data exist, it is difficult to estimate probabilities. In such cases, one approach is to survey individual opinions.

Under conditions of risk, the decision maker can use expected value analysis to help arrive at a decision. With this technique, the expected payoff of each known alternative is mathematically calculated based on its probability of occurrence. One potential shortcoming of expected value analysis is that it represents the average outcome if the event is repeated many times. That is of little help if the act occurs only once. For example, airplane passengers are not interested in average fatality rates; rather, they are interested in what happens on their particular flight.

## Uncertainty

When the decision maker has very little or no reliable information on which to evaluate the different possible outcomes, he or she is operating in a situation of uncertainty. Under a **situation of uncertainty,** the

**situation of uncertainty**
Situation that occurs when a decision maker has very little or no reliable information on which to evaluate the different possible outcomes.

decision maker has no knowledge concerning the probabilities associated with different possible outcomes. For example, a person who is going to New York and has not heard a weather forecast for New York will have no knowledge of the likelihood of rain and hence will not know whether or not to carry an umbrella.

If the decision maker has little or no knowledge about which state of nature will occur, one of several basic approaches may be taken. The first is to choose the alternative whose best possible outcome is the best of all possible outcomes for all alternatives. This is an optimistic, or gambling, approach and is sometimes called the **maximax approach.** A decision maker using this approach would not take the umbrella because the best possible outcome (being dry without being inconvenienced) could be achieved only with this alternative.

A second approach for dealing with uncertainty is to compare the worst possible outcomes for each alternative and select the one that is least bad. This is a pessimistic approach and is sometimes called the **maximin approach.** In the umbrella example, the decision maker would compare the worst possible outcome of taking an umbrella to that of not taking an umbrella. The decision maker would then decide to take an umbrella because it is better to be dry than wet.

A third approach is to choose the alternative with the least variation among its possible outcomes. This is a **risk-averting approach** and results in more effective planning. If the decision maker chooses not to take an umbrella, the outcomes can vary from being dry to being wet. Thus, the risk-averting decision maker would take an umbrella to ensure staying dry.

Figure 4.4 summarizes the different approaches to making a decision under conditions of uncertainty.

**maximax approach**

Selecting the alternative whose best possible outcome is the best of all possible outcomes for all alternatives; sometimes called the *optimistic* or *gambling approach* to decision making.

**maximin approach**

Comparing the worst possible outcomes for each alternative and selecting the one that is least undesirable; sometimes called the *pessimistic approach* to decision making.

**risk-averting approach**

Choosing the alternative with the least variation among its possible outcomes.

## figure 4.4

**POSSIBLE APPROACHES TO MAKING DECISIONS UNDER UNCERTAINTY**

| APPROACH | HOW IT WORKS | RELATED TO THE UMBRELLA EXAMPLE |
| --- | --- | --- |
| Optimistic or gambling approach (maximax) | Choose the alternative whose best possible outcome is the best of all possible outcomes for all alternatives. | Do not take umbrella |
| Pessimistic approach (maximin) | Compare the worst possible outcomes of each of the alternatives, and select the alternative whose worst possible outcome is least undesirable. | Take umbrella |
| Risk-averting approach | Choose the alternative that has the least variation among its possible alternatives. | Take umbrella |

# TIMING THE DECISION

To properly time a decision, the need for a decision must be recognized. That is not always easy. The manager may simply not be aware of what is going on, or the problem requiring a decision may be camouflaged. Some managers always seem to make decisions on the spot; others tend to take forever to decide even a simple matter. The manager who makes quick decisions runs the risk of making bad decisions. Failure to gather and evaluate available data, consider people's feelings, and anticipate the impact of the decision can result in a quick but poor decision. Just as risky is the other extreme: the manager who listens to problems, promises to act, but never does. Nearly as bad is the manager who responds only after an inordinate delay. Other familiar types are the manager who never seems to have enough information to make a decision, the manager who frets and worries over even the simplest decisions, and the manager who refers everything to superiors.

Knowing when to make a decision is complicated because different decisions have different time frames. For instance, a manager generally has more time to decide committee appointments than he or she has to decide what to do when three employees call in sick. No magic formula exists to tell managers when a decision should be made or how long it should take to make it. The important thing is to see the importance of properly timing decisions.

# PARTICIPATION IN DECISION MAKING

Most managers have opportunities to involve their subordinates and others in the decision-making process. One pertinent question is, Do groups make better decisions than individuals? Another is, When should subordinates be involved in making managerial decisions?

## Group or Team Decision Making

Everyone knows the old saying that two heads are better than one. Empirical evidence generally supports this view, with a few minor qualifications. Group performance is frequently better than that of the average group member.[5] Similarly, groups can often be successfully used to develop innovative and creative solutions to problems. Groups also often take longer to solve problems than does the average person.[6] Thus, group decisions are generally better when avoiding mistakes is more important than speed.

Group performance is generally superior to that of the average group member for two reasons. First, the sum total of the group's knowledge is greater. Second, the group has a much wider range of alternatives in the decision process.

Hot Topic is a retailer that takes pride in employee involvement. Their willingness to include employees in the decision-making process has strengthened the company. What are some potential downsides to this management approach?

**figure 4.5**

POSITIVE AND NEGATIVE
ASPECTS OF GROUP
(TEAM) DECISION
MAKING

| POSITIVE ASPECTS | NEGATIVE ASPECTS |
|---|---|
| 1. The sum total of the group's knowledge is greater. | 1. One individual may dominate or control the group. |
| 2. The group possesses a much wider range of alternatives in the decision process. | 2. Social pressures to conform can inhibit group members. |
| 3. Participation in the decision-making process increases the acceptance of the decision by group members. | 3. Competition can develop to such an extent that winning becomes more important than the issue itself. |
| 4. Group members better understand the decision and the alternatives considered. | 4. Groups have a tendency to accept the first potentially positive solution while giving little attention to other possible solutions. |

One aspect of group or team decision making compares the risk people will take alone with the risk they will take in a group. Laboratory experiments have shown that unanimous group decisions are consistently riskier than the average of the individual decisions.[7] This is somewhat surprising, since group pressures often inhibit the members. Possibly people feel less responsible for the outcome of a group decision than when they act alone. More recent research has found that groups make decisions best described as more polar than do individuals acting alone.[8] "More polar" means that groups tend to make decisions that are more extreme than those they would make as individuals. Figure 4.5 summarizes the positive and negative aspects of group decision making.

## PROGRESS CHECK QUESTIONS

5. List the different conditions under which managers make decisions.
6. Explain the difference between the *maximax* and *maximin* approaches to decision making.
7. What is the *risk-averting* approach to decision making?
8. Summarize the positive and negative aspects of group decision making.

## BARRIERS TO EFFECTIVE DECISION MAKING

Although it is desirable to study how to make decisions, managers must also work to remove barriers that limit the effectiveness of those decisions. Daniel Wheeler and Irving Janis identified four basic barriers to effective decision making. Barrier one is *complacency:* The

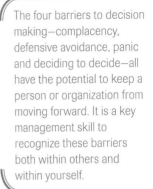

The four barriers to decision making—complacency, defensive avoidance, panic and deciding to decide—all have the potential to keep a person or organization from moving forward. It is a key management skill to recognize these barriers both within others and within yourself.

decision maker either does not see danger signs or opportunity or ignores data from the environment that would affect decision making. Barrier two is called *defensive avoidance:* The decision maker denies the importance of danger, the opportunity, or the responsibility for taking action. *Panic* is the third barrier: Frantic attempts to solve a problem rarely produce the best results. The final barrier is *deciding to decide:* Accepting the responsibility and challenge of decision making is critical to overall effectiveness.[9] All these barriers must be dealt with to create an environment that stimulates effective and creative decision making.

## MAKING CREATIVE DECISIONS

If the optimizing approach to decision making is based on unrealistic assumptions and the intuitive and satisfying approaches often result in less than optimal decisions, what can managers do to improve their decision-making process? One option that has produced positive results

## Getting Out of the Army

Jay Abbott is confident that his future will be secure and financially rewarding if he decides to remain in the army. He entered more than 10 years ago as a commissioned officer after completing his college education on an ROTC scholarship. At age 32, Jay has progressed to the rank of captain and is currently being considered for promotion to major. He has no reason to believe he will not be promoted. He has been successful in all his appointments, is well liked by everyone—his peers, superiors, and subordinates—and has an unblemished record.

The army had a lot of positive aspects, he kept reminding himself: He was already earning $40,000 a year, and with his nearly certain promotion, this would rise to $46,000. Also, he was being recommended for the army's command and general staff college. There was little chance he would not be approved; completing the program would make his future even brighter. If he stayed, he would be able to retire in just 10 more years (at age 42) with a permanent retirement income of half his final salary plus free medical and dental coverage. By then, he figured, he would probably be a lieutenant colonel with a base pay of about $61,000; at worst, he would retire a major. At 42, he would have plenty of time to devote to a second career if he so desired.

On the other hand, regardless of how attractive the benefits seemed, salaries in the armed services had not kept pace with the rising rate of inflation: Congress had held the lid on raises at less than 3 percent, and no changes in this position were evident for the next few years. In fact, Jay had read several newspaper articles indicating that Congress was considering reducing benefits for the armed services, the 20-year retirement specifically.

After doing some checking, Jay learned that the training and experience received in the army were valuable to civilian employers. Commissioned in the signal corps, he had vast experience in the area of telecommunications. He had recently completed a tour as an instructor in a service school. He had also been in many positions of leadership during his term in the army. At 32, he probably had more firsthand managerial experience than most civilian managers. He knew that large organizations were currently hiring young ex-military officers at salaries $10,000 to $15,000 higher than those of recent college graduates.

### Questions

1. What factors are prompting Jay to consider leaving the army?

2. What factors are encouraging him to stay?

3. Which factors do you think are more important? Why?

4. What would you advise Jay to do?

---

in numerous organizations is to encourage creative decisions and innovation at all levels within the organization. A recent study by PricewaterhouseCoopers found that almost half (45 percent) of lucrative ideas—whether breakthrough products or services, new uses for old ones, or ways to cut costs—came from employees.[10] The other half came from customers, suppliers, and competitors. This section discusses several techniques that can be used to foster creative decision making within an organization.

### The Creative Process

Creativity and innovation may seem similar but are actually quite different processes. **Creativity** is the thinking process involved in producing an idea or a concept that is new, original, useful, or satisfying to its creator or to someone else. **Innovation** refers to doing new things.

**creativity**

Coming up with an idea that is new, original, useful, or satisfying to its creator or to someone else.

**innovation**

Process of applying a new and creative idea to a product, service, or method of operation.

Creativity involves coming up with a new idea, whereas innovation involves implementing the new idea. The challenge for today's managers is to establish an environment that encourages both creativity and innovation. The most successful managers are not necessarily those that are personally very creative but those that establish environments that encourage creativity among the employees. The following five-step process is generally thought to help establish an environment for creative decision making:

1. *Preparation.* The manager investigates thoroughly to make sure that all parts of the problem are fully understood and that all facts and ideas relevant to the problem have been identified.
2. *Concentration.* The manager commits to solving the problem in a timely manner.
3. *Incubation of ideas and information.* The manager recognizes that the accepted way of solving a problem is not always the best way. (Allow the creative spark to catch fire.)
4. *Illumination.* The manager connects a problem with an acceptable solution. (This step is often called the *eureka connection.*)
5. *Verification.* The manager tests the solution and accepts the result.[11]

Although these steps often overlap, they provide a sound beginning point for the development of creative solutions that are critical to the success of the modern organization.

## Establishing a Creative Environment

Probably the single most important factor that influences creativity and innovation by organizational members is the climate, or environment, in which they work. Certainly a manager's boss can have an impact on the type of climate established, but ultimately it is the individual manager who sets the tone for his or her area of responsibility. If a manager is genuinely interested in creative ideas, most employees are aware of it. The opposite is also true: Most employees realize when a manager is not interested in creativity.

People-based management skills and positive leadership can encourage a climate of creativity. To avoid hindering creativity, the manager must:

- Instill trust—eliminate the fear of failure of an idea.
- Develop effective internal and external communication. Upward and lateral communication encourage innovation.
- Seek a mix of talent within the organization. A blend of different personality types and interactions encourages creative problem solving.

A creative work environment can have as much to do with people as it does job description.

- Reward useful ideas and solutions.
- Allow for some flexibility in the existing organizational structure so that new ideas and creative solutions will not be eliminated by tradition.

## PROGRESS CHECK QUESTIONS

9. What are the four barriers to effective decision making?
10. Explain the difference between creativity and innovation.
11. Which would be more important—a manager who is creative or a manager who knows how to encourage creativity among his employees? Why?
12. What steps can a manager take to avoid hindering creativity?

## Tools to Foster Creativity

In addition to establishing the proper environment, managers can use several techniques to encourage creativity. The following sections describe some of these techniques.

### Brainstorming

**brainstorming**
Presenting a problem to a group and allowing group members to produce a large quantity of ideas for its solution; no criticism is allowed initially.

Alex F. Osborn developed brainstorming as an aid to producing creative ideas for an advertising agency. Basically, **brainstorming** involves presenting a problem to a group of people and allowing them to present ideas for a solution to the problem. Brainstorming is intended to produce a large quantity of ideas or alternatives and generally follows a definite procedure.

In the first phase, members of the group are asked to present ideas off the tops of their heads. Group members are told that quantity rather than quality of ideas is the goal. Questions submitted by the group leader usually include, How can we use this differently? How can we change? How can we substitute this? or How can we combine this? Four basic rules for the first phase are as follows:

1. No criticism of ideas is allowed.
2. No praise of ideas is allowed.
3. No questions or discussion of ideas is allowed.
4. Combinations of and improvements on ideas that have been previously presented are encouraged.

During the second phase, the merits of each idea are reviewed. This review often leads to additional alternatives. Furthermore, alternatives with little merit are eliminated in this phase. In the third phase, one of the alternatives is selected, frequently through group consensus.

### Gordon Technique

William J. J. Gordon developed a technique for the consulting firm of Arthur D. Little, Inc., to spur creative problem solving. The technique was initially devised to get creative ideas on technical problems. The **Gordon technique** differs from brainstorming in that no one but the group leader knows the exact nature of the real problem under consideration. A key word is used to describe a problem area; the group then explores that area, using the key word as a starting point. For instance, the word *conservation* may be used to start a discussion on energy conservation. The key word would direct discussion and suggestions on conservation to other areas in addition to the one under question. Proponents of the Gordon technique argue that it generates better-quality ideas because the discussion is not limited to one particular area as is the case with brainstorming.

**Gordon technique**
Differs from brainstorming in that no one but the group leader knows the exact nature of the real problem under consideration. A key word is used to describe a problem area.

### Brainwriting

In the **brainwriting** approach, group members are presented with a problem situation and then asked to jot their ideas on paper without any discussion. The papers are not signed. The papers are then exchanged with others, who build on the ideas and pass the papers on again until all members have had an opportunity to participate.

**brainwriting**
Technique in which a group is presented with a problem situation and members anonymously write down ideas, then exchange papers with others, who build on ideas and pass them on until all members have participated.

## A Model for Creative Decision Making

This section presents a practical model that can lead to better and more creative decisions.[12] While this model incorporates parts of the rational

| STAGE | | ACTIVITY |
|---|---|---|
| 1 | Recognition | To investigate and eventually define a problem or decision situation. |
| 2 | Fact finding | |
| 3 | Problem finding | |
| 4 | Idea finding | To generate possible alternatives or solutions (ideas). |
| 5 | Solution finding | To identify criteria and evaluate ideas generated in stage 4. |
| 6 | Acceptance finding | To work out a plan for implementing a chosen idea. |

approach, its emphasis is on encouraging the generation of new ideas. Figure 4.6 outlines the stages of this model.

### Stage 1: Recognition

When a problem or a decision situation exists, it is useful to first describe the circumstances in writing. An effective approach is to simply write out the facts in narrative form. This stage should include a description of the present situation, as well as when and where pertinent events occurred or will occur.

### Stage 2: Fact Finding

After the decision situation has been described in written form, the next step is to systematically gather additional information concerning the current state of affairs. Questions asked in this stage usually begin with *who, what, where, when, how many, how much,* or similar words. The intent of the fact-finding stage is to organize available information about the decision situation.

### Stage 3: Problem Finding

The fact-finding stage is concerned primarily with the present and the past; the problem-finding stage is oriented toward the future. In a sense, this stage might be viewed as problem redefining or problem analysis. The overriding purpose of this stage is to rewrite or restate the problem in a manner that will encourage more creative solutions. In light of stages 1 and 2, the decision maker should attempt to restate the problem in several different ways, with the ultimate goal of encouraging a broader range of solutions. For example, the decision situation "Shall I use my savings to start a new business?" could be restated, "In what ways might I finance my new business?" The first statement elicits a much narrower range of possible solutions than does the second. Similarly, "Shall I fire this employee?" could be restated, "Should I transfer, punish, retrain, or fire this employee, or should I give him or her another chance?"

After listing several restatements of the problem, the decision maker should select the one that most closely represents the real problem and has the greatest number of potential solutions. At this point, the decision situation should be defined in a manner that suggests multiple solutions.

### Stage 4: Idea Finding

This stage aims to generate a number of different alternatives for the decision situation. In this stage, a form of brainstorming is used, following two simple rules: (1) no judgment or evaluation is allowed and (2) all ideas presented must be considered. The purpose of these rules is to encourage the generation of alternatives, regardless of how impractical they seem at first. A good approach is for the decision maker to list as many ideas as possible that relate to the problem. The decision maker should then go back and consider what might be substituted, combined, adopted, modified, eliminated, or rearranged to transform any of the previously generated ideas into additional ideas.

### Stage 5: Solution Finding

The purpose of this stage is to identify the decision criteria and evaluate the potential ideas generated in stage 4. The first step is for the decision maker to develop a list of potential decision criteria by listing all possibilities. Once a list of potential criteria has been developed, the decision maker should pare down the list by selecting the most appropriate criteria. Naturally, the decision maker should aim for a manageable number of criteria (normally fewer than seven). The next step is to evaluate each idea generated in stage 4 against the selected criteria. Usually many ideas from stage 4 can be eliminated by simple inspection. The remaining ideas should then be evaluated against each criterion using some type of rating scale. After each idea has been evaluated against all criteria, the best solution usually becomes obvious.

### Stage 6: Acceptance Finding

This final stage attempts to identify what needs to be done to successfully implement the chosen idea or solution. This stage not only addresses the *who, when, where,* and *how* questions but should also attempt to anticipate potential objections to the decision.

While the above model is certainly not perfect, it does encourage managers to go beyond bounded rationality and to make better decisions than they would by following the satisficing approach.

## Study Skills

### The Need to Succeed

We have a "need to succeed," and the objective of this exercise is to help identify the areas that you rate as *needing* the most attention to help improve your study preparation and execution effectiveness. (*Instructions: Put a number 1 next to the most important area you identify as needing improvement, a number 2 to the next important, a number 3 to the next important … until to reach the end of the list.*)

- Organization _____
- Time management _____
- Note taking _____
- Listening _____
- Writing _____
- Reading _____
- Prioritizing _____
- Memorization _____
- Test taking _____
- Motivation _____

## Going Abroad

You supervise 12 engineers. Their formal training and work experience are very similar, so you move them around on different projects. Yesterday, your manager informed you that an overseas affiliate has requested four engineers to go abroad on extended loan for six to eight months. For a number of reasons, he argued and you agreed, this request should be met from your group.

All your engineers are capable of handling this assignment; from the standpoint of present and future projects, there is no special reason any one engineer should be retained over any other. Somewhat complicating the situation is the fact that the overseas assignment is in a generally undesirable location.

**Questions**

1. How would you select who should go abroad on extended loan?
2. What are some major factors that would influence your decision process?
3. How would you communicate the news to those engineers selected for the assignment?
4. What would you do if any of the engineers requested not to be sent overseas?

*Source:* Victor H. Vroom, "A New Look at Managerial Decision Making," *Organizational Dynamics,* Spring 1973.

## PROGRESS CHECK QUESTIONS

13. Explain the three phases of the brainstorming process.
14. What is the major difference between brainstorming and the Gordon technique?
15. Explain how a brainwriting exercise works.
16. Explain the six stages of a creativity model.

# MANAGEMENT INFORMATION SYSTEMS

**management information systems (MISs)**

Integrated approach for providing interpreted and relevant data that can help managers make decisions.

**Management information systems (MISs),** also called *management reporting systems,* support the day-to-day operational and tactical decision-making needs of managers. MISs are designed to produce information needed for the successful management of a process, department, or business. An MIS provides information that managers have specified in advance as adequately meeting their information needs. Usually the information made available by an MIS is in the form of periodic reports, special reports, and outputs of mathematical simulations.

In the broader sense, management information systems have existed for many years, even before computers. However, in most people's mind, the term *MIS* implies the use of computers to process data that managers will use to make operational decisions. The information an MIS provides describes the organization or one of its major parts in terms of

## Tony sees things differently

"It looks to them like your new title is going to your head when all you want to do is be more available to help them."

Tanya's statement opened Tony's eyes. He had automatically assumed that his staff would understand what he was trying to do by changing the scheduling policy, but now he realized that all they had seen was a new policy posted on the staff notice board without any discussion or warning. Making an example of Matt had been more about protecting his own ego than about sending a message to the rest of the staff—Tony didn't want word of him being a "pushover" reaching Jerry Smith or, worse still, Dawn Williams, his regional manager.

He might have had the best intentions in getting more time to work with his people, but their reaction showed that they didn't see it that way. Now Tony was stuck. He had been considering filling Tanya's position as shift leader as an internal promotion (there were a couple of good people who were ready), but now he wasn't sure if he could count on them sticking around long enough to apply for the position.

He had really wanted to put his stamp on this Taco Barn to reassure Jerry and Dawn for the faith that they had shown in him, but Tony was certain that this potential mutiny wasn't what he had in mind at all. He still felt sure that there was a better way to do the schedule every week, and he really did want to free up more time to be in the restaurant with his staff, but all he had done was convince his staff—friends that he had worked with for years before his promotion—that he was on some sort of power trip. How could he get the message across that he was on their side without that message being seen as an admission that he made a big mistake in his first major decision as unit manager?

### QUESTIONS

1. Should Tony change the scheduling policy back to the way things were? Why or why not?

2. How do you think this new awareness will change Tony's management style?

3. Do you think he can rebuild his relationship with his staff? Why or why not?

4. What should Tony do now?

what has happened in the past, what is happening now, and what is likely to happen in the future.

It is important to note that an MIS is not the same as data processing. **Data processing** is the capture, processing, and storage of data, whereas an MIS uses those data to produce information for management in making decisions to solve problems. In other words, data processing provides the database of the MIS.

**Transaction-processing systems** substitute computer processing for manual record-keeping procedures. Examples include payroll, billing, and inventory record systems. By definition, transaction processing requires routine and highly structured decisions. It is actually a subset of data processing. Therefore, an organization can have a very effective transaction-processing system and not have an MIS.

Many MISs have been developed for use by specific organizational subunits. Examples of MISs intended to support managers in particular functional areas include operational information systems, marketing information systems, financial information systems, and human resource information systems. Several specific MISs used by organizational subunits are discussed in later chapters.

**data processing**

Capture, processing, and storage of data.

**transaction-processing systems**

Substitutes computer processing for manual recordkeeping procedures.

## CONCLUSION

Experienced managers are often most proud of the decisions they have made on the basis of a hunch or "gut instinct", without recognizing the important part played by experience in the development of that instinct that they trust so well. For new managers, decision making skills often represent the most valuable asset you bring to the role. Your product knowledge and job performance may win you the promotion, but with that new title comes the responsibility to make decisions. As we have seen in this chapter, organizations would do well to establish consistent policies on how decisions should be made and to determine what constitutes an acceptable level of risk in making those decisions. In the next chapter we review how those decision-making skills are put to work in making strategic choices for the management and future direction of a business.

## key terms

brainstorming 96
brainwriting 97
creativity 94
data processing 101
decision making 82
decision process 82
Gordon technique 97
innovation 94
intuitive approach 83
level of aspiration 86

management informa-
  tion systems
  (MISs) 100
maximax approach 90
maximin approach 90
optimizing 86
optimizing approach 84
principle of bounded
  rationality 85
problem solving 82

risk-averting
  approach 90
satisficing 86
situation of certainty 88
situation of risk 88
situation of
  uncertainty 89
transaction-processing
  systems 101

## review questions

1. What are the three stages in the decision-making process?
2. What criticisms can be made concerning the optimizing approach to decision making?
3. Describe the five-step process for creating an environment that fosters creative decision making.
4. Explain the role of a management information system.

## internet exercise

Research a business magazine (*BusinessWeek, Fast Company, Fortune,* or *Forbes*) or newspaper (*The Wall Street Journal* or *The New York Times*), and identify a significant business decision made by a major company.

1. What business and/or economic factors prompted the decision?
2. Did the managers involved satisfice or optimize?
3. What was their risk approach to the decision they made?
4. In your assessment, how creative was their decision?

## team exercise

### BENJAMIN FRANKLIN'S "T-CHART"

When faced with making a tough decision, Ben Franklin used a simple but effective step to help him arrive at what he saw as the "right" decision. He would draw a large letter T on a piece of paper, with + over the left side of the cross bar of the T (indicating the points in favor of making the choice—the pros) and a − over the right side of the cross bar of the T (indicating the points against making the choice—the cons). Whichever side of the list contained the most items determined the choice to be made.

Divide the group into two teams—one focusing on the pros and one on the cons of an important decision that the group as a whole selects. Take 10 minutes to fill your assigned side of the T-chart, and then answer the following questions:

1. How hard was it to agree on the important decision you would use?
2. What was the final verdict?
3. If you could add a relative importance weighting to each of the pros and cons so that one pro could be treated as being more important than another, would that change the outcome?
4. Should this be your only step in making an important decision? Why or why not?

# Avon: More Than Cosmetic Changes

*How Andrea Jung Is Trying to Stop the Sag by Getting Smarter about the Numbers*

In 2005, Avon Products Inc.'s success story turned ugly. After six straight years of 10 percent plus growth and a tripling of earnings under CEO Andrea Jung, the company suddenly began losing sales across the globe. Developing markets such as Central Europe and Russia, the engine of Avon's amazing run, stumbled just as sales in the U.S. and Mexico stalled. The global diversity that had long propped up the company's performance suddenly began to weigh it down. This dramatic turn of events hit investors by surprise. In May, Jung had predicted Avon would exceed Wall Street's already high expectations. By September, problems in China, Eastern Europe, and Russia were mounting, and Jung was backpedaling at full speed. Angry shareholders bailed out. The stock price, which had risen 181 percent during Jung's first 5½ years at the helm, plummeted 45 percent between April and October. Over the past 18 months, Jung has tried to figure out what went wrong and how to fix it. While it's far too soon to celebrate at Avon, the company is emerging from Wall Street's doghouse. Avon sells Skin So Soft and Anew skin-care products as well as makeup and other items through a network of 5 million independent representatives. Its stock had jumped 39 percent, to 36.65, by Feb. 27, from its lows of last August. Investors are happy about, among other things, Avon's progress signing up 399,000 new salespeople in China, where a fast-growing middle class is compelling enough to outweigh the government's tight regulation of direct sellers. Renewed growth in Central Europe and the U.S. is helping, too. For the fourth quarter of 2006, revenue rose 9 percent, to $2.6 billion, while net income stayed flat at $184 million.

## PAINFUL CUTS

An expert in building brands, Jung had no turnaround experience when she arrived in her job. At times she doubted that she could make the deep staff cuts needed to right the company. "I'd never done anything like that before," said the 48-year-old Jung. "My first reaction was: I get it. I see the numbers, but I just don't know if I, or we, have the stomach for it." One of Jung's most important moves has been forcing managers to make decisions based on fact rather than intuition. In the past year, she has reorganized Avon's management structure, taking away much of the independence from country managers, in favor of globalized manufacturing and marketing. Previously, Avon managers from Poland to Mexico ran their own plants, developed new products, and created their own ads, often relying as much on gut as numbers. In Jung's words they were "king or queen of every decision." Now Jung has trimmed out seven layers of management, bringing the total from 15 down to 8, and finally launched the kind of numbers-heavy return-on-investment analysis that most large consumer products companies have been doing for decades. That analysis is directed from New York headquarters by an executive team stocked with more people from the outside. Recent recruits have come from larger, more analytical consumer-products companies such as Gillette, Procter & Gamble, PepsiCo, and Kraft.

At the height of Jung's problems, in December 2005, management guru Ram Charan gave her a piece of pivotal advice. He advised Jung to go home that Friday night and imagine she had been fired. Then, he said, return Monday morning with the mindset of someone brought in from the outside. "If you can be that objective and blend in your institutional knowledge and relationships, you're going to have an advantage," he told her. A month later Jung was flying around the globe on a CEO road show, addressing audiences of her top 1,000 global managers. Her message: By the end of this year, one-quarter of you will be gone. "I put a lot of people in those jobs," says Jung, "You can imagine it was the toughest time to walk the halls."

## ANALYZE THIS

Avon's new executives and their new data were on display at the annual analysts' conference, held in New York in February 2007. Traditionally, this show was heavy on product announcements and ad clips. But this year's edition contained nearly four hours' worth of PowerPoint slides. In them, the company provided a detailed explanation of what had gone wrong in many of its 114 worldwide markets. One revelation: The roster of products for sale in Mexico had ballooned to 13,000. Another: Decreasing the payoffs for adding new representatives had stalled the U.S. business. Avon's new data-centric approach isn't just about creating a good set of slides, however. It's also helping to change Avon's marketing and product development. Avon sells many thousands of products, and 1,000 of those have been introduced in the past 12 months. Savings from centralized manufacturing and other initiatives are being put into advertising and research and development, a strategy Jung hopes will get earnings climbing again. Avon increased its ad budget from $136 million in 2005 to $249 million in 2006. This was a big factor in the company's 6 percent sales growth in 2006. Avon had planned to raise advertising to $200 million, but good returns on TV ads in Brazil, the U.S., and Russia, along with other marketing pushes, persuaded management to add a further $49 million, for a total increase of 83 percent. Avon is also doing more marketing to spark recruiting. Last year the company ran TV and newspaper ads supporting 1,400 recruiting events in China. In Russia the company sponsors a TV show featuring a character who sells Avon.

### Questions

1. Why did Andrea Jung feel unprepared to manage the turnaround of Avon?

2. How has Avon's global management structure changed during this turnaround process?

3. What are the potential advantages for an organization becoming more "data-centric"?

4. Do you think that Andrea Jung has managed a successful turnaround? Why or why not?

*Source:* Adapted from Nanette Byrnes, "The Corporation," *BusinessWeek Online,* March 12, 2007.

## Mulally, Ford's Most Important New Model

*To Help Turn Ford Around, Its New CEO Is First Attacking Its Deep-Rooted Bureaucracy, Forcing to Be Smarter and More Efficient*

With six concept and real production cars to show at the North American International Auto Show this week, Ford Motor is trying to make a statement to the world that the 103-year-old automaker, despite falling market share and deep financial losses, is serious about being around for a second century. As important as the vehicles are, however, the most important new model to be found in Detroit's Cobo Hall is the new CEO, Alan Mulally, who is just completing three months on the job after coming to the struggling automaker from Boeing.

Mulally hasn't earned his stripes as a "car guy" yet. In fact, as he walked around Ford's show cars in October shortly after arriving, one Ford designer showing him the Lincoln MKR concept car explained to him how important the C-pillar design would be in future Lincolns. "And what's the C-pillar?" the former Boeing executive asked. Such naiveté in front of assistants on the part of an auto industry ruler operating in a historically testosterone-filled business might have spelled a kind of social and political death by backroom chatter a decade ago.

Not now. Ford Motor's future is so precarious that even many hard-bitten veterans of the Detroit auto wars once quick to reject outsiders are embracing his methodical and hyperdisciplined coach approach to fixing the automaker. It's an approach that relies more on asking questions that haven't been asked before than it does on dictating sweeping brand repositioning or new product ideas.

### WEEDING OUT NEEDLESS COMPLEXITY

Mulally is doing nothing less than undoing a management scheme put into place by Henry Ford II almost 40 years ago—a system of regional territories around the world that has worn out the company's ability to compete in today's global industry and one that Chairman Bill Ford couldn't or wouldn't unwind. And Mulally is accelerating a shift begun in small ways under Bill Ford when he was CEO, before giving way to Mulally. For example, there is a new emphasis on lessening the power of Ford's historically powerful finance department, which too often compromised a model's competitiveness in the interest of saving a few dollars.

A phrase frequently uttered by Mulally these days, which now draws snickers from staff that have taken to respectfully impersonating his friendly delivery, sometimes with arm around shoulder, is, "I hear what you are saying, but I can't get there." Take that Lincoln concept car Mulally was shown a few months ago. The show car is built off the rear-wheel-drive-engineered Ford Mustang. Ford has another rear-drive-engineered car it could have chosen, the

Australian Falcon. Mulally's questions, said Ford President of the Americas Mark Fields, have centered not so much on the design, which he liked, but on why Ford had two separate platforms for rear-drive small and midsize cars like the Mustang and Falcon. Fields says the answer lies in Ford's past regional system whereby Ford Australia wouldn't want to jointly develop a chassis with Ford North America and vice versa.

When Mulally arrived at Ford in September 2006, that needless complexity was the first thing he zeroed in on. He also found multiple engineering and manufacturing platforms in development for the small sporty cars and for large SUVs and small vans. Most puzzling to him was that a global company trying to create manufacturing and efficiencies worldwide and fighting for its life had one product chief for North America and another for the rest of the world. Just three months into the job, the CEO who didn't know that the C-pillar is the vertical support behind the rear passenger door appointed one global product boss, Derrick Kuzack, and has him reporting to Mulally rather than Fields.

## NOT AFRAID TO APPLY THE BRAKES

Mulally isn't a complete beginner about cars. He speaks with knowledge and affection about a series of Nissan sports cars he owned in the 1970s whose engines ran hot in part because the fuel line, he says, was wrapped around the engine block in a way that wasn't ideal. One part of the car Mulally is definitely familiar with is the brakes. So far, he has slammed on them to postpone two big and potentially costly decisions that had been all but final before he took over—the sale of Ford's ailing British luxury brands, Jaguar and Land Rover, and the plan to build a new low-cost manufacturing complex in North America [likely Mexico] announced by Fields last year. Instead, he took Fields to Japan in late December for meetings with Toyota to discuss, among other issues, the possibility of a joint manufacturing project in North America.

## BRINGING ORDER TO A HOUSE OF LORDS

Ford has mortgaged its assets to borrow up to $23.4 billion to fund a massive restructuring plan and cover billions in losses expected until 2009. The company, which lost $7 billion in the first nine months of last year, expects to burn up $17 billion in cash during the next two years. Ford is expected to lose its status as No. 2 automaker by 2007 sales in the U.S. to Toyota.

Mulally, say Ford executives, has been appalled by the power the finance department has had on product decisions. When Ford launched its Fusion sedan a year ago, for example, it did so without a navigation system, satellite radio, or side air bags. The finance department forced the limits to keep the car's "piece cost" down. But it left the car short of equipment offered even on the lesser Hyundai Elantra. The new model on sale for the 2007 model year has side-curtain air bags, as well as satellite radio and an all-wheel-drive option. The same finance system kept, until now, a stability control system out of the Ford Escape, which has been in large part why the SUV has been left off *Consumer Reports'* recommended list, a key endorsement Fields says Ford must get more of.

Mulally's approach to management and communication hasn't been seen before in the halls of Ford, which have historically been the atmosphere of a kingdom with competing dukes. Regional chiefs with responsibility around the world meet weekly now instead of quarterly. Each manager has to represent progress on new products and financial goals with color-coded progress lines. If he or she is behind, the color is red.

## PLAINSPOKEN NEW GUY

But Mulally is still somewhat green about the job. Besides his C-pillar query, he recently had to ask what the name of the auto industry's lobby group is (Alliance of Automobile Manufacturers) and what NADA stands for (National Automobile Dealers Assn., which he will address in a keynote speech in February). He uttered the name of Lincoln's concept car for the Detroit Auto Show (which he has never attended until now), the MKR, but said the acronym very slowly and turned to Fields to see if he got it right. And when asked why Ford had the poorest corporate average fuel economy (CAFE) rating among major automakers, he asked one of Ford's public-relations managers, "Is that right?"

But the lack of experience is balanced with a refreshing frankness and plain communication that staffers appreciate. Before the company's announcement of its latest restructuring, he asked staff, "What are we saying about Jaguar?" Then-Ford Europe chief Mark Schultz rattled off a three-paragraph answer he planned to read to the media. The CEO responded: "I have no idea what you just said. . . . Are we keeping Jaguar? If so, let's just say that. If it changes, we'll let them know."

## "WORKING SMARTER" BUSINESS MODEL

And he is attacking, to the delight of many Ford executives, a system by which the automaker shifts managers as often as once a year. The company, for example, has had five heads of Ford Europe in as many years.

Key to Ford's comeback is not so much making do with fewer resources than its rival Toyota, but working smarter with what it has. Consider that Ford currently has different V6 gasoline engines for the U.S., South America, Europe, and Asia. And it has had three distinctly different small cars for the South American, European, and U.S. markets. "The cost and complexity of that duplication is ridiculous," says Mulally. Ford has recently committed to building one small car for all its world markets, with slight changes in sheet-metal designs to reflect local tastes.

That's to avoid the failure of trying to sell the same car around the world, which the company did in the 1980s and early '90s with the Ford Contour compact sedan. And the car's engineering will be sourced from one recently formed core engineering center in Michigan. "We wound up with so much duplication because Europe wanted to source from Europe and South America wanted to source from South America, and

so on," says Fields. "It's a business model that doesn't work, and we're paying the price for keeping it going as long as we did."

## DRIVE AND CURIOSITY

Mulally is shy about divulging details of his trip to Japan last month to visit Toyota Chairman Fujio Cho. Generally, he says, it was to discuss fuel-economy regulations and technology as well as "places where we could cooperate."

Mulally, who may be motivated to succeed at Ford in part because he got passed over twice for the CEO job at Boeing, has an almost kid-on-Christmas-morning curiosity about Ford. On a recent trip to Las Vegas, he rented a Ford Taurus, a car he has affection for from when he studied the car's development 20 years ago for Ford's production systems. Ford recently ceased production after turning the car into a rental fleet car. "I haven't had time to do the deep dive on why we stopped investing in it, but I'd like to," he says wistfully. "You know, Toyota used to be scared to death of Ford and the Taurus and thought we had this big plot hatching when we stopped investing in it to make it better. I wish we had."

## Questions

1. What messages is Alan Mulally trying to communicate to both Ford employees and Ford customers?

2. What challenges does he face in building his credibility as the new CEO of Ford Motor Company?

3. Give three examples of decisions that Mulally has made in his early days as the new CEO of Ford.

4. Ford Motor Company is currently in dire financial straits, having lost $12.7 billion in 2006, forcing them to borrow $23.4 billion to cover further losses expected through 2009. How do you think this desperate situation will affect Mulally's decision-making process?

*Source:* Adapted from David Kiley, "Autos," *Business-Week Online,* January 9, 2007.

# PLANNING AND STRATEGIC MANAGEMENT

**"Long range planning does not deal with future decisions, but with the future of present decisions."**

—Peter Drucker

## The World of Work: Tony tries a new approach

Tanya had helped Tony see the situation at the Taco Barn in a different way, and he was ready to try a different approach—an approach that involved two stages. In the first stage, rather than being rigid and refusing to make changes in the staffing schedule, Tony held a meeting of all the staff and explained that his fumbled attempt at improved efficiency was designed to give him more time to work with them in the restaurant, not just to make his life easier or theirs any harder. This admission seemed to calm everyone down, but it still left the problem of managing the individual scheduling needs of his crew. Tony knew he could play hardball and give his folks a "take-it-or-leave-it" choice on the shifts he gave them, but he was committed to these people and wanted them to continue to work for Taco Barn.

The second stage involved ordering some "project planning" training materials through the HR department at head office and scheduling enough training sessions to make sure everyone was able to view the materials. Tony waited until everyone had gone through the training before he made his announcement. The feedback on the training had been very positive— people found the material interesting, and several of his crew had started using some of the ideas in their jobs. However, no one had questioned why the entire crew had been put through the training. Now they were about the find out.

Tony announced in a very matter-of-fact manner in the next staff meeting that he was handing responsibility for the staffing schedule over to them. Kevin, their

**After studying this chapter, you will be able to:**

1. Define planning and distinguish between formal and functional plans.

2. Contrast strategic planning with operational planning.

3. Define the Management by Objectives (MBO) Process.

4. Define strategy and explain the strategic management process.

5. Define organizational mission and explain how mission relates to long- and short-range objectives.

6. Discuss the components of a SWOT analysis.

most experienced team member and next in line for Tanya's position as shift leader, was appointed as project leader, but Tony emphasized that he wanted everyone involved in the project and, more important, that he was expecting them not only to work the schedule out among themselves but also to work as a team and cover for each other in the event that they couldn't make it in for their assigned shift.

At first glance, this decision looked like Tony was just dumping the schedule headache in their laps, but he was gambling that they would get a clearer picture of the situation if they reviewed everyone's requests as a team, rather than individual employees simply forwarding their scheduling issues to him and leaving him to figure out how to make it work.

Plus, Tony thought, the planning exercise would be good experience for them, and if they do it well, there would be lots of other opportunities for planning exercises in the future.

**QUESTIONS**

1. Do you think the employees will see this as a growth opportunity or as Tony dumping more work on them? Explain your answer.

2. Do you think the employees will be able to manage the schedule as a team? Why or why not?

3. What happens if their first attempt at a schedule doesn't work?

4. Read "The Planning Process" section in this chapter, and suggest some approaches that Kevin could use in building the new schedule.

# THE PLANNING PROCESS

Planning is the process of deciding which objectives to pursue during a future time period and how to achieve those objectives. It is the primary management function and is inherent in everything a manager does. This chapter discusses the basics of the planning function and how this function relates to strategic management.

## Why Plan?

It is futile for a manager to attempt to perform any other management functions without having a plan. Managers who attempt to organize without a plan find themselves reorganizing on a regular basis. The manager who attempts to staff without a plan will be constantly hiring and firing employees. Motivation is almost impossible in an organization undergoing continuous reorganization and high employee turnover.

Planning enables a manager or an organization to actively affect rather than passively accept the future. By setting objectives and charting a course of action, the organization commits itself to "making it happen." This allows the organization to affect the future. Without a planned course of action, the organization is much more likely to sit back, let things happen, and then react to those happenings in a crisis mode.

Planning provides a means for actively involving personnel from all areas of the organization in the management of the organization. Involvement produces a multitude of benefits. First, input from throughout the organization improves the quality of the plans; good suggestions can come from any level in the organization. Involvement in the planning process also enhances the overall understanding of the organization's direction. Knowing the big picture can minimize friction among departments, sections, and individuals. For example, through planning, the sales department can understand and appreciate the objectives of the production department and their relationship to organizational objectives. Involvement in the planning process fosters a greater personal commitment to the plan; the plan becomes "our" plan rather than "their" plan. Positive attitudes created by involvement also improve overall organizational morale and loyalty.

Planning can also have positive effects on managerial performance. Studies have demonstrated that employees who stress planning earn high performance ratings from supervisors.[1] They have also shown that planning has a positive impact on the quality of work produced.[2] While some have proven inconclusive, several studies have reported a positive relationship between planning and certain measures of organizational success, such as profits and goals.[3] One explanation that would fit all the findings to date is that good planning, as opposed to the mere presence or absence of a plan, is related to organizational success.

Whether a business is locally owned or nationwide, management needs to create and implement formal plans.

A final reason for planning is the mental exercise required to develop a plan. Many people believe the experience and knowledge gained throughout the development of a plan force managers to think in a future- and contingency-oriented manner; this can result in great advantages over managers who are static in their thinking.

## Formal Planning

All managers plan. The difference lies in the methods they employ and the extent to which they plan. Most planning is carried out on an informal or casual basis. This occurs when planners do not record their thoughts but carry them around in their heads. A **formal plan** is a written, documented plan developed through an identifiable process. The appropriate degree of sophistication depends on the needs of the individual managers and the organization itself. The environment, size, and type of business are factors that typically affect the planning needs of an organization.

**formal plan**
Written, documented plan developed through an identifiable process.

## Functional Plans

Plans are often classified by function or use. The most frequently encountered types of **functional plans** are sales and marketing plans, production plans, financial plans, and personnel plans. Sales and marketing plans are for developing new products or services and selling both present and future products or services. Production plans deal with producing the desired products or services on a timely schedule. Financial plans deal primarily with meeting the financial commitments and capital expenditures of the organization. Personnel plans relate to the human resource needs of the organization. Many functional plans are interrelated and interdependent. For example, a financial plan would obviously be dependent on production, sales, and personnel plans.

**functional plans**
Originate from the functional areas of an organization such as production, marketing, finance, and personnel.

## The Planning Horizon: Short Range, Intermediate, and Long Range

**short-range plans**

Generally cover up to one year.

The length of the planning horizon is relative and varies somewhat from industry to industry, depending on the specific environment and activity. What may be long range when operating in a rapidly changing environment, such as the electronics industry, may be short range when operating in a relatively static environment, such as the brick manufacturing industry. In practice, however, **short-range plans** generally cover up to one year, whereas **long-range plans** span at least three to five years, with some extending as far as 20 years into the future. While long-range planning is possible at any level in the organization, it is carried out primarily at the top levels.

**long-range plans**

Typically span at least three to five years; some extend as far as 20 years into the future.

*Intermediate plans* cover the time span between short-range and long-range plans. From a pragmatic standpoint, intermediate plans generally cover from one to three or one to five years, depending on the horizon covered by the long-range plan. Usually intermediate plans are derived from long-range plans, and short-range plans are derived from intermediate plans. For example, if the long-range plan calls for a 40 percent growth in sales by the end of five years, the intermediate plan should outline the necessary steps to be taken over the time span covering one to five years. Short-range plans would outline what actions are necessary within the next year.

## Operational versus Strategic Plans

**strategic planning**

Formulation, proper implementation, and continuous evaluation of strategic plans; determines the long-run directions and performance of an organization. The essence of strategic management is developing strategic plans and keeping them current.

**Strategic planning** is equivalent to top-level, long-range planning. It is the planning process applied at the highest levels of the organization, covering a relatively long period and affecting many parts of the organization. **Operations** or **tactical planning** is short-range planning and concentrates on the formulation of functional plans. Production schedules and day-to-day plans are examples of operational plans.

However, the distinctions between strategic and operations planning are relative, not absolute. The major difference is the level at which the planning is done. Strategic planning is done primarily by top-level managers; operational planning is done by managers at all levels in the organization and especially by middle- and lower-level managers.

**operations or tactical planning**

Short-range planning; done primarily by middle- to lower-level managers, it concentrates on the formulation of functional plans.

## Contingency Plans

**contingency plans**

Address the what-ifs of the manager's job; get the manager in the habit of being prepared and knowing what to do if something does go wrong.

Regardless of how thorough plans are, there will always be things that go wrong. What goes wrong is often beyond the control of the manager. For example, the economy takes an unexpected dip, a machine breaks down, or the arrival of a new piece of equipment is delayed. When such things happen, managers must be prepared with a backup, a contingency, plan. **Contingency plans** address the what-ifs of the manager's job. Contingency planning gets the manager in the habit of being prepared and knowing what to do if something does go wrong. Naturally, contingency plans cannot be prepared for all possibilities. What managers should do is identify the most critical assumptions of the current plan and then develop contingencies for problems that have a reasonable chance of occurring. A good approach is to examine the current plan from the point of view of what could go wrong. Contingency planning is most needed in rapidly changing environments.

## Objectives

If you don't know where you're going, how will you know when you get there? **Objectives** are statements outlining what you are trying to achieve; they give an organization and its members direction and purpose. Few managers question the importance of objectives, only what the objectives should be.

> **objectives**
> Statements outlining what the organization is trying to achieve; give an organization and its members direction.

As discussed in Chapter 1, management is a form of work that involves coordinating an organization's resources—land, labor, and capital—toward accomplishing organizational objectives—the process centers around objectives. Management cannot be properly practiced without pursuing specific objectives. Managers today and in the future must concentrate on where they and their organizations are headed.

It is also important to realize that managers and employees at all levels in an organization should have objectives; everyone should know what he or she is trying to achieve. One key for organizational success is for the objectives at all different levels to mesh together.

### Long-Range Objectives

**Long-range objectives** generally go beyond the organization's current fiscal year. Long-range objectives must support and not conflict with the organizational mission. However, they may be quite different from the organizational mission, yet still support it. For instance, the organizational mission of a fast-food restaurant might be to provide rapid, hot-food service to a certain area of the city. One long-range objective might be to increase sales to a specific level within the next four years. Obviously, this objective is quite different from the organizational mission, but it still supports the mission.

> **long-range objectives**
> Go beyond the current fiscal year; must support and not conflict with the organizational mission.

### Short-Range Objectives

**Short-range objectives** should be derived from an in-depth evaluation of long-range objectives. Such an evaluation should result in a listing of priorities of the long-range objectives. Then short-range objectives can be set to help achieve the long-range objectives.

> **short-range objectives**
> Generally tied to a specific time period of a year or less and are derived from an in-depth evaluation of long-range objectives.

Regardless of your occupation, long- and short-range objectives are essential. What might be some of the differences in objectives for these two managers?

Objectives should be clear, concise, and quantified when possible. Affected personnel should clearly understand what is expected. Normally, multiple objectives should be used to reflect the desired performance of a given organizational unit or person. From a top-level perspective, objectives should span all major areas of the organization. A problem with one dominant objective is that it is often achieved at the expense of other desirable objectives. For example, if production is the only objective, quality may suffer in attempts to realize maximum production. While objectives in different areas may serve as checks on one another, they should be reasonably consistent among themselves.

Objectives should be dynamic; that is, they should be reevaluated as the environment and opportunities change. Objectives for organizations usually fall into one of four general categories: (1) profit oriented, (2) service to customers, (3) employee needs and well being, and (4) social responsibility. Even nonprofit organizations must be concerned with profit in the sense that they generally must operate within a budget. Another scheme for classifying organizational objectives is (1) primary, (2) secondary, (3) individual, and (4) societal. Primary objectives relate directly to profit. Secondary objectives apply to specific units of the organization (e.g., departmental objectives). Individual objectives directly concern the organization's employees. Finally, societal objectives relate to the local, national, and global communities. The following section outlines areas for establishing objectives in most organizations:[4]

1. *Profitability.* Measures the degree to which the firm is attaining an acceptable level of profits; usually expressed in terms of profits before or after taxes, return on investment, earnings per share, or profit-to-sales ratios.

2. *Markets.* Reflects the firm's position in its marketplace, expressed in terms of share of the market, dollar or unit volume in sales, or niche in the industry.

3. *Productivity.* Measures the efficiency of internal operations expressed as a ratio of inputs to outputs, such as number of items or services produced per unit of time.

4. *Product.* Describes the introduction or elimination of products or services; expressed in terms of when a product or service will be introduced or dropped.

5. *Financial resources.* Reflects goals relating to the funding needs of the firm; expressed in terms of capital structure, new issues of common stock, cash flow, working capital, dividend payments, and collection periods.

6. *Physical facilities.* Describes the physical facilities of the firm; expressed in terms of square feet of office or plant space, fixed costs, units of production, or similar measurements.

7. *Research and innovation.* Reflects the research, development, or innovation aspirations of the firm; usually expressed in terms of dollars to be expended.

8. *Organization structure.* Describes objectives relating to changes in the organizational structure and related activities; expressed in terms of a desired future structure or network of relationships.

9. *Human resources.* Describes the human resource assets of the organization; expressed in terms of absenteeism, tardiness, number of grievances, and training.

10. *Social responsibility.* Refers to the commitments of the firm regarding society and the environment; expressed in terms of types of activities, number of days of service, or financial contributions.

## Management by Objectives

One approach to setting objectives that has enjoyed considerable popularity is the concept of **management by objectives (MBO).** MBO is a philosophy based on converting organizational objectives into personal objectives. It assumes that establishing personal objectives elicits employee commitment, which leads to improved performance. MBO has also been called management by results, goals and control, work planning and review, and goals management. All these programs are similar and follow the same basic process.

MBO works best when the objectives of each organizational unit are derived from the objectives of the next higher unit in the organization.

**management by objectives (MBO)**

MBO is a philosophy based on converting organizational objectives into personal objectives. It assumes that establishing personal objectives elicits employee commitment, which leads to improved performance.

## First in the Market

Juan Peron is a process engineer employed by Vantage Engineering, Inc., and assigned to the research laboratory in the Advanced Products Division (APD). Vantage is a well-established manufacturer of military hardware. APD's general purpose is to conduct research to improve the company's military hardware products. However, the laboratory director was recently given permission to develop spin-off products for possible sale on the open market.

Juan spent his first year in APD assisting on various project assignments. At the end of that year, he was put in charge of a special project to research a chemically processed wood for specialty applications. During the initial stages of the project, Juan spent most of his time in the laboratory becoming familiar with the basic aspects of the treatment process. However, he soon tired of the long, tedious experimental work and became more and more eager to move quickly into the promotion and marketing of the product. This desire was soon realized. An article in a recent national trade publication had generated keen interest in a similar wood product, and as a result, Vantage immediately allocated several thousand dollars to the development and marketing of the chemically processed wood. Simultaneously, a minor reorganization occurred, placing Juan and his project under the direction of Greg Waites, a close friend of Juan's. Thus, Juan had an opportunity to get out of the lab and become involved in the more desirable promotion and marketing aspects.

Juan and Greg soon began traveling nationally, discussing the new product with potential customers. Traveling enabled Juan to spend less and less time in the lab, and as a result many of the experiments required to determine the performance characteristics of the new product were left unfinished. As the number of companies demonstrating an interest in purchasing small quantities for trial applications grew, Juan suggested to Greg that a small pilot plant be constructed. In response to Greg's concerns regarding the performance characteristics of the wood, Juan assured him the preliminary tests indicated the wood could be successfully produced. Juan contended that Vantage had to get a head start on the newly created market before everyone else got into the game, that they should build the pilot plant immediately to fill the sudden influx of orders and then worry about completing the performance tests. Greg, seeing the advantages of getting into the market first, finally agreed, and construction of the pilot plant began shortly thereafter.

During construction, Juan and Greg continued traveling to promote the wood. When the pilot plant was near completion, Juan went to Vantage's personnel department and requested that three laborers be hired to operate the plant. Juan intended to personally direct the

---

Thus, the objective-setting process requires involvement and collaboration among the various levels of the organization; this joint effort has beneficial results. First, people at each level become more aware of organizational objectives. The better they understand the organization's objectives, the better they see their roles in the total organization. Second, the objectives for an individual are jointly set by the person and the superior; there are give-and-take negotiating sessions between them. Achieving self-formulated objectives can improve motivation and, thus, job performance. MBO is discussed in further depth in Chapter 11.

## Policies

**policies**

Broad, general guides to action that constrain or direct the attainment of objectives.

To help in the objective-setting process, the manager can rely to some extent on policies and procedures developed by the organization. **Policies** are broad, general guides to action that constrain or direct objective

technical operations and thus saw no need to establish elaborate job descriptions for the positions.

A week later, Juan had his three employees. Due to a workload reduction in the Electronics Division of Vantage, the employees filling these positions had taken the laborer jobs to avoid being laid off. One had been a purchasing agent, and the others had been electronics technicians. At the beginning of the workday, Juan would drop by the plant and give directions to the crew for the entire day before departing to make sales calls. No formal leader had been appointed, and the three laborers, knowing little about the chemical process involved, were instructed to "use common sense and ingenuity."

A month after the plant operations had gotten under way, a major producer of archery bows requested an order for 70,000 bow handles to be delivered in time to be sold for the upcoming hunting season. It was too good to be true! Juan knew that if they accepted the order, the first year of operations would be guaranteed to be in the black. On receiving the product specifications, Juan persuaded Greg to sign the contract, arguing that they would be throwing all their hard work down the drain if they didn't. Subsequently, a crash program was established at the plant to get the order out on time.

One month after the final shipment of handles had been made, Juan hired a junior engineer, Libby Adams, to conduct the performance experiments that had been disbanded while the plant was getting the rush order out. Libby examined some of the experimental handles and discovered hairline cracks at various stress points that had not appeared during the initial examination. She immediately went to Juan's office to inform him of the problem and found Juan and Greg sitting there with a telegram from the archery company. It stated that several retail merchants had returned bows with hairline cracks in the handles and that the archery company would seek a settlement for its entire investment in the handles.

Vantage paid the settlement and subsequently canceled the wood project.

## Questions

1. What caused the wood project to fail?

2. Would a more effective strategy on the part of Juan and Greg have helped ensure the success of the project?

3. At what stage of the strategic management process did the breakdown occur?

4. What general observations can be made to prevent such a situation from occurring again?

*Source:* From Patricia Buhler, "Managing in the 90s," *Supervision,* May 1997. Reprinted by permission of © National Research Bureau.

---

attainment. Policies do not tell organizational members exactly what to do, but they do establish the boundaries within which they must operate. For example, a policy of "answering all written customer complaints in writing within 10 days" does not tell a manager exactly how to respond, but it does say it must be done in writing within 10 days. Policies create an understanding among members of a group that makes the actions of each member more predictable to other members.

Procedures and rules differ from policies only in degree. In fact, they may be thought of as low-level policies. A **procedure** is a series of related steps or tasks expressed in chronological order for a specific purpose. Procedures define in step-by-step fashion the methods through which policies are achieved. Procedures emphasize details. **Rules** require specific and definite actions to be taken or not to be taken in a given situation. Rules leave little doubt about what is to be done. They permit no flexibility or deviation. Unlike procedures, rules do not have to specify sequence. For example, "No smoking in the conference room"

**procedure**

Series of related steps or task expressed in chronological order for a specific purpose.

**rules**

Require specific and definite actions to be taken or not to be taken in a given situation.

is a rule. In reality, procedures and rules are subsets of policies. The primary purpose is guidance. The differences lie in the range of applicability and the degree of flexibility. A no-smoking rule is much less flexible than a procedure for handling customer complaints. However, a rule can have a clear relationship to an objective. For example, a no-smoking rule may help the organization reach a stated objective of "a cleaner and safer corporate environment."

---

## PROGRESS CHECK QUESTIONS

1. Distinguish between formal and functional planning.
2. What is the difference between strategic planning and operational planning?
3. What are the 10 areas for establishing objectives in most organizations?
4. What is management by objectives (MBO)?

---

# STRATEGY

**strategy**

Outlines the basic steps management plans to take to reach an objective or a set of objectives; outlines how management intends to achieve its objectives.

The word *strategy* originated with the Greeks about 400 B.C.; it pertained to the art and science of directing military forces.[5] A **strategy** outlines the basic steps that management plans to take to reach an objective or a set of objectives. In other words, a strategy outlines how management intends to achieve its objectives.

## Levels of Strategy

Strategies exist at three primary levels in an organization and are classified according to the scope of what they are intended to accomplish. The three levels are corporate, business, and functional strategies.

**corporate strategies**

Address which businesses an organization will be in and how resources will be allocated among those businesses.

### Corporate Strategies

Strategies that address which businesses the organization will be in and how resources will be allocated among those businesses are referred to as **corporate strategies.** Corporate strategies are sometimes called *grand strategies.* They are established at the highest levels in the organization, and they involve a long-range time horizon. Corporate strategies are concerned with the overall direction of the organization, specifically tied to mission statements, and generally formulated by top corporate management. Four basic corporate strategy types are recognized: growth, stability, defensive, and combination.

**growth strategies**

Used when the organization tries to expand, as measured by sales, product line, number of employees, or similar measures.

    **Growth strategies** are used when the organization tries to expand in terms of sales, product line, number of employees, or similar measures.

Under this concept, an organization can grow through concentration of current businesses, vertical integration, and diversification. Kellogg and McDonald's use concentration strategies—focusing on extending the sales of their current products or services—very successfully. A. G. Bass (maker of the famous "preppie" shoe, Bass Weejuns) believes vertical integration, in which a company moves into areas it previously served either as a supplier to or as a customer for its current products or services, to be a superior growth strategy. The final growth strategy is exemplified by Coca-Cola's purchase of Minute Maid Orange Juice in the early 1980s and its more recent purchase of Dasani spring waters. Diversification can take several forms, but concentric (in related fields) is the most common.

**Stability strategies** are used when the organization is satisfied with its present course. Management will make efforts to eliminate minor weaknesses, but generally its actions will maintain the status quo. Stability strategies are most likely to be successful in unchanging or very slowly changing environments. Growth is possible under a stability strategy, but it will be slow, methodical, and nonaggressive. Most organizations elect a stability strategy by default rather than by any conscious decision or plan.

**Defensive** or **retrenchment strategies** are used when a company wants or needs to reduce its operations. Most often they are used to reverse a negative trend or to overcome a crisis or problem. The three most popular types are *turnaround* (designed to reverse a negative trend and get the organization back to profitability), *divestiture* (the company sells or divests itself of a business or part of a business), and *liquidation* (the entire company is sold or dissolved).

**Combination strategies** are used when an organization simultaneously employs different strategies for different parts of the company. Most multibusiness companies use some type of combination strategy, especially those serving several different markets. Coca-Cola, for example, pursued a combination strategy in 1989 when it divested its Columbia Pictures division while expanding its soft-drink and orange juice businesses.

Figure 5.1 summarizes the major types and subtypes of corporate strategies.

**stability strategies**
Used when the organization is satisfied with its present course (status quo strategy).

**defensive or retrenchment strategies**
Used when a company wants or needs to reduce its operations.

**combination strategies**
Used when an organization simultaneously employs different strategies for different parts of the company.

| Corporate Strategies | Substrategies |
|---|---|
| 1. Growth strategies | Concentration |
| | Vertical integration |
| | Diversification |
| 2. Stability strategies | |
| 3. Defensive strategies | Turnaround |
| | Divestiture |
| | Liquidation |
| 4. Combination | |

**figure 5.1**

**MAJOR TYPES AND SUBTYPES OF CORPORATE STRATEGIES**

The New England Potato Chip Company has been a well-respected food company for many years. Recently the company has decided to expand into new markets to maintain an aggressive growth plan. To do this, it will need to attract new investors, and to accomplish that, it will need to show it is capable of producing a solid return on investments each year.

In keeping with these objectives, a policy has been introduced which reduces the finished products' inventory to a rock bottom level each June 30th, which is the end of the company's fiscal year. Why? The lower the inventory, the less money is tied up. This situation, in turn, tends to put the company in a better cash position at year end, which means that more money can be passed on to the stockholders as dividends.

As the recently hired production manager, Jane realizes there is a downside to this policy. With inventory levels on June 30 lower than at any other point during the year but with demand for potato chips higher than usual, the net result is an inability to meet the total customer demand for various types of potato chips. In fact, once inventory levels are reduced, it will take more than one month to get the process back to normal and running smoothly again.

The effect, Jane predicts, will be both lost sales at year end and a number of operations problems associated with a low-inventory situation.

For Jane, the dilemma is whether or not to confront senior management with these problems. What should Jane do?

**Source:** Adapted from "How to Keep the Chips from Falling?" Institute for Global Ethics, www.globalethics.org/resources/dilemmas/how_to_keep_the_chips.htm.

## Business Strategies

**Business strategies,** the second primary level of strategy formulation, are sometimes called competitive strategies. Business strategies focus on how to compete in a given business. Narrower in scope than a corporate strategy, a business strategy generally applies to a single business unit. Though usually situational in nature, most of these strategies can be classified as overall cost leadership, differentiation, or focus.[6]

*Overall cost leadership* is a strategy designed to produce and deliver the product or service for a lower cost than the competition. Cost leadership is usually attained through a combination of experience and efficiency. More specifically, cost leadership requires close attention to production methods, overhead, marginal customers, and overall cost minimization in such areas as sales and research and development (R&D). Achieving an overall low-cost position usually requires that the company develop some unique advantage or advantages over its competitors. Examples include a high market share, favorable access to raw materials, use of state-of-the-art equipment, or special design features that make the product easy to manufacture. Wal-Mart and Home Depot have adopted this strategy with great success.

*Differentiation* aims to make the product or service unique in its category, thus permitting the organization to charge higher-than-average prices. Differentiation can take many forms, such as design or brand image, quality, technology, customer service, or dealer network. The basic purpose of a differentiation strategy is to gain the brand loyalty of customers and a resulting lower sensitivity to price. Following a differentiation strategy does not imply that the business should have little

> Differentiation is what makes a product or company unique.

concern for costs but, rather, that the major competitive advantage sought is through differentiation.

Depending on what is required to achieve differentiation, a company may or may not find it necessary to incur relatively high costs. For example, if high-quality materials or extensive research is necessary, the resulting product or service may be priced relatively high. When this is the case, the idea is that the uniqueness of the product or service will create a willingness on the part of the customers to pay the premium price. While such a strategy can be very profitable, it may or may not preclude gaining a high share of the market. For example, Rolex demands a very high price for its watches and makes a profit, but it has a very small market share.[7] Ralph Lauren Polo sportswear and Mercedes-Benz are other examples of products that used a differentiation strategy. Differentiation can be achieved through a superior product (Microsoft), a quality image (Mercedes-Benz), or a brand image (Polo sportswear).

*Focus* is a third type of business strategy. Companies that use this method focus on, or direct their attention to, a narrow market segment. The segment may be a special buyer group, a geographical market, or one part of the product line. With a focus strategy, the firm serves a well-defined but narrow market better than competitors that serve a broader or less defined market. A "tall men's" clothing store is an example of a company following a focus strategy. Colgate-Palmolive, for example, has determined that to reach Hispanics successfully, it must capitalize on shared traits of this growing segment. Its 70 percent market share of toothpaste sold to Hispanics is largely attributed to understanding that three-quarters of Hispanics who watch TV or listen to radio do so with Spanish-language stations. Colgate-Palmolive has heavy sponsorship of favorite programs on these stations.[8]

### Functional Strategies

The third primary level of strategy is functional strategies. **Functional strategies** are narrower in scope than business strategies and deal with the activities of the different functional areas of the business—production, finance, marketing, human resources, and the like. Functional strategies support the business strategies and are primarily concerned with how-to issues. Usually functional strategies are in effect for a relatively short period, often one year or less. Figure 5.2 summarizes the different levels of strategies.

**functional strategies**
Concerned with the activities of the different functional areas of the business.

**figure 5.2**

**LEVELS OF STRATEGIES**

**Corporate Strategy**

Addresses which businesses an organization will be in and how resources will be allocated among those businesses; describes the way the organization will pursue its objectives.

**Business Strategy**

Focuses on how to compete in a given business.

**Functional Strategy**

Concerned with the activities of the different functional areas of the organization, short-range step-by-step methods to be used (tactics).

---

## PROGRESS CHECK QUESTIONS

5. What is the difference between a policy and a procedure?
6. Explain the three levels of strategy in an organization.
7. What are combination strategies?
8. How do functional strategies differ from business strategies?

---

# THE STRATEGIC MANAGEMENT PROCESS

## Strategic Management

**strategic management**

Formulation, proper implementation, and continuous evaluation of strategic plans; determines the long-run directions and performance of an organization. The essence of strategic management is developing strategic plans and keeping them current.

The rapid rate of change in today's business world is making it increasingly necessary that managers keep their plans current. **Strategic management** is the application of the basic planning process at the highest levels of the organization. Through the strategic management process, top management determines the long-run direction and performance of the organization by ensuring careful formulation, proper implementation, and continuous evaluation of plans and strategies. The essence of strategic management is developing strategic plans and keeping them current as changes occur internally and in the environment. It is possible to prepare a formal plan with a well-defined strategy and not practice strategic management. In such a situation, the plan could become outmoded as changes occur in the environment. Practicing strategic management does not ensure that an organization will meet all change successfully, but it does increase the odds.

Although guided by top management, successful strategic management involves many different levels in the organization. For example, top management may ask middle- and lower-level managers for input when formulating top-level plans. Once top-level plans have been finalized, different organizational units may be asked to formulate plans for their respective areas. A proper strategic management process helps ensure that plans throughout the different levels of the organization are coordinated and mutually supportive.

Organizations that consciously engage in strategic management generally follow some type of formalized process for making decisions and taking actions that affect their future direction. In the absence of a formal process, strategic decisions are made in a piecemeal fashion. An informal approach to strategy, however, does not necessarily mean the organization doesn't know what it is doing. It simply means the organization does not engage in any type of formalized process for initiating and managing strategy.

The strategic management process includes setting the organization's mission; defining what business or businesses the organization will be in; setting objectives; developing, implementing, and evaluating strategies; and adjusting these components as necessary. While the basic process is similar in most organizations, differences exist in the formality of the process, levels of managerial involvement, and degree of institutionalization of the process.

Although different organizations may use somewhat different approaches to the strategic management process, most successful approaches share several common components and a similar sequence. The strategic management process is composed of three major phases: (1) formulating the strategic plan, (2) implementing the strategic plan, and (3) evaluating the strategic plan. The **formulation phase** is concerned with developing the initial strategic plan. The **implementation phase** involves implementing the strategic plan that has been formulated. The **evaluation phase** stresses the importance of continuously evaluating and updating the strategic plan after it has been implemented. Each of these three phases is critical to the success of the strategic management process. A breakdown in any one area can easily cause the entire process to fail.

**formulation phase**
First phase in strategic management, in which the initial strategic plan is developed.

**implementation phase**
Second phase in strategic management, in which the strategic plan is put into effect.

**evaluation phase**
Third phase in strategic management, in which the implemented strategic plan is monitored, evaluated, and updated.

## Formulating Strategy

The formulation stage of the strategic management process involves developing the corporate- and business-level strategies to be pursued. The strategies ultimately chosen are shaped by the organization's internal strengths and weaknesses and the threats and opportunities the environment presents.

The first part of the formulation phase is to obtain a clear understanding of the current position and status of the organization. This includes identifying the mission, identifying the past and present strategies, diagnosing the organization's past and present performance, and setting objectives for the company's operation.

## figure 5.3

**OBJECTIVES OF THE COMPANY MISSION**

**Source:** Adapted from William R. King and David I. Cleland, *Strategic Planning and Policy* (New York: Van Nostrand Reinhold, 1978), p. 124.

1. To ensure harmony of purpose within the organization.
2. To provide a basis for motivating the use of the organization's resources.
3. To develop a basis, or standard, for allocating organizational resources.
4. To establish a general tone or organizational climate; for example, to suggest a businesslike operation.
5. To serve as a focal point for those who can identify with the organization's purpose and direction and to deter those who cannot do so from participating further in its activities.
6. To facilitate the translation of objectives and goals into a work structure involving the assignment of tasks to responsible elements within the organization.
7. To specify organizational purposes and the translation of these purposes into goals in such a way that cost, time, and performance parameters can be assessed and controlled.

### Identifying Mission

**mission**

Defines the basic purpose(s) of an organization: why the organization exists.

An organization's mission is actually the broadest and highest level of objectives. The **mission** defines the basic purpose or purposes of the organization (for this reason, the terms *mission* and *purpose* are often used interchangeably). Basically, an organization's mission outlines why the organization exists. A mission statement usually includes a description of the organization's basic products or services and a definition of its markets or sources of revenue. Figure 5.3 outlines the objectives of a typical mission statement. Figure 5.4 presents actual mission statements from three well-known companies.

## figure 5.4

**EXAMPLES OF MISSION STATEMENTS**

| COMPANY | MISSION STATEMENT |
| --- | --- |
| FedEx | FedEx Corporation will produce superior financial returns for its shareowners by providing high value-added logistics, transportation, and related information services through focused operating companies. Customer requirements will be met in the highest quality manner appropriate to each market segment served. FedEx Corporation will strive to develop mutually rewarding relationships with its employees, partners, and suppliers. Safety will be the first consideration in all operations. Corporate activities will be conducted to the highest ethical and professional standards. |
| Harley-Davidson | We fulfill dreams through the experience of motorcycling, by providing to motorcyclists and to the general public an expanding line of motorcycles and branded products and services in selected market segments. |
| Pfizer | We will become the world's most valued company to patients, customers, colleagues, investors, business partners, and the communities where we work and live. |

Defining *mission* is crucial. It is also more difficult than one might imagine. Over 50 years ago, Peter Drucker emphasized that an organization's purpose should be examined and defined not only at its inception or during difficult times but also during successful periods.[9] If the railroad companies of the early 1900s or the wagon makers of the 1800s had made their organizational purpose to develop a firm position in the transportation business, they might hold the same economic positions today that they enjoyed in earlier times.

Drucker argues that an organization's purpose is determined not by the organization itself but by its customers. Customer satisfaction with the organization's product or service defines the purpose more clearly than does the organization's name, statutes, or articles of incorporation. Drucker outlines three questions that need to be answered to define an organization's present business. First, management must identify the customers: where they are, how they buy, and how they can be reached. Second, management must know what the customer buys. For instance, does the Rolls-Royce owner buy transportation or prestige? Finally, what is the customer looking for in the product? For example, does the homeowner buy an appliance from Sears because of price, quality, or service?

Management must also identify what the future business will be and what it should be. Drucker presents four areas to investigate. The first is market potential: What does the long-term trend look like? Second, what changes in market structure might occur due to economic developments, changes in styles or fashions, or competition? For example, how have oil prices affected the automobile market structure? Third, what possible changes will alter customers' buying habits? What new ideas or products might create new customer demand or change old demands? Consider the impact of the cell phone on the demand for pay telephones. Finally, what customer needs are not being adequately served by available products and services? The introduction of overnight package delivery by FedEx is a well-known example of identifying and filling a current customer need.

### Identifying Past and Present Strategies

Before deciding if a strategic change is necessary or desirable, the past and present strategies used by the organization need to be clearly identified. General questions to be addressed include the following: Has past strategy been consciously developed? If not, can past history be analyzed to identify what inherent strategy has evolved? If so, has the strategy been recorded in written form? In either case, a strategy or a series of strategies, as reflected by the organization's past actions and intentions, can usually be identified.

## Diagnosing Past and Present Performance

To evaluate how past strategies have worked and determine whether strategic changes are needed, the organization's performance record must be examined. How is the organization currently performing? How has the organization performed over the last several years? Is the performance trend moving up or down? Management must address all of these questions before attempting to formulate any type of future strategy. Evaluating an organization's performance usually involves some type of in-depth financial analysis and diagnosis.

Once management has an accurate picture of the current status of the organization, the next step in formulating strategy is to decide what the long-, intermediate-, and short-range objectives should be in light of the current mission. However, these objectives cannot be accurately established without examining the internal and external environments. Thus, establishing the long- and intermediate-range objectives and analyzing the internal and external environments are concurrent processes that influence each other.

## Setting Objectives

Once the mission of the organization has been clearly established, the guidelines offered earlier in this chapter should be followed to determine the specific long- and short-range objectives of the different organizational units. In general, long-range organizational objectives should derive from the mission statement. These long-range organizational objectives should then lead to the establishment of short-range performance objectives for the organization. Derivative objectives are subsequently developed for each major division and department. This process continues down through the various subunits right down to the individual level.

---

### PROGRESS CHECK QUESTIONS

9. Define strategic management.
10. What are the three major phases of the strategic management process?
11. What is the purpose of an organization's mission?
12. Why is it important to diagnose past as well as present performance?

---

**SWOT**

An acronym for Strengths, Weaknesses, Opportunities, and Threats, business managers evaluate the performance of their department or the entire company using a SWOT analysis.

## SWOT Analysis

**SWOT** is an acronym for an organization's **s**trengths, **w**eaknesses, **o**pportunities, and **t**hreats. A SWOT analysis is a technique for evaluating an organization's internal strengths and weaknesses and its external opportunities and threats. A major advantage of using a SWOT analysis is that it provides a general overview of whether its overall situation is healthy or unhealthy.[10] The underlying assumption of a SWOT analysis is that managers can better formulate a successful strategy after they have carefully reviewed the organization's strengths and weaknesses in light of the threats and opportunities the environment presents.

An organization's strengths and weaknesses are usually identified by conducting an internal analysis of the organization. The basic idea of conducting an internal analysis is to perform an objective assessment of the organization's current strengths and weaknesses. What things does the organization do well? What things does the organization do poorly? From a resource perspective, what are the organization's strengths and weaknesses?

The threats and opportunities presented by the environment are usually identified by methodically assessing the organization's external environment. An organization's **external environment** consists of everything outside the organization, but the focus of this assessment is on the external factors that have an impact on its business. Such factors are classified by their proximity to the organization: They are either in its broad environment or in its competitive environment. Broad environmental factors are somewhat removed from the organization but can still influence it. General economic conditions and social, political, and technological trends represent major factors in the broad environment. Factors in the competitive environment are close to the organization and come in regular contact with it. Stockholders, suppliers, competitors, labor unions, customers, and potential new entrants represent members of the competitive environment.

> **external environment**
> Consists of everything outside the organization.

Managers use many different qualitative and quantitative methods for forecasting broad environmental trends. Qualitative techniques are based primarily on opinions and judgments, whereas quantitative techniques are based primarily on the analysis of data and the use of statistical techniques. Both methods can be helpful depending on the circumstances and the information available.

The five forces model of competition is a tool developed by Michael Porter to help managers analyze their competitive environment. This model suggests that the competitive environment can be assessed by analyzing the import of and interactions among five major forces in the competitive or industry environment: (1) suppliers, (2) buyers, (3) competitive rivalry among firms currently in the industry, (4) product or service substitutes, and (5) potential entrants into the industry.[11] By using this tool to access the competitive environment, managers can then better select the most appropriate business level strategy to pursue. Figure 5.5 summarizes the five forces model of competition.

An assessment of the external environment emphasizes the fact that organizations do not operate in a vacuum and are very much affected by

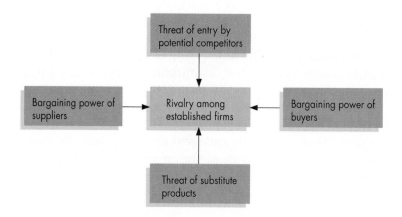

their surroundings. Figure 5.6 lists several factors that managers should consider when assessing an organization's strengths and weaknesses and the threats and opportunities posed by the environment. The most important result of a SWOT analysis is the ability to draw conclusions about the attractiveness of the organization's situation and the need for strategic action.

### Comparing Strategic Alternatives

The goal in this stage of the formulation process is to identify the feasible strategic alternatives (in light of everything that has been done up to this point) and then select the best alternative. Given the mission and long-range objectives, what are the feasible strategic alternatives? The results of the SWOT analysis also limit the feasible strategic alternatives. For example, the results of an internal financial analysis could severely restrict an organization's options for expansion. Similarly, the results of an external analysis of population trends might also limit an organization's expansion plans. Once a set of feasible alternatives has been defined, the final strategic choice must be made.

The evaluation and final choice of an appropriate strategic alternative involves the integration of the mission, objectives, internal analysis, and external analysis. In this phase, management attempts to select the corporate strategy that offers the organization its best chance to achieve its mission and objectives through actions that are compatible with its capacity for risk and its value structure. Once the corporate strategy has been identified, additional substrategies must be selected to support it.

In the case of diversified, multibusiness organizations, comparing strategic alternatives involves assessing the attractiveness of each business as well as the overall business mix. A **strategic business unit (SBU)** is a distinct business that has its own set of competitors and can be managed reasonably independently of other businesses within the organization.[12] The elements of an SBU vary from organization to organization

John implemented planning and strategic management to increase sales more than 40 percent. He discovered the advantages of a detailed plan versus the more laid back approach he'd used in the past.

**strategic business unit (SBU)**

Distinct business that has its own set of competitors and can be managed reasonably independently of other businesses within the organization.

## POTENTIAL INTERNAL STRENGTHS

- Core competencies in key areas
- Adequate financial resources
- Well-thought-of by buyers
- An acknowledged market leader
- Well-conceived functional area strategies
- Access to economies of scale
- Insulated (at least somewhat) from strong competitive pressures
- Proprietary technology
- Cost advantages
- Better advertising campaigns
- Product innovation skills
- Proven management
- Ahead on experience curve
- Better manufacturing capability
- Superior technological skills
- Other?

## POTENTIAL EXTERNAL OPPORTUNITIES

- Ability to serve additional customer groups or expand into new markets or segments
- Ways to expand product line to meet broader range of customer needs
- Ability to transfer skills or technological know-how to new products or businesses
- Integrating forward or backward
- Falling trade barriers in attractive foreign markets
- Complacency among rival firms
- Ability to grow rapidly because of strong increases in market demand
- Emerging new technologies

## POTENTIAL INTERNAL WEAKNESSES

- No clear strategic direction
- Obsolete facilities
- Subpar profitability because . . .
- Lack of managerial depth and talent
- Missing some key skills or competencies
- Poor track record in implementing strategy
- Plagued with internal operating problems
- Falling behind in R&D
- Too narrow a product line
- Weak market image
- Weak distribution network
- Below-average marketing skills
- Unable to finance needed changes in strategy
- Higher overall unit costs relative to key competitors
- Other?

## POTENTIAL EXTERNAL THREATS

- Entry of lower-cost foreign competitors
- Rising sales of substitute products
- Slower market growth
- Adverse shifts in foreign exchange rates and trade policies of foreign governments
- Costly regulatory requirements
- Vulnerability to recession and business cycle
- Growing bargaining power of customers or suppliers
- Changing buyer needs and tastes
- Adverse demographic changes
- Other?

but can be a division, a subsidiary, or a single product line. In a small organization, the entire company may be an SBU.

## Implementing Strategy

After the corporate strategy has been carefully formulated, it must be translated into organizational actions. Given that the corporate strategy and business-level strategies have been clearly identified, what actions must be taken to implement them? Strategy implementation involves everything that must be done to put the strategy in motion successfully.

## figure 5.6

**SWOT ANALYSIS—WHAT TO LOOK FOR IN SIZING UP A COMPANY'S STRENGTHS, WEAKNESSES, OPPORTUNITIES, AND THREATS**

***Source:*** From Arthur A. Thompson, Jr., and A. J. Strickland III, *Strategic Management: Concepts and Cases,* 8th ed, 1995, p. 94. Reproduced with permission of The McGraw-Hill Companies.

## Hudson Shoe Company

John Hudson's company, located in a midwestern city, was started some 50 years earlier by his father, now deceased. It has remained a family enterprise, with his brother David in charge of production, his brother Sam the comptroller, and his brother-in-law Bill Owens taking care of product development. Bill and David share responsibility for quality control; Bill often works with Sam on administrative matters and advertising campaigns. Many competent subordinates are also employed. The company has one of the finest reputations in the shoe industry. The product integrity is to be envied and is a source of great pride to the company.

During a vacation in Santo Oro, in Central America, John had decided to visit some importers of shoes. He spoke to several and was most impressed with Señor Lopez of Bueno Compania. After checking Lopez's bank and personal references, his impression was confirmed. Lopez said he would place a small initial order if the samples proved satisfactory. John immediately phoned his office and requested the company rush samples of its best-sellers to Lopez. These arrived a few days before John

left for home. Shortly after arriving home, John was pleased to receive an order for 1,000 pairs of shoes from Lopez.

John stayed in touch with Lopez by telephone; within two months after the initial order, Hudson Shoe received an order for 5,000 additional pairs of shoes per month. Business continued at this level for about two years until Señor Lopez visited the plant. He was impressed and increased his monthly order from 5,000 to 10,000 pairs of shoes.

This precipitated a crisis at Hudson Shoe Company, and the family held a meeting. They had to decide whether to increase their capacity with a sizable capital investment or drop some of their customers. They did not like the idea of eliminating loyal customers but did not want to make a major investment. David suggested they run a second shift, which solved the problem nicely.

A year later, Lopez again visited and left orders for 15,000 pairs per month. He also informed them that more effort and expense was now required on his part for a wide distribution of the shoes. In addition to his regular 5 percent commission, he asked John for an additional commission of $2 per pair of shoes. When John hesitated, Lopez assured

Necessary actions include determining and implementing the most appropriate organizational structure, developing short-range objectives, and establishing functional strategies.

### Organizational Factors

Not only does an organization have a strategic history; it also has existing structures, policies, and systems. Although each of these factors can change as a result of a new strategy, each must be assessed and dealt with as part of the implementation process.

Even though an organization's structure can always be altered, the associated costs may be high. For example, a reorganization may result in substantial hiring and training costs for newly structured jobs. Thus, from a practical standpoint, an organization's current structure places certain restrictions on strategy implementation.

The strategy must fit with current organizational policies, or the conflicting policies must be modified. Often past policies heavily influence the extent to which future policies can be altered. For example, A. T. Cross Company, manufacturer of world-renowned writing instruments,

him that Hudson could raise its selling price by $2 and nothing would be lost. John felt uneasy but went along because the business was easy, steady, and most profitable. A few of Hudson's smaller customers had to be dropped.

By the end of the next year, Lopez was placing orders for 20,000 pairs per month. He asked that Hudson bid on supplying boots for the entire police force of the capital city of Santo Oro. Hudson received the contract and, within a year, was supplying the army and navy of Santo Oro and three other Central American countries with their needs.

Again, several old Hudson customers could not get their orders filled. Other Hudson customers were starting to complain of late deliveries. Also, Hudson seemed to be less willing to accept returns at the end of the season or to offer markdown allowances or advertising money. None of this was necessary with its export business. However, Hudson Shoe did decide to cling to its largest domestic customer—the largest mail-order chain in the United States.

In June of the following year, Lopez made a trip to Hudson Shoe. He informed John that in addition to his $2 per pair, it would be necessary to give the minister of revenue $2 per pair if he was to continue granting import licenses. Moreover, the defense ministers, who approved the army and navy orders in each country where they did business, also wanted $2 per pair. Again, selling prices could be increased accordingly. Lopez informed John that shoe manufacturers in the United States and two other countries were most eager to have this business at any terms. John asked for 10 days to discuss this with his partners. Lopez agreed and returned home to await their decision. The morning of the meeting of the board of directors of the Hudson Shoe Company, a wire was received from the domestic chain stating it would not be buying from Hudson next season. John Hudson called the meeting to order.

### Questions

1. What were the objectives of Hudson Shoe?
2. What policies existed?
3. How would you evaluate John Hudson's plans?
4. What would you do if you were John Hudson?

has a policy of unconditionally guaranteeing its products for life. Because customers have come to expect this policy, Cross would find it difficult to discontinue it.

Similarly, organizational systems that are currently in place can affect how the strategy might best be implemented. These systems can be either formal or informal. Examples include information systems, compensation systems, communication systems, and control systems.

## Functional Strategies

As introduced earlier in this chapter, functional strategies are the means by which business strategies are operationalized. Functional strategies outline the specific short-range actions to be taken by the different functional units of the organization (production, marketing, finance, human resource, etc.) to implement the business strategies. The development of functional strategies generally requires the active participation of many levels of management. In fact, input by lower levels of management at the development stage is essential to the successful implementation of functional strategies.

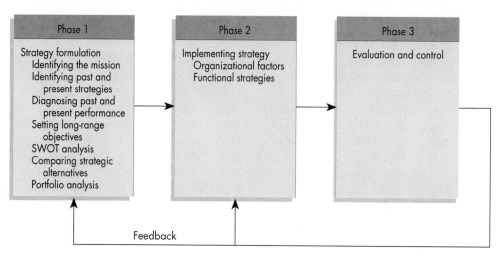

| Phase 1 | Phase 2 | Phase 3 |
|---|---|---|
| Strategy formulation<br>  Identifying the mission<br>  Identifying past and<br>    present strategies<br>  Diagnosing past and<br>    present performance<br>  Setting long-range<br>    objectives<br>  SWOT analysis<br>  Comparing strategic<br>    alternatives<br>  Portfolio analysis | Implementing strategy<br>  Organizational factors<br>  Functional strategies | Evaluation and control |

Feedback

**figure 5.7**

**THE STRATEGIC MANAGEMENT PROCESS**

## Evaluating and Controlling the Strategic Plan

After the strategic plan has been put into motion, the next challenge is to monitor continuously the organization's progress toward its long-range objectives and mission. Is the corporate strategy working, or should revisions be made? Where are problems likely to occur? The emphasis is on making the organization's managers aware of the problems that are likely to occur and of the actions to be taken if they do arise. As discussed earlier in this chapter, continuously evaluating and responding to internal and environmental changes are what strategic management is all about.

Figure 5.7 summarizes the strategic management process and its major components.

### PROGRESS CHECK QUESTIONS

13. Explain the term "SWOT analysis."
14. What are the five forces of competition?
15. What is an SBU?
16. What is the difference between a functional strategy and a business strategy?

## CONCLUSION

In Chapter 1 we defined management as "the process of deciding the best way to use an organization's resources to produce goods or provide services." In this chapter we have seen that making those decisions

# Tony fills a vacancy

The scheduling project worked remarkably well. There were a few grumbles at first that Tony was simply dumping one of his headaches onto them, but once the crew rolled up their sleeves and started working on the schedule, some amazing things started to happen. First, the problems and challenges that prevented individual employees from working specific shifts on specific days suddenly became manageable outside of the schedule. People started carpooling more; people traded babysitting duties for free to cover for each other; the more experienced crew members swapped stations on their assigned shift—all to make the schedule work and to make sure every shift was covered. Tony was true to his word and spent every available minute in the restaurant working with new employees and helping others get cross-trained in other areas of the Taco Barn system.

Kevin had done a great job in leading the scheduling project, and he was hoping that this would clinch his promotion to shift leader once Tanya left. She was scheduled to leave at the end of the week, and so far no decision had been announced.

After the lunch rush was over, Kevin received the request he had been waiting for—a private meeting with Tony in his office.

"Kevin, you've been a great crew member here, and you did a good job on that scheduling project."

Just like Tony to get straight to the point thought Kevin. "Thanks, Tony," he replied.

"I'm putting your name forward to Dawn as Tanya's replacement," said Tony, "but to do that I will need some supporting information. Your work record here speaks for itself, but Dawn likes to get a sense of people outside of their résumés, so I'd like you to write a little report for me."

"What kind of report?" asked Kevin, suddenly getting a little nervous.

"Taco Barn is always looking for future unit managers and regional managers, and I think you should be included in that group, Kevin. To convince Dawn of that, I'd like you to write a strategic planning document for this unit for the next three to five years. Nothing too complicated—where are we now and where do you think we should go in the next few years. Think you can do that?"

"Sure," answered Kevin, suddenly wishing he had paid more attention in his business classes at school.

"Great," said Tony. "Tanya's leaving at the end of the week, so if you can get it to me in a couple of days, I can have it on Dawn's desk in time to get you promoted before she leaves."

## QUESTIONS

1. Which should count more for Kevin's promotion: his leadership of the scheduling project or his length of employment with Taco Barn? Explain your answer.

2. Why is Tony making Kevin write the strategic planning report?

3. What information should Kevin put in his report?

4. Do you think Tony will be able to use any of the material in Kevin's report? Why or why not?

requires both an operational and a strategic perspective. While Henry Mintzberg's observations of managerial roles documented the extent to which managers have to function 'in the moment', the key to effective management is to plan ahead and proactively affect rather than passively accept the future. In the next chapter we will examine the importance of leadership as it relates to management and review how important it is to have an organizational culture that supports an environment in which effective management can occur.

## key terms

business strategies 122
combination strategies 121
contingency plans 114
corporate strategies 120
defensive or retrenchment strategies 121
evaluation phase 125
external environment 129
formal plan 113
formulation phase 125
functional plans 113
functional strategies 123

growth strategies 120
implementation phase 125
long-range objectives 115
long-range plans 114
management by objectives (MBO) 117
mission 126
objectives 115
operations or tactical planning 114
policies 118
procedure 119
rules 119

short-range objectives 115
short-range plans 114
stability strategies 121
strategic business unit (SBU) 130
strategic management 124
strategic planning 114
strategy 120
SWOT 128

## review questions

1. Why is it necessary to plan? How is most planning conducted?
2. Describe the differences between objectives, policies, procedures, and rules.
3. How would you respond to the following question from a manager: "How can I plan for next year when I don't even know what I'm going to do tomorrow?"
4. If strategic planning is an activity that originates from senior management, why should a front-line or middle manager be concerned with strategic planning?

## internet exercise

**IDENTIFYING MISSION STATEMENT COMPONENTS**

Using the Internet, select the mission statement of an organization of your choice, and identify the following components of the statement:

1. Customer and/or market
2. Product and/or service
3. Geographic domain

4. Technology

5. Concern for survival

6. Philosophy

7. Self-concept

8. Concern for public image

## team exercise

### ENVIRONMENTAL FORCES

Summarized below are the descriptions of two environmental forces that could have an influence on the automobile industry. Describe the threats and opportunities that might face General Motors as a result of these environmental forces.

### Social

Studies of social and economic trends present the auto industry with an enormous population of buyers who are predisposed to purchase and will have the financial means to buy new cars on a regular basis. Three demographic groups that will be particularly significant to the industry are baby boomers, women, and the elderly.

Maturing baby boomers will have far more disposable income available for automobile purchases, and a sizable upscale segment will favor luxury cars and sport-utility vehicles. Baby boomers and the elderly also will increase demand for recreational vehicles (RVs) while reducing the need for station wagons and minivans as their families mature. A large and growing blue-collar segment of the boomers, however, favors pickup trucks and Japanese cars.

Women will increasingly become more involved in new-car purchases and are expected to exercise as much power in the automotive market as men. Automotive marketing successes of the future will be generated by advertising that prominently features women.

The final dominant group, which represents a "graying of America," is buyers 55 and older. They constitute 25 percent of new-car buyers, and this statistic will increase. Older buyers will look for features that make driving safer and easier, including electronic systems to warn drivers who are getting drowsy, nonglare instrument panels, and simplified electronic controls.

### Technological

The rocketing price of gasoline has made efficiency a top priority with almost all buyers. The cars of tomorrow will be loaded with intelligent systems: smart computers that run the engine and transmission more efficiently, electronic suspension systems, radar obstacle detection to help drivers avoid accidents, and navigation systems that will help drivers avoid traffic jams while video screens indicate alternate routes. Self-tinting glass and infrared technology that enhances night vision also will be available. Antilock brakes, air bags, and traction control will become standard.

The use of space-age plastics will increase because they are lightweight, less expensive than steel, and noncorrosive. New techniques for making models and prototypes quickly and inexpensively using sophisticated computers are the wave of the future.

The extensive use of robotic technology in production will increase, and automobile manufacturers will develop cars for the future that will run on alternative fuels. The demand for electric and hybrid cars is expected to increase dramatically.

Divide the group into two teams, one representing General Motors (GM) and one representing Toyota. Each team will prepare a presentation documenting the degree to which their assigned organization has responded to these environmental forces and how they should proceed over the next three to five years.

## Electrolux Redesigns Itself

*Johan Hjertonsson's Drive for Change*

Johan Hjertonsson was lounging around his house outside Stockholm late one Saturday afternoon in 2003 when his boss, Electrolux CEO Hans Straberg called. "Hans said: 'We have a problem,'" recalls the 38-year-old Hjertonsson. "Things aren't moving fast enough." Sales were falling, products were taking too long to get to market, and consumers weren't sure why they should buy from Electrolux instead of the competition. Straberg told Hjertonsson: "I want you to fix this." In the past, the CEO of the giant Swedish appliance maker would have dealt with weak sales by turning to the company's army of engineers to power up a new line of products. But this time, Straberg chose a more radical approach. Instead of letting Electrolux engineers dominate the development process, he opted to go with another model—teams of designers, engineers, marketers, and salespeople working together to design consumer-friendly products. This model had been developed by Hjertonsson when he was marketing manager of the floor products and small appliance unit, which had been hit hard in the 1990s by cheaper Chinese products. The team-based approach became known as the Consumer Innovation Program. Hjertonsson reinvented his entire division, taking it from an engineer-driven, heavy manufacturer with full-scale operations in many countries to an integrated global company driven by teams and guided by consumer insights. He brought in innovation/design consultant IDEO to benchmark his program, then launched it in 2001. By then, the entire company was having

trouble from increasing Asian competition. In 2003, Hjertonsson, now head of Consumer Innovation, hired strategy consultant McKinsey & Co. to develop a questionnaire, which was sent to 500 managers. His team then followed up with 60 in-depth interviews. Four problems emerged: Managers didn't know enough about their customers, so they couldn't figure out what to develop; products were well-engineered but weren't filling consumer needs; R&D wasn't in sync with commercial product launches; and executives were afraid to take risks.

In early 2004, Straberg and Hjertonsson began a six-week road show, visiting hundreds of company managers to explain the Consumer Innovation Program. "The reaction was: 'I met my quota last month, I met my budget, what's the big deal?'" Hjertonsson says. The big deal, as managers quickly learned, was that Straberg wasn't just interested in monthly quotas. He wanted to reinvent the company, changing the way products were developed, brought to market, and sold. He was calling for a total business-model revolution, not evolution. Fast-forward to 2006, and Electrolux is morphing into a very different company. It uses a series of innovation methods to measure unmet consumer needs and how well new products meet them; how products are developed and launched; and whether the right product and marketing managers are in the right jobs. Hjertonsson simply calls this "talent management." Hjertonsson wields both carrots and sticks. Bonuses are based on how well managers adapt to the new system at

Electrolux. The evaluation process includes a series of 30 questions aimed at figuring out how well managers are adapting to the environment. Electrolux uses three basic measures. First there is what they call "value market share" which is the portion of the consumer's wallet going to Electrolux versus other competitors. It is determined by the volume of appliances multiplied by the average price. Electrolux also looks closely at growth of profit margins and at average prices. The purpose of all three of these metrics is to shift focus toward higher-value products and away from those products that have become "commoditized."

One of the biggest changes in Electrolux is the switch from using marketing surveys that ask consumers what they want to actually visiting consumers in their homes to see how they use their appliances. The new consumer-centric focus has caught the attention of designers such as Henrik Otto, 41, who was recruited by Straberg in August, 2004, from carmaker Volvo to be Electrolux's design chief. Otto had been using a similar approach at Volvo and found the challenge of applying the method at a completely different kind of company irresistible. He also saw similarities between designing cars and designing appliances. "It's not purely about price and performance anymore. It's about the satisfaction people get out of the products," he says. "Now, people want their personalities to be reflected by their appliances." Under Otto's leadership, the design department began asking "how do we make these products more emotional, and how do we get away from the boxy white look of home appliances?" Through home visits and interviews with more than 160,000 consumers worldwide, various types of core consumer profiles emerged. They were refined by Electrolux into four archetypes dubbed Anna, Catherine, Maria, and Monica to help the innovation teams visualize who they were developing products for. Catherine is a neatness freak, while Anna just wants to get the chores over as quickly as possible. Monica is superefficient and Maria is a homebody who dotes on her family. Hjertonsson says the personas cut across nationality, age, and socioeconomic groups.

Straberg is training 700 managers, including nearly all of his top execs, in the methods of the Consumer Innovation Program. Working in small groups that include designers, engineers, and marketers, the managers develop their prototype products. By working in multidisciplinary teams from the beginning, designers avoid developing products that can't be engineered, engineers avoid technological solutions that aren't visually appealing, and marketers can help shape products so that retailers are more likely to give them prominent play.

Electrolux is also using design thinking to relaunch older products. Countertop dishwashers and frost-free freezers in Europe are cases in point. Electrolux relaunched a mini-dishwasher about the size of a large microwave in Italy, aimed at households with one or two people. When these households have full-size dishwashers, they wait for them to be full, and run them only once or twice a week. That makes it harder to get dishes clean. It also means favorite mugs or plates can't be used every day. The Electrolux machine was marketed with the pitch that it allows those favorites to be used daily.

While Straberg and Hjertonsson have made progress reinventing Electrolux, they don't kid themselves that they are finished. Hjertonsson believes it will take "many, many years," to complete the transformation. "Once you are on this quest," he says, "it is a continuous journey rather than a race."

## Questions

1. What were the primary weaknesses in the product development process at Electrolux before Johan Hjertonsson arrived?

2. What are the features of the Consumer Innovation Program (CIP)?

3. What were the initial reactions of Electrolux employees to the CIP?

4. List the successes Hjertonsson has achieved in his reinvention of Electrolux.

*Source:* Adapted from Ariane Sains and Stanley Reed, *BusinessWeek Online,* November 27, 2006.

## Paul Pressler's Fall from the Gap

*Hailed on His Arrival, the Former CEO Is Now Viewed as "The Wrong Guy at the Wrong Time"*

When Paul S. Pressler arrived as the chief executive officer of Gap Inc. in the fall of 2002, he was exactly what the board wanted—or at least what it thought it wanted. The polished, good-looking Disney veteran was a hard-nosed operations wizard, not a dreamy fashion junkie. He seemed to be just the man to restore discipline to the floundering company. But over the next four years, Gap's performance came apart at the seams. On January 22, 2007 Pressler resigned.

The immediate postmortem analysis: He was a numbers guy who didn't appreciate the subtleties of the fashion business. That's true, but it's only part of the story. Pressler's problems involved more than just a few bad bets on colors and styles. According to 12 former employees interviewed by *BusinessWeek*, he also bungled some of the very things that were supposed to be his strengths, including cost-cutting campaigns, human resources initiatives, and supply chain streamlining efforts. One ex-employee characterizes Pressler's tenure as "total system failure."

Pressler's management shortcomings were particularly visible at the company's most important division: its flagship Gap brand. The story of his failed effort to fix this once-proud chain, insiders say, is a classic demonstration of what can

happen when a talented man is handed the wrong mission. "He is a skilled leader and he understands how to build a team, but unfortunately he didn't build a team for the particular challenges Gap faced," says a former insider. "Maybe he was the wrong guy at the wrong time."

In the wake of Pressler's departure, Gap is still reeling. Although shares ran up significantly following Pressler's arrival, increasing from about $10 a share in the fall of 2002 to more than $24 during the summer of 2004, they have traded in the $17-to-$20 range ever since. That's a steep fall for a retailer that, just a decade ago, seemed perfectly in step with American tastes. When the workplace went casual in the 1990s, Gap was at the ready with big selections of khaki pants. When fleece vests were popular a few years later, Gap had them in a rainbow of colors. Everyone seemed to own a classic Gap pocket T-shirt or two. Between 1989 and 2001, companywide sales rocketed from $1.6 billion to $13.7 billion. Those stunning results were driven in part by the breathtaking success of the Old Navy chain's inexpensive wares. At the same time the Banana Republic chain—which in 1989 shed its original safari theme in favor of a more sophisticated, urban style—also sizzled.

## ALIENATING LONGTIME CUSTOMERS

But by the end of 2001, the Gap brand and Old Navy were suffering sharp growing pains. Under Millard S. "Mickey" Drexler, the company's CEO at the time, the two chains overexpanded. Long-term debt ballooned from $780 million to $2 billion in 2001. At the same time, the usually trend-savvy Drexler oversaw a series of fashion missteps, in particular veering toward super-hip clothes that alienated longtime customers. Earnings sank, and in 2002, Drexler was pushed out. Along came Pressler. A 15-year Walt Disney Co. veteran, he had risen to the chairmanship of the company's amusement parks and resorts unit. By nature a methodical thinker, say people who worked under him at Disney, Pressler embraced market analyses and other research to help him understand consumer spending patterns. He also imposed strict cost controls that annoyed his creative staff.

Once at Gap, Pressler, who wore neat jeans, jackets, and a ready smile, came across as a likable and approachable manager. At the start, Pressler had the benefit of excellent timing: Clothing designed during Drexler's final year on the job was starting to appear in stores and did well. Sales rose at the Gap brand, and company-wide, for more than a year. Earnings shot up, too. Pressler went on a hiring spree, bringing in a handful of former Disney colleagues, including Chief Financial Officer Byron H. Pollitt Jr., who paid down debt and restored the company's credit rating to investment-grade status. Pressler also hired another ex-Disney co-worker, Eva Sage-Gavin, to lead human resources.

It was Gap's longstanding corporate culture that caught Pressler's attention early on. At the time, the no-nonsense corporate mantra was "Own it, do it, get it done." But Pressler thought this culture didn't sufficiently promote collaboration. He set out to promote a new environment built around the slogan "Purpose, Values, and Behaviors." Pamphlets promoting communication and teamwork landed on employees' desks. Posters and banners trumpeting the bland new slogans went up around headquarters. In the beginning, "people were very receptive" to the effort, says Alan J. Barocas, the company's former senior vice-president for real estate. "It was embraced." But eye-rolling started as the initiative began consuming a lot of time. Former employees say they had to sit through countless meetings, workshops, and role-playing seminars where Pressler and his HR executives discussed the new culture. Many staffers felt they were wasting their time in get-togethers that didn't address the crucial matter of creating and marketing clothes.

In 2003, Dressler kicked off a plan to remake the retailer's supply chain. One goal was to combine fabric purchases across all three of the company's brands, which had previously used separate suppliers. Pressler wanted to cut costs and speed the flow of merchandise from drawing board to store shelf. But the effort stumbled. Since all three brands sell jeans made of denim, in late 2003 they began purchasing it together. But the big buying deals yielded denim of a single quality, weave, and weight. That meant all three brands were limited to one kind of fabric even though, with their different audiences, they needed to be able to offer a selection of jeans. And with all that denim ordered in advance, there was less incentive for designers to keep their eyes open so they could jump on the next great style. Jeans made with material from the pooled purchases ended up largely falling flat, and the joint purchasing effort was abandoned.

## RAISING EYEBROWS

As part of the supply chain revamping, Pressler also tinkered with the way the Gap brand produced clothing samples. These prototypes had long been made at studios in Manhattan's Garment District. But Pressler moved sample-making to Asia, where the company's many suppliers are located. With that change, designers had to create patterns, ship them to Asia, get the samples back, make changes, and ship them back to be remade. While making samples in Asia was cheaper than in New York, it delayed the process. Aggravating matters, the company instituted a new cost-cutting rule: No overnight shipping to Asia without high-level approval.

The first clothes produced under Pressler's leadership of the Gap brand started to reach shelves in the spring of 2005. But even supported by an advertising blitz fronted by actress Sarah Jessica Parker, the brand's sales fell 4 percent that spring and summer. One sore spot was Pressler's directive to use the findings of the research staff, known as the consumer insights group, that he had created. Some designers and merchants didn't believe that the group's output—which included findings from consumer focus groups, polls, and surveys of customers and store employees—was particularly useful in the fashion business, because consumers aren't good at predicting what they'll buy in the future.

The constant disagreements delayed determining final designs. Ideas for any given season ping-ponged back and forth. Entire collections were made, and altered, and then reworked, sometimes several times over. In the 11th-hour crunch, staffers would end up falling back on lowest-common-denominator items, bland styles that they hoped would please everyone but risked pleasing no one.

By the end of 2005, speculation was widespread that Pressler, who'd won the nickname "Dead Man Walking" on Wall Street, would soon be on his way out. Sales declines at the Gap brand were widening, reaching an 8 percent drop in the first quarter of fiscal 2006. The tumult dragged on. Ad campaigns came and went, including commercials for black pants that used footage of Audrey Hepburn. They failed to reverse the sales declines that Wall Street had come to expect. In November 2006, the company's credit rating dropped back into junk territory, and holiday sales for the Gap brand plummeted 9 percent. It came as no great surprise when the company said Pressler and the board "have mutually agreed that Mr. Pressler will step down from his position." And it didn't come as much of a surprise when the company spelled out the qualifications for its next CEO: Gap is now seeking an executive who sounds like the opposite of Pressler, one with "deep retailing and merchandising experience, ideally in apparel," and who "understands the creative process."

## Questions

1. Why was Paul Pressler hired as the CEO of Gap?
2. What was Pressler's approach to the strategic management of Gap?
3. Where did Pressler go wrong?
4. What challenges will the new CEO of Gap be facing?

*Source:* Adapted from Louise Lee, *BusinessWeek Online,* February 26, 2007.

# LEADERSHIP AND CULTURE

"Leadership is the ability to get men to do what they don't want to do and like it."

—President Harry Truman

## The World of Work: Tony gets assigned to a project

Tony had put Kevin's name forward as a replacement for Tanya as shift leader at the Taco Barn. He had asked Kevin to write a report to support his application—a strategic plan for the next three to five years.

Kevin had done exactly as Tony had asked, and Dawn, the regional manager, was sufficiently impressed to confirm Kevin's appointment as the new shift leader. In fact, Dawn had been so impressed with the report idea that she asked Tony to come and see her at the regional offices.

"Tony, that idea of the strategic plan was very creative," said Dawn as they began their morning meeting.

"Thanks, Dawn—I really thought it would give Kevin a chance to show that he had some positive ideas to contribute—he's a really good team member,

and with the right encouragement, I think he could go far with Taco Barn."

"Speaking of people who could go far with Taco Barn," continued Dawn, "you seem to have filled Jerry's shoes very well, Tony—sales are up and your people are working well together—you've really hit the ground running."

Tony thought for a second and realized there was an opportunity here, "Thanks, Dawn. Jerry built a great crew, and he gave me some great advice before he took up his new position— 'If it ain't broke, don't try to fix it'—and I've tried to remember that." Tony did his best to look as serious as possible, even as the thought of his disastrous scheduling idea flashed across his mind—if only Dawn knew how close he had come to a mutiny over that one.

# objectives

**After studying this chapter, you will be able to:**

1 Define leadership, power, and authority.

2 Discuss leadership as it relates to management.

3 Explain leadership attitudes.

4 Describe the differences between a Theory X and a Theory Y manager.

5 Explain the differences between Transactional, Transformational, and Charismatic leadership styles.

6 Identify strategies for effectively managing corporate culture.

---

"Well," continued Dawn, "I think your unit is running well enough that we can pull you away for a week to work on a companywide project—what do you think?"

"Sounds great," answered Tony. "Kevin can cover things, and I can check in on a regular basis if he needs any help."

"Great," continued Dawn. "We're looking at developing a Leadership Development Program for the future leaders of this organization—people like you and Kevin. We've been working with a team of consultants, and they've suggested that before we start putting the program together, we really need to survey our employees to get a sense of what type of leaders we currently have in the organization, and what kind of organizational culture those leaders have created. Once we have that in place, then we can move on to looking at whether that culture and leadership style will take us to where we want to go in the future—what do you think?"

"Sounds great," responded Tony, wondering just how long the project would take and whether he could really answer those questions himself. What was his leadership style, and could he describe the culture of the Taco Barn organization?

## QUESTIONS

1. From what you know of Tony so far, how would you describe his leadership style? Refer to page 149 for some suggested classifications of different leadership styles.

2. How would you describe the organizational culture of the Taco Barn?

3. Do you think the consultants' recommendation of an employee survey is a good idea? Why or why not?

4. List six questions that you think should be included in the survey.

# POWER, AUTHORITY, AND LEADERSHIP

**power**

Ability to influence, command, or apply force; a measure of a person's potential to get others to do what he or she wants them to do, as well as to avoid being forced by others to do what he or she does not want to do.

**authority**

Legitimate exercise of power; the right to issue directives and expend resources; related to power but narrower in scope.

**leadership**

Ability to influence people to willingly follow one's guidance or adhere to one's decisions.

**leader**

One who obtains followers and influences them in setting and achieving objectives.

Before undertaking a study of leadership, a clear understanding must be developed of the relationships among power, authority, and leadership. **Power** is a measure of a person's potential to get others to do what he or she wants them to do, as well as to avoid being forced by others to do what he or she does not want to do. Figure 6.1 summarizes several sources of power in organizations. The use of or desire for power is often viewed negatively in our society because power is often linked to the concepts of punishment, dominance, and control.

Power can have both a positive and negative form. Positive power results when the exchange is voluntary and both parties feel good about the exchange. Negative power results when the individual is forced to change. Power in organizations can be exercised upward, downward, or horizontally. It does not necessarily follow the organizational hierarchy from top to bottom.

**Authority,** which is the right to issue directives and expend resources, is related to power but is narrower in scope. Basically, the amount of authority a manager has depends on the amount of coercive, reward, and legitimate power the manager can exert. Authority is a function of position in the organizational hierarchy, flowing from the top to the bottom of the organization. An individual can have power—expert or referent—without having formal authority. Furthermore, a manager's authority can be diminished by reducing the coercive and reward power in the position.

**Leadership** is the ability to influence people to willingly follow one's guidance or adhere to one's decisions. Obtaining followers and influencing them in setting and achieving objectives makes a **leader.** Leaders use power in influencing group behavior. For instance, political leaders often use referent power. Informal leaders in organizations generally combine referent power and expert power. Some managers rely only on authority, while others use different combinations of power.

## figure 6.1

**SOURCES OF POWER**

| ORGANIZATIONAL SOURCES | BASIS |
|---|---|
| Reward power | Capacity to provide rewards. |
| Coercive power | Capacity to punish. |
| Legitimate power | Person's position in the organizational hierarchy. |

| PERSONAL SOURCES | BASIS |
|---|---|
| Expert power | The skill, expertise, and knowledge an individual possesses. |
| Referent power | The personal characteristics of an individual that make other people want to associate with the person. |

# LEADERSHIP AND MANAGEMENT

Leadership and management are not necessarily the same but are not incompatible. Effective leadership in organizations creates a vision of the future that considers the legitimate long-term interests of the parties involved in the organization, develops a strategy for moving toward that vision, enlists the support of employees to produce the movement, and motivates employees to implement the strategy. Management is a process of planning, organizing, staffing, motivating, and controlling through the use of formal authority. In practice, effective leadership and effective management must ultimately be the same.

# LEADER ATTITUDES

Douglas McGregor developed two attitude profiles, or assumptions, about the basic nature of people. These attitudes were termed **Theory X** and **Theory Y;** they are summarized in Figure 6.2. McGregor maintained that many leaders in essence subscribe to either Theory X or Theory Y and behave accordingly. A Theory X leader would likely use a much

**figure 6.2**

**ASSUMPTIONS ABOUT PEOPLE**

*Source:* From D. McGregor and W. Bennis, *The Human Side of Enterprise,* 1/e, 1989. Reproduced with permission of The McGraw-Hill Companies.

**Theory X**

1. The average human being has an inherent dislike of work and will avoid it if possible.
2. Because of their dislike of work, most people must be coerced, controlled, directed, or threatened with punishment to get them to put forth adequate effort toward the achievement of organizational objectives.
3. The average human being prefers to be directed, wishes to avoid responsibility, has relatively little ambition, and wants security above all.

**Theory Y**

1. The expenditure of physical and mental effort in work is as natural as play or rest.
2. External control and the threat of punishment are not the only means for bringing about effort toward organizational objectives. Workers will exercise self-direction and self-control in the service of objectives to which they are committed.
3. Commitment to objectives is a function of the rewards associated with their achievement.
4. The average human being learns, under proper conditions, not only to accept but to seek responsibility.
5. The capacity to exercise a relatively high degree of imagination, ingenuity, and creativity in the solution of organizational problems is widely, not narrowly, distributed in the population.
6. Under the conditions of modern industrial life, the intellectual potential of the average human being is only partially utilized.

more authoritarian style of leadership than a leader who believes in Theory Y assumptions. The real value of McGregor's work was the idea that a leader's attitude toward human nature has a large influence on how that person behaves as a leader.[1]

The relationship between a leader's expectations and the resulting performance of subordinates has received much attention. Generally, it has been found that if a manager's expectations are high, productivity is likely to be high. On the other hand, if the manager's expectations are low, productivity is likely to be poor. McGregor called this phenomenon the **self-fulfilling prophecy.**

**self-fulfilling prophecy**
The relationship between a leader's expectations and the resulting performance of subordinates.

---

**PROGRESS CHECK QUESTIONS**

1. Define the terms power, authority, and leadership.
2. Explain the different expectations of Theory X and Theory Y managers.
3. Would you describe yourself as a Theory X or a Theory Y manager? Why?
4. Define the self-fulfilling prophecy of management.

---

## FRAMEWORK FOR CLASSIFYING LEADERSHIP STUDIES

Many studies have been conducted on leadership. One useful framework for classifying these studies is shown in Figure 6.3. *Focus* refers to whether leadership is to be studied as a set of traits or as a set of behaviors. *Traits* refer to what characteristics the leader possesses, whereas *behaviors* refer to what the leader does. The second dimension—*approach*—refers to whether leadership is studied from a universal or contingent approach. The universal approach assumes there is one best way to lead regardless of the circumstances. The contingent approach assumes the best approach to leadership is contingent on the situation. Each of the studies shown in Figure 6.3 is discussed in the following sections.

**figure 6.3**

**FRAMEWORK FOR CLASSIFYING LEADERSHIP STUDIES**

*Source:* Arthur G. Yago, "Leadership Perspectives in Theory and Practice," *Management Science,* March 1982, p. 316.

| | Approach | |
|---|---|---|
| **FOCUS** | **UNIVERSAL** | **CONTINGENT** |
| Traits | Trait theory | Fiedler's contingency theory |
| Behaviors | Leadership styles | Path–goal theory |
| | Ohio State studies | Situational theory |
| | Michigan studies | |
| | Managerial Grid | |

As a result of bad weather and supplier problems, you are behind schedule on a building project, and the owner of the company instructs you to hire some illegal immigrants to help get the project back on track. You are ordered to pay them in cash "under the table," and the owner justifies the decision as being "a one-off—besides, the Immigration and Naturalization Service has bigger fish to fry than a few undocumented workers on a building site! If we get caught, we'll pay the fine—it will be less than the penalty we would owe our client for missing our deadline on the project." What do you do?

**Source:** Andrew Ghillyer, *Business Ethics: A Real World Approach* (New York: McGraw-Hill, 2007), Chapter 3, page 47.

## Trait Theory

Early research efforts devoted to leadership stressed what the leader was *like* rather than what the leader did—a **trait theory** of leadership. Many personality traits (such as originality, initiative, persistence, knowledge, enthusiasm), social traits (tact, patience, sympathy, etc.), and physical characteristics (height, weight, attractiveness) have been examined to differentiate leaders.

At first glance, a few traits do seem to distinguish leaders from followers. These include being slightly superior in such physical traits as weight and height and in a tendency to score higher on tests of dominance, intelligence, extroversion, and adjustment. But the differences seem to be small, with much overlap.

Thus, the research in this area has generally been fruitless—largely because the traits related to leadership in one case usually did not prove to be predictive in other cases. In general, it can be said that traits may to some extent influence the capacity to lead. But these traits must be analyzed in terms of the leadership situation (described in detail later in this chapter).

> **trait theory**
> Stressed what the leader was like rather than what the leader did.

## Basic Leadership Styles

Other studies dealt with the style of the leader. They found three basic leadership styles: autocratic, laissez-faire, and democratic. The main difference among these styles is where the decision-making function rests. Generally, the **autocratic leader** makes more decisions for the group; the **laissez-faire leader** allows people within the group to make all decisions; and the **democratic leader** guides and encourages the group to make decisions. More detail about each of the leadership styles is given in Figure 6.4. The figure implies that the democratic style is the most desirable and productive. However, current research on leadership, discussed later in this chapter, does not necessarily support this conclusion. The primary contribution of this research was identifying the three basic styles of leadership.

> **autocratic leader**
> Makes most decisions for the group.

> **laissez-faire leader**
> Allows people within the group to make all decisions.

> **democratic leader**
> Guides and encourages the group to make decisions.

**149**

## figure 6.4

**RELATIONSHIP BETWEEN STYLES OF LEADERSHIP AND GROUP MEMBERS**

***Source:*** L. B. Bradford and R. Lippitt, "Building a Democratic Work Group," *Personnel* 22, no. 2, November 1945.

### Autocratic Style

*Leader*

1. The individual is very conscious of his or her position.
2. He or she has little trust and faith in members of the group.
3. This leader believes pay is a just reward for working and the only reward that will motivate employees.
4. Orders are issued to be carried out, with no questions allowed and no explanations given.

*Group members*

1. No responsibility is assumed for performance, with people merely doing what they are told.
2. Production is good when the leader is present, but poor in the leader's absence.

### Laissez–Faire Style

*Leader*

1. He or she has no confidence in his or her leadership ability.
2. This leader does not set goals for the group.

*Group members*

1. Decisions are made by whoever in the group is willing to do it.
2. Productivity generally is low, and work is sloppy.
3. Individuals have little interest in their work.
4. Morale and teamwork generally are low.

### Democratic Style

*Leader*

1. Decision making is shared between the leader and the group.
2. When the leader is required or forced to make a decision, his or her reasoning is explained to the group.
3. Criticism and praise are given objectively.

*Group members*

1. New ideas and change are welcomed.
2. A feeling of responsibility is developed within the group.
3. Quality of work and productivity generally are high.
4. The group generally feels successful.

It is important to have an established leadership style. It benefits both employees and employers.

## Ohio State Studies

A series of studies on leadership was conducted at Ohio State University to find out the most important behaviors of successful leaders. The researchers wanted to find out what a successful leader does, regardless of the type of group being led: a mob, a religious group, a university, or a business organization. To do this, they developed a questionnaire called the **Leader Behavior Description Questionnaire (LBDQ).** Both the original form and variations of it are still used today.

From the research, two leader behaviors emerged consistently as being the most important: consideration and initiating structure. The term **consideration** refers to the leader behavior of showing concern for individual group members and satisfying their needs. The term **initiating structure** refers to the leader behavior of structuring the work of group members and directing the group toward the achievement of the group's goals.

Since the Ohio State research, many other studies have been done on the relationship between the leader behaviors of consideration and initiating structure and their resulting effect on leader effectiveness. The major conclusions that can be drawn from these studies are:[2]

1. Leaders scoring high on consideration tend to have more satisfied subordinates than do leaders scoring low on consideration.
2. The relationship between the score on consideration and leader effectiveness depends on the group being led. In other words, a high score on consideration was positively linked with leader effectiveness for managers and office staff in a large industrial firm, whereas a high score on consideration was negatively linked with leader effectiveness for production foremen.
3. There is also no consistent relationship between initiating structure and leader effectiveness; rather, the relationship varies depending on the group that is being led.

## University of Michigan Studies

The Institute for Social Research of the University of Michigan conducted studies to discover principles contributing both to the productivity of a group and to the satisfaction derived by group members. The initial study was conducted at the home office of the Prudential Insurance Company in Newark, New Jersey.

Interviews were conducted with 24 managers and 419 non managerial employees. Results of the interviews showed that managers of high-producing work groups were more likely:

1. To receive general rather than close supervision from their superiors.
2. To like the amount of authority and responsibility they have in their job.
3. To spend more time in supervision.
4. To give general rather than close supervision to their employees.
5. To be employee-oriented rather than production-oriented.

Supervisors of low-producing work groups had basically opposite characteristics and techniques. They were production-oriented and gave close supervision.

Rensis Likert, then director of the institute, published the results of his years of research in the book *New Patterns of Management,* which is a classic in its field.[3] Likert believes there are four patterns or styles of

**leader behavior description questionnaire (LBDQ)**
Questionnaire designed to determine what a successful leader does, regardless of the type of group being led.

**consideration**
Leader behavior of showing concern for individual group members and satisfying their needs.

**initiating structure**
Leader behavior of structuring the work of group members and directing the group toward the attainment of the group's goals.

## Changes in the Plastics Division

Ed Sullivan was general manager of the Plastics Division of Warner Manufacturing Company. Eleven years ago, Ed hired Russell (Rusty) Means as a general manager of the Plastics Division's two factories. Ed trained Rusty as a manager and thinks Rusty is a good manager, an opinion based largely on the fact that products are produced on schedule and are of such quality that few customers complain. In fact, for the past eight years, Ed has pretty much let Rusty run the factories independently.

Rusty believes strongly that his job is to see that production runs smoothly. He feels that work is work. Sometimes it is agreeable, sometimes disagreeable. If an employee doesn't like the work, he or she can either adjust or quit. Rusty, say the factory personnel, "runs things. He's firm and doesn't stand for any nonsense. Things are done by the book, or they are not done at all." The turnover in the factories is low; nearly every employee likes Rusty and believes that he knows his trade and that he stands up for them.

Two months ago, Ed Sullivan retired and his replacement, Wallace Thomas, took over as general manager of the Plastics Division. One of the first things Thomas did was call his key management people together and announce some major changes he wanted to implement. These included (1) bring the operative employees into the decision-making process; (2) establish a planning committee made up of three management members and three operative employees; (3) start a suggestion system; and (4) as quickly as possible, install a performance appraisal program agreeable to both management and the operative employees. Wallace also stated he would be active in seeing that these projects would be implemented without delay.

After the meeting, Rusty was upset and decided to talk to Robert Mitchell, general manager of sales for the Plastics Division.

**Rusty:** *Wallace is really going to change things, isn't he?*

**Robert:** *Yeah, maybe it's for the best. Things were a little lax under Ed.*

**Rusty:** *I liked them that way. Ed let you run your own shop. I'm afraid Wallace is going to be looking over my shoulder every minute.*

**Robert:** *Well, let's give him a chance. After all, some of the changes he's proposing sound good.*

**Rusty:** *Well, I can tell you our employees won't like them. Having them participate in making decisions and those other things are just fancy management stuff that won't work with our employees.*

### Questions

1. What different styles of leadership are shown in this case?
2. What style of leadership do you think Wallace will have to use with Rusty?
3. Do you agree with Rusty? Why or why not?
4. If "products are produced on schedule and of such quality that few customers complain," why should there be any changes?

leadership or management employed by organizations. He has identified and labeled these styles as follows:

*System 1: Exploitative authoritative.* Authoritarian form of management that attempts to exploit subordinates.

*System 2: Benevolent authoritative.* Authoritarian form of management, but paternalistic in nature.

*System 3: Consultative.* Manager requests and receives inputs from subordinates but maintains the right to make the final decision.

*System 4: Participative.* Manager gives some direction, but decisions are made by consensus and majority, based on total participation.

Likert used a questionnaire to determine the style of leadership and the management pattern employed in the organization as a whole. The results of his studies indicated that system 4 was the most effective style of management and that organizations should strive to develop a management pattern corresponding to this system.

## The Managerial Grid

Robert Blake and Jane Mouton have also developed a method of classifying the leadership style of an individual.[4] The **Managerial Grid,** depicted in Figure 6.5, is a two-dimensional framework rating a leader on the basis of concern for people and concern for production. (Notice that these activities closely relate to the leader activities from the Ohio State studies—consideration and initiating structure.) A questionnaire is used to locate a particular style of leadership or management on the grid.

Blake and Mouton identified five basic styles of management using the Managerial Grid. *Authority-obedience*—located in the lower-right-hand corner (9,1 position)—assumes that efficiency in operations results from properly arranging the conditions at work with minimum interference from other people. The opposite view, *country club management*—located in the upper-left-hand corner (1,9)—assumes that proper attention to human needs leads to a comfortable organizational atmosphere and

> **managerial grid**
> A two-dimensional framework rating a leader on the basis of concern for people and concern for production.

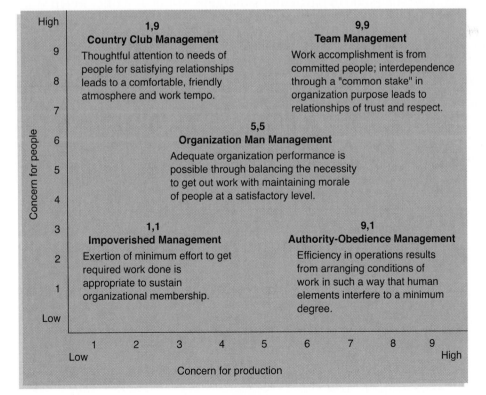

**figure 6.5**

**THE MANAGERIAL GRID**

***Source:*** Robert R. Blake and Jane Srygley Mouton, *The New Managerial Grid* ® (Houston: Gulf Publishing, 1978), p. 11. Copyright © 1978 by Gulf Publishing Company. Reproduced by permission.

### Basics of Career Planning Objectives

For students to become more focused on their career, basic questions need to be asked to help set the course of where the student would like to see his/her career reach.

To begin the process of planning career objectives, read the following questions and do your best to provide answers that will help you formulate your career aspirations:

- What is your ideal career job?
- What companies would you consider to be a good fit to the career job you are striving for?
- What skills do you have that might be a good fit to your ideal job?
- What desired salary and benefits do you expect from this career job?
- Are you willing to relocate?
- What is keeping you from obtaining this career job?

**contingency approach to leadership**

Focuses on the style of leadership that is most effective in particular situations.

workplace. *Team management*—in the upper-right-hand corner (9,9)—combines a high degree of concern for people with a high degree of concern for production. The other two styles on the grid are *impoverished management* (1,1) and *organization man management* (5,5). The Managerial Grid is intended to serve as a framework for managers to learn what their leadership style is and to develop a plan to move toward a 9,9 team management style of leadership.

## Contingency Approach to Leadership

The leadership studies discussed so far are similar in that they did not specifically address the complex differences between groups (such as production workers versus accountants) and their influences on leader behavior. To imply that a manager should be employee-oriented rather than production-oriented (Michigan studies) or that the manager should exhibit concern for both production and people (Blake and Mouton) does not say much about what the manager should do in particular situations. Nor does it offer much guidance for daily leadership situations. As a result, research began to focus on the style of leadership that is most effective in particular situations. This is called the **contingency approach to leadership.**

One of the first studies using the contingency approach was conducted by Fred Fiedler.[5] He studied the match between the leader's personality and the situation. Fiedler defined two basic leader personality traits—task and relationship motivation. Task-motivated leaders gain satisfaction from the performance of a task. Relationship-motivated leaders gain satisfaction from interpersonal relationships. Fiedler viewed task versus relationship as a leader trait that was relatively constant for any given person.

A scale, called the *least preferred co-worker scale* (LPC), was used to measure whether a person is a task- or relationship-oriented leader. Respondents were asked to think of all the people they had worked with and select the person with whom they could work least effectively. The respondents then described their least preferred co-worker on the LPC. A person who described a least preferred co-worker in fairly favorable terms was presumed to be motivated to have close interpersonal relations with others; Fiedler classified these people as *relationship-motivated* leaders. On the other hand, people who rejected co-workers with whom they had difficulties were presumed to be motivated to accomplish or achieve the task; they were classified as *task-oriented* leaders.

| SITUATION | 1 | 2 | 3 | 4 | 5 | 6 | 7 | 8 |
|---|---|---|---|---|---|---|---|---|
| Leader–member relations | Good | Good | Good | Good | Poor | Poor | Poor | Poor |
| Task structure | Structured | Structured | Unstructured | Unstructured | Structured | Structured | Unstructured | Unstructured |
| Position power | Strong | Weak | Strong | Weak | Strong | Weak | Strong | Weak |
| | *Favorable for leader* | | | | | | *Unfavorable for leader* | |

### figure 6.6

**FIEDLER'S CLASSIFICATION OF SITUATIONS**

**leader–member relations**
Degree to which others trust and respect the leader and the leader's friendliness.

**task structure**
Degree to which job tasks are structured.

**position power**
Power and influence that go with a job.

Fiedler next turned to the situation in which the leader was operating. He placed leadership situations along a favorable-unfavorable continuum based on three major dimensions: leader-member relations, task structure, and position power. **Leader-member relations** refer to the degree others trust and respect the leader and to the leader's friendliness. This compares somewhat to referent power. **Task structure** is the degree to which job tasks are structured. For example, assembly-line jobs are more structured than managerial jobs. **Position power** refers to the power and influence that go with a job. A manager who is able to hire, fire, and discipline has more position power. Position power compares to coercive, reward, and legitimate power. Using these three dimensions, an eight-celled classification scheme was developed. Figure 6.6 shows this scheme along the continuum.

Figure 6.7 shows the most productive style of leadership for each situation. In both highly favorable and highly unfavorable situations, a task-motivated leader was found to be more effective. In highly favorable situations, the group is ready to be directed and is willing to be told what to do. In highly favorable situations, the group welcomes having the leader make decisions and direct the group. In moderately favorable situations, a relationship-motivated leader was found to be more effective. In situation 7 (moderately poor leader-member relations, unstructured task, and strong position power), the task and relationship styles of leadership were equally productive.

### figure 6.7

**LEADERSHIP STYLE AND LEADERSHIP SITUATIONS**

| SITUATION | 1 | 2 | 3 | 4 | 5 | 6 | 7 | 8 |
|---|---|---|---|---|---|---|---|---|
| Leader–member relations | Good | Good | Good | Good | Poor | Poor | Poor | Poor |
| Task structure | Structured | Structured | Unstructured | Unstructured | Structured | Structured | Unstructured | Unstructured |
| Leader position power | Strong | Weak | Strong | Weak | Strong | Weak | Strong | Weak |
| | *Favorable for leader* | | | | | | *Unfavorable for leader* | |
| Most productive leadership style | Task | Task | Task | Relationship | Relationship | No data | Task or relationship | Task |

## Continuum of Leader Behaviors

Robert Tannenbaum and Warren Schmidt also contend that different combinations of situational elements require different styles of leadership. They suggest that there are three important factors, or forces, involved in finding the most effective leadership style: forces in the manager, the subordinate, and the situation. Furthermore, all these forces are interdependent.[6]

Figure 6.8 describes in detail the forces that affect leadership situations. Since these forces differ in strength and interaction in differing situations, one style of leadership is not effective in all situations.

In fact, Tannenbaum and Schmidt argue that there is a continuum of behaviors that the leader may employ, depending on the situation (see Figure 6.9). These authors further conclude that successful leaders are keenly aware of the forces that are most relevant to their behavior at a given time. Successful leaders accurately understand not only themselves but also the other persons in the organizational and social environment, and they are able to behave correctly in light of these insights.

**figure 6.8**

**FORCES AFFECTING THE LEADERSHIP SITUATION**

| FORCES IN THE MANAGER | FORCES IN THE SUBORDINATES | FORCES IN THE SITUATION |
| --- | --- | --- |
| Value system: How the manager personally feels about delegating, degree of confidence in subordinates. | Need for independence: Some people need and want direction, while others do not. | Type of organization: Centralized versus decentralized. |
| Personal leadership inclinations. Authoritarian versus participative. | Readiness to assume responsibility: Different people need different degrees of responsibility. | Work group effectiveness: How effectively the group works together. |
| Feelings of security in uncertain situations. | Tolerance for ambiguity: Specific versus general directions. | The problem itself: The work group's knowledge and experience relevant to the problem. |
| | Interest and perceived importance of the problem: People generally have more interest in, and work harder on, important problems. | Time pressure: It is difficult to delegate to subordinates in crisis situations. |
| | Degree of understanding and identification with organizational goals: A manager is more likely to delegate authority to an individual who seems to have a positive attitude about the organization. | Demands from upper levels of management. |
| | Degree of expectation in sharing in decision making: People who have worked under subordinate-centered leadership tend to resent boss-centered leadership. | Demands from government, unions, and society in general. |

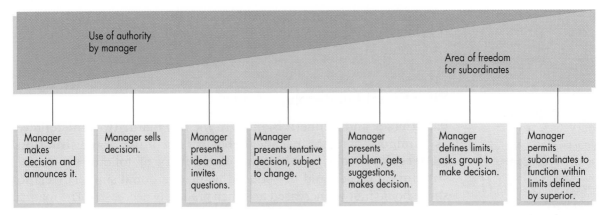

**figure 6.9**

**CONTINUUM OF LEADER BEHAVIOR**

***Source:*** Reprinted by permission of *Harvard Business Review*. Exhibit from "How to Choose a Leadership Pattern," by Robert Tannenbaum and Warren H. Schmidt, June 1973. Copyright © 1973 by the Harvard Business School Publishing Corporation; all rights reserved.

## Path-Goal Theory of Leadership

The **path-goal theory of leadership** attempts to define the relationships between a leader's behavior and the subordinates' performance and work activities. Leader behavior is acceptable to subordinates to the degree that they see it as a source of satisfaction now or as a step toward future satisfaction. Leader behavior influences the motivation of subordinates when it makes the satisfaction of their needs contingent on successful performance; and it provides the guidance, support, and rewards needed for effective performance (but that are not already present in the environment). The path-goal theory of leadership and the expectancy theory of motivation, which is described in more detail in Chapter 10, are closely related in that leader behaviors can either increase or decrease employee expectancies.

In path-goal theory, leader behavior falls into one of the four basic types: role classification, supportive, participative, and autocratic. *Role classification leadership* lets subordinates know what is expected of them, gives guidance as to what should be done and how, schedules and coordinates work among the subordinates, and maintains definite standards of performance. *Supportive leadership* has a friendly, approachable leader who attempts to make the work environment more pleasant for subordinates. *Participative leadership* involves consulting with subordinates and asking for their suggestions in the decision-making process. *Autocratic leadership* comes from a leader who gives orders that are not to be questioned by subordinates.

Under this theory, each of these leadership behaviors results in different levels of performance and subordinate satisfaction, depending on the structure of the work tasks. Role clarification leads to high satisfaction and performance for subordinates engaged in unstructured tasks. Supportive leadership brings the most satisfaction to those who work on highly structured tasks. Participative leader behavior enhances performance and satisfaction for subordinates engaged in ambiguous tasks.

**path-goal theory of leadership**

Attempts to define the relationships between a leader's behavior and the subordinates' performance and work activities.

Autocratic leadership behavior has a negative effect on both satisfaction and performance in both structured and unstructured task situations.

## Situational Leadership Theory

Paul Hersey and Kenneth Blanchard include maturity of the followers as an important factor in leader behavior.[7] According to the **situational leadership theory,** as the level of maturity of followers increases, structure (task) should be reduced while emotional support (relationship) should first be increased and then gradually decreased. The maturity level of the followers is determined by their relative independence, their ability to take responsibility, and their achievement-motivation level.

Figure 6.10 shows the cycle of the basic leadership styles that should be used by the leader, depending on the maturity of the followers. The situational leadership theory proposes that as the followers progress from immaturity to maturity, the leader's behavior should move from: (1) high task–low relationships to (2) high task–high relationships to (3) low task–high relationships to (4) low task–low relationships.

## Transactional, Transformational, and Charismatic Leaders

Another approach to the analysis of leadership has been based on how leaders and followers influence one another. Under this approach, leadership is viewed as transactional, transformational, or charismatic. **Transactional leadership** takes the approach that leaders engage in an unemotional bargaining relationship with their followers—management is simply done "by the book." Under this approach, the leader (manager):

1. Tells employees what they need to do to obtain rewards.
2. Takes corrective action only when employees fail to meet performance objectives.

**situational leadership theory**

As the level of maturity of followers increases, structure should be reduced while emotional support should first be increased and then gradually decreased.

**transactional leadership**

Takes the approach that leaders engage in bargaining relationship with their followers.

**transformational leadership**

Involves cultivating employee acceptance of the group mission.

**figure 6.10**

SITUATIONAL LEADERSHIP THEORY

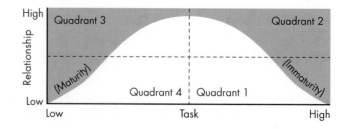

**Transformational leadership** involves cultivating employee acceptance of the group mission. The manager-employee relationship is one of mutual encouragement and is characterized by personality on the part of the leader, inspiration by the leader, consideration by the leader of individual needs, and intellectual motivation between the leader and followers. Transformational leaders go beyond management by the book and transform not only the situation but also the followers.

**Charismatic leadership** presents a unique situation in which the leader and followers develop a relationship based directly on the personality of that leader often in the face of a lack of any proven skills or experience. In contrast to the modern interpretation of charismatic leadership as a leader being polished and skilled at managing public relations, the traditional definition implies a specific set of circumstances. Charismatic leaders are often credited with the achievement of heroic feats (turning around ailing corporations, revitalizing aging bureaucracies, or launching new enterprises) by:[8]

The strength of a company is often based upon the strength of its leaders. What type of leader do you think has the greatest effect on employees?

**charismatic leadership**
Involves a leader who can successfully influence employee behavior on the strength of personality or a perceived charisma, without the formal power or experience to back it up.

1. Powerfully communicating a compelling vision of the future.
2. Passionately believing in their vision.
3. Relentlessly promoting their beliefs with boundless energy.
4. Putting forward creative "outside the box" ideas.
5. Inspiring extraordinary performance in followers by (a) expressing confidence in followers' abilities to achieve high standards and (b) building followers' trust, faith, and belief in the leader.

## PROGRESS CHECK QUESTIONS

5. Define the following leadership styles: autocratic, laissez-faire, and democratic.
6. Summarize the findings of both the Ohio State and University of Michigan leadership studies.
7. Explain the path-goal theory of leadership.
8. Explain the differences between transactional, transformational, and charismatic leadership styles.

# LESSONS FROM LEADERSHIP STUDIES

How can all these leadership theories be made relevant to the organization's need for effective managers? First, given the situational factors discussed in this chapter, it appears unlikely that a selection process will be developed to accurately predict successful leaders. The dynamic, changing nature of managerial roles further complicates the situation. Even if the initial process could select effective leaders, the dynamics of the managerial situation might make the selection invalid. Further, contrary to the conclusions of many studies, most leadership training today seems to assume there is one best way to lead. In reality, most leadership remains situational. Successful leaders recognize that effective leadership requires drawing on a range of skills and techniques, depending on the individual situation, not on a prescribed leadership model.

The effectiveness of any leadership style can often be determined by the environment or atmosphere of the organization itself. Are the employees happy and productive? Or are there problems with absenteeism and employee turnover? Do the employees feel valued? Do they contribute positive and creative ideas for the organizations' future growth? Or do they "punch in and punch out," waiting for the next paycheck?

Leadership is a key determinant of the atmosphere or culture of an organization, and the future success or failure of that organization can rest on the degree to which that culture supports or challenges the organization's ability to move forward in a competitive market.

# MANAGING CORPORATE CULTURE

The word *culture* is derived in a roundabout way from the Latin verb *colere,* which means "to cultivate."[9] In later times, *culture* came to indicate a process of refinement and breeding in domesticating a particular crop. The modern-day meaning draws on this agricultural derivation: It relates to society's control, refinement, and domestication of itself. A contemporary definition of **culture** is "the set of important understandings (often unstated) that members of a community share in common."[10]

**culture**

Set of important understandings (often unstated) that members of a community share.

Culture in an organization compares to personality in a person. Humans have fairly enduring and stable traits that help them protect their attitudes and behaviors. So do organizations. In addition, certain groups of traits or personality types are known to consist of common elements. Organizations can be described in similar terms. They can be warm,

How might the corporate cultures differ between an independent record store and a national chain?

aggressive, friendly, open, innovative, conservative, and so forth. An organization's culture is transmitted in many ways, including long-standing and often unwritten rules; shared standards regarding what is important; prejudices; standards for social etiquette and demeanor; established customs for relating to peers, subordinates, and superiors; and other traditions that clarify to employees what is and is not appropriate behavior. Thus, corporate culture communicates how people in the organization should behave by establishing a value system conveyed through rites, rituals, myths, legends, and actions. Simply stated, **corporate culture** means "the way we do things around here."[11]

> **corporate culture**
> Communicates how people in an organization should behave by establishing a value system conveyed through rites, rituals, myths, legends, and actions.

## Cultural Forms of Expression

Culture has two basic components: (1) substance, the meanings contained in its values, norms, and beliefs, and (2) forms, the practices whereby these meanings are expressed, affirmed, and communicated to members.[12]

## How Does Culture Originate?

There is no question that different organizations develop different cultures. What causes an organization to develop a particular type of culture? Many organizations trace their culture to one person who provided a living example of the major values of the organization. Robert Wood Johnson of Johnson & Johnson, Harley Procter of Procter & Gamble, Walt Disney of Walt Disney Company, Thomas J. Watson Sr. of IBM, and Phil Knight of Nike all left their imprints on the organizations they headed. Research indicates, however, that fewer than half of a new company's values reflect the values of the founder or chief executive. The rest appear to develop in response both to the environment in which the business operates and to the needs of the employees.[13] Four distinct factors contribute to an organization's culture: its history, its environment, its selection process, and its socialization processes.[14]

Executives at Walt Disney Company reportedly pick up litter on the grounds without thinking because of the Disney vision of an immaculate Disneyland.

### History

Employees are aware of the organization's past, and this awareness builds culture. Much of the "way things are done" is a continuation of how things have always been done. The existing values that a strong leader may have established originally are constantly and subtly reinforced by experiences.

The status quo is also protected by the human tendency to fervently embrace beliefs and values and to resist changes. Executives at Walt Disney Company reportedly pick up litter on the grounds without thinking because of the Disney vision of an immaculate Disneyland.

### Environment

Because all organizations must interact with their environments, the environment plays a role in shaping their cultures. Deregulation of the telecommunications industry in the 1980s dramatically altered its environment. Before deregulation, the environment was relatively risk averse and noncompetitive. Increases in costs were automatically passed on to customers. As a result of deregulation, the environment changed overnight to become highly competitive and much more dynamic. No longer sheltered by a regulated environment, the cultures of the telecommunications companies were forced to change.

### Staffing

Organizations tend to hire, retain, and promote people who are similar to current employees in important ways. A person's ability to fit in can be important in these processes. This "fit" criterion ensures that current values are accepted and that potential challengers of "how we do things" are screened out. Adjustment has to be carefully managed. For example, when Bill George took over Medronic, a leading producer of pacemakers, in 1991, he quickly found out that to survive in the rapidly growing high-tech health care business, he needed a change—but not at the expense of what had historically worked for the company. He opted for a merger with another company. The merger brought in "new blood" that was free-spirited and experimental in nature and teamed them with a highly disciplined, methodical existing culture. Though it was hard work, empowerment of people and a merger of cultures helped the company halve its development time and remain competitive in the industry.[15]

### Entry Socialization

**entry socialization**

Adaptation process by which new employees are introduced and indoctrinated into the organization.

While an organization's values, norms, and beliefs may be widely and uniformly held, they are rarely written down. The new employee, who is least familiar with the culture, is most likely to challenge it. It is therefore important to help the newcomer adopt the organization's culture. Companies with strong cultures attach great importance to the process of introducing and training new employees. This process is called **entry socialization.** Entry socialization not only reduces threats to the organization from newcomers but also lets new employees know what is

- Organizational members share clear values and beliefs about how to succeed in their business.
- Organizational members agree on which beliefs about how to succeed are most important.
- Different parts of the organization have similar beliefs about how to succeed.
- The rituals of day-to-day organizational life are well organized and consistent with company goals.

**figure 6.11**

**CHARACTERISTICS OF A STRONG CORPORATE CULTURE**

*Source:* Terrence E. Deal and Allan A. Kennedy, *Corporate Cultures: The Rites and Rituals of Corporate Life* (Reading, MA: Addison-Wesley, 1982).

expected of them. It may be handled in a formal or informal manner, as well as on an individual or group basis.

## Strong and Weak Corporate Cultures

A strong corporate culture is clearly defined, reinforces a common understanding about what is important, and has the support of management and employees. Such a culture contributes greatly to an organization's success by creating an understanding about how employees should behave. Figure 6.11 identifies the characteristics of a strong corporate culture.

Weak cultures have the opposite characteristics. In a weak corporate culture, individuals often act in ways that are inconsistent with the company's way of doing things. Figure 6.12 summarizes some characteristics of a weak culture.

## PROGRESS CHECK QUESTIONS

9. Define the term "culture."
10. Where does organizational culture originate?
11. Explain the four distinct factors that contribute to an organization's culture.
12. Summarize the characteristics of a weak organizational culture.

- Organizational members have no clear values or beliefs about how to succeed in their business.
- Organizational members have many beliefs as to how to succeed but cannot agree on which are most important.
- Different parts of the organization have fundamentally different beliefs about how to succeed.
- Those who personify the culture are destructive or disruptive and don't build on any common understanding about what is important.
- The rituals of day-to-day organizational life are disorganized or working at cross-purposes.

**figure 6.12**

**CHARACTERISTICS OF A WEAK CORPORATE CULTURE**

*Source:* Terrence E. Deal and Allan A. Kennedy, *Corporate Cultures: The Rites and Rituals of Corporate Life* (Reading, MA: Addison-Wesley, 1982).

## Identifying Culture

Researchers have identified seven characteristics that, taken together, capture the essence of an organization's culture:[16]

1. *Individual autonomy.* The degree of responsibility, independence, and opportunities for exercising initiative that individuals in the organization have.

2. *Structure.* The number of rules and regulations and the amount of direct supervision that is used to oversee and control employee behavior.

3. *Support.* The degree of assistance and warmth provided by managers to their subordinates.

4. *Identification.* The degree to which members identify with the organization as a whole rather than with their particular work group or field of professional expertise.

5. *Performance-reward.* The degree to which reward allocations (i.e., salary increases, promotions) in the organization are based on performance criteria.

6. *Conflict tolerance.* The degree of conflict present in relationships between peers and work groups, as well as the willingness to be honest and open about differences.

7. *Risk tolerance.* The degree to which employees are encouraged to be aggressive, innovative, and risk seeking.

Each of these traits should be viewed as existing on a continuum ranging from low to high. A picture of the overall culture can be formed by evaluating the organization on each of these characteristics.

There are as many distinct cultures as there are organizations. Most can be grouped into one of four basic types, determined by two factors: (1) the degree of risk associated with the organization's activities and (2) the speed with which the organization and its employees get feedback indicating the success of decisions. Figure 6.13 shows in matrix form the four generic types of culture.[17]

### Tough-Person, Macho Culture

**tough-person, macho culture**

Characterized by individuals who take high risks and get quick feedback on whether their decisions are right or wrong.

The **tough-person, macho culture** is characterized by individualists who regularly take high risks and get quick feedback on whether their decisions are right or wrong. Teamwork is not important, and every colleague is a potential rival. In this culture, the value of cooperation is ignored; there is no chance to learn from mistakes. People who do best in this culture are those who need to gamble and who can tolerate all-or-nothing risks because they need instant feedback. Companies that develop large-scale advertising programs for major clients would be characterized by the tough-person, macho culture; these advertising programs are usually high budget with rapid acceptance or failure.

| | | Degree of Risk | |
|---|---|---|---|
| | | **HIGH** | **LOW** |
| **Speed of Feedback** | Rapid | Tough-person, macho culture | Work-hard/play-hard culture |
| | Slow | Bet-your-company culture | Process culture |

figure 6.13

GENERIC TYPES OF
ORGANIZATION CULTURE

## Work-Hard/Play-Hard Culture

The **work-hard/play-hard culture** encourages employees to take few risks and to expect rapid feedback. In this culture, activity is the key to success. Rewards accrue to persistence and the ability to find a need and fill it. Because of the need for volume, team players who are friendly and outgoing thrive. Companies that are sales based such as real estate companies often have a work-hard/play-hard culture.

## Bet-Your-Company Culture

The **bet-your-company culture** requires big-stake decisions, with considerable time passing before the results are known. Pressures to make the right decisions are always present in this environment. Companies involved in durable goods manufacturing are often characterized by a bet-your-company culture.

## Process Culture

The **process culture** involves low risk coupled with little feedback; employees must focus on how things are done rather than on the outcomes. Employees in this atmosphere become cautious and protective. Those who thrive are orderly, punctual, and detail-oriented. Companies in regulated or protected industries often operate in this type of culture.

## Organizational Subcultures

In addition to its overall culture, organizations often have multiple subcultures. It is not uncommon for the values, beliefs, and practices to vary from one part of the organization to another. For example, newly acquired components of a company often have cultural differences that must be worked out over time. Global companies also tend to be faced with multiple cultures. Such factors as language, social norms, values, attitudes, customs, and religion naturally vary throughout the world.

The presence of different subcultures within an organization does not preclude the development of areas of commonality and compatibility.[18] For example, a company's emphasis on quality can be embedded in the local culture at sites throughout the world. At the same time, however, successful companies have learned to look at the compatibility of

**work-hard/play-hard culture**

Encourages employees to take few risks and to expect rapid feedback.

**bet-your-company culture**

Requires big-stakes decisions; considerable time passes before the results are known.

**process culture**

Involves low risk with little feedback; employees focus on how things are done rather than on the outcomes.

## The Way We Do Things

Fitzgerald Company manufactures a variety of consumer products for sale through retail department stores. For over 30 years, the company has held a strong belief that customer relations and a strong selling orientation are the keys to business success. As a result, all top executives have sales backgrounds and spend much of their time outside the company with customers. Because of the strong focus on the customer, management at Fitzgerald emphasizes new-product development projects and growth in volume. The company rarely implements cost reduction or process improvement projects.

Between 1975 and 1985, Fitzgerald's 10 percent share of the market was the largest in the industry. Profitability was consistently better than the industry average. However, in the last 10 years, the markets for many of Fitzgerald's products have matured, and Fitzgerald has dropped from market share leader to the number three company in the industry. Profitability has steadily declined since 1991, although Fitzgerald offers a more extensive line of products than any of its competitors. Customers are complaining that Fitzgerald's prices are higher than those of other companies.

In June 1996, Jeff Steele, president of Fitzgerald Company, hired Valerie Stevens of Management Consultants, Inc., to help him improve the company's financial performance. After an extensive study of Fitzgerald Company and its industry group, Valerie met with Jeff and said, "Jeff, I believe the Fitzgerald Company may have to substantially change its culture."

### Questions

1. Describe, in general terms, the corporate culture at Fitzgerald Company.

2. What's wrong with a business philosophy based on the belief "that customer relations and a strong selling orientation are the keys to business success"?

3. What does Valerie mean when she says Fitzgerald Company may have to change its culture? What are some of the necessary changes?

4. Discuss the problems the company may encounter in attempting to implement changes.

cultures when considering acquisitions and mergers and new locations. Extreme cultural differences can make it very difficult for an acquisition or an expansion to be successful.

### PROGRESS CHECK QUESTIONS

13. Which seven characteristics capture the essence of an organization's culture?

14. Explain the four basic types of organizational culture.

15. Think of the organization you currently work for (or one you have worked for in the past). Which of the four basic types of culture most accurately describes that organization? Provide an example to support your selection.

16. Define the term "organizational subculture."

## Changing Culture

Executives who have successfully changed organization cultures estimate that the process usually takes from 6 to 15 years.[19] Because organization culture is difficult and time-consuming to change, any attempts should be well thought-out.

Allan Kennedy, an expert on organization culture, believes only five reasons justify a large-scale cultural change:[20]

1. The organization has strong values that do not fit into a changing environment.
2. The industry is very competitive and moves with lightning speed.
3. The organization is mediocre or worse.
4. The organization is about to join the ranks of the very large companies.
5. The organization is small but growing rapidly.

Some organizations attempt to change their cultures only when they are forced to do so by changes in their environments or economic situations; others anticipate a necessary change. While massive cultural reorientation may be reasonable in most situations, it is usually possible to strengthen or fine-tune the current situation. A statement of corporate mission consistently reinforced by systems, structures, and policies is a useful tool for strengthening the culture.

Because of the cost, time, and difficulty involved in changing culture, many people believe it is easier to change, or physically replace, the people. This view assumes most organizations promote people who fit the prevailing norms of the organization. Therefore, the easiest if not the only way to change an organization's culture is to change its people.

## CONCLUSION

We have seen in this chapter that leadership and management are not necessarily the same, but are not incompatible. Effective leadership creates a vision of the future and builds an organizational culture that encourages all stakeholders in the organization to work together in the realization of that vision. In practice, that's easier said than done, since each stakeholder brings his or her unique perspective to the table. So the challenge lies in creating a culture that embraces those individual perspectives while, at the same time, conveying a consistent message to drive the organization forward. As we shall see in the next chapter, a critical component in meeting that challenge is the effective organization of the work performed in the organization.

# Taco Barn gets some surprising feedback

Tony found that he enjoyed the leadership survey project much more than he thought he would. Working with other unit managers and regional managers allowed him to get a much better sense of the organization as a whole—lots of creative and talented people but a remarkable difference in overall unit performance. Some units were very well run, and very profitable for the Taco Barn organization, but there were also some "problem children," with high employee turnover, poor financial performance, and, unfortunately, very poor customer service.

That difference in unit performance was directly reflected in the responses to the employee survey. Employees in smooth-running units seemed to be happy with their jobs and had a strong level of confidence in where the company was going. They felt that the company had a strong, customer-focused culture, and they felt valued as a part of the overall organizational team. However, employees in the struggling units took the opportunity to express their sense of frustration with the leadership and their feeling of isolation from any sense of culture within the Taco Barn family.

Tony felt fortunate that even though the responses were anonymous, those employees who could be identified from their comments as being from his unit responded very positively. He also felt sorry for the other members of the survey project whose employees didn't respond so positively.

Once the survey data were collected and analyzed, Dawn called a meeting to review what the data had to say about their region and about the Taco Barn organization as a whole.

"Okay folks, I think you would agree that we have some work to do here. We have some very happy employees and also some very unhappy ones. We honestly didn't expect the results to be all over the map like this—we don't appear to have a consistent leadership style, and we certainly don't have a clear organizational culture that the employees can identify with.

"You know that we are anticipating significant expansion in the coming years, and we can only achieve that if we start from a solid foundation. So, where do we go from here? What's the right leadership style for Taco Barn, and what kind of culture should the Taco Barn family have?"

## QUESTIONS

1. Should the leadership team have been surprised by the survey results? Why or why not?

2. Should they be pursuing a "right" leadership style? Why or why not?

3. If the Taco Barn doesn't have a clear sense of culture (as the survey results appear to indicate), where and how does it start to develop one?

4. What should the leadership of the Taco Barn organization do now?

## key terms

| | | |
|---|---|---|
| **authority** 146 | **culture** 160 | **leader-member relations** 155 |
| **autocratic leader** 149 | **democratic leader** 149 | |
| **bet-your-company culture** 165 | **entry socialization** 162 | **leadership** 146 |
| | **initiating structure** 151 | **Managerial Grid** 153 |
| **charismatic leadership** 159 | **laissez-faire leader** 149 | **path-goal theory of leadership** 157 |
| | **leader** 146 | |
| **consideration** 151 | **leader behavior description questionnaire (LBDQ)** 151 | **position power** 155 |
| **contingency approach to leadership** 154 | | **power** 146 |
| | | **process culture** 165 |
| **corporate culture** 161 | | |

**self-fulfilling
    prophecy** 148
**situational leadership
    theory** 158
**task structure** 155
**Theory X** 147

**Theory Y** 147
**tough-person, macho
    culture** 164
**trait theory** 149
**transactional
    leadership** 158

**transformational
    leadership** 158
**work-hard/play-hard
    culture** 165

## review questions

1. Discuss the following statement: Leaders are born and cannot be developed.
2. Explain what people mean when they use this statement: Leaders lead by example. Do you believe it? Explain your answer.
3. How is corporate culture originated and maintained?
4. List the five reasons that justify a large-scale cultural change.

## internet exercise

Visit the Web site of the Center for Creative Leadership (CCL) at www.ccl.org/leadership

1. What is the philosophy of the Center for Creative Leadership?
2. What are the mission and vision of the CCL?
3. Document one example of CCL's leadership research.
4. Select and summarize one of CCL's Custom Solutions Case Studies.

## team exercise

Divide the class into groups of three or four students. Each team must select an organization that will need to change its culture if it is to thrive in the future. Develop a PowerPoint presentation to be delivered to your fellow students outlining the following:

1. A brief assessment of the culture of your selected organization.
2. A summary of how that culture needs to change.
3. An explanation of why you think this change must occur.
4. Clear suggestions as to how that change could be implemented.

## Bertelsmann's New Web-Friendly CEO

*The German Media Conglomerate Will Soon Have a New Chief Who Fits the Company Profile—But His Internet Savvy Is Expected to Widen Its Reach*

**H**artmut Ostrowski was fit into a stereotype even before he was officially appointed chief executive–designate of German media company Bertelsmann on January 19, 2007. Numerous stories in the German and foreign press pegged Ostrowski, 48, as the typical Bertelsmann lifer, sensible enough to keep a low profile at a company that values mo- desty and loyalty and skilled at staying in good favor with family shareholders led by Liz Mohn.

There is cer- tainly an element of truth to that descr- iption of Ostrowski, who most recently served as chief of Bertelsmann's prof- itable but unglamor- ous Arvato printing and services divi- sion. In his former position, Ostrowski "was known for being discrete and reserved," says a former Arvato employee. "That is valued around Bertelsmann." But Ostrowski, the son of a plumber who has spent almost all his life in the area around Bertelsmann headquarters in the Westfalian burg of Gütersloh, could turn out to be a more aggres- sive chief executive than the cliché suggests.

EVSM0064430   Guetersloh.Germany. Corporate Headquarters of Bertelsmann AG. media conglomerate  10.03.2003 ©Thomas Pflaum / Visum / The Image Works

out as CEO of Bertel-smann in 2002, but like Middelhoff, Ostrowski could push Bertelsm- ann to better exploit the media possibilities of the Internet. The comp-any alrea-dy has a re- spectable presence on the Internet, but critics say it could do more. RTL Group, Bertels- mann's TV division, is No. 1 in broadcast- related Web sites in Germany, according to Nielsen/NetRatings. (RTL's holdings include the company that produces the *Pop Idol* casting shows.) But Bertelsmann's Internet stature is modest compared to rival News Corp., which purchased social-networking site MySpace in 2005.

Meanwhile, as with all media companies, Bertels- mann's traditional business such as Random House books, *Gruner + Jahr* maga- zines, and BMG music (now part of Sony BMG Music Entertainment) have suffered from the disruptive effects of the Internet, which drained away audiences and advertisers.

### TAKING IT TO THE EDGE

True, he won't be a flashy dealmaker in the mold of Thomas Middelhoff, who was thrown

### ON A BUDGET

Expect Ostrowski, who will officially succeed Gunter Thielen as Bertelsmann CEO on Jan. 1,

2008, to attack the online world more forcefully. Ostrowski won't make acquisitions on the scale of MySpace, preferring smaller assets with substance and solid cash flow, says one informed source.

Even if it were Ostrowski's style to make a big acquisition, Bertelsmann lacks the resources. It is too busy paying back $11.6 billion in debt, largely the result of the buyback last year of 25 percent of its own shares from outside investor Groupe Bruxelles Lambert. Instead, Ostrowski will look for reasonably priced acquisitions in areas such as broadband cable access or mobile TV.

In his current job running Arvato, Ostrowski is no stranger to the digital world. For example, Arvato provides the platform that British music company EMI Music uses to sell tunes over the Internet. In a joint venture with Warner Bros. Home Entertainment, Arvato also operates a video and movie download service called In2Movies.

## STABLE OF CLIENTS

In fact, Arvato has helped Bertelsmann keep growing even as the rest of the company struggled with crises in music and magazines. Continuing work begun by Thielen, who ran Arvato before becoming Bertelsmann's CEO, Ostrowski transformed what was once a printing company into an outsourcing powerhouse whose services often involve e-commerce.

Arvato runs customer-service centers for McDonald's and Nokia. It also handles shipping for Microsoft's Xbox in Europe and distributes digital content such as ringtones for mobile-phone operators Vodafone Group and T-Mobile International. Ostrowski inherits a company with solid, but not spectacular, profits. For the first nine months of 2006, Bertelsmann's operating profit rose 8.3 percent to $1.3 billion on sales of $17.6 billion. However, net income slipped 36 percent to $471 million, largely because of increased taxes and interest expenses. To deliver better growth than that, the reserved Ostrowski may have to behave more like a cocky Silicon Valley entrepreneur than a Bertelsmann lifer.

## Questions

1. How would you describe the organizational culture at Bertelsmann? Provide examples to support your description.

2. What kind of changes does Bertelsmann have to make in order to compete against rivals like News Corp.?

3. What challenges does Bertelsmann face in making those changes?

4. Do you think Ostrowski has the right leadership style to be the CEO of Bertelsmann? Why or why not?

*Source:* Adapted from Jack Ewing, "Bertelsmann's New Web-Friendly CEO," *BusinessWeek.com* Europe, January 19, 2007.

## Siemens' Culture Clash

*CEO Kleinfeld Is Making Changes, and Enemies—Including within the Ranks*

If things had turned out a little differently, Siemens Chief Executive Klaus Kleinfeld might already be on his way to executive stardom, like his role model Jack Welch. Just two years after Kleinfeld took over the Munich electronics and engineering behemoth, Siemens is on track to hit its aggressive internal earnings targets for the first time since 2000. In fact, it is expanding both sales and profits faster than Welch's former domain, General Electric Co. What's more, the company has a larger presence than GE in rapid-growth markets such as India. But instead of literary agents breaking down his door in pursuit of a book on management wisdom, Kleinfeld has angry employees demonstrating outside his window. He has gotten little applause for boosting 2006 sales by 16 percent and profits by 35 percent, and he faces questions about a bribery scandal that has sapped his authority even though he is not personally implicated.

Transforming Siemens was never going to be easy. With branches in 190 countries and $114 billion in sales last year, the company has long been respected for its engineering expertise but criticized for its sluggishness. And Germany, with its long-standing tradition of labor harmony and powerful workers' councils, is highly resistant to the kind of change Kleinfeld has tried to implement. That's one reason Siemens lags seriously in overall profits, with a margin of 3.5 percent compared with 12.6 percent for GE. Kleinfeld concedes that some people doubt Siemens can change its ways, but he counters: "It took less time than we originally planned to get that growth momentum started." Against the odds, in just two years Kleinfeld has managed a mighty restructuring. He has quoted the management precepts of Welch and has drawn on the GE playbook to realign Siemens as the world's leading provider of such infrastructure as airports, power plants, and medical equipment. He has pushed Siemens' 475,000 employees to make decisions faster and focus as much on customers as on technology. He spun off underperforming telecommunications-gear businesses and simplified the company's structure. And when one group of managers failed to deliver, he broke up an entire division.

## RESPECT AND RESENTMENT

Although restructuring has dominated his tenure, Kleinfeld isn't just a cost-cutter. The 49-year-old believes Siemens is perfectly positioned to profit from huge global shifts in population and wealth, and he spent $8.6 billion last year on acquisitions in areas such as medical diagnostics and wind power. As people in the developing world get richer, he says, Siemens will supply CT and MRI scanners to diagnose their illnesses. It will build switching systems and engines for their trains and subways. And it will sell them water-purification equipment, power plants, and machines to run mines and factories. Says Kleinfeld: "This Company is solving the biggest issues this planet has." Investors have warmed to Kleinfeld's vision. Siemens shares have risen 26 percent in the two years since he took over, vs. 6 percent for GE. But his tactics have made him a target for German resentment of globalization and the perceived heartlessness of U.S.-style management methods. When, in an attempt at openness, Kleinfeld invited workers to respond to his blog, they did—in spades. "I used to feel good in the Siemens family," one employee wrote. "But there's not much of that feeling left."

## HAPPY IN THE HEARTLAND

Kleinfeld downplays the influence of his three years in the U.S., a stint ordinary Germans view as a blot on his résumé. There's no question, though, that he counts those years among his best. "I liked it over there," says Kleinfeld, who served as CEO of Siemens' U.S. operations in 2002 and 2003. "Wherever I went, I made friends." And to this day, Kleinfeld's style is decidedly less German-centric than that of his predecessor, Heinrich von Pierer. Von Pierer played tennis with the Chancellor. Kleinfeld runs the New York Marathon. Von Pierer served

on a half-dozen boards of German companies. Kleinfeld does so for Citigroup, Alcoa, and the New York Metropolitan Opera. Von Pierer speaks English well but prefers German. Kleinfeld is totally fluent in English.

One of Kleinfeld's problems is that few inside Siemens can match his energy. The Old Guard tend to grumble that Kleinfeld is too impatient and demanding. Soon after taking office in January, 2005, he vowed that Siemens would finally achieve ambitious profit-margin goals established in 2000 for each unit. The targets range from 6 percent for auto parts to 13 percent for the top-performing medical-equipment division. Kleinfeld staked his job on the company hitting those numbers by April, 2007—which now looks likely, analysts say. His message: Everyone, including the boss, is accountable. "We commit to something, and we deliver," Kleinfeld says. "That is the culture we want to form." Communicating that culture change across such a sprawling enterprise is a massive challenge. The company's 11 main business units operate almost as separate entities, with their own boards and distinct corporate cultures, making it hard for directives from the top to filter down to the troops. One executive says Kleinfeld's biggest impact so far has been increased pressure to speak English throughout the company—hardly an earth-shattering reform. And while Siemens excels at technological breakthroughs, such as mobile phones with built-in music players, they have often failed because of poor marketing and a lack of focus on the consumers who use the products.

So how do you persuade Siemens' vaunted engineers to pay more attention to customers? Kleinfeld declared that he would personally visit Siemens' 100 biggest clients in his first 100 days in office. He wound up meeting more than 300 of them. Kleinfeld isn't shy about administering harsh medicine when he feels it's needed. That's something new at the 159-year-old company. At the end of 2005, it became clear that the Logistics & Assembly Systems Div., which made products such as sorting equipment used by the U.S. Postal Service, would deliver only a 2 percent profit margin. Most unpardonable in Kleinfeld's eyes was that the unit's managers waited too long to alert him to the problem. So Kleinfeld transferred the most profitable parts of the division, such as baggage-handling systems for airports, to other parts of Siemens. The rest was sold. Within weeks, an entire Siemens division with $1.9 billion in annual sales was vaporized.

## Questions

1. How would you describe the culture of Siemens before Kleinfeld's appointment as CEO?

2. How has the culture changed under his leadership? Provide examples to support your answer.

3. How would you categorize Kleinfeld's leadership style?

4. Do you think Kleinfeld's adoption of "U.S.-style management methods" was the right choice for Siemens? Why or why not?

*Source:* Adapted from Jack Ewing, "Global Business," *BusinessWeek Online,* January 29, 2007.

# ORGANIZING WORK

**"We tend to meet any new situation by re-organizing and a wonderful method it can be for creating the illusion of progress while producing confusion, inefficiency, and demoralization."**

—Petronius Arbiter

## The World of Work: Tony tries to delegate

All the time Tony was spending on the employee survey for the Leadership Development Program was stretching his schedule to the point where he was falling behind in some of his responsibilities at the restaurant. He didn't want to admit to Dawn that he couldn't manage all this extra work, but he was smart enough to realize that he needed some help, and so he called a few of his fellow unit managers for some advice.

That advice ranged from withdrawing from the survey project (not an option!) to simply letting the work pile up and getting to it when the survey was complete. Tony knew that the end of the survey project was only going to mark the beginning of the Leadership Development Program, which he was eager to be a part of, so there was no hope of putting off the work until a later date. In the end he took the advice of Fred Thompson, one of the veteran unit managers, who suggested that he "offload some of the work onto his people."

"HR calls it 'delegation,'" continued Fred, "but don't give them anything they can mess up because it'll be your job to clean it up. Stop trying to run everything, and give them some of the easier tasks to do: ordering, menus, time sheets. They'll appreciate the break in their regular routine, and if they do a good job, you know you've found some future shift leaders."

Tony liked Fred's idea, but he admitted to himself that he had gotten this far in his career by always

**After studying this chapter, you will be able to:**

1   Explain the importance and rationale behind organizing work.

2   Define division of labor.

3   Distinguish between power, authority, and responsibility.

4   Explain the concept of centralization versus decentralization.

5   Define empowerment.

6   Identify several reasons why managers are reluctant to delegate authority.

being better than the folks he worked with—working harder, longer, and always being willing to take on extra work from Jerry to learn more about how he ran the restaurant. Did he have anyone he could count on to do it as well as he could do it himself?

In the end, the decision was made for Tony as Dawn kept calling on him for more and more work in the employee survey. One day, Katie, one of his waitresses, reminded him that they were running low on stuff for the restaurant: napkins, condiments, and menu holders. Tony, distracted by a fast-approaching deadline for something he needed to give to Dawn, snapped back at Katie:

"Look Katie I'm really busy here—why don't you make up a list of what we need and call it in to our supplier, okay? Kevin can give you the number. Just don't spend too much."

**QUESTIONS**

1.  Why wouldn't Tony just withdraw from the survey project if it was affecting his work at the Taco Barn?

2.  What's wrong with Fred's interpretation of "delegation"?

3.  Did Tony give Katie clear directions? Why or why not?

4.  What should Tony have done here?

# ORGANIZING WORK

Most work today is accomplished through organizations. An **organization** is a group of people working together in some type of concentrated or coordinated effort to achieve objectives. As such, an organization provides a vehicle for implementing strategy and accomplishing objectives that could not be achieved by individuals working separately. The process of organizing is the grouping of activities necessary to achieve common objectives and the assignment of each grouping to a manager who has the authority required to supervise the people performing the activities.[1] Thus, organizing is basically a process of division of labor accompanied by appropriate delegation of authority. Proper organizing results in more effective use of resources.

The framework that defines the boundaries of the formal organization and within which the organization operates is the organization structure. A second and equally important element of an organization is the informal organization. The **informal organization** refers to the sum of the personal contacts and interactions and the associated groupings of people working within the formal organization.[2] The informal organization has a structure, but it is not formally and consciously designed.

## Reasons for Organizing

One of the primary reasons for organizing is to establish lines of authority. Clear lines of authority create order within a group. Absence of authority almost always leads to chaotic situations where everyone is telling everyone else what to do.

Second, organizing improves the efficiency and quality of work through synergism. *Synergism* occurs when individuals or groups work together to produce a whole greater than the sum of the parts. For example, synergism results when three people working together produce more than three people working separately. Synergism can result from division of labor or from increased coordination, both of which are products of good organization. Two organizations that appear to be very similar can experience very different levels of performance due to the synergy resulting from their organizational structures. Highly successful organizations generally achieve a high level of synergy as a result of the manner in which they are organized.

A final reason for organizing is to improve communication. A good organization structure clearly defines channels of communication among the members of the organization. Such a system also ensures more efficient communications.

Historically, the desire to organize led to the development of an organization. The use of an organization allows people to jointly

(1) increase specialization and division of labor, (2) use large-scale technology, (3) manage the external environment, (4) economize on transaction costs, and (5) exert power and control.[3] When designed and coordinated effectively, these characteristics help the organization serve its customers with a high degree of service and productivity.

## DIVISION OF LABOR

Employing a defined division of labor is important to Toyota's success. *Do you think this style of vertical labor would work as well in another industry?*

Organizing is basically a process of division of labor. The merits of dividing labor have been known for centuries. Labor can be divided either vertically or horizontally. Vertical division of labor is based on the establishment of lines of authority and defines the levels that make up the vertical organization structure. In addition to establishing authority, vertical division of labor facilitates the flow of communication within the organization. To illustrate how vertical division of labor can vary from company to company, consider the automobile industry in the early 1980s. At that time, Toyota had 5 levels between the chairperson and the first-line supervisor, whereas Ford had over 15.[4]

Horizontal division of labor is based on specialization of work. The basic assumption underlying horizontal division of labor is that by making each worker's task specialized, more work can be produced with the same effort through increased efficiency and quality. Specifically, horizontal division of labor can result in the following advantages:

1. Fewer skills are required per person.
2. The skills required for selection or training purposes are easier to supply.
3. Practice in the same job develops proficiency.
4. Primarily utilizing each worker's best skills promotes efficient use of skills.
5. Simultaneous operations are made possible.
6. More conformity in the final product results when each piece is always produced by the same person.

The major problem with horizontal division of labor is that it can result in job boredom and even humiliation of the employee. An extreme example of horizontal division of labor is the automobile assembly line. Most people working on an automobile assembly line do a small number of very simple tasks over and over again. It usually doesn't take long for these employees to become bored. Once employees become bored, their productivity often declines, absenteeism and lateness increase, and the

**job scope**

Refers to the number of different types of operations performed on the job.

**job depth**

Refers to the freedom of employees to plan and organize their own work, work at their own pace, and move around and communicate as desired.

**power**

Ability to influence, command, or apply force; a measure of a person's potential to get others to do what he or she wants them to do, as well as to avoid being forced by others to do what he or she does not want to do.

quality of work goes down. Solutions to the problems created by horizontal division of labor include a reexamination of job scope, implementing job rotation, and balancing job simplification with job depth.

**Job scope** refers to the number of different types of operations performed. In performing a job with narrow scope, the employee performs few operations and repeats the cycle frequently. The negative effects of jobs lacking in scope vary with the person performing the job, but they can include more errors and lower quality. Often job rotation, wherein workers shift in the planned sequence of activities, eliminates boredom and monotony and encourages multiple skills and cross training.

**Job depth** refers to the freedom of employees to plan and organize their own work, work at their own pace, and move around and communicate as desired. A lack of job depth can result in job dissatisfaction and work avoidance, which in turn can lead to absenteeism, lateness, and even sabotage.

Division of labor is not more efficient or even desirable in all situations. At least two basic requirements must exist for the successful use of division of labor. The first requirement is a relatively large volume of work. Enough volume must be produced to allow for specialization and keep each employee busy. The second requirement is stability in the volume of work, employee attendance, quality of raw materials, product design, and production technology.

---

### PROGRESS CHECK QUESTIONS

1. What is an informal organization?
2. Explain the term synergism.
3. What are the six advantages and the disadvantages of horizontal division of labor?
4. Explain the terms *job scope* and *job depth.*

---

**authority**

Legitimate exercise of power; the right to issue directives and expend resources; related to power but narrower in scope.

**responsibility**

Accountability for the attainment of objectives, the use of resources, and the adherence to organizational policy.

## POWER, AUTHORITY, AND RESPONSIBILITY

**Power** is the ability to influence, command, or apply force. Power is usually derived from the control of resources. **Authority** is power derived from the rights that come with a position and represents the legitimate exercise of power. Thus, authority is one source of power for a manager. Lines of authority link the various organizational components. Unclear lines of authority can create major confusion and conflict within an organization.

**Responsibility** is accountability for the achievement of objectives, the use of resources, and the adherence to organizational policy. Once responsibility is accepted, performing assigned work becomes an obligation. The term *responsibility* as used here should not be confused with the term *responsibilities* as in the context of defining job duties.

## Sources of Authority

As just mentioned, authority can be viewed as a function of position, flowing from top to bottom through the formal organization. According to this view, people hold authority because they occupy a certain position; once removed from the position, they lose their authority. Taking this theory one step further, one can say the American people, through the Constitution and laws, represent the ultimate source of authority in this country. The Constitution and laws guarantee the right of free enterprise. The owners of a free enterprise organization have the right to elect a board of directors and top management. Top management selects middle-level managers. This process continues down to the lowest person in the organization. This traditional view of authority is also called the *formal theory of authority*.

A second theory of authority was first outlined in 1926 by Mary Parker Follett and popularized in 1938 by Chester Barnard.[5] Called the *acceptance theory of authority*, this theory maintains that a manager's source of authority lies with his or her subordinates because they have the power to either accept or reject the manager's command. Presumably, if a subordinate does not view a manager's authority as legitimate, it does not exist. Both Follett and Barnard viewed disobeying a communication from a manager as a denial of authority by the subordinate. In summary, the acceptance theory of authority recognizes that subordinates play an active role in determining lines of authority and are not merely passive recipients in the process. This idea is somewhat similar to the contention that without followers you can have no leaders. Both elements must be present and mutually recognized for true structure to exist. Companies with a high degree of employee involvement, responsibility, and accountability appear to recognize acceptance theory as being beneficial for mutual support and encouragement between labor and management.

Power, authority, and responsibility are all part of the equation when factoring effective versus ineffective management. *What are some potential problems for a manager lacking power, authority, or responsibility?*

## Study Skills

### Can You Read This?

In the world of education, one cannot underestimate the importance of reading!

**Consider that:** More time is spent reading text material, class notes, written papers, and test questions than on any other part of the learning process.

**Understand that:** Poor reading skills might make passing a course difficult.

**Celebrate that:** Superior reading skills help a student become more efficient in the learning process and can become the bridge to converting obtained knowledge into a successful level of applied knowledge that usually equates to excellent grades during a student's academic career.

## A Good Manager?

Francis S. Russell is assistant general manager and sales manager for Webb Enterprises. At the moment, this self-styled perfectionist is sitting up in bed, checking his things-to-do (TTD) sheet for tomorrow. The TTD itemizes his daily activities, placing them on an exact time schedule. Never one to browbeat subordinates, Russell has his own special way of reminding people that time is money. Ever since the days when he was the best salesperson the company ever had, he had worked harder than the rest. It had paid off, too, because in only two years (when old Charlie retired), he was the heir apparent to the general managership. As this thought crossed Russell's mind, his immediate pride was replaced with a nagging problem. Where was he going to find the time to do all the things his position required? He certainly couldn't afford to just maintain the status quo. Then his mind forced him to plan tomorrow's activities, and the problem was pushed into the background for future consideration.

(We see below a portion of Russell's well-planned day below.)

### TTD—OCTOBER 16

**7:15** Breakfast with Johnson (Purchasing). Get information on his cataloging system. Maybe combine with sales department and avoid duplication.

**8:30** Meeting with Henry (assistant sales manager). Tell him exactly how the sales meeting for out-of-state representatives should be conducted. Caution—he's shaky on questions.

**9:15** Discuss progress on new office procedures manual with Charlie (general manager). (He's irritated because I've dragged my heels on this. Let him know I've got Newman working on the problem.)

**9:45** Assign Pat Newman the job of collecting data and sample copies regarding office manuals in other companies in our industry. Set up a system for him to use in analysis.

**10:45** Call on Acliff Printing. A potentially big customer. (As Russell jotted down some information on this client, he reflected that it was a shame no one else on his staff could really handle the big ones the way he could. This thought was pleasing and bothersome at the same time.)

**12:00** Lunch with J. Acliff (reservations at Black Angus).

**3:00** Meet with Frank Lentz (advertising assistant), and check his progress on the new sales campaign. (Russell thought about Lentz's usual wild ideas and hoped that he had followed the general theme and rough sketches he had prepared.)

**7:30** Chamber of Commerce meeting. (Look up Pierce Hansen—he may be able to help on the Acliff account.)

### Questions

1. Do you think Francis is a highly motivated employee trying to do a good job? Explain your answer.

2. What problems do you see concerning Francis's effectiveness as a manager?

3. What options are available to help Francis?

4. Assuming you were Charlie, the general manager, what solutions would you recommend?

## CENTRALIZATION VERSUS DECENTRALIZATION

There are limitations to the authority of any position. These limitations may be external, in the form of laws, politics, or social attitudes, or they may be internal, as delineated by the organization's objectives or by the job description. The tapered concept of authority states that the breadth and scope of authority become more limited as one descends the scalar chain (see Figure 7.1).

The top levels of management establish the shapes of the funnels in Figures 7.1 and 7.2. The more authority top management chooses to

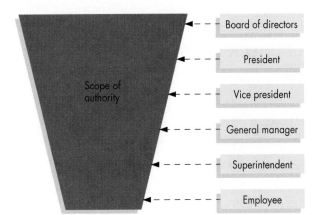

**figure 7.1**

TAPERED CONCEPT OF
AUTHORITY

delegate, the less conical the funnel becomes. The less conical the funnel, the more decentralized the organization. **Centralization** and **decentralization** refer to the degree of authority delegated by upper management. This is usually reflected by the numbers and kinds of decisions made by the lower levels of management. As they increase, the degree of decentralization also increases. Thus, an organization is never totally centralized nor totally decentralized; rather, it falls along a continuum ranging from highly centralized to highly decentralized. In Figure 7.2, the organization represented by the diagram on the left is much more centralized than that represented by the right-hand diagram.

The trend in today's organizations is toward more decentralization. Decentralization has the advantage of allowing for more flexibility and quicker action. It also relieves executives from time-consuming detail work. It often results in higher morale by allowing lower levels of management to be actively involved in the decision-making process. The major disadvantage of decentralization is the potential loss of control. Duplication of effort can also accompany decentralization.

**centralization**
Little authority is delegated to lower levels of management.

**decentralization**
A great deal of authority is delegated to lower levels of management.

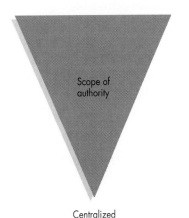

**figure 7.2**

CENTRALIZED VERSUS
DECENTRALIZED
AUTHORITY

**PROGRESS CHECK QUESTIONS**

5. Explain the terms *power, authority,* and *responsibility.*
6. What is the formal theory of authority?
7. What is the acceptance theory of authority?
8. What are the advantages and disadvantages of a decentralized structure?

# EMPOWERMENT

**empowerment**

Form of decentralization in which subordinates have authority to make decisions.

**Empowerment** is a form of decentralization that involves giving subordinates substantial authority to make decisions. Under empowerment, managers express confidence in the ability of employees to perform at high levels. Employees are also encouraged to accept personal responsibility for their work. In situations where true empowerment takes place, employees gain confidence in their ability to perform their jobs and influence the organization's performance. Under true empowerment, employees can bend the rules to do whatever they have to do to take care of the customer.[6] One result of empowerment is that employees demonstrate more initiative and perseverance in pursuing organizational goals. In order for empowerment to take root and thrive, the following four elements must be present:[7]

- *Participation.* Employees must be actively and willingly engaged in their respective job. They must want to improve their work processes and work relationship.
- *Innovation.* Employees must be given permission and encouragement to innovate and not do things the way they have always been done.
- *Access to information.* Employees at every level in the organization should make decisions about what kind of information they need to perform their job. This is different from traditional organizations where senior managers decide who gets what information.
- *Accountability.* Employees must be held accountable for their actions and the results achieved.

While the concept of empowerment looks relatively simple, it can be difficult to implement—especially in organizations where authority has traditionally flowed from top to bottom. Organizations can take several actions to help implement empowerment:[8]

- Whenever possible, restructure organizational units to be smaller, less complex, and less dependent on other units for decision making and action.
- Reduce to a minimum the number of hard rules for the organization.

# CASE INCIDENT 7.2

## The Vacation Request

Tom Blair has a week's vacation coming and really wants to take it the third week in May, which is the height of the bass fishing season. The only problem is that two of the other five members of his department have already requested and received approval from their boss, Luther Jones, to take off that same week. Afraid that Luther would not approve his request, Tom decided to forward his request directly to Harry Jensen, who is Luther's boss and who is rather friendly to Tom (Tom has taken Harry fishing on several occasions). Not realizing that Luther has not seen the request, Harry approves it. Several weeks pass before Luther finds out, by accident, that Tom has been approved to go on vacation the third week of May.

The thing that really bugs Luther is that this is only one of many instances in which his subordinates have gone directly to Harry and gotten permission to do something. Just last week, in fact, he overheard a conversation in the washroom to the effect that, "If you want anything approved, don't waste time with Luther—go directly to Harry."

### Questions

1. What should Harry have done?
2. Who is at fault, Harry or Tom?
3. Should Tom get his vacation? Why or why not?
4. What should Luther do to make sure this doesn't happen again?

---

- Emphasize a change throughout the organization that focuses on empowerment and personal accountability for delivering results.
- Provide the education and training necessary to enable people to respond to opportunities for improvement.

Accompanying the trend toward more decentralization in today's organizations is a trend toward increased empowerment of today's workforce. While some people believe that empowerment is praised loudly in public but seldom implemented, companies have experienced very positive results from having empowered their employees.

## Self-Managed Work Teams

One method for empowering employees is through the use of *self-managed work teams*. Self-managed work teams (also called *self-directed* or *self-regulated work teams*) are work units without a frontline manager and empowered to control their own work.[9] The philosophy behind any type of work team is that teams can contribute to improved performance by identifying and solving work-related problems. The basic idea is to motivate employees by having them participate in decisions that affect them and their work. Self-managed work teams are teams of employees who accomplish tasks within their area of responsibility without direct supervision. Each team makes its own job assignments, plans its own work, performs equipment maintenance, keeps records, obtains supplies, and makes selection decisions of new members into the work unit.

Kraft Foods has implemented many self-managed work teams. They maintain that the key to success in this workflow is open communication. What are some other things to keep in mind when creating self-managed work teams?

There is no doubt that the use of self-managed work teams has grown dramatically over the last several years and will continue to grow in the future. Self-directed work teams are discussed further in Chapter 9, which is devoted to understanding all forms of work teams.

# PRINCIPLES BASED ON AUTHORITY

Because authority is a key element in managing organizations, several key concepts are relevant. Delegation, unity of command, the scalar principle, and the span of management historically have been the most important of these concepts.

## Delegation: The Parity Principle

According to Herbert Engel, "As an abstract idea, delegation must be as old as the human race itself."[10] The allocation of specific duties to members of a group by a leader seems almost as natural as it is necessary. Delegation normally occurs when one needs something done that one either cannot or chooses not to do oneself. The decision may be based on situations, skills, time, established order, or the expansion and growth of responsibilities as dictated by the group or the organization. Managers can delegate responsibility to subordinates in the sense of making subordinates responsible to them. However, this delegation to subordinates makes managers no less responsible to their superiors. Delegation of responsibility does not mean abdication of responsibility by the delegating manager. Responsibility is not like an object that can be passed from individual to individual.

The **parity principle** states that authority and responsibility must coincide. Management must delegate sufficient authority to enable subordinates to do their jobs. At the same time, subordinates can be expected to accept responsibility only for those areas within their authority.

Subordinates must accept both authority and responsibility before the delegation process has been completed. Management sometimes expects employees to seek and assume responsibility they have not been asked to assume and then bid for the necessary authority. Such a system leads to guessing games that do nothing but create frustration and waste energy.

**parity principle**

States that authority and responsibility must coincide.

## career management

### Understanding that Results Matter

Good grades, a successful job, and healthy relationships are the results of good habits, and other positive results usually follow.

For better results as they relate to your career, read the list below. If good habits are followed and your skill at each of these areas improves, your career success would move forward with potentially exceptional results.

Work on the following for better career skills:

- Filling out job applications
- Improving your dress
- Knowing how to properly follow up your work
- Understanding the power of networking
- Enhancing your personal qualities
- Improving your attitude
- Improving skill development and usage
- Improving job dedication and completion
- Improving your life planning and balance skills
- Employing full use of education and additional training

A manager's resistance to delegating authority is natural. There are several reasons for this reluctance:

1. Fear that subordinates will fail in doing the task.
2. The belief that it is easier to do the task oneself rather than delegate it.
3. Fear that subordinates will look "too good."
4. Humans' attraction to power.
5. Comfort in doing the tasks of the previous job held.
6. Preconceived ideas about employees.
7. Desire to set the right example.

Despite all the reasons for not delegating, there are some very strong reasons for a manager to delegate. Several things occur when a manager successfully delegates. First, the manager's time is freed to pursue other tasks, and the subordinates gain feelings of belonging and being needed. These feelings often lead to a genuine commitment on the part of the subordinates. Second, delegation is one of the best methods for developing subordinates and satisfying customers. Pushing authority down the organization also allows employees to deal more effectively with customers. In its mid-1990s reengineering effort, Hallmark Cards, Inc., found that when you drive something from the top, you have to articulate clearly and communicate why it is being done.[11] By converting delegation to a shared vision, the organization has a much better chance of accomplishing its goals and objectives without resorting to adverse persuasion. Similarly, Taco Bell went from a $500 million regional company in 1982 to a $3 billion national company today because it recognized that the way to ultimately reach and satisfy customers was to empower its lower-level employees to make changes in operational strategies and tactics.[12] Successful delegation involves delegating matters that stimulate subordinates.

### How to Delegate

To successfully delegate, a manager must decide which tasks can be delegated. Figure 7.3 indicates the steps the manager can follow to analyze and improve the delegation process. Clearly defining objectives and standards, involving subordinates in the delegation process, and initiating training that defines and encourages delegation tend to improve the overall delegation process. Controlling the delegation requires that the delegating manager periodically check to ensure that things are going as planned. The frequency of these checks should be cooperatively decided by the delegating manager and the employees. Checks should not be so frequent as to stifle the employees, but they should be frequent enough to provide necessary support and guidance.

Probably the most vague part of the delegation process centers around the question of how much authority to delegate. As mentioned previously, management must delegate sufficient authority to allow the subordinate to perform the job. Precisely what can and cannot be delegated depends

**figure 7.3**

STEPS IN THE DELEGATION PROCESS

1. Analyze how you spend your time.
2. Decide which tasks can be assigned.
3. Decide who can handle each task.
4. Delegate the authority.
5. Create an obligation (responsibility).
6. Control the delegation.

on the commitments of the manager and the number and quality of subordinates. A rule of thumb is to delegate authority and responsibility to the lowest organization level that has the competence to accept them.

Failure to master delegation is probably the single most frequently encountered reason managers fail. To be a good manager, a person must learn to delegate.

The **exception principle** (also known as *management by exception*) states that managers should concentrate their efforts on matters that deviate significantly from normal and let subordinates handle routine matters. The exception principle is closely related to the parity principle. The idea behind the exception principle is that managers should concentrate on those matters that require their abilities and not become bogged down with duties their subordinates should be doing. The exception principle can be hard to comply with when incompetent or insecure subordinates refer everything to their superiors because they are afraid to make a decision. On the other hand, superiors should refrain from making everyday decisions that they have delegated to subordinates. This problem is often referred to as *micromanaging*.

**exception principle**

States that managers should concentrate on matters that deviate significantly from normal and let subordinates handle routine matters; also called *management by exception*.

## Unity of Command

The **unity of command principle** states that an employee should have one, and only one, immediate manager. The difficulty of serving more than one superior has been recognized for thousands of years. Recall the biblical quote, "No man can serve two masters." In its simplest form, this problem arises when two managers tell the same employee to do different jobs at the same time. The employee is thus placed in a no-win situation. Regardless of which manager the employee obeys, the other will be dissatisfied. The key to avoiding problems with unity of command is to make sure employees clearly understand the lines of authority that directly affect them. Too often managers assume employees understand the lines of authority when in fact they do not. All employees should have a basic understanding of the organizational chart for their company and where they fit on it. An organizational chart frequently clarifies lines of authority and the chain of command.

More times than not, problems relating to the unity of command principle stem from the actions of managers rather than the actions of employees. This happens most often when managers make requests of employees who do not work directly for them.

**unity of command principle**

States that an employee should have one, and only one, immediate manager.

## Scalar Principle

The **scalar principle** states that authority in the organization flows through the chain of managers one link at a time, ranging from the

**scalar principle**

States that authority in the organization flows through the chain of managers one link at a time, ranging from the highest to the lowest ranks; also called *chain of command*.

highest to the lowest ranks. Commonly referred to as the *chain of command,* the scalar principle is based on the need for communication and the principle of unity of command.

The problem with going around the scalar principle is that the link bypassed in the process may have very important information. For example, suppose Jerry goes directly above his immediate boss, Ellen, to Charlie for permission to take his lunch break 30 minutes earlier. Charlie, believing the request is reasonable, approves it, only to find out later that the other two people in Jerry's department had also rescheduled their lunch breaks. Thus, the department would be totally vacant from 12:30 to 1 o'clock. Ellen, the bypassed manager, would have known about the other rescheduled lunch breaks.

A common misconception is that every action must painstakingly progress through every link in the chain, whether its course is upward or downward. This point was refuted many years ago by Lyndall Urwick, an internationally known management consultant:

> *Provided there is proper confidence and loyalty between superiors and subordinates, and both parties take the trouble to keep the other informed in matters in which they should have a concern, the "scalar process" does not imply that there should be no shortcuts. It is concerned with authority, and provided the authority is recognized and no attempt is made to evade or to supersede it, there is ample room for avoiding in matters of action the childish practices of going upstairs one step at a time or running up one ladder and down another when there is nothing to prevent a direct approach on level ground.*[13]

As Henri Fayol stated years before Urwick, "It is an error to depart needlessly from authority, but it is an even greater one to keep to it when detriment to the business ensues."[14] Both Urwick and Fayol are simply saying that in certain instances, one can and should shortcut the scalar chain as long as one does not do so in a secretive or deceitful manner.

---

### PROGRESS CHECK QUESTIONS

 9.  What are the four elements that must be present for empowerment to thrive?
10.  What is a self-managed work team?
11.  What are the seven reasons for a manager's reluctance to delegate authority?
12.  What is the exception principle?

---

## Span of Management

The **span of management** (also called the *span of control*) refers to the number of subordinates a manager can effectively manage. Although the British World War I general Sir Ian Hamilton is usually credited for

**span of management**
Number of subordinates a manager can effectively manage; also called *span of control.*

A group of civil engineers is involved in a major construction project. Their duties include liaison with the architects and builders and the provision of advice on appropriate structural materials for different parts of the building. Unfortunately, the software package they are using to run the numbers has two major flaws—a bug that produces arithmetic errors in some calculations, and some incorrect information on the load bearing properties of some of the materials being used in the construction project. The project is behind schedule, and the developers are putting pressure on the builders to get caught up.

Halfway through the construction process, the building is unable to support the loads being placed upon it. A crane on the top floor crashes through several floors and kills a number of workers in the process. An analysis of the disaster shows that the arithmetic bug and the incorrect information on material strength combined to bring about the failure. In these circumstances, who has the greater ethical responsibility for the accident? The engineers who failed to recognize that the material information was incorrect? The developers whose tight schedules made checking the stress calculations impossible? Or the software developers, who supplied a faulty product?

*Source:* T. Forester and P. Morrison, *Computer Ethics: Cautionary Tales and Ethical Dilemmas in Computing*, 2nd ed. (Cambridge, MA: MIT Press, 2001) pp. 233–236.

developing the concept of a limited span of control, related examples abound throughout history. Hamilton argued that a narrow span of management (with no more than six subordinates reporting to a manager) would enable the manager to get the job accomplished in the course of a normal working day.[15]

In 1933, V. A. Graicunas published a classic paper that analyzed subordinate-superior relationships in terms of a mathematical formula.[16] This formula was based on the theory that the complexities of managing increase geometrically as the number of subordinates increases arithmetically.

Based on his personal experience and the works of Hamilton and Graicunas, Lyndall Urwick first stated the concept of span of management as a management principle in 1938: "No superior can supervise directly the work of more than five, or at the most, six subordinates whose work interlocks."[17]

Since the publication of Graicunas's and Urwick's works, the upper limit of five or six subordinates has been continuously criticized as being too restrictive. Many practitioners and scholars contend there are situations in which more than five or six subordinates can be effectively supervised. Their beliefs have been substantiated by considerable empirical evidence showing that the limit of five or six subordinates has been successfully exceeded in many situations.[18] Urwick has suggested these exceptions can be explained by the fact that senior workers often function as unofficial managers or leaders.[19]

In view of recent evidence, the span of management concept has been revised to state that the number of people who should report directly to any one person should be based on the complexity, variety, and proximity of the jobs, the quality of the people filling the jobs, and the ability of the manager.

**figure 7.4**

**FACTORS AFFECTING THE SPAN OF MANAGEMENT**

| FACTOR | DESCRIPTION | RELATIONSHIP TO SPAN OF CONTROL |
|---|---|---|
| Complexity | Job scope Job depth | Shortens span of control |
| Variety | Number of different types of jobs being managed | Shortens span of control |
| Proximity | Physical dispersion of jobs being managed | Lengthens span of control |
| Quality of subordinates | General quality of the employees being managed | Lengthens span of control |
| Quality of manager | Ability to perform managerial duties | Lengthens span of control |

While much effort is given to ensuring that a manager's span of management is not too great, the opposite situation is often overlooked. All too frequently in organizations, situations develop in which only one employee reports to a particular manager. While this situation might very well be justified under certain circumstances, it often results in an inefficient and top-heavy organization. The pros and cons of flat organizations (wide spans of management, few levels) versus tall organizations (narrow spans of management, many levels) are discussed at length in the next chapter. Figure 7.4 summarizes the factors affecting the manager's span of management.

## Workplace Changes in Organizations

Several changes are occurring in the workplace environment that can have an impact on how an entity might best be organized. Flextime, telecommuting, and job sharing are three such practices that are growing in popularity.

*Flextime*, or flexible working hours, allows employees to choose, within certain limits, when they start and end their workday. Usually the organization defines a core period (such as 10 a.m. to 3 p.m.) when all employees will be at work. It is then left to each employee to decide when to start and end the workday as long as the hours encompass the core period. Some flextime programs allow employees to vary the hours worked each day as long as they meet some specific total, which is usually 40 hours. The percentage of organizations offering flextime has increased dramatically over the last 15 years. A recent study by the Society for Human Resource Management found that 56 percent of employers offered some type of flextime in 2005.[20]

Flextime has the advantage of allowing different employees to accommodate different lifestyles and schedules. Other potential advantages include avoiding rush hours and having less absenteeism and tardiness. From the employer's viewpoint, flextime can have

A more flexible work environment is indicative of changing philosophies in business. *What are some of the advantages and disadvantages to allowing employees to work from home?*

the advantage of providing an edge in recruiting new employees and also retaining hard-to-find qualified employees. Also, organizations with flextime schedules have reported an average increase of 1 to 5 percent in productivity, as well as improved recruiting and retention.[21] On the downside, flextime can create communication and coordination problems for supervisors and managers.

*Telecommuting* is the practice of working at home or while traveling and being able to interact with the office, or working at a satellite office. Today's information technology (PCs, the Internet, cellular phones, etc.) has made telecommuting a reality for many companies. According to the International Telework Association and Council (ITAC), over 45 million Americans were working from their home in 2005 and over 20 million were working from their cars.[22] The earlier referenced survey by the Society for Human Resource Management found that 37 percent of its respondents offered some type of telecommuting.[23] Advantages of telecommuting include lower turnover, less travel time, avoiding rush hour, avoiding distractions at the office, being able to work flexible hours, and lower real estate costs for employers. Potential disadvantages of telecommuting are insurance concerns relating to the health and safety of employees working at home. Another drawback is that some state and local laws restrict just what work can be done at home. The dramatic rise in the price of gasoline has made telecommuting even more attractive to millions of Americans.

*Job sharing* is a relatively new concept whereby two or more part-time employees perform a job that would normally be held by one full-time employee. Job sharing can be in the form of equally shared responsibilities or split duties, or a combination of both. Approximately 19 percent of major firms in the United States offer some type of job sharing, according to the 2005 survey by the Society for Human Resource Management. Job sharing is especially attractive to people who want to work but not full time. A critical factor relating to job sharing is how benefits are handled. Often benefits are prorated between the part-time employees. Some organizations allow job-sharing employees to purchase full health insurance by paying the difference between their prorated benefit and the premium for a full-time employee.

## PROGRESS CHECK QUESTIONS

13. Explain the span of management (span of control).

14. Think of an organization you work for (or have worked for in the past). What is the span of management at your company?

15. Explain the following terms: flextime, telecommuting, and job sharing.

16. Would it be possible to introduce telecommuting at your company? Why or why not?

## Be careful what you wish for

Katie really liked working at the Taco Barn. Several of her friends worked there, and Tony had followed in Jerry's footsteps by being really flexible on her schedule so that she could meet her cheerleading and AP course commitments. So when Tony asked her to make up a list of things they needed in the restaurant and to place the order, Katie decided that she would show Tony what a smart choice he had made in giving her the task.

She had originally gone to him to remind him that they need napkins, condiments (salt and pepper), and some new tabletop menu holders to replace the ones that were cracked and chipped. Since Tony wanted her to make a list of everything they needed, Katie decided to make a detailed inspection of the restaurant before putting the order together. She came in half an hour before her regular shift and checked the restaurant from top to bottom. Not only did they need napkins, condiments, and a few menu holders, she noted, but they could also use some more silverware (they were always running so low on teaspoons that waiters and waitresses started hoarding them at their stations to make sure they had enough). Plus, several of the

trays were cracked, and a couple of the tray stands were wobbly. (What would Tony say if a tray full of food fell on the floor because the tray stand broke?) And so it went on—a few water jugs here, a couple of candleholders there—all designed to make the restaurant look as good as it possibly could.

Katie asked Kevin for the number and catalog for their vendor and placed the order—an order that was several hundred dollars more than their regular weekly order—as the salesperson was kind enough to point out to Katie. She replied:

"Tony is very busy on a project for our regional office right now, and he asked me to place the order. When will these items be delivered?"

### QUESTIONS

1. What was Katie's mistake here?
2. What contribution did Tony make to this situation?
3. How do you think Tony will react?
4. How would you have handled this situation?

## CONCLUSION

Organizing work is the process of dividing labor resources according to assigned tasks, and delegating the necessary authority to perform those tasks. Managers should be directly involved in all aspects of that process, but most importantly in establishing the lines of authority because without those clearly defined lines the organization can collapse into chaos very quickly. In the next chapter we'll review the options available to managers in defining the formal boundaries of an organization in order to establish the environment in which the work of the organization takes place.

## key terms

| | | |
|---|---|---|
| **authority** 180 | **empowerment** 184 | **job depth** 180 |
| **centralization** 183 | **exception principle** 188 | **job scope** 180 |
| **decentralization** 183 | **informal organization** 178 | **organization** 178 |

## review questions

1. What is the difference between horizontal and vertical division of labor?
2. Discuss two approaches to viewing the sources of authority.
3. What is the unity of command principle?
4. As a manager, would you prefer a relatively large (more than seven subordinates) or small (seven or fewer subordinates) span of management? Why? What are the implications of your choice?

## internet exercise

Visit the Web site of the Telework Coalition (TelCoa) at www.telcoa.org

1. What are the mission and vision of TelCoa?
2. Download and summarize IDC's 2007 white paper on "homeshoring."
3. Who were the 2007 Hall of Fame Award recipients?
4. How does telecommuting relate to business continuity planning?

## team exercise

The assistant sales manager of ABC Company has been in that job for six months. Due to poor sales over the past 18 months, the sales manager (his or her boss) has just been fired. The president of ABC then offers this job to the assistant sales manager subject to the following stipulations:

- You cannot increase the advertising budget.
- You must continue to let Metro-Media, Inc., handle the advertising.
- You cannot make any personnel changes.
- You will accept full responsibility for the sales for this fiscal year (which started two months ago).

Divide into two teams. Team 1 is in favor of taking the job offer. Team 2 wants to pass. Each team will have 30 minutes to prepare a presentation outlining the reasons for its decision.

## JetBlue's Fiasco Could Improve Flying

*As the Discount Airline Scrambles to Repair Its Business and Retain Customers, New Service Efforts Put Rivals on Notice: Changes Are Needed*

It's the new must-share video for airline executives. In a two-minute clip posted Feb. 20 on his company's home page, a contrite and fatigued JetBlue Airways Chief Executive David Neeleman apologizes to passengers for the airline's six-day meltdown and vows that such an operational disaster will "never again" befall the company and its passengers. Packed planes sat near empty gates, in some cases for 8, 9, and 10 hours. Irate passengers screamed at workers and security guards. A few JetBlue employees started to cry, according to media reports. It was the sort of operational catastrophe that no traveler or airline wants.

Neeleman, in the clip, said the company was going through "the most difficult time in our history." He added, "I wanted to assure you as the CEO of this company that the events that transpired last week, and the way that they transpired, will never happen again." In a later press release, Neeleman also apologized to employees, and promised "to get the right resources, tools, and support for them."

### PR OFFENSIVE

So what exactly went wrong at a business that bills itself as a "customer service" company that just happens to fly airplanes? In a word, everything. An organizational bias against flight cancellations—JetBlue scrubs the fewest flights in the industry—collided with an infrastructure too lean to manage the mix of poor weather and cascading flight delays and cancellations.

Now the New York–based company is jumping into a high-profile public relations campaign, hiring new staff, doling out refunds and free flights, and hoping the public doesn't turn away from what once was a runaway success story. Still, despite the shrill feel of its new "customer bill of rights" and no shortage of skeptics, JetBlue has a good shot at fulfilling Neeleman's pledge. What turned into a $30 million February disaster for JetBlue could, in the end, make the U.S. airline industry a more hospitable environment for passengers.

Why? Fear and fortuity. The airlines are petrified that politicians, itching to jump on the service issue, will try to impose new government mandates, so they may be more motivated than ever to make real changes. Neeleman looks like just the person to push for changes and make them industry practice. He's an industry outsider with a successful track record, the CEO most closely associated with a U.S. airline since Herb Kelleher of Southwest Airlines. The impatient, hands-on, get-'er-done CEO grasped the severity of the situation immediately and has, with a high-profile response, helped keep the issue in the public eye. He emitted a flood of daily apologies, declaring himself "mortified" by the operations and declining to defend his company's performance.

## CASH REFUNDS

JetBlue will deplane passengers on flights that have been sitting at least five hours, unless the pilot has been notified of a pending "wheels up" time. After arrival, passengers will get a refund, from $25 to the full amount of their round-trip ticket, if a flight waits for an open gate for more than 30 minutes. The airline's tab is $100 for departing flights delayed three to four hours, and for longer delays, a voucher for the full amount spent.

So far, the company has spent $14 million for refunds and chartering other airplanes to fly passengers and has committed $16 million in future free flights for affected customers. It will also spend heavily on newspaper ads, apologizing for the problems.

## DOMINO EFFECT

Canceled flights are a treacherous problem for airlines such as JetBlue. They tip off a series of costly events for hub-and-spoke carriers, like dominos toppling one after another. First, passengers need to be rebooked on later flights or, in certain cases, on other airlines that charge more expensive fares. Then jets aren't in the cities they need to be in, and are unable to collect additional groups of passengers that will not get to their final destination at the time they expected to arrive. Crew members don't get to the airport where they're needed for either another flight or for a return leg that must happen within employees' federally mandated work schedules. On top of that, the paying customer has been inconvenienced and is usually irritable, anxious, and exhausted.

## PROMISES, PROMISES

Still, many observers consider linking delays with penalty payments to be a very bad idea. If airline workers feel pressure to get a plane off the ground, saving their company a few bucks, it could set a troubling precedent in an industry where safety must be paramount. "It is supreme hubris to think that Congress could divine a set of passenger service standards that would deliver intended benefits without risking safety margins," Kevin Mitchell, chairman of the Business Travel Coalition, wrote on the group's site in response to JetBlue's troubles.

Chris Collins, the senior vice-president of operations at Denver-based Frontier Airlines and a former JetBlue operations manager, says, "It's the unintended consequences of forcing airlines to do something that really scares a lot of us in the industry. It has to be really thought out and understood." Whatever happens in Washington, Neeleman says JetBlue's bare-bones crew and customer-management systems will be corrected and augmented within 30 days, and its new customer bill of rights has been made retroactive to Feb. 14.

## Questions

1. JetBlue "bills itself as a 'customer service' company that just happens to fly airplanes." How did such a customer service company reach a point where passengers were trapped in planes "in some cases for 8, 9, and 10 hours"?
2. What is the domino effect of canceled flights for hub-and-spoke carriers?
3. Do you agree with David Neeleman's decision to make such a public apology and such an explicit commitment to a customer's bill of rights? Why or why not?
4. Do you think Neeleman's approach will be followed by other airlines? Why or why not?

*Source:* Adapted from: Justin Bachman, *BusinesWeek Online,* February 21, 2007.

## The Wiki Workplace

*Thanks in Part to Younger Workers, More Companies Are Using Social Computing Tools to Aid Collaboration and to Foster Innovation and Growth*

When Robert Stephens graduated from the University of Minnesota with a degree in computer science in 1994, he wanted to start a business consultancy. But hiring a staff of good consultants takes a lot of money, and Stephens had little, so he founded Geek Squad, a cheekily branded computer repair company that helps consumers navigate the increasing complexity of electronic gadgetry.

From humble origins, Geek Squad grew and grew. In 2002, after nearly a decade of profitable operations, the company was acquired by consumer electronics giant Best Buy.

At the time, Stephens had 60 employees and was booking $3 million in annual revenue. Today, working out of 700 Best Buy locations across North America, Geek Squad's 12,000 service agents clock nearly $1 billion in services and return some $280 million to the retailer's bottom line.

For Stephens, Geek Squad's meteoric success was exhilarating and challenging. How, for example, would he recruit and train an ever-growing number of employees, let alone keep them in the loop and gather their input into the business?

One day, Stephens asked his deputy director for counterintelligence at headquarters how things were going in the field. "I worry about those agents in Anchorage, Alaska," he said. "There are about 20 of them there, and I worry about them staying connected to the mission."

"Oh, those Anchorage guys, I talk to them all the time," the deputy director replied.

Prodded for details, he sheepishly told Stevens that they all play *Battlefield 2* online. "With each server, you can have 128 people simultaneously fighting each other in a virtual environment," said the director. "We wear headsets and use Ventrilo software so that we can talk over the Internet while we are running around fighting."

Stephens, who now joins in himself from time to time, says: "The agents taunt each other, saying, 'Hey, I see you behind the wall.' But then, while we're running along, rifles in our hands, one of the agents behind me will be like, 'Yeah, we just hit our revenue to budget,' and somebody else will be like, 'Hey, how do you reset the password on a Linksys router?'"

Welcome to the Wiki Workplace.

### RISE OF THE WIKI WORKPLACE

The information and communication technologies that are transforming media, culture, and the economy are also reshaping how companies and employees function. New social computing tools such as wikis and blogs put unprecedented communication power in the hands of employees.

Some companies worry about the risks of uncontrolled communications leaking out. But a growing number believe the new collaboration tools are good for innovation and growth—they help employees connect with more people, in more regions of the world, with less hassle and more enjoyment, than earlier generations of workplace technology.

Geek Squad is a case in point. Many thousands of Geeks are using a growing suite of collaboration technologies to brainstorm new products and services, manage projects, swap service tips, and socialize with their peers.

Best Buy CEO Brad Anderson says empowering employees to collaborate in unorthodox ways is all about "unleashing the power of human capital." As the retailer continues to crush its competition, it would seem that Anderson is onto something. Already North America's largest consumer electronics seller, the profitable company plans to open more than 100 new stores this year, while ailing competitors such as Circuit City are closing locations.

Much of this is due to a younger generation of workers who embrace Web-based tools in a way that often confounds older workers. Nourished on instant messaging, blogs, wikis, chat groups, playlists, peer-to-peer file sharing, and online multiplayer video games, the net generation will increasingly bring a heightened comfort with technology, inclination toward social connectivity, more emphasis on creativity and fun, and greater diversity to the companies they work for and to the companies they found themselves.

## BOTTOM-UP KNOWLEDGE CREATION

Some companies, like Geek Squad, are already finding that internal blogs and wikis help stimulate creative thinking and capture knowledge. One example: Typically, high-level strategy documents are formulated by a handful of people at the top of the corporate hierarchy. At Xerox, Chief Technology Officer Sophie VanDebroek turned the process inside out by setting up a wiki that would allow researchers in the R&D group to define collaboratively the company's technology strategy.

VanDebroek expects a more robust technology roadmap and a much stronger competitive strategy section as a result. "We'll get more content and knowledge in all of our areas of expertise," she says, "including everything from material science to the latest document services and solutions."

Another trailblazer is IBM, which in September, 2006, invited employees in more than 160 countries—along with their clients, business partners, and even family members—to join in a massive, wide-open brainstorming session it called the InnovationJam. More than 100,000 participants took part in a series of moderated online discussions taking place in two 72-hour sessions.

IBM expects the insights gleaned will transform industries, improve human health, and help protect the environment over the course of the coming decades. Chief Executive Sam Palmisano believes so strongly in the concept that he's committed up to $100 million to develop the ideas with the most social and economic potential.

## READY OR NOT

Wikis, blogs, and other tools will arrive in the workplace whether companies are ready or not, as younger employees tend to develop their own self-organized networks that cut across traditional corporate divisions. Increasingly these employees will be capable of interacting as a global, real-time workforce. Indeed, if Linux, Wikipedia, and other collaborative projects are any indication, it will often be easier and less expensive for workers to self-organize productively than to squeeze them into more traditional business units.

Could too much openness and self-organization in the workplace lead to disorganization, confusion, and lack of focus and direction? Not according to Google CEO Eric

Schmidt, whose employees are allowed plenty of self-direction.

"It doesn't feel like you have the kind of control over the way in which decisions are made that you might have had in a more traditional environment" Schmidt says. And yet he is convinced that self-organization is better. "You talk about the strategy, you get people excited, you tell people what the company's priorities are, and somehow it works out."

Clear goals, structure, discipline, and leadership in the organization will remain as important as ever and perhaps more so as self-organization and peer production emerge as organizing principles for the workplace. The difference today is that these qualities can emerge organically as employees seize the new tools to collaborate across departmental and organizational boundaries, and, yes, "the power of human capital" can be unleashed.

## Questions

1. Why are these new collaboration tools "good for innovation and growth"?

2. What are the potential benefits of "unleashing the power of human capital"?

3. Is there a downside to so much openness and self-organization?

4. Would blogs and wikis work at your company? Why or why not?

*Source:* Adapted from Don Tapscott, and Anthony D. Williams, The *BusinessWeek* Wikinomics Series, March 26, 2007.

# ORGANIZING STRUCTURE

**"Every company has two organizational structures: The formal one is written on the charts; the other is the everyday relationship of the men and women in the organization."**

—Harold S. Geneen

## The World of Work: Taco Barn takes customer service offshore

Taco Barn's leadership survey had uncovered many issues for the company to address, including a wide disparity in leadership styles and abilities in many of their unit managers. The Human Resource department was immediately tasked with the project of developing a new leadership-training course that would both help the more inexperienced unit managers improve their skills and also establish a more consistent leadership style among the Taco Barn managers.

At the same time, corporate announced a new customer service initiative called "Taco Barn to Go," as an attempt to reach customers who didn't want to sit and eat in the restaurant. With a toll-free central ordering number, customers could call in their order from the Taco Barn menu and pick up their food at their local restaurant within 30 minutes.

Tony was introduced to this new initiative at the regular monthly regional meeting for unit managers. His first reaction was very positive. Their competition had been offering a similar service for months now, and Tony felt that Taco Barn's response was long overdue. However, when the regional information technology specialist began his presentation to explain why the launch had taken so long to get off the ground, Tony found his enthusiasm for the new project rapidly disappearing.

Because there were so many choices on the Taco Barn menu—particularly side items—the company had decided not to use a Web site for the new "To Go" service. It felt it would be more customer-friendly to have a live person on the phone taking your order, just like the waiter would if you ate in the restaurant. Further research had shown that taking telephone orders at each restaurant would be disruptive to running the restaurant,

# LEARNING objectives

**After studying this chapter, you will be able to:**

1 Explain the purpose of an organization chart.

2 Describe factors and changes that affect an organization's structure.

3 Define a contingency approach.

4 Identify the different types of departmentalization.

5 Describe the different types of organizational structure, including a virtual organization.

6 Discuss the types and effective use of committees.

and that developing a central reservations center would be too expensive to build and maintain. The company then looked at contracting with a service to take orders on a per call basis, but even that was expensive.

The solution had been found after the regional IT specialist had returned from a conference on outsourcing manufacturing and service functions to overseas (a trend now referred to as "offshoring"). The IT specialist had attended a presentation by an Indian company that could maintain a call center for Taco Barn to take telephone orders during U.S. business hours, transmit those orders by computer to the closest Taco Barn, and do all that at less than half the cost quoted by U.S. vendors offering the same service.

The general reaction in the regional meeting was very positive. Corporate executives were pleased with both the potential cost savings and the prospect of a few magazine articles on how Taco Barn was using cutting-edge technology to serve their customers. Regional and unit managers were pleased not to have to handle the calls in the local restaurants. Tony, however, was not so sure.

## QUESTIONS

1. Do you think cost savings should be the primary decision factor for any new company initiative? Why or why not?

2. What are the potential benefits and challenges of outsourcing? Review the material on pages 208–209 for help on this.

3. Which issues will have to be addressed before this service will be ready to launch?

4. What do you think Tony's concerns are here?

# ORGANIZING STRUCTURE

**Organization structure** is the framework that defines the boundaries of the formal organization and within which the organization operates. The structure of an organization reflects how groups compete for resources, where responsibilities for profits and other performance measures lie, how information is transmitted, and how decisions are made. Many people believe a good manager or a competent employee should be able to perform well regardless of the organization structure and environment. They believe that if managers or employees are good enough, they can overcome any obstacles the organization structure presents. Others believe that given the right organization structure, anyone should be able to perform in an acceptable fashion. The truth lies somewhere in between. An appropriate organization structure certainly helps foster good performance.

# ORGANIZING GROWTH STAGES

Figure 8.1 shows in general terms the stages an organization goes through as it grows and matures. The craft or family stage is characterized by the absence of formal policies, objectives, and structure. The operations of the organization at this stage generally center on one individual and one functional area. During the entrepreneurial stage, the organization grows first at an increasing and then a decreasing rate. An atmosphere of optimism spreads through the entire organization as sales and profits rise rapidly. By the third stage of growth, the entrepreneur has been replaced by or evolved into a professional manager who performs the processes of planning, organizing, staffing, motivating, and controlling.[1] Profits are realized more from internal efficiency and less from external exploitation of the market. At this stage, the organization becomes characterized by written policies, procedures, and plans.

**figure 8.1**

**ORGANIZATION GROWTH AND CHANGE**

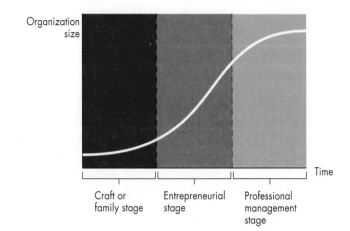

As the organization moves through the craft stage and into the entrepreneurial stage, an organization structure must be developed. This is a critical stage for the organization. If an appropriate structure is not established and utilized, the entrepreneur may lose control and the entire organization may collapse. An organization structure must be developed that allows the organization to adapt to change in its environment.

## ORGANIZING CHARTS

An organization chart uses a series of boxes connected with one or more lines to graphically represent the organization's structure. Each box represents a position within the organization, and each line indicates the nature of the relationships among the different positions. The organization chart not only identifies specific relationships but also provides an overall picture of how the entire organization fits together. As organizations become larger and more complex, it becomes increasingly difficult to represent all the relationships accurately.

## FACTORS AFFECTING ORGANIZATION

Several factors can affect which structure is the most appropriate for a given organization. A structure that is appropriate for a high-tech company that employs 50,000 people in eight countries will probably not be appropriate for a small retail business with just a dozen employees. Strategy, size, environment, and technology are some of the important factors found to be most closely related to organization structure.

### Strategy

A major part of an organization's strategy for achieving its objectives deals with how the organization is structured. An appropriate structure will not guarantee success, but it will improve the organization's chances for success. Business leaders, athletic coaches, and military leaders all stress that to succeed one must not only have a good strategy but also be prepared to win (mentally and structurally). In addition to clarifying and defining strategy through the delegation of authority and responsibility, the organization structure can either help or hinder strategy implementation.

In a groundbreaking study of organizational strategy, Alfred D. Chandler described a pattern in the evolution of organizational structures.[2] The pattern was based on studies of Du Pont, General Motors, Sears, and Standard Oil Company, with supporting evidence from many other firms. The pattern Chandler described was that of changing strategy, followed by administrative problems, leading to decline

Planning a strategy elevates a company from merely reacting to planning for the future.

in performance, revised structure, and a subsequent return to economic health. In summary, Chandler concluded that structure follows strategy; in other words, changes in strategy ultimately led to changes in the organization's structure. Chandler's work related particularly to growth and to the structural adjustments made to maintain efficient performance during market expansion, product line diversification, and vertical integration.

Although subsequent research has supported the idea of a relationship between strategy and structure, it is clear that strategy is not the only variable that has an impact on structure.[3] The process of matching structure to strategy is complex and should be undertaken with a thorough understanding of the historical development of the current structure and of other variables, including size, environment, and technology.

## Size

There are many ways to measure the size of an organization, but sales volume and number of employees are the most frequently used factors. While no hard-and-fast rules exist, certain characteristics generally relate to an organization's size. Small organizations tend to be less specialized (horizontal division of labor), less standardized, and more centralized. Larger organizations tend to be more specialized, more standardized, and more decentralized. Thus, as an organization grows in size, certain structural changes naturally occur.

## Environment

A landmark study relating organization to environment was conducted by Tom Burns and G. M. Stalker in the United Kingdom.[4] By examining some 20 industrial firms in both a changing industry and a more stable, established industry, Burns and Stalker focused on how a firm's pattern of organization was related to certain characteristics of the external environment. The researchers identified two distinct organizational systems. **Mechanistic systems** are characterized by a rigid definition of functional duties, precise job descriptions, fixed authority and responsibility, and a well-developed organizational hierarchy through which information filters up and instructions flow down. **Organic systems** are characterized by less formal job descriptions, greater emphasis on adaptability, more participation, and less fixed authority. Burns and Stalker found that successful firms in stable and established industries tended to be mechanistic in structure, whereas successful firms in dynamic industries tended to be organic in structure. See Figure 8.2 for a more complete evaluation of the structural differences between mechanistic and organic systems.

Paul Lawrence and Jay Lorsch conducted a later study dealing with organization structure and its environment.[5] Their original study included 10 firms in three different industrial environments. Reaching conclusions similar to those of Burns and Stalker, Lawrence and Lorsch found that to be successful, firms operating in a dynamic environment needed a relatively

**mechanistic systems**
Organizational systems characterized by a rigid delineation of functional duties, precise job descriptions, fixed authority and responsibility, and a well-developed organizational hierarchy through which information filters up and instructions flow down.

**organic systems**
Organizational systems having less formal job descriptions, greater emphasis on adaptability, more participation, and less fixed authority.

At the height of his powers as the chairman and CEO of the Walt Disney Company, Michael Eisner's activities were, in theory at least, overseen by a board of directors who were reported to be independent, objective, and committed to ensuring that Eisner ran the company in an ethical and professional manner. In reality, Eisner had personal and professional relationships with many of the board members:

- Irwin Russell, Eisner's personal lawyer, negotiated Eisner's lucrative contract and had a professional duty of loyalty to Eisner simultaneous to his duty to shareholders. Yet Russell was also the chairman of Disney's compensation committee.

- Director Robert Stern was Eisner's personal architect and was beholden to Eisner for an immense amount of work from Disney, including designing the new animation building.

- Reveta Bowers was the principal of the prestigious Center for Early Education in West Hollywood, a school attended by Eisner's sons and the children of other Disney executives, who also gave the school donations.

- Eisner had named Leo O'Donovan, a Jesuit priest and president of Georgetown University, to the board after Eisner's son Breck graduated from Georgetown. He gave Georgetown $1 million and his foundation financed a school scholarship.

- George Mitchell earned a $50,000 consulting fee in addition to his board stipend, and his law firm earned hundreds of thousands in legal fees representing Disney on various matters.

What's wrong with this picture? What should the Disney Company have done to ensure that the board could fulfill it's obligation to shareholders?

(For further information about Boards of Directors turn to page 223.)

***Source:*** James B. Stewart, *The Disney War* (New York: Simon & Schuster, 2005).

---

flexible structure, firms operating in a stable environment needed a more rigid structure, and firms operating in an intermediate environment needed a structure somewhere between the two extremes.

| Characteristics of Mechanistic and Organic Organizations | |
| --- | --- |
| **MECHANISTIC** | **ORGANIC** |
| Work is divided into narrow, specialized tasks. | Work is defined in terms of general tasks. |
| Tasks are performed as specified unless changed by managers in the hierarchy. | Tasks are continually adjusted as needed through interaction with others involved in the task. |
| Structure of control, authority, and communication is hierarchical. | Structure of control, authority, and communication is a network. |
| Decisions are made by the specified hierarchical level. | Decisions are made by individuals with relevant knowledge and technical expertise. |
| Communication is mainly vertical, between superior and subordinate. | Communication is vertical and horizontal, among superiors, subordinates, and peers. |
| Communication content is largely instructions and decisions issued by superiors. | Communication content is largely information and advice. |
| Emphasis is on loyalty to the organization and obedience to superiors. | Emphasis is on commitment to organizational goals and possession of needed expertise. |

**figure 8.2**

STRUCTURAL DIFFERENCES BETWEEN MECHANISTIC AND ORGANIC SYSTEMS

***Source:*** Adapted from Tom Burns and G. W. Stalker, *The Management of Innovation* (London: Tavistock, 1961), pp. 119–22.

## Who Dropped the Ball?

In October 2006, Industrial Water Treatment Company (IWT) introduced Kelate, a new product that was 10 times more effective than other treatments in controlling scale buildup in boilers. The instantaneous demand for Kelate required that IWT double its number of service engineers within the following year.

The sudden expansion caused IWT to reorganize its operations. Previously, each district office was headed by a district manager who was assisted by a chief engineer and two engineering supervisors. In 2007, this structure changed. The district manager now had a chief engineer and a manager of operations. Four engineering supervisors (now designated as group leaders) were established. They were to channel all work assignments through the manager of operations, while all engineering-related problems were to be handled by the chief engineer. Each group leader supervised 8 to 10 field service engineers (see Figure 8.3).

Bill Marlowe, district manager for the southeast district, has just received a letter from an old and very large customer, Sel Tex, Inc. The letter revealed that when Sel Tex inspected one of its boilers last week, it found the water treatment was not working properly. When Sel Tex officials contacted Wes Smith, IWT's service engineer for the area, they were told he was scheduled to be working in the Jacksonville area the rest of the week but would get someone else down there the next day. When no one showed up, Sel Tex officials were naturally upset; after all, they were only requesting the engineering service they had been promised.

Bill Marlowe, upset over the growing number of customer complaints that seemed to be crossing his desk in recent months, called Ed Jones, chief engineer, into his office and showed him the letter he had received from Sel Tex.

*Ed:* Why are you showing me this? This is a work assignment foul-up.

*Bill:* Do you know anything about this unsatisfactory condition?

*Ed:* Sure, Wes called me immediately after he found out. Their concentration of Kelate must have gone up, since they're getting corrosion and oxygen on their tubes. I told Peter Adinaro, Wes's group leader, about it, and I suggested he schedule someone to visit Sel Tex.

*Bill:* Okay, Ed, thanks for your help. [Bill calls Peter Adinaro into his office.] *Peter, two weeks ago Ed asked you to assign someone to visit Sel*

*Tex because of a tube corrosion problem they are having. Do you remember?*

*Peter:* Oh, sure! As usual, Wes Smith called Ed instead of me. I left a message for Dick to assign someone there because my whole group was tied up and I couldn't spare anyone. I thought Dick would ask another group leader to assign someone to check it out.

*Bill:* Well, thanks for your help. Tell Dick to come on in here for a second.

Dick Welsh, manager of operations, came into Bill's office about 20 minutes later.

*Bill:* Dick, here's a letter from Sel Tex. Please read it, and tell me what you know about the situation.

*Dick:* [After reading the letter] *Bill, I didn't know anything about this.*

*Bill:* I checked with Pete, Wes's group leader, and he tells me he left a message for you to assign someone since his group was all tied up. Didn't you get the message?

*Dick:* Have you taken a look at my desk lately? I'm flooded with messages. Heck, I'm the greatest message handler of all times. If I could schedule my people without having all the engineering headaches unloaded on me, I wouldn't have all these messages. Sure, it's possible that he left a message, but I haven't seen it. I will look for it, though. Anyway, that letter sounds to me like they've got an engineering problem, and Ed should contact them to solve it.

*Bill:* I'll write Sel Tex myself and try to explain the situation to them. You and I will have to get together this afternoon and talk over some of these difficulties. See you later, Dick.

### Questions

1. How has IWT's structure changed?
2. What problems does Bill Marlowe face?
3. Are the problems related to the way IWT is organized, or are they related to the employees?
4. How could these problems be resolved?

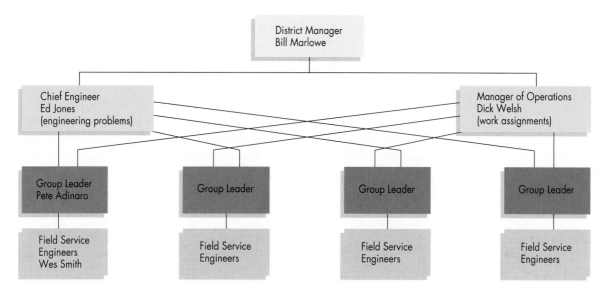

figure 8.3

PARTIAL ORGANIZATIONAL
CHART FOR IWT

## Organization and Technology

Numerous studies have also been conducted investigating potential relationships between technology and organization structure. One of the most important of these studies was conducted by Joan Woodward in the late 1950s.[6] Her study was based on an analysis of 100 manufacturing firms in the southeast Essex area of England. Woodward's general approach was to classify firms along a scale of "technical complexity" with particular emphasis on three modes of production: (1) unit or small-batch production (e.g., custom-made machines), (2) large-batch or mass production (e.g., an automotive assembly plant), and (3) continuous flow or process production (e.g., a chemical plant). The unit or small-batch production mode represents the lower end of the technical complexity scale, while the continuous flow mode represents the upper end.

After classifying each firm into one of the preceding categories, Woodward investigated a number of organizational variables. Some of her findings follow:

1. The number of levels in an organization increased as technical complexity increased.

2. The ratio of managers and supervisors to total personnel increased as technical complexity increased.

3. Using Burns and Stalker's definition of organic and mechanistic systems, organic management systems tended to predominate in firms at both ends of the scale of technical complexity, while mechanistic systems predominated in firms falling in the middle ranges.

4. No significant relationship existed between technical complexity and organizational size.

A few years later, Edward Harvey undertook a similar study.[7] Rather than using Woodward's technical complexity scale, Harvey grouped firms along a continuum from techniscal "diffuseness" to technical "specificity." Technically diffused firms have a wider range of products, produce products that vary from year to year, and produce more made-to-order products. Harvey's findings were similar to Woodward's in that he found significant relationships between technology and several organizational characteristics.

The general conclusion reached in the Woodward and Harvey studies was that a relationship clearly exists between organizational technology and a number of aspects of organization structure. Many additional studies have investigated the relationship between technology and structure. While they have reported some conflicting results, most studies have found a relationship between technology and structure.

---

## PROGRESS CHECK QUESTIONS

1. What is an organization chart?
2. Explain the stages an organization goes through as it grows and matures.
3. What are the four most important factors affecting organization structure?
4. Explain the differences between mechanistic and organic organizational systems.

---

# CHANGES AFFECTING ORGANIZATION STRUCTURE

In recent years, dramatic improvements in communication technology have introduced new ways of conducting business. These new practices have affected the structure of many organizations. Outsourcing has resulted from improved communication technology and is having an effect on the structure of many organizations.

**outsourcing**
Practice of subcontracting certain work functions to an outside organization.

**Outsourcing** is the practice of subcontracting certain work functions to an outside organization. Whether outsourcing is a response to downsizing, an attempt to cut costs, or an effort to increase service, it is a practice that will significantly affect the workplace and organizational charts. Work functions that are frequently being outsourced include accounting and finance functions, human resources, information technology, and even contract manufacturing. Dun and Bradstreet estimates that outsourcing, which began a mere 30 years ago, is now a $4 trillion a year business worldwide.[8] Outsourcing in the United States is expected to grow from $21.5 billion in 2004 to $32.6 billion in 2008.[9] It has been estimated that over 25 percent of the typical executive's budget goes to outsourcing supplies or services, and that is expected to grow considerably.[10] Outsourcing is a practice utilized by both large and small companies.

The International Association of Outsourcing Professionals estimates that almost 30 percent of all outsourcing in the United States is conducted by companies with less than $500 million in annual revenues.[11]

Outsourcing is an important business trend to understand. *What are some of the pros and some of the cons of outsourcing?*

Outsourcing has numerous potential benefits, including the following:[12]

- Allowing the organization to emphasize its core competencies by not spending time on routine areas that can be outsourced.

- Reducing operating costs by utilizing others who can do the job more efficiently.

- Accessing top talent and state-of-the-art technology without having to own it.

- Fewer personnel headaches.

- Improving resource allocation by allowing growth to take place more quickly.

Of course, there are potential drawbacks to outsourcing.[13] One overriding concern is that a large number of jobs are being lost to other countries through outsourcing. For example, it has been estimated that more than 3 million jobs will leave the United States by 2015.[14] Other specific drawbacks include:

- Loss of control and being at the mercy of the outside vendor.

- Loss of in-house skills.

- Threat to the morale of the workforce if too many areas are dominated by outside vendors.

- No guarantee that it will save money or provide higher service standards.

As with most management approaches, outsourcing is not a cure-all. Care must be taken that a long-term strategy evolves out of the use of outsourcing, not just a short-term fix to reduce costs. In the right situations, outsourcing can work well; but it almost always requires good management, good contracts, and realistic expectations.

## figure 8.4

**VARIABLES AFFECTING
APPROPRIATE
ORGANIZATION
STRUCTURE**

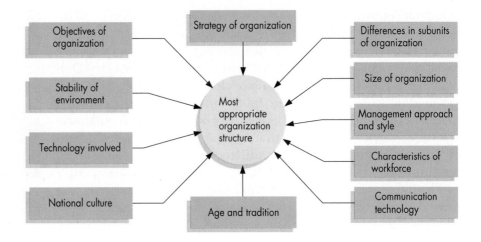

## Study Skills

### Write Your Own Ticket!

Can you identify the skill that can be monumental to your career?

#### Yes, it's writing.

In the competitive, global job market, the skill that can advance your career is exceptional writing capabilities.

What do great writing skills do for you? Consider that exceptional writing skills:

- Elevate your ability to communicate.
- Show a higher level of translating research into practical use.
- Show the ability to use language for multiple purposes, such as motivation, praise and conviction.

## A CONTINGENCY APPROACH

The previous discussions emphasize the fact that several factors affect an organization's structure. The knowledge that there is no one best way to organize (i.e., the design is conditional) has led to a contingency (situational) approach to organizing. Figure 8.4 shows the previously discussed variables and others that can help determine the most appropriate organization structure. The contingency approach should be viewed as a process of assessing these relevant variables and then choosing the most appropriate structure for the situation. Because most of the relevant variables are dynamic, management should periodically analyze and appraise the organization's structure in light of any relevant changes.

## DEPARTMENTALIZATION

**departmentalization**
Grouping jobs into related work units.

While thousands of different organization structures exist, almost all are built on the concept of departmentalization. **Departmentalization** involves grouping jobs into related work units. The work units may be related on the basis of work functions, product, geography, customer, technique, or time.

These two groups of employees work for the same company, but they serve very different functions.

## Work Functions

**Functional departmentalization** occurs when organization units are defined by the nature of the work. Although different terms may be used, most organizations have four basic functions: production, marketing, finance, and human resources. Production refers to the actual creation of something of value, either goods, services, or both. Marketing involves product or service planning, pricing the product or service with respect to demand, evaluating how to best distribute the good or service, and communicating information to the market through sales and advertising. Any organization, whether manufacturing or service, must provide the financial structure necessary for carrying out its activities. The human resource function is responsible for securing and developing the organization's people.

Each of these basic functions may be broken down as necessary. For instance, the production department may be split into maintenance, quality control, engineering, manufacturing, and so on. The marketing department may be grouped into advertising, sales, and market research. Figure 8.5 charts a typical functional departmentalization.

The primary advantage of functional departmentalization is that it allows for specialization within functions. It also provides for efficient use of equipment and resources, potential economies of scale, and ease of coordination within the function itself. However, functional departmentalization can have some negative effects, such as when members of a functional group develop more loyalty to the functional group's goals than to the organization's goals. For example, the marketing department might be overzealous in selling products even when production cannot meet any additional demand. If the group's goals and the organization's goals are not mutually supportive, such activity can lead to problems. Conflict may also develop among different departments striving for different goals. In addition, employees who are locked into their functions

> **functional departmentalization**
> Defining organization units in terms of the nature of the work.

**figure 8.5**

FUNCTIONAL
DEPARTMENTALIZATION

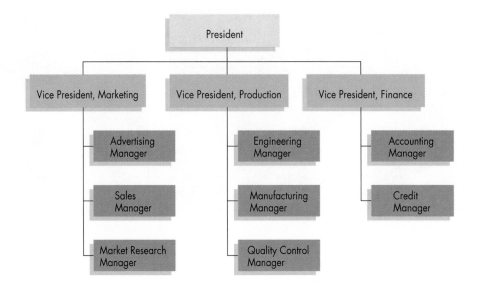

have a restricted view of the organization. Finally, the rather narrow functional scope of managers may be a disadvantage when a multidisciplinary approach would be more advantageous.

## Product

> **product departmentalization**
>
> Grouping all activities necessary to produce and market a product or service under one manager.

Under **product departmentalization,** all the activities needed to produce and market a product or service are usually under a single manager. This system allows employees to identify with a particular product and thus develop esprit de corps. It also facilitates managing each product as a distinct profit center. Product departmentalization provides opportunities for training for executive personnel by letting them experience a broad range of functional activities. Problems can arise if departments become overly competitive to the detriment of the overall organization. A second potential problem is duplication of facilities and equipment. Product departmentalization adapts best to large, multiproduct organizations. Figure 8.6 illustrates how a company might be structured using product departmentalization.

**figure 8.6**

PRODUCT
DEPARTMENTALIZATION

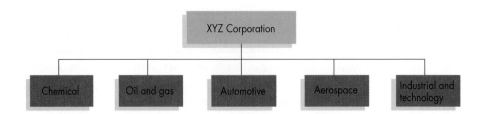

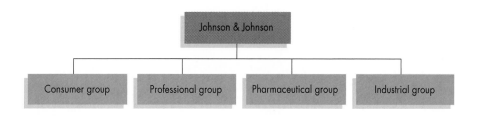

**figure 8.7**

CUSTOMER
DEPARTMENTALIZATION

## Geographic

**Geographic departmentalization** is most likely to occur in organizations that maintain physically isolated and independent operations or offices. Departmentalization by geography permits the use of local employees or salespeople. This can create customer goodwill and an awareness of local needs. It can also lead to a high level of service. Of course, having too many locations can be costly.

**geographic departmentalization**
Organization units by territories.

## Customer

**Customer departmentalization** is based on division by customers served. A common example is an organization that has one department to handle retail customers and one department to handle wholesale or industrial customers. Figure 8.7 shows departmentalization by customer for Johnson & Johnson. This type of departmentalization has the same advantages and disadvantages as product departmentalization. For example, if the professional group and the pharmaceutical group in Figure 8.7 became too competitive with each other for corporate resources, the organization's overall performance could suffer.

**customer departmentalization**
Organization units in terms of customers served.

## Other Types

Several other types of departmentalization are possible. Departmentalization by simple numbers is practiced when the most important ingredient for success is the number of employees. Organizing for a local United Way drive would be an example. Departmentalization by process or equipment is another possibility. A final type of departmentalization is by time or shift. Organizations that work around the clock may use this type of departmentalization.

## Hybrid Departmentalization

Typically, as an organization grows in size, it adds levels of departmentalization. A small organization may have no departmentalization at first. As it grows, it may departmentalize first on one basis, then another, and then another. For example, a large sales organization may use product departmentalization to create self-contained divisions; then each division might be further divided by geography and then by type

**hybrid departmentalization**
Occurs when an organization simultaneously uses more than one type of departmentalization.

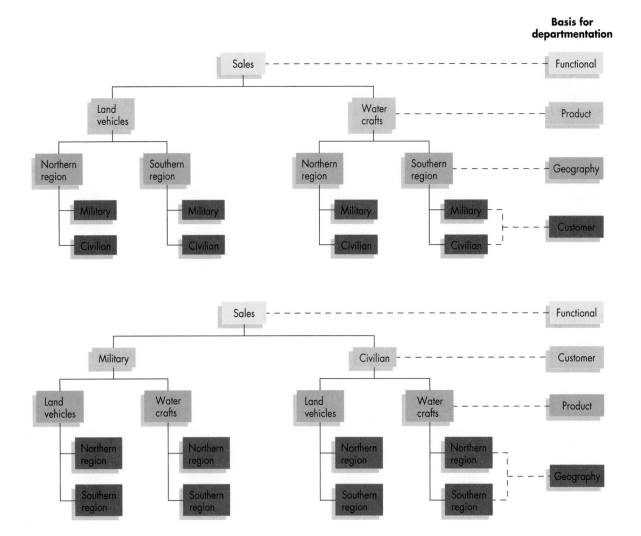

**Basis for departmentation**

## figure 8.8

**POSSIBLE DEPARTMENTALIZATION MIXES FOR A SALES ORGANIZATION**

of customer. **Hybrid departmentalization** occurs when an organization simultaneously uses more than one type of departmentalization. As Figure 8.8 illustrates, many different department mixes are possible for a given organization. Which one is best depends on the specific situation.

### PROGRESS CHECK QUESTIONS

5. What are the potential benefits and drawbacks of outsourcing?
6. Explain the contingency (situational) approach to organizing.
7. Explain the process of departmentalization.
8. Define the terms *geographic, customer,* and *hybrid departmentalization.*

# TYPES OF ORGANIZATIONAL STRUCTURES

There are several basic types of structures that organizations may use. Traditionally, these have been the line structure, the line and staff structure, or the matrix structure. Recently, new types of structures and organizations have evolved and are evolving to take advantage of the new communication and logistical technology available. These new structures include the horizontal structure and the virtual organization. Each type of structure is discussed in the following sections.

## Line Structure

In a *line organization,* authority originates at the top and moves downward in a line. All managers perform *line functions,* or functions that contribute directly to company profits. Examples of line functions include production managers, sales representatives, and marketing managers.

The most important aspect of the line structure is that the work of all organizational units is directly involved in producing and marketing the organization's goods or services. This is the simplest organization structure and is characterized by vertical links between the different levels of the organization. All members of the organization receive instructions through the chain of command. One advantage is a clear authority structure that promotes rapid decision making and prevents "passing the buck." A disadvantage is that it may force managers to perform too broad a range of duties. It may also cause the organization to become too dependent on one or two key employees who are capable of performing many duties. Because of its simplicity, line structure exists most frequently in small organizations. Figure 8.9 represents a simplified line structure.

## Line and Staff Structure

The addition of staff specialists to a line-structured organization creates a **line and staff structure.** As a line organization grows, staff assistance

**line and staff structure**
Organization structure that results when staff specialists are added to a line organization.

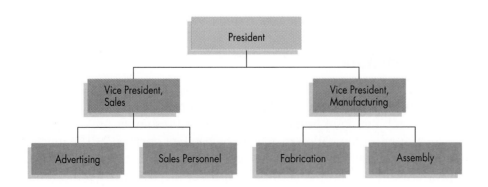

**figure 8.9**

**A SIMPLIFIED LINE STRUCTURE**

## figure 8.10

**A SIMPLIFIED LINE AND STAFF STRUCTURE**

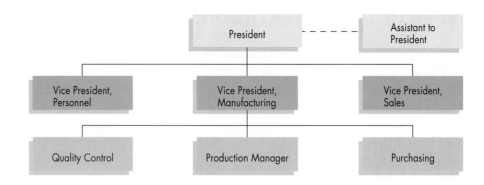

**staff functions**

Functions that are advisory and supportive in nature; designed to contribute to the efficiency and maintenance of the organization.

**line functions**

Functions and activities directly involved in producing and marketing the organization's goods or services.

often becomes necessary. **Staff functions** are advisory and supportive in nature; they contribute to the efficiency and maintenance of the organization. **Line functions** are directly involved in producing and marketing the organization's goods or services. They generally relate directly to the attainment of major organizational objectives, while staff functions contribute indirectly. Staff people are generally specialists in one field, and their authority is normally limited to making recommendations to line people. Typical staff functions include research and development, personnel management, employee training, and various "assistant to" positions. Figure 8.10 shows a simplified line and staff organization structure.

### Line and Staff Conflict

The line and staff organization allows much more specialization and flexibility than does the simple line organization; however, it sometimes creates conflict. Some staff specialists resent the fact that they may be only advisers to line personnel and have no real authority over the line. At the same time, line managers, knowing they have final responsibility for the product, are often reluctant to listen to staff advice. Many staff specialists think they should not be in a position of having to sell their ideas to the line. They believe the line managers should openly listen to their ideas. If the staff specialist is persistent, the line manager often resents even more that the staff "always tries to interfere and run my department." The staff specialist who does not persist often becomes discouraged because "no one ever listens."

## Matrix Structure

The matrix (sometimes called *project*) form of organization is a way of forming project teams within the traditional line and staff organization. A project is "a combination of human and nonhuman resources pulled together in a temporary organization to achieve a specified purpose."[15] The marketing of a new product and the construction of a new building are examples of projects. Because projects have a temporary life, a method of managing and organizing them was sought so that the existing organization structure would not be totally disrupted and would maintain some efficiency.

Under the **matrix structure,** those working on a project are officially assigned to the project and to their original or base departments. A manager is given the authority and responsibility to meet the project objectives in terms of cost, quality, quantity, and time of completion. The project manager is then assigned the necessary personnel from the functional departments of the parent organization. Thus, a horizontal-line organization develops for the project within the parent vertical-line structure. Under such a system, the functional personnel are assigned to and evaluated by the project manager while they work on the project. When the project or their individual work on it is done, the functional personnel return to their departments or begin a new project, perhaps with a new project team. Figure 8.11 shows a matrix structure.

A major advantage of matrix structure is that the mix of people and resources can readily be changed as project needs change. Other advantages include the emphasis placed on the project by use of a project team and the relative ease with which project members can move back into the functional organization once the project has ended. In addition, employees are

**matrix structure**

Hybrid organization structure in which individuals from different functional areas are assigned to work on a specific project or task.

## figure 8.11

**ILLUSTRATIVE MATRIX STRUCTURE**

***Source:*** From David Cleland and William King, *Systems Analysis and Project Management,* 3rd ed., 1983. Reproduced with permission of the McGraw-Hill Companies, Inc.

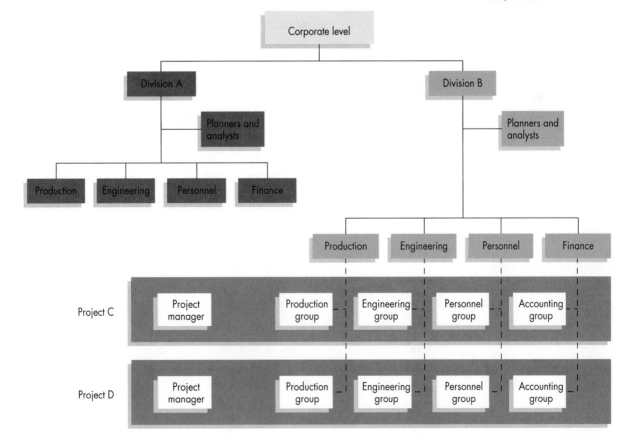

### Assessing Strengths and Weaknesses

Knowing our own strengths and weaknesses has great value. For one, we are able to be true to ourselves in how we approach our lives and the job(s) we are willing and able to do. The understanding of what we are good at allows us to work on the areas that need improvement. The very idea that we are honest in accepting our shortcomings and willing to work through the difficulties can create leads to internal exercises that we do to understand our strengths and weaknesses.

While it can be difficult to accept criticism or, at times, accept praise, we learn and grow into better, more productive workers when we learn and understand our strengths and weaknesses.

What might be your own personal strengths? Your weaknesses? What can you do to improve your weaknesses and better use your strengths? Do a self-evaluation, and find out how knowing strengths and weaknesses is knowing yourself!

challenged constantly, and interdepartmental cooperation develops along with expanded managerial talent due to the multitude of roles the project manager must undertake.

One serious problem with the matrix structure is that it can violate the principle of unity of command. A role conflict can develop if the authority of the project manager is not clearly delineated from that of the functional managers. In such a case, the people assigned to the project may receive conflicting assignments from the project manager and their functional managers. A second problem occurs when the personnel assigned to a project are still evaluated by their functional manager, who usually has little opportunity to observe their work on the project. Third, they defy tradition and put undue stress on communication networks.

## Horizontal Structure

A relatively new type of structure is the **horizontal structure** (also called *team structure*). The pure form of a horizontal structure consists of two core groups. One group is composed of senior management who are responsible for strategic decisions and policies. The second group is composed of empowered employees working together in different process teams. Figure 8.12 illustrates a basic horizontal structure. Characteristics of a horizontal organization include the following:

1. The organization is built around three to five core processes, such as developing new products, with specific performance goals assigned. Each process has an owner or champion.

**horizontal structure**

Consists of two groups. One group is composed of senior management who are responsible for strategic decisions and policies. The second group is composed of empowered employees working together in different process teams.

## figure 8.12

**HORIZONTAL STRUCTURE**

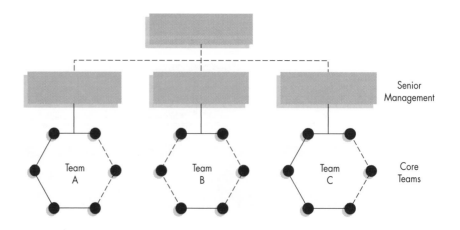

Senior Management

Team A

Team B

Team C

Core Teams

2. The hierarchy is flattened to reduce supervision.

3. Teams manage everything, including themselves. They're held accountable for performance goals.

4. Customers, not stock appreciation or profitability, drive performance.

5. Team performance, not just the individual, is rewarded. Staffers are encouraged to develop multiple skills and are rewarded for it.

6. Customer contact is maximized with employees.

7. Emphasis is on informing and training all employees. "Don't just spoon-feed information on a 'need to know' basis."[16]

As suggested above, the horizontal organization emphasizes customer satisfaction, rather than focusing on financial or functional goals. Information is processed at the local level by process teams. Local problems can often be resolved quickly by the process team, thus permitting the organization to operate with flexibility and responsiveness.[17]

Additional advantages of the horizontal organization include increased efficiency, improved work culture and morale, and more satisfied customers. Kraft Foods, Ford Motor Company, General Electric, British Airways, AT&T, Motorola, Saab, Tesco, and American Express Financial Advisors have all made efforts to implement a horizontal structure in at least a part of their organizations.

---

## PROGRESS CHECK QUESTIONS

9. How is a line and staff structure created?

10. Explain how the matrix organization structure works.

11. What is the major advantage of the matrix structure?

12. What are the seven characteristics of the horizontal organization structure?

---

# THE VIRTUAL ORGANIZATION

A **virtual organization** is one in which business partners and teams work together across geographical or organizational boundaries by means of information technology.[18] In a virtual organization, co-workers often do not see each other on a regular basis. Three common types of virtual organizations have been identified.[19]

**virtual organization**
Temporary network of independent companies— suppliers, customers, and even rivals—linked by information technology to share skills, costs, and access to one another's markets.

While these employees are actually working in a terminal, several Jet Blue customer service representatives work from home. This shift allows more employee freedom and reduces the overhead of office space. What are some of the pros and cons to allowing employees to use technology to escape traditional office confines?

One type exists when a group of skilled individuals form a company by communicating via computer, phone, fax, and video-conference. A second type occurs when a group of companies, each of which specializes in a certain function such as manufacturing or marketing, partner together. A third type occurs when one large company outsources many of its operations by using modern technology to transmit information to its partner companies so that it can focus on its specialty.

Virtual organizations create a network of collaborators that come together to pursue a specific opportunity. Once the opportunity has been realized, the collaborators usually disband and form new alliances to pursue new opportunities. Thus, virtual organizations are fluid, flexible, and constantly changing. Figure 8.13 illustrates a basic type of virtual organization.

Technology plays a central role in allowing virtual organizations to form. Integrated computer and communication technology are the means by which the different collaborators are put together. To illustrate one example of how a virtual organization might work, suppose you head a large company.[20] It's Christmas season, and your company needs an additional 100 customer service representatives. Once the Christmas rush is over, these additional service representatives won't be needed, so it makes no sense to hire permanent employees.

Instead, you hire 100 people who work at home and have their own computers. The physical location of these virtual employees doesn't matter; they can be in Cleveland, Hong Kong, or Singapore. The virtual employees dial into the company's database and become an extension of the company. Whenever a customer calls in, all information about that customer appears on the computer screen of the virtual employee handling the call; hence, the widely scattered employees can operate as if they are all at the same location. Once the Christmas rush is over, the collaboration is dissolved.

As outlined in Figure 8.14, virtual organizations have many potential benefits and challenges. Many people believe that some form of virtual organization is the wave of the future.

## figure 8.13

**VIRTUAL ORGANIZATION**

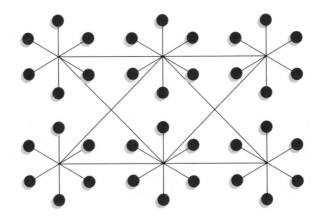

| BENEFITS | CHALLENGES |
|---|---|
| Increases productivity. | Leaders must move from a control model to a trust method. |
| Decreases the cost of doing business. | |
| Provides the ability to hire the best talent regardless of location. | New forms of communication and collaboration will be required. |
| Allows you to quickly solve problems by forming dynamic teams. | Management must enable a learning culture and be willing to change. |
| Allows you to more easily leverage both static and dynamic staff. | Staff reeducation may be required. |
| Improves the work environment. | It can be difficult to monitor employee behavior. |
| Provides better balance for professional and personal lives. | |
| Provides competitive advantage. | |

## figure 8.14

**BENEFITS AND CHALLENGES OF TRANSITIONING TO A VIRTUAL ORGANIZATION**

***Sources:*** Maggie Biggs, "Tomorrow's Workforce," *Infoworld,* September 18, 2000, p. 59; and Sonny Ariss, Nick Nykodym, and Aimee A. Cole-Laramore, "Trust and Technology in the Virtual Organization," *S.A.M. Advanced Management Journal,* Autumn 2002, pp. 22–25.

# TRENDS IN ORGANIZATION STRUCTURE

Several trends in organization structures have emerged over the last several decades. Beginning in the 1950s and 1960s, much attention was focused on the virtues of flat versus tall organization structures. A **flat structure** has relatively few levels and relatively large spans of management at each level; a **tall structure** has many levels and relatively small spans of management (see Figure 8.15). A classic study in this area was conducted by James Worthy.[21] Worthy studied the morale of over 100,000 employees at Sears and Roebuck during a 12-year period. His study noted that organizations with fewer levels and wider spans of management offered the potential for greater job satisfaction. A wide span of management also forced managers to delegate authority and develop more direct links of communication— another plus. On the other hand, Rocco Carzo and John Yanouzas found that groups operating in a tall structure had significantly better performance than those operating in a flat structure.[22] Other studies have also

**flat structure**
Organization with few levels and relatively large spans of management at each level.

**tall structure**
Organization with many levels and relatively small spans of management.

## figure 8.15

**FLAT VERSUS TALL STRUCTURES**

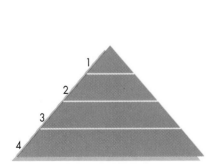

Span of management 8:1
Four levels
Flat structure

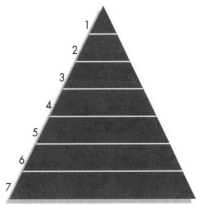

Span of management 5:1
Seven levels
Tall structure

shown conflicting results. Therefore, one cannot conclude that all flat structures are better than all tall structures, or vice versa.[23]

In general, Japanese organizations historically have had fewer middle managers and flatter structures than American organizations. For example, Toyota has historically had many fewer levels of management than has General Motors, Ford, or Chrysler. However, the downsizing many American organizations have experienced in the last several years has resulted in flatter structures with wider spans of control. Beginning in the early 1980s with the publication of the best-selling book *In Search of Excellence* by Thomas Peters and Robert Waterman, emphasis shifted to the concept of a simple form and a lean staff. Historically, as organizations grow and meet with success, they tend to evolve into increasingly complex structures. How this occurs varies; frequently, a major cause is an increase in staff positions, especially at high levels. Many managers seem to feel a need for more staff and a more complex structure as the organization grows. They seem inclined to equate staff size with success.

In their study, Peters and Waterman found that many of the best-performing companies had maintained simple structures with small staffs.[24] One reason is that a simple form with a lean staff allows an organization to adjust more rapidly to a fast-changing environment. It is also conducive to innovation. A simple form and a lean staff are naturally intertwined in that one breeds the other: A simple form requires fewer staff, and a lean staff results in a simple form.

More recently, many organizations have abandoned the more traditional line and staff structures in favor of horizontal structures and virtual organizations. All indications are that these trends will continue. As more and more employees become empowered, companies will put increased emphasis on managing through teams. Similarly, as communications technology continues to improve, many companies will evolve into virtual organizations.

## COMMITTEES

**committee**

Organization structure in which a group of people is formally appointed, organized, and superimposed on the line or line and staff structure to consider or decide certain matters.

Committees represent an important part of most traditional organization structures. A **committee** is a group of people formally appointed and organized to consider or decide certain matters. From a structural standpoint, committees are superimposed on the existing line, line and staff, or matrix structure. Committees can be permanent (standing) or temporary (ad hoc) and are usually in charge of, or supplementary to, the line and staff functions.

Teams are the counterpart to committees in nontraditional horizontal structures and virtual organizations. Because of their importance in today's organizations, the next chapter is devoted to understanding teams.

### Using Committees Effectively

Managers can do many things to avoid the pitfalls and increase the efficiency of a committee. The first step is to define clearly its functions, scope, and authority. Obviously, the members must know the purpose of

figure 8.16

**METHODS OF SELECTING COMMITTEES**

| METHOD | ADVANTAGES/DISADVANTAGES |
|---|---|
| Appointment of chairperson and members | Promotes sense of responsibility for all. May result in most capable members. Members may not work well together. |
| Appointment of chairperson who chooses members | Will probably get along well. Lack of sense of responsibility by members. May not be most capable or representative. |
| Appointment of members who elect chairperson | Lack of sense of responsibility by chairperson. May not choose best chairperson for the job. Election of chairperson may lead to split in the committee. |
| Volunteers | Will get those who have greatest interest in the outcome or those who are least busy. Lack of responsibility. Potential for splits among committee members is great. |

the committee to function effectively. If it is a temporary committee, the members should be informed of its expected duration. This will help avoid prolonging the life of the committee unnecessarily. Those responsible for establishing a committee should carefully communicate the limits of the committee's authority. This should be done very soon after the committee has been established.

In addition, careful thought should go into the selection of the committee members and chairperson. Size is always an important variable; generally, committees become more inefficient as they grow in size. A good rule of thumb is to use the smallest group necessary to get the job done. It is more important to select capable members than representative members. It is also important to pick members from the same approximate organizational level. Members from higher levels may inhibit the actions and participation of the other members. Figure 8.16 lists several methods for selecting committee members and chairpeople and outlines advantages and disadvantages for each method.

## Boards of Directors

A **board of directors** is really a type of committee that is responsible for reviewing the major policy and strategy decisions proposed by top management. A board of directors can be characterized as either an inside or an outside board. On an *inside board,* a majority of the members hold management positions in the organization; on an *outside board,* a majority of the members do not hold or have not held a position with the organization. While insiders who are members of a board ordinarily have other duties related to the strategic management process by virtue of their corporate position, the role the board plays as an entity should be basically the same for both types. Board members do not necessarily need to own stock (although many organizations require that they do); they should be chosen primarily for what they can and will contribute to the organization.

**board of directors**
Carefully selected committee that reviews major policy and strategy decisions proposed by top management.

A board of directors can play a vital role in the changing shape of a company. *What are some skills you believe a board of directors should have?*

Although most boards of directors restrict their inputs to the policy and strategy level and do not participate in the day-to-day operations of the organization, their degree of involvement varies widely from board to board. For many years, boards were used primarily as figureheads in many organizations, contributing little to the organization. However, this trend has been changing over the last several years. Recent lawsuits against boards of directors concerning their liabilities regarding the day-to-day operation of the organization have increased the risks of serving on boards.[25] Because of this, boards are becoming more active than they have been in the past. Moreover, some people now require liability insurance coverage before they will serve on a board of directors. An even more recent development is the tendency of shareholders to demand that the chairperson of the board be an outsider who is not employed in another capacity by the organization. Every diligent board of directors should address itself on behalf of the shareholders to this key issue: What is the standard of performance of the company's management—not what the company earned last year or this year, but what it *should* have earned?[26]

## CONCLUSION

Organization structure defines the boundaries of the formal organization and establishes the environment within which the organization operates. An appropriate organization structure helps ensure good performance, but the question as to whether a manager succeeds because of or in spite of an organization structure remains open for debate. This chapter has presented several different approaches to organization structure and offered different types of structure for your review. With all these options available, the key point to remember is that the organization structure should clearly establish who makes the decisions, how those decisions are made and where responsibility for performance lies. In the next chapter we'll review how the management of the people who work within the organization structure can mean the difference between success and failure.

### PROGRESS CHECK QUESTIONS

13. What are the potential benefits and challenges of a virtual organization?
14. List three types of virtual organization.
15. Explain the difference between flat and tall structures. Which is better? Why?
16. Why are boards of directors becoming more active than they have in the past?

## A New Organization Structure

Yesterday, Tom Andrews was officially promoted to his new job as hospital administrator for Cobb General Hospital. Cobb General is a 600-bed hospital located in a suburban area of Cincinnati. Tom is extremely excited about the promotion but at the same time has some serious doubts about it.

Tom has worked at Cobb General for three years and had previously served as the associate administrator of the hospital. Although associate administrator was his official job title, he was really more of an errand boy for the former administrator, Bill Collins. Because of Tom's educational background (which includes a master of hospital administration degree) and his enthusiasm for the hospital, Tom was offered the administrator's job last week after the hospital's board of directors had asked for Bill Collins's resignation.

Tom was now looking at the organization chart for the hospital, which had been pieced together over the years by Bill Collins (see Figure 8.17). In reality, each time a new unit had been added or a new function started, Bill merely had the person report directly to him. Tom is worried about his ability to handle all the people currently reporting to him in his new position.

### Questions

1. Do you think Tom has the necessary skills and experience for this position? Why or why not?

2. How would you describe Cobb General's current organizational structure?

3. Do you agree with Tom's concern? Why?

4. How would you redraw the organizational chart?

## figure 8.17

ORGANIZATION STRUCTURE—COBB GENERAL HOSPITAL

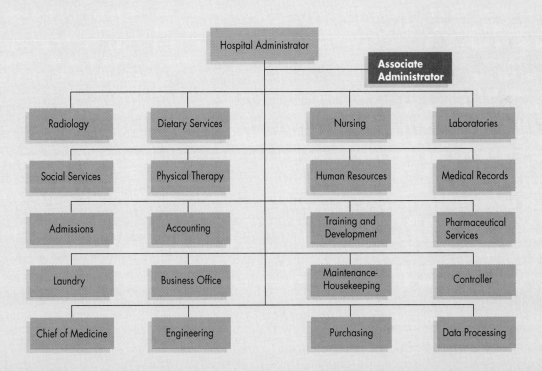

## "Taco Barn To Go"

Tony had not been convinced that the new "To Go" project would live up to everyone's high expectations. There were a couple of trade magazine articles featuring Taco Barn's use of "cutting-edge technology to deliver superior customer service," but they were printed when the project was still in the development stage. "Probably a good thing," thought Tony, since the implementation wasn't delivering the promised cost savings, at least not yet.

The "To Go" project had been all about costs savings, which was why the idea of using an Indian call center had been so attractive. The quoted cost per order processed had been less than half the number quoted by U.S. providers of the same service. However, as the project had progressed, it became clear that a lot of the setup costs to get the service off the ground had not been included in that quoted cost per order processed. Suddenly everything was going to cost more—sending Taco Barn personnel overseas to train the call center people on the Taco Barn restaurant concept and the intricacies of the menu from which customers would be ordering and bringing Indian call center managers to the United States to see Taco Barns in operation—all of this had to be paid for before the first order was taken.

To make sure costs were minimized, most of these expenses were scaled back. Call center managers were shown internal Taco Barn training videos rather than visiting the U.S. units; training of the call center personnel was handled by conference calls where Indian trainers were walked through the menu so that they could then train their people on how to take telephone orders. Call center managers assured Taco Barn executives that this would not be a problem, since they handled calls for many U.S. manufacturers and their products—computers, cellular phones, tech support and many other services.

A few weeks later, Tony received notice in an e-mail that his region had been selected as the pilot region for testing the "To Go" project and that it would start the following Friday. "Great," Tony said to himself, "start it on a busy night. Why not start it on Saturday night and really cause some confusion?"

Tony had never considered himself to be a pessimist, but the first night's trial run performed even worse than he had expected. Some customers called the central ordering number and then called the restaurant to make sure the order had come through. Other customers called the restaurant to complain that the "girl on the phone had a strange accent and didn't understand her." Still more customers complained that they couldn't switch out menu items like they did in their local Taco Barn.

On the restaurant's side of this experiment, orders came through with incorrect items or wrong numbers of items or items the restaurant didn't even serve. Some items never arrived at all, which caused much confusion and scrambling when the customer showed up 30 minutes after placing the order expecting to drive away with a freshly prepared meal.

After two weeks of trials, the "To Go" project was pulled from Tony's region, and all parties involved went back to the drawing board. Tony was left with a 15-page assessment report to fill out.

"Where do I start?" thought Tony.

### QUESTIONS

1. Where does Tony start here? What went wrong with the implementation of "Taco Barn To Go".

2. Could these mistakes have been anticipated? Why or why not?

3. How do you think Tony's local customers have been impacted by this project?

4. What should Taco Barn do now? Explain your answer.

## key terms

| | | |
|---|---|---|
| **board of directors** 223 | **geographic departmentalization** 213 | **organic systems** 204 |
| **committee** 222 | **horizontal structure** 218 | **organization structure** 202 |
| **contingency (situational) approach** 210 | **hybrid departmentalization** 213 | **outsourcing** 208 |
| **customer departmentalization** 213 | **line and staff structure** 215 | **product departmentalization** 212 |
| **departmentalization** 210 | **line functions** 216 | **staff functions** 216 |
| **flat structure** 221 | **matrix structure** 217 | **tall structure** 221 |
| **functional departmentalization** 211 | **mechanistic systems** 204 | **virtual organization** 219 |

## review questions

1. Describe the general relationship between an organization's strategy and its structure.
2. What factors contribute to potential conflict between line and staff personnel in a line and staff organization?
3. If you were an employee and your company embarked on a large-scale outsourcing program, how would you react?
4. Do you think virtual organizations are going to become more and more prominent in the future? Why or why not?

## internet exercise

Identify the most recent list of most admired companies as selected by *Fortune* magazine.

Select two companies from the top 10 and two companies from the bottom 10 on the list. Using Internet resources, determine how many outside directors and how many inside directors are serving each company.

1. Do these companies have a majority of inside or outside directors?
2. Are there any obvious differences in the composition of the boards of those companies from the top of the most admired list compared to those from the bottom of the list?
3. Do you think the trend is toward more inside or more outside directors? Why?
4. If you were a shareholder of any of these companies, would you prefer to have more inside or outside directors? Why?

## team exercise

Divide the class into two or three teams. Each team should select a company whose product is being sold in a highly competitive marketplace. On the assumption that the product has not been selling well against its competition, despite clear design and functionality advantages, it has been decided that there is a need to reorganize the sales division. You can make any reasonable assumptions you think are necessary to complete the following tasks:

1. Design what you think would be the best way to organize the sales (marketing) division of your company.
2. Design an alternative structure for your division.
3. Why do you prefer one structure over the other?
4. Design a matrix structure for this situation (if you did not use one in question 1 or 2). What would be the pros and cons of such a structure in this situation?

## China's First Global Capitalist

*Lenovo Chairman Yang Yuanqing Is Building a New Breed of Multinational*

Yang Yuanqing, 42, chairman of Lenovo Group Ltd., leads the world's third-largest PC company, with $13 billion in revenues. Last year, when Lenovo bought IBM PC Co., Yang stepped onto the world stage. He became the first Chinese executive to lead the takeover of an iconic Western business. In one swoop, he took on the world's leading technology companies. Now, as China's first truly global capitalist, he has a chance to help his homeland shed its image as a cheap manufacturing hub. But Yang Yuanqing may turn out to be much more. From the moment he was tapped at age 29 to shake up the struggling PC unit of Lenovo's predecessor company, Legend, Yang has defied the stereotype of a Chinese manager. Today he is emerging as the first of a hybrid class of leader, marrying the drive and creativity of Western management with the vast efficiencies of China's manufacturing operations.

The honeymoon after the IBM PC purchase is long over. This spring, Yang ran into a buzz saw of Washington Beltway politics when congressional concerns about security forced the State Dept. to change the way it used some of the 14,000 PCs it had ordered from Lenovo. Responding to worries that Chinese government snooping technology could be tucked into the machines, the department redirected some of them to less sensitive projects. There has been plenty of friction inside Lenovo, too. Last December, Yang and the board pushed out his second-in-command, former IBMer Steve Ward, in part because he was too slow to cut costs. Ward's replacement as CEO is the frenetic William J. Amelio, who formerly ran Asian operations for Dell Inc. It's an oddball management setup. Yang runs the company, and Amelio reports to him. But they share a lot of responsibilities for overseeing this sprawling organization on a near-equal basis. Lenovo sells products in no fewer than 66 countries and develops them at labs in China, the U.S., and Japan. Yang and Amelio also must mix the best people and traits of the old Lenovo with those of IBM. In essence, they're blending two national cultures and, to add to the stress, three corporate ones, since Amelio has been replacing some of the top executives from Lenovo and IBM with his own team, mostly from Dell. Rarely if ever has a corporate leader had to manage such a tangled web of relationships.

Yang's strategy is ambitious. Over the next couple of years, he wants to boost Lenovo's already dominant 35 percent market share in China while expanding to other emerging markets. In the West, he taps IBM for help in selling to large corporations. But for small and midsize businesses, Lenovo is now mimicking its China strategy and offering a new line of PCs through a host of retailers. Meanwhile, the company is retooling the old IBM PC Co. manufacturing supply chain to make it as efficient as Lenovo's China operations.

Former IBM engineers say things have changed for the better since the merger—and in ways you might not expect. Yang has kept research and development spending constant as a percentage of revenues. But because more of the work is being done in China, where engineers cost one-fifth what they do in the U.S., he gets more bang for the buck. He has also dedicated 20 percent of his R&D budget for cutting-edge ideas. Under U.S. management, the unit had become focused largely on cost cutting.

Figuring out exactly what role Yang should play in the company has been tricky. He engineered the IBM acquisition, yet during the transition seemed to fade into the background. Initial encounters between Yang and Amelio were tense. No wonder: They had been head-to-head competitors in the China market. Amelio recalls their first awkward one-on-one session at a Hong Kong hotel: "Here we were, two guys who have been trying to slit each other's throats talking about doing something together." At their second meeting, Yang surprised Amelio by pulling out a single sheet of paper listing the roles for Lenovo's chairman and CEO. His job included setting corporate and technology strategy and communicating with investors. Amelio's main task was running the PC business day-to-day. This is not the typical split between chairman and CEO—Yang would be much more hands-on, like a co-CEO. Amelio went along without complaint. Now they're a tag team. Yang goes deep on his specialties, which include marketing and distribution. Amelio, meanwhile, concentrates on fine-tuning the supply chain. Shortly after the IBM PC takeover, the board created a powerful strategy committee headed by Yang but packed with other strong voices, including company co-founder Liu Chuanzhi. At first, the committee met monthly; now, it meets just once a quarter.

Yang's big opportunity came in 2003, when he learned that IBM was interested in selling off its large but money-losing PC unit as part of its move to services. Yang saw this deal as a way for Legend, which was about to rebrand itself as Lenovo, to leap onto the world stage without having to grind it out country by country. But the entire board of directors lined up against Yang. Think about what he was asking the Lenovo elders to do: A $3 billion company based in China would be taking over a $10 billion global behemoth. IBM had practically invented the PC industry; if Big Blue couldn't make money selling these machines worldwide, how could little Lenovo hope to do any better? Yang and his team dug in. They made presentation after presentation to the board until the endless meetings took on the feel of a court trial. Eventually, Yang prevailed. He agreed to give up the CEO role to a more worldly Western executive and convinced the board that he could make the former IBM operations more profitable.

## Questions

1. How has Yang managed to defy the stereotype of a Chinese manager?

2. Explain how Yang and Amelio operate "as a tag team."

3. What problems are presented in "blending two national cultures and, to add to the stress, three corporate ones"?

4. How would you organize a company that "sells products in no fewer than 66 countries and develops them at labs in China, the U.S., and Japan"?

*Source:* Adapted from Steve Hamm and Dexter Roberts, "Global Business," *BusinessWeek*, December 11, 2006.

## Blueprint from India

*More Architecture Firms Are Offshoring*

Even in Las Vegas, a city not known for understatement, the overhaul of the Tropicana Casino & Resort is grandiose. When the $2 billion face-lift is completed in 2010, the hotel will have more than 10,200 rooms, a new convention center and shopping mall, parking for 6,200 cars, and multiple pools. That's great for gamblers, but it's a big challenge for the architects putting all the pieces together. "It's like building three mega-resorts at once," says Jim Stapleton, vice-president of Cincinnati-based FRCH Design Worldwide, the lead architect on the project. Adding to the complexity, gaming tables and sections of the hotel will remain open through the renovation. Worse, it's happening at a time when U.S. architects are in short supply.

Time to call India. In a cramped office in Kolkata, some 8,000 miles from the Strip, dozens of Indian architects spend their days and often nights generating plans for the Tropicana. They work for Cadforce Inc., a Marina del Rey (Calif.) startup that is helping bring offshore outsourcing to yet another U.S. sector. All told, Cadforce has some 150 designers and computer technicians in India and 41 in the U.S. working on a new hospital in San Diego, private homes, fast-food joints, and more. "The tidal wave of interest has just begun

in the last year," says Cadforce CEO Robert W. Vanech, a venture capitalist who founded the company in 2001. Cadforce is one of a growing number of companies jumping into the business. The $29 billion U.S. architecture industry ships about $100 million in work abroad each year, Cadforce estimates. Some 20 percent of U.S. firms say they are offshoring, according to a survey by Harvard University and the American Institute of Architects (AIA), while an additional 30 percent are considering doing so.

"Clients are demanding shorter and shorter turnarounds, smaller fees, and better details," says Harvard doctoral student David del Villar, who helped lead the study.

While the work isn't glamorous, many Indian architects say it's a great opportunity. Rather than developing complete designs, architects in these outsourcing shops tend to handle tasks such as turning schematic drawings into blueprints or making sure doors and pipes are aligned. These are essential jobs, but they're tedious and can take up 60 percent of the time spent designing a building. Nonetheless, 25-year-old Aditi Sengupta jumped at the opportunity to join Cadforce. "It's a chance to work with more space and nicer materials," she says. Digitization is one big force driving the trend. More architectural firms are adopting sophisticated computer tools that allow them to render entire buildings in 3D, simulate stress tests, and track all construction materials. That makes it easier to work remotely—and requires tech skills that can be hard to find in the U.S. "The challenge isn't cost. It's understanding the processes and systems," says Michael Jansen, CEO of Satellier, a New Delhi–based group with 300 staffers doing work for half of the top 30 U.S. architecture firms.

## JUST FOR NOW?

Not everyone is convinced the future of architecture lies offshore. AIA Chief Economist Kermit Baker thinks the outsourcing surge is largely the result of a cyclical talent crunch. He notes that the pay gap between U.S. and Indian architects isn't nearly as wide as in, say, software programming. Many American architects with 10 or 15 years of experience earn up to $60,000 annually—about four times what Indians take home. That compares with salary differentials of 8 to 10 times in software. "If the job market softens, there will be a lot less incentive to outsource," Baker predicts. Still, many firms say outsourcing pays. Acres Group Inc., a firm in Pasadena, Calif., that specializes in

fast-food restaurants, has been able to take on 75 percent more work by outsourcing some tasks to Cadforce. While Acres is saving money—President Robert Liu says he has been able to lower his fees by 30 percent—other factors are more important. "They do the most time-consuming, technical work," Liu says. "It allows me to do other things, like get more clients and concentrate on design."

## Questions

1. Describe the factors in the U.S. architectural industry that are driving this trend to send work overseas.

2. What are the potential benefits and challenges of offshoring in this manner?

3. If the availability of U.S. architects increases, will the amount of work sent offshore decrease? Why or why not?

4. Do you think these Indian architects will always work on the "tedious" portions of large designs? Why or why not?

*Source:* Reprinted with special permission from *Business Week Online*. Global Business, April 2, 2007, by Pete Engardio, with Nandini Lakshman in Kolkata.

# ORGANIZING PEOPLE

**"I will pay more for the ability to deal with people than any other ability under the sun."**

—John D. Rockefeller

## The World Of Work: Kevin makes a suggestion

Tony had promoted Kevin to shift leader after Tanya had announced her resignation. Kevin had proven to be a smart choice. He had done a great job on the scheduling project, and Tony was already grooming him for the management development program in anticipation of Dawn assigning Kevin to his own Taco Barn unit in the future.

Kevin was enthusiastic and constantly coming up with new ideas, and today was no exception. Tony was working on the produce order for the next day when Kevin knocked on the office door.

"Tony, do you have a couple of minutes?"

"Sure, Kevin, what do you need?"

"I'd like to run an idea by you about my shift crew. You know the scheduling project we worked on?"

"Yes," answered Tony, wondering where this conversation was headed.

"Well, they've been bitten by the bug, and now they want to work on some other projects as a team. To be honest, Tony, I know you gave me a lot of credit for that scheduling project, but they did most of the work, and I think they've got some really good ideas for improving our food ordering and our inventory management. How would you feel about letting them

**After studying this chapter, you will be able to:**

1    Outline the human resource planning process.

2    Define job analysis, job description, job specification, and skills inventory.

3    Distinguish between affirmative action and reverse discrimination.

4    Explain formal and informal work groups.

5    Discuss the concept of team building.

6    Define Groupthink.

---

meet for half an hour once or twice a week to work on their ideas? They'll have to come to you for budget approval if they want to spend any money, and I'll make sure that their work doesn't suffer—what do you think?"

Tony's first reaction was a brief panic that if his crew started coming up with all the new ideas, Dawn wouldn't have a reason for keeping him around, but he was impressed by Kevin's willingness to go to bat for his people and his support and confidence in their abilities.

"I think that's a great idea, Kevin," said Tony. "Ask them to pick a project, and give them a couple of weeks to work on it. Then we can look at what they come up with and see if it's worth putting it in front of Dawn for approval.

"Thanks, Tony—I think you'll be really surprised with what they come up with," said Kevin.

**QUESTIONS**

1. Why would Tony's first reaction to Kevin's idea be one of panic?

2. Why is Kevin supporting his people in this manner? What's in it for him?

3. Do you think Tony is making a mistake here? Why or why not?

4. Would this idea work at your company? Why or why not?

# STAFFING

The staffing function of management involves securing and developing people to perform the jobs created by the organizing function. The goal of staffing is to obtain the best available people for the organization and to develop the skills and abilities of those people. Obtaining the best available people generally involves forecasting personnel requirements and recruiting and selecting new employees. Developing the skills and abilities of an organization's employees involves employee development as well as the proper use of promotions, transfers, and separations. The staffing function is complicated by numerous government regulations. Furthermore, many of these regulations are subject to frequent change.

Unfortunately, many staffing activities have traditionally been conducted by human resource/personnel departments and have been considered relatively unimportant by line managers. However, securing and developing qualified personnel should be a major concern of all managers because it involves the most valuable asset of an organization: human resources.

# JOB ANALYSIS

**job analysis**

Process of determining, through observation and study, the pertinent information relating to the nature of a specific job.

**Job analysis** is the process of determining, through observation and study, the relevant information relating to the nature of a specific job. The end products of a job analysis are a job description and a job specification. A **job description** is a written statement that identifies the tasks, duties, activities, and performance results required in a particular job. The job description should be used to develop fair and comprehensive compensation and reward systems. In addition, the accuracy of the job description can help or hinder recruiters in their efforts to attract qualified applicants for positions within the company. A **job specification** is a written statement that identifies the abilities, skills, traits, or attributes necessary for successful performance in a particular job. In general, a job specification identifies the qualifications of an individual who could perform the job. Job analyses are frequently conducted by specialists from the human resource department. However, managers should have input into the final job descriptions for the jobs they are managing.

**job description**

Written statement that identifies the tasks, duties, activities, and performance results required in a particular job.

**job specification**

Written statement that identifies the abilities, skills, traits, or attributes necessary for successful performance in a particular job.

## Skills Inventory

**skills inventory**

Consolidates information about the organization's current human resources.

Through conducting job analysis, an organization defines its current human resource needs on the basis of existing or newly created jobs. A **skills inventory** consolidates information about the organization's current human resources. The skills inventory contains basic information about each employee of the organization, giving a comprehensive picture of the individual. Through analyzing the skills inventory, the organization can assess the current quantity and quality of its human resources.

Six broad categories of information that may be included in a skills inventory are:

1. Skills: education, job experience, training, etc.
2. Special qualifications: memberships in professional groups, special achievements, etc.
3. Salary and job history: present salary, past salary, dates of raises, various jobs held, etc.
4. Company data: benefit plan data, retirement information, seniority, etc.
5. Capacity of individual: scores on tests, health information, etc.
6. Special preferences of individual: location or job preferences, etc.

**Positive Attitude and Its Importance**

How would you respond to the question, "Are you a positive person?" What variables might come into play that affect your mental outlook? Have your life experiences been less than positive and, therefore, affected your attitude, making it more negative than positive? If you think about your disposition, how does it affect the following areas of your life?

- Schoolwork and effort
- Your current relationships
- Your current job
- Your effort to get things done
- The perception of how others look at you
- Your potential to excel in your life

Your attitude is the conduit to all the outcomes you encounter. A good attitude has positive results that help place you in a better light to all those you come in contact with!

The primary advantage of a computerized skills inventory is that it offers a quick and accurate evaluation of the skills available within the organization. Combining the information provided by the job analysis and the skills inventory enables the organization to evaluate the present status of its human resources.

Specialized versions of the skills inventory can also be devised and maintained. One example would be the management inventory, which would separately evaluate the specific skills of managers, such as strategy development, experiences (e.g., international experience or language skill), and successes or failures at administration or leadership.

In addition to appraising the current status of its human resources, the organization must consider anticipated changes in the current workforce due to retirements, deaths, discharges, promotions, transfers, and resignations. Certain changes in personnel can be estimated accurately and easily, whereas other changes are more difficult to forecast.

**Human resource planning (HRP),** also referred to as *personnel planning,* involves getting the right number of qualified people into the right job at the right time. Put another way, HRP involves matching the supply of people—internally (existing employees) and externally (those to be hired)—with the openings the organization expects to have for a given time frame.

HRP involves applying the basic planning process to the human resource needs of the organization. Once organizational plans are made and specific objectives set, the HRP process attempts to define the human resource needs to meet the organization's objectives.

The first basic question addressed by the planning process is, Where are we now? Human resource planning frequently answers this question by using job analysis and skills inventories.

**human resource planning (HRP)**

Process of getting the right number of qualified people into the right job at the right time. Also called *personnel planning.*

## Forecasting

The second basic question the organization addresses in the planning process is, Where do we want to go? **Human resource forecasting** attempts to answer this question with regard to the organization's human resource needs. It is a process that attempts to determine the future human resource needs of the organization in relation to the organization's objectives. Some of the many variables considered in forecasting human resource needs include sales projections, skills required in potential business ventures, composition of the present workforce, technological changes, and general economic conditions. Given the critical role human resources play in attaining organizational objectives, all levels of management should be involved in the forecasting process.

Human resource forecasting is often conducted largely on the basis of intuition; the experience and judgment of the manager are used to determine future human resource needs. This assumes all managers are aware of the future plans of the total organization. Unfortunately, this is not true in many cases.

## Transition

In the final phase of human resource planning, the transition, the organization determines how it can obtain the quantity and quality of human resources it needs to meet its objectives as reflected by the human resource forecast. The human resource forecast results in a statement of what the organization's human resource needs are in light of its plans and objectives. The organization engages in several transitional activities to bring its current level of human resources in line with forecast requirements. These activities include recruiting and selecting new employees, developing current or new employees, promoting or transferring employees, laying off employees, and discharging employees. Given the current trend of downsizing in many organizations, some human resource departments now maintain a replacement chart for each employee. This confidential chart shows a diagram of each position in the management hierarchy and a list of candidates who would be qualified to replace a particular person should the need arise. Generally, the coordination of all the activities mentioned earlier is delegated to a human resource or personnel department within the organization. Figure 9.1 shows the relationship between job analysis, skills inventory, and human resource planning.

## Legal Considerations

Due to discriminatory personnel practices by many organizations, government regulation now plays a vital role in human resource planning. The following paragraphs describe the significant government bills and laws that have affected human resource planning.

The **Equal Pay Act of 1963,** which became effective in June 1964, prohibits wage discrimination on the basis of sex. The law states,

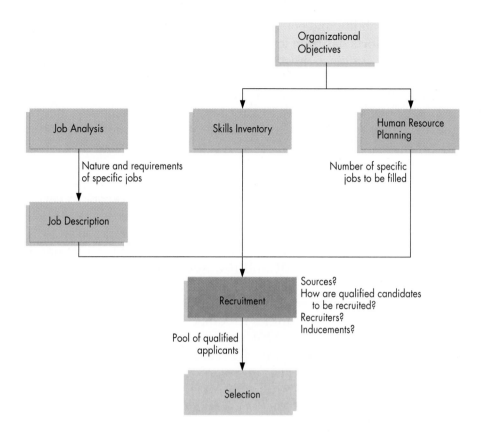

**figure 9.1**

RELATIONSHIP BETWEEN
JOB ANALYSIS, SKILLS
INVENTORY, HUMAN
RESOURCE PLANNING,
RECRUITMENT, AND
SELECTION

*No employer . . . shall . . . discriminate . . . between employees on the basis of sex by paying wages . . . at a rate less than the rate at which he pays wages to employees of the opposite sex . . . for equal work on jobs the performance of which requires equal skill, effort, and responsibility and which are performed under similar working conditions.*[1]

**Title VII of the Civil Rights Act of 1964** is designed to eliminate employment discrimination related to race, color, religion, sex, or national origin in organizations that conduct interstate commerce. The act as amended covers the following types of organizations:

1. All private employers of 15 or more employees.
2. All educational institutions, public and private.
3. State and local governments.
4. Public and private employment agencies.
5. Labor unions with 15 or more members.
6. Joint labor-management committees for apprenticeship and training.

Congress passed the Civil Rights Act to establish guidelines for ensuring equal employment opportunities for all people. **Equal employment opportunity** refers to the right of all people to work and to advance on the

**Title VII of the Civil Rights Act of 1964**
Designed to eliminate employment discrimination related to race, color, religion, sex, or national origin.

**equal employment opportunity**
The right of all people to work and to advance on the bases of merit, ability, and potential.

bases of merit, ability, and potential. One major focus of equal employment opportunity efforts has been to identify and eliminate discriminatory employment practices. Such practices are any artificial, arbitrary, and unnecessary barriers to employment when the barriers operate to discriminate on the basis of sex, race, or another impermissible classification.

The **Age Discrimination in Employment Act** went into effect on June 12, 1968. Initially it was designed to protect individuals 40 to 65 years of age from discrimination in hiring, retention, compensation, and other conditions of employment. In 1978, the act was amended, and coverage was extended to individuals up to age 70. Specifically, the act now forbids mandatory retirement at age 65 except in certain circumstances.

The **Rehabilitation Act of 1973** prohibits discrimination in hiring of individuals with disabilities by federal agencies and federal contractors. The **Americans with Disabilities Act (ADA) of 1990** gives individuals with disabilities sharply increased access to services and jobs. Both acts have given citizens with disabilities protection in the workplace and increased opportunities to compete for jobs.

The **Civil Rights Act of 1991** permits women, minorities, persons with disabilities, and persons who are religious minorities to have a jury trial and sue for punitive damages of up to $300,000 if they can prove they are victims of intentional hiring or workplace discrimination. The law covers all employers with 15 or more employees. Prior to the passage of this law, jury trials and punitive damages were not permitted except in intentional discrimination lawsuits involving racial discrimination. The law places a cap on the amount of damages a victim of nonracial, intentional discrimination can collect. The cap is based on the size of the employer.

A second aspect of this act concerned the burden of proof for companies with regard to intentional discrimination lawsuits. In a series of Supreme Court decisions beginning in 1989, the Court began to ease the burden-of-proof requirements on companies. This act, however, requires that companies provide evidence that the business practice that led to the discrimination was not discriminatory but was related to the performance of the job in question and consistent with business necessity.

The **Family and Medical Leave Act (FMLA)** was enacted in 1993 to enable qualified employees to take prolonged unpaid leave for family- and health-related reasons without fear of losing their jobs. Under the law, employees can use this leave if they are seriously ill, if an immediate family member is ill, or in the event of the birth, adoption, or placement for foster care of a child.

The results of discrimination are not always as obvious as hiring and firing practices. Communication, managerial and promotional career paths, and networking that are essential to employees' success in the workplace also can be affected by indirect discrimination. Figure 9.2 summarizes the laws related to equal employment opportunity.

| LAW | YEAR | INTENT | COVERAGE |
|---|---|---|---|
| Equal Pay Act | 1963 | Prohibits sexual-based discrimination in rates of pay for men and women working in the same or similar jobs. | Private employers engaged in commerce or in the production of goods for commerce and with two or more employees; labor organizations. |
| Title VII, Civil Rights Act (as amended in 1972) | 1964 | Prohibits discrimination based on race, sex, color, religion, or national origin. | Private employers with 15 or more employees for 20 or more weeks per year, educational institutions, state and local governments, employment agencies, labor unions, and joint labor–management committees. |
| Age Discrimination in Employment Act (ADEA) | 1967 | Prohibits discrimination against individuals who are 40 years of age and older. | Private employers with 20 or more employees for 20 or more weeks per year, labor organizations, employment agencies, state and local governments, and federal agencies with some exceptions. |
| Rehabilitation Act (as amended) | 1973 | Prohibits discrimination against persons with disabilities and requires affirmative action to provide employment opportunity for these individuals. | Federal contractors and subcontractors with contracts in excess of $2,500, organizations receiving federal financial assistance, federal agencies. |
| Vietnam-Era Veterans Readjustment Assistance Act | 1974 | Prohibits discrimination in hiring disabled veterans with 30 percent or more disability rating, veterans discharged or released for a service-connected disability, and veterans on active duty between August 5, 1964, and May 7, 1975. Also requires written affirmative action plans for certain employers. | Federal contractors and subcontractors with contracts in excess of $10,000. Employers with 50 or more employees and contracts in excess of $50,000 must have written affirmative action plans. |
| Pregnancy Discrimination Act (PDA) | 1978 | Requires employers to treat pregnancy just like any other medical condition with regard to fringe benefits and leave policies. | Same as Title VII, Civil Rights Act. |
| Immigration Reform and Control Act | 1986 | Prohibits hiring of illegal aliens. | Any individual or company. |
| Americans with Disabilities Act | 1990 | Increases access to services and jobs for persons with disabilities. | Private employers with 15 or more employees. |
| Civil Rights Act | 1991 | Permits women, minorities, persons with disabilities, and persons who are religious minorities to have a jury trial and to sue for punitive damages if they can prove intentional hiring and workplace discrimination. Also requires companies to provide evidence that the business practice that led to the discrimination was not discriminatory but was related to the position in question and consistent with business necessity. | Private employers with 15 or more employees. |
| Family and Medical Leave Act (FMLA) | 1993 | Enables qualified employees to take prolonged unpaid leave for family- and health-related reasons without fear of losing their jobs. | Private employers with 15 or more employees. |

**figure 9.2**

**SUMMARY OF EQUAL OPPORTUNITY LAWS**

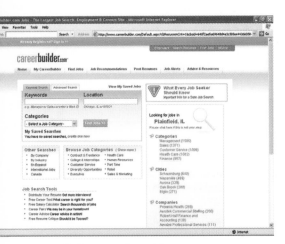

Online recruitment is on the rise. What are some pros and cons of these sorts of career searches?

**recruitment**

Seeking and attracting a supply of people from which qualified candidates for job vacancies can be selected.

**temporary help**

People working for employment agencies who are subcontracted out to businesses at an hourly rate for a period of time specified by the businesses.

**employee leasing companies**

Provide permanent staff at customer companies as listed in text.

# RECRUITMENT

**Recruitment** involves seeking and attracting a supply of people from which qualified candidates for job vacancies can be selected. The amount of recruitment an organization must do is determined by the difference between the forecasted human resource needs and the talent available within the organization. After the decision to recruit has been made, the sources of supply must be explored.

An organization that has been doing an effective job of recruiting employees has one of the best sources of supply for filling job openings: its own employees. Promotion from within is very popular with growing and dynamic organizations. If internal sources prove to be inadequate, external sources are always available. Though usually more costly and time consuming to pursue, external sources such as employment agencies, consulting firms, employee referrals, and employment advertisements can be valuable resources for an organization. Figure 9.3 summarizes the advantages and disadvantages of using internal and external sources for human resource needs.

One of the fastest-growing areas of recruitment is **temporary help** hired through employment agencies. The agency pays the salary and benefits of the temporary help; the organization pays the employment agency an agreed-upon figure for the services of the temporary help. The use of temporary help is not dependent on economic conditions. When an organization is expanding, temporary employees are used to supplement the current staff. When an organization is downsizing, temporary employees create a flexible staff that can be laid off easily and recalled when necessary. One obvious disadvantage of using temporary employees is their lack of commitment to the organization.

Unlike temporary agencies, which normally place people in short-term jobs at various companies, **employee leasing companies** and professional employer organizations (PEOs) provide permanent staff at customer companies, issue the workers' paychecks, take care of personnel matters, ensure compliance with workplace regulations, and provide various employee benefits.[2] In addition, highly skilled technical workers such as engineers and information technology specialists are supplied for long-term projects under contract between a company and a technical services firm.

## Legal Considerations in the Recruitment Process

The previously discussed legislation has also had a profound impact on the recruitment activities of organizations. For example, the courts have ruled reliance on word-of-mouth or walk-in methods of recruitment to be a discriminatory practice where females and minorities are not well represented at all levels within the organizations.[3]

| SOURCE | ADVANTAGES | DISADVANTAGES |
|---|---|---|
| Internal | • Company has a better knowledge of strengths and weaknesses of job candidate.<br>• Job candidate has a better knowledge of company.<br>• Morale and motivation of employees are enhanced.<br>• The return on investment that an organization has in its present workforce is increased. | • People might be promoted to the point where they cannot successfully perform the job.<br>• Infighting for promotions can negatively affect morale.<br>• Inbreeding can stifle new ideas and innovation. |
| External | • The pool of talent is much larger.<br>• New insights and perspectives can be brought to the organization.<br>• Frequently it is cheaper and easier to hire technical, skilled, or managerial employees from outside. | • Attracting, contacting, and evaluating potential employees is more difficult.<br>• Adjustment or orientation time is longer.<br>• Morale problems can develop among those employees within the organization who feel qualified to do the job. |

**figure 9.3**

**ADVANTAGES AND DISADVANTAGES OF INTERNAL AND EXTERNAL SOURCES**

The Equal Employment Opportunity Commission (EEOC) offers the following suggestions to help eliminate discrimination in recruitment practices:[4]

- Maintain a file of unhired female and minority applicants who are potential candidates for future openings. Contact these candidates first when an opening occurs.

- Utilize females and minorities in recruitment and in the entire human resource process.

- Place classified ads under "Help Wanted" or "Help Wanted, Male-Female" listings. Be sure the content of ads does not indicate any sex, race, or age preference or qualification for the job.

- Advertise in media directed toward women and minorities.

- All advertising should include the phrase "equal opportunity employer."

Research has shown that organizations that are aware of protective legislation and EEOC guidelines are more likely to promote diversity, conform to accepted hiring practices, be identity conscious in their recruitment efforts, and generally go beyond symbolic efforts to improve conditions for protected groups.[5] The diverse workplace is a reality, and growth-oriented companies use that fact as a positive rather than a negative influence on the staffing of their organizations.

# SELECTION

The selection process involves choosing from those available individuals the most likely to succeed in the job. The process is dependent on proper human resource planning and recruitment. Only when an adequate pool of qualified candidates is available can the selection process function effectively. The ultimate objective of the selection process is to match the requirements of the job with the qualifications of the individual.

## Who Makes the Decision?

The responsibility for hiring is assigned to different levels of management in different organizations. Often the human resource/personnel department does the initial screening of recruits, but the final selection decision is left to the manager of the department with the job opening. Such a system relieves the manager of the time-consuming responsibility of screening out unqualified and uninterested applicants. Less frequently, the human resource/personnel department is responsible for both the initial screening and the final decision. Many organizations leave the final choice to the immediate manager, subject to the approval of higher levels of management. In small organizations, the owner or the top manager often makes the choice.

An alternative approach is to involve peers in the selection decision. Traditionally, peer involvement has been used primarily with professionals and those in upper levels of management, but it is becoming more popular at all levels of the organization. With this approach, co-workers have an input into the final selection decision.

## Legal Considerations in the Selection Process

The selection process has been of primary interest to the government, as evidenced by the number of laws and regulations in effect that prohibit discrimination in the selection of employees. One action frequently required of organizations is the development of an affirmative action plan. An **affirmative action plan** is a written document outlining specific goals and timetables for remedying past discriminatory actions. All federal contractors and subcontractors with contracts over $50,000 and 50 or more employees are required to develop and implement written affirmative action plans, which are monitored by the Office of Federal Contract Compliance Programs (OFCCP). While Title VII and the EEOC require no specific type of affirmative action plan, court rulings have often required affirmative action when discrimination has been found.

A number of basic steps are involved in the development of an effective affirmative action plan. Figure 9.4 presents the EEOC's suggestions for developing an affirmative action plan.

Organizations without affirmative action plans will find it makes good business sense to identify and revise employment practices that have discriminatory effects before the federal government requires such

**affirmative action plan**
Written document outlining specific goals and timetables for remedying past discriminatory actions.

## Redundancies and Confidential Information

The company for which you are working is about to be restructured. Everyone knows that there will be some redundancies. You work for the director of human resources and have access to confidential information about the restructure, including the names of those scheduled to be made redundant.

One day at lunch, a colleague mentions that her boss is about to take on a heavy debt in order to buy a new house. It seems that he needs the space as his wife is due to have a third child in a few months' time.

You recognize the name as someone who has been identified to be made redundant. What are your choices here? Should you give this information to the director of human resources? Should you tell your colleague's boss before he buys the bigger house?

***Source:*** St. James Ethics Centre, "Ethical Dilemmas," www.ethics.org.au.

action. Increased legal action and the record of court-required affirmative action emphasize the advantage of writing and instituting an affirmative action plan.

However, the growing number of reverse discrimination suits may have a significant impact on affirmative action programs. **Reverse discrimination** is providing preferential treatment for one group (e.g., minority or female)

**reverse discrimination**

Providing preferential treatment for one group (e.g., minority or female) over another group (e.g., white male) rather than merely providing equal opportunity.

1. The chief executive officer of an organization should issue a written statement describing his or her personal commitment to the plan, legal obligations, and the importance of equal employment opportunity as an organizational goal.
2. A top official of the organization should be given the authority and responsibility to direct and implement the program. In addition, all managers and supervisors within the organization should clearly understand their own responsibilities for carrying out equal employment opportunity.
3. The organization's policy and commitment to the policy should be publicized both internally and externally.
4. Present employment should be surveyed to identify areas of concentration and underutilization and to determine the extent of underutilization.
5. Goals and timetables for achieving the goals should be developed to improve utilization of minorities, males, and females in each area where underutilization has been identified.
6. The entire employment system should be reviewed to identify and eliminate barriers to equal employment. Areas for review include recruitment, selection, promotion systems, training programs, wage and salary structure, benefits and conditions of employment, layoffs, discharges, disciplinary action, and union contract provisions affecting these areas.
7. An internal audit and reporting system should be established to monitor and evaluate progress in all aspects of the program.
8. Company and community programs that are supportive of equal opportunity should be developed. Programs might include training of supervisors regarding their legal responsibilities and the organization's commitment to equal employment and job and career counseling programs.

**figure 9.4**

**EEOC'S SUGGESTIONS FOR DEVELOPING AN AFFIRMATIVE ACTION PLAN**

***Source:*** *Affirmative Action and Equal Employment,* vol. 1 (Washington, DC: U.S. Equal Employment Opportunity Commission, 1974), pp. 16–64.

figure 9.5

**STEPS IN THE SELECTION PROCESS**

| STEPS IN SELECTION PROCESS | POSSIBLE CRITERIA FOR ELIMINATING POTENTIAL EMPLOYEE |
|---|---|
| • Preliminary screening from application form, résumé, employer records, etc. | Inadequate educational level or performance/experience record for the job and its requirements. |
| • Preliminary interview | Obvious disinterest and unsuitability for job and its requirements. |
| • Testing | Failure to meet minimum standards on job-related measures of intelligence, aptitude, personality, etc. |
| • Reference checks | Unfavorable reports from references regarding past performance. |
| • Employment interview | Inadequate demonstration of ability or other job-related characteristics. |
| • Physical examination | Lack of physical fitness required for job. |
| • Personal judgment | Intuition and judgment resulting in the selection of a new employee. Inadequate demonstration of ability or other job-related characteristics. |

**tests**

Provide a sample of behavior used to draw inferences about the future behavior or performance of an individual.

**aptitude tests**

Measure a person's capacity or potential ability to learn.

**psychomotor tests**

Measure a person's strength, dexterity, and coordination.

**job knowledge tests**

Measure the job-related knowledge possessed by a job applicant.

over another group (e.g., white male) rather than merely providing equal opportunity. The first real test case in this area was the *Bakke* case of 1978.[6] Allen Bakke, a white male, brought suit against the medical school of the University of California at Davis. He charged he was unconstitutionally discriminated against when he was denied admission to the medical school while some minority applicants with lower qualifications were accepted. The Supreme Court ruled in Bakke's favor but at the same time upheld the constitutionality of affirmative action programs.

## Selection Procedure

Figure 9.5 presents a suggested procedure for selecting employees. The preliminary screening and preliminary interview eliminate candidates who are obviously not qualified for the job. In the preliminary screening of applications, personnel data sheets, school records, work records, and similar sources are reviewed to determine characteristics, abilities, and the past performance of the individual. The preliminary interview is then used to screen out unsuitable or uninterested applicants who passed the preliminary screening phase.

## Testing

One of the most controversial areas of staffing is employment testing. **Tests** provide a sample of behavior that is used to draw inferences about the future behavior or performance of an individual. Many tests are available to organizations for use in the selection process.[7]

Tests used by organizations can be grouped into the following general categories: aptitude, psychomotor, job knowledge and proficiency, interests, psychological, and polygraphs.

**Aptitude tests** measure a person's capacity or potential ability to learn. **Psychomotor tests** measure a person's strength, dexterity, and coordination. **Job knowledge tests** measure the job-related knowledge possessed by a job applicant. **Proficiency tests** measure how well the applicant can do a sample of the work to be performed. **Interest tests** are designed to determine how a person's interests compare with the interests of successful people in a specific job. **Psychological tests** attempt to measure personality characteristics. **Polygraph tests,** popularly known as *lie detector tests,* record physical changes in the body as the test subject answers a series of questions. By studying recorded physiological measurements, the polygraph examiner then makes a judgment as to whether the subject's response was truthful or deceptive.

Would you submit to a polygraph test for your dream job?

Employment testing is legally subject to the requirements of validity and reliability. **Test validity** refers to the extent to which a test predicts a specific criterion. For organizations, the criterion usually used is performance on the job. Thus, test validity generally refers to the extent to which a test predicts future job success or performance. The selection of criteria to define job success or performance is a difficult process, and its importance cannot be overstated. Obviously, test validity cannot be measured unless satisfactory criteria exist.

**Test reliability** refers to the consistency or reproducibility of the results of a test. Three methods are commonly used to determine the reliability of a test. The first method, called *test-retest,* involves testing a group of people and then retesting them later. The degree of similarity between the sets of scores determines the reliability of the test. The second method, called *parallel forms,* entails giving two separate but similar forms of the test. The degree to which the sets of scores coincide determines the reliability of the test. The third method, called *split halves,* divides the test into two halves to determine whether performance is similar on both halves. Again, the degree of similarity determines the reliability. All these methods require statistical calculations to determine the degree of reliability of the test.

## Background and Reference Checks

Background and reference checks usually fall into three categories: personal, academic, and past employment. Contacting personal and academic references is generally of limited value, because few people will list someone as a reference unless they feel that that person will give them a positive recommendation. Previous employers are in the best

**proficiency tests**
Measure how well the applicant can do a sample of the work that is to be performed.

**interest tests**
Determine how a person's interests compare with the interests of successful people in a specific job.

**psychological tests**
Attempt to measure personality characteristics.

**polygraph tests**
Record physical changes in the body as the test subject answers a series of questions; popularly known as *lie detector tests.*

**test validity**
Extent to which a test predicts a specific criterion.

**test reliability**
Consistency or reproducibility of the results of a test.

position to supply the most objective information. However, the amount and type of information that a previous employer is willing to divulge varies. Normally, most previous employers will provide only the following information—yes or no to the question if this applicant worked there, what the employee's dates of employment were, and what position he or she held.[8]

If a job applicant is rejected because of information in a credit report or another type of report from an outside reporting service, the applicant must be given the name and address of the organization that developed the report. The reporting service is *not* required by law to give the person a copy of his or her file, but it *must* inform the person of the nature and substance of the information.

---

## PROGRESS CHECK QUESTIONS

1. What are the six broad categories of information that may be included in a skills inventory?
2. Explain the human resource planning (HRP) process.
3. Summarize the seven significant government bills and laws that have affected human resource planning.
4. What are the six general categories of tests that organizations use in the selection process?

---

# EMPLOYMENT INTERVIEW

The employment interview is used by virtually all organizations as an important step in the selection process. Its purpose is to supplement information gained in other steps in the selection process to determine the suitability of an applicant for a specific opening in the organization. It is important to remember that all questions asked during an interview must be job-related. Equal employment opportunity legislation has placed limitations on the types of questions that can be asked during an interview.

## Types of Interviews

**structured interview**
An interview conducted using a predetermined outline.

Organizations use several types of interviews. The **structured interview** is conducted using a predetermined outline. Through the use of this outline, the interviewer maintains control of the interview so that all relevant information on the applicant is covered systematically. Structured interviews provide the same type of information on all interviewees and allow systematic coverage of all questions deemed necessary by the organization. The use of a structured interview tends to increase reliability and accuracy.

Two variations of the structured interview are the semistructured and the situational interview. In the **semistructured interview,** the interviewer prepares the major questions in advance but has the flexibility to use such techniques as probing to help assess the applicant's strengths and weaknesses. The **situational interview** uses projective techniques to put the prospective employee in action situations that might be encountered on the job. For example, the interviewer may wish to see how the applicant might handle a customer complaint or observe certain important decision-making characteristics. With either method, however, interviewer bias must be guarded against.

**Unstructured interviews** are conducted without a predetermined checklist of questions. This type of interview uses open-ended questions, such as, "Tell me about your previous job." Interviews of this type pose numerous problems, such as a lack of systematic coverage of information, and are susceptible to the personal biases of the interviewer. This type of interview, however, does provide a more relaxed atmosphere.

Organizations have used three other interviewing techniques to a limited extent. The **stress interview** is designed to place the interviewee under pressure. In the stress interview, the interviewer assumes a hostile and antagonistic attitude toward the interviewee. The purpose of this type of interview is to detect whether the person is highly emotional. In the **board (or panel) interview,** two or more interviewers conduct the interview. The **group interview,** which questions several interviewees together in a group discussion, is also sometimes used. Board interviews and group interviews can involve either a structured or an unstructured format.

## Problems in Conducting Interviews

Although interviews have widespread use in selection procedures, they can pose a host of problems. The first and one of the most significant problems is that interviews are subject to the same legal requirements of validity and reliability as other steps in the selection process. Furthermore, the validity and reliability of most interviews are questionable. One reason seems to be that it is easy for the interviewer to become either favorably or unfavorably impressed with the job applicant for the wrong reasons.

Several common pitfalls may be encountered in interviewing a job applicant. Interviewers, like all people, have personal biases, and these biases can play a role in the interviewing process. For example, a qualified

**semistructured interview**
An interview in which the interviewer prepares the major questions in advance but has the flexibility to use such techniques as probing to help assess the applicant's strengths and weaknesses.

**situational interview**
Interview that uses projective techniques to put the prospective employee in action situations that might be encountered on the job.

**unstructured interviews**
Interviews conducted without a predetermined checklist of questions.

**stress interview**
An interview designed to place the interviewee under pressure.

**board (or panel) interview**
An interview in which two or more interviewers conduct the interview.

**group interview**
An interview which questions several interviewees together in a group discussion.

## The Employment Interview

Jerry Sullivan is the underwriting manager for a large insurance company located in the Southwest. Recently, one of his best employees had given him two weeks' notice of her intention to leave. She was expecting a baby soon, and she and her husband had decided she was going to quit work and stay home with her new baby and her other two young children.

Today, Jerry was scheduled to start interviewing applicants for this job. The first applicant was Barbara Riley. She arrived at the company's office promptly at 9 a.m., the time scheduled for her interview. Unfortunately, just before she arrived, Jerry received a phone call from his boss, who had just returned from a three-week vacation. He wanted Jerry to bring him up to date on what had been going on. The telephone conversation lasted 30 minutes. During that time, Barbara Riley was seated in the company's reception room.

At 9:30, Jerry went to the reception room and invited her into his office. The following conversation occurred:

*Jerry:* Would you like a cup of coffee?

*Barbara:* No, I've already had one.

*Jerry:* You don't mind if I have a cup, do you?

*Barbara:* No, go right ahead. [Jerry pauses and rings his secretary Dorothy Cannon.]

*Jerry:* Dorothy, would you fix me a cup of coffee?

*Dorothy:* I'll bring it in shortly. You have a call on line 1.

*Jerry:* Who is it?

*Dorothy:* It's Tom Powell, our IBM representative. He wants to talk to you about the delivery date on our new word processor.

*Jerry:* I'd better talk to him. [Turning to Barbara.] I'd better take this call. I'll only be a minute. [He picks up his phone.] Well, Tom, when are we going to get our machines?

This phone conversation goes on for almost 10 minutes. After hanging up, Jerry turns again to Barbara to resume the interview.

*Jerry:* I'm sorry, but I needed to know about those machines. We really do need them. We only have a short time, so why don't you just tell me about yourself.

At that point, Barbara tells Jerry about her education, which includes an undergraduate degree in psychology and an MBA, which she will be receiving shortly. She explains to Jerry that this will be her first full-time job. Just then the phone rings, and Jerry's secretary tells him that his next interviewee is waiting.

*Jerry:* [Turns to Barbara.] Thank you for coming in. I'll be in touch with you as soon as I interview two more applicants for this job. However, I need to ask you a couple of quick questions.

*Barbara:* OK.

*Jerry:* Are you married?

*Barbara:* I am divorced.

*Jerry:* Do you have children?

*Barbara:* Yes, two boys.

*Jerry:* Do they live with you?

*Barbara:* Yes.

*Jerry:* The reason I am asking is that this job requires some travel. Will this pose a problem?

*Barbara:* No.

*Jerry:* Thanks, and I'll be in touch with you.

## Questions

1. Outline the inadequacies of this interview.
2. What information did Jerry learn?
3. What do you think of Jerry's last questions?
4. What questions would you have asked? Why?

**halo effect**

Occurs when the interviewer allows a single prominent characteristic to dominate judgment of all other traits.

male applicant should not be rejected merely because the interviewer dislikes long hair on males.

Closely related is the problem of the **halo effect,** which occurs when the interviewer allows a single prominent characteristic to dominate judgment of all other traits. For instance, it is often easy to overlook other characteristics when a person has a pleasant personality. However, merely having a pleasant personality does not ensure that the person will be a qualified employee.

Overgeneralizing is another common problem. An interviewee may not behave exactly the same way on the job that she or he did during the interview. The interviewer must remember that the interviewee is under pressure during the interview and that some people just naturally become nervous during an interview.

Job interviews can vary as widely as the positions applied for, even within the same company. How would your preparation vary based on in interview at Sears' cosmetics department versus their juniors department?

## Conducting Effective Interviews

Problems associated with interviews can be partially overcome through careful planning. The following suggestions are offered to increase the effectiveness of the interviewing process.

First, careful attention must be given to the selection and training of interviewers. They should be outgoing and emotionally well-adjusted people. Interviewing skills can be learned, and the people responsible for conducting interviews should be thoroughly trained in these skills.

Second, the plan for the interview should include an outline specifying the information to be obtained and the questions to be asked. The plan should also include room arrangements. Privacy and some degree of comfort are important. If a private room is not available, the interview should be conducted in a place where other applicants are not within hearing distance.

Third, the interviewer should attempt to put the applicant at ease. The interviewer should not argue with the applicant or put the applicant on the spot. A brief conversation about a general topic of interest or offering the applicant a cup of coffee can help ease the tension. The applicant should be encouraged to talk. However, the interviewer must maintain control and remember that the primary goal of the interview is to gain information that will aid in the selection decision.

Fourth, the facts obtained in the interview should be recorded immediately. Generally, notes can and should be taken during the interview.

Finally, the effectiveness of the interviewing process should be evaluated. One way to evaluate effectiveness is to compare the performance ratings of individuals who are hired against assessments made during the interview. This cross-check can serve to evaluate the effectiveness of individual interviewers as well as that of the overall interviewing program.

## Study Skills

### Importance of Good Communication Skills!

What happens when you are faced with speaking in front of a large audience? Or speaking to a group of your peers? Or speaking one on one with your boss?

These situations constitute opportunities for displaying good communication skills, and improvement in any or all of these areas can greatly guide you to a level of confidence that can move you ahead of others in the business world.

How far can you take your communications skills? College course work is a great learning and proving ground for working on your communication skills. Your instructor or professor can be a good critic or mentor for helping you improve your communication skills by providing detailed evaluations of your writing and public speaking skills.

## Personal Judgment

The final step in the selection process is to make a personal judgment regarding which individual to select for the job. (Of course, it is assumed that at this point more than one applicant will be qualified for the job.) A value judgment using all the data obtained in the previous steps of the selection process must be made in selecting the best individual for the job. If previous steps have been performed correctly, the chances of making a successful personal judgment improve dramatically.

The individual making the personal judgment should also recognize that in some cases, none of the applicants is satisfactory. If this occurs, the job should be redesigned, more money should be offered to attract more qualified candidates, or other actions should be taken. Caution should be taken against accepting the "best" applicant if that person is not truly qualified to do the job.

# TRANSFERS, PROMOTIONS, AND SEPARATIONS

The final step in the human resource planning process involves transfers, promotions, and separations. A transfer involves moving an employee to another job at approximately the same level in the organization with basically the same pay, performance requirements, and status. Planned transfers can serve as an excellent development technique. Transfers can also be helpful in balancing varying departmental workload requirements. The most common difficulty relating to transfers occurs when a "problem" employee is unloaded on an unsuspecting manager. Training, counseling, or corrective discipline of the employee may eliminate the need for such a transfer. If the employee cannot be rehabilitated, discharge is usually preferable to transfer.

A promotion moves an employee to a job involving higher pay, higher status, and thus higher performance requirements. The two basic criteria used by most organizations in promotions are merit and seniority. Union contracts often require that seniority be considered in promotions. Many organizations prefer to base promotions on merit as a way to reward and encourage performance. Obviously, this assumes the organization has a method for evaluating performance and determining merit. An organization must also consider the requirements of the job in question, not just the employee's performance in previous jobs. Success in one job does not automatically ensure success in another job. Both past performance and potential must be considered.

A separation involves either voluntary or involuntary termination of an employee. In voluntary separations, many organizations attempt to determine why the employee is leaving by using exit interviews. This type of interview provides insights into problem areas that need to be corrected in the organization. Involuntary separations involve terminations and layoffs. Layoffs occur when there is not enough work for all employees. Laid-off employees are called back if and when the workload increases. A termination usually occurs when an employee is not performing his or her job or has broken a company rule. Terminations should be made only as a last resort. When a company has hired an employee and invested resources in the employee, termination results in a low return on the organization's investment. Training and counseling often are tried before firing an individual. However, when rehabilitation fails, the best action is usually termination because of the negative impact a disgruntled or misfit employee can have on others in the organization.

---

## PROGRESS CHECK QUESTIONS

5. Explain the six most common types of interviews.

6. What is the halo effect?

7. What five things should you do to increase the effectiveness of the interviewing process?

8. "Terminations should only be made as a last resort." Do you agree with this statement? Why or why not?

---

# UNDERSTANDING WORK GROUPS AND TEAMS

## Formal Work Groups

Management establishes **formal work groups** to carry out specific tasks. Formal groups may exist for a short or long period of time. A task force is an example of a formal group. These groups have a single goal, such as resolving a problem or designing a new product. A different type of formal work group is the *command*, or *functional*, group. This group consists of a manager and all the employees he or she supervises. Unlike a task group, the command group's work is ongoing and not confined to one issue or product.

> **formal work groups**
> Established by management to carry out specific tasks such as designing a new product or resolving a problem.

## Informal Work Groups

**Informal work groups** are formed voluntarily by members of an organization. They develop from personal contacts and interactions among people. Groups of employees who lunch together regularly and office cliques are examples of informal work groups. A special type of informal group is the *interest group*. Its members share a purpose or concern. For example, women executives might form a group to share ideas about issues that women in management face.

Work is a social experience. Employees interact while performing job duties in offices, factories, stores, and other workplaces. Friendships emerge naturally from these contacts. Informal groups formed around mutual interests fill importants social needs. In earlier centuries, groups like extended families, churches, and small towns met these needs. Today people socialize mostly with people they meet at work.

Informal work groups affect productivity, the morale of other employees, and the success of managers. They can be the result of—and can help create—a shared sense of loyalty. This is especially prevalent in high-risk occupations, such as firefighting and police work. Informal work groups often develop in areas where employees work close together (such as offices with cubicles) and among employees in the same field (such as accounting or graphic design). Employees may band together to share fears or complaints. In such cases, informal groups work against organization goals.

Studies have identified the power of informal work groups in organizations. The Hawthorne studies we reviewed in Chapter 2 discovered that groups may set their own productivity levels and pressure workers to meet them. In one group, workers who produced more or less than the acceptable levels met with name-calling, sarcasm, ridicule, and in some cases, a blow on the arm. The Hawthorne studies concluded that informal organizations with their own social systems exist within formal organizations.

In general, management does not recognize informal groups that revolve around friendships, interests, or shared working space and tasks. Yet an understanding of these groups can improve managers' work with formal groups. Employees join informal groups to meet a social need. They often gain great satisfaction from these groups. Managers seek to duplicate this satisfaction in formal work groups.

## Group Norms

**Group norms** are the informal rules a group adopts to regulate the behavior of group members. They may be extremely simple—a group that lunches together may maintain a rigid seating order. They may include expectations that group members will remain loyal to each other under any circumstances. Whatever the norms, group members are expected to hold to them. Members who break the rules often are shut out.

Norms don't govern every action in a group, only those important for group survival. For instance, a working group's norms would affect its productivity levels, operating procedures, and other work-related activities. Norms may not be written down or even spoken. Rather, group members use their actions to show new members how to behave.[9]

## Group Behavior

Think about the informal groups of friends and classmates you have belonged to at school or in your neighborhood. However they develop, informal work groups share similar behaviors. They include cohesiveness, conformity, and groupthink.

## Group Cohesiveness

**Group cohesiveness** is the degree of attraction among group members, or how tightly knit a group is. The more cohesive a group, the more likely members are to follow group norms. A number of factors affect the cohesiveness of informal work groups—size, success, status, outside pressures, stability of membership, communication, and physical isolation.[10]

> **group cohesiveness**
> Degree of attraction each member has for the group, or the "stick-togetherness" of the group.

Size is a particularly important factor in group cohesiveness. The smaller the group, the more cohesive it is likely to be. A small group allows individual members to interact frequently. Members of large groups have fewer chances to interact; therefore, these groups tend to be less cohesive.

Think about how two close friends operate when they study together. Because they know each other well and talk easily, they have no trouble working together. Now imagine three new people in the study session. Everyone might not agree on the best way to cover material. It may be hard to work with different people. This might cause the study group to fall apart.

Success and status affect group cohesiveness. The more success a group experiences, the more cohesive it becomes. Several factors contribute to a group's status. For instance, highly skilled work groups tend to have more status than less-skilled groups. Like groups that meet their goals, high-status groups tend to be more cohesive than other informal work groups. These relationships are circular—success and status bring about cohesiveness, and cohesiveness brings about status and success.

Outside pressures, such as conflicts with management, can increase group cohesiveness. If a group sees management's requests as a demand or threat, it becomes more cohesive. In these situations, members may develop an "us against them" mentality.

A stable membership and easy lines of communication improve group cohesiveness. Long-standing members know each other well and are familiar with group norms. Employees who work in the same area socialize easily. In a production line, however, conversation is difficult and groups are less cohesive.

Finally, physical isolation from other employees may increase group cohesiveness. The isolation forces workers into close contact with each other and strengthens bonds.

## Group Conformity

**group conformity**

Degree to which the members of the group accept and abide by the norms of the group.

**Group conformity** is the degree to which group members accept and follow group norms. A group generally seeks to control members' behavior for two reasons. First, independent behavior can cause disagreements that threaten a group's survival. Second, consistent behavior creates an atmosphere of trust that allows members to work together and socialize comfortably. Members are able to predict how others in the group will behave. Individual members tend to conform to group norms under certain conditions:

- When group norms are similar to personal attitudes, beliefs, and behavior.
- When they do not agree with the group's norms but feel pressure to accept them.
- When the rewards for complying are valued or the sanctions imposed for noncompliance are devalued.

### Group Pressure and Conformity

Researchers have studied the influence of group pressure on individual members. One study of group conformity took place at a textile firm in Virginia.[11] A textile employee began to produce more than the group norm of 50 units per day. After two weeks, the group started to pressure this worker to produce less, and she quickly dropped to the group's level. After three weeks, all the members of the group were moved to other jobs except for this worker. Once again, her production quickly climbed to double the group norm (see Figure 9.6).

## figure 9.6

**EFFECT OF GROUP NORMS ON A MEMBER'S PRODUCTIVITY**

***Source:*** Lester Coch and J.R.P. French, Jr., "Overcoming Resistance to Change," *Human Relations* (1948), pp. 519–20.

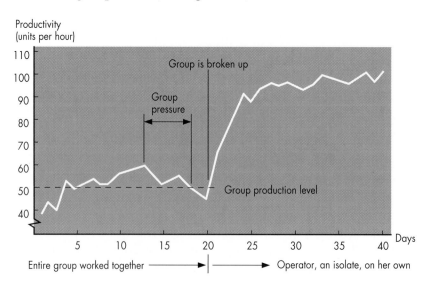

## Groupthink

When group members lose their ability to think as individuals and conform at the expense of their good judgment, **groupthink** occurs. Members become unwilling to say anything against the group or any member, even if an action is wrong.

Keeping a group together under any circumstance is a goal in itself. Groups with this goal believe that the group is indestructible and always right. Group members justify any action, stereotype outsiders as enemies of the group, and pressure unwilling members to conform. In business, groupthink is disruptive because it affects employees' ability to make logical decisions.[12]

> **groupthink**
>
> Dysfunctional syndrome where group members lose their ability to think as individuals and conform to group decisions at the expense of their individual good judgment.

### PROGRESS CHECK QUESTIONS

9. What are group norms?
10. What are the differences between formal and informal work groups?
11. What is the difference between group cohesiveness and groupthink?
12. Consider a group you work with in the organization you currently work for or one you have worked for in the past. How would you describe the norms of that group? Explain.

## The Importance of Teams

Teams play an important part in helping an organization meet its goals. Groups have more knowledge and information than individuals. They make communicating and solving problems easier. This creates a more efficient and effective company.

The importance of managing groups effectively is becoming recognized in the business world. Employees must work closely to improve

> A group's ability or inability to work as a unit is key to any company's success. How can you be a team player?

production and maintain a competitive edge. Changes in the workforce are bringing men and women from different backgrounds together. Managers must work with groups to overcome cultural and gender differences. These, and other factors, make managing work groups one of management's most important tasks.

## Influencing Work Groups

Studies at the Hawthorne plant, where researchers documented the existence of informal work groups, looked at the effects of various changes on workers' productivity. Researchers varied job factors, including the way workers were paid and supervised, lighting, the length of rest periods, and the number of hours worked. Productivity rose with each change.

This result led to the coining of the term Hawthorne effect. As you may remember from Chapter 2, the Hawthorne effect states that giving special attention to a group of employees changes the employees' behavior. The results of the studies show that when groups of employees are singled out for attention, they tend to work more efficiently.

## Building Effective Teams

Members of informal work groups often develop a shared sense of values and group loyalty. Formal groups rarely share these qualities because they are assigned to rather than voluntary. Managers are responsible for developing shared values and group loyalty in formal work groups.

**linchpin concept**

Holds that because managers are members of overlapping groups, they link formal work groups to the total organization.

The linchpin concept is one way of describing management's role in work groups. The **linchpin concept** holds that because managers are members of overlapping groups, they link formal work groups to the total organization. Managers improve communication and ensure that organizational and group goals are met. In other words, managers themselves are the linchpins (see Figure 9.7).

**team building**

Process of establishing a cohesive group that works together to achieve its goals.

Building effective formal work groups often is called team building. **Team building** is the process of establishing a cohesive group that works together to achieve its goals.[12] A team will be successful only if its members feel that working conditions are fair to all. A team can fail, even in a supportive organization, if a manager does not encourage fair play. The success of a group or team can be measured in the same way as the success of organizations. Successful organizations and groups both meet their goals by using their resources well. Managers encourage teamwork by selecting group members carefully, creating a positive work environment, building trust, and increasing group cohesiveness. Figure 9.8 describes three steps to use in building productive teams.

## Creating Groups

For a group to succeed, members must be able to perform the tasks assigned by management. Selecting the right individuals is key to the success of a group. The first step is to identify qualified people. Then

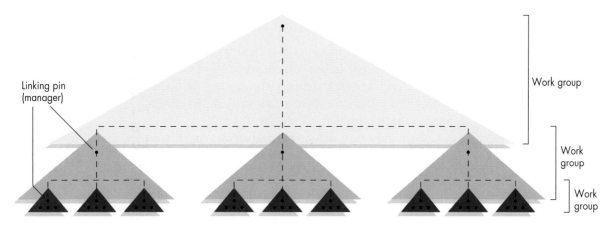

**figure 9.7**

**LINCHPIN CONCEPT**

***Source:*** From Renis Linkert, *New Patterns of Management*, 1/e, 1961, p. 104 Reproduced with permission of The McGraw-Hill Companies, Inc.

management must make the group attractive to these individuals. For most employees, a formal work group is attractive because it increases pay and offers some satisfaction. If employees see that joining a formal group can provide them with the same satisfaction that an informal group can, they are more likely to participate willingly. Environment also can be important to the success of a group. An important requirement for meeting group goals is a suitable place to work. How the office is laid out and other physical factors will affect the group's ability to work together successfully.

## Building Trust

Trust is essential among group members and between groups and management. A successful group effort means sharing responsibilities and making decisions together. Group members must feel that the entire group is willing and able to work together successfully to achieve goals. Without trust, groups can't set or stick to production norms.

Managers must have faith in their employees. They also must recognize the interests of the organization, the group, and the employees. Effective managers should become personally involved, take a real interest in group members, share information, and exhibit honesty.

**figure 9.8**

**STEPS FOR BUILDING PRODUCTIVE TEAMS**

**1. Selecting Individuals**

The first step in building an effective team is finding the right people. Group members need to have the right skills and the right personality fit.

**2. Building Trust**

The second step is to build trust among group members and between the group and management.

**3. Encouraging Group Cohesiveness**

The third step is to develop a cohesive group that conforms to group norms. Managers can improve group cohesiveness by keeping groups small, giving them clear goals, and rewarding them as a team.

## Influencing Group Cohesiveness and Conformity

Think about teams you have belonged to at school or summer camp. These successful teams often are highly competitive and eager to succeed. Effective work groups share these characteristics. Both types of groups also draw their primary satisfaction from a sense of accomplishment, which comes from a job well done.

Managers can affect formal group performance levels by studying the degree of group conformity. Formal groups must be cohesive and dedicated to high-performance norms in order to succeed. Managers can influence group cohesiveness by:

- Keeping groups small.
- Selecting group members carefully.
- Finding a good personality fit between new and old employees.
- Developing an office layout that improves communication.
- Creating clear goals.
- Inspiring group competition.
- Rewarding groups rather than individuals.
- Isolating groups from each other.

High individual performance with poor team performance is not what winning is about, either in sports or in business. Individuals must surrender their egos so that the end result is bigger than the sum of its parts. When this happens, the team works together like fingers on a hand.

## Phases in the Life of Teams

Effective work teams go through four phases of development: forming, norming, storming, and performing. Phase one (forming) occurs when the team members first come together. Uncertainty and anxiety are common feelings that members of the team experience. Therefore, the focus of the forming phase is for members of the team to get to know each other and have their questions answered. Phase two (storming) often involves a period of disagreement and intense discussion as members attempt to impose their individual viewpoints on the rest of the group. In phase three (norming), the team develops the informal rules that enable it to regulate the behavior of the team members. In phase four (performing), the team becomes an effective and high-performing team only if it has gone through the three previous phases.

**quality circle**
Composed of a group of employees (usually from 5 to 15 people) who are members of a single work unit, section, or department; the basic purpose of a quality circle is to discuss quality problems and generate ideas that might help improve quality.

## Quality Circles

One type of formal work group is the **quality circle.** A quality circle is a group of employees, usually from 5 to 15 people, from a single work unit (such as a department) that share ideas on how to improve quality. The goal of a quality circle is to involve employees in decision making. Membership is almost always voluntary, and members share a common bond—they perform similar tasks.

Japan has used quality circles since the early 1960s. The idea arrived in the United States after executives from Lockheed Corporation visited Japan in the 1970s and saw the circles in action. Lockheed used quality circles to improve quality and save several million dollars. Quality circles have benefits other than increasing employee participation.[13] They encourage communication and trust among members and managers. They are an inexpensive way to provide employees with training while giving them a sense of control over their work lives. Most important, however, they may solve problems that have been around for years. Quality circles create strong lines of communication. "Me" becomes "us" in a good quality circle.

## Self-Directed Work Teams

Another type of formal work group is the **self-directed work team** (SDWT). SDWTs are empowered to control the work they do without a formal supervisor. Each SDWT has a leader who normally comes from the employees on the team. Most of these teams plan and schedule their work, make operational and personnel decisions, solve problems, set priorities, determine what employee does what work, and share leadership responsibilities.

**self-directed work team**

Teams in which members are empowered to control the work they do without a formal supervisor.

## Virtual Work Teams

Virtual work teams were largely nonexistent a decade ago. Today, globalization, technology, and fast responses to customer needs have led organizations to establish virtual work teams. **Virtual work teams** are responsible for making or implementing important decisions for the business, mainly using technology-supported communication, with the team members working and living in different locations. It is likely that this form of work team over time will be more widely used.

**virtual work team**

Responsible for making or implementing important decisions for the business, mainly using technology-supported communication, with the team members working and living in different locations.

### PROGRESS CHECK QUESTIONS

13. Explain the Hawthorne effect.
14. List six ways in which managers can influence group cohesiveness.
15. What are the four phases of development for effective work teams?
16. Explain the difference between a quality circle and a self-directed work team.

## Groups and Leaders

When an informal group selects a leader, members choose the person most capable of satisfying the group's needs. The group gives this leader

# One of the Gang?

Recently, Ruth Brown was appointed as the supervisor of a group of word processors in which she was formerly one of the rank-and-file employees. When she was selected for the job, the department head told her the former supervisor was being transferred because she could not get sufficient work out of the group. He also said the reason Ruth was selected was that she appeared to be a natural leader, she was close to the group, and she knew the tricks they were practicing to restrict output. He told Ruth he believed she could lick the problem and he would stand behind her.

He was right about Ruth knowing the tricks. When she was one of the gang, not only did she try to hamper the supervisor, but she was the ringleader in the group's efforts to make life miserable for her. None of them had anything personal against the supervisor; all of them considered it a game to pit their wits against hers. There was a set of signals to inform the employees the supervisor was coming so that everyone would appear to be working hard. As soon as she left the immediate vicinity, everyone would take it easy. Also, the employees would act dumb to get the supervisor to go into lengthy explanations and demonstrations while they stood around. They complained constantly, and without justification, about the materials and the equipment.

At lunchtime, the employees would ridicule the company, tell the latest fast one they had pulled on the supervisor, and plan new ways to harass her. All of this seemed to be a great joke. Ruth and the rest of the employees had a lot of fun at the expense of the supervisor and the company. Now that Ruth has joined the ranks of management, it is not so funny. She is determined to use her managerial position and knowledge to win the group over to working for the company instead of against it. She knows that if this can be done, she will have a top-notch group. The employees know their stuff, have a very good team spirit, and, if they would use their brains and efforts constructively, could turn out above-average production.

Ruth's former colleagues are rather cool to her now, but this seems natural, and she believes she can overcome it in a short time. What concerns her is that Joe James is taking over her old post as ringleader of the group, and the group is trying to play the same tricks on her that it did on the former supervisor.

## Questions

1. Did the company make a good selection in Ruth? Explain.

2. What suggestions would you make to Ruth?

3. How do you think the team will react to "one of their own" as team leader?

4. Are work groups always opposed to working toward organizational goals? Explain.

---

authority and can take this authority away at any time. This leader needs strong communication skills, especially in setting objectives for the group, giving directions, and summarizing information.

To see how informal groups choose leaders, imagine a group of people shipwrecked on an island. The group's first goal is to find food, water, and shelter. The individual best equipped to help the group survive would naturally become the leader. Later, the group's goal might change to getting off the island. The original leader may no longer be the best person to help meet this new goal, and a new leader could emerge. The process may continue through several leaders.

## Gaining Acceptance

Managers assigned to formal work groups must work to gain acceptance as leaders. They generally do not have the same authority as leaders of informal groups. The formal authority granted by top management is no guarantee that a manager will effectively guide a group.

Think about how you respond to your teachers. You respect teachers who know their subject well, communicate information effectively, treat students with respect, and make fair judgments. Managers working with formal groups can use these same behaviors to gain the trust and respect of employees.

Managers must keep track of those changes within the organization that might affect the group. At times, they may have to modify group goals to meet new organizational goals. For example, an organization faced with strong competition may need to make decisions rapidly rather than rely on groups to come up with a solution. In these cases, managers must be ready to make immediate decisions for the group.

## Encouraging Participation

Building an effective team requires a nontraditional managerial approach. In a traditional organizational structure, managers direct the employees who work for them. As part of a team, however, managers encourage participation and share responsibility, acting more like a coach than a manager.

One way of encouraging team spirit is to provide the group with a vision. People who organize groups to support social causes often use this approach. For example, one person may rally a community around a project such as reclaiming a vacant lot for a park. In the business world, managers can offer team members the possibility of designing a state-of-the-art product or service.

Managers lead by example. Their attitude and performance become the standard for group norms. A manager who believes that a group must listen to and support all members might create a group of top managers who share this feeling. Employees who see managers functioning within a cohesive group are more likely to work effectively in groups themselves.

# CONCLUSION

Once management has identified and categorized the jobs to be performed in the organization, and then developed an organization structure for the performance of those jobs, the next task is to hire and develop the people who will do those jobs. In this chapter we have reviewed the importance of a carefully managed hiring process with detailed skills inventory (to determine what resources are on hand and what positions need to be filled); a thorough interview process (to identify the best candidates from the applicant pool); and the extensive legal framework that surrounds the management of human resources. In addition, we have considered the challenge for managers in hiring individuals who will ultimately work as a team within the organization, either within a specific department or as a group assigned to a specific project. In the next chapter we'll review the challenges and opportunities managers face in the development of a motivated and productive workforce.

## The Taco Barn survives the experiment

When the two weeks were up, Kevin and his shift crew asked for an opportunity to present their ideas to Tony: not just a written report, but a formal business presentation with a PowerPoint presentation and handouts supporting the business case for their ideas in considerable detail. Tony had to admit, he was impressed before he had even heard what they had to say.

The presentation took about 30 minutes, and everyone took part. They explained how they had come up with their ideas, where they had done the research to support their proposal, and how they had arrived at their final recommendations including proposed costs and potential savings to be achieved. Tony guessed that Kevin had told them that showing the material to Dawn would be the next step in the process, because their handouts had obviously been prepared with that end in mind—charts, spreadsheets, numbers, and all the supporting material.

At the end of the presentation Tony was so impressed that the only fitting response for him was to stand up and applaud his crew. The look of surprise and pride on their faces was priceless, and it took a moment for them to get over the shock. Then chaos broke out, and everyone started screaming and shouting about how nervous they had been, how uncertain they had been that he would like their ideas, and how much they appreciated the chance to do this, even if Dawn didn't take any of their suggestions.

Tony gave them a few minutes to blow off some steam, and then he spoke:

"You have done a wonderful job here, guys. I am really impressed with your creativity and your attention to detail. You've redesigned our ordering and modified the storeroom layout to make the deliveries easier. You've even worked out a better way to incorporate vendor specials into our menu that has the potential to save us a lot of money. I think Dawn is really going to be interested in that one."

Tony paused as the energy level bubbled over again. "So what other ideas do you and your team have, Kevin?"

### QUESTIONS

1. Why didn't Tony come up with all these ideas? If they were obvious to his crew, surely they should have been obvious to him as the unit manager?

2. How do you think this project will change the atmosphere at Tony's Taco Barn?

3. Do you think Dawn will adopt some of these ideas? Why or why not?

4. Would you want the opportunity to be involved in a project like this? Why or why not?

## key terms

## review questions

1. Describe the relationship between job analysis, skills inventory, and human resource planning.
2. What is equal employment opportunity?
3. Discuss some common pitfalls in interviewing.
4. Outline the conditions under which individual members of a group tend to conform to group norms.

## internet exercise

Visit the Web site of the HRM Guide at www.hrmguide.net. Answer the following questions:

1. What is the HRM Guide?
2. Select and summarize an article on work life balance under the "Employee Relations" HR topic.
3. Select and summarize a U.S. HR news article.
4. The HRM Guide is a network of HRM and other Web sites. Identify six other Web sites to which the HRM Guide can refer you.

## team exercise

### THE LAYOFF

Two years ago, your organization experienced a sudden increase in its volume of work. At about the same time, it was threatened with an equal employment opportunity suit that resulted in an affirmative action plan. Under this plan, additional women and minority members have been recruited and hired.

Presently, the top level of management in your organization is anticipating a decrease in volume of work. You have been asked to rank the clerical employees of your section in the event a layoff is necessary.

Below you will find biographical data for the seven clerical people in your section. Divide yourselves into two groups. Each group must rank the seven people according to the order in which they should be laid off; that is, the person ranked first is to be laid off first, and so on. Each group will then present its rankings back to their peers, along with the justification for the assigned ranking of each employee.

*Burt Green:* White male, age 45. Married, four children; five years with the organization. Reputed to be an alcoholic; poor work record.

*Nan Nushka:* White female, age 26. Married, no children, husband has a steady job; six months with the organization. Hired after the affirmative action plan went into effect; average work record to date. Saving to buy a house.

*Johnny Jones:* Black male, age 20. Unmarried; one year with organization. High performance ratings. Reputed to be shy—a "loner"; wants to start his own business some day.

*Joe Jefferson:* White male, age 24. Married, no children but wife is pregnant; three years with organization. Going to college at night; erratic performance attributed to work-study conflicts.

*Livonia Long:* Black female, age 49. Widow, three grown children; two years with the organization. Steady worker whose performance is average.

*Ward Watt:* White male, age 30. Recently divorced, one child; three years with the organization. Good worker.

*Rosa Sanchez:* Hispanic female, age 45. Six children, husband disabled one year ago; trying to help support her family; three months with the organization. No performance appraisal data available.

**Questions**

1. What criteria did you use for ranking the employees?
2. What implications does your ranking have in the area of affirmative action?
3. How hard was it to reach consensus as a group in this exercise?
4. How would you feel if you were ranked in your organization in the same manner?

## One Company's Delicate Balancing Act

*At Baxter Export, Employees and Managers Confront Work-Family Chaos*

As the afternoon crashes in around her office, as voice mail and e-mail stream in from Saudi Arabia, Oman, and Panama, as conference calls drone on, one inevitability stares Debbie DeBree square in the face: At 5:30 p.m., she has to have dinner on the table.

By then, her husband, Mark, will have picked up 3-year-old Ashley from day care and Adam, 7, from grade school before heading to the first of his two night jobs. Zachary, 15, gets home on his own now. After dinner comes Adam's weekly Cub Scout meeting, where Debbie presides as den mother. The kids are in bed by 9, and Debbie soon after. She'll rise at 4:30 to start breakfast and get the kids going.

And that's just Monday. The rest of the week, a cacophonous maze of alternating work schedules, schools, errands, and kids' activities, simply defies summary. Chaotic? Exhausting? Truly. But "we're kind of used to it," DeBree says. "This is our life."

There are 85 lives at Baxter Export Corp., the international logistics unit at Baxter International Inc.'s Deerfield (Ill.) headquarters where DeBree is based. Few are extraordinary, but none is "normal." Brian Kaspari, for one, juggles family responsibilities with his wife, Pamela, whose job as a police dispatcher requires her to rotate shifts every two weeks.

Elizabeth Bergman and her flight attendant husband, Eric, work complementary schedules—and rarely see each other—to avoid putting 2-year-old Emily in day care.

Like any workplace, Baxter Export is the sum of its employees: Bergman's, Kaspari's, and DeBree's personal lives are enmeshed inextricably with their jobs, the jobs of co-workers, and the unit's business. Last-minute customer orders, superfluous memoranda, or a colleague's sick day all take their toll on the delicate balance. Likewise, the ups and downs of families affect productivity, quality, and corporate profits.

### NO EASY FIX

An 18-month study by Baxter International of 1,000 employees, published this year, revealed that among salaried employees, most work-life tensions were driven by the need for greater balance and the desire for flexibility. At Baxter Export, with 30 percent of its employees telecommuting, job-sharing or working part-time, flexibility has become the norm. But many employees still have trouble striking a satisfactory balance between job and home. There's a solution, but it is no easy fix: The division is entering a thorough restructuring that is altering not just its own jobs and processes but also those throughout the corporation.

Baxter Export's willingness to grapple openly with such issues makes it a revealing laboratory of social change. Its parent, a $5.4 billion maker of health-care products, ranks 19th on *BusinessWeek's* survey, winning employees' plaudits for its supportive culture and alternative work arrangements. "Shared values," rooted in the notion of mutual respect, are reprised relentlessly in internal communications. The company's 42-year-old president, Harry M. Kraemer Jr., begins his widely read monthly financial reports with tales from his own dual-career, three-child family. Workers, he says, "need to know we're all in the same boat."

Even so, the competing pressures of a globally competitive business on the one hand and the two-income family on the other have converged here, forcing many people into inventive, intense arrangements. For Jackie Demo, the workday begins at 6:30 a.m. Like other operations analysts, who typically make between $30,000 and $40,000 a year, she helps support Baxter's briskly growing international business, managing the flow of catheters, dialysis solutions, and intravenous tubes to subsidiaries and customers around the world. She chose to start at daybreak because she can both better communicate with customers in South Africa and New Zealand and pick up her daughter Kaleen, 5, from day care by 4 p.m. Demo, 37, who started at Baxter in 1981, initiated the arrangement four years ago. "I was working overtime, often until 7 p.m. I'd get home in time to give Kaleen her bottle, then put her to sleep. I said: 'This is ridiculous.'"

At home, while microwaving dinner, Demo looks in on her mother-in-law, Elaine, in a basement apartment, then fields a call from the hospice agency that coordinates her care. Diagnosed with terminal cancer last spring, Elaine needs round-the-clock attention. After trying to provide it themselves, with help from family members, Demo and her husband, Joe, hired a live-in health aide several months ago.

Demo's flexible hours and at least one day a week telecommuting ease the burden. Still, the demands of looking after a child and an ill parent—not to mention Joe's small graphics business—prove draining. When heavy rains flooded Joe's office recently, Jackie stayed up until midnight cleaning 75 T-shirts scheduled to go to a customer that week. Joe often doesn't eat until 9 p.m., then stays up late paying bills. "Some nights we cry, and sometimes we snipe at each other," Jackie admits.

## GROUP ETHIC

John Lindner, the front-line manager who oversees Demo, Kaspari, DeBree, and 11 others, is convinced that acknowledging and easing such tensions is good business. Although he doesn't work at home himself, he believes that his people are 10 percent more productive on the days they telecommute. Baxter's willingness to accommodate problems, he adds, also pays off in higher commitment. Still, telecommuters are held to rules that limit disruption. They can't work more than two days a week out of the office; more than that reduces contact with co-workers and erodes the group ethic. Everyone has to be in the office on Wednesdays for meetings. They must pay for call-waiting for their home phones—Latin American customers, especially, don't like voice mail. And they have to share their company-provided laptop PCs: DeBree and co-worker Linda Barry swap theirs at church every Sunday.

With all their flexibility, though, Baxter Export's employees still struggle to find balance. Most spend 45 to 50 hours a week on the job—longer, some say, than they would like. Kaspari checks his office voice mail twice after he gets home and often spends an hour or more dealing with urgent customer issues. As for Demo, the onset of her mother-in-law's cancer and subsequent chemotherapy coincided with a six-week stretch of 14-hour days for a special project, though she says the office actually provided emotional respite through the ordeal.

In the scheme of things, of course, a 50-hour week for white-collar workers hardly is unusual. But the question of balance isn't lost on Griff Lewis, the executive who presides over Baxter Export. "We think they work too much," he says of his employees. More than that, he recognizes that his unit's volume is growing at 12 percent to 15 percent a year, and he does not have the budget to add corresponding staff. Just to keep people's hours reasonable, much less reduce them, he has to find ways to lift productivity—rethinking processes, redesigning jobs, eliminating unnecessary tasks.

That means moving, over the next five years, to an automated allocation system that requires overseas customers, rather than Baxter Export analysts, to prepare demand forecasts and enter orders. That would route orders directly to U.S. warehouses and, as a result, lop three days' work off each analyst's monthly load. Within two years, Lewis expects to standardize procedures across the 120 countries his department serves, eliminating extraneous tasks and allowing employees to address mostly exceptional orders and higher-level issues.

Already, such schemes have relieved the 60-hour weeks that were commonplace a few years back, employees say. Yet Lewis' putative makeover is complicated by his division's web of relationships with the many units of its global parent. Baxter's U.S. manufacturing, for instance, maintains as little inventory as possible—so when demand overseas spikes above expectations, Lewis' analysts can't always find product easily. If managers in Brazil cram in last-minute orders to meet quarterly quotas, someone in Deerfield has to work late to meet requirements on time.

Can Brazil change? Can everyone? That's what it will take, ultimately, for DeBree, Kaspari, and Demo to have easier lives. They have support, in name and in practice, from manager Lindner up to President Kraemer. Now the rest of Baxter will try to adjust to new schedules, changed systems, and altered strategies. If everyone pulls together, Debbie DeBree's kids can eat on time.

## Questions

1. Why would Baxter Corporation make the effort to restructure in order to manage the work-life tensions of its employees? What does it stand to gain?

2. Do you agree with Baxter's concern that "more than two days a week out of the office . . . reduces contact with co-workers and erodes the group ethic"? Why or why not?

3. Baxter's plan to move to an automated allocation system will require its overseas customers to enter orders and forecast demand—work formerly done by Baxter employees. Is that an appropriate solution to employee work-life tensions? Why or why not?

4. Consider the company you work for (or one you have worked for in the past). Would you say that the company is concerned about your work-life tensions? Explain your answer.

*Source:* Adapted from Keith H. Hammonds "One Company's Delicate Balancing Act", *BusinessWeek Online,* September 15, 1997.

# Smashing the Clock

*Inside Best Buy's Radical Reshaping of the Workplace*

One afternoon last year, Chap Achen, who oversees online orders at Best Buy Co. shut down his computer, stood up from his desk, and announced that he was leaving for the day. It was around 2 p.m., and most of Achen's staff were slumped over their keyboards, deep in a post-lunch, LCD-lit trance. "See you tomorrow," said Achen. "I'm going to a matinee." Under normal circumstances, an early-afternoon departure would have been totally un-Achen. After all, this was a 37-year-old corporate comer whose wife laughs in his face when he utters the words "work-life balance." But at Best Buy's Minneapolis headquarters, similar incidents of strangeness were breaking out all over the ultramodern campus. In employee relations, Steve Hance had suddenly started going hunting on workdays, a Remington 12-gauge in one hand, a Verizon LG in the other. In the retail training department, e-learning specialist Mark Wells was spending his days chasing around the country following rocker Dave Matthews. Single mother Kelly McDevitt, an online promotions manager, started leaving at 2:30 p.m. to pick up her 11-year-old son Calvin from school. Scott Jauman, a Six Sigma black belt, began spending a third of his time at his Northwoods

cabin. At most companies, going AWOL during daylight hours would be grounds for a pink slip. Not at Best Buy. The nation's leading electronics retailer has embarked on a radical— if risky—experiment to transform a culture once known for killer hours and herd-riding bosses. The endeavor, called ROWE, for "results-only work environment," seeks to demolish decades-old business dogma that equates physical presence with productivity. The goal at Best Buy is to judge performance on output instead of hours. Hence workers pulling into the company's amenity-packed headquarters at 2 p.m. aren't considered late. Nor are those pulling out at 2 p.m. seen as leaving early. There are no schedules. No mandatory meetings. No impression-management hustles. Work is no longer a place where you go, but something you do. It's O.K. to take conference calls while you hunt, collaborate from your lakeside cabin, or log on after dinner so you can spend the afternoon with your kid. Best Buy did not invent the post-geographic office. Tech companies have been going bedouin for several years. At IBM, 40 percent of the workforce has no official office; at AT&T, a third of managers are untethered. Sun Microsystems Inc. calculates that it's saved $400 million over six years in real estate costs by allowing nearly half of all employees to work anywhere they want. And this trend seems to have legs. A recent Boston Consulting Group study found that 85 percent of executives expect a big rise in the number of unleashed workers over the next five years. In fact, at many companies the most innovative new product may be the structure of the workplace itself. But arguably no big business has smashed the clock quite so resolutely as Best Buy. The official policy for this post-face-time, location-agnostic way of working is that people are free to work wherever they want, whenever they want, as long as they get their work done. "This is like TiVo for your work," says the program's co-founder, Jody Thompson. By the end of 2007, all 4,000 staffers working at corporate will be on ROWE. Starting in February, the new work environment will become an official part of Best Buy's recruiting pitch as well as its orientation for new hires. And the company plans to take its clockless campaign to its stores—a high-stakes challenge that no company has tried before in a retail environment. Another thing about this experiment: It wasn't imposed from the top down. It began as a covert guerrilla action that spread virally and eventually became a revolution. So secret was the operation that Chief Executive Brad Anderson only learned the details two years after it began transforming his company. Such bottom-up, stealth innovation is exactly the kind of thing Anderson encourages. The Best Buy chief aims to keep innovating even when something is ostensibly working. "ROWE was an idea born and nurtured by a handful of passionate employees," he says. "It wasn't created as the result of some edict."

The CEO may have bought in, but there has been plenty of opposition inside the company. Many execs wondered if the program was simply flextime in a prettier bottle. Others felt that working off-site would lead to longer hours and destroy forever the demarcation between work and personal time. Cynics thought it was all a PR stunt dreamed up by Machiavellian operatives in human resources. And as ROWE infected one department after the other, its supporters ran into old-guard saboteurs, who continue to plot an overthrow and spread warnings of a coming paradise for slackers. Then again, the new work structure's proponents say it's helping Best Buy overcome challenges. And thanks to early successes, some of the program's harshest critics have become true believers. With gross margins on electronics under pressure, and Wal-Mart Stores Inc. and Target Corp. shouldering into Best Buy territory, the company has been moving into services, including its Geek Squad and "customer centricity" program in which salespeople act as technology counselors. But Best Buy was afflicted by stress, burnout, and high turnover. The hope was that ROWE, by freeing employees to make their own work-life decisions, could boost morale and productivity and keep the service initiative on track. It seems to be working. Since the program's implementation, average voluntary turnover has fallen drastically, and Best Buy notes that productivity is up an average 35 percent in departments that have switched to ROWE. Employee engagement, which measures employee satisfaction and is often a barometer for retention, is way up too, according to the Gallup Organization, which audits corporate cultures. ROWE may also help the company pay for the customer centricity campaign. The endeavor is hugely expensive because it involves tailoring stores to local markets and training employees to turn customer feedback into new business ideas. By letting people work off-campus, Best Buy figures it can reduce the need for corporate office space, perhaps rent out the empty cubicles to other companies, and plow the millions of dollars in savings into its services initiative. Phyllis Moen, a University of Minnesota sociology professor who researches work-life issues, is studying the Best Buy experiment in a project sponsored by the National Institutes of Health. She says most companies are stuck in the 1930s when it comes to employees' and managers' relationships to time and work. "Our whole notion of paid work was developed within an assembly line culture," Moen says. "Showing up was work. Best Buy is recognizing that sitting in a chair is no longer working."

### Questions

1. Why is Best Buy's ROWE program considered to be such a radical move?

2. What are the potential benefits of the ROWE program?

3. Consider your current job (or one you have held in the past). Would this kind of program work there? Why or why not?

4. Do you think such employment flexibility would improve your productivity and morale? Explain your answer.

*Source:* Adapted from Michelle Conlin, **"Inside Best Buy's Radical Reshaping of the Workplace,"** *BusinessWeek Online,* December 11, 2006.

# MOTIVATING PEOPLE

**"Management is nothing more than motivating other people."**

—Lee Iacocca

## The World of Work: Employee of the month—again!

"And the employee of the month is . . ." Tony paused for dramatic effect. "Kelly Stevens!"

The round of applause that followed was very unenthusiastic. Probably, Tony thought, because Kelly had been voted employee of the month three times in the last six months, and this was her fourth award.

That was one of the biggest challenges in running a single unit like this—the part-time staff weren't around enough to really make a memorable impact and so the pool of candidates for the award typically ended up being the small core of full-time crew members. They had tried to modify the program a few months ago by recognizing specific examples of excellent customer service observed by the manager or shift leaders, but that had backfired when people started going out of

their way to "create" opportunities for memorable service. The most blatant example, Tony recalled, had been when one of their new servers took orders from a table of eight that were totally off the standard menu and had to be cooked to order using ingredients purchased very rapidly from the food market down the block! That was definitely service above and beyond the norm, but when the server charged them all standard prices, Tony had to step in and control his enthusiasm.

On the day after the employee of the month award, Tony called his staff into a brief meeting and proposed a new idea:

"I know everyone is working hard here, and the company is committed to rewarding you for that, but

274

# LEARNING objectives

**After studying this chapter, you will be able to:**

1  Define motivation.

2  Discuss the equity approach to motivation.

3  Explain the hierarchy of needs.

4  Discuss the expectancy approach to motivation.

5  Discuss the motivation-hygiene approach to motivation.

6  Define job satisfaction and organizational morale.

---

the employee of the month award doesn't work for such a small crew of full-timers. I'd like to explore some other ways of recognizing all your efforts—ways that include the part-time team members as well as the full-time ones. More important, I'm looking for ways to offer incentives that really mean something to you—not just the plaque on the wall and the designated parking space—something that you will enjoy receiving long after the award is given.

"Since you'll be the ones receiving the awards, I'd like you to propose some ideas for what those awards should be," continued Tony. "I'm not going to put you on the spot now for ideas, but I would like you to write some down and put them in the suggestion box in the break room. We'll give it a few days and then we'll look at what everyone came up with—okay?"

## QUESTIONS

1. Why does Tony feel that the employee of the month award isn't working?

2. What's the value in asking the Taco Barn employees for their ideas?

3. What ideas do you have for recognizing employee performance?

4. Consider the organization you currently work for or one you have worked for in the past. How did that organization recognize employee performance?

# MOTIVATING EMPLOYEES

Statements and questions such as the following are often expressed by managers: Our employees are just not motivated. Half the problems we have are due to a lack of personal motivation. How do I motivate my employees?

The problem of motivation is not a recent development. Research conducted by William James in the late 1800s indicated the importance of motivation.[1] James found that hourly employees could keep their jobs by using approximately 20 to 30 percent of their ability. He also found that highly motivated employees will work at approximately 80 to 90 percent of their ability. Figure 10.1 illustrates the potential influence of motivation on performance. Highly motivated employees can bring about substantial increases in performance and substantial decreases in problems such as absenteeism, turnover, tardiness, strikes, and grievances.

The word **motivation** comes from the Latin word *movere*, which means to move. Numerous definitions are given for the term. Usually included are such words as *aim, desire, end, impulse, intention, objective,* and *purpose*. These definitions normally include three common characteristics of motivation. First, motivation is concerned with what activates human behavior. Second, motivation is concerned with what directs this behavior toward a particular goal. Third, motivation is concerned with how this behavior is sustained.

Motivation can be analyzed using the following connecting sequence:

$$\text{Needs} \rightarrow \text{Drives or motives} \rightarrow \text{Achievement of goals}$$

In motivation, needs produce motives, which lead to the accomplishment of goals. Needs are caused by deficiencies, which can be either physical or psychological. For instance, a physical need exists when an individual goes without sleep for 48 hours. A psychological need exists when an individual has no friends or companions. Individual needs will be explored in much greater depth later in this chapter.

**motivation**

Concerned with what activates human behavior, what directs this behavior toward a particular goal, and how this behavior is sustained.

**figure 10.1**

**POTENTIAL INFLUENCE OF MOTIVATION ON PERFORMANCE**

**Source:** P. Hersey and K. H. Blanchard, *Management of Organizational Behavior: Utilizing Human Resources,* 4th ed., Prentice Hall, 1982.

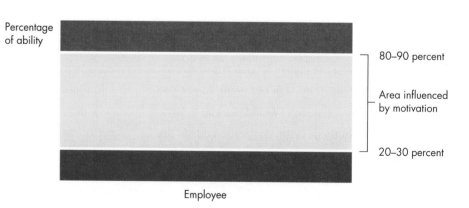

A motive is a stimulus that leads to an action that satisfies the need. In other words, motives produce actions. Lack of sleep (the need) activates the physical changes of fatigue (the motive), which produces sleep (the action or, in this example, inaction).

Achievement of the goal satisfies the need and reduces the motive. When the goal is reached, balance is restored. However, other needs arise, which are then satisfied by the same sequence of events. Understanding the motivation sequence in itself offers a manager little help in determining what motivates employees. The approaches to analyzing motivation described in this chapter help to provide a broader understanding of what motivates people. They include the following: scientific management, equity, hierarchy of needs, achievement-power-affiliation, motivation-hygiene, expectancy, and reinforcement.

## IMPORTANCE OF TRUST IN MANAGEMENT

The importance of trust in management by employees cannot be stressed enough as being absolutely essential for the success (or failure) for all motivational efforts. Without trust in management, all organizational efforts to motivate employees for improved performance is suspect. The presence of trust gives management credibility when asking for more productivity from employees.

## EQUITY APPROACH

**Equity theory** is based on the idea that people want to be treated fairly in relationship to others. **Inequity** exists when a person perceives his or her job inputs and rewards to be less than the job inputs and outcomes of another person. The important point to note in this definition is that it is the person's *perception* of inputs and rewards, not necessarily the actual inputs and rewards. Furthermore, the other person in the comparison can be an employee in the person's work group or in another part of the organization, which forms the employee's internal equity perception. Likewise, an employee may compare his or her inputs and rewards to others outside the company in like jobs.

**Inputs** are what an employee perceives are his or her contributions to the organization (i.e., education, intelligence, experience, training, skills, and the effort exerted on the job). Outcomes are the rewards received by the employee (i.e., pay, rewards central to the job, seniority benefits, and status). Equity theory also suggests that the presence of inequity in a person creates tension in a person that is directly relative to the size of the inequity. Furthermore, the tension will motivate the person to achieve equity or reduce inequity. The strength of the motivation varies directly with the amount of inequity. A person might take several actions to reduce inequity:

**equity theory**
Motivation theory based on the idea that people want to be treated fairly in relationship to others.

**inequity**
Exists when a person perceives his or her job inputs and outcomes to be less than the job inputs and outcomes of another person.

**inputs**
What an employee perceives are his or her contributions to the organization (e.g., education, intelligence, experience, training skills, and the effort exerted on the job).

## An Informative Coffee Break

On a Monday morning, April 28, George Smith was given the news that effective May 1, he would receive a raise of 13 percent. This raise came two months before his scheduled performance appraisal. His manager, Tom Weeks, informed him that the basis for the raise was his performance over the past several months and his value to the company. He was told that this was an "above average" increase.

On the next day, Tuesday, a group of George's co-workers were having their regular morning coffee break. The conversation slowly made its way around to salary increases. One member of the group shared that she had received a performance review in April, but she had yet to receive any indication of a salary increase. George made a comment about the amount of any such increases, specifically questioning the range of increase percentages. Another co-worker immediately responded by saying how surprised he was in getting an across-the-board 12 percent increase last Friday. Another co-worker confirmed that he too had received a similar salary increase. Shocked by this information, George pressed for information, only to learn that several people had received increases of "around" 11 to 13 percent. Confused and angry, George excused himself, went back to his office, and closed the door.

That evening, George wrestled with his conscience concerning that morning's discussion. His first impression of his raise was that it had been given based on performance. He felt he was being singled out for recognition for his hard work and his value to the organization. Now he wasn't so sure. Several questions were bothering him:

1. Why did his boss present the raise to him as a merit increase when it was the same as everyone else's?
2. Did individual job performance really count for that much in salary increases in his department?
3. Did his boss hide the truth regarding the raise?
4. Can he trust his boss in the future?
5. Will future salary increases be averaged across the board too?

### Questions

1. Do you think George is right to be this upset? Why or why not.
2. How do you think the information George discovered during that morning coffee break will affect his performance from now on?
3. How would you react if you were George? Why?
4. What can Tom Weeks do to regain George's trust?

---

1. Increase inputs on the job if his or her inputs are low relative to the other person. For example, a person might work harder to increase his or her inputs on the job.
2. Reduce inputs if they are high relative to the other person's inputs and to his or her own outcomes.
3. Quit the job.
4. Request a pay increase.

---

### PROGRESS CHECK QUESTIONS

1. What are the three common characteristics of management?
2. Why is trust in management so important for any motivational efforts?
3. What is equity theory?
4. Define the term *inputs*.

# HIERARCHY OF NEEDS

The **hierarchy of needs** is based on the assumption that individuals are motivated to satisfy a number of needs and that money can directly or indirectly satisfy only some of these needs. The need hierarchy is based largely on the work of Abraham Maslow.[2] The hierarchy of needs consists of the five levels shown in Figure 10.2.

The **physiological** needs are basically the needs of the human body that must be satisfied in order to sustain life. These needs include food, sleep, water, exercise, clothing, shelter, and so forth.

**Safety** needs are concerned with protection against danger, threat, or deprivation. Since all employees have (to some degree) a dependent relationship with the organization, safety needs can be critically important. Favoritism, discrimination, and arbitrary administration of organizational policies are all actions that arouse uncertainty and therefore affect the safety needs.

The third level of needs is composed of the **social** needs. Generally categorized at this level are the needs for love, affection, belonging—all are concerned with establishing one's position relative to others. This need is satisfied by the development of meaningful personal relations and by acceptance into meaningful groups of individuals. Belonging to

**hierarchy of needs**
Based on the assumption that individuals are motivated to satisfy a number of needs and that money can directly or indirectly satisfy only some of these needs.

**physiological**
Needs of the human body that must be satisfied in order to sustain life.

**safety**
Protection against danger, threat, or deprivation.

## figure 10.2

**HIERARCHY OF NEEDS**

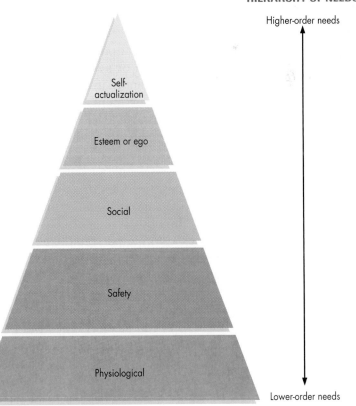

**Self-actualization needs:**
1. Self-fulfillment of potential.
2. Doing things for the challenge of accomplishment.
3. Intellectual curiosity.
4. Creativity and aesthetic appreciation.
5. Acceptance of reality.

**Esteem (or ego) needs:**
1. Recognition and prestige.
2. Confidence and leadership.
3. Competence and success.
4. Strength and intelligence.

**Social needs:**
1. Acceptance.
2. Feeling of belonging.
3. Membership in group.
4. Love and affection.
5. Group participation.

**Safety needs:**
1. Security and safety.
2. Protection.
3. Comfort and peace.
4. No threats or danger.
5. Orderly and neat surroundings.
6. Assurance of long-term economic well-being.

**Physiological needs:**
1. Food and thirst.
2. Sleep.
3. Health.
4. Body needs.
5. Exercise and rest.

Higher-order needs

Self-actualization

Esteem or ego

Social

Safety

Physiological

Lower-order needs

The span from the lowest to highest level in Maslow's hierarchy is fairly significant. Simple everyday activities can feel vastly different, depending on specific need-requirements. Which needs do you feel are fulfilled in your own life?

**social**

Categorized as needs for love, affection, belonging—all are concerned with establishing one's position relative to others.

**esteem**

Influences the development of various kinds of relationships based on adequacy, independence, and the giving and receiving of indications of esteem and acceptance.

**self-actualization or self-fulfillment**

Highest-order need is concerned with the need of people to reach their full potential in applying their abilities and interests to functioning in their environment.

organizations and identifying with work groups are means of satisfying these needs in organizations.

The fourth level of needs is composed of the **esteem** needs. The esteem needs include both self-esteem and the esteem of others. These needs influence the development of various kinds of relationships based on adequacy, independence, and the giving and receiving of indications of esteem and acceptance.

The highest-order need is concerned with the need for **self-actualization** or **self-fulfillment**—that is, the need of people to reach their full potential in applying their abilities and interests to functioning in their environment. This need is concerned with the will to operate at the best possible level. The need for self-actualization or self-fulfillment is never completely satisfied; one can always reach one step higher.

The hierarchy of needs adequately describes the general order or ranking of most people's needs. However, there are several other possibilities to be considered. First, although the needs of most people are arranged in the sequence shown in Figure 10.2, differences in the sequence can occur, depending on an individual's experience, culture, social upbringing, and numerous other personality aspects. Second, the strength or potency of a person's needs may shift back and forth under different situations. For instance, during bad economic times, physiological and safety needs might tend to dominate an individual's behavior; in good economic times, higher-order needs might dominate an individual's behavior.

The unconscious character of the various needs should be recognized. In addition, there is a certain degree of cultural specificity of needs. In other words, the ways by which the various needs can be met tend to be controlled by cultural and societal factors. For example, the particular culture may dictate one's eating habits, social life, and numerous other facets of life.

Finally, different methods can be used by different individuals to satisfy a particular need. Two individuals may be deficient in relation to the same physiological need; however, the way in which each chooses to satisfy that need may vary considerably.

As far as motivation is concerned, the thrust of the hierarchy of needs is that the lowest-level unsatisfied need causes behavior. The hierarchy represents what Maslow thought was the order in which unsatisfied needs would activate behavior.

Many of today's organizations are applying the logic of the needs hierarchy. For instance, compensation systems are generally designed to satisfy the lower-order needs—physiological and safety. On the other hand, interesting work and opportunities for advancement are designed to appeal to higher-order needs. So the job of a manager is to determine the need level an individual employee is attempting to satisfy and then provide the means by which the employee can satisfy that need. Obviously, determining the need level of a particular person can be difficult. All people do not operate at the same level on the needs hierarchy. All people do not react similarly to the same situation.

Little research has been conducted to test the validity of the hierarchy of needs theory. Its primary value is that it provides a structure for analyzing needs and, as will be seen later in this chapter, is used as a basis for other theories of motivation.

> ### Make an Impression That Counts!
>
> From the very beginning of our careers, we learn how important a first impression is when we interview, begin a new job, join a sports team, or have a first day of school.
>
> In the world of establishing a career, first impressions really count. Your positive attitude can let others know you are mentally prepared and ready to make healthy contributions to the work environment. Getting off to a good start can open doors and position you as a leader.
>
> How do you make a good first impression? Try being prepared, positive, and mentally and physically ready. As the saying goes, "You only get one chance to make a first impression."

## ACHIEVEMENT-POWER-AFFILIATION APPROACH

While recognizing that people have many different needs, David C. McClelland developed the achievement-power-affiliation approach to motivation, which focuses on three needs: (1) need to achieve, (2) need for power, and (3) need for affiliation.[3] The use of the term *need* in this approach is different from the hierarchy of needs approach in that, under this approach, the three needs are assumed to be learned, whereas the needs hierarchy assumes that needs are inherent.

The *need for achievement* is a desire to do something better or more efficiently than it has been done before—to achieve. The *need for power* is basically a concern for influencing people—to be strong and influential. The *need for affiliation* is a need to be liked—to establish or maintain friendly relations with others.

The *need for achievement* is a powerful motivator for many employees. Is it a motivator you think you would respond to?

This approach assumes that most people have developed a degree of each of these needs, but the level of intensity varies among people. For example, an individual may be high in the need for achievement, moderate in the need for power, and low in the need for affiliation. This individual's motivation to work will vary greatly from that of another person who has a high need for power and low needs for achievement and affiliation. An employee with a high need for affiliation would probably respond positively to demonstrations of warmth and support by a manager; an employee with a high need for achievement would likely respond positively to increased responsibility. Finally, under this approach to motivation, when a need's strength has been developed, it motivates behaviors or attracts employees to situations where such behaviors can be acted out. However, this does not satisfy the need; it is more likely to strengthen it further. Figure 10.3 describes this approach to motivation.

## Motivation–Hygiene Approach

Another approach to work motivation was developed by Frederick Herzberg and is referred to by several names: the **motivation-hygiene,** two-factor, or motivation-maintenance approach.[4] Initially, the development of the approach involved extensive interviews with approximately 200 engineers and accountants from 11 industries in the Pittsburgh area. In the interviews, researchers used what is called the critical incident method. This involved asking subjects to recall work situations in which they had experienced periods of high and low motivation. They were asked to recount specific details about the situation and the effect of the experience over time.

Analysis of the interviewees' statements showed that different factors were associated with good and bad feelings. The findings fell into two major categories. Those factors that were most frequently mentioned

**figure 10.3**

ACHIEVEMENT-POWER-AFFILIATION NEEDS

**1. The Need for Power**

Some people are strongly motivated by the need for power. They are likely to be happiest in jobs that give them control over budgets, people, and decision making.

**2. The Need for Achievement**

Other people are strongly motivated by the need for achievement. They are likely to be happiest working in an environment in which they can create something new.

**3. The Need for Affiliation**

Some people are strongly motivated by the need for affiliation. These people usually enjoy working with other people. They are motivated by the prospect of having people like them.

in association with a favorably viewed incident concerned the work it-self. These factors were achievement, recognition, responsibility, ad-vancement, and the characteristics of the job. But when subjects felt negatively oriented toward a work incident, they were more likely to mention factors associated with the work environment. These included status; interpersonal relations with supervisors, peers, and subordi-nates; technical aspects of supervision; company policy and administra-tion; job security; working conditions; salary; and aspects of their personal lives that were affected by the work situation.

The latter set of factors was called *hygiene* or *maintenance* factors because the researchers thought that they are preventive in nature. In other words, they do not produce motivation but can prevent motivation from occurring. Thus, proper attention to maintenance factors is a nec-essary but not sufficient condition for motivation. The first set of factors were called *motivators*. The researchers contended that these factors, when present in addition to the maintenance factors, provide true motivation.

In summary, the motivation-hygiene approach contends that moti-vation comes from the individual, not from the manager. At best, proper attention to the maintenance factors keeps an individual from being highly dissatisfied but does not make that individual motivated. Both hygiene and motivator factors must be present in order for true motiva-tion to occur. Figure 10.4 lists some examples of hygiene and motivator factors.

Job enrichment programs have been developed in an attempt to solve motivational problems by using the motivation-maintenance theory. Unlike **job enlargement,** which merely involves giving an em-ployee more of a similar type of operation to perform, or **job rotation,** which is the practice of periodically rotating job assignments, **job enrichment** involves an upgrading of the job by adding motivator factors. Designing jobs that provide for meaningful work, achieve-ment, recognition, responsibility, advancement, and growth is the key to job enrichment.

**motivation–hygiene**

An approach to work motivation that associates factors of high-low motivation with either the work environment or the work itself.

**job enlargement**

Giving an employee more of a similar type of operation to perform.

**job rotation**

The practice of periodically rotating job assignments within the organization.

**job enrichment**

Upgrading the job by adding motivator factors.

| HYGIENE FACTORS (ENVIRONMENTAL) | MOTIVATOR FACTORS (JOB ITSELF) |
| --- | --- |
| Policies and administration | Achievement |
| Supervision | Recognition |
| Working conditions | Challenging work |
| Interpersonal relations | Increased responsibility |
| Personal life | Opportunities for advancement |
| Money, status, security | Opportunities for personal growth |

**figure 10.4**

**MOTIVATION-HYGIENE FACTORS**

## figure 10.5

**COMPARISON OF THE HIERARCHY OF NEEDS WITH THE MOTIVATION-HYGIENE APPROACH**

**Hierarchy of needs**

Self-actualization

Esteem or ego

Social

Safety

Physiological

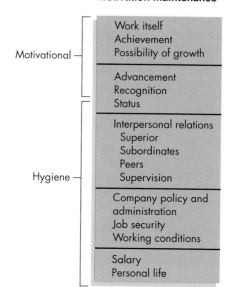

**Motivation maintenance**

Motivational —
- Work itself
- Achievement
- Possibility of growth

- Advancement
- Recognition
- Status

Hygiene —
- Interpersonal relations
  - Superior
  - Subordinates
  - Peers
  - Supervision

- Company policy and administration
- Job security
- Working conditions

- Salary
- Personal life

As can be seen from Figure 10.5, the motivation-hygiene approach is very closely related to the hierarchy of needs approach to motivation and so is subject to many of the same criticisms.

What does a manager do in using the motivation-hygiene theory when the manager has an employee that is not performing well? First, all hygiene factors should be checked to ensure that they are satisfactory. Then a motivation should be applied that meets the individual's needs and drives.

## PROGRESS CHECK QUESTIONS

5. Why is self-actualization or self-fulfillment at the top of Maslow's hierarchy of needs?

6. How does McClelland's achievement-power-affiliation approach to motivation differ from Maslow's hierarchy of needs approach?

7. Explain the statement: "Proper attention to maintenance factors keeps an individual from being highly dissatisfied but does not make that individual motivated."

8. Explain the terms *job enlargement, job rotation,* and *job enrichment.*

**expectancy approach**
Based on the idea that employee, beliefs about the relationship among effort, performance, and outcomes as a result of performance and the value employees place on the outcomes determine their level of motivation.

## Expectancy Approach

The **expectancy approach** to motivation was developed by Victor Vroom and is based on the idea that employee beliefs about the relationship among effort, performance, and outcomes as a result of performance and the value employees place on the outcomes determine their level of motivation.[5] Figure 10.6 outlines the expectancy approach to motivation.

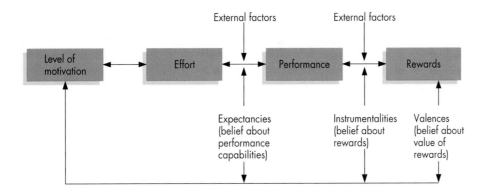

**figure 10.6**

**EXPECTANCY APPROACH**

The expectancy approach suggests that an employee's level of motivation depends on three basic beliefs: expectancy, instrumentality, and valence. **Expectancy** refers to the employee's belief that his or her effort will lead to the desired level of performance. **Instrumentality** refers to the employee's belief that achieving the desired level of performance will lead to certain rewards. **Valence** refers to the employee's belief about the value of the rewards. External factors are beyond the employee's control and often negatively influence expectancies and instrumentalities because they introduce uncertainty into the relationship. Company policies and efficiency of the equipment being used are examples of external factors.

The following example is intended to illustrate the expectancy approach. Assume John Stone is an insurance salesman for the ABC Life Insurance Company. John has learned over the years that he completes one sale for approximately every six calls he makes. John has a high expectancy about the relationship between his effort and performance. Since John is on a straight commission, he also sees a direct relationship between performance and rewards. Thus, his expectation that increased effort will lead to increased rewards is relatively high. Further, suppose that John's income is currently in a high tax bracket such that he gets to keep, after taxes, only 60 percent of his commissions. This being the case, he may not look on the additional money he gets to keep (the outcome) as being very attractive. The end result is that John's belief about the value of the additional money (valence) may be relatively low. Thus, even when the expectation of receiving the additional money is high, his motivation to do additional work may be relatively low.

Each of the separate components of the expectancy approach can be affected by the organization's practices and management. The expectancy that increased effort will lead to increased performance can be positively influenced by providing proper selection, training, and clear direction to the workforce. The expectancy that increased performance will lead to desired rewards is almost totally under the control of the organization. Does the organization really attempt to link rewards to performance? Or are rewards based on some other variable, such as

**expectancy**

Employee's belief that his or her effort will lead to the desired level of performance.

**instrumentality**

Employee's belief that attaining the desired level of performance will lead to desired rewards.

**valence**

Employee's belief about the value of the rewards.

seniority? The final component—the preference for the rewards being offered—is usually taken for granted by the organization. Historically, organizations have assumed that whatever rewards are provided will be valued by employees. Even if this were true, some rewards are certainly more valued than others. Certain rewards, such as a promotion that involves a transfer to another city, may be viewed negatively. Organizations should solicit feedback from their employees concerning the types of rewards that are valued. Since an organization is going to spend a certain amount of money on rewards (salary, fringe benefits, and so on), it should try to get the maximum return from its investment.

## Reinforcement Approach

Developed by B. F. Skinner, the general idea behind the reinforcement approach to motivation is that the consequences of a person's present behavior influence his or her future behavior.[6] For example, behavior that leads to a positive consequence is likely to be repeated, while behavior that leads to a negative consequence is unlikely to be repeated.

The consequences of an individual's behavior are called *reinforcement*. Basically, four types of reinforcement exist—positive reinforcement, avoidance, extinction, and punishment. These are summarized in Figure 10.7. **Positive reinforcement** involves providing a positive consequence as a result of desired behavior. **Avoidance,** also called *negative reinforcement,* involves giving a person the opportunity to avoid a negative consequence by exhibiting a desired behavior. Both positive reinforcement and avoidance can be used to increase the frequency of desired behavior.

**Extinction** involves providing no positive consequences or removing previously provided positive consequences as a result of undesirable behavior. In other words, behavior that no longer pays is less likely to be repeated. **Punishment** involves providing a negative consequence as a result of undesired behavior. Both extinction and punishment can be used to decrease the frequency of undesired behavior.

The current emphasis on the use of reinforcement theory in management practices is concerned with positive reinforcement. Examples include

**positive reinforcement**

Providing a positive consequence as a result of desirable behavior.

**avoidance**

Giving a person the opportunity to avoid a negative consequence by exhibiting a desirable behavior. Also called *negative reinforcement.*

**extinction**

Providing no positive consequences or removing previously provided positive consequences as a result of undesirable behavior.

**punishment**

Providing a negative consequence as a result of undesirable behavior.

## figure 10.7

**TYPES OF REINFORCEMENT**

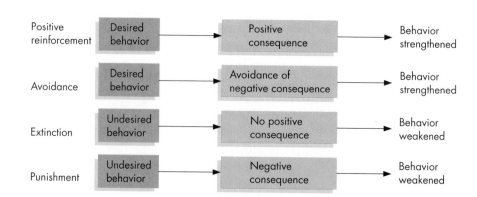

increased pay for increased performance, and praise and recognition when an employee does a good job. Generally, several steps are to be followed in the use of positive reinforcement. These steps include:

1. Selecting reinforcers that are strong and durable enough to establish and strengthen the desired behavior.
2. Designing the work environment in such a way that the reinforcing events are contingent on the desired behavior.
3. Designing the work environment so that the employee has the opportunity to demonstrate the desired behavior.

The key to successful positive reinforcement is that rewards must result from performance. Several suggestions for the effective use of reinforcement have been proposed. These include the following:

1. All people should not be rewarded the same. In other words, the greater the level of performance by an employee, the greater should be the rewards.
2. Failure to respond to an employee's behavior has reinforcing consequences.
3. A person must be told what can be done to be reinforced.
4. A person must be told what he or she is doing wrong.
5. Reprimands should not be issued in front of others.
6. The consequences of a person's behavior should be equal to the behavior.

In addition, positive reinforcement generally is more effective than negative reinforcement and punishment in producing and maintaining desired behavior.

## Study Skills

### Importance of Study Partners
*What has been your experience using a study partner?*

Consider the advantages:

- Study partners help you schedule and participate in study time.
- They keep you focused on the right amount of study time and frequency required to keep on top of the course requirements.
- Study partners are a great sounding board to the learning process, helping to fill in the gaps of what might be complicated subject materials.

However, there are some disadvantages:

- Study partners sometimes have other obligations that crowd study time, and scheduling time becomes complicated and nonproductive.
- Study partners sometimes have issues with an instructor or other students and allow these distractions to become a higher priority of discussion than the subject material.

## PROGRESS CHECK QUESTIONS

9. What is the expectancy approach to motivation?
10. Explain the terms *instrumentality* and *valence.*
11. Explain the difference between positive reinforcement and avoidance.
12. What are the six key points to remember in the effective use of reinforcement?

## The Long-Term Employee

Bill Harrison is 57 years old and has been with Ross Products for 37 years. He has been on a top-paying machine-operator job for the last 20 years. Bill is quite active in community affairs and takes a genuine interest in most employee activities. He is very friendly and well liked by all employees, especially the younger ones, who often come to him for advice. He is extremely helpful to these younger employees and never hesitates to help when asked. When talking with the younger employees, Bill never talks negatively about the company.

Bill's one shortcoming, as his supervisor Alice Jeffries sees it, is his tendency to spend too much time talking with other employees. This not only causes Bill's work to suffer but also, perhaps more important, hinders the output of others. Whenever Alice confronts Bill with the problem, Bill's performance improves for a day or two. It never takes long, however, for Bill to slip back into his old habit of storytelling and interrupting others.

Alice considered trying to have Bill transferred to another area where he would have less opportunity to interrupt others. However, Alice concluded she needs Bill's experience, especially since she has no available replacement for Bill's job.

Bill is secure in his personal life. He owns a nice house and lives well. His wife works as a librarian, and their two children are grown and married. Alice has sensed that Bill thinks he is as high as he'll ever go in the company. This doesn't seem to bother him since he feels comfortable and likes his present job.

### Questions

1. What approach to motivation would you use to try to motivate Bill? Explain in detail what you would do.

2. Suppose Alice could transfer Bill. Would you recommend that she do it?

3. How do you think the other employees would respond if Alice fired Bill?

4. If Bill's behavior doesn't change, what are Alice's options?

## Integrating the Approaches to Motivation

There are many ways to look at motivation. Each approach emphasizes different contributors to motivation or sees the same contributors from a different perspective (see Figure 10.8). No single approach provides all the answers, so it is sometimes necessary to utilize more than one approach.

## Job Satisfaction

**job satisfaction**
An individual's general attitude about his or her job.

**Job satisfaction** is an individual's general attitude about his or her job. The five major components of job satisfaction are (1) attitude toward work group, (2) general working conditions, (3) attitude toward company, (4) monetary benefits, and (5) attitude toward supervision. Other major components that should be added to these five are the individual's attitudes toward the work itself and toward life in general. The individual's health, age, level of aspiration, social status, and political and social activities can all contribute to job satisfaction. Therefore, job satisfaction is an attitude that results from other specific attitudes and factors.

**organizational morale**
An individual's feeling of being accepted by, and belonging to, a group of employees through common goals, confidence in the desirability of these goals, and progress toward these goals.

Job satisfaction refers to the individual's mind-set about the job. This mind-set may be positive or negative, depending on the individual's mind-set concerning the major components of job satisfaction. Job satisfaction is not synonymous with organizational morale. **Organizational morale**

Jon Bennett is the human resource manager of ABC Industries, a small, privately owned, metal fabrication company. After three years of trying, Jon has finally convinced the owners of the company that a performance bonus incentive system, tied to specific cost and revenue targets, will help with employee productivity and help to reduce the employee turnover problems they've been experiencing over the past year.

The new program is launched in an all-staff meeting and the employees are told that if the company hits the cost and revenue targets, they will receive their bonus checks at the annual holiday party held on the last Saturday before Christmas.

The response from the ABC employees is very positive. They become very cost conscious, and productivity increases dramatically. Several new process ideas are proposed which save the company tens of thousands of dollars in the first six months. However, in the last quarter of the year, ABC's biggest competitor, XYZ Industries, drops its prices significantly and manages to steal two of ABC's largest clients. XYZ doesn't have better products or better service, but they offer prices that Jon is convinced are below XYZ's cost of production, just to win the business away from ABC.

As a result, ABC misses its revenue targets for the year. The company grew at a rate of 8 percent instead of the planned 15 percent. Despite Jon's requests for the owners to consider the cost savings and new process ideas achieved by the employees, the owners decide that the incentive bonuses will not be paid out, and they cancel the holiday party as an additional cost-saving measure.

1. Do you agree with the owners' decision not to pay out the bonuses? Why or why not?

2. How do you think the employees will react?

3. What could the owners have done to salvage the situation and maintain the increased levels of productivity and creativity at ABC Industries?

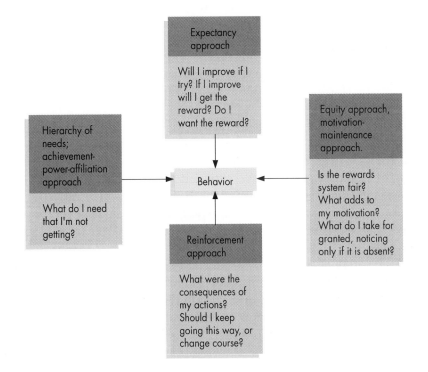

## figure 10.8

**THE RELATIONSHIP BETWEEN DIFFERENT MOTIVATION APPROACHES**

J.M. Smucker, the company best known for Smucker's Jams and Jellies, is ranked as one of the best companies to work for. Execs have claimed that the fantastic smell in the factory contributes to well-above-average employee morale.

refers to an individual's feeling of being accepted by and belonging to a group of employees through common goals, confidence in the desirability of these goals, and progress toward these goals. Morale is related to group attitudes, whereas job satisfaction is more of an individual attitude. However, the two concepts are interrelated in that job satisfaction can contribute to morale and morale can contribute to job satisfaction.

## The Satisfaction-Performance Controversy

For many years, managers have believed for the most part that a satisfied worker will automatically be a good worker. In other words, if management could keep all the workers "happy," good performance would automatically follow. Many managers subscribe to this belief because it represents "the path of least resistance." Increasing employees' happiness is far more pleasant for the manager than confronting employees with their performance if a performance problem exists.

Research evidence generally rejects the more popular view that employee satisfaction leads to improved performance. The evidence does, however, provide moderate support for the view that performance causes satisfaction. The evidence also provides strong indications that (1) rewards constitute a more direct cause of satisfaction than does performance and (2) rewards based on current performance directly impact subsequent performance.[7]

Research has also investigated the relationship between intrinsic and extrinsic satisfaction and performance for jobs categorized as being either stimulating or nonstimulating.[8] The studies found that the relationship did vary, depending on whether the job was stimulating or nonstimulating. These and other studies further emphasize the complexity of the satisfaction-performance relationship. One relationship that has been clearly established is that job satisfaction does have a positive impact on turnover, absenteeism, tardiness, accidents, grievances, and strikes.[9]

In addition, recruitment efforts by employees are generally more successful if the employees are satisfied. Satisfied employees are preferred simply because they make the work situation a more pleasant environment. So even though a satisfied employee is not necessarily a high performer, there are numerous reasons for cultivating satisfied employees.

A wide range of both internal and external factors affect an individual's level of satisfaction. The top portion of Figure 10.9 summarizes the major factors that determine an individual's level of satisfaction (or dissatisfaction). The lower portion of the figure shows the organizational behaviors generally associated with satisfaction and dissatisfaction. Individual satisfaction leads to organizational commitment, while

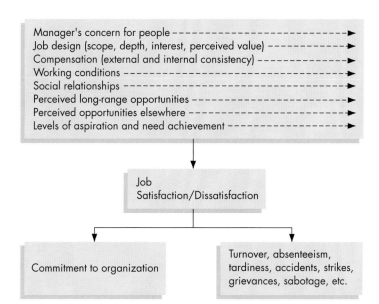

figure 10.9

**DETERMINANTS OF
SATISFACTION AND
DISSATISFACTION**

dissatisfaction results in behaviors detrimental to the organization (turnover, absenteeism, tardiness, accidents, etc.). For example, employees who like their jobs, supervisors, and other job-related factors will probably be very loyal and devoted employees. However, employees who strongly dislike their jobs or any of the job-related factors will probably be disgruntled and will often exhibit these feelings by being late, absent, or by taking more covert actions to disrupt the organization.

---

## PROGRESS CHECK QUESTIONS

13. What are the five major components of job satisfaction?

14. Define the term *organizational morale*.

15. Consider the organization you currently work for or one you have worked for in the past. How would you describe the morale of that organization? Explain.

16. Explain the difference between satisfaction and motivation.

---

# CONCLUSION

Satisfaction and motivation are not identical. Motivation is a drive to perform, whereas satisfaction reflects the individual's attitude or happiness with the situation. The factors that determine whether an individual

# You can't please everyone

As promised, Tony gave his crew a few days to put forward some ideas for recognizing employee performance, and then he emptied the suggestion box from the break room. He was hoping for something simple and straightforward, such as gift certificates or cash awards in their paychecks. Unfortunately, what he found in the suggestion box responses was not so simple.

Some wanted gift certificates from specific companies like grocery stores or electronic stores; others wanted certificates they could use at a store of their choice; others wanted certificates for specific services like a spa day or a car detailing; others just wanted the cash (some in their paychecks and others in cold, hard cash); and some even wanted to keep the current employee of the month award, as long as Kelly Stevens didn't keep winning it! Some didn't ask for money at all—they wanted a day off with pay. Others felt that the award was more trouble than it was worth every month and suggested that the whole program be scrapped in favor of a big staff party at the end of the year or even a minivacation paid for by Taco Barn.

As he read through all the suggestions, Tony started noticing a clear pattern. They were supposed to be anonymous suggestions, but Tony knew his people well enough to recognize a lot of the handwriting, and it was this that helped him identify the pattern. Those older employees with families and the younger single moms had fairly simple requests, such as gift certificates from the grocery store or cash in their paychecks. The younger, part-time employees, most of whom were still in school or college, wanted the gift certificates for the electronics store or to put more music on their iPods. Those with no kids or two incomes coming in wanted the treats like a spa day or their car detailed.

Tony was pleased on the one hand that they had put so much thought into their suggestions, but on the other hand he was disappointed to learn that the employee of the month award had meant so little to so many of his crew. He really did want them to be motivated by the chance to win these employee recognition awards, but how was he going to make sure that everybody got what they wanted?

## QUESTIONS

1. Were the suggestions that Tony received really that surprising? Why or why not?

2. How do these suggestions relate to Abraham Maslow's hierarchy of needs?

3. Was it a good idea to create the expectation that the employees could pick their own award? Why or why not?

4. What should Tony do now?

is satisfied with the job differ from those that determine whether the individual is motivated. Satisfaction is largely determined by the comfort offered by the environment and the situation. Motivation, on the other hand, is largely determined by the value of rewards and their contingency on performance. The result of motivation is increased effort, which in turn increases performance if the individual has the ability and if the effort is properly directed. The result of satisfaction is increased commitment to the organization, which may or may not result in increased performance. This increased commitment will normally result in a decrease in problems, such as absenteeism, tardiness, turnover, and strikes. In the next chapter we'll review what happens when the ideal world of satisfied and motivated employees working in a smoothly-running organization doesn't quite materialize and managers need to step-in and monitor the performance of the company more closely.

## key terms

## review questions

1. Explain the motivation sequence.
2. What is job satisfaction?
3. Discuss the satisfaction-performance controversy.
4. From a managerial standpoint, what are the real benefits of having satisfied employees?

## internet exercise

Visit the Web site of Outward Bound Professional at www.outward-boundpro.org.

1. What does Outward Bound Professional do?
2. What kind of outcomes can you expect from an Outward Bound event?
3. Review and summarize one of the case studies under the category of "Personal and Professional Review."

## team exercise

### DOES MONEY MOTIVATE?

You will be divided into two groups (or an equal number of smaller groups). Each group will be assigned one of the two following statements:

1. Money is the primary motivator of people.
2. Money is not the primary motivator of people.

Prepare for a debate with another group on the validity of the statement that your group has been assigned. You will be debating a group that has the opposing viewpoint.

At the end of the debate, answer the following questions:

1. Summarize the key points of your viewpoint.

2. Summarize the key points of the opposing group's viewpoint.

3. Did the information shared in the debate change your opinion? Why or why not?

4. Your viewpoint was chosen for you according to the team to which you were assigned. How did the team reach agreement in its debating viewpoint? Explain your answer.

## Seagate's Morale-athon

*Inside the Tech Giant's $9,000-a-Head Team-Building Blowout in New Zealand*

**P**lenty of companies try to motivate the troops, but few go as far as Seagate Technology. In February the $9.8 billion maker of computer storage hardware flew 200 staffers to New Zealand for its sixth annual Eco Seagate—an intense week of team-building topped off by an all-day race in which Seagaters had to kayak, hike, bike, swim, and rappel down a cliff. The tab? $9,000 per person. Correspondent Sarah Max went along for the bonding.

**SUNDAY "DON'T BE TOO COOL TO PARTICIPATE."** It's cocktail hour, and nervous getting-to-know-you chatter floats around the Queenstown chalet, where we've arrived by gondola. Staffers from a dozen countries are talking and gazing out at a stupendous mountain view of The Remark-

ables. The employees have been chosen from 1,200 who tried to get into Eco Seagate. (The company employs a total of 45,000.) There are no age limits: The oldest racer this year is 62. In the first of many embarrassing exercises, four "tribes," each made up of 10 athletically, regionally, and operationally diverse teams, are asked to imitate the sound of the New Zealand birds for which their group has been named: Ruru,

Kia, Tui, or Weka. "You're going to think some of this is pretty dumb," CEO Bill Watkins tells the crowd. "Just get involved. Don't be too cool to participate." This event, or social experiment, is Watkins' pet project. He dreamed up Eco Seagate as a way to break down barriers, boost confidence, and, yes, make staffers better team players. "Some of you will learn about teamwork because you have a great team," he says. "Some of you will learn because your team is a disaster."

**MONDAY BOOT CAMP IT AIN'T.** "Oh, what a beautiful morning. Oh, what a beautiful day," croons Malcolm Mc-Leod of Australia's Motivation Worldwide. "Now get out there and stretch." Dressed in referee garb, Malcolm and his gang of "stripies" have helped Eco Seagate run smoothly since the first one in 2000. Over the years the outing has evolved from just a race to a tightly organized event with a streamlined message. Each morning, Watkins or one of his top executives gives a presentation on a key attribute of a strong team, such as trust, healthy conflict, commitment, accountability. That lesson carries over to the afternoon, when tribes go off to learn orienteering, rappelling, mountain biking, or kayaking. Today we're up at 5:45 for the "optional" pre-dawn stretch. But this isn't exactly boot camp. For Eco Seagate the company has taken over Rydges Lakeland Resort in Queenstown, a mountain village on the South Island. All participants have their own comfy rooms. The stretch takes place in a park across the street. Seagate CFO Charles Pope, 50, and his Shark Attack team are among the throng bending and groaning in the dark. "I don't like to schmooze for the sake of schmoozing," says Pope, who was initially opposed to the event because, for one thing, it costs a lot of money— about $1.8 million this year. That's a lot of hard drives. But it represents a fraction of the company's $40 million training-and-development budget. In the afternoon, the tribes head out for physical training. I'm "embedded" with the Rurus, who today will learn the most essential but least exciting skill of adventure racing— navigation—in the rolling hills overlooking Lake Wakatipu. The Five Elements team has done some team-building already: "We've been e-mailing almost every day since we got matched up," says Karri Barry, 37, a cash manager in Scotts Valley, Calif., where Seagate is headquartered. When the team gets maps and compasses today, they know that Choon Keong "C.K." Neo, 33, a quality manager in Singapore, will be the navigator, thanks to a stretch in his nation's military.

**TUESDAY TESTING THE LIMITS.** Watkins is pacing the stage of the hotel conference room, giving his morning pep talk. The speech: unscripted and emotional. The look: shaggy hair, cargo shorts, and trail-running shoes. Today he's wearing a backpack with the head of a large toy kiwi bird sticking out the top. Yesterday each team was given one of these stuffed animals, its "sixth team member," and warned that one person must be in physical contact with it at all times. Many teams have strapped on the birds, dressed them, and even named them. Anyone caught without a bird will lose 15 green

Eco tokens, which teams earn throughout the week and will use on race day to buy better maps, skip a checkpoint, or take a bridge over a frigid, fast-moving river. At the rappel site, Pope's teammate Tish Sanchez earns an extra token for volunteering to rappel off a bridge, her fear of heights be damned. The climbing instructors stay close. Still, Sanchez has to step out over the ledge and hang her life on a harness. "You can do it, Tish," says Pope encouragingly, standing on the bridge and looking down at his white-faced teammate. It's slow going at first, but halfway down, the usually reserved info tech manager starts yelling out: "Whoo-hoo!"

**WEDNESDAY "SEAGATE IS POWERFUL. SEAGATE IS POWERFUL."** Wearing war paint, headbands, and makeshift grass skirts, each tribe is performing its own uniquely choreographed *haka*—a Maori chant typically performed by native New Zealanders—in a competition worth 50 tokens to the winning tribe, as judged by a panel of Maoris. The chant—*Moanaketi roopu kaha. Moanaketi roopu kaha*—is said to mean: "Seagate is powerful. Seagate is powerful." But it could just convey: "What a bunch of nutcases." "For me the race is anticlimactic," says COO David Wickersham, 49. "You learn so much about yourself in the first four days and, personally, I'm surprised by how people let their guard down." Tonight there's no question that people have shed their inhibitions. They've also shed some of their clothing: The men are shirtless, the women sport bathing suits and tank tops with skirts improvised from fabric of their team's color.

**THURSDAY "THE HARDEST YET."** "How much water will there be on the course?" "Will we have wet suits?" "Did you say this could take us 10 hours?" The night before the big test, Nathan Faavae, an adventure-racing superstar, is being bombarded with questions. He spent months studying maps and bushwhacking around Queenstown to design the course. "This will be the hardest Eco Seagate yet," says Faavae, who's a first-timer but tested the course with several veterans. He hands out bags filled with a map, jerseys, life jackets, and a radio.

**FRIDAY TIME TO WALK THE WALK—AND SWIM THE SWIM.** Here's the plan: The 40 teams are dropped on an island in the middle of Lake Wakatipu between 6 and 7 a.m. A conch sounds, and the teams race to their kayaks and paddle 1.5 miles to shore. Then, navigating with a compass, they trek over 4.3 miles of hilly terrain, mountain-bike 10.5 miles of rocks and ruts, then rappel 160 feet into a canyon for a hypothermic swim and hike. Here's the reality: a ragged day of pain and suffering. At the finish line they find portable showers, dry clothes, and tables laden with grilled meats and salads. Miraculously, all 40 teams make it, carrying their silly kiwi birds. I hang out near the beer, certain that exhausted Seagaters will have some critical things to say about Watkins' cockamamie event. Instead they gush about how they loved it.

## Questions

1. Two hundred staffers at $9,000 per head is an expensive tab for a motivation event. What does Seagate hope to get for its investment?

2. Twelve hundred employees applied to be one of the two hundred. What does that say about the culture of Seagate?

3. Seagate spends over $40 million each year on training and development. Is that a worthwhile investment of funds? Why or why not?

4. Would you apply to take part in Eco Seagate? Why or why not?

*Source:* Adapted from Sarah Max, "Managing," *BusinessWeek,* April 3, 2006.

## Becoming a Chief Inspiration Officer

*Employees Want to Know They're Making a Difference in People's Lives, Says Entergy's CEO. Katrina Gave His Troops a Chance to Shine.*

Wayne Leonard is the CEO of Entergy, America's third largest electric-utility company, which serves Arkansas, Louisiana, Mississippi, and Texas. Leonard's actions during Hurricanes Katrina and Rita offer an inspiring case study for people seeking to improve their leadership communications skills. In August 2005, Katrina knocked out power to more than 1 million of Entergy's 2.7 million customers. Approximately 1,500 Entergy employees were displaced, and many of them saw their homes destroyed or severely damaged. One lineman and his friends were caught in rising water. They fled to an attic and used a two-by-four to break through the roof. The very next day, after being rescued, that lineman joined his fellow workers to turn the lights back on for Entergy's customers.

His story wasn't unusual. It was common to see crews working 16-hour days for more than a week, while they were unable to check on their own homes. By the end of the first week, power was restored to 550,000 people. And nearly everyone had power restored by the end of September—a remarkable achievement by all accounts.

**SIMPLE MISSION.** Within a month of Katrina, Hurricane Rita knocked out power to more than three-quarters of a million Entergy customers. The company was hit by two massive natural disasters in a row, and yet its employees showed devotion, commitment, and a level of teamwork that would be the envy of any corporation in America. CEO Wayne Leonard has consistently cultivated a culture based on a simple mission—to leave this world a better place than the company found it. In other words, for Entergy employees, their work represents more than a paycheck. "Our employees know that what they do makes a real difference in people's lives," Leonard told me during a recent interview. "We don't just provide electricity. We cool their homes in the summer and warm their homes in the winter. We allow people to cook their food. We clean the environment and educate their children. We do a lot more than make electricity and money." If Entergy's displaced employees had viewed their role as just another job instead of a mission to provide hope to those in need, its customers might have remained in the dark a lot longer.

**PASSION AND POWER.** Entergy won numerous awards for its handling of the crisis, as did Leonard himself. It's easy to see why. Leonard wrote a string of emotional and optimistic e-mails to all of his employees in the days and weeks after Katrina. The correspondence reflects the power of a mission consistently and passionately conveyed. Here are some excerpts: "In every man and woman's life, there is a defining moment. It is a brief intersection of circumstances and choices that define a person for better or worse, a life of unfilled potential or a life that mattered, that made a difference. It is true of individuals and it is true of business. We have great passion for the difference we make in other's lives. We provide a commodity that sustains life. But, more importantly, we provide the most precious commodity of all—hope." "The task before us is awesome, but not insurmountable. We will be challenged at every turn, but this is what has always defined Entergy. We are at our best when the challenge is greatest. . . . Our response to this crisis will make the people we call Entergy remembered and revered for all time. . . . We are bruised, but not broken. We are saddened, but not despondent. We are at that remarkable place in time where the hearts, minds, and souls of the good cross with challenge and opportunity to set the course of history. We define ourselves here and now for all to see, everywhere." "Future generations will stand in awe at what you have endured and accomplished. Books will be written. Stories will be handed down. Some fall or spring day, the sun will be out, the temperature will be in the 70s, and you'll be sitting on the front porch content with the knowledge that you were not only there, but you stood tall and you didn't break or bend. Maybe it wasn't the life you envisioned, but in many ways it was better. Stronger, more courageous, more selfless than you ever even imagined you might be. You see things like this on television or in history books and ask 'how did they do it?' Now, you can tell them, because you did it. You were in the game. Maybe you were or maybe you weren't a 'superstar' growing up. But I know this. You are now."

**"A GREAT CAUSE."** While some leaders motivate by fear and greed, Leonard believes the best motivation is appreciation. "It goes back to whether you believe people are basically good or not, Leonard says. "I know in my heart that people are basically good. People want to know that what they do makes a difference. And in our business, it does make a difference. We need to remind people of that fact and reinforce that message. When you show people that you really do appreciate them, they will do anything in the world for you when times get tough."

**THE BIG PICTURE.** People want more than a paycheck. They want to believe that what they're doing is adding up to a great cause. It's up to you to communicate that vision. If not, how do you expect to get the best in people? You can't. Just as Entergy's employees believe in the power of their mission, your employees should be inspired by the true value behind your service, product, company, or cause. Think hard about what you provide. Go beyond the surface. The people who surround you eight, nine, 10 hours a day or more are looking to you for inspiration. As a leader in your company or industry, it's up to you to craft a bold vision and to passionately promote the vision as something larger than the individual. That's the secret to getting the most out of your colleagues and employees. It works for Leonard. It can work for you.

### Questions

1. What is Entergy's mission?

2. "People want more than a paycheck." Explain this statement.

3. CEO Wayne Leonard "believes the best motivation is appreciation." How does Entergy's approach to motivation reflect that statement?

4. Think of the organization you currently work for (or one you have worked for in the past). Does the organization's mission inspire you? Why or why not?

*Source:* Adapted from Carmine Gallo, "Viewpoint," *BusinessWeek*, April 20, 2006.

# MANAGEMENT CONTROL

"To persuade is more trouble than to dominate, and the powerful seldom take this trouble if they can avoid it."

—Charles Horton Cooley

## The World of Work: Managing by objectives

When Tony had worked as a shift crew leader for Jerry Smith, his annual performance review had consisted of a brief meeting, a review of his successes for the year, and the notification of what his raise would be—usually a cost of living increase plus a little extra if the company was having a good year. For Tony, that had always been enough. Jerry was a good manager and always made himself available to his people, so there was never a need to have any major discussions about issues that had been stewing for a while. Jerry kept an open door policy, and if you needed to talk something over, you just asked for some time to sit down with him and work it through. That always worked both ways. If Jerry saw something that he didn't like, he would pull you aside and talk to you about it there and then, in private, without embarrassing you in front of your workmates.

Now that Tony was the unit manager for this Taco Barn, he wanted to do things a little differently. It wasn't that Jerry's approach didn't work. He had been and still was a fantastic mentor to Tony, but, Tony thought, this was his crew now, and he wanted to put his stamp on things. Plus the changes Tony had in mind weren't that dramatic. He felt strongly that several members of his unit crew had real potential and promising futures with the Taco Barn organization. He wanted them to start thinking of themselves in the same way, and he had begun to think that the annual performance reviews were a way to start that process. One of his business professors had talked about a process called management by objectives (MBO), where you worked with your people in the development of clear goals to be achieved each year. Tony thought that by helping his people work on specific

**After studying this chapter, you will be able to:**

**1** Explain why management controls are necessary.

**2** Describe the control pyramid.

**3** Differentiate between preliminary, concurrent, and postaction controls.

**4** List the four basic types of financial ratios.

**5** Explain the determinants of performance.

**6** Describe the major performance appraisal methods.

goals, they could move that much closer to their potential, both personally and professionally.

The reviews were always done on the anniversary of your hire date with the company, and over the next two weeks, over a dozen of his full-time folks were due for their reviews—a perfect time to get going on this new approach, Tony thought. Kevin, Tony's new shift leader, was first on the list.

A week before the anniversary of Kevin's hire date with the company, Tony asked to meet with him after the lunch rush was over. They met on a regular basis, so Kevin saw no need to be nervous about the request, but Tony's opening question caught Kevin by surprise.

"Kevin, you know how happy we are with your work here at Taco Barn—both Dawn and I think you have a great future with the organization. For that reason, I'd like to do your performance review a little differently this year. I'd like you to come to your review

meeting with some goals that you'd like to achieve over the coming year. They can be work-related and personal goals if you'd like. We'll then incorporate those goals into a plan for the year and then review your achievement of those goals at next year's performance review. How does that sound?"

## QUESTIONS

1. Why does Tony think that incorporating MBO will be a positive move for his restaurant? Review page 315 for some guidance on this.

2. How do you think Kevin will respond to this request?

3. What challenges can you see in adopting the MBO approach?

4. If your boss made the same request of you as Tony is making of Kevin, how would you respond?

# CONTROLLING

**control**

Process of ensuring that organizational activities are going according to plan; accomplished by comparing actual performance to predetermined standards or objectives, then taking action to correct any deviations.

The basic premise of organizations is that all activities will function smoothly; however, the possibility that this will not be the case gives rise to the need for control. **Control** simply means knowing what is actually happening in comparison to set standards or objectives and then making any necessary corrections. The overriding purpose of all management controls is to alert the manager to an existing or a potential problem before it becomes critical. Control is accomplished by comparing actual performance to predetermined standards or objectives and then taking action to correct any deviations from the standard. However, control is a sensitive and complex part of the management process.

Controlling is similar to planning. It addresses these basic questions: Where are we now? Where do we want to be? How can we get there from here? But controlling takes place after the planning is completed and the organizational activities have begun. Whereas most planning occurs before action is taken, most controlling takes place after the initial action has been taken. This does not mean control is practiced only after problems occur. Control decisions can be preventive, and they can also affect future planning decisions.

# WHY PRACTICE MANAGEMENT CONTROL?

As we just noted, management controls alert the manager to potentially critical problems. At top management levels, a problem occurs when the organization's goals are not being met. At middle and lower levels, a problem occurs when the objectives for which the manager is responsible are not being met. These may be departmental objectives, production standards, or other performance indicators. All forms of management controls are designed to give the manager information regarding progress. The manager can use this information to do the following:

1. *Prevent crises.* If a manager does not know what is going on, it is easy for small, readily solvable problems to turn into crises.
2. *Standardize outputs.* Problems and services can be standardized in terms of quantity and quality through the use of good controls.
3. *Appraise employee performance.* Proper controls can provide the manager with objective information about employee performance.
4. *Update plans.* Even the best plans must be updated as environmental and internal changes occur. Controls allow the manager to compare what is happening with what was planned.
5. *Protect the organization's assets.* Controls can protect assets from inefficiency, waste, and pilferage.

## The Control Pyramid

The control pyramid provides a method for implementing controls in the organization.[1] The idea is to implement simple controls first and then move to more complex controls at a later time. The first area to be considered using this method would be *foolproof controls,* which deal with repetitive acts and require little thought (e.g., turning off lights). Surprisingly, many of these acts and controls already exist in an organization's normal course of business. The second area to consider is *automatic controls,* where a feedback loop can exist without much human interaction (e.g., regulation of plant temperature). These systems require monitoring, but the control can be machine- or computer-based. The third area is *operator controls,* which require a human response (e.g., a salesperson checking records). The key to this form of control is to make it meaningful for the controller. The fourth area is *supervisory control,* the layer that controls the person or persons implementing the controls (e.g., a department head checking an employee's reports). The organization must make sure that this form of control gets results and is not redundant. The final area is *informational controls* (e.g., report summaries). This is the ultimate feedback loop, wherein the manager must pull together all the information provided by the other controls.[2] Seeing the process as a whole helps the manager get a feel for how interrelated the control process is and how it must be synchronized. Figure 11.1 shows how these different types of controls relate to each other.

Informational controls are the final feedback loop wherein the manager must pull together all the information provided by other controls.

## Where Should Control Reside?

For years, it was believed that control in organizations is a fixed commodity that should be only in the hands of top management. This viewpoint

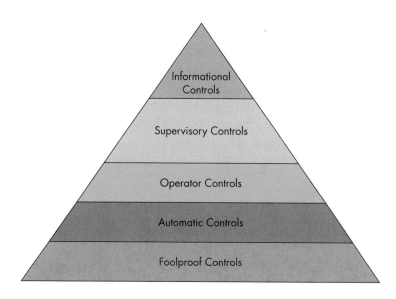

Informational Controls

Supervisory Controls

Operator Controls

Automatic Controls

Foolproof Controls

## figure 11.1

**THE CONTROL PYRAMID**

*Source:* From Joseph Juran, *Managerial Breakthrough,* 4th Edition, p. 205, 1995. Reproduced with permission of The McGraw-Hill Companies, Inc.

naturally favored a highly centralized approach to decision making and controlling. However, as decentralized organizations have become more common, controls have been pushed farther and farther down the hierarchy. It is now recognized that where the controls reside is an important factor in how much control is desirable.

James Champy, author of *Reengineering Management,* believes the modern approach to control should involve more "enabling" or learning to control at lower levels.[3] Supporting this idea, Leon Royer, director of Learning Services at 3M, found that learning and enabling go hand in hand. Lower-level employees are valuable controllers if they are allowed to learn how to control.[4] The difficulty with enabling, however, is that it means senior management must be willing to relinquish control. One reason for pushing controls down in the organization is that the controllers then are close to the actual situations that require control.

Building on this material, evidence favors relatively tight controls as long as they are placed as far down in the organization as possible.[5] This approach has several advantages. First, it keeps higher-level managers from getting too involved in details. Second, it shows why the control is necessary. Third, it elicits commitment from lower-level managers. When controls are spread through many levels of an organization, caution must be taken to ensure that there are no disagreements about how the controls are distributed. In other words, managers at every level should clearly understand their authority and responsibility.

## TYPES OF CONTROL

**behavior or personal control**
Based on direct, personal surveillance.

There are two categories of control methods: behavior control and output control. **Behavior** or **personal control** is based on direct, personal surveillance. The first-line supervisor who maintains a close personal watch over employees is using behavior control. **Output** or **impersonal control** is based on the measurement of outputs. Tracking production records and monitoring sales figures are examples of output controls.

**output or impersonal control**
Based on the measurement of outputs.

Research shows that these two categories of control are not substitutes for each other in the sense that a manager uses one or the other.[6] The evidence suggests that output control occurs in response to a manager's need to provide an accurate measure of performance. On the other hand, behavior control is exerted when performance requirements are well known and personal surveillance is needed to promote efficiency and motivation. In most situations, organizations need to use a mix of output and behavior controls because each serves different organizational needs.

### Preliminary, Concurrent, or Postaction Control?

**preliminary control**
Method of exercising control to prevent a problem from occurring.

In general, methods for exercising control can be described as preliminary, concurrent, or postaction. **Preliminary control** methods, sometimes called *steering controls,* attempt to prevent a problem from occurring. Requiring prior approval for purchases of all items over a certain dollar value is an example. **Concurrent controls,** also called *screening controls,* focus on things that happen as inputs are being transformed into outputs. They are designed to detect a problem as it occurs. Personal observation of customers being served is an example of a concurrent control. **Postaction control** methods are designed to detect existing problems after they occur but before they reach crisis proportions. Written or periodic reports represent postaction control methods. Most controls are based on postaction methods.

**concurrent controls**

Focuses on process as it occurs; designed to detect a problem as it occurs.

**postaction control**

Designed to detect an existing or a potential problem before it gets out of hand.

## Budgetary Control

Budgets are probably the most widely used control devices. A **budget** is a statement of expected results or requirements expressed in financial or numerical terms. Budgets express plans, objectives, and programs of the organization in numerical terms. Preparation of the budget is primarily a planning function; however, its administration is a controlling function.

**budget**

Statement of expected results or requirements expressed in financial or numerical terms.

Many different types of budgets are in use. Figure 11.2 outlines some of the most common types. Some may be expressed in terms other than dollars. For example, an equipment budget may be expressed in numbers of machines; material budgets may be expressed in pounds, pieces, gallons, and so on. Budgets not expressed in dollars can usually be translated into dollars for inclusion in an overall budget.

While budgets are useful for planning and control, they are not without their dangers. Perhaps the greatest danger is inflexibility. This is a special threat to organizations operating in an industry with rapid change and high competition. Rigidity in the budget can also lead to ignoring organizational goals for budgetary goals. The financial manager who won't go $5 over budget to make $500 is a classic example. Budgets can hide inefficiencies. The fact that a certain expenditure has been made in the past often becomes justification for continuing the practice even when the situation has greatly changed. Managers may also "pad" budgets

| TYPE OF BUDGET | PURPOSE |
|---|---|
| Revenue and expense budget | Provides details for revenue and expense plans. |
| Cash budget | Forecasts cash receipts and disbursements. |
| Capital expenditure budget | Outlines specific expenditures for plant, equipment, machinery, inventories, and other capital items. |
| Production, material, or time budget | Expresses physical requirements of production, or material, or the time requirements for the budget period. |
| Balance sheet budgets | Forecasts the status of assets, liabilities, and net worth at the end of the budget period. |

**figure 11.2**

**TYPES AND PURPOSES OF BUDGETS**

(build in extra cost items) because they anticipate that their budgets will be cut by superiors. Since the manager is never sure how severe the cut will be, the result is often an inaccurate, if not unrealistic, budget.

The answer to effective budget control may be to make the manager and any concerned employees accountable for their budgets. Performance incentives can be tied to budget control, accuracy, and fulfillment. In other words, if it is worth budgeting, it is worth budgeting right! Others believe budgets should also be tied not only to financial data but also to customer satisfaction. Budgeting for what it takes to satisfy the customer would be the rule of thumb for this logic. Managers can get so hung up on measuring themselves by sticking to their own sets of rules, focusing internally, and watching their budgets that they forget their customers.[7] Yet the customer is what business is all about. Generally managers meet on a periodic basis (usually monthly or quarterly) with accounting officials to discuss planned finances versus actual expenses.

## Zero-Base Budgeting

**zero-base budgeting**

Form of budgeting in which the manager must justify each area of a budget. Each year the activity is identified, evaluated, and ranked by importance.

Zero-base budgeting was designed to stop basing this year's budget on last year's budget. **Zero-base budgeting** requires each manager to justify an entire budget request in detail. The burden of proof is on each manager to justify why any money should be spent. Under zero-base budgeting, each activity under a manager's discretion is identified, evaluated, and ranked by importance. Then each year every activity in the budget is on trial for its life and is matched against all the other claimants for an organization's resources.

---

### PROGRESS CHECK QUESTIONS

1. What is the overriding purpose of all management controls?
2. Explain the five layers of the control pyramid.
3. What are the five most common types of operational budgets?
4. Explain zero-base budgeting.

---

## Financial Controls

In addition to budgets, many managers use other types of financial information for control purposes. These include balance sheets, income statements, and financial ratios. Regardless of the type of financial information used, it is meaningful only when compared with either the historical performance of the organization or the performances of similar organizations. For example, knowing that a company had net income of $100,000 last year doesn't reveal much by itself. However, when compared to last year's net income of $500,000 or to an industry average of $500,000, much more can be determined about the company's performance.

### Financial Ratio Analysis

Financial ratios can be divided into four basic types: profitability, liquidity, debt, and activity ratios. *Profitability ratios* indicate the organization's operational efficiency, or how well the organization is being managed. Gross profit margin, net profit margin, and return on investment (ROI) are all examples of profitability ratios. *Liquidity ratios* are used to judge how well an organization will be able to meet its short-term financial obligations. The current ratio (current assets divided by current liabilities) and the quick ratio (current assets minus inventories divided by current liabilities) are examples of liquidity ratios. *Debt* (sometimes called *leverage*) *ratios* measure the magnitude of owners' and creditors' claims on the organization and indicate the organization's ability to meet long-term obligations. The debt to equity ratio and total debt to total assets ratio are two common debt ratios. *Activity ratios* evaluate how effectively an organization is managing some of its basic operations. Asset turnover, inventory turnover, average collection period, and accounts receivable turnover represent some commonly used activity ratios.

As mentioned earlier, financial ratios are meaningful only when compared to past ratios and to ratios of similar organizations. Also, financial ratios reflect only certain specific information, and therefore they should be used in conjunction with other management controls. Figure 11.3 presents a summary of several financial ratio calculations.

### Sarbanes-Oxley Act of 2002

On July 30, 2002, President Bush signed into law the Sarbanes-Oxley Act of 2002. The Sarbanes-Oxley Act, which has been called the most dramatic change to federal securities laws since the 1930s, radically redesigned federal regulation of public company corporate governance and reporting obligations. The law also significantly tightens accountability standards for corporate directors and officers, auditors, securities, analysts, and legal counsel. The purpose of the act is to prevent the kind of accounting and financial maneuvering that caused the meltdowns experienced at such companies as Enron and WorldCom. Figure 11.4 summarizes the major points of the law.

One major concern related to the Sarbanes-Oxley Act is its hefty compliance costs. A 2004 survey by Financial Executives International (FEI) reported that large public companies spent thousands of hours and an average of $4.4 million each to comply with the Sarbanes-Oxley Act.[8] The costs stem largely from a 66 percent increase in external costs for consulting, software, and other vendors and a 58 percent increase in the fees charged by external auditors. In response to concerns about the costs of complying

| RATIO | CALCULATION | PURPOSE |
|---|---|---|
| **Profitability Ratios** | | |
| Gross profit margin | $\dfrac{\text{Sales} - \text{Cost of goods sold}}{\text{Sales}} \times 100$ | Indicates efficiency of operations and product pricing |
| | $\dfrac{\text{Net profit after tax}}{\text{Sales}} \times 100$ | Indicates efficiency after all expenses are considered |
| Return on assets (ROA) | $\dfrac{\text{Net profit after tax}}{\text{Total assets}} \times 100$ | Shows productivity of assets |
| Return on equity (ROE) | $\dfrac{\text{Net profit after tax}}{\text{Stockholders' equity}} \times 100$ | Shows earnings power of equity |
| **Liquidity Ratios** | | |
| Current ratio | $\dfrac{\text{Current assets}}{\text{Current liabilities}}$ | Shows short-run debt-paying ability |
| Quick ratio | $\dfrac{\text{Current assets} - \text{Inventories}}{\text{Current liabilities}}$ | Shows short-term liquidity |
| **Debt Ratios** | | |
| Debt to equity | $\dfrac{\text{Total liabilities}}{\text{Stockholders' equity}}$ | Indicates long-term liquidity |
| Total debt to total assets (debt ratio) | $\dfrac{\text{Total liabilities}}{\text{Total assets}}$ | Shows percentage of assets financed through borrowing |
| **Activity Ratios** | | |
| Asset turnover | $\dfrac{\text{Sales}}{\text{Total assets}}$ | Shows efficiency of asset utilization |
| Inventory turnover | $\dfrac{\text{Cost of goods sold}}{\text{Average inventory}}$ | Shows management's ability to control investment in inventory |
| Average collection period | $\dfrac{\text{Receivables} \times 365 \text{ days}}{\text{Annual credit sales}}$ | Shows effectiveness of collection and credit policies |
| Accounts receivable turnover | $\dfrac{\text{Annual credit sales}}{\text{Receivables}}$ | Shows effectiveness of collection and credit policies |

**figure 11.3**

**SUMMARY OF FINANCIAL RATIO CALCULATIONS**

for smaller businesses, the Securities and Exchange Commission delayed implementation of key sections of the act until 2007 for companies with less than $75 million in market capitalization.[9]

## Direct Observation

A store manager's daily tour of the facility or a company president's annual visit to all branches are examples of control by direct observation. Although time-consuming, personal observation is sometimes the only way to get an

**figure 11.4**

**MAJOR POINTS OF THE
SARBANES-OXLEY ACT
OF 2002**

The SEC will direct the NYSE and NASDAQ to prohibit listing any public company whose audit committee does not comply with a new list of requirements affecting auditor appointment, compensation, and oversight. The audit committee must consist solely of independent directors.

CEOs and CFOs must certify in each periodic report containing financial statements that the report fully complies with Sections 13(a) and 15(d) of the Securities Exchange Act of 1934 and that the information fairly presents the company's financial condition and results of operations.

Certifying officers will face penalties for false certification of $1,000,000 and/or up to 10 years' imprisonment for "knowing" violation and $5,000,000 and/or up to 20 years' imprisonment for "willing" violation.

No public company may make, extend, modify, or renew any personal loan to its executive officers or directors, with limited exceptions.

The act sets a deadline for insiders to report any trading in their companies' securities to within two business days after the execution date of the transaction.

Each company must disclose "on a rapid and current basis" additional information about the company's financial condition or operations as the SEC determines is necessary or useful to investors or in the public interest.

All annual reports filed with the SEC containing financial statements must include all material corrections identified by a public accounting firm.

The act creates several new crimes for securities violations, including:

- Destroying, altering, or falsifying records with the intent to impede or influence any federal investigation or bankruptcy proceeding.
- Knowing and willful failure by an accountant to maintain all audit or workpapers for five years.
- Knowingly executing a scheme to defraud investors in connection with any security.

accurate picture of what is really happening. One hazard is that employees may misinterpret a superior's visit and consider such action interfering or eavesdropping. A second hazard is that behaviors change when people are being watched or monitored. Another potential inaccuracy lies in the interpretation of the observation. The observer must be careful not to read into the picture events that did not actually occur. Visits and direct observation can have positive effects when viewed by employees as a display of the manager's interest.

## Written Reports

Written reports can be prepared on a periodic or an as-necessary basis. There are two basic types of written reports: analytical and informational. Analytical reports interpret the facts they present; informational reports present only the facts. Preparing a report is a four- or five-step process, depending on whether it is informational or analytical. The steps are (1) planning what is to be done, (2) collecting the facts, (3) organizing the facts, (4) interpreting the facts (this step is omitted with informational

Visits and direct observations by managers can have positive effects when viewed by employees as a display of the managers' interest. Why might an employee view a visit as a negative event?

### Make Good Career Planning Habits a Life Skill

If you are truly sincere about finding a successful career, you will find sooner than later that a positive outcome comes from your own work and hard efforts. While there are courses and professionals who can help you along the way, ultimately your successful career will happen because of your commitment to the skills and habits that are required to move you from an average achiever to a high achiever.

Separate the planning functions into career preparation and career execution. *Career preparation* involves all the activities that can help you on career and job research, improving reading and writing skills, assessing strengths and weaknesses, learning job and industry terminology, and establishing career goals and objectives. *Career execution* involves establishing high levels of skills in filling out job applications, interviewing, career etiquette, résumé writing, personal planning, and effective communication.

reports), and (5) writing the report.[10] Most reports should be prepared for the benefit of the reader and not the writer. In most cases, the reader wants useful information not previously available.

## Electronic Monitors

Today, a number of different types of electronic devices can be used to monitor what is going on. Examples include electronic cash registers that keep a record of what items are sold and when; video cameras that record employee and customer movements; phones that record how long each customer was engaged; and Internet programs that track where and how long an employee or customer is at certain Internet sites.

## Balanced Scorecard

The balanced scorecard (BSC) system is a measurement and control system that is similar to management by objectives and based on the idea that financial measures alone do not adequately indicate how an organization or organizational unit is performing. BSC attempts to balance traditional financial measures with measures relating to customer service, internal processes, and potential for learning and innovation. The idea is to balance these four categories of measures on both the short and long term.

A significant advantage of BSC is that it is based on participation and commitment at all levels within the organization. Under BSC, operational managers develop scorecards at every level in the organization so that each manager can see how his or her job duties relate to and contribute to the higher-level objectives and strategies. The key is that the scorecards at one level are derived from the scorecards at the next level up. Once the scorecards have been developed, managers and employees use them to periodically assess how they are doing and what, if any, corrective actions should be taken.

While BSC is relatively new, its use has grown significantly in the last several years and is expected to increase at a rapid rate.[11]

## Management Information Systems

As discussed in Chapter 4, management information systems (MISs) are computerized systems designed to produce information needed for successful management of a process, department, or business. Usually, the information provided by an MIS is in the form of periodic reports, special reports, and outputs of mathematical simulations.[12]

## Audits

**Audits** can be conducted by either internal or external personnel. External audits are normally done by outside accountants and are limited to financial matters. Most are conducted to certify that the organization's accounting methods are fair, are consistent, and conform to existing practices. Internal audits are performed by the organization's own personnel.

An audit that looks at areas other than finance and accounting is known as a management audit. **Management audits** attempt to evaluate the overall management practices and policies of the organization. They can be conducted by outside consultants or inside staff; however, a management audit conducted by inside staff can easily result in a biased report.

## Break-Even Charts

**Break-even charts** depict graphically the relationship of volume of operations to profits. The break-even point (BEP) is the point at which sales revenues exactly equal expenses. Total sales below the BEP result in a loss; total sales above the BEP result in a profit.

Figure 11.5 shows a typical break-even chart. The horizontal axis represents output; the vertical axis represents expenses and revenues. Though not required, most break-even charts assume there are linear relationships and all costs are either fixed or variable. Fixed costs do not vary with output, at least in the short run. They include rent, insurance, and administrative salaries. Variable costs vary with output. Typical variable costs include

**audits**
Method of control normally involved with financial matters; also can include other areas of the organization.

**management audits**
Attempt to evaluate the overall management practices and policies of the organization.

**break-even charts**
Depict graphically the relationship of volume of operations to profits.

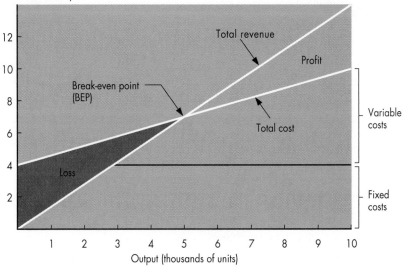

**figure 11.5**

**BREAK-EVEN CHART**

## "Bird-Dogging" the Employee

Ace Electronics, Inc., is a small company located in Centerville. It is owned and operated by Al Abrams, a highly experienced electronics person who founded the company.

Ace's basic product is a walkie-talkie that is sold primarily to the U.S. military. The walkie-talkie units are relatively simple to produce; Ace merely purchases the parts—cables, wires, transistors, and so on—and assembles them with hand tools. Due to this moderate level of complexity, Ace employs semiskilled workers at low wage rates.

Although Ace has made a profit each year since it started production, Al Abrams was becoming increasingly concerned. Over the past six years, he had noticed a general decline in employee morale; furthermore, he had observed a decline in his employees' productivity and his company's profit margin.

As a result of his concern, Al asked his supervisors to keep a closer watch on the workers' hour-to-hour activities. In the first week, they discovered two workers in the restroom reading magazines. This "bird-dogging" technique, as management called it, or "slave driving," as the workers called it, failed to increase either production or productivity.

Al recognized that the lack of performance on the part of some employees was affecting the production of everyone. This phenomenon was caused by the balanced assembly line under which the walkie-talkies were assembled. If an employee next to a normally productive employee did not work fast enough, walkie-talkies would back up on the line. Instead of having a backup, however, the assembly line was usually readjusted to the production rate of the slower employees.

In addition, another situation developed to lower productivity and increase unit costs. Ace was required by the government to meet monthly production and delivery schedules. If it failed, a very substantial financial penalty could result. In recent years, the production and delivery schedule had become more difficult to meet. For the last eight months, Al had scheduled overtime to meet the production and delivery schedule and thus avoid the financial penalty. This overtime increased unit production costs and caused another problem: Many employees began to realize that if they worked more slowly at the beginning of the month, they could receive more overtime at the end of the month. Even the senior employees were slowing down to increase their overtime wages.

Al was very reluctant to fire employees, especially senior employees. Even if he was inclined to do so, it was difficult to catch employees slowing down or provide any reasonable evidence for such a rash action. Al was frustrated and perplexed.

### Questions

1. Describe in detail the control dilemma at Ace Electronics.
2. Are Al Abrams and the employees getting the same feedback? Why or why not?
3. Al is avoiding a substantial financial penalty from the government by paying the overtime in order to meet delivery schedules. Does that justify the decision to pay the overtime? Why or why not?
4. What should Al do?

direct labor and materials. The purpose of the chart is to show the break-even point and the effects of changes in output. A break-even chart is useful for showing whether revenue and costs are running as planned.

### PROGRESS CHECK QUESTIONS

5. Explain the following ratios: productivity, liquidity, debt, and activity.
6. Describe the five steps in the written report process.
7. Explain the balanced scorecard (BSC) system.
8. Define the term *break-even point*.

# APPRAISING PERFORMANCE

## Understanding Performance

**Performance** refers to the degree of accomplishment of the tasks that make up an employee's job. It reflects how well an employee is fulfilling the requirements of the job. Often confused with effort, which refers to energy expended, performance is measured in terms of results. Because many organizations have become very results-oriented in the last decade, more and more emphasis is being placed on managing performance.

> **performance**
> Degree of accomplishment of the tasks that make up an employee's job.

## Determinants of Performance

Job performance is the net effect of an employee's effort as modified by abilities, role perceptions, and results produced. This implies that performance in a given situation can be viewed as resulting from the interrelationships among effort, abilities, role perceptions, and results produced.

> **effort**
> Results from being motivated; refers to the amount of energy an employee uses in performing a job.

    **Effort,** which results from being motivated, refers to the amount of energy an employee uses in performing a job. **Abilities** are personal characteristics used in performing a job. Abilities usually do not fluctuate widely over short periods of time. **Role perception** refers to the direction in which employees believe they should channel their efforts on their jobs. The activities and behavior employees believe are necessary in the performance of their jobs define their role perceptions. The results produced are usually measured by standards created by the degree of achievement of management-directed objectives.

> **abilities**
> Personal characteristics used in performing a job.

> **role perception**
> Direction in which employees believe they should channel their efforts on their jobs.

## Performance Appraisal Process

Performance appraisal systems that are directly tied to an organization's reward system provide a powerful incentive for employees to work diligently and creatively toward achieving organizational objectives. When properly conducted, performance appraisals not only let employees know how well they are presently performing but also clarify what needs to be done to improve performance.[13]

    **Performance appraisal** is a process that involves determining and communicating to employees how they are performing their jobs and establishing a plan for improvement. Some of the more common uses of performance appraisals are to make decisions related to merit pay increases, promotions, layoffs, and firings. For example, the present job performance of an employee is often the most significant consideration for determining whether to promote the person. While successful performance in the present job does not necessarily mean an employee will be an effective performer in a higher-level job, performance appraisals do provide some predictive information.

> **performance appraisal**
> Process that involves determining and communicating to employees how they are performing their jobs and establishing a plan for improvement.

Performance appraisal information can also provide needed input for determining both individual and organizational training and development needs. For example, it can be used to identify individual strengths and weaknesses. The data can then be used to help determine the organization's overall training and development needs. For an individual employee, a completed performance appraisal should include a plan outlining specific training and development needs.

Another important use of performance appraisals is to encourage performance improvement. In this regard, performance appraisals are used as a means of communicating to employees how they are doing and suggesting needed changes in behavior, attitude, skill, or knowledge. This type of feedback clarifies for employees the job expectations the manager holds. Often, the feedback must be followed by coaching and training by the manager to guide an employee's work efforts.

To work effectively, performance appraisals must be supported by documentation and a commitment by management to make them fair and effective. Typical standards for the performance appraisal process are that it be fair, accurate (facts, not opinions, should be used), include as much direct observation as possible, be consistent, and contain as much objective documentation as possible. The amount and types of documentation necessary to support decisions made by management vary, but the general rule of thumb is to provide enough varied documentation to allow anyone evaluating the performance of an employee to generally come to the same conclusion as the manager.

An additional concern in organizations is how often to conduct performance appraisals. No real consensus exists on this question, but the usual answer is as often as necessary to let employees know what kind of job they are doing and, if performance is not satisfactory, the measures they must take to improve. For many employees, this cannot be accomplished through one annual performance appraisal. Therefore, it is recommended that for most employees, informal performance appraisals should be conducted two or three times a year in addition to the annual performance appraisal.

## PERFORMANCE APPRAISAL METHODS

An early method of performance appraisal used in the United States was described as follows:

> *On the morning following each day's work, each workman was given a slip of paper informing him in detail just how much work he had done the day before, and the amount he had earned. This enabled him to measure his performance against his earnings while the details were fresh in his mind.*[14]

This method of performance appraisal was effective in that it gave immediate feedback and tied pay to performance. Since then the number and variety of performance appraisal methods have dramatically increased. The following sections describe the performance appraisal methods used in businesses today.

## Goal Setting, or Management by Objectives

Management by objectives (MBO) was discussed in Chapter 5 as an effective means for setting objectives. In addition to being a useful method for directing the organization's objective-setting process, management by objectives can also be used in the performance appraisal process. The value of linking the MBO program to the appraisal process is that employees tend to support goals if they agree the goals are acceptable and if they expect to be personally successful in their efforts. Employee acceptance (by giving the employee a stake in the MBO process) is certainly a powerful motivator for considering the MBO process. The typical MBO process consists of the following:

1. Establishing clear and precisely defined statements of objectives for the work an employee is to do.
2. Developing an action plan indicating how the objectives are to be achieved.
3. Allowing the employee to implement the action plan.
4. Appraising performance based on objective achievement.
5. Taking corrective action when necessary.
6. Establishing new objectives for the future.

If an employee is to be evaluated on the objectives set in the MBO process, several requirements must be met. First, objectives should be quantifiable and measurable; objectives whose attainment cannot be measured or at least verified should be avoided if possible. Objectives should also be challenging, yet achievable, and they should be expressed in writing and in clear, concise language. Figure 11.6 lists sample objectives that meet these requirements.

## Production Standards

The **production standards approach** to performance appraisal is most frequently used for employees who are involved in physically producing a product and is basically a form of objective setting for these employees. It involves setting a standard or an expected level of output and then comparing each employee's performance to the standard. Generally, production standards should reflect the normal output of an average person.

**production standards approach**

Performance appraisal method most frequently used for employees who are involved in physically producing a product; is basically a form of objective setting for these employees.

The production standards approach would work for this employee. Name some industries for which that standard of measurement might prove problematic.

**figure 11.6**

**SAMPLE OBJECTIVES**

> To answer all customer complaints in writing within three days of receipt of complaint.
> To reduce order-processing time by two days within the next six months.
> To implement the new computerized accounts receivable system by August 1.

Production standards attempt to answer the question of what is a fair day's output. Several methods can be used to set production standards. Figure 11.7 summarizes some of the more common methods.

An advantage of the production standards approach is that the performance review is based on highly objective factors. Of course, to be effective, the standards must be viewed by the affected employees as being fair. The most serious criticism of production standards is a lack of comparability of standards for different job categories.

## Essay Appraisal

**essay appraisal method**

Requires the manager to describe an employee's performance in written narrative form.

The **essay appraisal method** requires the manager to describe an employee's performance in written account form. Instructions are often provided to the manager as to the topics to be covered. A typical essay appraisal question might be, "Describe, in your own words, this employee's performance, including quantity and quality of work, job knowledge, and ability to get along with other employees. What are the employee's strengths and weaknesses?"

The primary problem with essay appraisals is that their length and content can vary considerably (depending on the manager) and the method can be very subjective (whereas objective measures are more defendable). For instance, one manager may write a lengthy statement describing an employee's potential and saying little about past performance; another manager may concentrate on the employee's past performance. Thus, essay appraisals are difficult to compare. The writing

**figure 11.7**

**FREQUENTLY USED METHODS FOR SETTING PRODUCTION STANDARDS**

| METHOD | AREAS OF APPLICABILITY |
|---|---|
| Average production or work | When tasks performed by all employees are the same or approximately the same. |
| Performance of specially selected employees | When tasks performed by all employees are basically the same, and it would be cumbersome and time-consuming to use the group average. |
| Time study | Jobs involving repetitive tasks. |
| Work sampling | Noncyclical types of work in which many different tasks are performed and there is no set pattern or cycle. |
| Expert opinion | When none of the more direct methods (described above) applies. |

skill of a manager can also affect the appraisal. An effective writer can make an average employee look better than the actual performance warrants.

## Critical-Incident Appraisal

The **critical-incident appraisal** method requires the manager to keep a written record of incidents, as they occur, involving job behaviors that illustrate both satisfactory and unsatisfactory performance of the employee being rated. As they are recorded over time, the incidents provide a basis for evaluating performance and providing feedback to the employee.

The main drawback to this approach is that the manager is required to jot down incidents regularly, which can be a burdensome and time-consuming task. Also, the definition of a critical incident is unclear and may be interpreted differently by different managers. Some believe this method can lead to friction between the manager and employees when the employees think the manager is keeping a "book" on them.

> **critical-incident appraisal**
> Requires the manager to keep a written record of incidents, as they occur, involving job behaviors that illustrate both satisfactory and unsatisfactory performance of the employee being rated.

## Graphic Rating Scale

With the **graphic rating scale** method, the manager assesses an employee on factors such as quantity of work, dependability, job knowledge, attendance, accuracy of work, and cooperativeness. Graphic rating scales include both numerical ranges and written descriptions. Figure 11.8 (p. 318) gives an example of items that might be included on a graphic rating scale that uses written descriptions.

The graphic rating scale method is subject to serious weaknesses. One potential weakness is that managers are unlikely to interpret written descriptions in the same manner because of differences in background, experience, and personality. Another potential problem relates to the choice of rating categories. It is possible to choose categories that have little relationship to job performance or omit categories that have a significant influence on job performance.

> **graphic rating scale**
> Requires the manager to assess an employee on factors such as quantity of work, dependability, job knowledge, attendance, accuracy of work, and cooperativeness.

## Checklist

With the **checklist** method, the manager answers yes or no to a series of questions concerning the employee's behavior. Figure 11.9 (p. 318) lists some typical questions. The checklist can also have varying weights assigned to each question.

Normally, the scoring key for the checklist method is kept by the human resource department; the manager is generally not aware of the weights associated with each question. But because the manager can see the positive or negative connotation of each question, bias can be introduced. Additional

> **checklist**
> Requires the manager to answer yes or no to a series of questions concerning the employee's behavior.

**Quantity of work** (the amount of work an employee does in a workday)

|  (   )  |  (   )  |  (   )  |  (   )  |  (   )  |
|---|---|---|---|---|
| Does not meet requirements. | Does just enough to get by. | Volume of work is satisfactory. | Very industrious, does more than is required. | Superior production record. |

**Dependability** (the ability to do required jobs with a minimum of supervision)

|  (   )  |  (   )  |  (   )  |  (   )  |  (   )  |
|---|---|---|---|---|
| Requires close supervision; is unreliable. | Sometimes requires prompting. | Usually completes necessary tasks with reasonable promptness. | Requires little supervision; is reliable. | Requires absolute minimum of supervision. |

**Job knowledge** (information that an employee should have on work duties for satisfactory job performance)

|  (   )  |  (   )  |  (   )  |  (   )  |  (   )  |
|---|---|---|---|---|
| Poorly informed about work duties. | Lacks knowledge of some phases of job. | Moderately in-formed; can answer most questions about the job. | Understands all phases of job. | Has complete mastery of all phases of job. |

**Attendance** (faithfulness in coming to work daily and conforming to work hours)

|  (   )  |  (   )  |  (   )  |  (   )  |  (   )  |
|---|---|---|---|---|
| Often absent without good excuse, or frequently reports for work late, or both. | Lax in attendance or reporting for work on time, or both. | Usually present and on time. | Very prompt; regular in attendance. | Always regular and prompt; volunteers for overtime when needed. |

**Accuracy** (the correctness of work duties performed)

|  (   )  |  (   )  |  (   )  |  (   )  |  (   )  |
|---|---|---|---|---|
| Makes frequent errors. | Careless; often makes errors. | Usually accurate; makes only average number of mistakes. | Requires little supervision; is exact and precise most of the time. | Requires absolute minimum of supervision; is almost always accurate. |

**figure 11.8**

**SAMPLE ITEMS ON A GRAPHIC RATING SCALE EVALUATION FORM**

drawbacks to the checklist method are that it is time-consuming to assemble the questions for each job category; a separate listing of questions must be developed for each job category; and the checklist questions can have different meanings for different managers.

**figure 11.9**

**SAMPLE CHECKLIST QUESTIONS**

|  | YES | NO |
|---|---|---|
| 1. Does the employee lose his or her temper in public? | ____ | ____ |
| 2. Does the employee play favorites? | ____ | ____ |
| 3. Does the employee praise people in public when they have done a good job? | ____ | ____ |
| 4. Does the employee volunteer to do special jobs? | ____ | ____ |

# Ranking Methods

When it becomes necessary to compare the performance of two or more employees, ranking methods can be used. Three of the more commonly used ranking methods are alternation, paired comparison, and forced distribution.

### Alternation Ranking

In the alternation ranking method, the names of the employees to be evaluated are listed down the left side of a sheet of paper. The manager is then asked to choose the most valuable employee on the list, cross that name off the left-hand list, and put it at the top of the column on the right side of the paper. The manager is then asked to select and cross off the name of the least valuable employee from the left-hand column and move it to the bottom of the right-hand column. The manager then repeats this process for all of the names on the left-hand side of the paper. The resulting list of names in the right-hand column gives a ranking of the employees from most to least valuable.

### Paired Comparison Ranking

The paired comparison ranking method is best illustrated with an example. Suppose a manager is to evaluate six employees. The names of the employees are listed on the left side of a sheet of paper. The manager then compares the first employee with the second employee on a chosen performance criterion, such as quantity of work. If the manager thinks the first employee has produced more work than the second employee, she or he places a check mark by the first employee's name. The first employee is then compared to the third, fourth, fifth, and sixth employees on the same performance criterion. A check mark is placed by the name of the employee who produced the most work in each of these paired comparisons. The process is repeated until each employee has been compared to every other employee on all of the chosen performance criteria. The employee with the most check marks is considered to be the best performer. Likewise, the employee with the fewest check marks is the lowest performer. One major problem with the paired comparison method is that it becomes unwieldy when comparing large numbers of employees.

### Forced Distribution

The forced distribution method requires the manager to compare the performances of employees and place a certain percentage of employees at various performance levels. It assumes the performance level in a group of employees is distributed according to a bell-shaped, or "normal," curve. Figure 11.10 illustrates how the forced distribution method works. The manager is required to rate 60 percent of the employees as meeting expectations, 20 percent as exceeding expectations, and 20 percent as not meeting expectations.

## figure 11.10

**FORCED DISTRIBUTION CURVE**

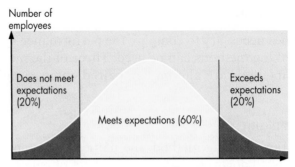

One problem with the forced distribution method is that for small groups of employees, a bell-shaped distribution of performance may not be applicable. Even if the distribution approximates a normal curve, it is probably not a perfect curve. This means some employees will probably not be rated accurately. Also, ranking methods differ dramatically from the other methods in that one employee's performance evaluation is a function of the performance of other employees in the job.

### Multirater Assessment (or 360-Degree Feedback)

**multirater assessment or 360-degree feedback**

Method of performance appraisal that uses input from an employee's managers, peers, customers, suppliers, or colleagues.

The final method of performance appraisal is called **multirater assessment or 360-degree feedback.** Typically, an employee's performance appraisal is conducted by his or her manager. With multirater assessment, the process of evaluation is expanded to other individuals who have knowledge of the employee's work performance. Co-workers, subordinates, customers, or any other individual who is familiar with the employee's work performance is asked to complete a questionnaire on the employee's work performance. Thus, an evaluation is made by those individuals who are familiar with the employee's work performance. These individuals can come from inside or outside the organization or from individuals that are higher or lower in the organizational structure.

In addition to the above, the person that is being evaluated does a self-evaluation using the same form that the evaluators use. When all these questionnaires are completed, a circle (360 degrees) of evaluations exists. Normally the questionnaires are rather lengthy. The human resource department compiles the results of the questionnaires and provides the results to the employee who is being evaluated. The employee gets to see how his or her opinion differs from those of the group doing the assessment.[15]

## SELECTING A PERFORMANCE APPRAISAL METHOD

Whatever performance appraisal method an organization uses, it must be job-related. Therefore, before selecting a performance appraisal method, job analyses must be conducted and job descriptions

| AREA OF INFORMATION | CONTENTS |
|---|---|
| Job title and location within company | |
| Organizational relationship | A brief explanation of the number of persons supervised (if applicable) and the job title(s) of the position(s) supervised; a statement concerning supervision received. |
| Relation to other jobs | Describes and outlines the coordination required by the job. |
| Job summary | Condensed explanation of the content of the job. |
| Information concerning job requirements | Varies greatly from job to job and from organization to organization; typically includes information on such topics as machines, tools, and materials; mental complexity and attention required; physical demands; and working conditions. |

**figure 11.11**

**INFORMATION PROVIDED BY JOB ANALYSIS**

written. Normally, job analyses are performed by trained specialists with the organization's human resource department or by outside consultants. Figure 11.11 summarizes the information a job analysis provides.

Job analysis involves not only determining job content but also reporting the results of the analysis. One product of a job analysis is a job description, a formal written document, usually one to three pages long, that should include the following:

- Date written.
- Job status (full or part time).
- Job title.
- Supervision received (to whom the jobholder reports).
- Supervision exercised (who reports to this employee).
- Job summary (a synopsis of the job responsibilities).
- Detailed list of job responsibilities.
- Principal contacts (in and outside the organization).
- Competency or position requirements.
- Required education or experience.
- Career mobility (position or positions employee may qualify for next).

After a job description is written, the most appropriate performance appraisal method can be determined.[16]

Your company has recently made a sizable investment in radio frequency identification (RFID) technology to help it better manage inventory control and product shipment to customers. By attaching RFID tags to product containers, you can now accurately record item quantities in the warehouse (helping to reduce the chance of items being out of stock). With the appropriate transmission signal on your delivery trucks, you can also track the shipments on the way to customers and provide an accurate delivery time—all this with a wafer-thin electronic chip embedded in the tag.

As an added bonus from the RFID equipment vendor for this substantial order, your company has also been provided with new employee ID tags that also have a wafer-thin electronic chip embedded inside them. The company announced the move as a new building security measure without mentioning that the technology now allows the location of every employee on site to be tracked in real time.

**Questions**

1. How comfortable are you with this ability to track your location?

2. Do you see the RFID tag as an invasion of your privacy? Why or why not?

3. How do you think the employees would react if they knew about this capability?

## POTENTIAL ERRORS IN PERFORMANCE APPRAISALS

**leniency**

Grouping of ratings at the positive end of the scale instead of spreading them throughout the scale.

**central tendency**

Occurs when performance appraisal statistics indicate that most employees are evaluated similarly as doing average or above-average work.

**recency**

Occurs when performance evaluations are based on work performed most recently, generally work performed one to two months before evaluation.

Several common errors have been identified in performance appraisals. **Leniency** is the grouping of ratings at the positive end of the performance scale instead of spreading them throughout the scale. **Central tendency** occurs when performance appraisal statistics indicate that most employees are evaluated similarly as doing average or above-average work. **Recency** occurs when performance evaluations are based on work performed most recently, generally work performed one to two months before evaluation. Leniency, central tendency, and recency errors make it difficult, if not impossible, to separate the good performers from the poor performers. In addition, these errors make it difficult to compare ratings from different managers. For example, it is possible for a good performer who is evaluated by a manager committing central tendency errors to receive a lower rating than a poor performer who is rated by a manager committing leniency errors.

Another common error in performance appraisals is the halo effect.[17] This occurs when managers allow a single prominent characteristic of an employee to influence their judgment on each separate item in the performance appraisal. It often results in the employee receiving approximately the same rating on every item.

Personal preferences, prejudices, and biases can also cause errors in performance appraisals. Managers with biases or prejudices tend to look for employee behaviors that conform to their biases. Appearance, social status, dress, race, and sex have influenced many performance

Appearance, social status, dress, race, and sex have influenced many performance appraisals. Name a better way to evaluate employees.

appraisals. Managers have also allowed first impressions to influence later judgments of an employee. First impressions are only a sample of behavior; however, people tend to retain these impressions even when faced with contradictory evidence.

## PROGRESS CHECK QUESTIONS

 9. Define performance appraisal.

10. List the six steps of the management by objectives (MBO) process.

11. List three of the more commonly used ranking methods.

12. Explain the four most common errors in the performance appraisal process.

## The College Admissions Office

Bob Luck was hired to replace Alice Carter as administrative assistant in the admissions office of Claymore Community College. Before leaving, Alice had given a month's notice to the director of admissions, hoping this would allow ample time to locate and train her replacement. Alice's responsibilities included preparing and mailing transcripts at the request of students, mailing information requested by people interested in attending the college, answering the telephone, assisting students or potential enrollees who came to the office, and general supervision of clerical personnel and student assistants.

After interviewing and testing many people for the position, the director hired Bob, mainly because his credentials were good and he made a favorable impression. Alice spent many hours during the next 10 days training Bob. He appeared to be quite bright and seemed to quickly pick up the procedures involved in operating a college admissions office. When Alice left, everyone thought Bob would do an outstanding job.

However, little time had elapsed before people realized that Bob had not caught on to his job responsibilities. Bob seemed to have personal problems that were severe enough to stand in the way of his work. He asked questions about subjects that Alice had covered explicitly; he

should have been able to answer these himself if he had comprehended her instructions.

Bob appeared to constantly have other things on his mind. He seemed to be preoccupied with such problems as his recent divorce, which he blamed entirely on his ex-wife, and the distress of his eight-year-old daughter, who missed her father terribly. His thoughts also dwelled on his search for peace of mind and some reasons for all that had happened to him. The director of admissions was aware of Bob's preoccupation with his personal life and his failure to learn the office procedures rapidly.

### Questions

1. Could Alice Carter have done anything differently here? Why or why not?

2. What would you do at this point if you were the director of admissions?

3. Do you think Bob should keep his job? Why or why not?

4. Describe how you might effectively use a performance appraisal in this situation.

# CONDUCTING EFFECTIVE PERFORMANCE APPRAISALS

A promising approach to conducting effective performance appraisals is to improve the skills of managers. Suggestions on the specific training managers should receive are often vague, but they usually emphasize that managers should be given training to observe behavior more accurately and judge it fairly.

More research is needed before a definitive set of topics for manager training can be established. However, at a minimum, managers should receive training in (1) the performance appraisal method(s) of the company, (2) the importance of the manager's role in the total appraisal process, (3) the use of performance appraisal information, and (4) the communication skills necessary to provide feedback to the employee.

General dos and don'ts of the performance appraisal process can help managers to not only prevent but also reduce the errors that always seem to plague the process. The dos include the following:

1. Base performance appraisal on job performance only and not other factors unrelated to the job.

2. Use only those rating scales that are relevant to the job itself and are indicators of objective performance and attainment.

3. Sincerely work at the appraisal interview process.

4. Be problem solving oriented.

The don'ts include the following:

1. Don't criticize. Be proactive.

2. Carefully avoid the halo effect and leniency errors.

3. Dominate conversations about performance. Encourage employees to speak and to address issues in the evaluation process themselves.

4. Avoid general prescriptions to fix performance. Always present concrete and realizable objectives. Performance goals are the foundation of productivity.

# PROVIDING FEEDBACK THROUGH THE APPRAISAL INTERVIEW

After one of the previously discussed methods for developing an employee's performance appraisal has been used, the results must be communicated to the employee. Unless this interview is properly conducted, it can and frequently does result in an unpleasant experience for both manager and employee. Following are some of the more important factors influencing success or failure of appraisal interviews:

- The more employees participate in the appraisal process, the more satisfied they are with the appraisal interview and with the manager and the more likely they are to accept and strive to meet performance improvement objectives.

- The more a manager uses positive motivational techniques (e.g., recognizing and praising good performance), the more satisfied the employee is likely to be with the appraisal interview and with the manager.

- The mutual setting by the manager and the employee of specific performance improvement objectives results in more improvement in performance than does a general discussion or criticism.

- Discussing and solving problems that may be hampering the employee's current job performance improve the employee's performance.

- Areas of job performance needing improvement that are most heavily criticized are less likely to be improved than similar areas of job performance that are less heavily criticized.

## Study Skills

### Importance of Doing Your Own Work

Do the pressures of being a student get you in trouble?

When learning becomes dependent upon the assistance of others or other sources, students face internal and external pressures of honesty and validity of their own work.

A key term, *plagiarism*, now comes into play. Plagiarism is presenting someone else's work as your own.

This misuse of the learning process can lull a student into a false sense of knowing the subject of study, and plagiarism can jeopardize a student's integrity and cause a character flaw that carries over into other areas of the student's life.

Learn the valuable lessons school provides— sacrifice, hard work, and honesty—and look for the payoff in all phases of your life!

- The more employees are allowed to voice their opinions during the interview, the more satisfied they will be with the interview.
- The amount of thought and preparation employees independently devote before the interview increases the benefits of the interview.
- The more the employee perceives that performance appraisal results are tied to organizational rewards, the more beneficial the interview will be.

The interviewer must also be aware that many employees are skeptical about the appraisal process because of its potential association with punishment. Research has shown that this most often happens because the employee does not trust the manager's motivation; the feedback is unclear; the employee does not respect the manager's judgment; the feedback is inconsistent with the opinions of others; and the employee has had negative past experiences with the evaluation, appraisal, or feedback process. Most of these problems can be overcome by simply accentuating the positive as the basis for the interview, feedback, and correction processes.[18]

---

### PROGRESS CHECK QUESTIONS

13. Describe the four areas of training needed by managers before conducting performance appraisals.
14. What are the four dos of the appraisal process?
15. What are the corresponding don'ts of the process?
16. Describe at least five important factors that can influence the success or failure of performance appraisal.

---

## DEVELOPING PERFORMANCE IMPROVEMENT PLANS

Earlier in this chapter, we stated that a completed performance appraisal should include a performance improvement plan. This important step is often ignored. However, managers must recognize that an employee's development is a continuous cycle of setting performance goals, providing training necessary to achieve the goals, assessing performance as to the accomplishment of the goals, and then setting new, higher goals. A performance improvement plan consists of the following components:

1.  *Where are we now?* This question is answered in the performance appraisal process.
2.  *Where do we want to be?* This requires the evaluator and the person being evaluated to mutually agree on the areas that can and should be improved.
3.  *How does the employee get from where he or she is now to where he or she wants to be?* This component is critical to the performance improvement plan. Specific steps to be taken must be agreed on. The steps may include the training the employee will need to improve his or her performance and should also include how the evaluator will help the employee achieve the performance goals.

## CONCLUSION

The responsibility of managers to control the running of the organization simply means that they should know what is actually happening in comparison to established standards or performance objectives, and then make any corrections where necessary. With clearly established standards in place, the control mechanisms can serve as an early warning system to alert managers when a problem exists or, even better, before a problem even occurs. To be effective and comprehensive in their coverage of the organization, those control mechanisms must address both the work performance of the personnel in the organization and the systems and processes required to produce the product or service that the organization delivers to its customers. In the next chapter we'll review the importance of managing both the design and the control of those systems and processes.

## Kevin gets some goals

Kevin took a few days to think about Tony's question. The first day had been taken up with worrying about what was really going on here. Kevin had never been asked to do this in any of his other jobs. His annual review had always been the same—a brief chat with the boss; here's what you're doing well; here's something you could improve on; keep up the good work; and here's your pay raise. Simple and predictable, thought Kevin.

Now Tony wanted goals and, more than that, goals for which Kevin would be held accountable over the next year. What was he looking for? Was he looking for Kevin to learn Spanish (something they had talked about because of their growing Latino customer base) or finally finish his bachelor's degree or maybe take some more of the management training courses that the company was always offering at the regional meetings?

Suddenly, Kevin realized how excited he was at the prospect of committing to doing something new over the next year and committing to it in writing rather than just talking about it. He started to make a list of what he wanted to do, taking the extra time to make notes for Tony on how the restaurant would benefit if it gave him the time off to do them or, better yet, if it was willing to help him cover the costs of doing them. Before he knew it, he had two pages of ideas. Some of them would take longer than a year to achieve, but many of them could be started right away and be done a lot sooner, which would allow Kevin to show progress toward his goals long before the next annual review. The management courses could be taken at the regional meeting next month, and the local college started Spanish classes for beginners every other month. "I wonder if Tony realized what he was letting himself in for when he started this," Kevin said to himself.

### QUESTIONS

1. Kevin had no problem coming up with ideas for personal and professional goals. Do you think he'll get to do them all? Why or why not?

2. Do you think Tony is expecting this kind of response from every one of his people? Why or why not?

3. What challenges will Tony face if everyone is as creative as Kevin in setting goals?

4. What can Tony do to manage this situation?

## key terms

## review questions

1. Describe the two categories of control methods.
2. Outline the major points of the Sarbanes-Oxley Act of 2002.
3. Identify at least three uses of performance appraisal information.
4. Outline at least three factors that influence the success or failure of performance appraisal interviews.

## internet exercise

Visit the Web site www.360-feedback.com, and answer the following questions:

1. What are the pros and cons of this appraisal tool?
2. Why is coaching an important part of the 360-feedback process?
3. How do you know if your company is ready to start using 360 feedback?
4. Would 360 feedback work in your organization? Why or why not?

## team exercise

### DEBATING THE SARBANES-OXLEY ACT

The major points of the Sarbanes-Oxley Act of 2002 are summarized in Figure 11.4 on page 309. Divide the class into two groups (or an even number of smaller groups). Carefully study Figure 11.4, and develop an argument either supporting the rise and necessity of the act or in opposition to the act. Your instructor may allow you to gather additional information through library or Internet research. Summarize your argument points in outline form, and be prepared to debate classmates who take the other side of the argument. Once the debates are completed, answer the following questions:

### Questions

1. Summarize the key points of your argument.
2. Summarize the key points of the opposing group's argument.
3. Did the information shared in the debate change your opinion? Why or why not?
4. Your viewpoint was chosen for you according to the team to which you were assigned. How did the team reach agreement in debating its viewpoint? Explain your answer.

## How Bob Iger Unchained Disney

The Walt Disney Co. has been racking up enviable numbers. It's posting record earnings, and the stock price has been defying gravity like Disneyland's Big Thunder Mountain Railroad. So the Oscar for Disney's turnaround goes to . . . CEO Bob Iger. No, wait, to his predecessor Michael Eisner. No, both. We'll explain. Ignore for the moment the splash Iger made last year when he repaired relations with Steve Jobs and took control of Pixar, the Apple Inc. founder's animation hit factory. Most of the good news at Disney since Iger's promotion—the resurrection of ABC, the $2 billion *Pirates of the Caribbean* franchise, rising attendance at Disney's U.S. theme parks—are the payoff of plans laid during the Eisner era. And though Iger was deeply involved in the revival at

ABC, he is the first to give his predecessor credit: "It was because of Michael that I was able to hit the ground running," he says. On the other hand, those record profits deserve a second look. Yes, net income soared 33 percent in fiscal 2006, to $3.4 billion, while revenues climbed 7 percent to $34.3 billion. But Disney had a one-of-a-kind year in 2006, with two box-office smashes in *Cars* and *Pirates of the Caribbean: Dead Man's Chest* that by themselves gave Disney earnings a huge pop. That sets the bar high for Disney this year. While another *Pirates* film is due out this summer, along with Pixar's *Ratatouille*, Thomson Financial projects net income growth in 2007 of 12 percent vs. 24 percent for the media sector as a whole. To buffer the company against the hit-and-miss characteristics of the movie business, Iger will need to complete an ongoing revival of the Paris and Hong Kong theme parks, keep ABC's momentum going, and encourage the Pixar team to make more than one film a year. He must also make Disney nimbler and capable of moving quickly to seize the digital day.

It's on that final challenge that Iger has made the most progress. Behind the scenes he has tipped Eisner's centrally planned company on its end, hacking away at the bureaucracy and unshackling a group of veteran executives to plot their own courses. Putting Disney movies and ABC shows on the iPod is not just groundbreaking. It's a reflection of a faster-moving and more aggressive Disney. However, rather than throwing Eisner's people out just because he could, Iger has kept the team largely intact, and by surrounding himself with smart people, including Jobs and the Pixar crew, and letting them get on with it, Iger has re-created a can-do culture at Disney.

Even so, to this day, Iger won't speak ill of Eisner. "I think fondly of Michael. I learned a lot from him," he says. "In a way, he founded the modern Walt Disney." What Iger tactfully leaves unsaid is that during the final years of Eisner's otherwise brilliant two-decade run, Disney lost its animating spirit. To say the culture was poisonous doesn't begin to capture the company's dysfunction. Eisner left behind a place where division chiefs were afraid to make decisions—the last thing the company needed when such rivals as News Corp. and Viacom Inc. were boldly staking out territory on the Web. Iger recognized that the problem wasn't the people running the show. It was the work environment—and he set about changing it. One of the first things Iger did was make the Monday morning meetings less autocratic. Where Eisner held court, Iger encourages a conversation. And he made a point of visiting the troops—for example spending half a day at Buena Vista Games Inc., talking to game developers in town for a brainstorming session. Iger has also reached out to former Disney people who can help him chart a new strategic direction. One regular dinner companion is former studio chief Jeffrey Katzenberg. Disney rece-ntly agreed to air a *Shrek* Christmas special produced by Katzenberg's DreamWorks Animation.

## "WHERE'S MY WOW?"

If Eisner struggled to rise above the petty and personal, Iger sees the big picture. He doesn't dump on people's ideas. Eisner famously wrote: "Where's my wow?" on subordinates' proposals he didn't like. And where Eisner got involved in every aspect of the creative process, from the color of the carpets at the theme park hotels to Tuesday morning script sessions, Iger lets his people take the lead. Nowhere has he given up more control than at Disney's animation unit. That's amazing given that the Mouse House was built on animation. In a good year it provides as much as one-third of the studio's profits. But with Disney animators turning out a steady stream of clunkers, Iger has given Jobs's Pixar team carte blanche. With Pixar creative guru John Lasseter installed as Disney's new chief creative officer, the newcomers laid off 160 people and reassigned executives. Last year, Lasseter and former Pixar President Ed Catmull, who is now president of Disney Animation, delayed the Christmas release of Disney's *Meet the Robinsons* movie until March 2007 to rework it.

However, Iger's hands-off style may yet prove to have its limits. The Pixar people decided, for example, not to release a Tinker Bell animated DVD later this year because they wanted time to make it better, even though the release had been timed to coincide with a new Disney promotion of toys based on fairy characters. And the quality-first attitude of the Pixarites, which could generate bigger box office, might also mean fewer animated movies each year. They're not big on sequels, either. That means less opportunity for tie-ins with merchandise, the theme parks, and Broadway plays.

If one thing separates Iger from other media moguls like Rupert Murdoch and Sumner M. Redstone, it's his belief that he doesn't need to go out and acquire a MySpace.com or YouTube Inc. While he hasn't ruled out buying an online property, Iger says he has the right content and world-class brands—Disney, ESPN, ABC—to lure eyeballs. The rollout in coming weeks of a reimagined

Disney.com is central to Iger's plan to boost the company's online fortunes. The reconfigured site, which draws 21 million unique visitors each month, now features social networking and streamed TV shows aimed at young kids—another way to capitalize on that family vibe. The hope is that the site will get visitors to stay longer, allowing Disney to surpass the $700 million in digital revenues it projects for this year. Ultimately, Iger wants to go directly to consumers on the Web, supplementing the company's existing deals with cable and satellite providers. "Why not be there ourselves?" he says. It's a question Iger will continue to wrestle with as he remakes Disney.

## Questions

1. How is Bob Iger's approach to managerial control different from Michael Eisner's?

2. Iger had the chance to start with a new leadership team, but he chose to keep Eisner's team almost intact. From a control perspective, was that the right decision? Why or why not?

3. "Iger lets his people take the lead." How do you balance that approach with managerial control?

4. Do you think Iger's approach will be successful? Why or why not?

*Source:* Adapted from Ronald Grover, *BusinessWeek* Entertainment, February 5, 2007.

## Fear of Firing

*How the Threat of Litigation Is Making Companies Skittish about Axing Problem Workers*

**W**ould you have dared fire Hemant K. Mody? In February 2003, the longtime engineer had returned to work at a General Electric Co. facility in Plainville, Conn., after a two-month medical leave. He was a very unhappy man. For much of the prior year, he and his superiors had been sparring over his performance and promotion prospects. According to court documents, Mody's bosses claimed he spoke disparagingly of his co-workers, refused an assignment as being beneath him, and was abruptly taking days off and coming to work late. But Mody was also 49, Indian born, and even after returning from leave continued to suffer a major disability: chronic kidney failure that required him to receive daily dialysis. The run-ins resumed with his managers, whom he had accused flat out of discriminating against him because of his race and age. It doesn't take an advanced degree in human resources to recognize that the situation was becoming increasingly unstable. But Mody's bosses were fed up. They axed him in April 2003. The situation collapsed last July. Following a six-day

trial, a federal court jury in Bridgeport, Conn., found GE's termination of Mody to be improper and awarded him $11.1 million, including $10 million in punitive damages. But the award wasn't for discrimination. The judge found those claims so weak that Mody wasn't allowed to present them. Instead, jurors concluded that Mody had been fired in retaliation for complaining about bias. GE is seeking to have the award overturned.

If this can happen to GE, a company famed for its rigorous performance reviews, with an HR operation that is studied worldwide, it can happen anywhere. It has never been easier for U.S. workers to go to court and allege that they've been sacked unfairly. Over the past 40 years federal, state, and local lawmakers have steadily expanded the categories of workers who enjoy special legal protection—a sprawling group that now includes women, minorities, gays, whistleblowers, the disabled, people over 40, employees who have filed workers' compensation claims, and workers who have been called away for jury duty or military service, among others. Factor in white men who believe that they are bias victims—so-called reverse-discrimination lawsuits —and it's difficult to find someone who doesn't have some capacity to claim protected status.

## THESE WORKERS WIELD A POTENT WEAPON

They can force companies to prove in court that there was a legitimate business reason for their termination. And once a case is in court, it's expensive. A company can easily spend $100,000 to get a meritless lawsuit tossed out before trial. And if a case goes to a jury, the fees skyrocket to $300,000, and often much higher. The result: Many companies today are gripped by a fear of firing. Terrified of lawsuits, they let unproductive employees linger, lay off coveted workers while retaining less valuable ones, and pay severance to screwups and even crooks in exchange for promises that they won't sue. The fear of firing is particularly acute in the HR and legal departments. They don't directly suffer when an underperformer lingers in the corporate hierarchy, but they may endure unpleasant indirect consequences if that person files a lawsuit.

This set of divergent incentives puts line managers in a tough position. When they finally decide to get rid of the underperforming slob who plays PC solitaire all day in her cubicle, it can be surprisingly tough to do. But it's often the supervisors themselves who bear much of the blame when HR says someone can't be shown the door. That's because most fail to give the kind of regular and candid evaluations that will allow a company to prove poor performance if a fired employee hauls them into court. Honest, if harsh, reviews not only offer legal cover, but they're also critical for organizations intent on developing top talent.

When Mody signed GE's job application in 1998, the form said his employment was "at will" and "the Company may terminate my employment at any time for any reason." Well, not exactly. The notion that American workers are employed "at will"—meaning, as one lawyer put

it, you can be fired if your manager doesn't like the color of your socks—took root in the laissez-faire atmosphere of the late 19th century, and as an official matter is still the law of the land in every state, save Montana. For most American workers now, their status as at-will employees has been transformed by a succession of laws growing out of the civil rights movement in the 1960s that bar employers from making decisions based on such things as race, religion, sex, age, and national origin. This is hardly controversial. Even the legal system's harshest critics find little fault with rules aimed at assuring that personnel decisions are based on merit. And most freely acknowledge that it is much easier to fire people in the U.S. than it is in, say, most of Western Europe. Mass layoffs, in fact, are a recurring event on the American corporate scene. Yet even in these situations, RIFs (for "reduction in force") are carefully vetted by attorneys to assess the impact on employees who are in a legally protected category. And these days the majority of American workers fall into one or more such groups. Mody, for example, belonged to three because of who he was (age, race, and national origin) and two more because of things he had done (complained of discrimination and taken medical leave). That doesn't mean such people are immune from firing. But it does mean a company will have to show a legitimate, nondiscriminatory business reason for the termination, should the matter ever land in court.

## Questions

1. Why are many companies now afraid of terminating unproductive employees?
2. Why do supervisors "bear much of the blame when HR says someone can't be shown the door"?
3. Can managers really fire employees "at will"?
4. The judge threw out Mody's claim of discrimination. Do you think Mody has a valid case for retribution? Why or why not?

*Source:* Adapted from Michael Orey, *BusinessWeek Online,* April 27, 2007.

# OPERATIONS CONTROL

> "Just because it can be counted doesn't mean it counts and just because it counts doesn't mean it can be counted."

> —Albert Einstein

## The World of Work: Taco Barn goes Japanese

Kevin's success with the MBO project gave Tony an idea.

"If one employee could be that insightful and creative in planning his own future, how many new ideas could we come up with if we gave every employee the chance to contribute their ideas? Not just a simple suggestion box, which usually gathers more gum wrappers than employee suggestions, but a real plan to improve the restaurant based on the ideas of the employees who work here—the folks who cook the food, serve the food, and listen to our customers."

On his next regular lunch meeting with his mentor and former boss Jerry Smith, Tony put the idea forward for Jerry's feedback.

"I think it's a great idea, Tony," said Jerry. "You've got a bright group over there, and I'm sure they'll surprise you with some really creative ideas. In fact, I just came back from a leadership conference where they had a presentation on this very topic—it's a philosophy called *kaizen* and it comes from Japanese companies that commit to continuously reinventing their operations, even when they're already the market leader in their industry. Toyota has become a global car company as a direct result of its kaizen practices."

Tony figured he would have to go back and do some web searching on Toyota and kaizen, but never one to miss an opportunity, he decided to take full advantage of Jerry's recent conference trip:

# objectives

**CHAPTER 12**

**After studying this chapter, you will be able to:**

1. Understand the basic requirements for controlling operating costs.

2. Define quality from the perspective of an operations manager.

3. Explain the concept of Total Quality Management (TQM).

4. Define the following terms: *continuous improvement, kaizen, six sigma, lean manufacturing,* and *quality at the source.*

5. Explain the purpose of the Malcolm Baldrige Award.

6. Explain the concept of just-in-time (JIT) inventory.

---

"That sounds really interesting, Jerry. What else did you pick up at the conference?"

"They had this great exercise that might help you get your group into the spirit of being creative," continued Jerry. "It's called *stand in the circle.* You get your team to stand in a circle drawn on the floor. They each have a pad with at least 30 lines on it. You then give them 30 minutes to come up with 30 ideas to improve the company. They can be as wild and crazy as they want, but the ideas have to be improvements on the way things are currently done. The 30-minute time limit is supposed to help focus their energy. Then you meet as a group and review the ideas and decide, as a group, which ones will be implemented and how soon that will be done. The instructor made us do the exercise on the experience we were having

at our hotel. You would be amazed how many ideas we generated—a couple of people even asked for extra paper!"

Tony thought this over for a while and decided, "I think that might just work for us—thanks, Jerry."

## QUESTIONS

1. How did Kevin's performance on the MBO project inspire Tony to consider kaizen?

2. If the employee suggestion box only collects gum wrappers, why should this exercise be any different?

3. What kind of ideas do you think Tony's team will come up with?

4. Would this exercise work at your company? Why or why not?

# OPERATIONS CONTROL

There are two aspects to an effective operating system: design and control. The two aspects are related in that after a system has been designed and implemented, day-to-day operations must be controlled. With respect to efficient operation, the system processes must be monitored; quality must be assured; inventories must be managed; and all of these tasks must be accomplished within cost constraints. In addition to ensuring that things do not get out of control, good operations control can be a substitute for resources. For example, good quality control can reduce scrap and wasted materials, thus cutting costs. Similarly, effective inventory control can reduce the investment costs in inventories.

Effective operations control is attained by applying the basic control concepts to the operations function of the organization. Operations controls generally relate to one of three areas: costs, quality, or inventories.

# CONTROLLING OPERATIONS COSTS

**variable overhead expenses**

Expenses that change in proportion to the level of production or service.

**fixed overhead expenses**

Expenses that do not change appreciably with fluctuations in the level of production or service.

Ensuring that operating costs do not get out of hand is one of the primary jobs of the operations manager. The first requirement for controlling costs is to understand the organization's accounting and budgeting systems. Operations managers are primarily concerned with costs relating to labor, materials, and overhead. Figure 12.1 describes the major components of each of these costs. **Variable overhead expenses** change with the level of production or service. **Fixed overhead expenses** do not change appreciably with the level of production or service.

Normally, operations managers prepare monthly budgets for each of the major cost areas. Once the budgets have been approved by higher levels of management, they are put into effect. By carefully monitoring

## figure 12.1

**BUDGET COSTS: THE BASIS FOR COST CONTROL**

***Source:*** N. Gaither, *Production and Operations Management* (Fort Worth: Dryden Press, 1980).

| TYPE OF COST | COMPONENTS |
|---|---|
| Direct labor—variable | Wages and salaries of employees engaged in the direct generation of goods and services. This typically does not include wages and salaries of support personnel. |
| Materials—variable | Cost of materials that become a tangible part of finished goods and services. |
| Production overhead—variable | Training new employees, safety training, supervision and clerical, overtime premium, shift premium, payroll taxes, vacation and holiday, retirement funds, group insurance, supplies, travel, repairs and maintenance. |
| Production overhead—fixed | Travel, research and development, fuel (coal, gas, or oil), electricity, water, repairs and maintenance, rent, depreciation, real estate taxes, insurance. |

the ensuing labor, material, and overhead costs, the operations manager can compare actual costs to budgeted costs. The methods used to monitor costs naturally vary, but typically they include direct observation, written reports, break-even charts, and so on.

Usually a cost control system indicates only when a particular cost is out of control; it does not address the question of *why* it is out of control. For example, suppose an operations manager determines from the monthly cost report that the labor costs on product X are exceeding budget by 20 percent. The manager must then attempt to determine what is causing the cost overrun. The causes could be many, including unmotivated employees, several new and untrained employees, low-quality raw materials, or equipment breakdowns. The wise manager not only investigates the cause but also plans for prevention. The logical conclusion of a monitoring process is the implementation of prevention measures.[1]

Determining the cause may require only a simple inspection of the facts, or it may call for an in-depth analysis. Whatever the effort required, the operations manager must ultimately identify the source of the problem and then take the necessary corrective action. If the same cost problems continue to occur, chances are the manager has not correctly identified the true cause of the problem or the necessary corrective action has not been taken.

## QUALITY MANAGEMENT

**Quality** is a relative term that means different things to different people. The consumer who demands quality may have a different concept from the operations manager who demands quality. The consumer is concerned with service, reliability, performance, appearance, and so forth. The operations manager's primary concern is that the product or service specifications be achieved, whatever they may be. For the operations manager, quality is determined in relation to the specifications or standards set in the design stages. Thus, the design quality refers to the inherent value of the product or service in the marketplace.[2] Figure 12.2 lists the six common dimensions of design quality.

**quality**

For the operations manager, quality is determined in relation to the specifications or standards set in the design stages – the degree or grade of excellence specified.

| DIMENSION | MEANING |
|---|---|
| Performance | Primary product or service characteristics |
| Features | Added touches; bells and whistles; secondary characteristics |
| Reliability/durability | Consistency of performance over time; probability of failing; useful life |
| Serviceability | Ease of repair |
| Aesthetics | Sensory characteristics (sound, feel, look, and so on) |
| Reputation | Past performance and other intangibles (perceived quality) |

## figure 12.2

**THE DIMENSIONS OF DESIGN QUALITY**

***Source:*** From Richard B. Chase, F. Robert Jacobs, and Nicholas J. Aquilano, *Operations Management for Competitive Advantage,* 11th ed., 2002. Reproduced with permission of The McGraw-Hill Companies, Inc.

## Study Skills

### Make Good Study Habits a Life Skill!

A good week of school does not make a college career.

The key to long-term success is the ability to consistently produce. Achieving an "A" average throughout your school career indicates your ability to handle the obligations that you must keep and manage with a high level of success!

If your mission is to stay on course, then use the following as a reminder of the method that can best help you do so. Implement the BORD principle as follows: *Balance* your responsibilities in a series of priorities, become *organized* in your daily activities, set a regular *routine* to make all this a normal operating process, and, finally, through *discipline,* all the troubles and difficulties you will encounter can be kept to a minimum.

The quality of an organization's goods and services can affect the organization in many ways. Some of the most important of these areas are (1) loss of business, (2) liability, (3) costs, and (4) productivity.[3] The reputation of an organization is often a direct reflection of the perceived quality of its goods or services. In today's legalistic environment, an organization's liability exposure can be significant and the associated costs can be high. Higher-quality goods and services generally have less liability exposure than lower-quality goods and services. In addition to liability costs, quality can affect other costs, including scrap, rework, warranty, repair, replacement, and other similar costs. Productivity and quality are often closely related.[4] Poor-quality equipment, tools, parts, or subassemblies can cause defects that hurt productivity. Similarly, high-quality equipment, tools, parts, and subassemblies can boost productivity.

Because of the many different ways quality can affect an organization, it is often difficult to determine precisely the costs associated with different quality levels. Also, it must be realized that consumers and customers are willing to pay for quality only up to a point. In response, many firms have instituted a total customer response program in which quality in the workplace is transferred to dealings with customers. To implement the program, firms must (1) develop a new attitude toward customers, (2) reduce management layers so that managers are in contact with customers, (3) link quality and information systems to customer needs and problems, (4) train employees in customer responsiveness, (5) integrate customer responsiveness throughout the entire distribution channel, and (6) use customer responsiveness as a marketing tool.[5]

## Quality Assurance

For years, the responsibility for quality in almost all organizations rested with a quality control department.[6] The idea under this approach was to identify and remove defects or correct mistakes before they got to the customer. Some systems emphasized finding and correcting defects at the end of the line; others focused on detecting defects during the production process. Both approaches focused on only the production part of the process; they gave little or no consideration to the design of the products/services or to working with suppliers. Suppliers were usually treated as adversaries.

Today's quality management emphasizes the prevention of defects and mistakes rather than finding and correcting them. The idea of

1. Create and publish to all employees a statement of the aims and purposes of the company or other organization. The management must demonstrate constantly their commitment to this statement.
2. Learn the new philosophy, top management and everybody.
3. Understand the purpose of inspection, for improvement of processes and reduction of cost.
4. End the practice of awarding business on the basis of price tag alone.
5. Improve constantly and forever the system of production and service.
6. Institute training.
7. Teach and institute leadership.
8. Drive out fear. Create trust. Create a climate for innovation.
9. Optimize toward the aims and purposes of the company the efforts of teams, groups, and staff.
10. Eliminate exhortations for the workforce.
11a. Eliminate numerical quotas for production. Instead learn and institute methods for improvement.
11b. Eliminate management by objective. Instead learn the capabilities of processes and how to improve them.
12. Remove barriers that rob people of pride of workmanship.
13. Encourage education and self-improvement for everyone.
14. Take action to accomplish the transformation.

**figure 12.3**

**DEMING'S 14 POINTS**

***Source:*** Deming, W. Edwards, *Out of the Crisis,* pp. 23-24. "The 14 Points," Copyright © W. Edwards Deming Institute, by permission of MIT Press.

"building in" quality as opposed to "inspecting it in" is also known as *quality assurance*. This approach views quality as the responsibility of all employees rather than the exclusive domain of a quality control department. Furthermore, suppliers are treated as partners.

While there have been many individuals who have championed the prevention approach to quality, W. Edwards Deming is perhaps most responsible. Deming was a statistics professor at New York University in the 1940s who went to Japan after World War II to assist in improving quality and productivity. While he became very much revered in Japan, Deming remained almost unknown to U.S. business leaders until the 1980s when Japan's quality and productivity attracted the attention of the world. Figure 12.3 presents a list compiled by Deming of 14 points he believed are needed to achieve quality in any organization. The underlying philosophy of Deming's work in this area is that the cause of poor quality and low productivity is the system and not the employees. He also stressed that it is management's responsibility to correct the system so that the desired results can be achieved.

## Total Quality Management

Total quality management (TQM) is a management philosophy that emphasizes "managing the entire organization so that it excels in all dimensions of products and services that are important to the customer."[7] TQM, in essence, is an organizationwide emphasis on quality as defined by the customer. Under TQM, everyone from the CEO on down to the lowest-level employee must be involved. TQM can be summarized by the following actions:[8]

1. Find out what customers want. This might involve the use of surveys, focus groups, interviews, or some other technique that integrates the customer's voice in the decision-making process.

2. Design a product or service that will meet (or exceed) what customers want. Make it easy to use and easy to produce.

3. Design a production process that facilitates doing the job right the first time. Determine where mistakes are likely to occur, and try to prevent them. When mistakes do occur, find out why so that they are less likely to occur again. Strive to mistake-proof the process.

4. Keep track of results, and use those results to guide improvement in the system. Never stop trying to improve.

5. Extend these concepts to suppliers and to distribution.

As stated previously, TQM is an organizationwide emphasis on quality as defined by the customer. It is not a collection of techniques but a philosophy or way of thinking about how people view their jobs and quality throughout the organization.

## PROGRESS CHECK QUESTIONS

1. What are the two aspects to an effective operating system?
2. Why is quality a relative term?
3. Explain the term *total quality management (TQM)*.
4. List the 14 points that Deming believed are needed to achieve quality in an organization.

## Implementing TQM

Today's managers are bombarded with advice and literature telling them how to implement TQM. Three of the most popular approaches for implementing TQM are the Deming method, the Juran method, and the Crosby method, each named after the person who championed the respective approach. These three men, W. Edwards Deming, Joseph M. Juran, and Philip Crosby, are known as the "quality gurus." The Deming method emphasizes statistical quality control through employee empowerment. The Juran method emphasizes the reformulation of attitudes, comprehensive controls, and annual objective reviews. The Crosby method emphasizes conformance to requirements and zero defects. All these approaches are sound; however, the best approach for implementing TQM is to custom-tailor the process for each application. In a study conducted by Frank Mahoney, the following initiatives were those most often cited by senior executives who had successfully implemented TQM.[9]

A major part of any total quality management is to keep customers satisfied. This often involves integrating the customers' voice in the decision-making process.

1. Demonstrate top-down commitment and involvement-push.
2. Set *tough* improvement goals, not just stretch goals.
3. Provide appropriate training, resources, and human resource backup.
4. Determine critical measurement factors; benchmark and track progress.
5. Spread success stories, especially those about favorable benchmarking; always share financial progress reports.
6. Identify the costs of quality and routes to improvement; prove the case that quality costs decline with quality progress.
7. Rely on teamwork, involvement, and all-level leadership.
8. Respect the "gurus," but tailor every initiative for a good local fit.
9. Allow time to see progress, analyze the system's operation, reward contributions, and make needed adjustments.
10. Finally, recognize that the key internal task is a culture change and the key external task is a new set of relationships with customers and suppliers.

Although it would seem to make good sense to transform an organization in the direction of total quality management, there is still resistance from the traditionalists. Figure 12.4 compares traditional organizations with those using TQM. The most often cited barriers to adopting TQM are (1) a lack of consistency of purpose on the part of management, (2) an emphasis on short-term profits, (3) an inability to modify personnel review systems, (4) mobility of management (job hopping), (5) lack of commitment to training and failure to instill leadership that is change oriented, and (6) excessive costs.[10]

## Specific Approaches for Improving Quality

*Continuous improvement, kaizen, quality at the source, six sigma,* and *lean manufacturing* are all terms that have particular relevance to TQM. Each approach is discussed in the following paragraphs.

# Production Problems

Braddock Company of Sea Shore City fabricates stamped metal parts used in the production of wheelbarrows. Braddock fabricates two basic styles of wheelbarrow trays: One is for a deep, four-cubic-foot construction model, and the other is for a shallow, two-cubic-foot homeowner model. Braddock's process is simple. (Braddock presently maintains about 7 days' worth of the large metal sheets for the construction model and about 10 days' worth of the smaller sheets for the homeowner model.) Raw metal sheets are picked up from inventory and fed into a large machine that bends and shapes the metal into the desired tray. The trays are then inspected and packaged, 10 to a box, for shipping.

In the past few days, Braddock has been experiencing quality problems with both tray styles. Undesirable creases have been forming in the corners following the stamping operation. However, the problem with the construction model tray is more pronounced and appeared almost three full days before it did on the homeowners model.

Several incidents have occurred at Braddock during the past week that Hal McCarthy, the operations manager, thinks may have a bearing on the problem. Shorty McCune, a machine operator and labor activist, was accused of drinking on the job and released a few days before the problem began. Since his release, Shorty has been seen in and around the plant talking to several other employees. About two weeks ago, Braddock also began receiving raw metal from a new supplier because of an attractive price break.

The only inspection the company performs is the postfabrication inspection.

## Questions

1. What do you think is causing Braddock's problem?
2. Why is the problem more pronounced on the construction model than on the homeowner model?
3. How can Braddock eliminate its problem?
4. What systems or processes should Braddock put in place to make sure this doesn't happen again?

## figure 12.4

**COMPARISON OF TRADITIONAL ORGANIZATIONS WITH THOSE USING TQM**

**Source:** From William J. Stevenson, *Production and Operations Management* 4th ed., 1992, p.107. Reproduced with permission of The McGraw-Hill Companies, Inc.

| ASPECT | TRADITIONAL | TQM |
|---|---|---|
| Overall mission | Maximize return on investment | Meet or exceed customer satisfaction |
| Objectives | Emphasis on short term | Balance of long term and short term |
| Management | Not always open; sometimes inconsistent objectives | Open; encourages employees' input; consistent objectives |
| Role of manager | Issue orders; enforce | Coach, remove barriers, build trust |
| Customer requirements | Not highest priority; may be unclear | Highest priority; important to identify and understand |
| Problems | Assign blame; punish | Identify and resolve |
| Problem solving | Not systematic; by individuals | Systematic; by teams |
| Improvement | Erratic | Continual |
| Suppliers | Adversarial | Partners |
| Jobs | Narrow, specialized; much individual effort | Broad, more general; much team effort |
| Focus | Product oriented | Process oriented |

**Continuous improvement** in general refers to an ongoing effort to make improvements in every part of the organization relative to all of its products and services.[11] With regard to TQM, it means focusing on continuous improvement in the quality of the processes by which work is accomplished. The idea here is that the quest for better quality and better service is never-ending.

**Kaizen** is a philosophy for improvement that originated in Japan and that has recently enjoyed widespread adoption throughout the world. Many people consider *kaizen* and *continuous improvement* to be one and the same; others consider kaizen to be a subset of or a particular type of continuous improvement. The word *kaizen* comes from two Japanese words: *kai,* meaning "change," and *zen,* meaning "good."[12] Hence, *kaizen* literally means "good change," and in today's context it describes a process of continuous and relentless improvement. Kaizen is not based on large technical leaps but on the incremental refining of existing processes. Kaizen is basically a system of taking small steps to improve the workplace. It is based on the belief that the system should be customer-driven and involve all employees through systematic and open communication. Under kaizen, employees are viewed as the organization's most valued asset. This philosophy is put into practice through teamwork and extensive employee participation. In summary, kaizen applies the principles of participatory management toward incremental improvement of the current methods and processes. Kaizen does not focus on obtaining new and faster machines but rather on improving the methods and procedures used in the existing situation.

**Quality at the source** refers to the philosophy of making each employee responsible for the quality of his or her work.[13] In effect, this approach views every employee as a quality inspector for his or her own work. A major advantage of this approach is that it removes the adversarial relationship that often exists between quality control inspectors and production employees. It also encourages employees to take pride in their work.

**Six sigma** is both a precise set of statistical tools and a rallying cry for continuous improvement.[14] Six sigma was pioneered by Motorola during the 1980s and literally means, in statistical terms, six standard deviations from the mean. The philosophy of six sigma is that in order to realize the very high level of quality demanded by six sigma (most processes traditionally have used three sigma), the entire production or service system must be examined and improved. Customer focus and data-driven rigor are at the heart of six sigma. Six sigma addresses the question, "What does the customer want in the way of quality?" The answer to this question is then translated into statistical terms and rigorously analyzed.

Although it's most often thought of as applying to manufacturing processes, six sigma can be applied to any business process where the quality of the result may be quantified and the results of each process tracked.[15] Processes such as shipping, pickup and delivery of goods, order taking, and credit management readily lead themselves to six sigma.

**continuous improvement**
Refers to an ongoing effort to make improvements in every part of the organization relative to all of its products and services.

**kaizen**
"Good change"; a process of continuous and relentless improvement.

**quality at the source**
The philosophy of making each employee responsible for the quality of his or her own work.

**six sigma**
Literally means, in statistical terms, six standard deviations from the mean. In order to realize the very high level of quality demanded by six sigma (most processes traditionally have used three sigma), the entire production or service system must be examined and improved.

**Lean manufacturing** is a systematic approach to identifying and eliminating waste and non-value-added activities.[16] The essence of lean manufacturing is to look at the entire production or service process to eliminate waste or unnecessary activities wherever possible.

All of the above terms (*continuous improvement, kaizen, quality at the source, six sigma,* and *lean manufacturing*) are approaches for improving quality of the product or service offered. These approaches are not mutually exclusive but rather are complementary; the differences are that each offers a different emphasis. It should also be pointed out that each of these approaches can be applied in nonmanufacturing environments, such as service, education, and government.

As stated earlier, TQM is an organization-wide emphasis on quality as defined by the customer. It is not a collection of techniques but a philosophy or way of thinking about how people view their jobs and quality through the organization.

## Reengineering

Some people confuse the concept of reengineering with TQM. **Reengineering,** also called *business process engineering,* is "the search for and implementation of radical change in business processes to achieve breakthrough results in costs, speed, productivity, and service."[17] Unlike TQM, reengineering is not a program for making marginal improvements in existing procedures. Reengineering is rather a onetime concerted effort, initiated from the top of the organization, to make major improvements in processes used to produce products or services. The essence of reengineering is to start with a clean slate and redesign the organization's processes to better serve its customers.

## Other Quality Standards

While TQM is a highly effective, organizationwide philosophy about quality, there are other techniques and approaches that organizations may adopt to encourage quality. Most of these can be used alone or in conjunction with TQM. Quality circles were discussed in Chapter 9. Three additional approaches are discussed below.

### ISO 9000

**ISO 9000** is a set of quality standards created in 1987 by the International Organization for Standardization (ISO), in Geneva, Switzerland. ISO is currently composed of the national standards bodies of over 152 countries with the major objective of promoting the development of standardization and facilitating the international exchange of goods and services. The American National Standards Institute (ANSI) is the member body representing the United States in the ISO.

Originally the ISO published five international standards designed to guide internal quality management programs and to facilitate external quality assurance endeavors. The original 1987 standards were slightly revised in 1994. In essence, ISO 9000:1994 outlined the quality system requirements necessary to meet quality requirements in varying situations. ISO 9000:1994 focused on the design and operation processes, not on the end product or service. ISO 9000:1994 required extensive documentation in order to demonstrate the consistency and reliability of the processes being used. In summary, ISO 9000:1994 certification did not relate to the quality of the actual end product or service, but it guaranteed that the company had fully documented its quality control procedures. While ISO issues the standards, it does not regulate the program internally; regulation is left to national accreditation organizations such as the U.S. Register Accreditation Board (RAB). RAB and other such boards then authorize registrars to issue ISO 9000 certificates.

New ISO 9000 standards were implemented beginning fall 2000. The new standards emphasize international organization and in-house performance, rather than engineering, as the best way to deliver a product or service. In essence the new ISO 9000:2000 focuses more on continuous improvement and customer satisfaction. ISO 9000:2000, like its predecessor, is really a series of interrelated standards. In ISO 9000:2000 there are three interrelated standards. ISO 9000:2000 deals with fundamentals and vocabulary; ISO 9001:2000 states the requirements for the new system; and ISO 9004:2000 provides guidance for implementation. Because ISO 9001:2000 represents the heart of the new standards, this entire set of standards is sometimes referred to as ISO 9001:2000 as opposed to ISO 9000:2000.

Organizations previously certified under ISO 9000:1994 are required to update their quality systems in order to meet the new standard's requirement. As of December 31, 2004, 670,399 organizations in 154 countries had been certified in ISO 9001:2000.[18] This represented an increase of 35 percent over the previous year.

Mary made a concerted effort to implement quality control systems while managing her design firm. The financial rewards have been substantial.

### ISO 14000

Sparked by the success of ISO 9000, ISO developed a similar series of international standards for environmental management. **ISO 14000** is a series of voluntary international standards covering environmental management tools and systems.[19] While many countries have developed environmental management system standards, these standards are often not compatible. The goal of ISO 14000 is to provide international environmental standards that are compatible. Similar to ISO 9000, which does not prescribe methods to integrate quality processes into an organization, ISO 14000 does not prescribe environmental policies. ISO 14000 does provide an international standard for environmental management systems so that organizations

> **ISO 14000**
> Addition to the ISO 9000 to control the impact of an organization's activities and outputs on the environment.

will have a systematic framework for their environmental activities. ISO 14000 focuses heavily on strategic issues such as setting goals and developing policies. ISO 14000 certification requires compliance in four organizational areas:[20] (1) implementation of an environmental management system, (2) assurance that procedures are in place to maintain compliance with laws and regulations, (3) commitment to continual improvement, and (4) commitment to waste minimization and prevention of pollution.

Although the ISO 14000 series will ultimately include 20 separate standards covering everything from environmental auditing to environmental labeling to assessing life cycles of products, ISO 14001 is the first standard released. ISO 14001, Environmental Management Systems–Specification with Guidance for Use, is the standard companies will use to establish their own environmental management systems. As of December 31, 2004, 90,569 companies in 127 countries had been certified for ISO 14001.[21] This represents an increase of 37 percent over the previous year.

### Zero Defects

| |
|---|
| **zero-defects program** |
| Increasing quality by increasing everyone's impact on quality. |

The name *zero defects* is somewhat misleading in that this approach doesn't literally try to cut defects or defective service to zero. Such an approach would obviously be very cost ineffective in many situations. A **zero-defects program** attempts to create a positive attitude toward the prevention of low quality. The objective of a zero-defects program is to heighten awareness of quality by making everyone aware of his or her potential impact on quality. Naturally, this should lead to more attention to detail and concern for accuracy.

Most successful zero-defects programs have the following characteristics:

1. Extensive communication regarding the importance of quality—signs, posters, contests, and so on.
2. Organizationwide recognition—publicly granting rewards, certificates, and plaques for high-quality work.
3. Problem identification by employees—employees point out areas where they think quality can be improved.
4. Employee goal setting—employees participate in setting quality goals.[22]

---

## PROGRESS CHECK QUESTIONS

5. Who are the quality gurus?
6. Explain the term *kaizen*.
7. What is ISO 14000?
8. Explain the term *zero defects*.

## The Malcolm Baldrige National Quality Award

The **Malcoln Baldrige National Quality Award,** named after the 26th U.S. Secretary of Commerce, was established by Congress in 1987 to enhance the competitiveness of U.S. organizations. The Award promotes performance excellence as an integral part of organizational management practices, publicizes successful performance strategies, and recognized the quality and performance achievements of U.S. organizations.

Six types of organizations are eligible to apply for the award: manufacturing, service, small business, education, health care, and nonprofit. In October 2004, President Bush signed into law legislation that authorized NIST to expand the Baldrige Award program to include nonprofit organizations. Any organization headquartered in the United States or its territories may apply for the award, including U.S. subunits of foreign companies.

The Awards's *Criteria for Performance Excellence,* which comprise seven categories (Leadership; Strategic Planning; Customer and Market Focus; Measurement, Analysis, and Knowledge Management; Workforce Focus; Process Management; and Results), are used by thousands of organizations as a general performance excellence model. This model is designed to improved overall organizational effectiveness and capabilities, and help deliver ever-improving value to customers, resulting in marketplace success.

The Malcolm Baldrige Award is administered to companies and organizations that excel in customer service. Why is the recognition associated with this Award good for businesses?

## Types of Quality Control

Quality control relating to the inputs or outputs of the system is referred to as **product quality control** (sometimes called *acceptance control*). Product quality control is used when the quality is being evaluated with respect to a batch of products or services that already exists, such as incoming raw materials or finished goods. Product quality control lends itself to acceptance sampling procedures, in which some portion of a batch of outgoing items (or incoming materials) is inspected to ensure that the batch meets specifications with regard to the percentage of defective units that will be tolerated in the batch. With acceptance sampling procedures, the decision to accept or reject an entire batch is based on a sample or group of samples.

**Process quality control** concerns monitoring quality while the product or service is being produced. Process control relates to the control of the equipment and processes used during the production process. Under process control, periodic samples are taken from a process and compared to a predetermined standard. If the sample results are acceptable, the process is allowed to continue. If the sample results are not acceptable, the process is halted and adjustments are made to bring the machines or processes back under control.

**Malcolm Baldrige Award**
Recognition of U.S. companies' achievements in performance excellence.

**product quality control**
Relates to inputs or outputs of the system; used when quality is evaluated with respect to a batch of existing products or services.

**process quality control**
Concerns monitoring quality while the product or service is being produced.

**acceptance sampling**

Statistical method of predicting the quality of a batch or a large group of products by inspecting a sample or group of samples.

**Acceptance sampling** is a method of predicting the quality of a batch or a large group of products from an inspection of a sample or group of samples taken from the batch.

Acceptance sampling is used for one of three basic reasons:

1. The potential losses or costs of passing defective items are not great relative to the cost of inspection; for example, it would not be appropriate to inspect every match produced by a match factory.
2. Inspection of some items requires destruction of the product being tested, as is the case when testing prepared food items.
3. Sampling usually produces results more rapidly than does a census.

Acceptance sampling draws a random sample of a given size from the batch or lot being examined. The sample is then tested and analyzed. If more than a certain number (determined statistically) are found to be defective, the entire batch is rejected, as it is deemed to have an unacceptably large percentage of defective items. Because of the possibility of making an incorrect inference concerning the batch, acceptance sampling always involves risks. The risk the producer is willing to take of rejecting a good batch is referred to as the *producer's risk*. The risk of accepting a bad batch is referred to as the *consumer's risk*. Obviously, one would desire to minimize both the producer's risk and the consumer's risk. However, the only method of simultaneously lowering both of these risks is to increase the sample size, which also increases the inspection costs. Therefore, the usual approach is to decide on the maximum acceptable risk for both the producer and the consumer and design the acceptance sampling plan around these risks.

**process control chart**

Time-based graphic display that shows whether a machine or process is producing items that meet pre-established specifications.

A **process control chart** is a time-based graphic display that shows whether a machine or a process is producing output at the expected quality level. If a significant change in the variable being checked is detected, the machine is said to be out of control. Control charts do not attempt to show why a machine is out of control, only whether it is out of control.

The most frequently used process control charts are called *mean* and *range charts*. Mean charts (also called *X-charts*) monitor the mean or average value of some characteristic (dimension, weight, etc.) of the items produced by a machine or process. Range charts (also called *R-charts*) monitor the range of variability of some characteristic (dimension, weight, etc.) of the items produced by a machine or process.

The quality control inspector, using control charts, first calculates the desired level of the characteristic being measured. The next step is to calculate statistically the upper and lower control limits, which determine how much the characteristic can vary from the desired level before the machine or process is considered to be out of control. Once

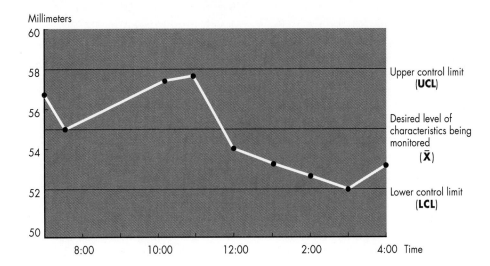

figure 12.5

**MEAN CHART**

the control chart has been set up, the quality control inspector periodically takes a small sample from the machine or process outputs. Depending on the type of chart being used, the mean or range of the sample is plotted on the control chart. By plotting the results of each sample on the control chart, it is easy to identify quickly any abnormal trends in quality. Figure 12.5 shows a sample mean chart. A range chart looks like a mean chart; the only difference is that the range, as opposed to the mean, of the characteristic being monitored is plotted.

A mean or range chart used by itself can easily lead to false conclusions. For example, the upper and lower control limits for a machined part might be 0.1000 millimeter and 0.0800 millimeter, respectively. A sample of four parts of 0.1200, 0.1100, 0.0700, and 0.0600 would yield an acceptable mean of 0.0900; yet every element of the sample is out of tolerance. For this reason, when monitoring variables, it is usually desirable to use mean and range charts simultaneously to ensure that a machine or a process is under control.

## PROGRESS CHECK QUESTIONS

9. What was the purpose of the Malcolm Baldrige National Quality Improvement Act?
10. Explain the difference between *product* quality control and *process* quality control.
11. What is acceptance sampling?
12. What is the purpose of a process control chart?

## The Purchasing Department

The buyers for a large airline company were having a general discussion with the manager of purchasing in her office Friday afternoon. The inspection of received parts was a topic of considerable discussion. Apparently, several parts had recently been rejected six months or more after being received. Such a rejection delay was costing the company a considerable amount of money, since most of the items were beyond the standard 90-day warranty period. The current purchasing procedures state that the department using the parts is responsible for the inspection of all parts, including stock and non-stock items. The company employs an inspector who is supposedly responsible for inspecting all aircraft parts, in accordance with FAA regulations. However, the inspector has not been able to check those items purchased as nonaircraft parts because he is constantly overloaded. Furthermore, many of the aircraft parts are not being properly inspected because of insufficient facilities and equipment.

One recent example of the type of problem being encountered was the acceptance of a batch of plastic forks that broke easily when in use. The vendor had shipped over 100 cases of the forks of the wrong type. Unfortunately, all the purchase order specified was "forks." Another example was the acceptance of several cases of plastic cups with the wrong logo. The cups were put into use for in-flight service and had to be used because no other cups were available. A final example was the discovery that several expensive radar components in stock were found to be defective and with expired warranty. The components had to be reordered at almost $900 per unit.

It was apparent that the inspection function was inadequate and unable to cope with the volume of material being received. Purchasing would have to establish guidelines as to which material should or should not be inspected after being processed by the material checker. Some of the buyers thought the material checker (who is not the inspector) should have more responsibility than simply checking quantity and comparing the packing sheet against purchase orders. Some believed the checker could and should have caught the obvious errors in the logo on the plastic cups. Furthermore, if the inspector had sampled the forks, they would have been rejected immediately. As for the radar tubes, they should have been forwarded by the inspector to the avionics shop for bench check after being received. Such a rejection delay was costing the company a considerable amount of money, since most of the items were beyond the standard 90-day warranty period. The current purchasing procedures state that the department using the parts is responsible for the inspection before the part is placed in stock. Some buyers thought the inspector should be responsible for inspection of all materials received, regardless of its function or usage. It was pointed out, however, that several landing gears had been received from the overhaul/repair vendor and tagged by the inspector as being acceptable. These gears later turned out to be defective and unstable and had to be returned for repair. This generated considerable discussion concerning the inspector's qualifications, testing capacity, workload, and responsibility for determining if the unit should be shop-checked.

Much of the remaining discussion centered around what purchasing should recommend for the inspection of material. One proposal was that everything received be funneled through the Inspection Department. Another proposal was that all material be run through inspection except as otherwise noted on the purchase order. Other questions were also raised. If purchasing required all material to be inspected, would this require additional inspection personnel? Who would be responsible for inspection specifications? Furthermore, who should determine which items should be shop-checked?

The meeting was finally adjourned until the following Friday.

### Questions

1. Why is the inspection of received parts such a concern for the airline?

2. What do you think of the current system of inspection?

3. Do you think the inspector is at fault? Explain.

4. What would you suggest should happen at the meeting next Friday?

# INVENTORY CONTROL

Inventories serve as a buffer between different rates of flow associated with the operating system. **Inventories** are generally classified into one of three categories, depending on their location within the operating system: (1) raw material, (2) in process, or (3) finished goods. Raw material inventories serve as a buffer between purchasing and production. In-process inventories are used to buffer differences in the rates of flow through the various production processes. Finished-goods inventories act as a buffer between the final stage of production and shipping.

Inventories add flexibility to the operating system and allow the organization to do the following:

1. Purchase, produce, and ship in economic lot sizes rather than in small jobs.

2. Produce on a smooth, continuous basis even if the demand for the finished product or raw material fluctuates.

3. Prevent major problems when forecasts of demand are in error or when unforeseen slowdowns or stoppages in supply or production occur.

If it were not so costly, every organization would attempt to maintain very large inventories to facilitate purchasing, production scheduling, and distribution. However, many costs are associated with carrying inventory. Potential inventory costs include such factors as insurance, property taxes, storage costs, obsolescence costs, spoilage, and the opportunity cost of the money invested in the inventory. The relative importance of these costs depends on the specific inventory being held. For example, with women's fashions, the obsolescence costs are potentially high. Similarly, the storage costs for dangerous chemicals may be high. Thus, management must continually balance the costs of holding the inventory against the costs of running short of raw materials, in-process goods, or finished goods.

## Just-in-Time Inventory Control

**Just-in-time inventory control (JIT)** was pioneered in Japan but has become popular in the United States. JIT systems are sometimes referred to as *zero inventory systems, stockless systems,* or *kanban systems.* JIT is

**inventories**

Quantity of raw materials, in-process goods, or finished goods on hand; serves as a buffer between different rates of flow associated with the operating system.

**just-in-time inventory control (JIT)**

Inventory control system that schedules materials to arrive and leave as they are needed.

actually a philosophy for production to ensure that the right items arrive and leave as they are needed. Traditionally, incoming raw materials are ordered in relatively few large shipments and stored in warehouses until needed for production or for providing a service.

Under JIT, organizations make smaller and more frequent orders of raw materials. JIT depends on the elimination of setup time between the production of different batches of different products. JIT can be viewed as an operating philosophy whose basic objective is to eliminate waste. In this light, waste is "anything other than the minimum amount of equipment, materials, parts, space, and workers' time which are absolutely essential to add value to the product or service."[23]

The JIT philosophy applies not only to inventories of incoming raw materials but also to the production of subassemblies or final products. The idea is not to produce an item or a subassembly until it is needed for shipment. JIT is called a *demand pull system* because items are produced or ordered only when they are needed (or pulled) by the next stage in the production process. Figure 12.6 summarizes the benefits of JIT. One potential hazard is that the entire production line can be shut down if the needed parts or subassemblies are not available when needed. JIT has been successfully implemented by many American companies, including Hewlett-Packard, Motorola, Black & Decker, General Motors, Ford, Chrysler, General Electric, Goodyear, and IBM.[24]

Despite the popularity of JIT in American business, it is not a quick fix for all the quality and operations problems a company may face. In fact, JIT may take many years to really catch hold in a company. Beginning in the early 1960s, it took Toyota over 20 years to fully implement the concept.[25] Although JIT was a key to Toyota's lean production system, it also exposed many defects in the inventory system, because JIT enables easier detection of defective inventory. Fixing these forms of defects (finding where and how the defects occurred) is sometimes time-consuming and difficult to accomplish.

**figure 12.6**

**BENEFITS OF JIT SYSTEM**

***Source:*** N. Gaither, *Production and Operations Management* (Fort Worth: Dryden Press, 1992).

1. Inventory levels are drastically lowered.
2. The time it takes products to go through the production facility is greatly reduced. This enables the organization to be more flexible and more responsive to changing customer demands.
3. Product/service quality is improved and the cost of scrap is reduced because defective parts and services are discovered earlier.
4. With smaller product batches, less space is occupied by inventory and materials-handling equipment. This also allows employees to work closer together, which improves communication and teamwork.

You are in the middle of the monthly meeting with the area account manager for XYZ Corporation, the company that produces one of the key components in your best-selling product. He suddenly asks if he can tell you something off the record. You are understandably curious and answer, "Sure." He says that his company is about to raise prices on your key component by 25 percent because it has inside information that its competitor is experiencing production problems with its component and would be unable to take additional orders from XYZ customers who wanted to switch vendors in response to the 25 percent price increase.

Based on this information, your account manager strongly advises you to place a large order to beat the 25 percent price increase.

1. Would you place a large order? Why?
2. If XYZ's competitor then announced a new version of its product that was much better than XYZ's component, what would you do?
3. Would you suspect that the area account manager had set you up? Why or why not?
4. What if the 25 percent price increase never came? What would you do then?

Tom Peters offers a new twist on JIT. He believes that instead of using JIT just to assist suppliers in improving their products (i.e., resulting in fewer defective parts), a company can push JIT forward in the distribution channel to proactively seek out opportunities to assist customers (using some variant of JIT as a marketing strategy) and link them to the company's processes. In other words, by examining and solving customers' problems by supplying them with exactly what they need, the company not only improves its quality control but also builds ties to its customer base.[26]

## Tracking Inventory

Before computers, tracking inventory was a tedious and time-consuming task. It was difficult to keep accurate inventory records. Employees recorded every sale and purchase, and a bookkeeper would subtract all sales and add all purchases at the end of the week. This determined how much inventory remained in stock. However, employees often forgot to record transactions. Bookkeepers frequently made mistakes computing figures. Both kinds of errors made it difficult for businesses to know how much inventory they actually had in stock.

### Bar-Code Technology

Technology has improved inventory tracking. Most items are marked with *bar codes*, patterns of bars and spaces that an electronic scanner recognizes. Bar coding has reduced errors in tracking inventory. When a company purchases or sells an item, an employee scans the item's bar code. A computer program recognizes the information contained in the bar code and automatically adds or subtracts the item from inventory.

Bar-code technology has changed the way businesses track inventory. What are some advantages and disadvantages to this tracking system?

### Physical Inventory

**physical inventory**

Counting the number of units of inventory a company holds in stock.

Even if computers track inventory, managers need to take physical inventory. A **physical inventory** involves counting the number of units of inventory a company holds in stock. Most businesses perform a physical inventory once or twice a year.

Managers need to conduct physical inventories because actual inventory is often different from the level of inventory tracked. The discrepancy may reflect errors or unauthorized withdrawals, including theft. Managers who do not adjust their inventory occasionally may experience shortages.

## Independent versus Dependent Demand Items

**independent demand items**

Finished goods ready to be shipped out or sold.

**dependent demand items**

Subassembly or component parts used to make a finished product; their demand is based on the number of finished products being produced.

**Independent demand items** are finished goods or other end items. For the most part, independent demand items are sold or shipped out as opposed to being used in making another product. Examples of independent demand environments include most retail shops, book publishing, and hospital supplies.[27] **Dependent demand items** are typically subassemblies or component parts that will be used in making a finished product. In these cases, the demand for the items depends on the number of finished products being produced. An example is the demand for wheels for new cars. If the car company plans to make 1,000 cars next month, it knows it must have 5,000 wheels on hand (allowing for spares).[28] With independent demand items, forecasting plays an important role in inventory stocking decisions. With dependent demand items, inventory stocking requirements are determined directly from the production plan.

## ABC Classification System

**ABC classification system**

Method of managing inventories based on their total value.

One of the simplest and most widely used systems for managing inventories is the ABC approach. The **ABC classification system** manages inventories based on the total value of their usage per unit of time. In many organizations, a small number of products or materials, group A, account for the greatest dollar value of the inventory; the next group of items, group B, accounts for a moderate amount of the inventory value; and group C accounts for a small amount of the inventory value. Figure 12.7 illustrates this concept. The dollar value reflects both the cost of the item and the item's usage rate. For example, an item might be put into group A through a combination of either low cost and high usage or high cost and low usage.

Grouping items in this way establishes appropriate control over each item. Generally, the items in group A are monitored very closely; the items in group B are monitored with some care; and the items in group C are checked only occasionally. Items in group C are usually not subject to the detailed paperwork of items in groups A and B. In an automobile service station, gasoline would be considered a group A item and monitored daily. Tires, batteries, and transmission fluid would be group B items and might be checked weekly or biweekly. Valve stems,

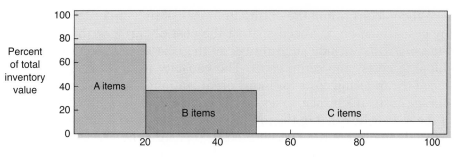

**figure 12.7**

**ABC INVENTORY CLASSIFICATION**

Shows the inventory value for each group versus the group's portion of the total list.

**Source:** From Richard B. Chase, F. Robert Jacobs, and Nicholas J. Aquilano, *Operation Management for Competitive Advantage*, 11th ed., 2002. Copyright © 2004. Reproduced with permission of The McGraw-Hill Companies, Inc.

windshield wiper blades, radiator caps, hoses, fan belts, oil and gas additives, car wax, and so forth would be group C items and might be checked and ordered only every two or three months.[29]

One potential shortcoming of the ABC method is that although the items in group C may have very little cost or usage value, they may be critical to the operation. It is possible, for instance, for an inexpensive bolt to be vital to the production of a costly piece of machinery. One way to handle items such as this is to designate them as group A or B items regardless of their cost or usage value. The major advantage of the ABC method is that it concentrates on controlling those items that are most important to the operation.

With computer technology and information systems becoming increasingly commonplace in small and medium-size firms, the ABC method can be computerized and categories can be monitored or changed with greater skill and accuracy. An additional value of computerizing the operation and control of the classification system is the power it brings to ordering cycles and stock control.

## Safety Stocks

Most organizations maintain **safety stocks** to accommodate unexpected changes in demand and supply and allow for variations in delivery time. The optimal size of the safety stock is determined by the relative costs of an out-of-stock item versus the costs of carrying the additional inventory. The cost of an out-of-stock item is often difficult to estimate. For example, the customer may choose to go elsewhere rather than wait for the product. If the product is available at another branch location, the out-of-stock cost may be simply the cost of shipping the item from one location to another.

**safety stocks**

Inventory maintained to accommodate unexpected changes in demand and supply and allow for variations in delivery time.

## The Order Quantity

Most materials and finished products are consumed one by one or a few units at a time; however, because of the costs associated with ordering, shipping, and handling inventory, it is usually desirable to purchase materials and products in large lots or batches.

When determining the optimal number of units to order, the ordering costs must be balanced against the cost of carrying the inventory. *Ordering costs* include such things as the cost of preparing the order, shipping costs, and setup costs. The capacity to order online has reduced the ordering costs for many organizations. *Carrying costs* include storage costs, insurance, taxes, obsolescence, and the opportunity costs of the money invested in the inventory. The smaller the number of units ordered, the lower the carrying costs (because the average inventory held is smaller) but the higher the ordering costs (because more orders must be placed). The optimal number of units to order, referred to as the **economic order quantity (EOQ),** is determined by the point at which ordering costs equal carrying costs, or where total cost (ordering costs plus carrying costs) is at a minimum.

The greatest weakness of the EOQ approach is the difficulty in accurately determining the actual carrying and ordering costs. However, research has shown that the total costs associated with order sizes that are reasonably close to the economic order quantity do not differ appreciably from the minimum total costs associated with the EOQ.[30] Thus, as long as the estimated carrying and ordering costs are in the ballpark, this approach can yield meaningful results. Variations of this basic model have been developed to take into account such things as purchase quantity and other special discounts.

**economic order quantity (EOQ)**

Optimal number of units to order at one time determined by the point at which ordering costs equal carrying costs, or where total cost (ordering costs plus carrying costs) is at a minimum.

---

## PROGRESS CHECK QUESTIONS

13. What are the three categories of inventory classification?
14. Explain the difference between *dependent* and *independent* demand items.
15. Explain the ABC classification system for inventory management.
16. How do you calculate the economic order quantity (EOQ) when placing purchase orders for materials or products?

---

## CONCLUSION

After an operating system has been designed and implemented, it must be monitored on a daily basis to ensure quality and operational efficiency. To do that, managers must have a clear sense of what product (or service) quality means to their organization, and they must also be able to control every element of the process including minimizing waste in the production process and controlling the cost of the inventory needed to supply materials to that process. In the next chapter we'll step back from these operational management issues and examine some of the "big picture" challenges that managers are facing today.

# Kaizen power—Handle with care!

Tony followed Jerry's instructions to the letter and got his team together to "stand in the circle." At first there were a few laughs and a few comments about square dancing and who didn't shower that morning, but once the group figured out that Tony was serious about the exercise, they got down to business. It took a while for them to start filling up their pads, but soon the competitive spirit started to kick in. Just as Jerry had predicted, a couple of them even asked for extra paper (which earned them several boos and comments from the team members who were still working on their first page!).

When the exercise was completed, the team met to review its ideas, and Tony was literally overwhelmed by the range and imagination of the ideas presented. He had given them fairly basic instructions and encouraged them to go as far out into left field as they wanted to find their ideas. Now he was beginning to have second thoughts because they had really taken him at his word. Ideas to change the theme of the restaurant entirely, to automate the restaurant, to bring in a live DJ, and to start featuring flamenco dancers during dinner were some of the more routine ones. Some of the more obvious ones included a

pay raise for the staff (which Tony explained wasn't a new idea, just a regular request), some new menu items, lower menu prices, and even higher menu prices.

Altogether the exercise generated close to two thousand ideas. When they had read all the ideas through, Kevin commented, "Wow, Tony, I guess you should be careful what you ask for, eh?" Then Tony got the question he had been dreading as soon as he had seen the size of the list: "Okay, Tony, which one are we going to implement first?"

## QUESTIONS

1. Is a list of "close to two thousand ideas" a successful outcome for Tony? Or has he created a monster here?

2. What do you think the reaction of the employees would be if none of the ideas were implemented?

3. If Tony encouraged his team to go as far out into left field as they wanted, how many of these new ideas are going to be practical? Why?

4. Where do you think Tony should start first? Why?

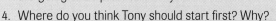

## key terms

## review questions

1. Name the three major categories of costs that usually concern operations managers from a control standpoint. Give an example from each category.
2. What is the difference between *fixed* and *variable* overhead expenses?
3. What are the six common dimensions of design quality? Provide an example of each dimension.
4. Define six sigma and lean manufacturing. How are they related?

## internet exercise

Visit the Web site of the Malcolm Baldrige National Quality Award (MBNQA) at www.quality.nist.gov, and answer the following questions:

1. How did the MBNQA come into existence?
2. Why would organizations consider applying for the MBNQA?
3. What are the three stages of the award process?
4. Who were the 2007 recipients of the MBNQA?

## team exercise

### KAIZEN

Organize into groups of three to four students. Agree as a group on a target industry (e.g., airlines, fast food, health care, retail, or telecommunications). Once you have selected your target industry, take 10 minutes to list 15 things that companies in that industry could do to improve their customer service. Remember, these must be new ideas, not something that one company is doing which you think other companies in the industry should copy. Stop after 10 minutes and review your list. Then take 15 minutes to come up with another 15 improvements. Be prepared to report your ideas back to your class.

### Questions

1. How did you arrive at your selection of a target industry?
2. How long did it take you to come up with your first 15 improvement ideas?
3. What were the major challenges in coming up with the second 15 improvement ideas?
4. What do you think you would find if you did this exercise in your current organization?

## Staying Paranoid at Toyota

*Fearful of "Big-Company Disease," the No. 1 Carmaker Keeps Scrambling to Retool Itself*

If there's one thing a company can learn from Toyota Motor Corp., it's the power of paranoia. Consider that Toyota just two months ago overtook General Motors Corp. as the world's biggest carmaker. As Detroit bled, Toyota pulled down a record $15 billion in profits in 2006. Still, its executives in Japan and North America are worried that they'll be spoiled by success. "The scariest symptom of 'big-company disease' is that complacency will breed," Toyota President Katsuaki Watanabe told *BusinessWeek* in an interview. So Toyota is giving itself a dose of strong medicine, meant as both a cure for current ills and as preventive mainte-nance. The company's U.S. management has just laun-ched its most far-reaching initiative in 50 years of doing business here. Called EM2, for "Everything Matters Exponentially," it's a total re-examination of product planning, customer service, sales and marketing, and even the car dealers the company doesn't directly own. Si-multaneously, Toyota is retraining all of its U.S. factory workers. Company executives also expect sales growth to slow. The concept of continuous improvement, or kaizen, remains part of Toyota's DNA. But "the challenge is [how to] sustain that paranoia," says Ranjay Gulati, a professor at Northwestern's Kellogg School of Management.

### OLDER, MORE SETTLED

The corporate world is littered with once-unbeatable companies done in by arrogance and inertia, from Motorola to K-Mart. Toyota needs only to look at its Big Three U.S. competi-tors for evidence. Executives inside Toyota talk about the example of Ford Motor Co., which in the late 1990s threatened to overtake GM and reaped massive profits, yet lost its focus on products and customers and is now fighting to survive. Toyota, too, has real reasons for con-cern. The company's headlong stretch for sales growth is creating quality is-sues. Recalls have tripled over the past three years, and the top-selling Toyota brand slipped in the latest J.D. Power & Associates Inc. study of quality. Dealerships continue to score poorly in customer satisfaction sur-veys that rate the overall car-buying experience. And despite hits like the Prius, Toyota's customer list is gradually getting older, which is the sad fate that befell struggling Detroit brands such as Buick and Oldsmobile. Toyota is light-years from following Detroit into ruin, but for more than a year Toyota executives at the North American headquarters in Torrance, Calif., have been thinking hard about how to stay un-satisfied. A brainstorming session last July in the office of James Lentz, executive vice-president of Toyota Motor Sales, produced

EM2. Lentz and his team have spent the 12 months since figuring out where problems could emerge and where they can improve. They tapped 50 managers from every discipline in the company's U.S. operations. These "EM2 experts" are now charged with examining budgets, looking at where people are deployed, and what's getting top results. Since EM2 launched only a couple of months ago, the company is ironing out the details, but already some priorities have emerged. One glaring problem: customer satisfaction. Toyota owners love their vehicles. But they gripe about what happens when they're buying the car and getting it serviced. Toyota ranked 28th out of 36 vehicle brands on the overall customer experience in J.D. Power's 2006 ranking.

## FINDING DENTS

Over the past few months the company has taken the unprecedented step of directly surveying car salesmen to see how they handle customers. They're also asking them about the customer-service attitudes of their bosses, the dealers. Consider World Toyota, a shop in Atlanta that routinely did poorly in customer-satisfaction surveys. In March, Toyota sent five people to observe the dealership and survey employees, down to the guys who wash the cars. They concluded that the dealer wasn't doing a good enough job of inspecting cars before delivering them—sometimes handing the buyer keys to a car with dents and scratches—and that there was too much emphasis on the sale and not enough on the customer. Drastic changes have been made: employees there have had their compensation tied to customer-service scores and top managers now inspect every car before delivery. The dealership now has top scores in every category of customer satisfaction.

Toyota is also taking a hard look at its famous factories. The originator of lean manufacturing, Toyota is the corporate gold standard for quality and efficiency, and its methods have been studied and copied by giants like GM and Boeing Co. But rampant growth has stretched the company's engineers and workers, and recalls have begun to occur more frequently in Japan and the U.S. Since the company has grown so fast, the engineers who once trained factory supervisors and workers are too busy to make house calls in every country where Toyota makes cars.

Toyota still ranks among the top makers in quality studies, but it is slipping. So its people are going back to school. At a new training center outside Toyota's manufacturing headquarters in Georgetown, Ky., even workers with 15 years of experience are being retrained on a mocked-up assembly line. There, Toyota will take its workers, Japanese-style, through the nitty-gritty of putting a bolt into an air gun and putting it into a car. Toyota has hired engineers at locations nearer factories, so they can drop in on the plant floor to solve problems more often. The attention to detail is fanatical. In one exercise, workers must put on a glove and massage the door of a Camry in a soft, circular motion in search of about a dozen dents and dings. They have to locate each one, even the subtlest defect, or else it's back to school. All 30,000 of Toyota's North American workers must either go through the training or learn from someone who did. This may take a few years but with Detroit on its knees, Toyota has time to work on its problems.

## Questions

1. Explain the purpose of Toyota's EM2 program.

2. What are Toyota's "reasons for concern"?

3. Do you think the EM2 program will succeed? Why or why not?

4. Would a program like EM2 work in your organization? Why or why not?

*Source:* Adapted from David Welch, "The Corporation," *BusinessWeek,* July 2, 2007.

# A Dynamo Called Danaher

*The Rales brothers' Sprawling Conglomerate Makes Everything—Especially Money*

**D**anaher Corp. is not nearly as big, famous, or influential as conglomerates such as General Electric, Berkshire Hathaway, or 3M. It owns such a mundane and sprawling portfolio of sleepy, underloved industrial businesses— companies that make dental surgery implements, multimeters, drill chucks, servomotors, and wrenches, just to name a few— that it seems deliberately assembled to be as unsexy as possible. But despite its low profile, Danaher is probably the best-run conglomerate in America. It's clearly the best performing: Over 20 years, it has returned a remarkable 25 percent to shareholders annually, far better than GE (16 percent), Berkshire Hathaway (21 percent), or the Standard & Poor's 500-stock index (12 percent).

The Washington (D.C.) company is the brainchild of the obsessively private brothers Steven M. and Mitchell P. Rales. They have turned Danaher from a mere acquisition vehicle into a true-blue, cash-producing, publicly owned industrial manufacturer. In the process, the Rales brothers have become two of the richest people in the U.S., worth more than $2 billion apiece. In 2006, Danaher posted revenues of nearly $10 billion and net profit margins of 16 percent, truly astounding for a company still in such Old Economy businesses as heavy-truck braking systems and hand tools.

## THE ANTI-BUFFETTS

Think of Danaher as the anti-Berkshire Hathaway. Warren Buffett runs his empire like a benevolent curator. The Rales and their management team are "the polar opposites" of that model, says Ann Duignan, an analyst at Bear, Stearns & Co. These conglomerateurs have built their portfolio not by buying undervalued companies and holding them but by imposing on them the "Danaher Business System." DBS, as it's called, is a set of management tools borrowed liberally from the famed Toyota Production System. In essence, it requires every employee, from the janitor to the president, to find ways every day to improve the way work gets done. Such quality-improvement—programs and lean manufacturing methods have been standard practice for manufacturers for years. The difference at Danaher: The company started lean manufacturing in 1987, one of the earliest U.S. companies to do so, and it has maintained a cultish devotion to making it pay off. Even before a deal is done, the DBS team, made up of managers throughout the company steeped in training, works with the acquisition target to inject a heavy dose of Danaher DNA. For employees at the newly acquired companies, it can be a jarring experience. It wouldn't be at all unusual for a Danaher manager clutching a clipboard, a tape measure, and a stopwatch, in a search for wasted motion, to tick off how many steps a data analyst has to take to get to the copier. Danaher also isn't afraid to swing the ax; it has, at times, bought certain product lines and closed the rest of a company.

Danaher's portfolio—with more than 600 subsidiary companies—reflects a move away from its hand-tool legacy to more technologically advanced products. The newest of its four units, accounting for 23 percent of sales, specializes in medical technologies. It includes Sybron, a dental-equipment maker, and Leica Microsystems, which makes high-end microscopes for pathology labs. Its most profitable division, professional instrumentation, includes Fluke, known to engineers for products such as multimeters. The company's industrial-tools division, though it only accounts for about 14 percent of sales, houses Danaher's most well-known brand, Craftsman hand tools. The rest of Danaher's business comes from industrial technologies, including machinery components and product-id devices, such as Accu-Sort package scanners.

After a group of managers in one of their divisions, Jacobs Vehicle Systems, found early success by mimicking Toyota Motor Corp.'s lean manufacturing, the brothers decided to implement the Toyota system companywide. The process breaks from the traditional "batch-and-queue"manufacturing system, in which big lots of product are assembled in discrete steps. In a lean environment, a company moves a smaller flow of items through production. Wasteful steps are easier to spot. And if a mistake creeps into the process, it won't affect a huge amount of inventory and can be fixed quickly.

In a typical Danaher factory, floors are covered with strips of tape indicating where everything should be, from the biggest machine to the humblest trash can. Managers determine the most efficient place for everything, so a worker won't have to walk an extra few yards to pick up a tool, for instance. The lean attitude permeates the culture at Danaher—only 40 people work in the Washington corporate headquarters, at a company of 40,000.

## Questions

1. How is Danaher able to generate such large profits on "such Old Economy businesses as heavy-truck braking systems and hand tools"?

2. What is lean manufacturing?

3. Do you think that Danaher's use of the kaizen philosophy has greater effect when it is selecting the companies to purchase or when it owns the companies? Explain your answer.

4. Consider the organization you currently work for or one you have worked for in the past. How easy would it be to introduce the kaizen philosophy in that organization? Explain your answer.

*Source:* Adapted from Brian Hindo, "Managing," *BusinessWeek Online,* February 19, 2007.

PART FOUR

# the future of management

## 13 Contemporary Issues

## 14 Management in the 21st Century

# CONTEMPORARY ISSUES

**"There is no way to make people like change. You can only make them feel less threatened by it."**

—Frederick O'R. Hayes

## The World of Work: The Taco Barn melting pot

Dawn Williams, the regional manager for Taco Barn, called the quarterly meeting to order and jumped straight into the first item on the agenda, listed as "Diversity and Succession Planning."

"As I look around this room," began Dawn, "I see a lot of talented, loyal, and dedicated unit managers who have worked hard to build successful careers with the Taco Barn organization." Dawn paused as a wave of murmured agreement filled the room. "However," she continued, "the senior leadership team has become concerned that those common traits of dedication and loyalty are being overshadowed by another, less attractive feature of our unit management team, and that's our lack of diversity." This time there was no wave of murmured agreement.

"This is a very powerful team," continued Dawn, "but this is also a predominantly white male team, and the company is concerned that we're sending the wrong message to both our customers and our younger employees who are looking at the opportunities for promotion ahead of them."

Tony looked around the room and saw the significance of Dawn's point. Of the 24 unit managers in Dawn's region, there were three African American and four Hispanic males but only two females (both white), with the remainder being white males, including Tony himself.

"Before anybody gets carried away," continued Dawn, "there's no question of racism or discrimination here, and we're not doing this in fear of a lawsuit or anything like that. Each of you has been promoted on

**After studying this chapter, you will be able to:**

**1** Define diversity and explain how it applies to management.

**2** Define global management.

**3** Compare and contrast importing and exporting.

**4** Identify protectionism.

**5** Explain how to manage change and the change process.

**6** Explain the process of organizational development.

CHAPTER

13

your proven leadership abilities and that will always be our number one concern. What we are going to do, however, is to start actively encouraging all of our employees, regardless of race or gender, to consider opportunities for promotion within this organization. To make those opportunities as real as possible, our current vacancies will be revisited in favor of a more diverse leadership team. To put it bluntly guys, this team has to reflect the diversity of our workforce and our customer base, and so we're going to start hiring on that basis."

Tony found himself raising his hand with a question without even being aware of the choice. "Excuse me Dawn," Tony asked, "So are you saying that someone's race and or gender will now count for more than their work skills?"

"No, Tony," Dawn answered. "What we are saying is that if two equally skilled applicants are in the running for the same position, we will want the final selection to be reflective of a more diverse leadership team than the one we currently have in place in this region."

**QUESTIONS**

1. Why has diversity become a focus for the Taco Barn corporation?

2. Do you agree with Tony's concerns about the new initiative? Why or why not?

3. Tony's mentor, Jerry Smith, was one of the original supporters of the plan. Do you think that will influence Tony's decision? Why or why not?

4. What do you think Taco Barn should do to increase diversity in the company? Explain your answer.

# DIVERSITY AND MANAGEMENT

For many years, the managers of most large- and medium-sized U.S. organizations were almost exclusively white males. As recently as the 1960s and 1970s, women in the workforce filled primarily service and support roles, acting as secretaries, teachers, salesclerks, and waitresses, for instance. Many minority workers were confined to menial jobs, such as custodial work and manual labor. In the last two decades of the twentieth century, however, more and more women and minorities have joined the workforce. They also have attained positions as high-level managers in organizations of all sizes. Furthermore, they presently serve in senior-level management jobs in the federal, state, and local governments.

Despite these changes, most senior managers in the country are still white men. The problems women and minorities have had winning promotions to senior management positions gave rise to the term glass ceiling. This is the invisible barrier that prevents women and minorities from moving up in the organizational hierarchy. As in many other fields, such as sports and space exploration, the glass ceiling is steadily becoming a window of opportunity. Top managers, especially CEOs, are highly visible and often inseparable from their companies. It also can be the spark that is needed to trigger more promotions of women to senior managerial positions. As businesses and government agencies downsize, or lay off workers to cut costs, many of those opting for attractive retirement benefits are senior white males. Their departure opens the door for women and minorities eager to move into the highest ranks of management.

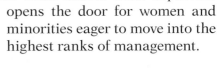

Cracker Barrel Restaurants have been fighting allegations of discrimination for more than 15 years. Their continued problems highlight why companies want to avoid these sorts of accusations.

## What Is Diversity?

Diversity in the workforce means including people of different genders, races, religions, nationalities, ethnic groups, age groups, and physical abilities. The increasing diversity of the workplace represents a major social change in the United States.

The trend toward greater diversity is expected to continue over the next 50 years, as the proportion of nonwhites and immigrants in the U.S. population grows. In fact, diversity is increasing so quickly in the United States that the percentage of

A colleague of yours is on an annual contract that is soon due to be renewed. During your time of working together you have become friends with him even though, as an African American, he was originally hired as part of an increased workforce diversity campaign (in preference to your brother-in-law who didn't offer the necessary diversity bonus). You are aware that your friend's wife has recently become pregnant with their second child.

However, while he tries hard and means well, your colleague is really quite incompetent at his job. You frequently need to work harder to try to compensate for this and have been aware of him covering up some relatively serious mistakes.

1. Your boss has asked for your advice as to whether or not your friend's contract should be renewed. What will you tell your boss?

2. Would your answer be different if diversity wasn't a factor? Why or why not?

3. How would you convince your boss that your feedback wasn't influenced by sour grapes over the decision not to hire your brother-in-law?

4. If the company requires a specific hiring ratio for employee diversity, is the diversity factor worth keeping an incompetent employee? Why or why not?

**Source:** Adapted from St. James Ethics Centre, "Ethical Dilemmas: The Ethics of an Incompetent Colleague," www.ethics.org.au.

non-Hispanic whites is projected to fall from 68 percent in 2010 to just 52.8 percent by 2050 (see Figure 13.1).

## Reasons for Creating a Diverse Workforce

Companies are seeking diverse workforces because of the following reasons:

- Employee population is increasingly diverse.
- Customer population is increasingly diverse.
- Retaining top talent means recruiting individuals from all backgrounds.
- Increasing diversity minimizes the risk of litigation.

By creating a culture that is open to different behavioral styles and that incorporates a wide range of views, diversity can improve decision making.

| DEMOGRAPHIC GROUP | 2010 | 2020 | 2030 | 2040 | 2050 |
|---|---|---|---|---|---|
| Non-Hispanic white | 68.0 | 64.3 | 60.6 | 56.6 | 52.8 |
| Non-Hispanic black | 12.6 | 12.9 | 13.1 | 13.3 | 13.6 |
| Hispanic | 13.8 | 16.3 | 18.9 | 21.7 | 24.5 |
| Non-Hispanic American Indian, Eskimo, and Aleut | 0.7 | 0.8 | 0.8 | 0.8 | 0.9 |
| Non-Hispanic Asian and Pacific Islander | 4.8 | 5.7 | 6.6 | 7.5 | 8.2 |
| Total | 100.0 | 100.0 | 100.0 | 100.0 | 100.0 |

**figure 13.1**

**PROJECTED U.S. POPULATION, BY DEMOGRAPHIC GROUP, 2000–2050 (PERCENT OF POPULATION)**

**Source:** U.S. Census Bureau, www.census.gov/populations/ nations/nsrh/nprh9600.txt.

## figure 13.2

**THE CHANGING AMERICAN WORKPLACE**

Advances in civil rights and demographic changes in the United States have made the workplace much more diverse than it was 30 years ago. Today, managers must understand how to work with people from diverse backgrounds.

**1. The Workplace in the 1960s**

Until the 1970s, white males dominated most businesses in the United States. For the most part, managers managed people who came from backgrounds that were similar to their own.

**2. The Workplace in the Year 2006**

By the year 2006, most workplaces included women and minorities. Increasing diversity has helped companies understand the needs of their increasingly diverse customer bases.

**3. The Workplace in the Mid-Twenty-First Century**

By the middle of the twenty-first century, minorities will make up almost half of the population. In response to these changes, the workplace is expected to become even more diverse than it is today.

Greater diversity allows an organization to respond not only to diverse groups of employees but also to diverse groups of customers (see Figure 13.2).

Another dimension of diversity is related to the increasing globalization of many companies. As companies become more global, diversity must be defined in global and not just Western terms. Defining diversity in global terms means looking at all people and everything that makes them different from one another, as well as the things that make them similar. Differentiating factors often go beyond race and language and may include such things as values and customs.

A multicultural workplace presents challenges for both employees and supervisors. For example, religious holidays, which are celebrated at different times throughout the year by Muslims, Christians, Jews, and other religious groups, have the potential to be a source of conflict among employees. Supervisors need to be sensitive to the needs of their employees when it comes to religious holidays. On the other hand, employees should be responsible about arranging to take these days off.

What challenges and contributions does the increasingly diverse workforce present? From an overall viewpoint, organizations must get away from the tradition of fitting employees into a single corporate mold. Everyone will not look and act the same. Organizations must create new human resource policies to explicitly recognize and respond to the unique needs of individual employees.

Greater diversity will create specific challenges but also make some important contributions. Communication problems are certain to occur, including misunderstandings among employees and managers as well as the need to translate verbal and written materials into several languages. Solutions to these problems will require additional training involving work in basic skills such as writing and problem solving. An increase in organizational divisions will require that increasing amounts of time be dedicated to dealing with special interest and advocacy groups.

In addition to creating the above challenges, greater diversity presents new opportunities. Diversity contributes to creating an organization culture that is more tolerant of different behavioral styles and wider views. This often leads to better business decisions. Another potential payoff is a greater responsiveness to diverse groups of customers.

---

### PROGRESS CHECK QUESTIONS

1. Why are organizations seeking diverse workforces?
2. Why are religious holidays a challenge for managers of a diverse workforce?
3. What are the challenges of increased diversity?
4. How diverse is the organization you work for (or one you have worked for in the past)? Explain your answer.

---

## GLOBAL MANAGEMENT

Over the past 50 years, companies from all over the world have begun operating globally. Nike operates factories in Vietnam and Indonesia. The Gap owns stores in Canada, France, Germany, Great Britain, and Japan. Perrier and Evian sell bottled water in dozens of countries outside of France. Nokia, a Finnish company, dominates the cellular phone market. Consumers everywhere own products made in other countries.

**International trade** consists of the exchange of goods and services by different countries. It includes the purchase of American blue jeans in China and the purchase of Belgian chocolate in the United States.

> **international trade**
> The exchange of goods and services by different countries.

Most of the world today depends on international trade to maintain its standard of living. American manufacturers sell automobiles, heavy machinery, clothing, and electronic goods abroad. Argentine cattle ranchers ship beef to consumers in dozens of foreign countries. Saudi Arabian oil producers supply much of the world with oil. In return, they purchase food, cars, and electronic goods from other countries.

Countries trade for several different reasons. One country may not be able to produce a good it wants. France, for example, cannot produce oil because it has no oil fields. If it wants to consume oil, it must trade with oil-producing countries. Countries also may trade because they have an advantage over other countries in producing particular goods or services.

### Absolute Advantage

Different countries are endowed with different resources. Honduras, for example, has fertile land, a warm and sunny climate, and inexpensive labor. Compared with Honduras, Great Britain has less fertile soil, a colder and rainier climate, and more expensive labor. Given the same combination of inputs (land, labor, and capital), Honduras would produce

**absolute advantage**

The ability to produce more of a good than another producer with the same quantity of inputs.

much more coffee than Great Britain. It has an absolute advantage in the production of coffee. An **absolute advantage** is the ability to produce more of a good than another producer with the same quantity of inputs.

## Comparative Advantage

**law of comparative advantage**

Producers should produce the goods they are most efficient at producing and purchase from others the goods they are less efficient at producing.

Countries need not have an absolute advantage in the production of a good to trade. Some countries may be less efficient at producing *all* goods than other countries. Even countries that are not very efficient producers are more efficient at producing some goods than others, however. The **law of comparative advantage** states that producers should produce the goods they are most efficient at producing and purchase from others the goods they are less efficient at producing. According to the law of comparative advantage, individuals, companies, and countries should specialize in what they do best.

## EXPORTING AND IMPORTING

**exports**

Goods and services that are sold abroad.

International trade takes place when companies sell the goods they produce in a foreign country or purchase goods produced abroad. Goods and services that are sold abroad are called **exports.** Goods and services that are purchased abroad are called **imports.**

**imports**

Goods and services purchased abroad.

The United States is the largest exporter in the world, exporting about $700 billion worth of goods and services a year. It also is the world's largest importer, purchasing about $900 billion worth of foreign goods and services annually.

### Exports

Exports represent an important source of revenue for many companies. Northwest Airlines, for example, earns about a third of its revenues outside the United States. IBM earns almost 40 percent of its revenues abroad.

#### Why Do Companies Export?

About 95 percent of the world's consumers live outside the United States. Companies that sell their products exclusively within the United States miss out on the opportunity to reach most of the world's consumers. To increase their sales, companies like Procter & Gamble spend millions of dollars trying to identify what customers in foreign countries want.

**diversification**

When a company engages in a variety of operations.

Companies also seek out export markets in order to diversify their sources of revenue. **Diversification** is engaging in a variety of operations. Businesses like to diversify their sales so that sluggish sales in one market can be offset by stronger sales elsewhere.

#### How Do Companies Identify Export Markets?

To determine if there is sufficient demand for their products or services overseas, companies analyze demographic figures, economic data, country reports, consumer tastes, and competition in the markets they are considering. Business managers contact the International Trade Administration of the U.S. Department of Commerce, foreign consulates and embassies, and foreign and international trade organizations. They also visit the countries they are considering and conduct surveys in order to assess consumer demand.

Businesses also need to find out what restrictions they may face as exporters. All countries require exporters to complete certain kinds of documents. Some countries also insist that foreign companies meet specific requirements on packaging, labeling, and product safety. Some also limit the ability of exporters to take money they earn from their exports out of the country.

## Imports

American companies import billions of dollars worth of goods and services every year. They import consumer goods, such as television sets and automobiles, and industrial goods, such as machines and parts. They import raw materials, such as petroleum, and food products, such as fruits and vegetables. They import these goods in order to use them to produce other goods or to sell them to customers.

### Imports of Materials

Many companies import some or all of the materials they use in order to reduce their production costs. Manufacturers of appliances, for example, import steel from Japan because it is less expensive than steel manufactured in the United States.

Some companies use imports because domestically made materials are not available or their quality is not as good as that of imported goods. Jewelry designers import diamonds and emeralds, which are not produced in the United States. Fashion designers use imported cashmere wool, which is softer than domestic wool.

### Imports of Consumer Goods

Companies also import products that they can resell in their own countries. Automobile dealers import cars and trucks from Europe and Asia. Wholesalers and retailers import clothing from Thailand, electronic goods from Japan, and cheese from France.

Companies import these goods because consumers want to purchase them. Some of these goods, such as garments from Asia, are less expensive than domestically manufactured products. Others, such as Saabs and Volvos, are popular despite costing more than domestically produced goods.

## The Trade Balance

The **balance of trade** is the difference between the value of the goods a country exports and the value of the goods it imports. A country that

**balance of trade**

Difference between the value of the good a country exports and the value of the goods it imports.

exports more than it imports runs a *trade surplus*. A country that imports more than it exports runs a *trade deficit*.

For many years the United States has run a trade deficit. This means that the value of the goods and services it buys from other countries exceeds the value of the goods and services it sells to other countries. Other countries, such as China, have run huge trade surpluses. In these countries, the value of exports exceeds the value of imports.

## Foreign Exchange

Companies that purchase goods or services from foreign countries must pay for them with foreign currency. If a U.S. company purchases goods from Japan, for example, it must pay for them in yen. If it purchases goods from Switzerland, it must pay for them in Swiss francs.

Companies purchase foreign currency from banks, which convert each currency into dollars. The value of one currency in terms of another is the foreign exchange rate.

Exchange rates can be quoted in dollars per unit of foreign currency or units of foreign currency per dollar. The exchange rate for the Swiss

Due to foreign exchange rates, the same sweater will cost the buyer different amounts depending on whether it is purchased at Harrod's in London or Macy's in New York. What are some possible benefits to money carrying different values in different countries?

franc, for example, might be 1.5 to the dollar. This means that 1 dollar is worth 1.5 Swiss francs and 1 Swiss franc is worth 1/1.5 dollar, or $0.67.

Most exchange rates fluctuate from day to day. Managers involved in international trade must follow these fluctuations closely, because they can have a dramatic effect on profits. Consider, for example, an American electronics store that wants to purchase 10 million yen worth of Japanese stereos, camcorders, and cameras. If the exchange rate of the yen is 115 to the dollar, the U.S. company must pay $86,956 to purchase 10 million yen worth of Japanese equipment (10 million yen divided by 115 yen per dollar). If the value of the yen rises so that a dollar is worth only 100 yen, the company would have to spend $100,000 to purchase the same value of Japanese goods (10 million yen divided by 100 yen per dollar).

**tariff**

Government-imposed taxes charged on goods imported into a country.

**quotas**

Restrictions on the quantity of a good that can enter a country.

## PROTECTIONISM

International trade can benefit all trading partners. It also may hurt some domestic producers, however. A U.S. manufacturer of watches may find it difficult to compete with a Taiwanese producer, which pays workers a fraction of what workers in the United States earn. Competition from the Taiwanese producer may force the U.S. company out of business.

To help domestic manufacturers compete against foreign companies, governments sometimes impose protectionist measures, such as tariffs, quotas, and other types of restrictions. All these measures reduce the volume of international trade.

### Tariffs

A **tariff** is a tax on imports. The purpose of a tariff is to raise the price of foreign goods in order to allow domestic manufacturers to compete. The United States imposes tariffs on many goods. This means that a Korean company that sells men's shirts in the United States must pay an import tax on every one of its shirts that enters the country. The purpose of this tax is to make it more difficult for foreign manufacturers to compete with American companies in the United States.

### Quotas

**Quotas** are restrictions on the quantity of a good that can enter a country. The United States imposes quotas on many kinds of goods. For example, it allows just 1.6 million tons of raw sugar to enter the country from abroad. This quota raised the price of raw sugar, making goods that use sugar, such as candy and cold cereal, more expensive. It hurt American companies and individuals that consume sugar, but it helped American companies and individuals that produce sugar.

## Embargoes

**embargo**

Involves stopping the flow of exports to or imports from a foreign country.

An **embargo** is a total ban on the import of a good from a particular country. Embargoes usually are imposed for political rather than economic reasons. Since 1961, for example, the United States has imposed an embargo on Cuba, whose regime it opposes. This embargo bans the importation of goods from Cuba and the export of U.S. goods to Cuba.

## Free Trade Areas

**free trade area**

A region within which trade restrictions are reduced or eliminated.

To promote international trade and limit protectionism, countries create free trade areas. A **free trade area** is a region within which trade restrictions are reduced or eliminated.

The largest free trade area in the world is in North America. Under the terms of the **North American Free Trade Agreement (NAFTA)** of 1994, businesses in the United States, Mexico, and Canada can sell their products anywhere in North America without facing major trade restrictions.

**North American Free Trade Agreement (NAFTA)**

NAFTA allows businesses in the United States, Mexico, and Canada to sell their products anywhere in North America without facing major trade restrictions.

Consumers in all three countries have benefited from lower prices on North American imports. The price of a blouse imported from Canada or a pair of shoes imported from Mexico, for example, is lower than it used to be, because the price no longer includes a tariff.

Many producers have also benefited from NAFTA by increasing their exports within North America. American grain farmers, for example, have increased their sales to Mexico as a result of NAFTA. U.S. automobile sales to Mexico also have risen.

NAFTA has forced some American workers to lose their jobs, however. Sara Lee laid off more than a thousand American workers after it moved some of its operations to Mexico. Many other companies have also reduced their workforces in this country to take advantage of lower labor costs south of the border.

The *European Union* (*EU*) is a union of 27 European countries, known as member states. Figure 13.3 provides a list of the member states by date when they joined. A key activity of the EU is the establishment of a common single market within the member states.

## DOING BUSINESS GLOBALLY

Thousands of U.S. businesses, large and small, participate in the global marketplace. Some companies, such as Benetton, build factories in foreign countries or set up retail outlets overseas. Others, such as Harley-Davidson, export their products throughout the world and import materials from other countries.

figure 13.3

**MEMBER STATES AND
DATE OF JOINING**

| YEAR | COUNTRY |
|------|---------|
| 1952 | Belgium, France, West Germany, Italy, Luxembourg, The Netherlands (founding members) |
| 1973 | Denmark, Ireland, United Kingdom |
| 1981 | Greece |
| 1986 | Portugal, Spain |
| 1990 | East Germany (reunites with West Germany and becomes part of the EU) |
| 1995 | Austria, Finland, Sweden |
| 2004 | Cyprus, Czech Republic, Estonia, Hungary, Latvia, Lithuania, Malta, Poland, Slovakia, Slovenia |
| 2007 | Bulgaria, Romania |

## Forms of International Operations

Companies can sell their products or services in foreign countries in various ways. Small companies often work through local companies, which are familiar with local markets. Large companies often establish sales, manufacturing, and distribution facilities in foreign countries.

### Working through a Foreign Intermediary

Companies that are not willing or able to invest millions of dollars in operations abroad often export their products through foreign intermediaries. A **foreign intermediary** is a wholesaler or agent that markets products for companies wanting to do business abroad. In return for a commission, the agent markets the foreign company's product.

Working through a foreign intermediary saves a company the expense of setting up facilities in a foreign country. It also ensures that the company is represented by someone familiar with local conditions. Foreign intermediaries usually work for many foreign companies at a time, however. Thus, they are not likely to devote as much time to a single company's products as the company's own sales force would.

**foreign intermediary**
A wholesaler or agent that markets products for companies wanting to do business abroad.

### Signing a Licensing Agreement with a Foreign Company

Another way companies can reach foreign consumers is by licensing a foreign company to sell their products or services abroad. A **licensing agreement** is an agreement that permits one company to sell another company's products abroad in return for a percentage of the company's revenues.

TGI Friday's, a Dallas-based restaurant company, has used licensing agreements to expand its operations overseas. Signing such agreements enabled it to open branches in Singapore, Indonesia, Malaysia, Thailand, Australia, and New Zealand. Without such agreements, it might not have been able to penetrate those markets.

**licensing agreement**
An agreement that permits one company to sell another company's products abroad in return for a percentage of the company's revenues.

**strategic alliance**
When companies pool resources and skills in order to achieve common goals.

## Forming a Strategic Alliance

Some companies can expand into foreign markets by forming *strategic alliances* with foreign companies. A **strategic alliance** involves pooling resources and skills in order to achieve common goals. Companies usually form strategic alliances to gain access to new markets, share research, broaden their product lines, learn new skills, and expand cross-cultural knowledge of management groups.

One of the largest strategic alliances in recent years has been the Star Alliance between major airlines started in 1997 by Air Canada, Lufthansa, Scandinavian Airlines, Thai Airways, and United Airlines. By 2006 the alliance had grown to 38 members divided among full, regional, and alliance membership categories, running almost 17,000 daily flights to over 800 airports in more than 150 countries worldwide.

**multinational corporation (MNC)**
Business that maintains a presence in two or more countries, has a considerable portion of its assets invested in and derives a substantial portion of its sales and profits from international activities, considers opportunities throughout the world, and has a worldwide perspective and orientation.

## Becoming a Multinational Corporation

Companies willing to make a significant financial commitment often establish manufacturing and distribution facilities in foreign countries. A business with such facilities is known as a **multinational corporation (MNC)** (see Figure 13.4).

Businesses become multinational corporations for several reasons. Some do so in order to sell their products or services in other countries. McDonald's, for example, maintains restaurants in 116 foreign countries. Sales to customers in these countries represent half of the company's total revenue.

Companies also expand abroad in order to take advantage of inexpensive labor costs. For example, Tarrant Apparel, a U.S. manufacturer of blue jeans, weaves most of its fabric in Mexico. It also has most of its jeans sewn in Mexico, where labor is cheaper than in the United States.

**figure 13.4**

**MULTINATIONAL CORPORATIONS**

There are many ways for companies to do business globally. Multinational corporations often purchase their materials abroad or manufacture or assemble their products abroad. They also sell their products in foreign countries.

1. **Imported Materials**
   Multinational corporations may import materials used to manufacture their products. General Motors (GM), the largest automobile producer in the United States, works with more than 30,000 suppliers worldwide. Many of these suppliers are overseas.
2. **International Production**
   Multinational companies may produce their products in other countries. GM has manufacturing, assembly, or component operations in 50 countries. It operates abroad in order to improve service or reduce costs.
3. **International Sales**
   Multinational companies sell their products in other countries. GM cars and trucks are sold in Africa, Asia and the Pacific, Europe, the Middle East, and North America. Foreign sales represent a significant share of the company's total sales.

## Challenges of Working in an International Environment

Working for a multinational corporation presents many challenges. Managers must learn to deal with customers, producers, suppliers, and employees from different countries. They must become familiar with local laws and learn to respect local customs. They must try to understand what customers and employees want in countries that may be very different from the United States.

## Understanding Foreign Cultures

Business managers from different countries see the world differently. Japanese managers, for example, tend to be more sensitive to job layoffs than American managers. Asian and African managers often have different views about the role of women in the workplace than American managers do.

Managers who work in foreign countries need to be aware of different cultural attitudes. They also need to understand business customs in different countries (see Figure 13.5). Not knowing how to act in a foreign country can cause managers embarrassment, and it can cause them to miss out on business opportunities. Showing up for a business meeting without a tie might be acceptable in Israel, for example, but it would be completely out of place in Switzerland. Demonstrating great respect to a superior would be appreciated in Indonesia, but it would send the wrong signal in the Netherlands, where equality among individuals is valued.

## Coalitions of Cooperating Countries and Trading Blocs

International businesses must also deal with coalitions of cooperating countries that are established to improve the economic conditions of the member countries. One coalition is the European Union. The European Union's member countries are listed in Figure 13.3. Its purpose is to reduce tariffs on goods sold among member countries. Also, it is an attempt to eliminate the fiscal, technical, and border barriers between

**figure 13.5**

**EXAMPLES OF FOREIGN BUSINESS PRACTICES**

| COUNTRY | BUSINESS PRACTICE |
| --- | --- |
| China | Food is extremely important. All business transactions require at least one and usually two evening banquets. The first banquet is given by the host, the second by the guest. |
| Indonesia | Even foreigners are expected to arrive late to social occasions. It is generally appropriate to arrive about 30 minutes after the scheduled time. |
| Singapore | Businesspeople exchange business cards in a formal manner, receiving the card with both hands and studying it for a few moments before putting it away. |
| Saudi Arabia | Businesspeople greet foreigners by clasping their hand, but they do not shake hands. |
| Switzerland | Business is conducted very formally. Humor and informality are inappropriate. |

member countries that over several decades have increased the costs of goods and services in Europe and reduced the international competitiveness of European companies. Europe was to be a single market with exciting potential for multinational corporations. Many problems still exist in implementing the changes necessary for Europe to become one market. The democratic movement in Eastern Europe, the reunification of Germany, and the breakup of the Soviet Union have resulted in some of those countries and republics joining the European Union.

Another coalition is the Organization of Petroleum Exporting Countries (OPEC), which includes many of the oil-producing countries of the world. Its purpose is to control oil prices and production levels among member countries. Today, OPEC's effectiveness is limited because several member countries sell and produce at levels considerably different from official OPEC standards.

Today, three large trading blocks exist: European Union; the North American Alliance of the United States, Canada, and Mexico (NAFTA); and Pacific Asia (Pacific Rim countries), with Japan being the dominant country in that region. Other members of the Pacific Rim trading bloc are China, Korea, Taiwan, Indonesia, Malaysia, the Philippines, Thailand, Hong Kong, and Singapore. The three large trading blocs will provide many opportunities and pose many threats for multinational organizations.

## Political Changes

One of the most dramatic illustrations of how political changes influence the international business environment was the breakup of the Soviet Union and the fall of communist governments in Eastern Europe in the early 1990s. In addition, the political and economic upheavals in Bulgaria, Hungary, Poland, Romania, and the countries formerly known as Czechoslovakia and Yugoslavia have caused significant changes in how these countries conduct their own international business activities and how they relate to businesses from foreign countries.

## Human Rights and Ethics

Should multinational firms close their plants in countries where human rights abuses are common and accepted ethical boundaries are violated? This is a valid issue, but U.S. managers must remember that business ethics have not yet been globalized; the norms of ethical behavior continue to vary widely even in Western capitalist countries. Thus, questions such as, Should Coca-Cola establish minimum labor standards for all of its bottlers around the world to prevent abuses of workers in certain countries? seem highly appropriate in the United States. However, such questions present dilemmas for multinational firms that are accompanied by ethical predicaments and hard choices. In each situation, the multinational firm must strike a balance among the values and ideals of all its various publics. No clear and easy choices exist.

## Imposed Quotas

A labor union official was alleged to have made the following statement:

Foreign imports of textiles have cost American jobs and tax revenues. In order to slow down the disruptive impacts on American society, quotas should be placed on imports into the United States for those goods and product lines that are displacing significant percentages of U.S. production and employment.

### Questions

1. Do you agree with the union official? Explain.
2. Do you believe import quotas should be established for certain industries? Which ones?
3. Does the United States benefit or lose from international business activity?
4. What do you think the response from other countries could be if the United States did impose import quotas?

## PROGRESS CHECK QUESTIONS

5. What is the balance of trade?
6. List and explain three examples of protectionism.
7. Explain the positive and negative aspects of NAFTA.
8. List and explain four forms of international operations.

## Managing Change

In his book *Thriving on Chaos,* Tom Peters stresses the importance of change to the modern corporation: "To up the odds of survival, leaders at all levels must become obsessive about change." He adds, "Change must become the norm, not cause for alarm."[1] Similarly, Jack Welch, the well-known former CEO of GE, has been quoted as saying, "When the rate of change on the outside exceeds the rate of change on the inside, the end is in sight."[2] What does *change* mean from these perspectives? Simply put, it means that unless managers have changed something, they have not earned their paychecks. This bold view is somewhat foreign to many organizations today.

Today, managing change and dealing with its impact on the corporate culture are essential skills that the manager must master if the organization is to compete globally. Furthermore, the manager must learn these skills rapidly, since change is occurring at an ever-increasing rate. The new bottom line for the twenty-first century will be to assess each and every action in light of its contribution to an increased corporate capacity for change.

Organizations today are beset by change. Many managers find themselves unable to cope with an environment or

Change isn't always drastic. At one time wearing jeans to work was considered taboo by many companies that now embrace casual Fridays. How might a culture shift of this kind impact a more conservative manager?

### Job Interviewing – Make It Count!

The job interview . . . what an opportunity to impress!! Interviewing for jobs are a growing process that young adults must learn from. Mistakes will happen but can become knowledge for future interviews that might have better opportunities and bigger implications to your future career.

The importance of job interviews is the entire experience that awaits you. A particular company has opened its doors for the right person to walk through it and if you understand the interviewing process, that "right" person can be you.

Therefore, come to an interview prepared to be hired. Ask good questions, take notes, research the perspective company, use good posture and good eye contact. These listed interview procedures might seem basic but more often than not, are not carried out by most prospective new hires. If you are poised, focused and confident about the hiring opportunity and carry out the basic interview practices, your odds of being hired are increased significantly!

an organization that has become substantially different from the one in which they received their training and gained their early experience. Other managers have trouble transferring their skills to a new assignment in a different industry. A growing organization, a new assignment, changing customer needs, changing employee expectations, and changing competition may all be encountered by today's managers. To be successful, managers must be able to adapt to these changes.

## Change as a Global Issue

One of the driving pressures for change is the desire to compete globally. Since America's global trading partners (notably Japan, China, and Europe) have adopted change as an essential ingredient of their long-term strategies, corporate America must follow suit. When asked about change in the international environment, Eric A. Cronson, vice president and managing director of Thomas Group Europe, commented, "Change has to be radical—if you stay in your comfort zone, you will not be internationally competitive."[3] Similarly, Joseph V. Marulli, president of information services at Eunetcom, commented at an international conference on change, "Transformation has to be in the leader's heart, in your heart, and in the hearts of all the senior people."[4] From comments such as these, the manager must understand that the challenge to compete is really the challenge to change.

**technological changes**
Changes in such things as new equipment and new processes.

**environmental changes**
All non-technological changes that occur outside the organization.

**internal changes**
Budget adjustments, policy changes, personnel changes, and the like.

## Types of Change

Change as it applies to organizations can be classified into three major categories: (1) technological, (2) environmental, and (3) internal to the organization. **Technological changes** include such things as new equipment and new processes. The technological advances since World War II have been dramatic, with computers and increased speed of communication being the most notable. **Environmental changes** are all the nontechnological changes that occur outside the organization. New government regulations, new social trends, and economic changes are all examples of environmental change. An organization's **internal changes** include such things as budget adjustments, policy changes, diversity adjustments, and personnel changes. Figure 13.6 lists several examples of each major type of change affecting today's organizations.

figure 13.6

**TYPES OF CHANGES
AFFECTING
ORGANIZATIONS**

| TECHNOLOGICAL | ENVIRONMENTAL | INTERNAL |
| --- | --- | --- |
| Machines | Laws | Policies |
| Equipment | Taxes | Procedures |
| Processes | Social trends | New methods |
| Automation | Fashion trends | Rules |
| Computers | Political trends | Reorganization |
| New raw materials | Economic trends | Budget adjustment |
| Robots | Interest rates | Restructuring of jobs |
| | Consumer trends | Personnel |
| | Competition | Management |
| | Suppliers | Ownership |
| | Population trends | Products/services sold |

Any of the three types of changes can greatly affect a manager's job. Both technological and environmental changes occur outside an organization and can create the need for internal change. Internal change can also occur because of performance issues (such as conflict, quality, lack of productivity, and so forth) or as a result of regular self-assessment as part of the strategic management process.

Any of the three types of change can create the need for unplanned change or planned change. Since managers can control planned change, they should be periodically analyzing which changes are necessary. Thus, by being proactive rather than reactive, managers can have much more control over the change process.

---

**PROGRESS CHECK QUESTIONS**

9. Explain the quotation: "When the rate of change on the outside exceeds the rate of change on the inside, the end is in sight."

10. In what ways do managers often struggle in dealing with change?

11. Is change a global issue? Why or why not?

12. What are the three major categories of change as it applies to organizations?

---

# THE CHANGE PROCESS

As first discussed in the late 1940s by social psychologist Kurt Lewin, change is a function of the forces that support or promote the change and those forces that oppose or resist the change (Lewin referred to this approach as *force field analysis*). Change forces introduce something different about the organization over time. Resistance forces support the status quo, or keeping things as they are. The sum total of these forces determines the extent to which a change will be successfully implemented.

## Lewin's Three-Step Model for Change

Lewin developed a three-step model for successfully implementing change:

1. Lewin's first step, *unfreezing*, deals with breaking down the forces supporting or maintaining the old behavior. These forces can include such variables as the formal reward system, reinforcement from the work group, and the individual's perception of what is proper role behavior.
2. The second step, *presenting a new alternative*, involves offering a clear and attractive option representing new patterns of behavior.
3. The third step, *refreezing*, requires that the change behavior be reinforced by the formal and informal reward systems and by the work group. It is in this step that the manager can play a pivotal role by positively reinforcing employee efforts to change.

Implicit in Lewin's three-step model is the recognition that the mere introduction of change does not ensure the elimination of the prechange conditions or that the change will be permanent. Unsuccessful attempts to implement lasting change can usually be traced to a failure in one of Lewin's three steps.

## Resistance to Change

Most people claim to be modern and up to date. However, their first reaction is usually to resist change. This is almost always true when the change affects their jobs. Resistance to change is a natural, normal reaction; it is not a reaction observed only in troublemakers. For example, most employees are apprehensive when there is a change in their immediate manager. It is usually not that the employees dislike the new manager, but rather that they don't know what he or she will be like. All change requires adjustment; in fact, the adjustment may concern employees more than the actual change.

Because organizations are composed of individuals, often there is organizational resistance to change. Organizational resistance to change occurs when the organization, as an entity, appears to resist change. For example, obsolete products or services and inappropriate organization structure are often the result of organizational resistance to change.

### Reasons for Resisting Change

Employees resist change for many reasons. Some of the most frequent reasons are as follows.

1. *Fear of the unknown.* It is natural human behavior to fear the unknown. With many changes, the outcome is not foreseeable. When

it is, the results are often not made known to all the affected employees. For example, employees may worry about and resist a new computer if they are not sure what its impact will be on their jobs.Similarly, employees may resist a new manager simply because they don't know what to expect. A related fear is the uncertainty employees may feel about working in a changed environment. They may fully understand the change yet really doubt whether they will be able to handle it. For example, an employee may resist a change in procedure because of a fear of being unable to master it.

2. *Economics.* Employees fear any change they think threatens their jobs or incomes. The threat may be real or only imagined. In either case, the result is resistance. For example, a salesperson who believes a territory change will result in less income will resist the change. Similarly, production workers will oppose new standards they believe will be harder to achieve.

There is a reason "fear of the unknown" is listed first as a reason to resist change. More often than not, innovation is a long-term benefit with a short-term inconvenience. Why would this sort of resistance pose a greater obstacle than more tangible factors like money?

3. *Fear that skills and expertise will lose value.* Everyone likes to feel valued by others, and anything that has the potential to reduce that value will be resisted. For example, an operations manager may resist implementation of a new, more modern piece of equipment for fear the change will make him or her less needed by the organization.

4. *Threats to power.* Many employees, and especially managers, believe a change may diminish their power. For example, a manager may perceive a change to the organization's structure as weakening his or her power within the organization.

5. *Additional work and inconvenience.* Almost all changes involve work, and many result in personal inconveniences to the affected employees. If nothing else, they often have to learn new ways. This may mean more training, school, or practice. A common reaction by employees is that "it isn't worth the extra effort required."

6. *Threats to interpersonal relations.* The social and interpersonal relationships among employees can be quite strong. These relationships may appear unimportant to everyone but those involved. For example, eating lunch with a particular group may be very important to the involved employees. When a change, such as a transfer, threatens these relationships, the affected employees often resist. Employees naturally feel more at ease when working with people they know well. Also, the group may have devised methods for doing the work

based on the strengths and weaknesses of group members. Any changes in the group would naturally disrupt the routine.

### Reducing Resistance to Change

As discussed previously, most employees' first reaction to change is resistance. However, how employees perceive the change's impact greatly affects their reaction to the change. While many variations are possible, four basic situations usually occur:

1. If employees cannot foresee how the change will affect them, they will resist the change or be neutral at best. Most people shy away from the unknown, believing that change may make things worse.
2. If employees perceive that the change does not fit their needs and hopes, they will resist the change. In this instance, employees are convinced the change will make things worse.
3. If employees see that the change is inevitable, they may first resist and then resign themselves to the change. The first reaction is to resist. Once the change appears imminent, employees often see no other choice but to go along with it.
4. If employees view the change as being in their best interests, they will be motivated to make the change work. The key here is for the employees to feel sure the change will make things better. Three out of four of these situations result in some form of resistance to change. Also, the way in which employees resist change can vary greatly. For example, an employee may not actively resist a change but may never actively support it. Similarly, an employee may mildly resist by acting uninterested in the change. At the other extreme, an employee may resist by trying to sabotage the change.

Figure 13.7 summarizes how employees might respond to change. Before a manager can reduce resistance to a change, she or he must try to determine how the employees will react to the change. The following steps are recommended before issuing a change directive.

1. Determine the response needed from the employee to accomplish the task effectively.
2. Estimate the expected response if the directive is simply published or orally passed to the employee (as many are).
3. If a discrepancy exists between the needed response and the estimated response, determine how the two responses can be reconciled (opposition is never an acceptable response).[5]

The following paragraphs present several suggestions for reducing resistance to change and helping employees to accept and even commit themselves to change.

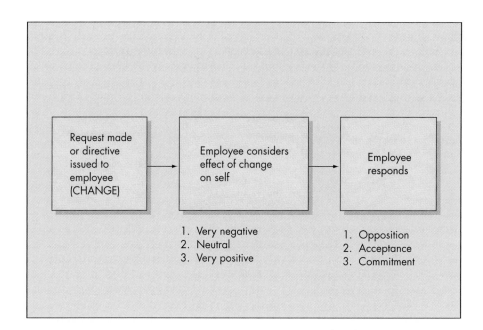

**figure 13.7**

**EMPLOYEE RESPONSE MODEL**

**Source:** Waldron Berry, "Overcoming Resistance to Change," *Supervisory Management,* February 1983.

**Build Trust** If employees trust and have confidence in management, they are much more likely to accept change. If an air of distrust prevails, change is likely to be strongly resisted. Management's day-to-day and long-term actions determine the degree of trust among employees. Managers can go a long way toward building trust if they discuss upcoming changes with employees and actively involve employees in the change process.

**Discuss Upcoming Changes** Fear of the unknown is one of the major barriers to change. This fear can be greatly reduced by discussing any upcoming changes with the affected employees. During this discussion, the manager should be as open and honest as possible. The manager should explain not only what the change will be but also why the change is being made. The manager should also outline the impact of the change on each affected employee. Figure 13.8 presents a classical approach to change resistance that can help a manager who is attempting to explain and discuss an upcoming change.

**Involve the Employees** Involving employees means more than merely discussing the upcoming changes with them. The key is to involve employees personally in the entire change process. It is natural for employees to want to go along with a change they have helped devise and implement. A good approach is to ask for employees' ideas and input as early as possible in the change process.

**Make Sure the Changes Are Reasonable** The manager should always do everything possible to ensure that any proposed changes are reasonable. Often proposals for changes come from other parts of the

| APPROACH | COMMONLY USED IN SITUATIONS | ADVANTAGES | DRAWBACKS |
|---|---|---|---|
| Education + communication | Where there is a lack of information or inaccurate information and analysis. | Once persuaded, people will often help with the implementation of the change. | Can be time-consuming if lots of people are involved. |
| Participation + involvement | Where the initiators do not have all the information they need to design the change, and where others have considerable power to resist. | People who participate will be committed to implementing change, and any relevant information they have will be integrated into the change plan. | Can be time-consuming if participators design an inappropriate change. |
| Facilitation + support | Where people are resisting because of adjustment problems. | No other approach works as well with adjustment problems. | Can be time-consuming and expensive and still fail. |
| Negotiation + agreement | Where someone or some group will clearly lose out in a change, and where that group has considerable power to resist. | Sometimes it is a relatively easy way to avoid major resistance. | Can be too expensive in many cases if it alerts others to negotiate for compliance. |
| Manipulation + co-optation | Where other tactics will not work or are too expensive. | It can be a relatively quick and inexpensive solution to resistance problems. | Can lead to future problems if people feel manipulated. |
| Explicit + implicit coercion | Where speed is essential and the change initiators possess considerable power. | It is speedy and can overcome any kind of resistance. | Can be risky if it leaves people mad at the initiators. |

## figure 13.8

**METHODS OF OVERCOMING RESISTANCE TO CHANGE**

organization. These proposals are sometimes not reasonable because the originator is unaware of all the pertinent circumstances.

**Avoid Threats** The manager who attempts to force change through the use of threats is taking a negative approach. This is likely to decrease rather than increase employee trust. Most people resist threats or coercion. Such tactics also usually have a negative impact on employee morale.

**Follow a Sensible Time Schedule** A manager can often influence the timing of changes. Some times are doubtless better than others for making certain changes. If nothing else, the manager should always use common sense when proposing a time schedule for implementing a change.

Most of the above suggestions for reducing resistance to change relate to the manner in which management communicates a change. It is often not the change itself that determines its acceptability but rather the manner in which the change is implemented. The importance of the manager's role in this process was reinforced by the finding of a late 1990s study conducted by Watson Wyatt Worldwide. The study of more than 9,000 working Americans concluded that the three biggest barriers to managing change are (1) lack of management visibility and support, (2) inadequate management skills, and (3) employee resistance to change.[6] It is interesting to note that two relate directly to management and only one relates directly to employees.

### Leading Change

Today's competitive world requires that managers at all levels be constantly looking for improvements via change. This fact, coupled with the realization that most people's natural reaction is to resist change, means that successful change implementation requires that managers make a conscious effort to lead change efforts. John Kotter has developed the eight-step method for leading change shown in Figure 13.9.[7] Each of these steps is discussed in the following paragraphs.

**Establish a Sense of Urgency**  Because so many large and small companies have a tendency to become complacent, managers must constantly be on the lookout for needed change. Success and the comfort of doing everything the same way are two frequently encountered reasons that organizations become complacent. Successful managers are constantly looking for the need to change, and once a need is identified, they establish an urgency for making it happen.

**Create a Guiding Coalition**  Most successful change efforts require the participation and support of several managers and employees from many different levels in the organization. A group or coalition of managers

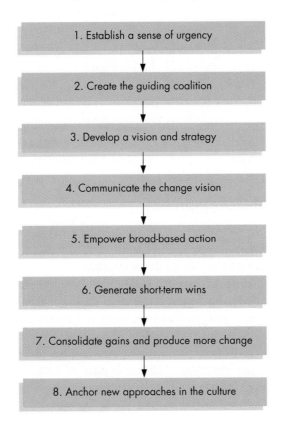

1. Establish a sense of urgency

2. Create the guiding coalition

3. Develop a vision and strategy

4. Communicate the change vision

5. Empower broad-based action

6. Generate short-term wins

7. Consolidate gains and produce more change

8. Anchor new approaches in the culture

**figure 13.9**

**MODEL FOR LEADING CHANGE**

***Source:*** Reprinted by permission of Harvard Business School Press. From *Leading Change,* by J. Kotter. Boston, MA 1996. Copyright © 1996 by the Harvard Business School Publishing Corporation; all rights reserved.

and employees must be formed to lead the change. Most major changes are initiated by top management, but to be successful they must eventually involve middle managers, supervisors, and employees.

**Develop a Vision and Strategy**  As discussed earlier in this chapter, most people are much more accepting of change when they can visualize its ultimate impact. Therefore, it is important that change leaders develop a clear image of what the results of the change will be and what the transition process will involve.

**Communicate the Change Vision**  Change leaders should use every available means to communicate the change vision to organizational members and affected parties. All too often managers assume that employees have the same vision about a change that they do. The best approach is to use multiple channels and opportunities to communicate the change vision.

**Empower Broad-Based Action**  The idea here is to actively involve managers and employees at all levels in the change process. Eliminate obstacles to the change process and empower employees to take the actions necessary to implement the change.

**Generate Short-Term Wins**  Once the successes associated with a change are seen, even those who initially resisted will usually get on board. The key here is to not wait for the ultimate realization of the vision but rather to recognize and celebrate numerous small successes along the way. Take the opportunity to publicly recognize successes and the people responsible. Everyone likes to be a member of a winning team.

**Consolidate Gains and Produce More Change**  Don't rest on your laurels along the way. Maintain the ultimate vision, and don't get sidetracked or satisfied with the small successes. As you approach the original ultimate vision, look for new projects and changes.

**Anchor New Approaches in the Culture**  Take actions to ensure that the organization and its members don't slowly revert back to the old ways. Emphasize the positive results of the changes, and continually give credit to those who participated in the change process.

## Organizational Development

The previous sections emphasized the change process from the viewpoint of individual managers. This section looks at the change process from the viewpoint of the entire organization.

**organizational development (OD)**

Organizationwide, planned effort, managed from the top, to increase organizational performance through planned interventions.

**Organizational development (OD)** is an organizationwide, planned effort managed from the top, with a goal of increasing organizational performance through planned interventions in the organization. In particular, OD looks at the human side of organizations. It seeks to change attitudes, values, and management practices in an effort to improve organizational performance. The ultimate goal of OD is to structure the organizational environment so that managers and employees can use their skills and abilities to the fullest.

An OD effort starts with a recognition by management that organizational performance can and should be improved. Following this, most OD efforts include the following phases: diagnosis, change planning, intervention/education, and evaluation.

## Diagnosis

The first decision to be made in the OD process is whether the organization has the talent and available time necessary to conduct the diagnosis. If not, an alternative is to hire an outside consultant. Once the decision has been made regarding who will do the diagnosis, the next step is to gather and analyze information. Some of the most frequently used methods for doing this are the following.

1. *Review available records.* The first step is to review any available records or documents that may be pertinent. Personnel records and financial reports are two types of generally available records that can be useful.

2. *Survey questionnaires.* The most popular method of gathering data is through questionnaires filled out by employees. Usually the questionnaires are intended to measure employee attitudes and perceptions about certain work-related factors.

3. *Personal interviews.* In this approach, employees are individually interviewed regarding their opinions and perceptions and certain work-related factors. This method takes more time than the survey questionnaire method but can result in better information.

4. *Direct observation.* In this method, the person conducting the diagnosis observes firsthand the behavior of organizational members at work. One advantage of this method is that it allows observation of what people actually do as opposed to what they say they do.

In the diagnosis stage, one should collect data for a reason. A plan for analyzing the data should be developed even before the data are collected. Too often data are collected simply because they are available and with no plan for analysis.

## Change Planning

The data collected in the diagnosis stage must be carefully interpreted to determine the best plan for organizational improvement. If a similar diagnosis has been done in the past, it can be revealing to compare the data and look for any obvious differences. Because much of the collected data are based on personal opinions and perceptions, there will always be areas of disagreement. The key to interpreting the data is to look for trends and areas of general agreement. The end result of the change-planning process is to identify specific problem areas and outline steps for resolving the problems.

### Intervention/Education

The purpose of the intervention/education phase is to share the information obtained in the diagnostic phase with the affected employees and help them realize the need for change. A thorough analysis in the change-planning phase often results in the identification of the most appropriate intervention/education method to use. Some of the most frequently used intervention/education methods are discussed next.

**Direct Feedback**  With the **direct feedback** method, the change agent communicates the information gathered in the diagnostic and change-planning phases to the involved parties. The change agent describes what was found and what changes are recommended. Then workshops are often conducted to initiate the desired changes.

**Team Building**  The objective of team building is to increase the group's cohesiveness and general group spirit. Team building stresses the importance of working together. Some of the specific activities used include (1) clarifying employee roles, (2) reducing conflict, (3) improving interpersonal relations, and (4) improving problem-solving skills.[8] Team building was discussed in depth in Chapter 9.

**Sensitivity Training**  **Sensitivity training** is designed to make one more aware of oneself and one's impact on others. Sensitivity training involves a group, usually called a *training group* or *T-group,* that meets and has no agenda or particular focus. Normally the group has between 10 and 15 people who may or may not know one another. With no planned structure or no prior common experiences, the behavior of individuals in trying to deal with the lack of structure becomes the agenda. While engaging in group dialogue, members are encouraged to learn about themselves and others in the nonstructured environment.

Sensitivity training has been both passionately criticized and vigorously defended as to its relative value for organizations. In general, the research shows that people who have undergone sensitivity training tend to show increased sensitivity, more open communication, and increased flexibility.[9] However, the same studies indicate that while the outcomes of sensitivity training are beneficial in general, it is difficult to predict the outcomes for any one person.

### Evaluation

Probably the most difficult phase in the OD process is the evaluation phase.[10] The basic question to be answered is, Did the OD process produce the desired results? Unfortunately, many OD efforts begin with admirable but overly vague objectives such as improving the overall health, culture, or climate of the organization. Before any OD effort can be evaluated, explicit objectives must be determined. Objectives of an OD effort should be outcome oriented and should lend themselves to the development of measurable criteria.

A second requirement for evaluating OD efforts is that the evaluation effort be methodologically sound. Ideally, an OD effort should be evaluated

**direct feedback**

Process in which the change agent communicates the information gathered in the diagnostic and change-planning phases to the involved parties.

**sensitivity training**

Method used in OD to make one more aware of oneself and one's impact on others.

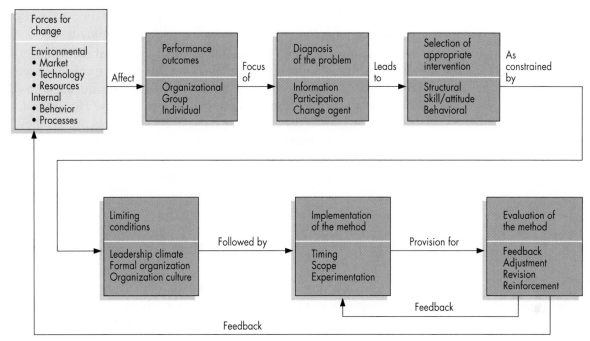

**figure 13.10**

**MODEL FOR THE MANAGEMENT OF ORGANIZATIONAL DEVELOPMENT**

***Source:*** James L. Gibson, John M. Ivancevich, and James H. Donnelly, Jr., *Organizations* (Burr Ridge, IL: Richard D. Irwin, 1994), p. 668.

using hard, objective data. One approach is to compare data collected before the OD intervention against data collected after the OD intervention. An even better approach is to compare "before" and "after" data with similar data from a control group. When using this approach, two similar groups are identified, an experimental group and a control group. The OD effort is then implemented with the experimental group but not with the control group. After the OD intervention has been completed, the before and after data from the experimental group are compared with the before and after data from the control group. This approach helps to rule out changes that may have resulted from factors other than the OD intervention. Figure 13.10 summarizes the OD process.

## Managing Innovation

The concept of innovation was briefly introduced in Chapter 4 as part of the discussion on creativity. Innovation refers to doing new things that inherently involve change. Many management experts today believe that innovation is an organization's best sustainable source of growth, competitive advantage, and new wealth.[11]

Because what worked in the past may not work today, many organizations are having to create new ways to foster innovation. Robert Tucker, author of the international best-seller *Managing the Future,* believes that organizations that successfully innovate in the future must embrace four essential principles. These four principles are discussed below.

1. An organization's approach to innovation must be comprehensive. Innovation cannot be confined to a few departments or to a small

group of "innovations." Innovation must permeate the entire organization, and it must encompass all aspects of organization.

2. Innovation must include systematic, organized, and continual search for new opportunities. Traditionally, top management was the only organizational entity concerned with such questions as, What do these developments mean to our company? How could we take advantage of these developments? What threats are on the horizon that we must respond to now if we are going to capitalize on this development? The rapid pace of change today dictates much broader participation than just top management in these decisions.

3. Organizations must involve everyone in the innovation process. Up until very recent times, many employees were not asked or expected to innovate in their jobs. In some instances, employees were encouraged *not* to innovate. The dormant creativity of employees across the organization must be tapped.

4. An organization must work constantly on improving its climate for innovation. As used here, climate refers to the "feeling in the air" you get when you work for or visit an organization. Does the feeling in the air foster innovation and encourage employees to take risks? What happens when someone fails? Innovative climates expect a certain degree of failure, learn from failures, and share the learning throughout the organization. As the old saying goes, if you haven't failed, you haven't taken sufficient risks. Organizations with favorable climates for innovation provide the context for people to collaborate in groups, teams, divisions, and departments without boundaries of fear.

As the rate of change increases for today's organizations, the ability to innovate becomes more and more critical. By subscribing to the above principles, managers at all levels can positively affect an organization's ability to innovate and remain competitive.

## The Learning Organization

If organizations are to encourage change and innovation, they must establish environments that support these actions. Learning organizations establish such an environment. A learning organization has been defined as an organization skilled at creating, acquiring, and transferring knowledge, and in modifying behavior to reflect the new knowledge.[12] Peter Senge, whose book *The Fifth Discipline* popularized the learning organization, has identified five principles for creating a learning organization:[13]

1. *Systems thinking.* Managers must learn to see the big picture and not concentrate only on their part; they

Jack Welch, former CEO for General Electric, led his company to the forefront of employee learning. What are some lessons a front-line manager can learn from his approach to management?

## The Way We Do Things

Fitzgerald Company manufactures a variety of consumer products for sale through retail department stores. For over 30 years, the company has held a strong belief that customer relations and a strong selling orientation are the keys to business success. As a result, all top executives have sales backgrounds and spend much of their time outside the company with customers. Because of the strong focus on the customer, management at Fitzgerald emphasizes new-product development projects and growth in volume. The company rarely implements cost reduction or process improvement projects.

Between 1975 and 1985, Fitzgerald's 10 percent share of the market was the largest in the industry. Profitability was consistently better than the industry average. However, in the last 10 years, the markets for many of Fitzgerald's products have matured, and Fitzgerald has dropped from market share leader to the number three company in the industry. Profitability has steadily declined since 1991, although Fitzgerald offers a more extensive line of products than any of its competitors. Customers are complaining that Fitzgerald's prices are higher than those of other companies.

In June 1996, Jeff Steele, president of Fitzgerald Company, hired Valerie Stevens of Management Consultants, Inc., to help him improve the company's financial performance. After an extensive study of Fitzgerald Company and its industry group, Valerie met with Jeff and said, "Jeff, I believe the Fitzgerald Company has to come to terms with its capacity for change."

### Questions

1. Describe, in general terms, the current state of the Fitzgerald Company.

2. What does Valerie mean when she says the Fitzgerald Company has to come to terms with its capacity for change? What are some of the necessary changes?

3. Discuss the problems the company may encounter in attempting to implement changes.

4. Do you think the changes will work? Why or why not?

---

must learn to recognize the effects of one level of learning on another.

2. *Personal mastery.* Individual managers and employees must be empowered to experiment, innovate, and explore.

3. *Mental models.* Managers and employees should be encouraged to develop mental models as ways of stretching their minds to find new and better ways of doing things.

4. *Shared vision.* Managers should develop and communicate a shared vision that can be used as a framework for addressing problems and opportunities.

5. *Team learning.* Team learning is the process of aligning a team so as to avoid wasted energy and to get the desired results.

Honda, Corning, and General Electric are examples of companies that have become good learning organizations.[14] In these organizations, learning, in whatever form, becomes an inescapable way of life for both managers and employees alike. These and other learning organizations are gaining the commitment of their employees at all levels by continually expanding their capacity to learn and change.

## Tony builds a rainbow coalition

Tony thought about Dawn's lecture on diversity for a few days before calling his mentor, Jerry Smith. "Are you giving the same instructions to the unit managers in your region Jerry?" Tony asked, half-expecting this whole thing to be a problem unique to Dawn's region.

"Absolutely," answered Jerry. "This isn't about some quota or lawsuit, Tony. We have to make sure that our restaurants reflect the communities in which they operate. We've been doing that to some degree by hiring workers from those communities, but if all our managers are the same color and same gender, how does that look? You know as well as I do that we don't discriminate in this company, but our customers and suppliers don't know that. If they don't see a diverse leadership team, they'll draw their own conclusions, and who knows where it will go from there? How would you like to overhear a conversation where someone is considering applying for our management-training program and their friend tells them not to bother because 'Taco Barn only hires white managers'? That's what this is about Tony."

"I still have a problem with this Jerry," continued Tony. "So are we going to start replacing our existing managers to make sure we're more diverse? I'm one of those white managers—should I be worried about my job too?"

"Of course not, Tony," Jerry replied. "You're doing a great job there, and the company would be crazy to let you go. All we're looking to do here is make sure that our employees and our customers know that Taco Barn promotes its people based on ability. We have always been an equal opportunity employer, and we want our leadership team to be more reflective of that. Why don't you bring the issue up at the next unit staff meeting and see what your people have to say about it?"

Tony took Jerry's advice and put the issue on the agenda at his next staff meeting. To his surprise, the response was overwhelmingly positive. He knew they were on the right track when one of his youngest and brightest team leaders, Caroline, an African American, spoke up and said:

"This has been a long time coming, Tony. We all know you've got our backs here, and you've always been willing to support us in learning new skills, but it won't hurt to see a few brothers and sisters running the place—gives us something to aim for you know?

### QUESTIONS

1. Jerry feels that the diversity issue is simply good business. Do you agree? Why or why not?

2. What does Tony's position as "one of those white managers" have to do with his concerns about the company's new diversity initiative?

3. What do you think will happen the first time Tony has to choose between two equally talented applicants of different races? Explain your answer.

4. Do you agree with Taco Barn's approach to diversity? Why or why not?

---

## PROGRESS CHECK QUESTIONS

13. Explain Kurt Lewin's three-step model for change.

14. List the six most frequently used reasons employees use to resist change.

15. List six things a manager can do to reduce resistance to change and help employees to accept and even commit themselves to change.

16. What are the four phases of an organizational development effort?

## CONCLUSION

In this chapter we have reviewed an assorted mixture of topics. We have seen that managers are currently being challenged by internal issues (building and managing a diverse workforce), external issues (management on a global scale), and the increasingly complex issue of organizational change as a constant feature of modern corporations. What does this mean for the day-to-day working life of a modern manager? At the operational level, nothing can be taken for granted. As soon as a new process or policy is tested and approved, it will be liable to change— either as a result of an internal decision, or in direct response to a change in the organization's external environment (customers, competitors, or other stakeholders). Successful managers are adapting to this new world and building an organizational  culture in which employees are motivated by the challenge of constant change and respond positively to it as an opportunity for creative and rewarding work.

## key terms

**absolute advantage** 372
**balance of trade** 373
**direct feedback** 392
**diversification** 372
**embargo** 376
**environmental changes** 382
**exports** 372
**foreign intermediary** 377
**free trade area** 376
**imports** 372

**internal changes** 382
**international trade** 371
**law of comparative advantage** 372
**licensing agreement** 377
**multinational corporation (MNC)** 378
**North American Free Trade Agreement (NAFTA)** 376

**organizational development (OD)** 390
**quotas** 375
**sensitivity training** 392
**strategic alliance** 378
**tariff** 375
**technological changes** 382

## review questions

1. Define glass ceiling, and give examples of how it affects women and minorities.
2. Define international trade.
3. What does foreign exchange mean?
4. What is organizational development?
5. What principles can organizations follow to innovate successfully?
6. What is a learning organization?

## internet exercise

### FREE TRADE

Free trade agreements, such as the North American Free Trade Agreement (NAFTA) and the General Agreement on Tariffs and Trade (GATT), may reduce trade restrictions within a designated region, as well as allow for increased sales and lower-priced goods. However, much criticism has also been voiced by consumer, labor, health, and environmental groups, such as the Alliance for Democracy, Public Citizen in Washington, D.C., and the Fair Trade Network. They believe that unrestricted, "corporate-managed" trade will do more harm than good.

Do research on the Internet to answer the following questions:

1. Be prepared to discuss either the positives or negatives of NAFTA and GATT.

2. Document the purpose of either Alliance for Democracy or the Fair Trade Network.

## team exercise

### CHANGE IN THE AIRLINE INDUSTRY

Many organizations have had to change the way they do business since the tragic events of September 11, 2001. The airline industry has certainly been one of the most affected industries. Your instructor will divide the class into groups of four to six students per group. Once the groups have been formed, each group should respond to the following:

1. Identify the major changes that have been implemented by or in the airline industry since September 11, 2001.

2. Does your group feel that these changes are positive or negative for the flying public? For airline employees?

3. Why does the group feel that these changes were not implemented before the tragic events took place?

After each group has answered the above questions, your instructor will ask each group to share their answers with the class.

## One Case against Wal-Mart

*In a Case with Wide-Ranging Implications, a Jury Rules for a Pharmacist Who Claimed Gender Discrimination and Defamation*

On June 19, Cynthia Haddad and her husband, Bill, walked across Wendell Avenue from the Berkshire Superior Court to the public library in Pittsfield, Mass., to talk. There they waited as a jury in the Park Square courthouse deliberated over the lawsuit Haddad had filed against her former employer Wal-Mart Stores for gender discrimination and defamation. As they exited the library hand-in-hand, the sun shone, filling Haddad with an impending sense of closure. "It was the first day of the rest of our lives no matter what the verdict," says the 45-year-old mother of four. "My story was told and I did the fight. My life would go on after that."

Shortly thereafter, Haddad was in tears. The jury awarded her nearly $2 million in punitive and compensatory damages. "It vindicated me," says Haddad. "It started to bring life back into me. Someone listened."

### UNDER FIRE

The dispute was over why Haddad had been dismissed by Wal-Mart, after more than 10 years as a pharmacist with the company. Haddad believed she was fired from the Pittsfield store in retaliation for her complaints about being paid less than male pharmacy managers and about the disappearance of controlled drugs from the pharmacy. Wal-Mart contended that Haddad was dismissed for violating company policies and failing to secure the pharmacy. The company also argued that Haddad wasn't entitled to the same pay as the other pharmacy managers, who were in fact male, because she wasn't actually a manager.

Wal-Mart is likely to appeal, and the verdict may be overturned. Of course, even if Wal-Mart loses, $2 million is barely a blip on the radar for a company that took in more than $355 billion in revenues in its most recent fiscal year. Still, Haddad's victory comes at a difficult time for Wal-Mart, with the company struggling to defend its reputation on a number of fronts. Wal-Mart has come under fire for the wages and benefits that it provides workers and for its impact on small, local retailers.

## POTENTIAL IMPACT

Haddad's success may also have ramifications beyond her particular case. Wal-Mart is facing a separate lawsuit, a massive class action over gender discrimination, and one of the lead attorneys in that case says that Haddad's victory may give him the opportunity to broaden his case. The case, *Dukes v. Wal-Mart Stores*, charges the company with a pattern of gender discrimination in promotion, pay, training, and job assignment on behalf of 1.5 million to 2 million women who have worked at Wal-Mart's retail stores and wholesale clubs since 1998. In addition to the *Dukes* class action, there are more than 75 legal proceedings pending against the company, according to filings with the Securities & Exchange Commission. The majority pertains to complaints about wages and off-the-clock work.

Haddad is an example of how one employee, backed by a team of determined attorneys, pulled out a legal victory against the giant retailer. She benefited from having a long track record at the company, complete with strong employee evaluations over many years. Even more important, her lawyers, Richard Fradette and David Belfort, were able to track down key witnesses who could put Haddad's treatment in context, especially male pharmacists who formerly or currently worked at Wal-Mart and who had faced markedly different treatment.

When Haddad started working at Wal-Mart in 1993, it was the realization of a life-long dream. She had wanted to become a pharmacist ever since she had developed a crush in the eighth grade on one of the pharmacists in her hometown. She worked for the company on quite good terms for the next 10 years.

## PIZZA AND POPSICLES

But in 2003, Haddad complained about not receiving the same level of bonuses and pay as other pharmacy managers, who were male. She says she had agreed to serve as a pharmacy manager on a temporary basis, but ended up staying in the position for 13 months. Haddad eventually received her bonuses in two installments. Wal-Mart says that because Haddad was not officially a pharmacy manager, she was not entitled to the extra $1 per hour that such managers receive.

It was in April, 2004, that Haddad was terminated and escorted from her Wal-Mart store. According to trial materials, Haddad was dismissed for "failure to secure the pharmacy, leaving a technician alone in the pharmacy." Haddad says the statement refers to a technician's theft of a medicine for treating ulcers, called Prevacid, that took place while she was on duty 18 months before.

## EXPERT TESTIMONY

In June of 2007, Haddad got her day in court. To counter Wal-Mart's claim that Haddad was fired for failing to secure the pharmacy, attorneys Belfort and Fradette had tracked down male pharmacists from the store who had also been on duty when thefts occurred. Pharmacist Richard Blackbird, who replaced Haddad as pharmacy manager and has since left Wal-Mart, said he was never disciplined for a technician's theft of Vicodin that took place under his watch. He also said the technician left voluntarily rather than being fired.

Fradette and Belfort also called in economics and psychology experts and pointed to Haddad's performance evaluations, in which several supervisors praised her as "a huge asset to the department" and "a very reliable pharmacist" who has "done a great job keeping the department together," according to trial exhibits.

## BREAKING THE CHAIN

Wal-Mart, in its response, took issue with a number of the claims by Haddad's lawyers. The company, in court filings, denied that Haddad received "excellent reviews throughout her employment." It also denied that the termination had anything to do with Haddad's complaints, and stuck to its contention that Haddad was terminated for violating company policy by leaving a technician alone in the pharmacy.

If the ruling stands, Haddad will be entitled to $1 million in punitive damages, $95,000 in back pay, $733,307 in front pay, and $125,000 for emotional distress. The jury found Wal-Mart guilty of defamation, but did not award Haddad any money for that charge. Separately, her attorneys plan to seek legal fees from Wal-Mart.

Haddad says she brought the case to clear her name, rather than for the money. "The hard part is I have four children and each one of them has children in their class whose parents are pharmacists," says Haddad. "Now I'm just getting phone calls from people who haven't spoken to me."

Haddad, whose husband is also a pharmacist, now works at the independent Lenox Village Integrative Pharmacy in Lenox, Mass. "Kind of leery of chains," she explains with a smile.

### Questions

1. What is Cynthia Haddad's dispute with Wal-Mart?

2. What is Wal-Mart's version of what happened?

3. In the end, the difference on pay came down to $1 an hour, which Wal-Mart could easily have settled. Why do you think it chose to present its case in court?

4. What do you think the consequences of this verdict will be for Wal-Mart? Why?

*Source:* Adapted from Emily Keller, "Top News," *BusinessWeek,* June 28, 2007.

## Remade in the USA

*Sony's Comeback May Ride on Its Yankee Know-How*

Once little more than a sales and marketing arm, Sony's U.S. consumer electronics unit has become key to their worldwide turnaround efforts. At the same time, Sony's U.S. chiefs are increasingly empowered to reject products conceived in Japan that they believe won't fly stateside, including a recently introduced Walkman whose screen they deemed too small to make a dent in the U.S. against Apple Inc.'s dominant iPod. Sure, Japan remains the center of Sony's creative universe. More than 80 percent of the company's 225 designers are based there. And many products that become hits in the U.S. are still dreamed up in Sony labs across the Pacific. Yet executives in the U.S. now enjoy an unprecedented degree of influence in shaping everything from a gadget's styling to the software that makes it tick.

The American-made gizmos may prove critical to the hoped-for turnaround. The company appears to be pulling out of a nearly decade-long sales and profit slump. Consumer electronics either conceived or improved in the U.S. have helped lessen losses in other divisions, such as film and music. For the company as a whole, sales for the fiscal year that began on Apr. 1, 2007 could reach an all-time high of $75 billion, yielding an operating profit of $3.4 billion. Credit the leadership of Chairman Howard K. Stringer. The former chief of Sony Corp. of America—and the first Westerner to lead the entire company—is two years into a push to revitalize Sony and restore its reputation as the leader of the cutthroat consumer electronics business, which still accounts for nearly 70 percent of the company's revenues. One big element of his strategy is tailoring products to differing tastes across the globe.

Sony has endured a string of commercial flops in recent years, from its online music store to movie disks for the PlayStation Portable handheld. And the company that gave the world the Walkman—and as a result owned the personal audio business for years—boasts no real category-killers today. Sony's portable digital audio and video players haven't come close to the market dominance of the iPod. And the PlayStation 3 video-game console has yet to match the buzz or sales of rival machines from Microsoft Corp. and Nintendo.

Since Stringer's appointment, Sony's U.S. unit has become an important incubator for new products and services. And the early success of U.S. initiatives has prompted the company to start offering similar products elsewhere. In France and Britain, Sony is now marketing VAIO PCs with built-in cellular broadband access. That strategy, initiated in the U.S., helps boost razor-thin PC margins because Sony collects a fee from cellular carriers every time a user activates the wireless service. The Mylo, a handheld Web-browsing and text-messaging gadget aimed at teens that was designed jointly in Japan and the U.S., was recently introduced in Japan after initial American sales exceeded expectations. Now the company is deciding whether to offer the Portable Reader for digital books—a gizmo revamped extensively in the U.S.—in Europe later this year.

The U.S. center is also tweaking designs to boost the appeal of Sony products to American buyers. For retailer Target Corp., Sony's Santa Monica, California, design center created the $99 Liv music system whose wood-like trim and environment-friendly packaging is a nod to American design trends. Tim Schaaf, a 15-year Apple veteran who defected to Sony in late 2005,

replaced the clunky keyboard on the $350 Portable Reader for digital books with easy-to-understand buttons and added an MP3 player. "In Japan they have a lot of innovative ideas," says the center's director, Alex Arie. "But that doesn't mean every idea fits into the U.S. market and consumer lifestyle."

## Questions

1. What ssteps is Sony taking to tailor "products to differing tastes across the globe"?
2. Provide at least three examples of such product tailoring.
3. Why is Howard K. Stringer's appointment as chairman of Sony Corporation significant?
4. Do you think Stringer's strategy will work? Why or why not?

*Source:* Adapted from Cliff Edwards and Kenji Hall, "Global Business," *BusinessWeek* May 7, 2007.

# MANAGEMENT IN THE 21ST CENTURY

"In truth, I believe that there is no such thing as a growth industry. There are only companies organized and operated to create and capitalize on growth opportunities. Industries that assume themselves to be riding some automatic growth escalator invariably descend into stagnation."

—Theodore Leavitt

## The World of Work: Taco Barn becomes socially responsible

Tony was beginning to dread the regional meetings. Lately, every meeting produced a major policy change for the organization that usually had a direct impact on his responsibilities as a unit manager. He appreciated that the leadership team was trying to stay ahead of a very aggressive growth plan for Taco Barn in a very competitive market, but a simple meeting to review seasonal menu items once in a while wouldn't hurt, would it?

As soon as Tony walked into the conference room he realized that this meeting would be no exception—Dawn obviously had major news to share. The walls were covered with full-color posters showing fresh produce, farms, people from various countries around the world, and newspaper columns blown up to poster size on one specific topic—how businesses are becoming more socially responsible.

The meeting started 15 minutes late—probably so that folks could take the time to read the posters, thought Tony—but Dawn wasted no time in getting right to the point:

"Starting next month, we are launching a major repositioning initiative to portray Taco Barn as a more socially responsible organization. You've all seen what the competition has been doing—healthier menu choices, recyclable packaging materials, and supporting local farmers and vendors in their food purchases—and it's time that we got on the same page before these guys start to steal our customers.

## LEARNING objectives

**After studying this chapter, you will be able to:**

**1** Discuss how managers might manage in the future.

**2** Identify how technology impacts the managerial role.

**3** Review the challenges of managing a virtual team.

**4** Discuss social responsibility and organization's code of ethics.

**5** Identify laws pertaining to ethics in business.

**6** Explain social responsibility.

---

"I realize that you've all been making individual strides in this area in your own units, but we want to approach this as an organizationwide initiative to show both the sincerity of our commitment to this and the extent to which the entire organization is behind it," continued Dawn. "We're not looking for a few pet projects or public relations exercises here, guys. We want to show real creativity and innovation in approaching this issue so that we have a strong message to share with our customers and our stakeholders. The plan is to give a lot of coverage to this in our annual report next quarter, so we have to get going. Go back to your units, and get your teams involved in this. We're starting with a full social audit and we'll reconvene in two weeks to start brainstorming some ideas. Remember—full involvement from everyone in the company is expected."

On the drive back to his restaurant, Tony thought about how his team would react to this new project.

### QUESTIONS

1. What is a social audit and how is it done? Refer to page 422 for guidance on this.

2. Is Taco Barn simply following a trend here, or is there evidence that this is a real commitment on the part of the organization? Explain your answer.

3. How will these new rules impact Tony's job as a unit manager?

4. How do you think your organization (or an organization you have worked for in the past) would react to this kind of policy change?

As we saw in Chapter 2, there is little doubt that significant changes occurred in the twentieth century in all facets of American organizations and the manner in which they are managed. From a management perspective, what changes are likely to occur as we move further into the twenty-first century?

The authors of the book *Beyond Workplace 2000* made some interesting projections as to what organizations and management might look like in the twenty-first century.

- Most American companies will find that they no longer can gain a competitive advantage from further improvements in quality, service, cost, or speed, since the gap between rivals on these traditional measures of performance will all but close.

- Every American business and every employee who works for an American business will be forced to become agile, flexible, and highly adaptive, since the product or service they will provide and the business processes they will employ will be in a constant state of change.

- Every American company will be forced to develop a much better understanding of what it does truly well and will invest its limited resources in developing and sustaining superiority in that unique knowledge, skill, or capability.

- Organizational structures will become extremely fluid. No longer will there be departments, units, divisions, or functional groups in most American businesses. There will only be multi-disciplinary and multiskilled teams, and every team will be temporary.

- There will be a meltdown of the barrier between leader and follower, manager and worker. Bosses, in the traditional sense, will all but disappear. While there will be a few permanent leaders external to work and project teams, these people will act more as coordinators of team activities than as traditional leaders.[1]

Other, even more recent, projections about organizations and management in the future reinforce the central theme that future organizations will be more fluid and less rigid than in the past.[2]

Looking back on these predictions from 2008, one thing for certain is that the rate of change has continued to accelerate, and both organizations and managers will be required to adapt to these changes in the future.

This chapter identifies three key areas that will dominate the future of management in the coming years: the growth of technology, the continued rise in virtual management, and the increased focus on ethical and social responsibilities.

# THE GROWTH OF TECHNOLOGY

It wasn't that long ago that many of the phrases and terms we now take for granted were brand new in our business vocabulary. The term *cyberspace* wasn't coined until the mid 1980s, and *e-commerce* (the abbreviated form of *electronic commerce*) hasn't been around that long either—it was only as recently as 1994 that the first banner ad was placed on one of those newfangled Web sites everyone was talking about at the time.

In the two decades since the prefix *e-* started taking over our lives, technology has totally transformed our world. The world of business, and the role of a manager in business, has changed beyond all recognition. We now conduct business B2B (business to business), B2C (business to consumer), and even C2C (consumer to consumer) through electronic marketplaces such as eBay. Technology has condensed both time and space in the life of a manager:

- Complex calculations can now be processed in seconds.
- Information can be sent to multiple recipients anywhere in the world at the stroke of a computer key via electronic mail (e-mail).
- Vast amounts of information can be accessed through various search engines that can track down more data on a topic than you could ever use.
- *Google* is now a verb, even though the original selection of the name for the search engine was a spelling mistake. (The original spelling was reputed to be *googol*, a mathematical term representing $10^{100}$—1 followed by 100 zeroes—but the domain name *google.com* was available, and so an urban legend was born.)
- Bricks-and-mortar stores have been replaced by clicks-and-mortar online vendors who may never see a customer in person. The largest book vendor in the world, Amazon.com, has no retail outlets at all.

Technology has changed the way we approach the world. Even things as hands on as movie watching have found online homes. What are some other industries that are using technology in creative ways?

- Traditional vendors now devote as many resources to their Web presence as they do to their physical storefront presence.

- Cell phones and PDAs now carry more functionality than a room full of computers, and if the law attributed to Intel cofounder Gordon Moore holds true, the computing capacity of integrated circuits will continue to double every two years (more commonly quoted as 18 months) for the foreseeable future.

---

## PROGRESS CHECK QUESTIONS

1. Define the term *cyberspace*.
2. What is electronic commerce?
3. What is Moore's law, and who was Moore?
4. Explain the terms B2B, B2C, and C2C.

---

In the workplace, technology has pushed the development of management processes built around information rather than raw materials. One example of an information management process is enterprise resource planning (ERP), which involves the interconnection of all the functional departments of an organization on one common framework. It is designed to give everyone in the organization instant access to the information they need to make key decisions in managing the organization's efficient performance. Developed from materials resource planning (the management of raw materials through a production process), ERP offers the promise of improved efficiency through the deliberate elimination of waste and rework. With current and accurate data available for all key decision points, the company is no longer required to commit significant resources based on projections—now it can use hard data.

For customers, ERP technology has advanced into customer relationship management (CRM) technology, which promised the capacity for organizations to track every interaction, or , 'touch point' with their customers and for customers to know the whereabouts of their order in the manufacturing and/or delivery process at any time, in real time. As a car buyer ordering a custom combination of colors, materials, and features, CRM offers the ability to log on and see exactly where your car is on the assembly line—definitely an impressive feat of technical wizardry, but questionable as to the payoff for what has amounted to a significant investment in hardware and software for the company to deliver that service.

# VIRTUAL MANAGEMENT

Technological advancement has produced a business environment in which the traditional organizational framework of functional departments dispersed by geographic location has been replaced by a complex network of suppliers, partners and collaborators that interact in the delivery of the organizations products and/or services from vast distances over an electronic platform. For managers, this presents a unique set of challenges:

1. How do you manage a team that may be spread across 50 states or 20 countries?
2. The technology may be there to support conference calls or "webinars" or videoconferences, but how do you build a team when the team members never meet in person?
3. Outsourcing offers tremendous cost savings when you take advantage of lower labor costs in other countries, but how much of your proprietary information are you willing to share with this new partner in order to make the new relationship work?
4. If your company has grown on the basis of a high-quality product that you designed and manufactured in house and you must now transfer that production overseas in order to maintain your profit margins, how do you know you can maintain that quality while working through a third-party vendor?

As we learned in Chapter 8, a virtual organization is one in which business partners and teams work together across geographic or organizational boundaries by means of information technology.[3] In a virtual organization, co-workers often do not see each other on a regular basis, if ever. Figure 14.1 illustrates a basic type of virtual organization.

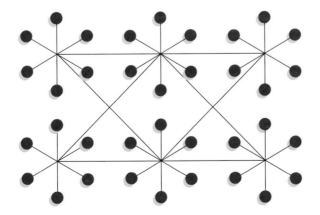

## figure 14.1

**VIRTUAL ORGANIZATION**

**figure 14.2**

**BENEFITS AND
CHALLENGES OF
TRANSFORMING
TO A VIRTUAL
ORGANIZATION**

*Sources:* Maggie Biggs,
"Tomorrow's Workforce," *Infoworld,*
September 18, 2000, p. 59; and
Sonny Ariss, Nick Nykodym, and
Aimee A. Cole-Laramore, "Trust
and Technology in the Virtual
Organization," *S.A.M. Advanced
Management Journal,* Autumn
2002, pp. 22–25.

| BENEFITS | CHALLENGES |
|---|---|
| Increases productivity. | Leaders must move from a control model to a trust method. |
| Decreases the cost of doing business. | New forms of communication and collaboration will be required. |
| Provides the ability to hire the best talent regardless of location. | Management must enable a learning culture and be willing to change. |
| Allows you to quickly solve problems by forming dynamic teams. | Staff re-education may be required. |
| Allows you to more easily leverage both static and dynamic staff. | It can be difficult to monitor employee behavior. |
| Improves the work environment. | |
| Provides better balance for professional and personal lives. | |
| Provides competitive advantage. | |

Technology has played a central role in allowing virtual organizations to form, and with each advancement in technological sophistication, the potential for more complex virtual organizations becomes achievable. The project-based organizations that were formed and disbanded according to the length of the project that brought them into existence have now been replaced by organizations that are designed to be *virtual* on a permanent basis. Shared server technology allows offices on opposite sides of the globe to work on the same document, often simultaneously, and the advances in web technology and video conferencing now make business trips an expensive luxury rather than a necessity. Product and functional specialists can now be accessed from anywhere in the world on a part-time or contract basis, without the need to hire them as full-time employees and relocate them to the office where their services are needed most. As outlined in Figure 14.2, virtual organizations have many potential benefits and challenges. How many of those challenges do you think can be addressed by advances in technology now or in the future?

## PROGRESS CHECK QUESTIONS

5. What is a virtual organization?
6. What are some of the challenges managers face in a virtual organization?
7. What are the three common types of virtual organizations?
8. Can the technology of videoconferences replace the human interaction of meeting with stakeholders in person? Why or why not?

## Virtual Organization Creates Virtual Convention

The Real Estate Cyberspace Society (RECS) (www.recyber. com) was founded in 1996 in Boston as a completely, virtual organization. The for-profit society developed a system for delivering audiotapes and newsletters to help real estate professionals who were interested in using technology and the Internet to improve their businesses. After September 11, 2001, the society's staff accurately predicted that member and exhibitor participation would decline at traditional in-person events. Leveraging its online experiences, the society's leaders decided to produce an online convention in April 2002. The event was highly successful with some 22,000 real-estate professionals attending across five days. The attendees registered for the convention, listened to speakers, networked, and visited exhibitor booths—all online.

In April 2004, the convention was extended from five to seven days and 42,000 real-estate professionals attended. During the seven days of the convention, participants could go to the exposition and view the exhibits at any time and have live chats with exhibitors. Each day four national speakers were showcased. Attendees could listen to these speakers and print out their handouts at any time during the scheduled 24-hour day. The convention also featured three keynote speakers. Participants unable to attend the keynote sessions live could retrieve slides, hear the talk, and get the handouts online at their own convenience.

### Questions

1. How is it possible to attend an entire convention online?

2. Visit the Real Estate Cyberspace Society (RECS) at www.recyber.com. How has the organization of the convention changed since it was first created?

3. What are the four key advantages that RECS offers to its members?

4. Would you attend an online convention in your industry? Why or why not?

*Source:* John M. Peckham III, "Virtual Society, Virtual Convention," *Association Management*, December 2004, p. 55.

# ETHICS AND SOCIAL RESPONSIBILITY

Individuals make personal decisions about what they believe is right or wrong. These decisions are based on their ethics. **Ethics** are a set of moral principles or values that govern behavior. All individuals develop their own set of ethical rules, which help them decide how to behave in different situations.

Like individuals, businesses develop ethics to help them determine how to behave. These ethics reflect a company's beliefs about what actions are appropriate and fair among people.

The role of ethics in management decisions is difficult. Management issues often are emotionally charged, and many types of ethical problems may arise in business situations. What should managers do if they are aware of unethical practices in their businesses? Should they blow the whistle and risk their jobs? Should they quit and allow unethical practices to continue? Should they ignore the practices? These are only a few of the difficult ethical decisions managers face.[6]

> **ethics**
> A set of moral principles or values that govern behavior.

# CODES OF ETHICS

To help managers know how to respond ethically to different business situations, many companies have developed codes of ethics. A **code of ethics** is a document that outlines the principles of conduct to be used in making decisions within an organization. Most corporations in the United States have codes of ethics.

## Content of Ethical Codes

Codes of ethics are formal documents that are shared with all employees. Some of the areas they cover include the following:

- Honesty.
- Adherence to the law.
- Product safety and quality.
- Health and safety in the workplace.
- Conflicts of interest.
- Employment practices.
- Selling and marketing practices.
- Financial reporting.
- Pricing, billing, and contracting.
- Trading in securities and using confidential information.
- Acquiring and using information about competitors.
- Security.
- Payments to obtain business.
- Political activities.
- Protection of the environment.

Merely establishing a code of ethics does not prevent unethical behavior. To be effective, codes of ethics must be enforced. In fact, ethical codes that are not enforced probably do more harm than good. For this reason, it is important that companies discipline employees who violate their codes of ethics.

## Behaving Ethically

Businesspeople regularly make ethical decisions. These decisions have important consequences for both individuals and their companies. Behaving unethically can hurt, or even end, a businessperson's career. It can cause a company to lose millions of dollars or even go out of business altogether. Behaving ethically helps employees gain the trust of the people with whom they work. It can also help businesses gain the trust of customers, suppliers, and others.

## Behaving Honestly

In many situations, the ethical course of action is clear-cut. Ethical employees never steal from their employers. They never lie about the hours they work. They never falsify documents. Employees who engage in any of these actions threaten their careers. They also risk causing severe damage to their employers.

### Employee Theft

Employers trust their employees not to steal from them. Employees who behave ethically do not violate that trust.

Dishonest employees steal from their employers in a variety of ways. Some embezzle money or steal supplies or inventory from their employers. Some accept bribes from people who want to do business with their company. Others submit false expense accounts.

### Lying about Hours Worked

Employees who behave ethically are honest about the hours they work. Employees who work at home, for example, accurately report how long they work. They do not take advantage of the fact that their managers cannot check to see if they are actually at their desks.

Ethical employees also show up at work unless they are ill or need to be away from their jobs for a legitimate reason. They do not pretend to be sick in order to stay home when they should be at work.

### Falsifying Records

One of the worst ethical lapses an employee can commit is falsifying records. This can cause very grave damage to a company's reputation. It can even cause people to become ill or die. A manager at a pharmaceutical company, for example, who falsifies records documenting the side effects of the drugs the company produces can cause people who take the drug to die. A production supervisor who falsifies documents to indicate that computer parts were checked can cause his company to sell defective products. Years of excellent corporate performance can be wiped out by these kinds of unethical actions.

## Dealing with Ethical Dilemmas

Ethical dilemmas are situations in which the ethical course of action is not clear. Such situations arise regularly in the business world. Consider the following examples:

Many employees don't realize it, but surfing the Internet or taking care of personal matters during business hours is a form of employee theft. How would a good manager strike a balance between facilitating employee needs and maintaining a productive work environment?

## figure 14.3

**SOLVING ETHICAL DILEMMAS**

*Source:* L. Nash, "Ethics without the Sermon," *Harvard Business Review* 59 (1981), p. 78.

1. Have you defined the problem accurately?
2. How would you define the problem if you stood on the other side of the fence?
3. Whom could your decision or action injure? Can you discuss the problem with the affected parties before you make your decision?
4. Are you confident that your position will be as valid over a long period of time as it seems now?
5. Could you disclose without qualm your decision or action to your boss, your CEO, the board of directors, your family, and society as a whole?

1. Your boss informs you confidentially that one of your friends is going to be fired. Your friend is about to buy a house. Should you warn your friend that he is about to be fired, even though you promised your boss that you would not?

2. Your colleague has been violating your company's code of ethics by accepting expensive gifts from a salesperson who does business with your company. Should you notify your supervisor?

3. One of your employees has not been performing her job properly. You know that she has been having serious personal problems, and you have tried to be understanding. However, your entire staff is suffering because of poor performance by this key team member. What should you do?

One way of approaching ethical dilemmas like these is to answer the series of questions shown in Figure 14.3. Talking to people you trust can also help you develop solutions to ethical problems. Figure 14.4 explains some of the ethical problems in business.

## figure 14.4

**ETHICAL PROBLEMS IN THE BUSINESS WORLD**

Having a code of ethics and a personal sense of what is right and wrong can help business managers choose the right course of action.

**1. Normal Interactions between Business Acquaintances**

Many interactions between people doing business together are considered a normal part of doing business. Managers often take clients out to lunch or invite them to play golf, for example. These kinds of interactions help businesspeople get to know each other.

**2. Questionable Interactions between Business Acquaintances**

Some interactions between business acquaintances are questionable. A manager who sends a client an expensive gift, for example, could be seen as trying to bribe the client into doing business with his or her company. Businesses often provide their employees with guidelines on the types of gifts they consider acceptable.

**3. Illegal Interactions between Business Acquaintances**

Paying bribes to attract business is unethical and illegal. Managers who engage in this kind of activity could face legal action and go to jail.

# LAWS RELATING TO ETHICS IN BUSINESS

Over the years, various laws have been enacted that directly relate to the issue of ethics in business. These laws apply to competitive behavior, corporate governance, consumer protection, and environmental protection.

## Competitive Behavior

Since the late nineteenth century the federal government has regulated companies to make sure that they do not engage in anticompetitive behavior. All companies operating in the United States must abide by these laws. Enforcement of these laws is handled by the Antitrust Division of the Justice Department and by the Federal Trade Commission.

### The Sherman Act

As you learned in Chapter 2, the Sherman Antitrust Act of 1890 makes it illegal for companies to monopolize trade. Under the law, mergers can be prohibited if the new company that results from the merger will control too large a share of the market. The purpose of the law is to ensure that companies remain able to compete fairly.

### The Clayton Act

The Clayton Act of 1914 makes it illegal to charge different prices to different wholesale customers. This means that a manufacturer of steel, for example, cannot charge one price to General Motors and another price to Chrysler.

The Clayton Act also bans the practice of requiring a customer to purchase a second good. Manufacturers of computer hardware, for example, cannot require customers to purchase software as well.

### The Wheeler-Lea Act

The Wheeler-Lea Act of 1938 bans unfair or deceptive acts or practices, including false advertising. Under the act, businesses must inform consumers of possible negative consequences of using their products. Labeling of cigarette packages is an example of the kind of disclosure required by the Wheeler-Lea Act.

---

**Winning Resumes . . . It's All About You!!**

Writing a resume can be a strange exercise when first done because often times we are not use to describing ourselves, our job experiences, our education, and our accomplishments. However, writing a resume is indeed all about you and the more there is to write about, the more a potential company can learn about you and the unique reasons they might hire you over other potential job candidates.

When writing your resume, companies that are hiring new employees are looking for goal orientated, leader-driven individuals who can be responsible and be good examples of their company with good upside for further training and development. Does this look like you?

Begin now to see where you have made accomplishments in your career and how that translates into desired skills for perspective companies you would like to work for. Remember, winning resumes are the ones that show the perspective employer who you really are and how that translates to a smart hire for them!

## Corporate Governance

The Public Company Accounting Reform and Investor Protection Act (Sarbanes-Oxley Act) was passed in 2002. The act is commonly abbreviated *SOX*. SOX includes requirements for auditor independence, restriction on firms engaging accounting firms for both auditing and consulting services, independence of firms' board committees, management's assessment of internal controls, and personal certification of financial reports by firms' CEOs and CFOs. Retaliation for whistle-blowing and altering or destroying documents to impede a federal investigation is generally illegal. Under SOX, employees can file complaints with the Occupational Safety and Health Administration (OSHA) if they have been retaliated against by their employer for reporting suspected corporate fraud or other activities related to fraud against shareholders.

### PROGRESS CHECK QUESTIONS

9. What are ethics?
10. What is a code of ethics?
11. Does establishing a code of ethics prevent unethical behavior? Why or why not?
12. What is an ethical dilemma, and what challenges does it prevent in a business environment?

## Consumer Protection

Several laws protect consumers in the United States against unethical and unsafe business practices. These laws cover food and drugs, other manufactured products, and loans.

### Food and Drugs

The Federal Food, Drug, and Cosmetic Act of 1938 bans the sale of impure, improperly labeled, falsely guaranteed, and unhealthful foods, drugs, and cosmetics. The law is enforced by the Food and Drug Administration (FDA), which has the power to force manufacturers to stop selling products it considers unsafe.

### Consumer Products

The Consumer Product Safety Commission (CPSC) was established in 1972. It establishes minimum product safety standards on consumer products. If a product is found to be defective, the Consumer Product Safety

Commission has the authority to force the manufacturer to recall the product. For example, in 1999 the CPSC recalled a quarter of a million Nike water bottles. The bottles were recalled because the cap was not attached properly, possibly causing users to choke.

### Loans

A series of laws protects U.S. consumers against unfair lending practices. Under the Truth in Lending Act of 1968, creditors are required to let consumers know how much they are paying in finance charges and interest. The Equal Credit Opportunity Act of 1975 prohibits creditors from making credit decisions on the basis of discriminatory practices.

Several companies, including Purina, were forced to recall massive amounts of pet food when one of their suppliers, Menu Foods, produced tainted foods. In this case, the recall was voluntary. Is there ever an instance in which not recalling a tainted product would be an acceptable practice?

## Environmental Protection

Since the late 1960s, environmental protection has been an important social and economic issue in the United States. This concern has been reflected in the many laws designed to protect the environment.

### The National Environmental Policy Act of 1969

The key piece of legislation in environmental protection is the National Environmental Policy Act of 1969. This law created the Environmental Protection Agency (EPA), whose mission is to protect human health and safeguard the air, water, and land.

Since 1969, many environmental laws affecting businesses have been passed. These laws include the Clean Air Act, the Toxic Substances Control Act, and the Clean Water Act. All these laws are enforced by the EPA.

### The Clean Air Act of 1970

The Clean Air Act of 1970 is the comprehensive federal law that regulates air emissions. The original act set maximum air pollution standards for each of the 50 states. In 1990, the act was amended to deal with problems of acid rain, ground-level ozone, stratospheric ozone depletion, and toxic substances in the air.

### The Toxic Substances Control Act of 1976

The Toxic Substances Control Act of 1976 was enacted to give the EPA the ability to track the 75,000 industrial chemicals currently produced in or imported into the United States. The EPA screens these chemicals and can require reporting or testing of those that may pose an environmental or human health hazard.

### The Clean Water Act of 1977

The Clean Water Act of 1977 gives the EPA the authority to set standards on the type and quantity of pollutants that industries can put into bodies of water. The law makes it illegal to discharge any pollutant into navigable waters unless a permit is obtained.

## Ethical Standards and Culture

Standards of business ethics differ around the world. This means that business practices that are acceptable in one country may be considered unethical in others.

Business managers working in foreign countries must be aware of these different ethical standards. They must set guidelines for their companies on how to operate both within their own culture and in other cultures.

## Corporate Gift Giving

Gift-giving customs differ around the world. In some cultures, gifts are expected; failure to present them is considered an insult. In Japan, for example, lavish gift giving is an important part of doing business. Gifts are usually exchanged at the first meeting.

In the United States, government officials are not allowed to accept expensive gifts from businesses. Regardless of local practices, American managers operating abroad must abide by the standards set in the United States.

## Intellectual Property

**intellectual property**
Ownership of ideas such as inventions, books, movies, and computer programs gives creators of the intellectual property the exclusive right to market and sell their work.

**Intellectual property** refers to ownership of ideas, such as inventions, books, movies, and computer programs. In many countries, including the United States, creators of intellectual property have the exclusive right to market and sell their work. These rights are guaranteed through patent, trademark, and copyright laws. These types of protection ensure that only the creators of intellectual property profit from their work.

Intellectual property protection is very important to business. Without such laws, a computer company could market a best-selling game created by another computer company. A pharmaceutical company could manufacture and sell drugs developed by another drug company.

Although the United States has tough laws governing intellectual property, enforcing those laws is a problem, particularly in the software industry. In 1999, the Justice Department, the FBI, and the Customs Service began cracking down on piracy and counterfeiting of computer software and other products in the United States.

Rules concerning intellectual property rights differ in some countries. In China and India, for example, the government does not enforce such rights. As a result, some Chinese companies copy and sell foreign computer programs. Some publishers in India reprint foreign textbooks, selling them as if they had published them themselves. In the United

States, someone who engages in this practice is guilty of plagiarism and can be sued in a court of law.

# SOCIAL RESPONSIBILITY

**Social Responsibility** refers to the obligation that individuals or businesses have to help solve social problems. Most companies in the United States feel some sense of social responsibility.[7]

Businesses' concept of their role in society has changed dramatically over the past century. Views toward social responsibility evolved through three distinct schools of thought: profit maximization, trusteeship management, and social involvement.

> **social responsibility**
> The obligation that individuals or businesses have to help solve social problems.

## Profit Maximization

In the nineteenth and early twentieth centuries, business owners in the United States believed that their role was simply to maximize the profits their companies earned. Dealing with social problems was not considered a legitimate business activity.

> **stakeholders**
> The people—employees, customers, suppliers, and the community—who are affected by the actions of a business.

## Trusteeship Management

Thinking about the role of business changed in the 1920s and 1930s, when a philosophy known as *trusteeship management* became popular. This philosophy recognized that owners of businesses had obligations to do more than just earn profits. They also had obligations to their employees, their customers, and their creditors. Most businesspeople continued to hold this view until the 1960s.

## Social Involvement

During the 1960s, many people began to believe that corporations should use their influence and financial resources to address social problems. They believed corporations should help solve problems such as poverty, crime, environmental destruction, and illiteracy.

According to this view, businesses should be responsible corporate citizens, not just maximizers of profit. Businesses have obligations to all the people affected by their actions, known as stakeholders. **Stakeholders** include a company's employees, customers, suppliers, and the community.

## Study Skills

### Keep a Journal!

The more productive way to improve your learning habits and see the necessary methods to make personal changes for improvement is to keep a journal!

What is required to keep a journal? When do I use it and how often do I write in it are all questions that you might have regarding this personal learning and life-changing skill.

A notebook and a pen, or a word document on your computer are all that's required to get started. How often you write & what you write about is up to you. You can start with your thoughts about your day and as you become more comfortable with putting your thoughts on paper (or on screen) you will begin to learn more & more about yourself.

The benefits of keeping a journal are many and the payoff can have dramatic results! Start your journal soon! You do not want to miss the story that unfolds!

*Idol Gives Back* took charity to a whole new level. The television program partnered with several mainstream companies, including Allstate and ExxonMobil, to raise more than $75 million in charitable funds. How can this example of corporate social responsibility be applied on a more local scale?

Since the 1960s, corporations have increasingly demonstrated their commitment to social change. One example of this commitment is the increased diversity in the workplace. Over the past 45 years, most corporations have made efforts to diversify their workforces by hiring and promoting more women and minorities. Many businesses also have established workshops to help their employees understand people from different backgrounds.

## Measuring Social Responsibility

Corporations demonstrate their sense of social responsibility in various ways. Performance in each of these areas is measured as part of a social audit.

### Philanthropy and Volunteerism

One way a company demonstrates its sense of social responsibility is by contributing time and money to charitable, cultural, and civic organizations. Corporate philanthropy, or efforts to improve human welfare, can take many forms. Computer giant Compaq (now merged with Hewlett-Packard), for example, provides technology, product, and cash contributions to organizations throughout the United States. It also has planted seedlings in Australia, supported an institute for people with disabilities in India, and refurbished a school in Brazil. All these activities reflect the company's sense of social responsibility.

Some companies grant employees paid time off to participate in charitable activities. Many high-tech companies, for example, allow their employees to volunteer for the U.S. Tech Corps, which sends employees from technology companies to work in public schools. Other corporations allow employees time off to donate blood, participate in food and clothing drives, or raise money for such causes as the United Way.

Many corporations also donate money by matching charitable donations made by their employees. In this way companies both encourage employee giving and make their own contributions to philanthropic causes.

### Environmental Awareness

Another way companies demonstrate their sense of social responsibility is by limiting the damage their operations cause to the environment. They do so by creating production processes that are as environmentally friendly as possible.

Businesses also can affect the environment by establishing policies that reduce pollution. Encouraging employees to carpool, for example, reduces toxic emissions and conserves gasoline. Using biodegradable products also helps protect the environment.

You are the line manager for a team of people in your company in the finance sector. One of your key staff members is excellent at her job and is known for her ability to generate a high amount of income for the company—none of your other staff members comes close to her in terms of this.

You are aware that your company's competitors have made attempts to head hunt this staff member, which she has so far rejected, much to your relief as your department is heavily reliant upon her abilities and you are paid bonuses based on your department's profitability.

However, you are certain that this staff member is submitting fraudulent expense claims, sometimes several hundred or even thousands of dollars more than she has actually spent—a tiny fraction of the profits she is generating, but fraudulent nonetheless.

1. Should the high amount of income this staff member generates for the company justify looking the other way over these fraudulent expense claims? Why or why not?

2. What would your action be if she weren't such a star performer? Why?

3. How would you go about bringing this to the attention of your boss?

4. Do you think the company would terminate this employee? Why or why not?

**Source:** Adapted from St. James Ethics Centre, "Ethical Dilemmas: How Much Should Valuable People Get Away with Things?" www.ethics.org.au.

### Sensitivity to Diversity and Quality of Work Life

One of the most important ways a company can demonstrate its sense of social responsibility is through its workforce. Socially responsible businesses maintain ethnically diverse workforces that reflect the societies in which they operate. McDonald's, for example, has created a diverse work environment. At least 70 percent of McDonald's restaurant management and 25 percent of the company executives are minorities and women.

Companies also can demonstrate their social responsibility by adopting policies that contribute to the quality of life of their workers. Flexible work hours, for example, allow workers to better meet family needs. On-site day care centers make life easier for employees with young children.

## Actions Necessary to Implement Social Responsibility

The biggest obstacle to organizations assuming more social responsibility is pressure by financial analysts and stockholders who push for steady increases in earnings per share on a quarterly basis. Concern about immediate profits makes it difficult to invest in areas that cannot be accurately measured and still have returns that are long run in nature. Furthermore, pressure for short-term earnings affects corporate social behavior; most companies are geared toward short-term profit goals. Budgets, objectives, and performance evaluations are often based on short-run considerations. Management may state a willingness to lose some short-term profit to achieve social objectives. However, managers who sacrifice profit and seek to justify these actions on the basis of corporate social goals may find stockholders unsympathetic.

Organizations should also carefully examine their cherished values and short-run profits to ensure that these concepts are in tune with the values held by society. This should be a constant process, because the values society holds are ever-changing.

Organizations should reevaluate their long-range planning and decision-making processes to ensure that they fully understand the potential social consequences. Plant location decisions are no longer merely economic matters. Environmental impact and job opportunities for disadvantaged groups are examples of other factors to consider.

Organizations should seek to aid both governmental agencies and voluntary agencies in their social efforts. This should include technical and managerial help as well as monetary support. Technological knowledge, organizational skills, and managerial competence can all be applied to solving social problems.

Organizations should look at ways to help solve social problems through their own businesses. Many social problems stem from the economic deprivation of a fairly large segment of our society. Attacking this problem could be the greatest social effort of organizations.

Another major area in which businesses are active is corporate philanthropy. Corporate philanthropy involves donations of money, property, or work by organizations to socially useful purposes. Many companies have directed their philanthropic efforts toward education, the arts, and the United Way. Contributions can be made directly by the company, or a company foundation can be created to handle the philanthropic program.

## Conducting a Social Audit

**social audit**

A method used by management to evaluate the success or lack of success of programs designed to improve the social performance of the organization.

One method of measuring the success of a firm is to conduct a social audit. A **social audit** allows management to evaluate the success or lack of success of programs designed to improve the social performance of the organization. Rather than looking exclusively at economic and financial measures, the social audit can be a beginning point for encouraging environmental and social strategies that really work.

One suggested method for accomplishing the social audit and reacting to the information includes the following steps:

1. Examine social expectations, sensitivity, and past responses.
2. Examine and then set social objectives and meaningful priorities.
3. Plan and implement strategies and objectives in each program area.
4. Set budgets for resources necessary for social action and make a commitment to acquire them.
5. Monitor accomplishments or progress in each program area.

To ensure that stockholders, stakeholders, and the general public know about the commitment and accomplishments of social programs,

## Shameless Exploitation in Pursuit of the Common Good

Newman's Own was supposed to be a tiny boutique operation—parchment labels on elegant wine bottles of antique glass. We expected train wrecks along the way and got, instead, one astonishment followed by another astonishment followed by another. . . . A lot of the time we thought we were in first gear we were really in reverse, but it didn't seem to make any difference. We anticipated sales of $1,200 a year and a loss, despite our gambling winnings, of $6,000. But in these twenty years we have earned over $175 million, which we've given to countless charities. How to account for this massive success? Pure luck? Transcendental meditation? Machiavellian manipulation? Aerodynamics? High colonics? We haven't the slightest idea.

In 1978, Paul Newman and A.E. Hotchner decided that rather than just distribute Paul's own salad dressing at Christmas to neighbors, they would offer it to a few local stores. Freewheeling, irreverent entrepreneurs, they conceived of their venture as a great way to poke fun at the mundane method of traditional marketing. Much to their surprise, the dressing was enthusiastically received. What had started as a lark quickly escalated into a full-fledged business, the first company to place all-natural foods in supermarkets. From salad dressing to spaghetti sauce, to popcorn, and lemonade, Newman's Own became a major player in the food business. The company's profits were originally donated to medical research, education, and the environment, and eventually went to the creation of the eight Hole in the Wall Gang camps for children with serious illnesses, serving over 13,000 children per year.

### Questions

1. What makes Newman's Own such a positive example of corporate social responsibility?

2. What other products are now included in the Newman's Own line?

3. If the organization used only all-natural ingredients and did not donate their after-tax profits to charity, would they still be held in such high regard? Why or why not?

4. Provide an example of something that your organization (or an organization you have worked for in the past) could do to be more socially responsible. Explain your answer.

*Source:* www.newmansown.com; and P. Newman and A. E. Hotchner, *Shameless Exploitation in Pursuit of the Common Good: The Madcap Business Adventure by the truly Oddest Couple* (New York: Random House, 2003).

most large corporations publish their successes in their annual reports. These firms make social responsibility an integral part of their mission statements. True commitment goes beyond the self-serving and selective nature of public relations. Most experts agree that socially responsible firms will eventually be rewarded by their markets and stakeholders.

## PROGRESS CHECK QUESTIONS

13. What is social responsibility?

14. What are the three schools of thought from which social responsibility was developed?

15. Explain the terms *philanthropy* and *volunteerism*.

16. List the five steps of a social audit.

# It costs money to be socially responsible

The social audit of Taco Barn operations revealed that the company was more involved in socially responsible activities than most people thought. The company was an active recycler at every restaurant and at the regional and national headquarters. Donation of surplus food to community food banks was widespread and well coordinated. The company kept track of how many pounds of food were being donated and how many meals were being provided to the homeless based on those donations.

Opportunities for improvement were identified in the area of stakeholder relationships—both in how Taco Barn worked with its suppliers on building its socially responsible message into every aspect of the company's operation and in how the company supported the local business community in purchasing supplies from local vendors.

On these issues Dawn chose to look to the unit managers, including Tony, for ideas on how they could get more involved in their local communities. On the weekly conference calls that took place between the regional meetings, several of Tony's fellow unit managers had raised concerns about the impact of this new policy on their profit margins:

"It's going to cost me real money to be socially responsible—buying local produce in smaller quantities is going to cost a lot more than getting it from our wholesaler. Are our customers really going to care where we buy our tomatoes?"

Tony had already made up his mind on that question, and the answer was a definite yes! When he had reviewed this new initiative at his staff meeting, the response from his people had been overwhelming. The younger crew members were thrilled and many commented that "it was about time." The older crew members also spoke up about how much their lives were going to improve now that they could give straight answers to customers who asked that very question: Where did Taco Barn buy its tomatoes? Was it from a local farm, or were they shipped in? What else did they buy locally?

The only concern they expressed was whether or not the company was making a serious commitment here or was it just a short-term initiative? Tony had asked the same question of Dawn Williams and his mentor Jerry Smith, and he had been happy with the response he received from them:

"Tony, it's a whole new business world out there. Our customers are expecting more from us, and we fully intend to deliver on those expectations."

## QUESTIONS

1. Are the unit managers' concerns about increased costs valid? Why or why not?

2. How do you think Tony's crew members would react if the company did go back on this new commitment to social responsibility?

3. What options does Taco Barn have in managing the increase in costs from this new initiative?

4. Based on the information shared in this case, do you think Taco Barn will follow through on all these commitments? Why or why not?

# CONCLUSION

How many years do you have to serve before you can be considered to be an experienced or *veteran* manager? If you had asked that question as recently as ten years ago, you would have received an answer that required you to think in decades rather than years. Today, the pace of change in business has become so fast that managers can look at their organizations and see dramatic changes occurring in months as opposed to years. Managers now consider themselves to be veterans after surviving a new product implementation, a company-wide layoff, or the ever-popular merger with a former competitor. New products and new divisions can appear and old divisions can disappear in the blink of an eye. Just when you think you have the competition on the run, they come up with a new product that puts them years ahead of you in the marketplace, or, even worse, a new competitor shows up with a product that makes your best-selling product obsolete! Welcome to management in the 21st century. The breakneck pace of change will make your head spin, but if you can rise to the challenge and grasp every opportunity to deliver inventive solutions with the help of a motivated and creative team of people who look to you for guidance and leadership, I can guarantee that you will never be bored!

## key terms

**code of ethics**  412       **intellectual property**  418       **social responsibility**  419
**ethics**  411                 **social audit**  422                  **stakeholders**  419

## review questions

1. How has technological growth impacted the role of a manager?
2. What are the challenges involved in running a virtual business?
3. Identify the laws that deal with ethical issues in business.
4. What are the three ways in which corporations can demonstrate a sense of social responsibility?

## internet exercise

1. Locate the Web site of Business for Social Responsibility (BSR). What is the stated mission of BSR? What does BSR do? List four benefits that BSR claims that corporations can achieve through its corporate social responsibility (CSR) programs? List four well-known companies that are members of BSR.

2. Locate the Web site of IdealsWork. What is the goal of the Ideals-Work organization? What services does the organization offer? How does the mission of the BSR differ from that of IdealsWork?

3. Locate the Web site of Corporate Social Responsibility newswire (CSRWire). What does CSRWire do? List four CSRWire members, and explain the services they receive from CSRWire. Find the CSRWire events page, and identify the next scheduled event. Briefly summarize the location and planned agenda for the event. If the event has a Web site, visit the site and record the name of one of the keynote speakers.

*Source:* A. Ghillyer, *Business Ethics: A Real World Approach,* (New York: McGraw-Hill, 2007), p. 71.

## team exercise

### WHERE DO YOU STAND?

Divide the class into groups (a maximum of six), and have each group select one of the following situations. Decide how you would respond. Be prepared to justify your position in a class discussion and to share how you arrived at your decision.

### Situation 1: Family versus Ethics

Jim, a 56-year-old middle manager with children in college, discovers that the owners of his company are cheating the government out of several thousand dollars a year in taxes. Jim is the only employee in a position to know this. Should Jim report the owners to the Internal Revenue Service at the risk of endangering his own livelihood, or should he disregard the discovery to protect his family's livelihood?

### Situation 2: The Roundabout Raise

When Joe asks for a raise, his boss praises his work but says the company's rigid budget won't allow any further merit raises for the time being. Instead, the boss suggests the company "won't look too closely at your expense accounts for a while." Should Joe take this as authorization to pad his expense account because he is simply getting the money he deserves through a different route, or should he not take this roundabout "raise"?

### Situation 3: The Faked Degree

Bill has done a sound job for over a year; he got the job by claiming to have a college degree. Bill's boss learns Bill actually never graduated. Should his boss dismiss him for a false résumé? Should he overlook the false claim, since Bill is otherwise conscientious and honorable and dismissal might ruin Bill's career?

### Situation 4: Sneaking Phone Calls

Helen discovers that a co-worker makes about $100 a month in personal long-distance telephone calls from an office telephone. Should Helen report the employee or disregard the calls, since many people make personal calls at the office?

### Situation 5: Cover-Up Temptation

José discovers that the chemical plant he manages is creating slightly more water pollution in a nearby lake than is legally permitted. Revealing the problem will bring negative publicity to the plant, hurt the lakeside town's resort business, and scare the community. Solving the problem will cost the company well over $100,000. It is unlikely that outsiders will discover the problem. The violation poses no danger whatever to people; at most, it will endanger a small number of fish. Should José reveal the problem despite the cost to his company, or should he consider the problem as a mere technicality and disregard it?

### Situation 6: Actual Salary

Dorothy finds out that the best-qualified candidate for a job really earned only $18,000 a year in his last job, not the $28,000 he claimed. Should Dorothy hire the candidate anyway, or should she choose someone considerably less qualified?

## Outsourcing: Beyond Bangalore

*Companies Are Increasingly Sending IT Work to Hubs outside India. They're Saving Money but Facing a Whole New Raft of Challenges*

After 10 months of working with software developers in Bangalore, India, Bill Wood was ready to call it quits. The local engineers would start a project, get a few months' experience, and then bolt for greener pastures, says the U.S.-based executive. Attrition rose to such a high level that year that Wood's company had to replace its entire staff, some positions more than once. "It did not work well at all," recalls Wood, vice-president of engineering at Ping Identity, a

to 14 percent a year, turnover is increasing, and an influx of workers is straining city resources. Even Indian outsourcing pioneers Tata Consultancy Services, Wipro Technologies, and Infosys Technologies, which have helped foreign companies shift software development and other IT operations to Bangalore, are starting to expand into smaller Indian cities, as well as China. "Overall, in terms of productivity and quality of life, beyond Bangalore is better," says

maker of Internet security software for corporations. Frustrated, Wood began searching for a partner outside India. He scoured 15 companies in 8 different countries, including Russia, Mexico, Argentina, and Vietnam.

That path is being trod by a lot of executives, eager for new sources of low-cost, high-tech talent outside India. Many are fed up with the outsourcing hub of Bangalore, where salaries for info tech staff are growing at 12 percent

Wipro Chief Information Officer Laxman Badiga. "Bangalore is getting more crowded, and the real infrastructure is getting stretched."

### THE SEARCH FOR LOWER COSTS

Make no mistake: India remains an IT outsourcing powerhouse, with $17.7 billion in software and IT services exports in 2005, compared with $3.6 billion for China and $1 billion for Russia, according to trade organizations in each country. And India's outsourcing industry is still growing at a faster pace than that of Russia and other wannabe Bangalores.

Yet many companies can't resist the lure of cheaper labor. "Ninety percent of all outsourcing deals in the market today have been structured around cost improvement only," says Linda Cohen, vice-president of sourcing research at consulting firm Gartner. By the third year of an outsourcing deal, after all the costs have been squeezed out, companies get antsy to find a new locale with an even lower overhead.

But moving IT operations into developing countries like Vietnam or China can also pose big risks, such as insurmountable language and cultural differences, geopolitical instability, and the risk of stolen intellectual property. "You keep following the money, but how often are you going to move people around?" asks Cohen. Even the routine day-to-day management of an offshore team can require significant project management expertise. "If you don't have experience and don't do it well, it can negate savings," says Barry Rubenstein, program manager of application outsourcing and offshore services at IDC.

## MIX OF OUTSOURCING LOCATIONS

Plenty of providers are ready to help clients overcome those obstacles. Companies including Accenture, EDS, IBM Global Services, and Genpact are building global networks, comprised of operations in a variety of cities, aimed at giving customers a mix of worker skills and labor costs. "We tailor where you want your people, based on the premium you want to pay," says Charlie Feld, executive vice-president of portfolio development at EDS.

Continental Airlines, for instance, uses an EDS center in India for development of some software that runs on mainframes, but the airline handles some finance work through an EDS office in Brazil. Accenture uses its global network of facilities in a similar fashion. "Today we are about 35 percent in high-cost locations, such as the U.S. and Britain; 20 percent in medium-cost locations like Spain, Ireland, and Canada; and about 45 percent in low-cost locations like the Philippines, India, China, and Eastern Europe," says Jimmy Harris, global managing director of infrastructure outsourcing at Accenture.

## THREAT TO U.S. WORKERS

And while a technically skilled global labor force is a boon to companies, the picture isn't so rosy for U.S. workers. Instead of competing with just India, now U.S. IT workers will need to go up against workers all over the world. In 2005, about 24 percent of North American companies used offshore providers to meet some of their software needs, according to Forrester Research. Over the next five years, spending on offshore IT services is set to increase at a compound annual growth rate of 18 percent, according to IDC.

The effect in the U.S. is that starting salaries in the engineering field—when adjusted for inflation—have stayed constant or decreased in the past five years or so, says Vivek Wadhwa, executive in residence at Duke University. "It doesn't make much sense to get into programming anymore," says Wadhwa, who worries that a lack of talent in certain industries, such as telecom, along with the outsourcing of research and development will erode U.S. competitiveness. But U.S. companies say that hiring programmers in India, who might make a fifth of what programmers do in the U.S., allows the companies to survive in a globally competitive economy.

### Questions

1. Why are companies starting to look outside India for outsourcing partners?

2. What is the lure of cheap labor?

3. Why is it difficult to move IT outsourcing into developing countries?

4. What is the impact of this global outsourcing trend on U.S. workers?

*Source:* Adapted from Rachael King, "CEO Guide to Technology," *BusinessWeek Online*, December 11, 2006.

## Online Extra: Calling the Ethics Cops

*A Growing Army of Corporate Monitors Is Helping Companies Police Their Dealings and Adjudicate Ethical Quandaries*

Corporate America is a surprisingly corrupt place. The high-profile scandals may have been just the tip of the iceberg. Graft, self-dealing, dishonesty, sexual harassment, and other unethical activity is strikingly common, according to recent surveys by search firm Hudson Highland Group and the Ethics Resource Center. The outfits found that between 31 percent and 52 percent of U.S. workers have witnessed co-workers operating unethically. But that could change. One byproduct of the scandals is growth in the ranks of ethics officers. A professional group for in-house corporate cops, the Ethics & Compliance Officer Assn., began with just 16 founding members in 1992, grew to 600 three years ago and has since doubled to 1,250. For the unethical these days, says Keith T. Darcy, executive director of the Waltham (Mass.)-based ECOA, "there are no secrets and no places to hide." Companies are finding improprieties very expensive. "The greatest threat to any publicly traded company is a well-publicized scandal," says Zachary W. Carter, a former U.S. attor-

ney for the Eastern District of New York and former judge in the Criminal Court of New York who now sits on the board of Marsh & McLennan. The insurance brokerage giant early last year agreed to pay $850 million to settle allega-tions of price-fixing and collusion leveled by New York Attorney General Eliot Spitzer.

**TOO MUCH POWER?** Since mid-2002, a corporate task force of the U.S. Justice Dept. has helped secure more than 700 corporate fraud convictions, with more than 100 chief executives and presidents convicted, along with more than 80 vice-presidents and more than 30 chief financial officers. In all, over the last four years, the task force has brought charges against a stunning 1,300 defendants. In some companies, courts have given outsiders exceptional clout to forestall more wrongdoing. Some outside monitors can probe as they wish and even fire suspect employees at will. Former SEC Chairman Richard C. Breeden can do just that at KPMG, the accounting firm that was caught up in an embarrassing tax-shelter sales scandal. Such exceptional powers are provoking a backlash. Corporate defense lawyers at the National Assn. of Criminal Defense Lawyers grumble that Breeden can become "the prosecutor, judge, and jury" at KPMG. And David B. Pitofsky, a former federal prosecutor now in private practice, argues that outside monitors in general should only "monitor and report" on company behavior, leaving action to the courts.

**"PRINCIPLES-BASED APPROACH."** But backers of aggressive corporate self-policing say ethics officers must be free to scrutinize everything in a company. Only then could they stand in the way of another Enron, argues Lee S. Richards III, an independent examiner at software company CA (formerly Computer Associates), which was caught up in an accounting scandal in recent years. Inside ethics officers "are in a position to prevent scandals of all sizes and shapes," adds Richards. He says they must have senior status in their companies, be able to look into "every nook and cranny," and take problems over the CEO's head to the board, if needed. Smart managers will give ethics honchos a long leash. Spitzer and other regulators are taking an ever-more expansive view on what is unacceptable. So in-house supercops like Eric R. Dinallo, who left Spitzer's office to become head of regulatory matters and affairs for Morgan Stanley, take a broad "principles-based approach," instead of hewing narrowly to the stated rules. Dinallo argues that practices that "just don't, in fact, feel right" probably aren't.

**STRICT RULES.** Ethics officers run training programs that spell out what's acceptable in dealings both internally and outside. They advise on ethical quandaries, such as when gifts are appropriate. And they monitor hotlines set up so whistle-blowers can draw attention to wrongdoing. "The rules are strict, and I don't apologize for that," says Susan E. Shepard, a former prosecutor and former commissioner of investigation for New York City who joined Nortel Networks as chief ethics and compliance officer last February. Nortel brought her on after it ousted CEO Frank Dunn and a clutch of other executives in 2004 amid disclosures of financial misreporting. Much of the dishonesty occurs at lower levels. Shepard tells of thefts in 2003 at Nortel in which equipment worth more than $1 million was stolen from a company lab affected by layoffs. Employees walked out the door with the gear, unchallenged. When her staff early last year reviewed an investigation of the thefts, she was stunned that controls on taking equipment out were still lax. That's not so anymore, the ethics chief says. In another case, a Nortel staffer was leaking company information to her husband, who worked for a competitor; the staffer has been canned. "When intellectual property is your product, you have to protect it," Shepard says.

**SENDING A MESSAGE.** Patrick J. Gnazzo, the new compliance chief at CA and formerly vice-president for business practices with United Technologies warns of a more everyday sort of corruption. Vendors or other business associates try to curry favor through improper gifts. Once, he says, an outside colleague seeking business at United Technologies sent a manager an oar and promised to send on the canoe if they could just meet to talk. The manager tipped Gnazzo to the obvious bribe. "He didn't get the canoe, and he gave me the oar, and I sent it back," Gnazzo recalls. For ethics officers to do their jobs well, the commitment must come from the top, ethics experts say. Top managers at Morgan Stanley recently sent a powerful message, for instance, by firing a research analyst and three sales staffers after they took clients to an Arizona strip club last November. The firm in mid-2004 paid $54 million to settle a gender-discrimination case where complaints had been raised about male-only outings. These firings reflect management's commitment to do the right thing, says Paul Shechtman, a court-appointed outside monitor who oversees Morgan Stanley's compliance with the settlement. Says Shechtman, "The decision was entirely theirs and made at very senior levels, and was made without much debate."

**OUTSIDE ENFORCEMENT.** But the job can still take intestinal fortitude; especially since ethics officers could easily make enemies. "The ethics officer of today, I believe, has to be somebody who is prepared to be fired," says Jeff Benjamin, the top ethics official at pharmaceutical giant, Novartis. Only a Pollyanna could believe all managers will do the right thing all the time without the threat of the law on their necks. "Self-policing can be enormously beneficial," says monitor Shechtman. "[But] I don't think anybody thinks the corporate world can do without police anymore than the rest of the world can do without police." And yet, self-policing by well-equipped ethics officers certainly can't hurt. So long as people will be tempted to stray, these ethics officers will be in hot demand.

## Questions

1. Why are companies "finding improprieties very expensive"?
2. What is the ECOA?
3. What kind of stature should an ethics officer hold within an organization?
4. Provide an example of "a more everyday sort of corruption" other than the one given in the case study.

*Source:* Adapted from Joseph Weber, "Legal Affairs," *BusinessWeek*, February 13, 2006.

# glossary

**ABC classification system** (p. 356) Method of managing inventories based on their total value.

**Abilities** (p. 313) Personal characteristics used in performing a job.

**Absolute advantage** (p. 372) The ability to produce more of a good than another producer with the same quantity of inputs.

**Acceptance sampling** (p. 350) Statistical method of predicting the quality of a batch or a large group of products by inspecting a sample or group of samples.

**Affirmative action plan** (p. 244) Written document outlining specific goals and timetables for remedying past discriminatory actions.

**Age Discrimination in Employment Act** (p. 240) Passed in 1968, initially designed to protect individuals ages 40 to 65 from discrimination in hiring, retention, and other conditions of employment. Amended in 1978 to include individuals up to age 70. Specifically, forbids mandatory retirement at age 65 except in certain circumstances.

**Americans with Disabilities Act (ADA) of 1990** (p. 240) Gives individuals with disabilities sharply increased access to services and jobs.

**Aptitude tests** (p. 246) Measure a person's capacity or potential ability to learn.

**Audits** (p. 311) Method of control normally involved with financial matters; also can include other areas of the organization.

**Authority** (p. 146, 180) Legitimate exercise of power; the right to issue directives and expend resources; related to power but narrower in scope.

**Autocratic leader** (p. 149) Makes most decisions for the group.

**Avoidance** (p. 286) Giving a person the opportunity to avoid a negative consequence by exhibiting a desirable behavior. Also called *negative reinforcement.*

**Balance of trade** (p. 373) Difference between the value of the good a country exports and the value of the goods it imports.

**Behavior or personal control** (p. 304) Based on direct, personal surveillance.

**Bet-your-company culture** (p. 165) Requires big-stakes decisions; considerable time passes before the results are known.

**Board (or panel) interview** (p. 249) An interview in which two or more interviewers conduct the interview.

**Board of directors** (p. 223) Carefully selected committee that reviews major policy and strategy decisions proposed by top management.

**Brainstorming** (p. 96) Presenting a problem to a group and allowing group members to produce a large quantity of ideas for its solution; no criticism is allowed initially.

**Brainwriting** (p. 97) Technique in which a group is presented with a problem situation and members anonymously write down ideas, then exchange papers with others, who build on ideas and pass them on until all members have participated.

**Break-even charts** (p. 311) Depict graphically the relationship of volume of operations to profits.

**Budget** (p. 305) Statement of expected results or requirements expressed in financial or numerical terms.

**Business ethics** (p. 16) The application of standards of moral behavior to business situations - in other words, 'doing the right thing' in a business transaction.

**Business strategies** (p. 122) Focus on how to compete in a given business.

**Central tendency** (p. 322) Occurs when performance appraisal statistics indicate that most employees are evaluated similarly as doing average or above-average work.

**Centralization** (p. 183) Little authority is delegated to lower levels of management.

**Charismatic leadership** (p. 158) Involves a leader who can successfully influence employee behavior on the strength of personality or a perceived charisma, without the formal power or experience to back it up.

**Checklist** (p. 317) Requires the manager to answer yes or no to a series of questions concerning the employee's behavior.

**Civil Rights Act of 1991** (p. 240) Permits women, minorities persons with disabilities, and persons who are religious minorities to have a jury trial and sue for punitive damages if they can prove intentional hiring and workplace discrimination. Also requires companies to provide evidence that the business practice that led to the discrimination was not discriminatory but was related to the performance of the job in question and consistent with business necessity.

**Closed system** (p. 39) By contrast closed systems do not interact with their external environments.

**Code of ethics** (p. 412) A document that outlines the principles of conduct to be used in making decisions within an organization.

**Combination strategies** (p. 121) Used when an organization simultaneously employs different strategies for different parts of the company.

**Committee** (p. 222) Organization structure in which a group of people is formally appointed, organized, and superimposed on the line or line and staff structure to consider or decide certain matters.

**Communication** (p. 56) The act of exchanging information.

**Conceptual skills** (p. 10) Involves understanding the relationship of the parts of a business to one another and to the business as a whole.

**Concurrent controls** (p. 305) Focuses on process as it occurs; designed to detect a problem as it occurs.

**Consideration** (p. 151) Leader behavior of showing concern for individual group members and satisfying their needs.

**Contingency approach to leadership** (p. 154) Focuses on the style of leadership that is most effective in particular situations.

**Contingency approach to management** (p. 40) Theorizes that different situations and conditions require different management approaches.

**Contingency plans** (p. 114) Address the what-ifs of the manager's job; get the manager in the habit of being prepared and knowing what to do if something does go wrong.

**Continuous improvement** (p. 345) Refers to an ongoing effort to make improvements in every part of the organization relative to all of its products and services.

**Control** (p. 302) Process of ensuring that organizational activities are going according to plan; accomplished by comparing actual performance to predetermined standards or objectives, then taking action to correct any deviations.

**Controlling** (p. 7) Measuring performance against objectives, determining the causes of deviations, and taking corrective action where necessary.

**Corporate culture** (p. 161) Communicates how people in an organization should behave by establishing a value system conveyed through rites, rituals, myths, legends, and actions.

**Corporate strategies** (p. 120) Address which businesses an organization will be in and how resources will be allocated among those businesses.

**Creativity** (p. 94) Coming up with an idea that is new, original, useful, or satisfying to its creator or to someone else.

**Critical-incident appraisal** (p. 317) Requires the manager to keep a written record of incidents, as they occur, involving job behaviors that illustrate both satisfactory and unsatisfactory performance of the employee being rated.

**Culture**   (p. 160) Set of important understandings (often unstated) that members of a community share.

**Customer departmentalization**   (p. 213) Organization units in terms of customers served.

**Data processing**   (p. 101) Capture, processing, and storage of data.

**Decentralization**   (p. 183) A great deal of authority is delegated to lower levels of management.

**Decision making**   (p. 82) In its narrowest sense, the process of choosing from among various alternatives.

**Decision process**   (p. 82) Process that involves three stages: intelligence, design, and choice.

**Defensive or retrenchment strategies**   (p. 121) Used when a company wants or needs to reduce its operations.

**Democratic leader**   (p. 149) Guides and encourages the group to make decisions.

**Departmentalization**   (p. 210) Grouping jobs into related work units.

**Dependent demand items**   (p. 356) Subassembly or component parts used to make a finished product; their demand is based on the number of finished products being produced.

**Direct feedback**   (p. 392) Process in which the change agent communicates the information gathered in the diagnostic and change-planning phases to the involved parties.

**Diversification**   (p. 372) When a company engages in a variety of operations.

**Diversity**   (p. 15) Including people of different genders, races, religions, nationalities, ethnic groups, age groups, and physical abilities.

**Economic order quantity (EOQ)**   (p. 358) Optimal number of units to order at one time determined by the point at which ordering costs equal carrying costs, or where total cost (ordering costs plus carrying costs) is at a minimum.

**Effort**   (p. 313) Results from being motivated; refers to the amount of energy an employee uses in performing a job.

**E-mail**   (p. 67) The abbreviated version of 'electronic mail' refers to the system of sending and receiving messages over an electronic communications system.

**Embargo**   (p. 376) Involves stopping the flow of exports to or imports from a foreign country.

**Employee leasing companies**   (p. 242) Provide permanent staff at customer companies as listed in text.

**Empowerment**   (p. 184) Form of decentralization in which subordinates have authority to make decisions.

**Entry socialization**   (p. 162) Adaptation process by which new employees are introduced and indoctrinated into the organization.

**Environmental changes**   (p. 382) All non-technological changes that occur outside the organization.

**Equal employment opportunity**   (p. 239) The right of all people to work and to advance on the bases of merit, ability, and potential.

**Equal Pay Act of 1963**   (p. 238) Prohibits wage discrimination on the basis of sex.

**Equity theory**   (p. 277) Motivation theory based on the idea that people want to be treated fairly in relationship to others.

**Essay appraisal method**   (p. 316) Requires the manager to describe an employee's performance in written narrative form.

**Esteem**   (p. 280) Influences the development of various kinds of relationships based on adequacy, independence, and the giving and receiving of indications of esteem and acceptance.

**Ethics**   (p. 411) A set of moral principles or values that govern behavior.

**Evaluation phase**   (p. 125) Third phase in strategic management, in which the implemented strategic plan is monitored, evaluated, and updated.

**Exception principle**   (p. 188) States that managers should concentrate on matters that deviate significantly from normal and let subordinates handle routine matters; also called *management by exception.*

**Expectancy approach** (p. 284) Based on the idea that employee, beliefs about the relationship among effort, performance, and outcomes as a result of performance and the value employees place on the outcomes determine their level of motivation.

**Expectancy** (p. 285) Employee's belief that his or her effort will lead to the desired level of performance.

**Exports** (p. 372) Goods and services that are sold abroad.

**External environment** (p. 129) Consists of everything outside the organization.

**Extinction** (p. 286) Providing no positive consequences or removing previously provided positive consequences as a result of undesirable behavior.

**Family and Medical Leave Act (FMLA)** (p. 240) Enables qualified employees to take prolonged unpaid leave for family- and health-related reasons without fear of losing their jobs.

**Fixed overhead expenses** (p. 338) Expenses that do not change appreciably with fluctuations in the level of production or service.

**Flat structure** (p. 221) Organization with few levels and relatively large spans of management at each level.

**Foreign intermediary** (p. 377) A wholesaler or agent that markets products for companies wanting to do business abroad.

**Formal plan** (p. 113) Written, documented plan developed through an identifiable process.

**Formal work groups** (p. 253) Established by management to carry out specific tasks such as designing a new product or resolving a problem.

**Formulation phase** (p. 125) First phase in strategic management, in which the initial strategic plan is developed.

**Free trade area** (p. 376) A region within which trade restrictions are reduced or eliminated.

**Functional departmentalization** (p. 211) Defining organization units in terms of the nature of the work.

**Functional plans** (p. 113) Originate from the functional areas of an organization such as production, marketing, finance, and personnel.

**Functional strategies** (p. 123) Concerned with the activities of the different functional areas of the business.

**Functions of management** (p. 35) Fayol's summary of the key responsibilities of a manager - planning, organizing, commanding, coordinating, and controlling.

**Geographic departmentalization** (p. 213) Organization units by territories.

**Glass ceiling** (p. 16) Refers to a level within the managerial hierarchy beyond which very few women and minorities advance.

**Gordon technique** (p. 97) Differs from brainstorming in that no one but the group leader knows the exact nature of the real problem under consideration. A key word is used to describe a problem area.

**Grapevine** (p. 66) Informal channels of communication within an organization.

**Graphic rating scale** (p. 317) Requires the manager to assess an employee on factors such as quantity of work, dependability, job knowledge, attendance, accuracy of work, and cooperativeness.

**Group cohesiveness** (p. 255) Degree of attraction each member has for the group, or the "stick-togetherness" of the group.

**Group conformity** (p. 256) Degree to which the members of the group accept and abide by the norms of the group.

**Group interview** (p. 249) An interview which questions several interviewees together in a group discussion.

**Group norms** (p. 254) Informal rules a group adopts to regulate group members' behavior.

**Groupthink** (p. 257) Dysfunctional syndrome where group members lose their ability to think as individuals and conform to group decisions at the expense of their individual good judgment.

**Growth strategies** (p. 120) Used when the organization tries to expand, as measured by sales, product line, number of employees, or similar measures.

**Halo effect** (p. 250) Occurs when the interviewer allows a single prominent characteristic to dominate judgment of all other traits.

**Hawthorne effect** (p. 37) The positive behavior change demonstrated by employee when managers pay attention to them.

**Hedgehog concept** (p. 44) Drawn from Isaiah Berlin's essay "The Hedgehog and the Fox" in which "The fox knows many things but the hedgehog knows only one". In other words, great companies develop a simple core concept that guides all their future strategies, as opposed to chasing every new management fad or policy implementation.

**Hierarchy of needs** (p. 279) Based on the assumption that individuals are motivated to satisfy a number of needs and that money can directly or indirectly satisfy only some of these needs.

**Horizontal structure** (p. 218) Consists of two groups. One group is composed of senior management who are responsible for strategic decisions and policies. The second group is composed of empowered employees working together in different process teams.

**Human relations skills** (p. 10) Are the ability to understand and work well with people. These skills enable managers to direct the social aspects of the work as well as the productivity of the work being performed.

**Human resource forecasting** (p. 238) Process that attempts to determine the future human resource needs of the organization in light of the organization's objectives.

**Human resource planning (HRP)** (p. 237) Process of getting the right number of qualified people into the right job at the right time. Also called *personnel planning*.

**Hybrid departmentalization** (p. 213) Occurs when an organization simultaneously uses more than one type of departmentalization.

**Implementation phase** (p. 125) Second phase in strategic management, in which the strategic plan is put into effect.

**Imports** (p. 372) Goods and services purchased abroad.

**Independent demand items** (p. 356) Finished goods ready to be shipped out or sold.

**Industrial Revolution** (p. 28) Starting in 1860, the U.S. Industrial Revolution encompassed the period when the United States began to shift from an almost totally farming-based society to an industrialized society.

**Inequity** (p. 277) Exists when a person perceives his or her job inputs and outcomes to be less than the job inputs and outcomes of another person.

**Informal organization** (p. 178) Aggregate of the personal contacts and interactions and the associated groupings of people working within the formal organization.

**Informal work groups** (p. 254) Groups formed voluntarily by members of an organization, based on personal contact and interaction to the workplace.

**Initiating structure** (p. 151) Leader behavior of structuring the work of group members and directing the group toward the attainment of the group's goals.

**Innovation** (p. 94) Process of applying a new and creative idea to a product, service, or method of operation.

**Inputs** (p. 277) What an employee perceives are his or her contributions to the organization (e.g., education, intelligence, experience, training skills, and the effort exerted on the job).

**Instrumentality** (p. 285) Employee's belief that attaining the desired level of performance will lead to desired rewards.

**Intellectual property** (p. 418) Ownership of ideas such as inventions, books, movies, and computer programs gives creators of the intellectual property the exclusive right to market and sell their work.

**Interest tests** (p. 247) Determine how a person's interests compare with the interests of successful people in a specific job.

**Internal changes**　(p. 382) Budget adjustments, policy changes, personnel changes, and the like.

**International trade**　(p. 371) The exchange of goods and services by different countries.

**Internet**　(p. 67) A global collection of independently operating, but interconnected, computers.

**Interpersonal communication**　(p. 57) An interactive process between individuals that involves sending and receiving verbal and nonverbal messages.

**Intranet**　(p. 68) A private, corporate, computer network that uses Internet products and technologies to provide multimedia applications within organizations.

**Intuitive approach**　(p. 83) Approach used when managers make decisions based largely on hunches and intuition.

**Inventories**　(p. 353) Quantity of raw materials, in-process goods, or finished goods on hand; serves as a buffer between different rates of flow associated with the operating system.

**ISO 14000**　(p. 347) Addition to the ISO 9000 to control the impact of an organization's activities and outputs on the environment.

**ISO 9000**　(p. 346) A set of quality standards for international business with the major objective of promoting the development of standardization and facilitating the international exchange of goods and services.

**Job analysis**　(p. 236) Process of determining, through observation and study, the pertinent information relating to the nature of a specific job.

**Job depth**　(p. 180) Refers to the freedom of employees to plan and organize their own work, work at their own pace, and move around and communicate as desired.

**Job description**　(p. 236) Written statement that identifies the tasks, duties, activities, and performance results required in a particular job.

**Job enlargement**　(p. 283) Giving an employee more of a similar type of operation to perform.

**Job enrichment**　(p. 283) Upgrading the job by adding motivator factors.

**Job knowledge tests**　(p. 246) Measure the job-related knowledge possessed by a job applicant.

**Job rotation**　(p. 283) The practice of periodically rotating job assignments within the organization.

**Job satisfaction**　(p. 288) An individual's general attitude about his or her job.

**Job scope**　(p. 180) Refers to the number of different types of operations performed on the job.

**Job specification**　(p. 236) Written statement that identifies the abilities, skills, traits, or attributes necessary for successful performance in a particular job.

**Just-in-time inventory control (JIT)**　(p. 353) Inventory control system that schedules materials to arrive and leave as they are needed.

**Kaizen**　(p. 345) "Good change"; a process of continuous and relentless improvement.

**Laissez-faire leader**　(p. 149) Allows people within the group to make all decisions.

**Law of comparative advantage**　(p. 372) Producers should produce the goods they are most efficient at producing and purchase from others the goods they are less efficient at producing.

**Leader behavior description questionnaire (LBDQ)**　(p. 151) Questionnaire designed to determine what a successful leader does, regardless of the type of group being led.

**Leader**　(p. 146) One who obtains followers and influences them in setting and achieving objectives.

**Leader-member relations**　(p. 155) Degree to which others trust and respect the leader and the leader's friendliness.

**Leadership**　(p. 146) Ability to influence people to willingly follow one's guidance or adhere to one's decisions.

**Leading**　(p. 7) Directing and channeling human behavior toward the accomplishment of objectives.

**Lean manufacturing**　(p. 346) A systematic approach to identifying and eliminating waste and non-value-added activities.

**Leniency**　(p. 322) Grouping of ratings at the positive end of the scale instead of spreading them throughout the scale.

**Level of aspiration**　(p. 86) Level of performance that a person expects to attain; determined by the person's prior successes and failures.

**Licensing agreement** (p. 377) An agreement that permits one company to sell another company's products abroad in return for a percentage of the company's revenues.

**Linchpin concept** (p. 258) Holds that because managers are members of overlapping groups, they link formal work groups to the total organization.

**Line and staff structure** (p. 215) Organization structure that results when staff specialists are added to a line organization.

**Line functions** (p. 216) Functions and activities directly involved in producing and marketing the organization's goods or services.

**Long-range objectives** (p. 115) Go beyond the current fiscal year; must support and not conflict with the organizational mission.

**Long-range plans** (p. 114) Typically span at least three to five years; some extend as far as 20 years into the future.

**Malcolm Baldrige Award** (p. 349) Recognition of U.S. companies' achievements in performance excellence.

**Management audits** (p. 311) Attempt to evaluate the overall management practices and policies of the organization.

**Management by objectives (MBO)** (p. 117) MBO is a philosophy based on converting organizational objectives into personal objectives. It assumes that establishing personal objectives elicits employee commitment, which leads to improved performance.

**Management information systems (MISs)** (p. 100) Integrated approach for providing interpreted and relevant data that can help managers make decisions.

**Management** (p. 4) The process of deciding the best way to use an organization's resources to produce goods or provide services.

**Managerial grid** (p. 153) A two-dimensional framework rating a leader on the basis of concern for people and concern for production.

**Matrix structure** (p. 217) Hybrid organization structure in which individuals from different functional areas are assigned to work on a specific project or task.

**Maximax approach** (p. 90) Selecting the alternative whose best possible outcome is the best of all possible outcomes for all alternatives; sometimes called the *optimistic* or *gambling approach* to decision making.

**Maximin approach** (p. 90) Comparing the worst possible outcomes for each alternative and selecting the one that is least undesirable; sometimes called the *pessimistic approach* to decision making.

**Mechanistic systems** (p. 204) Organizational systems characterized by a rigid delineation of functional duties, precise job descriptions, fixed authority and responsibility, and a well-developed organizational hierarchy through which information filters up and instructions flow down.

**Middle management** (p. 5) Responsible for implementing and achieving organizational objectives; also responsible for developing departmental objectives and actions.

**Mission** (p. 126) Defines the basic purpose(s) of an organization: why the organization exists.

**Motivation** (p. 276) Concerned with what activates human behavior, what directs this behavior toward a particular goal, and how this behavior is sustained.

**Motivation-hygiene** (p. 283) An approach to work motivation that associates factors of high-low motivation with either the work environment or the work itself.

**Multinational corporation (MNC)** (p. 378) Business that maintains a presence in two or more countries, has a considerable portion of its assets invested in and derives a substantial portion of its sales and profits from international activities, considers opportunities throughout the world, and has a worldwide perspective and orientation.

**Multirater assessment or 360-degree feedback** (p. 320) Method of performance appraisal that uses input from an employee's managers, peers, customers, suppliers, or colleagues.

**North American Free Trade Agreement (NAFTA)** (p. 376) NAFTA allows businesses in the United States, Mexico, and Canada to sell their products anywhere in North America without facing major trade restrictions.

**Objectives** (p. 115) Statements outlining what the organization is trying to achieve; give an organization and its members direction.

**Open system** (p. 39) Under the systems approach to management, the organization is seen as an open system that is influenced by its internal and external environmental factors. The organization then, in turn, influences these same internal and external environmental factors; as a result, a dynamic relationship is created.

**Operations or tactical planning** (p. 114) Short-range planning; done primarily by middle- to lower-level managers, it concentrates on the formulation of functional plans.

**Optimizing approach** (p. 84) Includes the following steps: recognize the need for a decision; establish, rank, and weigh criteria; gather available information and data; identify possible alternatives; evaluate each alternative with respect to all criteria; and select the best alternatives.

**Optimizing** (p. 86) Selecting the best possible alternative.

**Organic systems** (p. 204) Organizational systems having less formal job descriptions, greater emphasis on adaptability, more participation, and less fixed authority.

**Organization structure** (p. 202) The framework that defines the boundaries of the formal organization and within which the organization operates.

**Organization** (p. 178) Group of people working together in some concerted or coordinated effort to attain objectives.

**Organizational development (OD)** (p. 390) Organizationwide, planned effort, managed from the top, to increase organizational performance through planned interventions.

**Organizational morale** (p. 288) An individual's feeling of being accepted by, and belonging to, a group of employees through common goals, confidence in the desirability of these goals, and progress toward these goals.

**Organizing** (p. 7) Grouping activities, assigning activities, and providing the authority necessary to carry out the activities.

**Output or impersonal control** (p. 304) Based on the measurement of outputs.

**Outsourcing** (p. 208) Practice of subcontracting certain work functions to an outside organization.

**Parity principle** (p. 186) States that authority and responsibility must coincide.

**Path-goal theory of leadership** (p. 157) Attempts to define the relationships between a leader's behavior and the subordinates' performance and work activities.

**Perception** (p. 59) The mental and sensory processes an individual uses in interpreting information received.

**Performance appraisal** (p. 313) Process that involves determining and communicating to employees how they are performing their jobs and establishing a plan for improvement.

**Performance** (p. 313) Degree of accomplishment of the tasks that make up an employee's job.

**Physical inventory** (p. 356) Counting the number of units of inventory a company holds in stock.

**Physiological** (p. 279) Needs of the human body that must be satisfied in order to sustain life.

**Planning** (p. 7) Process of deciding what objectives to pursue during a future time period and what to do to achieve those objectives.

**Policies** (p. 118) Broad, general guides to action that constrain or direct the attainment of objectives.

**Polygraph tests** (p. 247) Record physical changes in the body as the test subject answers a series of questions; popularly known as *lie detector tests*.

**Position power** (p. 155) Power and influence that go with a job.

**Positive reinforcement** (p. 286) Providing a positive consequence as a result of desirable behavior.

**Postaction control** (p. 305) Designed to detect an existing or a potential problem before it gets out of hand.

**Power** (p. 146, 180) Ability to influence, command, or apply force; a measure of a person's potential to get others to do what he or she wants them to do, as well as to avoid being forced by others to do what he or she does not want to do.

**Preliminary control** (p. 304) Method of exercising control to prevent a problem from occurring.

**Principle of bounded rationality** (p. 85) Assumes people have the time and cognitive ability to process only a limited amount of information on which to base decisions.

**Problem solving** (p. 82) Process of determining the appropriate responses or actions necessary to alleviate a problem.

**Procedure** (p. 119) Series of related steps or task expressed in chronological order for a specific purpose.

**Process control chart** (p. 350) Time-based graphic display that shows whether a machine or process is producing items that meet pre-established specifications.

**Process culture** (p. 165) Involves low risk with little feedback; employees focus on how things are done rather than on the outcomes.

**Process quality control** (p. 349) Concerns monitoring quality while the product or service is being produced.

**Product departmentalization** (p. 212) Grouping all activities necessary to produce and market a product or service under one manager.

**Product quality control** (p. 349) Relates to inputs or outputs of the system; used when quality is evaluated with respect to a batch of existing products or services.

**Production standards approach** (p. 315) Performance appraisal method most frequently used for employees who are involved in physically producing a product; is basically a form of objective setting for these employees.

**Professional manager** (p. 38) A career person who does not necessarily have a controlling interest in the company for which he or she works. Professional managers realize their responsibility to three groups: employees, stockholders, and the general public.

**Proficiency tests** (p. 247) Measure how well the applicant can do a sample of the work that is to be performed.

**Psychological tests** (p. 247) Attempt to measure personality characteristics.

**Psychomotor tests** (p. 246) Measure a person's strength, dexterity, and coordination.

**Punishment** (p. 286) Providing a negative consequence as a result of undesirable behavior.

**Quality at the source** (p. 345) The philosophy of making each employee responsible for the quality of his or her own work.

**Quality circle** (p. 260) Composed of a group of employees (usually from 5 to 15 people) who are members of a single work unit, section, or department; the basic purpose of a quality circle is to discuss quality problems and generate ideas that might help improve quality.

**Quality** (p. 339) For the operations manager, quality is determined in relation to the specifications or standards set in the design stages – the degree or grade of excellence specified.

**Quotas** (p. 375) Restrictions on the quantity of a good that can enter a country.

**Recency** (p. 322) Occurs when performance evaluations are based on work performed most recently, generally work performed one to two months before evaluation.

**Recruitment** (p. 242) Seeking and attracting a supply of people from which qualified candidates for job vacancies can be selected.

**Reengineering** (p. 346) Searching for and implementing radical change in business processes to achieve breakthroughs in costs, speed, productivity, and service.

**Rehabilitation Act of 1973** (p. 240) Prohibits discrimination in hiring of persons with disabilities by federal agencies and federal contactors.

**Responsibility** (p. 180) Accountability for the attainment of objectives, the use of resources, and the adherence to organizational policy.

**Reverse discrimination** (p. 245) Providing preferential treatment for one group (e.g., minority or female) over another group (e.g., white male) rather than merely providing equal opportunity.

**Risk-averting approach** (p. 90) Choosing the alternative with the least variation among its possible outcomes.

**Role perception** (p. 313) Direction in which employees believe they should channel their efforts on their jobs.

**Role** (p. 6) Set of behaviors associated with a particular job.

**Rules** (p. 119) Require specific and definite actions to be taken or not to be taken in a given situation.

**Safety stocks** (p. 357) Inventory maintained to accommodate unexpected changes in demand and supply and allow for variations in delivery time.

**Safety** (p. 279) Protection against danger, threat, or deprivation.

**Satisficing** (p. 86) Selecting the first alternative that meets the decision maker's minimum standard of satisfaction.

**Scalar principle** (p. 188) States that authority in the organization flows through the chain of managers one link at a time, ranging from the highest to the lowest ranks; also called *chain of command.*

**Scientific management** (p. 31) Philosophy of Frederick W. Taylor that sought to increase productivity and make the work easier by scientifically studying work methods and establishing standards.

**Self-actualization or self-fulfillment** (p. 280) Highest-order need is concerned with the need of people to reach their full potential in applying their abilities and interests to functioning in their environment.

**Self-directed work team** (p. 261) Teams in which members are empowered to control the work they do without a formal supervisor.

**Self-fulfilling prophecy** (p. 148) The relationship between a leader's expectations and the resulting performance of subordinates.

**Semantics** (p. 58) The science or study of the meanings of words and symbols.

**Semistructured interview** (p. 249) An interview in which the interviewer prepares the major questions in advance but has the flexibility to use such techniques as probing to help assess the applicant's strengths and weaknesses.

**Senior management** (p. 4) The highest level of management, it establishes the goals, or objectives, of the organization, decides what actions are necessary to meet those goals, and decides how to use the organization's resources. Senior managers concentrate on setting the direction the company will follow.

**Sensitivity training** (p. 392) Method used in OD to make one more aware of oneself and one's impact on others.

**Short-range objectives** (p. 115) Generally tied to a specific time period of a year or less and are derived from an in-depth evaluation of long-range objectives.

**Short-range plans** (p. 114) Generally cover up to one year.

**Situation of certainty** (p. 88) Situation that occurs when a decision maker knows exactly what will happen and can often calculate the precise outcome for each alternative.

**Situation of risk** (p. 88) Situation that occurs when a decision maker is aware of the relative probabilities of occurrence associated with each alternative.

**Situation of uncertainty** (p. 89) Situation that occurs when a decision maker has very little or no reliable information on which to evaluate the different possible outcomes.

**Situational interview** (p. 249) Interview that uses projective techniques to put the prospective employee in action situations that might be encountered on the job.

**Situational leadership theory** (p. 158) As the level of maturity of followers increases, structure should be reduced while emotional support should first be increased and then gradually decreased.

**Six sigma** (p. 345) Literally means, in statistical terms, six standard deviations from the mean. In order to realize the very high level of quality demanded by six sigma (most processes traditionally have used three sigma), the entire production or service system must be examined and improved.

**Skills inventory** (p. 236) Consolidates information about the organization's current human resources.

**Social audit**   (p. 422) A method used by management to evaluate the success or lack of success of programs designed to improve the social performance of the organization.

**Social responsibility**   (p. 419) The obligation that individuals or businesses have to help solve social problems.

**Social**   (p. 280) Categorized as needs for love, affection, belonging—all are concerned with establishing one's position relative to others.

**Soldiering**   (p. 31) Describes the actions of employees who intentionally restrict output.

**Span of management**   (p. 189) Number of subordinates a manager can effectively manage; also called *span of control*.

**Stability strategies**   (p. 121) Used when the organization is satisfied with its present course (status quo strategy).

**Staff functions**   (p. 216) Functions that are advisory and supportive in nature; designed to contribute to the efficiency and maintenance of the organization.

**Staffing**   (p. 7) Determining human resource needs and recruiting, selecting, training, and developing human resources.

**Stakeholders**   (p. 419) The people—employees, customers, suppliers, and the community—who are affected by the actions of a business.

**Strategic alliance**   (p. 378) When companies pool resources and skills in order to achieve common goals.

**Strategic business unit (SBU)**   (p. 130) Distinct business that has its own set of competitors and can be managed reasonably independently of other businesses within the organization.

**Strategic management**   (p. 124) Formulation, proper implementation, and continuous evaluation of strategic plans; determines the long-run directions and performance of an organization. The essence of strategic management is developing strategic plans and keeping them current.

**Strategic planning**   (p. 114) Formulation, proper implementation, and continuous evaluation of strategic plans; determines the long-run directions and performance of an organization. The essence of strategic management is developing strategic plans and keeping them current.

**Strategy**   (p. 120) Outlines the basic steps management plans to take to reach an objective or a set of objectives; outlines how management intends to achieve its objectives.

**Stress interview**   (p. 249) An interview designed to place the interviewee under pressure.

**Structured interview**   (p. 248) An interview conducted using a predetermined outline.

**Supervisory management**   (p. 5) Manages operative employees; generally considered the first level of management.

**SWOT**   (p. 128) An acronym for Strengths, Weaknesses, Opportunities, and Threats, business managers evaluate the performance of their department or the entire company using a SWOT analysis.

**System**   (p. 39) A system is an assemblage or combination of things or parts forming a complex or unitary whole.

**Tall structure**   (p. 221) Organization with many levels and relatively small spans of management.

**Tariff**   (p. 375) Government-imposed taxes charged on goods imported into a country.

**Task structure**   (p. 155) Degree to which job tasks are structured.

**Team building**   (p. 258) Process of establishing a cohesive group that works together to achieve its goals.

**Technical skills**   (p. 10) Involves being able to perform the mechanics of a particular job.

**Technological changes**   (p. 382) Changes in such things as new equipment and new processes.

**Temporary help**   (p. 242) People working for employment agencies who are subcontracted out to businesses at an hourly rate for a period of time specified by the businesses.

**Test reliability**   (p. 247) Consistency or reproducibility of the results of a test.

**Test validity**   (p. 247) Extent to which a test predicts a specific criterion.

**Tests** (p. 246) Provide a sample of behavior used to draw inferences about the future behavior or performance of an individual.

**Theory X** (p. 39) Argues there is a simple division of management styles that capture what are fundamentally different ways of managing people. Theory X managers manage in a very controlling and authoritative manner.

**Theory Y** (p. 39) Managers believe employees can be trusted to meet production targets without being threatened, and that they will often seek additional responsibilities because they enjoy the satisfaction of being creative and increasing their own skills. As a result they manage in a democratic and participative manner.

**Theory Z** (p. 40) Attempts to integrate American and Japanese management practices by combining the American emphasis on individual responsibility with the Japanese emphasis on collective decision making, slow evaluation and promotion, and holistic concern for employees.

**Time and motion study** (p. 33) In order to find the 'one best way' to perform a task, Frederick Winslow Taylor began to measure individual tasks within jobs–measuring both the time taken to do the task and observing the motions involved. This area of research has since been incorporated into *ergonomics*.

**Title VII of the Civil Rights Act of 1964** (p. 239) Designed to eliminate employment discrimination related to race, color, religion, sex, or national origin.

**Tough-person, macho culture** (p. 164) Characterized by individuals who take high risks and get quick feedback on whether their decisions are right or wrong.

**Trait theory** (p. 149) Stressed what the leader was like rather than what the leader did.

**Transactional leadership** (p. 158) Takes the approach that leaders engage in bargaining relationship with their followers.

**Transaction-processing systems** (p. 101) Substitutes computer processing for manual record-keeping procedures.

**Transformational leadership** (p. 158) Involves cultivating employee acceptance of the group mission.

**Unity of command principle** (p. 188) States that an employee should have one, and only one, immediate manager.

**Unstructured interviews** (p. 249) Interviews conducted without a predetermined checklist of questions.

**Valence** (p. 285) Employee's belief about the value of the rewards.

**Variable overhead expenses** (p. 338) Expenses that change in proportion to the level of production or service.

**Virtual organization** (p. 219) Temporary network of independent companies—suppliers, customers, and even rivals—linked by information technology to share skills, costs, and access to one another's markets.

**Virtual work team** (p. 261) Responsible for making or implementing important decisions for the business, mainly using technology-supported communication, with the team members working and living in different locations.

**Work-hard/play-hard culture** (p. 165) Encourages employees to take few risks and to expect rapid feedback.

**Zero-base budgeting** (p. 306) Form of budgeting in which the manager must build justify each area of a budget. Each year the activity is identified, evaluated, and ranked by importance.

**Zero-defects program** (p. 348) Increasing quality by increasing everyone's impact on quality.

# photo credits

## CHAPTER 6

Page 150   © Royalty-Free/Corbis
Page 159   © Digital Vision/PunchStock
Page 161 (left)   © Royalty-Free/Corbis
Page 161 (right)   © Ryan McVay/Getty Images
Page 162   © Robert Holmes/Corbis
Page 170   © Thomas Pflaum/Visum/The Image Works
Page 172   © AP Photo/Uwe Lein

## CHAPTER 7

Page 179   © Michael S. Yamashita/Corbis
Page 181   © Helen King/Corbis
Page 185   © Getty Images
Page 191   © Steve Prezant/Corbis
Page 195   © AP Photo/Damian Dovarganes
Page 197   © Getty Images

## CHAPTER 8

Page 203   © Digital Vision
Page 209   © Comstock/Corbis
Page 211 (left)   © John A. Rizzo/Getty Images
Page 211 (right)   © Jim Craigmyle/Corbis
Page 220   © AP Photo/Rick Maiman
Page 224   © Royalty-Free/Corbis
Page 229   © AFP/Getty Images
Page 231   © Getty Images

## CHAPTER 9

Page 242   Courtesy of CareerBuilder.com
Page 247   © Anna Clopet/Corbis
Page 251   © AP Photo/Paul Sakuma
Page 257 (left)   © BananaStock/PunchStock
Page 257 (right)   © Image Source/Corbis
Page 268   © David P. Hall/Corbis
Page 271   © The McGraw-Hill Companies, Inc./Andrew Resek, Photographer

## CHAPTER 10

Page 280 (left)   © Dirk Linder/Corbis
Page 280 (right)   © moodboard/Corbis
Page 282   © Randy Fairs/Corbis
Page 290   © AP Photo/Lisa Poole
Page 295   © Rob Casey/Brand X/Corbis
Page 298   © RF/Corbis

## CHAPTER 11

Page 303   © Image Source/PunchStock
Page 309   © Ryan McVay/Getty Images
Page 315   © Royalty-Free/Corbis
Page 323 (top left)   © RCWW, Inc./Corbis
Page 323 (top right)   © Macduff Everton/Corbis
Page 323 (bottom left)   © Hugh Sitton/zefa/Corbis
Page 323 (bottom right)   © Push Pictures/Corbis
Page 330   © Carl & Ann Purcell/Corbis
Page 333   © Fotostudio FM/zefa/Corbis

## CHAPTER 12

Page 343   © Somos Images/Corbis
Page 347   © moodboard/Corbis
Page 349   Courtesy of NIST, National Institute of Standards and Technology
Page 355   © Spike Mafford/Getty Images
Page 361   © Car Culture/Corbis
Page 363   © PRNewsFoto/Sears, Roebuck and Co.

## CHAPTER 13

Page 368   © PRNewsFoto/Cracker Barrel Old Country Store, Inc.
Page 374 (left)   © Christopher Pillitz/Getty Images
Page 374 (right)   © The McGraw-Hill Companies, Inc./John Flournoy, Photographer
Page 381   © T. Kruesselmann/Corbis
Page 385   © Ryan McVay/Getty Images
Page 394   © Louie Psihoyos/Corbis
Page 399   © The McGraw-Hill Companies, Inc./John Flournoy, Photographer
Page 402   © PRNewsFoto/Sony

## CHAPTER 14

Page 407 (left)   Reproduced by permission of Netflix, Inc., Copyright © 2007 Netflix, Inc. All rights reserved.
Page 407 (right)   Courtesy of fandango
Page 413   © Pixland/Corbis
Page 417   © Royalty-Free/Corbis
Page 420   © Getty Images for Fox
Page 428 (left)   © Brand X Pictures/PunchStock
Page 428 (right)   © Royalty-Free/Corbis
Page 430   © C. Lee/PhotoLink/Getty Images

# references

## Chapter 1

1. Throughout this book, the terms *objectives* and *goals* will be used interchangeably.

2. Henry Mintzberg, "The Manager's Job: Folklore and Fact," *Harvard Business Review,* March–April 1990, pp. 163–76.

3. Ibid.

4. See Robert L. Katz, "The Skills of an Effective Administrator," *Harvard Business Review,* September–October 1987, pp. 90–102.

5. Adapted from Earnest R. Archer, "Things You Lose the Right to Do When You Become a Manager," *Supervisory Management,* 35 (July 1990): pp. 8–9.

## Chapter 2

1. Daniel Wren, *The Evolution of Management Thought,* 2nd ed. (New York: Ronald Press, 1979), p. 90.

2. Alfred D. Chandler Jr., "The Beginnings of 'Big Business' in American Industry," *Business History Review,* Spring 1959, p. 3.

3. Harry Kelsey and David Wilderson, "The Evolution of Management Thought" (unpublished paper, Indiana University, Bloomington, IN, 1974), p. 7.

4. Henry R. Towne, "The Engineer as Economist," *Transactions, ASME* 7 (1886), pp. 428–32.

5. *Scientific Management: Address and Discussions at the Conference on Scientific Management at the Amos Truck School of Administration and Finance* (Norwood, MA: Plimpton Press, 1912), pp. 32–35.

6. John F. Mee, *Management Thought in a Dynamic Economy* (New York: New York University Press, 1963), p. 411.

7. John F. Mee, "Seminar in Business Organization and Operation" (unpublished paper, Indiana University, Bloomington, IN), p. 5.

8. Wren, *The Evolution of Management Thought,* pp. 136–40.

9. Henry L. Gantt, *Organizing for Work* (New York: Harcourt Brace Jovanovich, 1919), p. 15.

10. Daniel A. Wren, "Henri Fayol as Strategist: A Nineteenth Century Corporate Turnaround," *Management Decision,* vol. 39, issue 5–6, 2001, pp. 475–87; and Daniel A. Wren, Arthur G. Bedeian, and John D. Breeze, "The Foundations of Henri Fayol's Administrative Theory," *Management Decision,* vol. 40, issue 9, 2002, pp. 906–18.

11. For a detailed description of the Hawthorne studies, see Fritz G. Roethlisberger and William J. Dickson, *Management and the Worker* (Cambridge, MA: Harvard University Press, 1939).

12. For example, see Alex Carey, "The Hawthorne Studies: A Radical Criticism," *American Sociological Review,* June 1967, pp. 403–16.

13. Henry C. Metcalf and L. Urwick, eds., *Dynamic Administration: The Collected Papers of Mary Parker Follett* (New York: Harper & Row, 1940), p. 21.

14. Chester I. Barnard, *The Functions of the Executive* (Cambridge, MA: Harvard University Press, 1938).

15. Richard A. Johnson, Fremont E. Kast, and James E. Rosenzweig, *The Theory of Management Systems* (New York: McGraw-Hill, 1963), p. 3.

16. Douglas McGregor, *The Human Side of Enterprise* (New York, McGraw-Hill, 1960).

17. William C. Ouchi, *Theory Z* (Reading, MA: Addison-Wesley, 1981).

18. Thomas J. Peters and Robert H. Waterman Jr., *In Search of Excellence* (New York: Harper &Row, 1982).

19. For a criticism of *In Search of Excellence,* see Daniel T. Carroll, "A Disappointing Search for Excellence," *Harvard Business Review,* November–December 1983, pp. 78–88.

20. Richard B. Chase and Nicholas J. Aquilano, *Production and Operations Management: A Life Cycle Approach* 6th ed. (Homewood, IL: Richard D. Irwin, 1992), pp. 186–87.

21. Jim Collins and Jerry I. Porras, *Built to Last: Successful Habits of Visionary Companies* (New York: Collins, 2004).

22. Jim Collins, *Good to Great: Why Some Companies Make the Leap . . . and Others Don't* (New York: Collins, 2001).

## Chapter 3

1. For additional information, see Mandy Thatcher, "The Grapevine: Communication Tool or Thorn in Your Side?" *Strategic Communication Management,* August 2003, pp. 30–34.

2. For more information on the Internet, see Rachel Singer Gordon, "The Oxford Dictionary of the Internet," *Library Journal,* December 2001, p. 12.

3. For more information, see Darlene Fichter, "Making Your Intranet Live Up to Its Potential," *Online,* January–February 2006, pp. 51–53.

## Chapter 4

1. Herbert A. Simon, *The New Science of Management Decision* (New York: Harper & Row, 1960), p. 2.

2. George S. Odiorne, *Management and the Activity Trap* (New York: Harper & Row, 1974), pp. 128–29; and George S. Odiorne, *The Change Resisters* (Englewood Cliffs, NJ: Prentice Hall, 1981), pp. 15–25.

3. Odiorne, *Management and the Activity Trap,* pp. 142–44.

4. Herbert A. Simon, *Model of Man* (New York: John Wiley & Sons, 1957), p. 198.

5. Irving Lorge, David Fox, Joel Davitz, and Martin Brenner, "A Survey of Studies Contrasting the Quality of Group Performance and Individual Performance, 1930–1957," *Psychological Bulletin,* November 1958, pp. 337–72; Frederick C. Miner, Jr., "Group versus Individual Decision Making: An Investigation of Performance Measures, Decision Strategies, and Process Losses/Gains," O*rganizational Behavior and Human Performance,* February 1984, pp. 112–24; and Alan S. Blinder and John Morgan, "Are Two Heads Better Than One? Monetary Policy by Committee," *Journal of Money, Credit, and Banking,* October 2005, p. 789.

6. M. E. Shaw, "A Comparison of Individuals and Small Groups in the National Solution of Complex Problems," *American Journal of Psychology,* July 1932, pp. 491–504; Lorge et al., "A Survey of Studies"; and W. E. Watson, K. Kumar, and L. K. Michaelson, "Cultural Diversity's Impact on Interaction Process and Performance: Comparing Homogeneous and Diverse Task Groups," *Academy of Management Journal,* June 1993, pp. 590–602.

7. M. Wallach, N. Kogan, and D. J. Bem, "Group Influence on Individual Risk Taking," *Journal of Abnormal and Social Psychology,* August 1962, pp. 75–86; and N. Kogan and M. Wallach, "Risk Taking as a Function of the Situation, the Person, and the Group," in *New Directions of Psychology,* Vol. 3, ed. G. Mardler (New York: Holt, Rinehart & Winston, 1967).

8. D. G. Meyers, "Polarizing Effects of Social Interaction", in *Group Decision Making,* ed. H. BranStatter, J. Davis, and G. Stock-Kreichgauer (New York: Academic Press, 1982).

9. Daniel D. Wheeler and Irving L. Janis, *A Practical Guide for Making Decisions* (New York: Macmillan, 1980), pp. 17–36.

10. Anne Fisher, "Get Employees to Brainstorm Online," *Fortune,* November 29, 2004, p. 72.

11. Graham Walles, *The Art of Thought* (New York: Harcourt Brace Jovanovich, 1976), p. 80.

12. The basis for this model and much of this discussion were contributed by Bruce Meyers, associate professor of management at Western Illinois University.

## Chapter 5

1. J. J. Hemphill, "Personal Variables and Administrative Styles," in *Behavioral Science and Educational Administration* (Chicago: National Society for the Study of Education, 1964), chap. 8.

2. A. L. Comrey, W. High, and R. C. Wilson, "Factors Influencing Organization Effectiveness: A Survey of Aircraft Workers," *Personnel Psychology* 8 (1955), pp. 79–99.

3. For a discussion of these studies, see John A. Pearce II, Elizabeth B. Freeman, and Richard D. Robinson Jr., "The Tenuous Link between Formal Strategic Planning and Financial Performance," *Academy of Management Review,* October 1987, pp. 658–73; and Mike Schraeder, "A Simplified Approach to Strategic Planning," *Business Process Management Journal* 8, no. 1 (2002), pp. 11–21.

4. Anthony Raia, *Managing by Objectives* (Glenview, IL: Scott, Foresman, 1974), p. 38.

5. George A. Steiner, *Top Management Planning* (New York: Macmillan, 1969), p. 237.

6. Michael E. Porter, *Competitive Strategy: Techniques for Analyzing Industries and Competitors* (New York: Free Press, 1980).

7. Porter, *Competitive Strategy,* pp. 37–38.

8. Patricia Braus, "What Does 'Hispanic' Mean?" *American Demographics,* June 1993, pp. 46–49, 58.

9. Peter F. Drucker, *The Practice of Management* (New York: Harper & Row, 1954), p. 51.

10. Arthur A. Thompson Jr., John E. Gamble, and A. J. Strickland III, *Strategy: Core Concepts, Analytical Tools, Readings* (Burr Ridge, IL: McGraw-Hill/Irwin, 2006), p. 85.

11. Porter, *Competitive Strategy.*

12. George A. Steiner, John B. Miner, and Edmond R. Gray, *Management Policy and Strategy,* 2nd ed. (New York: Macmillan, 1982), p. 189.

## Chapter 6

1. For another view on Theory X and Theory Y, see T. C. Carbone, "Theory X and Theory Y Revisited," *Managerial Planning,* May–June 1981, pp. 24–27. See also Michael P. Bobie and William Eric Davis, "Why So Many Newfangled Management Techniques Quickly Fail," *Journal of Public Administration Research and Theory,* July 2003, p. 239.

2. Victor H. Vroom, "Leadership," in *Handbook of Industrial and Organizational Psychology,* ed. Marvin D. Dunnette (Skokie, IL: Rand McNally, 1976), p. 1531.

3. Rensis Likert, *New Patterns of Management* (New York: McGraw-Hill, 1961).

4. Robert R. Blake and Jane Srygley Mouton, *The New Managerial Grid* (Houston: Gulf Publishing, 1978); and Robert R. Blake and Jane S. Mouton, "How to Choose a Leadership Style," *Training and Development Journal,* February 1982, pp. 38–45.

5. Fred E. Fiedler, *A Theory of Leadership Effectiveness* (New York: McGraw-Hill, 1967).

6. Robert Tannenbaum and Warren Schmidt, "HBR Highlights: Excerpts from How to Choose a Leadership Pattern," *Harvard Business Review,* July–August 1986, p. 131.

7. Paul Hersey and Kenneth Blanchard, "Life-Cycle Theory of Leadership," *Training and Development Journal,* June 1979, pp. 94–100. See also George William Yeatrey, *Hersey and Blanchard's Situational Leadership Theory: Applications in the Military* (Ft. Lauderdale, FL: Nova Southeastern University, 2002).

8. Excerpted from Jane M. Howell and Bruce J. Avolio, "The Ethics of Charismatic Leadership," *Academy of Management Executives,* 6 no. 2 (1992).

9. Roy Wagner, *The Invention of Culture,* rev. ed. (Chicago: University of Chicago Press, 1981), p. 21.

10. Vijay Sathe, "Implications of Corporate Culture: A Manager's Guide to Action," *Organizational Dynamics,* Autumn 1983, p. 6.

11. Terrence E. Deal and Allan A. Kennedy, *Corporate Cultures: The Rites and Rituals of Corporate Life* (Reading, MA: Addison-Wesley, 1982), p. 4.

12. Harrison M. Trice and Janice M. Beyer, "Studying Organizational Cultures through Rites and Ceremonials," *Academy of Management Review* 9, no. 4 (1984), p. 645.

13. "The Corporate Culture Vultures," *Fortune,* October 17, 1983, p. 72.

14. Stephen P. Robbins, *Essentials of Organizational Behavior* (Englewood Cliffs, NJ: Prentice Hall, 1984), pp. 174–76.

15. Ron Stodghill, "One Company, Two Cultures," *BusinessWeek,* January 22, 1996, p. 88.

16. Robbins, *Essentials of Organizational Behavior,* p. 171. © 1984; reprinted by permission of Prentice Hall, Inc.

17. This section is drawn from Deal and Kennedy, *Corporate Cultures,* pp. 107, 129–35.

18. Arthur A. Thompson Jr., and A. J. Strickland III, *Strategic Management: Concepts and Cases,* 13th ed. (New York: McGraw-Hill/Irwin, 2003), p. 423.

19. "The Corporate Culture Vultures," p. 70.

20. Ibid.

## Chapter 7

1. Harold Koontz and Cyril O'Donnell, *Management: A Systems and Contingency Analysis of Managerial Functions,* 6th ed. (New York: McGraw-Hill, 1976), p. 274.

2. Chester L. Barnard, *Functions of the Executive* (Cambridge, MA: Harvard University Press, 1938), pp. 114–15.

3. Gareth R. Jones, *Organizational Theory* (Reading, MA: Addison-Wesley, 1995), p. 9.

4. Thomas J. Peters and Robert H. Waterman Jr., *In Search of Excellence* (New York: Harper & Row, 1982), p. 313.

5. Mary Parker Follett, *Freedom and Co-ordination* (London: Management Publication Trust, 1949), pp. 1–15 (the lecture reproduced in *Freedom and Co-ordination* was first delivered in 1926); and Barnard, *Functions,* p. 163.

6. John Tschol, "Empowerment: The Key to Customer Service," *American Salesman,* November 1997, pp. 12–15.

7. John H. Dobbs, "The Empowerment Environment," *Training & Development,* February 1993, pp. 53–55.

8. Robert B. Shaw, "The Capacity to Act: Creating a Context for Empowerment," in *Organizational Architecture: Designs for Changing Organizations,* ed. David A. Nadler, Marc S. Gerstein, and Robert B. Shaw (San Francisco: Jossey-Bass, 1992), p. 169.

9. Renee Beckhams, "Self-Directed Work Teams: The Wave of the Future?" *Hospital Material Management Quarterly,* August 1998, pp. 48–60.

10. Herbert M. Engel, *How to Delegate* (Houston: Gulf, 1983), p. 6.

11. Michael Hammer and James Champy, *Reengineering the Corporation* (New York: Harper Business, 1993), pp. 168, 180–81.

12. Ibid., pp. 180–81.

13. L. F. Urwick, *The Elements of Administration* (New York: Harper & Row, 1943), p. 46.

14. Henri Fayol, *General and Industrial Management* (London: Sir Isaac Pitman & Sons, 1949), p. 36; first published in 1916.

15. Sir Ian Hamilton, *The Soul and Body of an Army* (London: Edward Arnold, 1921), p. 229.

16. V. A. Graicunas, "Relationship in Organization," *Bulletin of the International Management Institute* (Geneva: International Labour Office, 1933); reprinted in *Papers on the Science of Administration,* ed. L. Gulick and L. F. Urwick (New York: Institute of Public Administration, 1937), pp. 181–87.

17. L. F. Urwick, "Scientific Principles and Organizations," *Institute of Management Series No. 19* (New York: American Management Association, 1938), p. 8.

18. For a brief discussion of such situations, see Leslie W. Rue, "Supervisory Control in Modern Management," *Atlanta Economic Review,* January–February 1975, pp. 43–44.

19. L. F. Urwick, "V. A. Graicunas and the Span of Control," *Academy of Management Journal,* June 1974, p. 352.

20. Carolyn Hirshman, "Share and Share Alike," *HR Magazine, September 2005, pp. 52–57.*

21. Brian Gill, "Flextime Benefits Employees and Employers," *American Printer,* February 1998, p. 70; and Leah Carlson, "Firms Balance Workplace Flexibility and Business Demands," *Employee Benefit News,* April 1, 2005, p. 1.

22. www.workingfromanywhere.org/. Accessed on November 8, 2005.

23. Carolyn Hirshman, op.cit.

## Chapter 8

1. Alan Filley and Robert House, *Managerial Process and Organizational Behavior* (Glenview, IL: Scott, Foresman, 1969), pp. 443–55.

2. A. D. Chandler, *Strategy and Structure* (Cambridge, MA: MIT Press, 1962).

3. Some relevant research includes J. Child, "Organization Structure, Environment, and Performance: The Role of Strategic Choice," *Sociology* 6 (1972), pp. 1–22; R. Rumelt, *Strategy, Structure, and Economic Performance* (Boston: Harvard Business School, Division of Research, 1974); and Stephen P. Robins, *Organization Theory: Structure, Design, and Application* (Englewood Cliffs, NJ: Prentice Hall, 1990).

4. Tom Burns and G. M. Stalker, *The Management of Innovation* (London: Tavistock Institute, 1962).

5. Paul Lawrence and Jay Lorsch, "Differentiation and Integration in Complex Organizations," *Administrative Science Quarterly,* June 1967, pp. 1–47; and Paul Lawrence and Jay Lorsch, Organization and Environment (Homewood, IL: Richard D. Irwin, 1969). Originally published in 1967 by Division of Research, Graduate School of Business Administration, Harvard University.

6. Joan Woodward, *Industrial Organization: Theory and Practice* (London: Oxford University Press, 1965).

7. Edward Harvey, "Technology and the Structure of Organizations," *American Sociological Review,* April 1968, pp. 247–59.

[8] "Outsourcing Trends to Watch in '05,", *Fortune,* March 21, 2005, pp. C1–C10.

[9] Michelle V. Rafter, "Promise Fulfilled," *Workforce Management,* September 2005, pp. 51–54.

[10] *Fortune,* op cit.

[11] Michael Corbett, "The Outsourcing Solution," *Fortune Small Business,* September 2005, p. 115.

[12] Laure Edwards, "When Outsourcing Is Appropriate," *Wall Street and Technology,* July 1998, pp. 96–98; and "Outsourcing: What's In, What's Out," *Employee Benefits,* October 6, 2003, p. 39.

[13] Ibid.

[14] Kathleen Madigan and Michael J. Mandel, "Outsourcing Jobs: Is It Bad?" *BusinessWeek,* August 25, 2003, p. 36.

[15] David Cleland and William King, *Systems Analysis and Project Management,* 3rd ed. (New York: McGraw-Hill, 1983), p. 187.

[16] Cliff McGoon, "After Downsizing … Then What?" *Communication World,* May 1994, pp. 16–19.

[17] Ronald K. Chung, "The Horizontal Organization: Breaking Down Functional Silos," *Business Credit,* May 1994, pp. 21–24; and Barbara Crawford-Cook, "Breaking Down Silos," *Canadian HR Reporter,* May 31, 2004, pp. 11–12.

[18] Joyce Chutchian-Ferranti, "Virtual Corporation," *ComputerWorld,* September 1999, p. 33.

[19] Ibid., p. 37.

[20] This example is drawn from Samuel E. Bleecker, "The Virtual Organization," *Futurist,* March–April 1994, p. 9.

[21] James Worthy, "Organization Structure and Employee Morale," *American Sociological Review* 15 (1956), pp. 169–79.

[22] Rocco Carzo Jr. and John Yanouzas, "Effects of Flat and Tall Organization Structure," *Administrative Science Quarterly* 114 (1969), pp. 178–91.

[23] Dan R. Dalton, William D, Todor, Michael J. Spendolini, Gordon J. Fielding, and Lyman W. Porter, "Organization Structure and Performance: A Critical Review," *Academy of Management Review,* January 1980, pp. 49–54.

[24] Thomas J. Peters and Robert W. Waterman Jr., *In Search of Excellence* (New York: Harper & Row, 1982), pp. 306–17.

[25] Richard M. Miller, "The D&O Liability Dilemma," *Chief Executive,* November–December 1988, pp. 34–39; and Pamela W. Mason, "Portfolio D&O Insurance Can Leave Outside Directors in the Cold," *Venture Capital Journal,* October 1, 2005, p. 1.

[26] Harold Geneen, *Managing* (Garden City, NY: Doubleday, 1984), p. 259.

## Chapter 9

[1] "Equal Pay for Equal Work under the Fair Labor Standards Act," *Interpractices Bulletin* (Washington, DC: U.S. Department of Labor, 1967), Title 29, pt. 800.

[2] Jane Ester Bahls, "Employment for Rent," *Nation's Business,* June 1991, p. 36.

[3] *Parham v. Southwestern Bell Telephone Company,* 433 F.2d 421 (8th Cir. 1970).

[4] *Affirmative Action and Equal Employment,* vol. 1 (Washington, DC: U.S. Equal Employment Opportunity Commission, 1974), pp. 30–31.

[5] Alison M. Konrad and Frank Linnehan, "Formalized HRM Structures: Coordinating Equal Employment Opportunity or Concealing Organizational Practices?" *Academy of Management Journal* 38, no. 3 (1995), p. 787.

[6] *University of California Regents v. Bakke,* 483 U.S. 265 (1978).

[7] For a detailed description of a large number of tests, see *The Sixteenth Mental Measurements Yearbook,* edited by Robert A. Spics and Barbara S. Meke (Lincoln, NE: Buros Institute/ University of Nebraska Press, 2005).

[8] See Edward C. Andler, *The Complete Reference Checking Handbook: The Proven (and Legal) Way to Prevent Hiring Mistakes* (New York: AMACOM, 2003).

[9] David Greatbatch and Timothy Clark, "Displaying Group Cohesiveness, Humour and Laughter in the Public Lectures of Management Gurus," *Human Relations,* December 2000, p. 15.

[10] Lester Coch and John R. P. French Jr., "Overcoming Resistance to Change," *Human Relations,* 1948, pp. 519–20.

[11] Bones, Chris, "Group-Think Doesn't Unite, It Divides," *Human Resources,* October 2005, p. 24.

[12] See Paul E. Brauchle and David W. Wright, "Fourteen Team-Building Tips," *Training and Development Journal,* January 1992, pp. 32–36. Also see Mahmoud Salem, Harold Lazarus, and Joseph Cullen, "Developing Self-Managing Teams: Structure and Performance," *Journal of Management Development* 11 (1992), pp. 24–32.

[13] Helene, Fuhlfelder, "It's All about Improving Performance," *Quality Progress,* February 2000, pp. 49–53.

## Chapter 10

[1] Cited in Paul Hersey and Kenneth H. Blanchard, *Management of Organizational Behavior: Utilizing Human Resources,* 4th ed. (Englewood Cliffs, NJ: Prentice Hall, 1982), p. 4.

[2] Abraham H. Maslow, *Motivation and Personality,* 2nd ed. (New York: Harper & Row, 1970).

[3] David C. McClelland, *The Achievement Motive* (New York: Halsted Press, 1976).

[4] Frederick Herzberg, Bernard Mausner, and Barbara Snyderman, *The Motivation to Work* (New York: John Wiley & Sons, 1959).

[5] Victor H. Vroom, *Work and Motivation* (New York: John Wiley & Sons, 1967).

[6] B. F. Skinner, *Science and Human Behavior* (New York: Macmillan, 1953); and B. F. Skinner, *Beyond Freedom and Dignity* (New York: Knopf, 1972).

Charles N. Greene, "The Satisfaction-Performance Controversy," *Business Horizons,* October 1972, p. 31. Also see D. R. Norris and R. E. Niebuhr, "Attributional Influences on the Job Performance–Job Satisfaction Relationship," *Academy of Management Journal,* June 1984, pp. 424–31.

[7] Greene, "The Satisfaction-Performance Controversy," p. 40.

[8] John M. Ivancevich, "The Performance to Satisfaction Relationship: A Causal Analysis of Stimulating and Nonstimulating Jobs," *Organizational Behavior and Human Performance* 22 (1978), pp. 350–64.

[9] Donald P. Schwab and Larry L. Cummings, "Theories of Performance and Satisfactions: A Review," *Industrial Relations,* October 1970, pp. 408–29. Also see Locke, "Job Satisfaction," p. 1343, for a complete summary of the related research.

## Chapter 11

[1] J. M. Juran, *Managerial Breakthrough,* rev. ed. (New York: McGraw-Hill, 1995), pp. 203–205.

[2] Ibid.

[3] James Champy, *Reengineering Management* (New York: Harper Business, 1995), p. 130; and James Champy, "Ambition: Root of Achievement," *Executive Excellence,* March 2000, pp. 5–6.

[4] Champy, *Reengineering Management,* p. 130.

[5] Timothy J. McMahon and G. W. Perritt, "Toward a Contingency Theory of Organizational Control," *Academy of Management Journal,* December 1973, pp. 624–35.

[6] William G. Ouchi and Mary Ann Maguire, "Organizational Control: Two Functions," *Administrative Science Quarterly,* December 1975, pp. 559–71; and William G. Ouchi, "The Transmission of Control through Organizational Hierarchy," *Academy of Management Journal,* June 1978, pp. 174–76.

[7] Champy, *Reengineering Management,* p. 140.

[8] "Sarbanes-Oxley Act Improves Investor Confidence, But at a Cost," *The CPA Journal,* October 2005, p. 19.

[9] Deborah Solomon, "Corporate Governance: At What Price? Critics Say the Cost of Complying with Sarbanes-Oxley Is a Lot Higher Than It Should Be," *Wall Street Journal,* October 17, 2005, p. R3.

[10] C. W. Wilkinson, Dorothy Wilkinson, and Gretchen Vik, *Communicating through Letters and Reports,* 9th ed. (Homewood, IL: Richard D. Irwin, 1986).

[11] William Stratton, Raef Lawson, and Toby Hatch, "Scorecarding as a Management Coordination and Control System," *Cost Management,* May–June 2004, pp. 36–42.

[12] James A. Seen, *Information Technology in Business,* 2nd ed. (Englewood Cliffs, NJ: Prentice Hall, 1998), p. 615; and Raymond McLeod Jr., *Management Information Systems,* 4th ed. (New York: Macmillan, 1990), p. 30.

[13] Patricia M. Buhler, "The Performance Appraisal Process," *Supervision,* November 2005, pp. 14–17.

[14] Frederick W. Taylor, *Scientific Management* (New York: Harper & Row, 1911), p. 52.

[15] See for instance Arthur Morgan, "360 Degree Feedback: A Critical Enquiry," *Personnel Review,* 2005, pp. 663–82. Also, see Roger Siler, "Getting Results with 360 Assessments," *Law Enforcement Technology,* September 2005, pp. 148–56.

[16] Noel Amerpohl, "Who Writes Your Job Description?" *Pro,* October–November 2005, pp. 8–11.

[17] See John W. Rogers, "Halo Effect," *Forbes,* September 26, 2005, p. 246.

[18] Linda Henman, "Putting the Praise in Appraisals," *Security Management,* August 2005, pp. 28–32.

## Chapter 12

[1] Y. S. Chang, George Labovitz, and Victor Rosansky, *Making Quality Work* (New York: Harper Business, 1993), p. 65.

[2] Richard B. Chase, F. Robert Jacobs, and Nicholas J. Aquilano, *Operations Management for Competitive Advantage,* 11th ed. (New York: McGraw-Hill/Irwin, 2006), p. 322.

[3] William J. Stevenson, *Production/Operations Management,* 4th ed. (Burr Ridge, IL: Richard D. Irwin, 1993), p. 99.

[4] Ibid., p. 100.

[5] Tom Peters, *Thriving on Chaos* (New York: Alfred A. Knopf, 1987), pp. 118–19.

[6] Parts of this section were drawn from Stevenson, *Production/Operations Management,* p. 101.

[7] Chase, Jacobs, and Aquilano, *Operations Management for Competitive Advantage,* p. 320.

[8] Stevenson, *Production/Operations Management,* pp. 104–105.

[9] Adapted from Francis X. Mahoney and Carl G. Thor, *The TQM Trilogy* (New York: AMACOM, 1994), pp. 132–37. Excerpted by permission of the publisher. All rights reserved.

[10] Ibid., p. 134.

[11] Richard B. Chase and Nicholas J. Aquilano, *Production and Operations Management: A Life Cycle Approach,* 6th ed. (Homewood, IL: Richard D. Irwin, 1992), p. 196; other parts of this section are drawn from this source.

[12] Vivienne Walker, "Kaizen—The Art of Continual Improvement," *Personnel Management,* August 1993, pp. 36–38.

[13] Stevenson, *Production/Operations Management,* p. 105.

[14] Erik Einset and Julie Marzano, "Six Sigma Demystified," *Tooling and Production,* April 2002, p. 43.

[15] Ken Cowman, "Six Sigma: What, Where, When, Why and How," *Materials Management and Distribution,* October 2005, p. 69.

[16] Esther Durkalski, "Lean Times Call for Lean Concepts," *Official Board Markets,* October 26, 2002, p. 38.

[17] Thomas B. Clark, "Business Process Reengineering," working paper, Georgia State University, November 1997, p. 1.

[18] www.iso.org/iso/en/commcentre/pressreleases/2005Ref967.html. Accessed on November 23, 2005.

[19] Ibid.

[20] Ibid.

[21] Ibid.

[22] Chase and Aquilano, *Production and Operations Management,* pp. 654–55.

[23] Nicholas J. Aquilano and Richard B. Chase, *Fundamentals of Operations Management,* (Homewood, IL: Richard D. Irwin, 1991), p. 586.

[24] Norman Gaither, *Production and Operations Management,* 5th ed. (Fort Worth: Dryden Press, 1992), p. 377.

[25] Jeremy Main, *Quality Wars,* (New York: Free Press, 1994), p. 115.

[26] Peters, *Thriving on Chaos,* p. 117.

[27] Chase and Aquilano, *Production and Operations Management,* p. 481.

[28] Stevenson, *Production/Operations Management,* p. 585.

[29] Chase, Jacobs, and Aquilano, *Operations Management for Competitive Advantage,* p. 611.

[30] John F. Magee, "Guides to Inventory Policy: I. Functions and Lot Size," *Harvard Business Review,* January–February 1956, pp. 49–60.

## Chapter 13

[1] Tom Peters, *Thriving on Chaos* (New York: Alfred A. Knopf, 1987), p. 464.

[2] Lon Matejczyk, "Commentary: Everyone Responsible for Ensuring Change," *The Colorado Springs Business Journal,* October 21, 2005, p. 1.

[3] "The 1995 *Business Week* Europe Forum of Financial Directors," *Business Week,* January 15, 1996.

[4] Ibid.

[5] Waldron Berry, "Overcoming Resistance to Change," *Supervisory Management,* February 1983, pp. 25–30.

[6] Margaret Boles and Brenda Paik Sunoo, "Three Barriers to Managing Change," *Work-force,* January 1998, p. 25.

[7] John Kotter, *Leading Change* (Boston: Harvard Business School Press, 1996).

[8] Arthur G. Bedeian, *Management* (Hinsdale, IL: Dryden Press, 1986).

[9] Michael Beer, "The Technology of Organizational Development," in *Handbook of Industrial and Organizational Psychology,* ed. Marvin D. Dunnette (New York: John Wiley & Sons, 1983), p. 941; and Michael Beer, *Organizational Change and Development: A Systems View* (Santa Monica, CA: Goodyear Publishing, 1980), pp. 194–95.

[10] Much of this section is drawn from David E. Terpstra, "The Organization Development Evaluation Process: Some Problems and Proposals," *Human Resource Management,* Spring 1981, p. 24.

[11] Much of this section is drawn from Robert B. Tucker, "Innovation Discipline," *Executive Excellence,* September 2001, pp. 3–4; Robert B. Tucker, "Innovation: The New Core Competency," *Strategy and Leadership,* January–February 2001, pp. 11–14; and Robert B. Tucker, "Generating Ideas," *Executive Excellence,* December 2003, p. 19.

[12] David Garvin, "Building a Learning Organization," *Harvard Business Review,* July 1993, p. 78.

[13] Peter M. Senge, *The Fifth Discipline: The Art and Practice of the Learning Organization* (New York: Doubleday, 1990); and Peter M. Senge, "Learning Organizations," *Executive Excellence,* September 1991, pp. 7–8.

[14] Garvin, "Building a Learning Organization."

## Chapter 14

[1] Joseph H. Boyett and Jimmie T. Boyett, *Beyond Workplace 2000* (New York: Penguin Books, 1995), pp. xiii–xiv.

[2] Peter Senior, "Where Organization and Management May Be Headed," *Consulting to Management,* June 2004, pp. 50–56.

[3] Joyce Chutchian-Ferranti, "Virtual Corporation," *ComputerWorld,* September 1999, p. 33.

[4] Ibid., p. 37.

[5] This example is drawn from Samuel E. Bleecker, "The Virtual Organization," *Futurist,* March–April 1994, p. 9.

[6] See Dennis W. Organ, "Business Ethics 101?" *Business Horizons,* January–February 2003, pp. 1–2.

[7] For additional information, see Ronald Paul Hill, Debra Stephens, and Iain Smith, "Corporate Social Responsibility: An Examination of Individual Firm Behavior," *Business and Society Review,* September 2003, pp. 339–64.

# Index